T0139964

Lecture Notes of the Institute for Computer Sciences, Social Informatics and Telecommunications Engineering 492

The LNICST series publishes ICST's conferences, symposia and workshops.

LNICST reports state-of-the-art results in areas related to the scope of the Institute.
The type of material published includes

- Proceedings (published in time for the respective event)
- Other edited monographs (such as project reports or invited volumes)

LNICST topics span the following areas:

- General Computer Science
- E-Economy
- E-Medicine
- Knowledge Management
- Multimedia
- Operations, Management and Policy
- Social Informatics
- Systems

Shangguan Longfei · Priyantha Bodhi
Editors

Mobile and Ubiquitous Systems: Computing, Networking and Services

19th EAI International Conference, MobiQuitous 2022
Pittsburgh, PA, USA, November 14–17, 2022
Proceedings

 Springer

Editors
Shangguan Longfei
University of Pittsburgh
Pittsburgh, PA, USA

Priyantha Bodhi
Microsoft Research
Redmond, WA, USA

ISSN 1867-8211 ISSN 1867-822X (electronic)
Lecture Notes of the Institute for Computer Sciences, Social Informatics
and Telecommunications Engineering
ISBN 978-3-031-34775-7 ISBN 978-3-031-34776-4 (eBook)
https://doi.org/10.1007/978-3-031-34776-4

This Springer imprint is published by the registered company Springer Nature Switzerland AG
The registered company address is: Gewerbestrasse 11, 6330 Cham, Switzerland

Preface

We are delighted to introduce the proceedings of the 19th European Alliance for Innovation (EAI) International Conference on Mobile and Ubiquitous Systems: Computing, Networking and Services (MobiQuitous). This conference, which was held online, November 14–17, 2022, brought together researchers, developers, and practitioners around the world who are leveraging and developing mobile computing technology for a smarter world.

The technical program of MobiQuitous 2022 consisted of 38 full papers, including 36 regular papers and 2 short papers. The conference sessions were Session 1 – Internet of Things; Session 2 – security and privacy; Session 3 – human-centric computing (i); Session 4 – human-centric computing (ii); Session 5 – drone applications and edge computing; Session 6 – wireless networks; Session 7 – mobile and human computer interactions. Apart from the high-quality technical paper presentations, the technical program also featured two keynote speeches, one poster and demo session, and one workshop session. The two keynote speakers were Andreas Mueller from Bosch, Germany, and Tao Gu from Macquarie University, Australia. The workshop was Innovative Technologies for the Healthcare Empowerment (InnovTech4Health), which aimed to address critical health problems using mobile and wearable devices.

Coordination with the steering chairs, Imrich Chlamtac, Bruno Kessler, Takahiro Hara, and Tao Gu, was essential for the success of the conference. We sincerely appreciate their constant support and guidance. It was also a great pleasure to work with such an excellent organizing committee team for their hard work in organizing and supporting the conference. In particular, the Technical Program Committee, led by our TPC Co-Chairs, Longfei Shangguan from University of Pittsburgh and Bodhi Priyantha from Microsoft Research, Redmond completed the peer-review process of technical papers and made a high-quality technical program. We are also grateful to the Conference Manager, Radka Vasileiadis, for her support and to all the authors who submitted their papers to the MobiQuitous 2022 conference and InnovTech4Health workshop

We strongly believe that the MobiQuitous conference provides a good forum for all researchers, developers, and practitioners to discuss all science and technology aspects that are relevant to smart grids. We also expect that future MobiQuitous conferences will be as successful and stimulating, as indicated by the contributions presented in this volume.

Wei Gao
Mahanth Gowda

Organization

Steering Committee

Imrich Chlamtac	University of Trento, Italy
Takahiro Hara	Osaka University, Japan
Tao Gu	RMIT University, Australia

Organizing Committee

General Chair

Wei Gao   University of Pittsburgh, USA

General Co-chair

Mahanth Gowda   Pennsylvania State University, USA

TPC Chairs and Co-chairs

Longfei Shangguan	University of Pittsburgh, USA
Bodhi Priyantha	Microsoft Research, USA

Sponsorship and Exhibit Chair

Di Wang   Microsoft, USA

Local Chair

Boyuan Yang   University of Pittsburgh, USA

Workshops Chairs

Jian Liu	University of Tennessee, USA
V. P. Nguyen	UT Arlington, USA

Publicity and Social Media Chairs

Lei Wang   Peking University, China
Song Fang   University of Oklahoma, USA
Guohao Lan   TU Delft, The Netherlands

Publications Chair

Linke Guo   Clemson University, USA

Web Chair

Suryoday Basak   Pennsylvania State University, USA

Posters and PhD Track Chairs

Rui Zhang   University of Delaware, USA
Jie Xiong   UMass Amherst, USA
Ashutosh Dhekne   Georgia Tech, USA

Panels Chairs

Chen Qian   UC Santa Cruz, USA
Vivek Jain   Bosch Research, USA

Technical Program Committee

Christian Becker   University of Mannheim, Germany
Zhichao Cao   Michigan State University, USA
Jagmohan Chauhan   University of Southampton, UK
Tao Chen   City University of Hong Kong, China
Klaus David   University of Kassel, Germany
Xiaoran Fan   Google, USA
Stefan Fischer   University of Lübeck, Germany
Francesco Flammini   Mälardalen University, Sweden
Jean Philippe Georges   Université de Lorraine, France
Xiuzhen Guo   Tsinghua University, China
Martin Henze   RWTH Aachen University, Germany &
                                    Fraunhofer FKIE, Germany
Beihong Jin   Institute of Software, Chinese Academy of
                                    Sciences, China

Poster and Demo Sessions

Audio Content and Crowdsourcing: A Subjective Quality Evaluation of Radio Programs Streamed Online

Przemysław Falkowski-Gilski ⓘ

Faculty of Electronics, Telecommunications and Informatics, Gdansk University
of Technology, Narutowicza 11/12, 80-233 Gdansk, Poland
przemyslaw.falkowski@eti.pg.edu.pl

Abstract. Radio broadcasting has been present in our lives for over 100 years. The transmission of speech and music signals accompanies us from an early age. Broadcasts provide the latest information from home and abroad. They also shape musical tastes and allow many artists to share their creativity. Modern distribution involves transmission over a number of terrestrial systems. The most popular are analog FM (Frequency Modulation) and digital DAB+ (Digital Audio Broadcasting plus). It is worth mentioning that the same content is delivered simultaneously in several techniques, referred to as simulcasting. In addition, the vast majority of radio stations broadcast the same audio content online as well. Their signals are available through dedicated mobile applications for popular mobile devices running the Android or iOS operating system. In turn, other broadcasters offer content through their own website or third-party services associating several radio programs. Such a situation may be observed both on the local (regional) and national (state) market all around the world in America, Europe, Asia, etc.

When it comes to terrestrial radio, contrary to analog FM broadcasting, digital signals are grouped into a set, referred to as the multiplex ensemble. It should be emphasized that the costs associated with regular broadcasting of radio programs are much lower in case of the digital standard. The entire process and fees related to the collection and processing of audio signals and associated additional data, as well as the formation and emission of the multiplex collective signal, can be distributed among several or even a dozen shareholders. The total net bitrate can be flexibly distributed depending on the broadcaster's profile and target audience, played music genre, etc., according to the established needs.

Another approach related to the digital broadcasting of radio signals is the on-demand availability of content in the form of the so-called podcast. The listener is able to choose a previously recorded material through the web browser or a mobile application. Considering the number of available radio programs and the broad range of content they create, this form seems perfectly justified. In case of broadcasting radio programs online, referred to as streaming, speech and music signals and associated multimedia (e.g., album cover, author information, etc.) are available live in real-time. Of course, the transmission medium is different. For this reason, taking into account the ubiquity of mobile and wireless devices, it was decided to carry out research on the subjective evaluation of the quality of radio programs streamed online.

The research was conducted in April 2022 on a group of 45 participants aged 20–35 in a crowdsourcing manner. This approach is based on the fact that users are dispersed and can consume content and utilize available resources with their own device. During the tests no specific equipment, with given parameters or a given class, was assigned to receive and listen to radio programs. There was also no specific time imposed, e.g. the hour of the highest audience, so-called primetime. All participants were asked to devote several minutes to each selected radio program, available from the dedicated national radio Player platform. This online platform offers 9 radio programs broadcasted on a regular basis. Some of them are available simultaneously in the FM and DAB+ standard.

During the study, users were asked to familiarize themselves with the possibilities of the Player broadcast service, and then to listen to each radio program for several minutes during the day with their own reception equipment. The aim was to determine the overall quality of each broadcast considering the individual profile and target group of every station. The test results were saved in an online form and then processed to define the overall 5-point mean opinion score (MOS).

After the listening session, participants were asked to answer a number of questions, including an indication of the number and type of radio receivers they owned. Based on provided answers, it can be indicated that the analog FM standard is still dominant. As it turned out, most of the respondents are motorized, with only 6% of users having a DAB+ receiver in the cockpit of their vehicle. It should be noted that the majority of new cars sold have a build-in receiver compatible with the digital standard. In order to unlock the DAB+ signal reception function, it is necessary to purchase an appropriate package at a car dealership. As it turned out, almost a quarter of people use the so-called Internet radio, either with a mobile application, web browser, or an external portal or service. Spotify and YouTube dominated among the majority of responses.

Obtained results clearly show that it is possible to further improve the quality of provided streaming radio broadcast services available online. On the other hand, further actions would seem advisable, e.g., through a wider support for scientific research, various activities and campaigns, and a closer cooperation with the automotive industry. Outcomes of this analysis describe the changes that have occurred in case of broadcasting radio programs and associated voice and music content in analog FM and digital DAB+ and online streaming standards. The ubiquity of wireless networks, as well as the availability of mobile devices, have changed the needs and expectations of users. The audience's requirements for reliable, high-quality services have significantly increased.

Conclusions show the possibility for further improvement and development of radio transmission services and associated content. The outcomes constitute a valuable support for public and private broadcasters in terms of optimizing the management of available resources. It is worth noting that the process of digitizing radio is far from over, as new broadcasters emerge each year on the market. With the availability and popularity of mobile devices and wireless access media, thanks to the global network, basically anyone and everywhere can become a content creator and even a broadcaster in the web.

Keywords: Broadcasting · Crowdsourcing · Mobile devices · Multimedia · Quality evaluation · Simulcasting · Streaming

Comparing Apples and Oranges: A Mobile User Experience Study of iOS and Android Consumer Devices

Przemysław Falkowski-Gilski[1] ⓘ and Tadeus Uhl[2] ⓘ

[1]Faculty of Electronics, Telecommunications and Informatics, Gdansk University of Technology, Narutowicza 11/12, 80-233 Gdansk, Poland
[2]Faculty of Economics and Transport Engineering, Maritime University of Szczecin, Waly Chrobrego 1-2, 70-500 Szczecin, Poland
przemyslaw.falkowski@eti.pg.edu.pl
t.uhl@pm.szczecin.pl

Abstract. With the rapid development of wireless networks and the spread of broadband access around the world, the number of active mobile user devices continues to grow. Each year more and more terminals are released on the market, with the smartphone being the most popular among them. They include low-end, mid-range, and of course high-end devices, with top hardware specifications. They do vary in build quality, utilized type of material, screen size and screen technology, but the biggest differentiator relates with the CPU (Central Processing Unit), GPU (Graphical Processing Unit), RAM (Random-Access Memory), as well as integrated wireless connectivity modules. Another issue is the type of installed software, particularly the OS (Operating System).

Nowadays, two operating systems share approx. 90% of the mobile market, that is iOS from Apple and Android from Google. The first one is a closed environment, dedicated only to devices coming from one manufacturer. The fragmentation and distribution of different OSs is very low. The price range of different smartphone versions is quite high for a typical user. The second one is an open environment, available on numerous devices coming from various manufacturers. Additionally, this OS may be changed or modified by any interested third-party, which would like to implement, e.g., their own GUI (Graphical User Interface), etc. The fragmentation and distribution of different OSs is very large. The price range of smartphones available on the market is vast. The question remains which option proofs better in terms of quality for the end user.

One may assume that if a given solution is intended as a dedicated one, meaning that it is designed to operate on a limited number of, i.e., hardware configurations, it should prove to be more effective. The battery lifetime, stability and efficiency is expected to be high. If some solution is universal, meaning that it could operate on barely any hardware configuration, it would eventually prove to be less effective, less stable, and with a lower expected battery lifetime. This aspect would surely be an interesting hypothesis to investigate.

Currently, many operators and providers are investing in deploying 5G network infrastructure. This technology brings wider bandwidths with higher throughput for both downlink and uplink, with smaller delay and latency. However, still a vast majority of mobile devices is compatible with 3G and 4G cellular network technology. Not to mention network coverage issues, where LTE (Long-Term Evolution) is the leading solution for urban environments.

This paper aims to investigate the mobile user experience related with iOS and Android-powered smartphones. As we know, the term quality can be understood in many different ways. One focus on the technical side, described as QoN (Quality of Network) and QoS (Quality of Service), related with parameters such as: available bandwidth, throughput for downlink and uplink, as well as delay and latency of the connection. Others focus on the user side, described as QoE (Quality of Experience), related with end user judgements like: availability, responsiveness and reliability. In other words, users perceive the term quality as a mixture of subjective factors compared to previous experience.

In this work, we present an evaluation carried out under real-time operating conditions at a university campus, considering the overall performance of the LTE cellular network. The study involved 14 mobile devices, including 7 iOS and 7 Android smartphones, with all of them compatible with the LTE standard. The research scenario was based on the crowdsourcing approach, in which the utilized devices consisted of personal student's equipment, which they used during everyday activities. The measurements were carried out using a custom-build application. This mobile application enabled to gather information about the wireless connection, including: download and upload speeds, delay, as well as the ID (Identification) of the serving base station.

For each OS and every device, the measurement campaign was carried out in an indoor environment. Each person performed his or her measurements at 10 unique points, evenly distributed throughout a single floor of the chosen building, with more than 30 measurements per point. Obtained data were initially stored in the build-in memory of each mobile device, after which it was transferred in a wired manner onto a hard drive of a desktop PC for further processing and analysis purposes.

Obtained results have shown an observable difference between the closed and restricted iOS system and devices operating on it, and the open and fragmented Android system and its powered device. In case of download speeds, the results for iOS were close one to another with generally higher throughputs compared to Android which had a greater spread. For iOS, the mean value ranged from approx. 19 to 100 Mbps, with a median value oscillating from approx. 20 to 89 Mbps. Whereas for Android it varied between approx. 24 to 102 Mbps and approx. 21

to 107 Mbps, respectively. When it comes to upload speeds, results were quite similar comparing one group of devices to the other. For iOS it ranged from approx. 9 to 26 Mbps (mean) and 9 to 22 Mbps (median), whereas in case of Android it was equal to approx. 10 to 23 Mbps (mean) and 9 to 20 Mbps (median). Ping values were also most often lower for iOS, with both mean and median values oscillating from approx. 16 to 33 ms. Whereas, in case of Android devices the mean value fluctuated from approx. 16 to 36 ms, and the median varied from approx. 16 to 37 ms.

According to our findings, iOS-powered devices have a noticeable advantage when it comes to utilizing offered network resources. Probably, this is related with a higher optimization of the hardware-software aspect, linked with lesser fragmentation in terms of build-in components and version of the operating system.

Keywords: Mobile devices · Multimedia · Quality of experience · Quality of Network · Quality of Service · Wireless networks

Estimating the Area of Radio Signal Sources Activity in a Heterogeneous Sensor Network to Improve Battlefield Situational Awareness

Malon Krzysztof and Skokowski Paweł

Institute of Communications Systems, Faculty of Electronics, Military University
of Technology, Warsaw, Poland
krzysztof.malon@wat.edu.pl
pawel.skokowski@wat.edu.pl

Abstract. Over the last few years, military operational scenarios have changed significantly. Nowadays, conflicts concern asymmetric urban and suburban combat scenarios instead of classical open field warfare. Therefore, situation awareness knowledge is crucial to support the mission planning and operational phase. The article demonstrates how radio signal source localization - estimated using radio detectors - can be used for situational awareness of armed forces in an urban and suburban environment. Using the proposed approach, one can increase efficiency on the battlefield. Furthermore, the presented results of the estimated area of radio signal sources activity for an exemplary urban area indicate the legitimacy of a cooperative approach to the problem. Additionally, by combining results with those coming from heterogeneous sensors network (e.g., image or video recognition), one can get added functionalities to support applications like Blue Force Tracking (BFT), Red Force Tracking (RFT), and jammer localization. Finally, the research results were used to formulate conclusions and plan future work.

A cooperative detection result based on multiple sensors increases detection efficiency compared to the single detector solution. Additional information is the location of individual detectors, thanks to which it is possible to estimate the area of radio signal source presence. More sensors limit the estimated area. The zones from individual detectors must have common parts. Their geographical distribution greatly influences the effectiveness of radio detectors. In this article, we do not indicate a specific type of detector used but focus on the results of their work and the possibility of using them to estimate the presence of radio signal sources.

In the case of a known area, it is possible to use Digital Terrain Maps (DTM). Knowing the site-specific elements, one can get a more accurate link budget - closely to the real conditions. The estimated areas of radio signal source activity take irregular shapes depending on the topography and indicate the estimated locations of the transmitters much more precisely. Figure 1 presents the research results with the estimated area of radio signal sources activity (marked in gray) by 4 independent detectors. The percentage (given in brackets) shows the ratio of calculated radio signal activity region reference to a whole area. Figure 2 shows the simulation of aggregating the results from several detectors - the cooperative sensing result. As one can see, information from more detectors limits the area in which the radio transmitter is potentially located. To increase the localization efficiency of the radio sensor network, one can use a mobile detector integrated with an Unmanned Aerial Vehicle (UAV) platform.

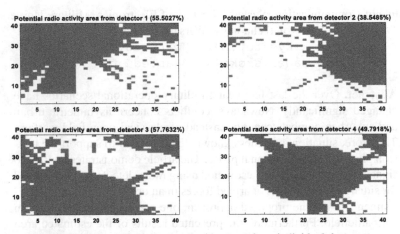

Fig. 1. Radio activity areas (marked in gray) from individual detectors.

Combining the results from different sensor types in heterogeneous network (e.g., image recognition and radio activity), it is possible to obtain complete situational awareness. One of the applications of a heterogeneous sensor network with radio detectors may be the identification, location, and tracking of enemy troops (RFT). In this situation, radio sensors monitor foe radio transmissions and, following the presented method, estimate the area of the emission source.

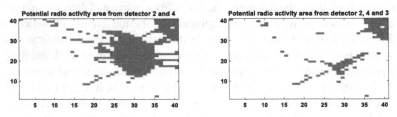

Fig. 2. Radio activity areas (marked in gray) from cooperative result.

The figures show that more sensors and knowledge about the region (DTM) significantly limit the estimated radio activity area. In addition, information from heterogeneous network detectors, e.g., image recognition and databases, provides different kinds of information, increasing situational awareness. A similar procedure can be used to detect and locate the source of the jammer. Knowing the parameters of the radio equipment used by our armed forces, it is also possible to support the tracking of our troops, the so-called Blue Force Tracking (BFT).

The article presents the concept of using radio detectors cooperating to monitor the detection spectrum of radio activity sources and estimate the area of their location. The obtained results confirm the correctness of the assumptions that the cooperative approach significantly increases the quality of situational awareness. Furthermore, thanks to the use of a heterogeneous sensor network and the combination of results from different types of detectors, it is possible to build a complete situational awareness that enables the support of various functionalities important from the point of view of operational activities on the battlefield. Finally, the authors plan to conduct research for more sensors and to combine information with the results of image recognition.

Keywords: Cooperative sensing · Heterogenous sensor network · Localization

Forest Protection as a Context-Aware System

Radosław Klimek

AGH University of Science and Technology, al. Mickiewicza 30, 30-059 Krakow, Poland
rklimek@agh.edu.pl

Abstract. A forest fire protection system may be considered successfully as acontext-aware system, which responds pro-actively to occurring threats, both in the phase of the routine monitoring of a forest area, as well as during a fire extinguishing action. The proposed system assumes the distribution of the network of detectors in forest sectors, which send basic parameters concerning the surroundings and weather. The information is processed in accordance with the multi-agent system architecture, and the obtained smart decisions, which support users, are the result of the proposed context processing.

Keywords: Forest protection · Context-aware system · Smart decision

1 Introduction

The essential aspects of forest protection involve both the assessment of fire threats and fire monitoring. These phases have different objectives. The first one is to prevent a fire onset, take proper actions and support foresters and forest patrols, and the other one, if the fire is already on, is to limit forest losses by calling professional firefighting crews to respective forest sectors and supporting such crews. A system corresponding to these objectives has been proposed, which integrates fully with the postulates of pervasive computing, pro-activeness and ambient intelligence.

2 System Presentation

The entire forest area is divided into sectors, see Fig. 1, which are equipped with detectors which provide the reading of numerous environmental and weather parameters, and which may be treated as contextual data, including the concentration of a carbon dioxide and aerosols in the air, which are typical for combustion processes. Contextual data are pre-filtered and pre-categorised [1], which is aimed at coping with their prospective complexity. The risk assessment of a given forest sector is determined based on McArthur Forest Fire Danger Index [2], $FDDI = 2e^{((-0.45 + 0.987 * log(f_D) - 0.0345 * H + 0.338 * T_c + 0.0234 * v_w))}$, where: f_D – forest bed dryness coefficient, H – air humidity coefficient, T_c – current temperature, v_W – wind speed, which is reflected in the risk scale: 1 – low, 2 – moderate, 3 – high, 4 – very high, and 5 – extreme. Whereas, fire classification is slightly more complex, it considers the influence of combustibility, wind, temperature, humidity and others, w hich leads to the following scale: 0 – non-combusted, 1 – early fire, 2 – medium fire, 3 – full fire, 4 – extreme fire, 5 – completely extinguished or combusted.

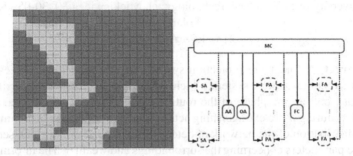

Fig. 1. Forest division into sectors (left) and agent system architecture(right). Left: The red squares indicate a fire threat. Right: MA (Managing Agent) – initiation of the system and agents, SA (Sensor Agent) – reading and sending measurement data from respective sectors, AA (Analyst Agent) – analysis of the data from SA, PA (PatrolAgent) – ground patrol, fire monitoring and protection, OC (Overseer Controller Agent) – forester, assigning tasks for PAs, FA (Firefighter Agent) – fire brigade, fire extinguishing, FC (Fire Controller Agent) – commander, assigning tasks for FAs, solid ovals mean permanent agents and dashed ovals show agents which may exist temporarily. Solid and dashed lines show agents' constructions and destructions, respectively

The distribution of detectors in sectors and operating many objects in the monitored forest, with different functions but requiring cooperation, integrates well with the Multi-agent system (MAS) idea, see Fig. 1. The planned system conducts agentification by means of specialisation and tasks automisation, and balancing between respective system tasks and activities. Furthermore, we plan to adapt a calculation [3] operating on contextual data to the specificity of our system. A basic object here is a simple detectoror a live object, specified as $Entity = \langle ID, N, L, T, C, P, S \rangle$, where ID is an object identifier, N – its name, L – location, T – type, C – context, P – profile, and S – state. Then, by including the defined activities $Activity$, and possible events $Event$, together with relationships $Relationship$, we obtain the following results $Summary = \langle ID, E, D_L \rangle$, where: ID – an identifier of forest protection or fire extinguishing operation, E – an identifier of a participating object, D_L – a risk or fire degree according to the scale accepted above.

3   Conclusions

The proposed manner of processing contextual data is new and coherent, and it allows for supplying smart decisions for forest workers and fire fighters. System validation will be carried out in simulations.

References

1. Klimek, R.: Exploration of human activities using message streaming brokers and automated logical reasoning for ambient-assisted services. IEEE Access **6**, 27127–27155 (2018). https://doi.org/10.1109/ACCESS.2018.2834532
2. Noble, I.R., Gill, A.M., Bary, G.A.V.: McArthur's fire-danger meters expressed as equations. Aust. J. Ecol. **5**, 201–203 (1980)
3. Pradeep, P., Krishnamoorthy, S., Pathinarupothi, R.K., Vasilakos, A.V.: Leveraging context-awareness for internet of things ecosystem: representation, organization, and management of context. Comput. Commun. **177**, 33–50 (2021)

Mobile Networks' Analysis in Terms of QoS Performance Assessment

Dariusz Zmysłowski(ID), Jan M. Kelner(ID) and Przemysław Falkowski-Gilski(ID)

Institute of Communications Systems, Faculty of Electronics, Military University of Technology, Warsaw, Poland
Faculty of Electronics, Telecommunications and Informatics, Gdansk University of Technology, Gdansk, Poland
dariusz.zmyslowski@wat.edu.pl
jan.kelner@wat.edu.pl
przemyslaw.falkowski@eti.pg.edu.pl

Abstract. Quality of service (QoS) assessment is one of the basic processes carried out by mobile network operators (MNOs) and regulators of the telecommunications market. Usually, professional companies carry out measurements for various country areas and use cases (scenarios). In this paper, we show exemplary measurement results carried out in drive tests in the vicinity of the Polish capital by a professional company. The measurement campaign included two MNOs and three use cases, i.e., voice calls, video live streaming from YouTube, and web browsing. Various parameters of the received signals and QoS metrics were recorded during the measurements, e.g., reference signal received power, signal-to-interference-plus-noise ratio, mean opinion score (MOS), video MOS, and throughput. One of the MNOs provides services using Universal Mobile Telecommunications Service (UMTS) and Long-Term Evolution (LTE) technologies, while another is based only on LTE technology. The presented results show that higher QoS metrics were obtained for the LTE network than one using UMTS/LTE technologies.

Keywords: Quality of Service (QoS) · Quality of Experience (QoE) · Mobile network · Drive test · Measurements · Long-Term Evolution (LTE) · Mean Opinion Score (MOS) · Video MOS · Throughput

1 Introduction

The development of digital telecommunications forced the introduction of two new and crucial processes that did not exist in analog systems, i.e., synchronization and quality of service (QoS) assessment. The introduction of a QoS management system in cellular systems was conducive to developing and variety of telecommunications services, including multimedia. In Global System for Mobile Communications (GMS), i.e., second generation (2G) systems, only voice calls were available. With the introduction of the General Packet Radio Service (GPRS), the era of packet data transmission began, which allowed for unlimited access to Internet resources and related services. The widespread use of Internet Protocol (IP) in mobile telephony has led to the displacement of typical voice calls to services based on this protocol, such as Voice over IP (VoIP) or Voice over Long-Term Evolution (VoLTE).

The analysis of QoS and quality of experience (QoE) in mobile networks is one of the fundamental processes implemented by both mobile network operators (MNOs) and telecommunications market regulators. For this purpose, both MNOs and regulators use specialized companies that deal with the implementation of QoS measurements. Such measurements are usually carried out by standards defined by the European Telecommunications Standards Institute (ETSI), the International Telecommunication Union (ITU), or the 3rd Generation Partnership Project (3GPP). Measurements often use specialized hardware and software with implemented standards and measurement methodologies for specific QoS metrics [1, 2].

2   Problem Solution

In this paper, we present the results of the measurement campaign aimed at assessing QoS in the mobile networks of two Polish MNOs, operating in particular in the third (3G) and fourth generation (4G) standards, i.e. Universal Mobile Telecommunications Service (UMTS) and Long-Term Evolution (LTE), respectively. The measurements were carried out by the professional measurement company Systemics-PAB Group on behalf of the Polish regulator, i.e., the Office of Electronic Communications (UKE). The measurement campaign was carried out in urban and suburban areas near Piaseczno, Konstancin Jeziorna, and Gora Kalwaria, south of the Polish capital, Warsaw.

The measurements were performed with the use of a professional test-bed by Rohde & Schwarz, which consisted of SwissQual Diversity Smart Benchmarker Rel. 20.3 with SwissQual QualiPoc software installed in Samsung Galaxy S20 + 5G (SM-G986BDS) terminals. These terminals support the carrier aggregation technology and all bands used by MNOs in Poland. Additionally, a passive scanner, Rohde & Schwarz TSME6, was used to evaluate the quality and strength of reference signals in the UMTS and LTE networks. The scanner supports all frequency bands used in cellular networks.

The research was carried out for several scenarios related to the provided services, including voice calls, live streaming video from YouTube, and browsing websites. To make the measurements more realistic, each scenario was implemented in several variants, e.g., the duration and the number of repetitions of the video transmission were variable. Different metrics were recorded for each scenario to assess QoS, e.g., mean opinion score (MOS), video MOS (VMOS), and throughput for voice calls, video streaming, and web browsing (i.e., data transmission), respectively. Parameters that testify to the quality of the radio channel, i.e., the power and quality of reference signals, were additionally measured with a scanner. In the case of LTE, these parameters are reference signal received power (RSRP) and signal-to-interference-plus-noise ratio (SINR). The performed measurements of QoS metrics and signal parameters are the basis for the correlation analysis between them [3, 4] and the multi-criteria assessment of MNOs in terms of QoS and QoE [2].

The conducted studies allow for a comparative assessment of two MNOs in terms of QoS. In this paper, we present an analysis of the results for two MNOs in terms of the measurement scenarios and recorded QoS metrics. One of the important factors assessed in the research is network capacity, which translates into the availability of services provided by the MNO.

The analysis of the use of various standards of mobile networks (2G–4G and fifth generation (5G)) showed that for GSM and UMTS, the number of measurement samples collected is much smaller than for LTE or 5G. One of the MNOs has dropped out of UMTS, and the radio resources used early by this network are now used by the LTE network. In this case, the analysis of the results shows that the QoS at this MNO is better. This is especially true in drive tests when handover is being performed between base stations that provide services under two different standards. The number of dropped connections during handover at the MNO, which maintains two mobile network standards, was greater than the MNO based only on LTE.

Figure 1 depicts exemplary results from our study. In this case, it is the percentage utilization of different technologies from UMTS, LTE, and LTE–carrier aggregation (CA) for 2 ÷ 4 bands to the hybrid configurations during a single session for the web browsing scenario. We analyzed the throughput for individual MNOs for the entire scenario and the sets of measurement bins with the selected technology.

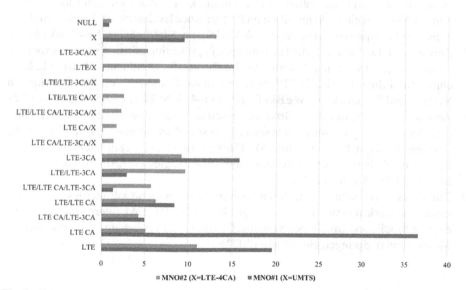

Fig. 1. Percentage utilization of different technologies by two MNOs during a single session for web browsing scenario.

3 Summary

The analysis of the obtained results shows that the QoS assessment is very important from the viewpoint of the provided services and the development of mobile networks. The next generations of mobile network standards offer more and more capacity but also better security and QoS control mechanisms. Thanks to this, also the QoE on the user's side is better and better assessed. The increase in QoS in subsequent generations of communication systems is also conducive to developing new services offered to network users.

Acknowledgements. This work was financed by the Military University of Technology under Research Project no. UGB/22-740/2022/WAT on "Modern technologies of wireless communication and emitter localization in various system applications".
The authors would like to thank the President of UKE, Dr. Jacek Oko, for providing the measurement data made by the Systemics-PAB Group company, which implemented QoS assessment campaigns in mobile networks on behalf of UKE.

References

1. Mongay Batalla, J., Sujecki, S., Oko, J., Kelner, J.M.: Cost-effective measurements of 5G radio resources allocation for telecom market regulator's monitoring. In: 2022 19th ACM International Symposium on Performance Evaluation of Wireless Ad Hoc, Sensor and Ubiquitous Networks (PE-WASUN), pp. 83–90. ACM, New York (2022).
2. Zmysłowski, D., Kelner, J.M.: The concept of application of the Wroclaw taxonomy for QoS assessment in mobile networks. In: Decker, S., Domínguez Mayo, F.J., Marchiori, M., Filipe, J. (eds.) 2022 18th International Conference on Web Information Systems and Technologies (WEBIST), pp. 485–494. SCITEPRESS, Setúbal (2022)
3. Zmysłowski, D., Kelner, J.M.: Drive test-based correlation assessment of QoS parameters for exemplary measurements scenario in suburban environment. In: Decker, S., Domínguez Mayo, F.J., Marchiori, M., Filipe, J. (eds.) 2022 18th International Conference on Web Information Systems and Technologies (WEBIST), pp. 485–494. SCITEPRESS, Setúbal (2022)
3. Zmysłowski, D., Kelner, J.M.: Relationships between QoS/QoE metrics in selected mobile network measurement campaign. In: 2022 19th EAI International Conference on Mobile and Ubiquitous Systems: Computing, Networking and Services (EAI MobiQuitous). Springer, Heidelberg (2022)

Relationships Between QoS/QoE Metrics in Selected Mobile Network Measurement Campaign

Dariusz Zmysłowski and Jan M. Kelner

Institute of Communications Systems, Faculty of Electronics, Military University of Technology, Warsaw, Poland
dariusz.zmyslowski@wat.edu.pl
jan.kelner@wat.edu.pl

Abstract. Modern mobile networks provide access to a variety of services. On the one hand, mobile network operators (MNOs) are required to ensure adequate network coverage, on the other hand, the provided services should be performed at an appropriate level. Introducing the assessment and management system quality of service (QoS) is designed to fulfill the second task. In this paper, we present a correlation analysis of QoS metrics and radio signal parameters for a web browsing scenario. This research is based on the measurement campaign carried out in the vicinity of Warsaw, the Polish capital. The measurements were carried out for two MNOs by a professional company that deals with QoS assessment in mobile networks. One of the MNOs provides services using Universal Mobile Telecommunications Service (UMTS) and Long-Term Evolution (LTE) technologies, while another is based only on LTE technology. For calculations, we used the Pearson correlation coefficient and linear regression. The obtained results indicate which of the analyzed metrics are characterized by a strong, medium, and weak correlation.

Keywords: Quality of Service (QoS) · Quality of Experience (QoE) · Mobile network · Drive test · Measurements · Correlation analysis · Pearson correlation coefficient · Web browsing

1 Introduction

The quality of services in mobile networks is currently of intense importance both for telecommunications infrastructure operators, their end-users (subscribers and subscribers of the services), and regulators of telecommunications markets. For the mobile network operator (MNO), knowledge of quality of service (QoS) and experience (QoE) is a valuable tool for assessing the network and the level of provided services but is also used to determine the causes of network failures, unavailability of services, and performance fluctuations. In addition, MNOs can use the conclusions from the statistical analysis of QoS and QoE measurements to assess the performance of devices and networks offered by suppliers at the stage of proof of concept (PoC) pilot studies of new network solutions.

QoS indicators are getting you to research, analyze and evaluate the technical aspects of the functioning of the network providing services in terms of meeting the requirements that initially had been set. By analyzing the values of QoE key performance indicators (KPIs), one can characterize the service state in a given network from the user's perspective. Using the possibility to assess QoS and QoE parameters is also essential for telecommunications market regulators. They can indicate to end-users the current service state offered by individual networks and compare them from the user's perspective. The market regulators may also conduct studies on how MNOs are in line with declarations submitted in auction and concession procedures of network and service development, their scope, range, and quality [1, 2].

In this paper, we evaluate the correlation between radio signal parameters and QoS metrics. Such an assessment may be the basis for modeling one of the parameters based on the other [3]. The authors of [4] propose an innovative approach to service selection that not only considers QoS correlations of services but also accounts for QoS correlations of user requirements. On the other hand, the correlational analysis of QoS metrics allows for the selection of uncorrelated ones for the assessment of MNOs in the broader aspect of the provided QoS and QoE [2].

2 Problem Solution

Correlation is one of the fundamental tools used in the analysis and processing of data and signals. The correlation analysis allows you to find similarities and relationships between two variables, properties, features, signals, or processes. The correlation methods are also used in QoS research and methods that can approximate service composition. The purpose of using correlation analyses is to determine the optimal path of service delivery [3].

The main concern of our work was to research the correlation between parameters of radio signals of mobile networks such as reference signal received power (RSRP) and signal-to-interference-plus-noise ratio (SINR) for Long-Term Evolution (LTE) technology, reference signal code power (RSCP) and downlink carrier-to-interference ratio (EC/IO) for Universal Mobile Telecommunications Service (UMTS) technology, average throughput (Th), throughput for first second of transmission (Th1s), and different time metrics of QoS, e.g., time (TD) and session duration (SC), first round trip time (RTT1), average round trip time for rest transmission (RTT2), time to first byte (T1B), time to 50% of volume (T50V), time to first 500 kB of transmission (T500kB).

The basis of the performed correlation analysis are measurements made by a professional company Systemics-PAB Group for the Polish regulator of the telecommunications market, i.e., the Office of Electronic Communications (UKE). The measurements were carried out near Warsaw within one week time for mobile networks of two MNOs (i.e., MNO#1 and MNO#2) that operating in particular in the third (3G) and fourth generation (4G) standards, i.e. UMTS and LTE, respectively [3, 5].

The measurements were performed using a professional test-bed by Rohde & Schwarz, which consisted of SwissQual Diversity Smart Benchmarker Rel. 20.3 with SwissQual QualiPoc software installed in Samsung Galaxy S20 + 5G (SM-G986BDS) terminals. These terminals support the carrier aggregation technology and all bands used by MNOs in Poland. A passive scanner, Rohde & Schwarz TSME6, was used to evaluate the quality and strength of reference signals in the UMTS and LTE networks. The scanner supports all frequency bands used in cellular networks [3].

In this paper, we focus on the issue of QoS assessment in mobile networks. Based on the measurements made during drive tests, the relationships between QoS metrics and parameters that define the received signal power and quality in mobile networks, i.e., RSRP and SINR or RSCP and EC/IO, are analyzed. The analysis was carried out for selected measurement scenarios of browsing websites. In our studies, we use the Pearson correlation coefficient (PCC) and linear regression between parameters. The determined PCCs for the parameter pairs indicated a relationship between the signal parameters (i.e., radio signal power and quality) or the QoS metrics like throughput and time data transmission ones. Deviations and regression lines for the metrics' pairs with significant PCCs were determined. Exemplary results of correlation analysis for MNO#1 and LTE technology, we show in the following Table 1.

Table 1. PCCs for MNO#1 and LTE technology.

Scale [PCC]	0.00÷0.09	0.10÷0.19	0.20÷0.29	0.30÷0.39	0.40÷0.49	0.50÷0.59	0.60÷0.69	0.70÷0.79	0.80÷0.89	0.90÷0.99	1.00
PCC	TD	RTT1	RTT2	T1B	T50V	T500kB	Th1s	Th	SD	RSRP	SINR
SINR	−0.18	−0.12	−0.31	−0.15	−0.26	−0.31	0.26	0.27	−0.19	0.67	1.00
RSRP	−0.15	−0.11	−0.30	−0.12	−0.24	−0.28	0.21	0.23	−0.16	1.00	
SD	1.00	0.12	0.52	0.46	0.81	0.53	−0.48	−0.42	1.00		
Th	−0.40	−0.09	−0.29	−0.49	−0.42	−0.67	0.77	1.00			
Th1s	−0.45	−0.10	−0.26	−0.58	−0.46	−0.57	1.00				
T500kB	0.49	0.31	0.45	0.73	0.67	1.00					
T50V	0.80	0.02	0.58	0.45	1.00						
T1B	0.41	0.40	0.26	1.00							
RTT2	0.50	0.29	1.00								
RTT1	0.06	1.00									
TD	1.00										

3 Summary

The carried-out correlation analysis of the data recorded during the test drive shows that the mentioned QoS metrics and signal parameters are related. The strong correlation we may see between time metrics (e.g., TD-SD, TD-T50V, T1B-T500kB), throughput (i.e., Th-Th1s) or signal parameters (e.g., SINR-RSRP for LTE). Between some QoS metrics and radio signal parameters, the correlation is from medium to weak. On the one hand, a better quality of the channel and received signal translates into a higher level of provided QoS, which is an obvious conclusion. However, the relations between these metrics are not trivial and are characterized by a certain spread. Its determination is possible by assessing the linear regression between these parameters. For small absolute PCC values, the relationship between the metrics is usually nonlinear. On the other hand, the Shannon formula shows that capacity, (and indirectly also throughput) is closely related to signal quality (i.e., SINR) and bandwidth. Therefore, the radio resources enabled by MNO for users to realize the service should additionally consider in the correlation analysis between QoS and signal parameters. Our future studies will be focused on the search for non-linear relationships between the analyzed parameters.

Only the data sets in which all the discussed parameters were determined were used in the correlation analysis. The analysis of incomplete data that was not considered also showed that the amount of rejected data was smaller in one of the MNOs that provided services only via the LTE network compared to the other, which used switching between UMTS and LTE technologies. This proves that the resignation from UMTS technology in favor of using its radio resources by LTE is more effective from the viewpoint of the MNOs and users.

The obtained results allow, on the one hand, to model changes in QoS metrics based on the values of signal parameters (e.g., RSRP or SINR). On the other hand, the conducted analysis allows limiting the number of correlated parameters considered in the assessment of QoS-related phenomena or processes.

Acknowledgements. This work was financed by the Military University of Technology under Research Project no. UGB/22-740/2022/WAT on "Modern technologies of wireless communication and emitter localization in various system applications".

The authors would like to thank the President of UKE, Dr. Jacek Oko, for providing the measurement data made by the Systemics-PAB Group company, which implemented QoS assessment campaigns in mobile networks on behalf of UKE.

References

1. Mongay Batalla, J., Sujecki, S., Oko, J., Kelner, J.M.: Cost-effective measurements of 5G radio resources allocation for telecom market regulator's monitoring. In: 2022 19th ACM International Symposium on Performance Evaluation of Wireless Ad Hoc, Sensor and Ubiquitous Networks (PE-WASUN), pp. 83–90. ACM, New York (2022)
2. Zmysłowski, D., Kelner, J.M.: The concept of application of the Wroclaw taxonomy for QoS assessment in mobile networks. In: Decker, S., Domínguez Mayo, F.J., Marchiori, M., Filipe, J. (eds.) 2022 18th International Conference on Web Information Systems and Technologies (WEBIST), pp. 485–494. SCITEPRESS, Setúbal, Portugal (2022).
3. Zmysłowski, D., Kelner, J.M.: Drive test-based correlation assessment of QoS parameters for exemplary measurements scenario in suburban environment. In: Decker, S., Domínguez Mayo, F.J., Marchiori, M., Filipe, J. (eds.) 2022 18th International Conference on Web Information Systems and Technologies (WEBIST), pp. 485–494. SCITEPRESS, Setúbal, Portugal (2022).

4. Li, D., Ye, D., Gao, N., Wang, S.: Service selection with QoS correlations in distributed service-based systems. IEEE Access **7**, 88718–88732 (2019)

5. Zmysłowski, D., Kelner, J.M., Falkowski-Gilski P.: Mobile networks' analysis in terms of QoS performance assessment. In: 2022 19th EAI International Conference on Mobile and Ubiquitous Systems: Computing, Networking and Services (EAI MobiQuitous). Springer, Heidelberg (2022)

Contents

Wireless Networks

Mobile and Human Computer Interactions

Internet of Things (IoT)

Devising a Vibration-Based Fault Detection System for Textile Machinery

Md. Harunur Rashid Bhuiyan[1]([✉]), Iftekhar Morshed Arafat[1],
Masfiqur Rahaman[2], Tarik Reza Toha[1], and Shaikh Md. Mominul Alam[1]

[1] Bangladesh University of Textiles, Dhaka, Bangladesh
`201718004@tmdm.butex.edu.bd`
[2] Bangladesh University of Engineering and Technology, Dhaka, Bangladesh

Abstract. The textile sector is the backbone of the economy of many developing countries in South Asia. Diverse machinery fault caused by intensive production schedules during operation is a major concern for industries in this sector. There exist several systems in the state-of-the-art literature for detecting textile machinery faults where faulty output is already produced before machine fault detection. In this study, we propose a vibration-based machinery fault detection system for the textile industry. We use a highly sensitive accelerometer to detect even the tiniest vibration changes. Using the accelerometer, we produce a data set by creating six artificial faults in the machine and measuring the vibration of the machine during those faults. Next, we perform Fast Fourier analysis to derive the machine frequency and statistical analysis to detect vibration variation during different faults. We find that there is a change in the machine frequency and vibration respectively during different faults. Then, we run eight different machine learning algorithms to detect the type of fault in the machine. We measure the precision, recall, and F1 score of our machine learning models through ten-fold cross-validation. We get the highest F1 score of 98.9% using the Decision Tree classifier. Finally, we construct a real device by implementing our trained machine learning model in Arduino to identify machine faults which demonstrate the utility of our proposed approach in real scenarios.

Keywords: machine-learning · vibration · FFT · textile-machinery

1 Introduction

The textile and clothing industries are the main source of foreign currency for developing south Asian countries. Bangladesh is the world's second-largest apparel garment exporter in the global textile market [14]. This sector contributes 80% of all exports [11] in this country. The textile industry consists of robust machinery like spinning, weaving, and finishing machinery and delicate machinery like knitting and dyeing machinery. Textile machinery consists of different mechanical components which contribute to the production of fabric.

© ICST Institute for Computer Sciences, Social Informatics and Telecommunications Engineering 2023
Published by Springer Nature Switzerland AG 2023. All Rights Reserved
S. Longfei and P. Bodhi (Eds.): MobiQuitous 2022, LNICST 492, pp. 3–20, 2023.
https://doi.org/10.1007/978-3-031-34776-4_1

Damage or absence of any of these components can result in the production of faulty fabric [16]. Some of these components are tiny and it is difficult to detect if any fault occurs in them. This can result in a stoppage of machines and loss of production.

Vibration has always been a primary concern of the maintenance department of any textile factory. It is one of the significant reasons for machinery health degradation [18]. Typically there is a standard amount of vibration for every machine. The core concept of vibration-based fault detection is that any structural fault in a machine results in a change in the structural dynamics which changes the machine vibration [3]. Existing vibration-based fault detection systems [2,5,20] are trained with only a small amount of data set. Hence, they lack accuracy. Existing photoelectric-based fault detection approaches [29,30] are not suitable for the industry since they are expensive and difficult to implement. Moreover, there are approaches to detecting textile machine fault indirectly through detecting the fabric fault [10,12,15,17,28]. However, these approaches are not real-time and can not detect machine faults until the produced fabric is damaged.

In this paper, we use a sensitive accelerometer to measure the vibration of a machine on three different axes. Then, we create six different frequently occurring faults in the machine artificially. We measure the machine vibration during each fault. We store the data on a computer. We create a data set from the vibration data during different faults. First, we analyze if there is any difference in vibration due to machine fault. For this, we use Fast Fourier Analysis which gives us information about the machine frequency during each fault. We also perform statistical analysis to detect the difference in vibration during the faults. We find that there is a significant difference in machine frequency during the faults and also a difference in vibration value. Next, we use our data set to train eight different machine learning algorithms. Furthermore, we evaluate the accuracy of the trained models by calculating the precision, recall, and F1 score of each trained machine-learning model. Then we take the model with the best accuracy and use that to make an Arduino library. We install the library in Arduino to build a real device that can detect machine faults in real time by measuring machine vibration.

Based on our work, we make the following contributions:

- We measure the machinery vibration by a highly sensitive ADXL-345 accelerometer on three different axes such as X, Y, and Z. The sensor can measure the tiniest vibration which is important because our experimented machine has a very minimum amount of vibration.
- We prepare a machinery fault data set by creating six artificial faults in a real textile machine and measuring the vibration during those faulty conditions.
- We conduct a Fast Fourier analysis of the machinery vibration data, which separates the vibration signal wave into its components on different frequencies. From this analysis, we find the actual frequency of the machine. Besides, we find that the machine frequency changes during faulty conditions.
- We conduct the statistical analysis of the data which gives information on vibration variation during different faults. From both the Fast Fourier and

statistical analysis we find that there is a significant difference in vibration during different faults.
- We train different machine learning algorithms by our prepared data set and use ten-fold cross-validation to measure the precision, recall, and F1 score of our model. Here, we find that the Decision Tree classifier algorithm delivers a 98.9% F1 score while detecting different faults.
- We construct a real machine fault detection device by implementing our trained machine learning model in Arduino. This device can detect textile machinery faults in real-time in factory scenarios.

2 Background and Related Work

The textile industry runs on three shifts per day and each shift spans eight hours. Due to the long working hour of the machinery, most of the machinery becomes fatigued and personnel maintaining these machineries also become inattentive. As a result, different faults occur in the machinery and due to the busy schedule often maintenance team reaches the machine very late. This problem can be solved only when there is a proper fault detection system for the machinery. Among all the machinery in the textile industry, the knitting machine is the most delicate one. It has very tiny components. Hence, whenever a small fault occurs in the machinery, it is really difficult to identify it with the naked eye although its impact on fabric quality can be significantly harmful. Circular weft knitting machines typically have latch needles. The needle does the main function of the knitting action which is loop formation. The sinkers in the weft knitting machine hold down the old loop while the needle knocks over the new loop. This function is known as 'holding down' [1]. If there is any fault in these components the production of fabric will not occur properly and the produced fabric will become faulty. Moreover, if the production rate is high, a huge amount of knit fabric will be defective. So, it is necessary to identify the fault in these components as soon as possible. The purpose of our research is to develop a system that can detect even the tiniest of defects in the machinery just by measuring its vibration in real time.

2.1 Vibration-Based Fault Detection

Mohamad et al., proposed a diagnostic method using a combination of nonlinear dynamic analysis and computational intelligence techniques in a vibration-based fault diagnosis in nonlinear systems [20]. But the proposed system did not have real industry data for developing the system. Mainghai et al., proposed a system where a piezoelectric type accelerometer is used for diagnosing the faults on a hydraulic brake system of a light motor vehicle done on nine fault conditions and one good condition [2]. They also used the machine learning approach. However, only 55 data were used for testing every fault condition. Bhuiyan et al., proposed a wireless vibration-based machinery health monitoring system that used a simple vibration sensor for data collection [5]. However, no-fault analysis was done in the proposed system. Senapathy et al., proposed a vibration-based condition monitoring of rotating machinery [24]. However, the system can only detect if there is any fault in the machinery. It can not detect the type of fault. Han et al., proposed a real-time monitoring system of textile equipment based on MQTT [9]. However, this system requires a huge amount of storage for every machine which is quite inapplicable in the industry sector. 10 sets of 10000 ingots need 130GB per day; excessive data transmission will affect the read-write performance of MySQL, resulting in data loss. Patange et al., proposed a machine learning-based milling cutter condition monitoring system [22]. However, readings from various premade or known faulty conditions of the machine were not taken in this approach. Peeters et al., proposed envelope spectrum sparsity indicators for bearing and gear vibration-based condition monitoring [23]. However, this system can not detect the type of fault in the machinery. Mauricio et al., proposed a vibration-based condition monitoring system for wind turbine gearboxes [19]. However, the system is not tested on real experimentation. Rather it is evaluated based on publicly available data.

2.2 Photoelectric-Based Fault Detection

Zhang et al., proposed a photoelectric detector-based needle fault detection system in a circular knitting machine [29]. The proposed system uses a photoelectric detector that collects the laser signal reflected by the needle and a charge-coupled device camera takes a photo of the defective needle for identification. However, this approach to fault identification is quite expensive and difficult to implement. Furthermore, this device may create a hindrance in the swift workflow of the worker. Zhang et al., also proposed a machine vision-based needle fault detection that was very accurate [30]. But this system required a high-brightness linear supplementary lighting source. This makes the system unrealistic for application in a real-factory scenario. Iftikhar et al., proposed an intelligent automatic fault detection technique incorporating image processing and fuzzy logic [13]. However, the system can only detect machine faults that are visible from the outside.

2.3 Fabric Defect-Based Machine Fault Detection

Several researchers use fabric defect identification for identifying machine faults. A local neighborhood analysis window on the fabric image was used by Kure et al. [17]. He introduced the image variation coefficient that can identify fabric defects. Furthermore, it indirectly gives feedback on the stitch state. Hannay et al., [10] established a fabric defect image database. He performed a shearlet transformation on the fabric image so that he can obtain high-dimensional feature vectors that correspond to defects in the images. Jia et al., fabric defect inspection based on isotropic lattice segmentation [15]. Guanghua et al., proposed a fabric defect identification by a deep convolutional generative adversarial network (DCGAN) [12]. Zhang et al., proposed a fabric defect identification algorithm based on the Gabor filter that can identify machine fault by detecting fabric fault [28]. These approaches can identify machine faults by identifying a fabric fault. But these systems fail when there is a machine fault without occurring any fabric fault. Furthermore, these systems are not real-time. Fouda et al., proposed an online quality control system for a single jersey circular knitting machine [8]. However, this system can not detect machine faults if there is no laddering effect on the produced fabric.

2.4 Machine Learning-Based Fault Detection

Caggiano et al., proposed a machine learning-based image processing for online defect recognition in additive manufacturing [6]. The system detects machine faults by detecting a material defect. Sobie et al., proposed a system for machine learning-based bearing fault detection [25]. In the work, training data for the machine learning algorithm is generated by the information gained from the high-resolution simulation of roller bearings. No real experimentation with bearing was done here for fault detection. Delli et al., proposed an automated process monitoring system in 3D printing by supervised machine learning [7]. In this paper SVM (Support Vector Machine) algorithm was used to classify the parts into the 'good' or 'defective' categories. From identifying the defect, the machine defect was identified. Nasrabadi et al., proposed a CNN-based condition monitoring system for turbine blades [27]. However, this approach fails to detect the type of fault in the machinery. Nisha [21] et al., proposed a fabric defect detection system through image pre-processing, feature extraction, and defect detection and classification by the multi-SVM algorithm. It identifies the presence of any machine fault by identifying fabric faults like an oil stain, ink stain, soil stain, etc. Bandara et al., proposed an automatic fabric defect detection system which in terms indicates machine fault [4]. It detects fabric faults through image pre-processing and Neural Networks.

The major problem with these approaches is, that these systems can detect machine faults only after a defective output is generated. Furthermore, they do not give information on which machine part is defective. In contrast, our system can detect machine faults before the generation of faulty output because it directly detects the machine's fault.

3   Proposed Methodology

In this section, we discuss the construction and working algorithm of our system.

3.1   System Design

Our device consists of one ADXL345 accelerometer, one DS-3231 real-time clock, and an Arduino Uno R3 as a controller module. The block diagram of our device is shown in Fig. 1. The accelerometer senses the vibration data of the machine and gives outputs as acceleration on the X, Y, and Z-axis.

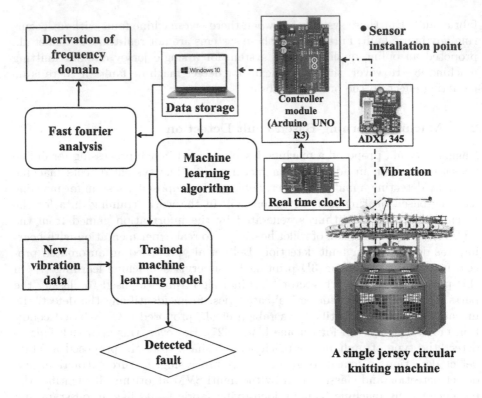

Fig. 1. Block diagram of our proposed system

Sensor. In our previous approach [5], we used the SW-420 vibration sensor. The problem regarding this sensor is, this sensor only gives numerical values indicating the intensity of vibration. It does not show any direction of vibration or any unit of vibration. In the case of the piezo sensor, they require an additional arrangement for measuring vibration, since the signal from the piezo sensor is very low. In order to get more meaningful vibration data, we use ADXL345 accelerometer in this approach. It is a three-axis acceleration measurement system and it has a choosable measurement range of either $\pm 2\,g$, $\pm 4\,g$, $\pm 8\,g$, or $\pm 16\,g$. It measures two types of acceleration. These are dynamic acceleration that results from motion or shock and static acceleration, such as gravity which broadens its application as a tilt sensor. The sensor itself is a poly silicon-surface-micro machined structure that is built on the top of a silicon wafer [26]. It consists of independent fixed plates and plates attached to the moving mass. When vibration occurs, the acceleration deflects the beam and unbalances the differential capacitor, which results in sensor output.

We use PuTTy software for data storage. It is a free and open-source terminal emulator. It can also be used as a serial console and network file transfer application. PuTTy software provides support for several network protocols, including

SCP, SSH, Telnet, login, and raw socket connection. For data collection from Arduino, the software has to be able to connect to the serial port. PuTTy software can connect to the Arduino serial port. The software shows the real-time data on the monitor and saves the data into a text, CSV file. Which can be later used to analyze the data.

Machine Learning. We use the stored raw accelerometer data to train the machine learning algorithms. For each condition 2000 sample data for each axis; in total 3 axes, 6000 sample data were stored for each condition (2000 data for each axis). In total, 42000 sample data was taken on the circular knitting machine under 7 conditions. The sampling rate was 50.

Data Labeling. First, we label the data according to the fault during which the vibration was measured. We use the following labels: Machine_ok, Needle_missing, Broken_hook, Broken_latch, Sinker_missing, Faulty_sinker, Broken_butt_sinker. For each fault, 6000 data points are given on 3 axes (on each axis 2000 data points).

Machine Learning Algorithm. We input the categorized labeled data in eight different machine learning algorithms.
Features: Vibration acceleration on X, Y, and Z axis as input. The type of fault as output.
The algorithms that are used are Decision Tree Classifier, Random Forest Classifier, Support Vector Machine, K Nearest Neighbors, Nearest Centroid, K Nearest Neighbors, Stochastic Gradient Descent, Gaussian Naive Bayes, and Gradient Boosting.

Evaluation of Machine Learning Models. We use ten-fold cross-validation to evaluate our machine learning algorithms by calculating precision, recall, and F1 score. First, the dataset is divided into ten folds. The cross-validation method takes a random fold as the test dataset and takes the remaining nine folds as the training dataset. It then fits a model on the training set and evaluates it based on the test set. Then it takes another fold as the test set and the remaining nine folds as the training set and so on. This process continues until all the folds are taken as a test set. Hence, it gives us ten evaluation results of the model. Finally, we find the mean precision, recall, and F1 scores of the ten test results of the cross-validation.

3.2 Algorithm

We implement our system on one of the most common machinery of the textile industry: the knitting machine. Firstly, we set the ADXL 345 accelerometer on the machine. Then we run the machine in a normal condition. We use PuTTy software for real-time monitoring and storing of the data. After saving

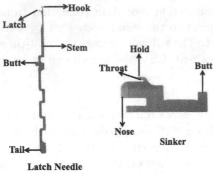

(a) Parts of needle and sinker

(b) Data collection on Saad Knitwear Limited

Fig. 2. Parts of the knitting machine's basic components and experimentation on the weft circular knitting machine

the data for almost 2 min, we stop the machine. We use a sampling rate of 50 samples/second. Then we open the upper cover of the cylinder and take out a needle. Then we start the machine again and monitor and store the vibration data in the same manner. We repeat this process for different conditions such as replacing a proper needle with a hook broken needle or a latch broken needle, replacing a sinker with a faulty sinker or butt broken sinker, and running the machine while a sinker is missing. Then we do a Fast Fourier analysis of the data to find out the frequency of the vibration measured under different conditions. We also do a statistical analysis to find the difference in vibration in different conditions. After that, we label the data according to the respective condition. We use the data set to train eight different machine-learning algorithms. We test the precision, recall, and F1 scores of these trained machine-learning models by ten-fold cross-validation.

4   Experimental Evaluation

In this section, we discuss the experimentation and the analysis of experimented data.

4.1   Industrial Data Collection

We go to the Saad Knitwear Limited knit fabric production section. There we test our device on a circular knitting machine (Fig. 2b) for experimental evaluation and preparation of the data set. We artificially create six different faults in the needle and sinker (the faults are shown in Fig. 3) and measure the vibration during these conditions. The parts of the needle and sinker are shown in Fig. 2a. A significant change in vibration during any fault makes the fault detectable

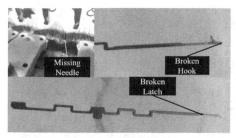

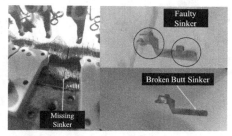

(a) Artificially created needle faults   (b) Artificially created sinker faults

Fig. 3. Artificial faults created on needle and sinker for experimentation

through monitoring of vibration data. The faults that were chosen for experimentation are missing needle, broken needle hook, Broken needle latch, missing sinker, faulty sinker, and butt broken sinker. The reason for choosing these faults is because these faults occur frequently in the knitting machine during normal operation. Furthermore, these faults can create defective fabric which results in a reduction in production efficiency.

Normal Condition. Firstly, we measure the vibration by our device in the normal condition of the circular knitting machine. Then we do the Fast Fourier Analysis of the vibration acceleration on the Z-axis. From the FFT, we plot the acceleration vs frequency graph (Fig. 4a). In this condition, the knitting machine will produce fabric without any fault.

Missing Needle. Then we take a needle out of the machine cylinder. For that, we first remove the cam guiding the needle path. After that, we remove a needle and restart the machine. We measure the vibration and then do an fft on the sensor data (Fig. 4b). If a needle is missing in the knitting machine during production, it can cause an empty straight line on the fabric, resulting in defective fabric and production wastage.

Broken Needle Hook. A broken needle hook can cause severe problems in production by producing drop stitches in the knitted fabric. We replace a perfect needle with the hook broken needle, and then measure the machine's vibration. Then fft of the vibration is done (Fig. 4c).

Broken Needle Latch. A needle latch is used for enclosing the hook during the loop formation of the knitting cycle. We break the latch of the needle and replace a perfect needle in the machine with this latch broken needle. The absence of a latch in the needle can result in absence of loop formation which can finally result in a drop stitch. We measure the machine vibration in this condition and do fft (Fig. 4d).

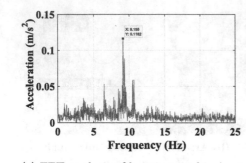

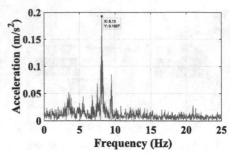

(a) FFT analysis of knitting machine's vibration data in normal condition

(b) FFT analysis of knitting machine's vibration data in needle missing condition

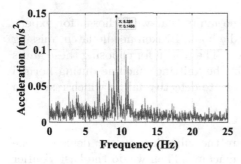

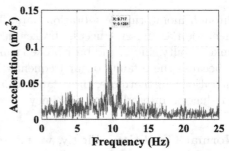

Fig. 4. FFT analysis of knitting machine's vibration data in normal condition and different needle faults

Missing Sinker. Sometimes due to workers' unawareness, sinkers can be found missing from the sinker ring of the circular knitting machine. Since sinkers perform the important function of 'holding down' in weft knitting machines, their absence can cause a heavy fault in the produced fabric. We deliberately take a sinker out of the sinker rail. Then we test and analyze the vibration by Fast Fourier transform (Fig. 5a).

Faulty Sinker. A faulty sinker may fail to perform its function properly. Which will hamper the knitting cycle since it will not perform the holding-down function properly. As a result, defective fabric will be produced. We deliberately bend a sinker on two sides. After that, we replace a perfect sinker with this faulty sinker and restart the machine. Then we follow the same procedure as other conditions (Fig. 5b).

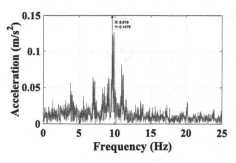

(a) FFT analysis of knitting machine's vibration data in sinker missing condition

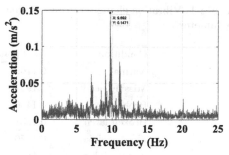

(b) FFT analysis of knitting machine's vibration data in faulty sinker condition

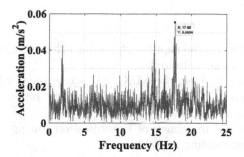

(c) FFT analysis of knitting machine's vibration data in sinker's butt broken condition

Fig. 5. FFT analysis of knitting machine's vibration data in different sinker faults

Butt Broken Sinker. Due to misalignment, the sinkers' butt can be broken. When a sinker butt is broken, it fails to follow the cam track resulting in fault in the fabric. We intentionally break the butt of a sinker and replace that sinker with a perfect sinker for the machine. Finally, we measure the vibration to see if there is any change in total machine vibration due to this fault (shown in Fig. 5c)

4.2 Statistical Analysis

To further evaluate our data set, we perform statistical analysis on our data. We calculate different parameters of our data: mean, median, standard deviation, kurtosis, skewness, minimum and maximum value. Next, we check if there is a difference in these values during different faults.

Table 1. Vibration changes during different faults based on acceleration and frequency parameter

Condition	Acceleration (m/s^2)	Frequency (Hz)
Normal	0.1162	9.155
Missing needle	0.1927	8.13
Broken hook	0.1456	9.326
Broken latch	0.1251	9.717
Missing sinker	0.1476	9.619
Faulty sinker	0.1471	9.692
Broken butt sinker	0.0554	17.65

4.3 Findings

In this section, we discuss the significant findings that we got from the experimentation on Saad knitwear limited.

We find vibration data from the ADXL 345 accelerometer in the acceleration (m/s^2) unit. We then do the Fast Fourier Transform on the data and get the frequency component of the data.

The acceleration and frequency of the vibration during different faults are shown for clear understanding in Table 1.

Comparison Regarding Needle. Firstly we analyze the data from the acceleration values that are expressed in m/s^2. From the acceleration data, we see the strength of the occurring vibration. From Table 1, we plot Fig. 6a. There we see that the vibration measured in acceleration rises when we take out a needle from the cylinder. The acceleration falls a bit after the missing needle spot is replaced with a needle that has a broken hook. However, the vibration still stays higher than in normal condition. Finally, after we replace the hook broken needle with a latch broken needle, the vibration falls a bit more while still being higher than normal vibration. Overall, we see a clear distinction in the acceleration caused by vibration during different faults.

Then we analyze the data based on frequency values that are derived from Fast Fourier Analysis. The frequency values express the no of vibration cycles per second. In other words, it expressed the intensity of the machine vibration. We plot Fig. 6b from the data of Table 1. The vibration frequency drops significantly when we take out a needle from the cylinder. The frequency rises significantly again after we replace the empty needle spot with a hook broken needle. The frequency rises further when the hook broken needle is replaced with a latch broken needle.

From the two graphs in Fig. 6 we can see that during a needle fault, while the acceleration increases the frequency of the vibration decreases, and when the acceleration decreases the frequency increases. We can detect the needle faults in a weft circular knitting machine by observing these changes in vibration acceleration and frequency.

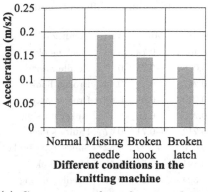

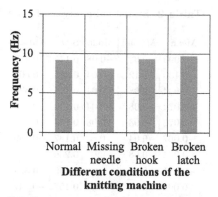

(a) Comparison of acceleration due to vibration during different needle faults obtained from FFT

(b) Comparison of vibration frequency data during different needle faults obtained from FFT

Fig. 6. Comparison of vibration data during different needle faults obtained from Fast Fourier Analysis

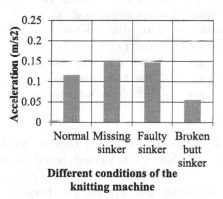

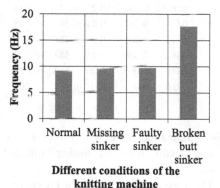

(a) Comparison of acceleration due to vibration during different sinker faults obtained from FFT

(b) Comparison of vibration frequency data during different sinker faults obtained from FFT

Fig. 7. Comparison of vibration data during different sinker faults obtained from Fast Fourier Analysis

Comparison Regarding Sinker. We plot Fig. 7 from the data of Table 1. In the case of sinker faults, Fig. 7a shows that the acceleration due to vibration rises significantly when we take out a sinker from the sinker ring of the circular knitting machine. The acceleration falls on a very tiny amount after the sinker's missing spot is replaced with a faulty sinker. However, the vibration acceleration

Table 2. Statistical analysis of the vibration data during different faults

Axis	Mean	Median	Mode	S.D	Kurtosis	Skewness	Min	Max	Condition
X	−0.090	−0.08	−0.08	0.175	0.439	−0.402	−0.78	0.43	Machine ok
	−0.130	−0.12	−0.04	0.215	−0.602	−0.078	−0.75	0.47	Needle missing
	−0.084	−0.08	−0.04	0.194	−0.328	−0.287	−0.71	0.43	Broken hook
	−0.074	−0.08	−0.04	0.193	−0.291	0.249	−0.67	0.47	Broken latch
	−0.072	−0.08	−0.08	0.184	−0.333	−0.235	−0.63	0.47	Sinker missing
	−0.067	−0.04	0	0.187	−0.169	−0.212	−0.71	0.47	Faulty sinker
	−0.064	−0.08	−0.04	0.266	0.036	−0.030	−1.22	0.82	Sinker butt broken
Y	−0.011	0	0	0.149	0.394	0.191	−0.51	0.55	Machine ok
	0.006	0	−0.04	0.157	−0.147	0.304	−0.39	0.59	Needle missing
	−0.011	0	−0.12	0.189	−0.486	0.194	−0.47	0.59	Broken hook
	−0.013	−0.04	−0.08	0.200	−0.478	0.117	−0.59	0.59	Broken latch
	−0.020	−0.04	−0.08	0.203	−0.507	0.041	−0.63	0.55	Sinker missing
	−0.013	−0.04	−0.04	0.210	−0.562	0.091	−0.55	0.55	Faulty sinker
	−0.399	−0.39	−0.12	0.407	−0.683	−0.005	−1.49	0.67	Sinker butt broken
Z	−0.001	0.010	0.05	0.332	−0.151	−0.162	−0.970	0.870	Machine ok
	0.000	−0.001	−0.2	0.423	−0.948	0.058	−1.021	0.979	Needle missing
	−0.001	0.017	0.24	0.405	−0.848	−0.016	−1.003	0.997	Broken hook
	0.001	0.030	0.3	0.427	−0.804	−0.031	−1.110	1.170	Broken latch
	0.001	−0.008	0.34	0.433	−0.963	−0.028	−1.108	1.172	Sinker missing
	0.005	−0.005	0.30	0.446	−0.927	−0.022	−1.305	1.135	Faulty sinker
	−0.001	−0.002	−0.04	0.281	0.008	−0.033	−1.022	1.058	Sinker butt broken

falls significantly when the faulty sinker is replaced with a butt broken sinker. Hence, we can detect any sinker fault in the machine by monitoring the vibration data.

Then we analyze the data based on the frequency of Fig. 7b. The frequency of the vibration rises slightly when a sinker is taken out of the machine. The frequency rises a very tiny amount when the sinker missing spot is replaced with a faulty sinker. The frequency rises significantly after the faulty sinker is replaced with a butt-broken sinker.

During the sinker faults, as the acceleration due to vibration increased the frequency or the intensity of the vibration decreased. And the frequency of the vibration increased when the acceleration due to vibration decreased. The faults of the sinker in a weft circular knitting machine can be detected by observing these changes in vibration data.

Result of Statistical Analysis. Table 2 shows some statistical analysis of our dataset. We see that, on three different axes, there is a significant change in the different parameters such as mean, median, kurtosis, skewness, etc. of the vibration data. As we artificially create a fault in the machine, the machine's vibration changes. Hence, feeding this data to any machine learning algorithm can help in detecting the machine fault by measuring its vibration.

Table 3. Evaluation of our machine learning models

ML Algorithm	Precision (%)	Recall (%)	F1 score (%)
DecisionTree Classifier	99.4	98.3	98.9
Gradient Boosting	100	39.5	56.5
Random Forest Classifier	48.3	28.6	36.8
K Nearest Neighbors	28.1	26.3	26.6
Gaussian Naive Bayes	24.0	26.0	24.0
Support Vector Machine	21.0	23.0	20.0
Stochastic Gradient Descent	12.3	22.1	13.9
Nearest Centroid	16.2	54.2	24.5

Accuracy of ML Models. Through cross-validation, we find the highest precision in the Gradient Boosting classifier and highest recall and F1 score in the Decision Tree Classifier algorithm, and the lowest in the Nearest Centroid algorithm. The precision, recall, and F1 scores of the machine learning model in different algorithms are shown in Table 3. The reason for finding the highest recall and F1 score and very high precision is the type of our data set. Our data set has discontinuous data which are very suitable for the Decision Tree Classifier algorithm. The recall and F1 scores in Random Forest Classifier were low because this algorithm works well with high dimensional data which has a large number of features. However, our data set has only 3 features. The number of estimators used was five. The support vector machine has low precision, recall, and F1 score for the same reason as the random forest algorithm. SVM also works well with high-dimensional data. Since our data is low dimensional, SVM has low accuracy. We use the linear kernel for SVM as it gives better accuracy than using other kernels. For the K Nearest Neighbor Classifier highest accuracy is found when the number of neighbors is one.

4.4   Fault Detection for Other Machinery

This methodology can be used to detect the fault in other machinery. The vibration is largely dependent on the unique structure of every machine. To implement this system, first, a fault data set have to be prepared by measuring the machine vibration during different fault. Then we have to train different machine learning algorithms using this data set and use those trained models to detect machine faults.

5   Real-Device Construction

To construct a device that can detect the machine's fault in real-time, we need to apply the machine learning algorithm in Arduino. We use the micromlgen library in python to get the raw code of different machine-learning algorithms according

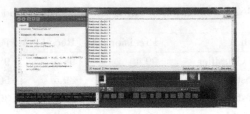

Fig. 8. Application of machine learning model in Arduino Uno

to our data set. We use that code to produce a header file that can be used to make an Arduino library. We use that library in Arduino. The Arduino then can detect machine faults on spot and show the machine fault in the serial monitor. This device only consists of an Arduino Uno and an accelerometer. Hence, by using this low-resource device, the maintenance personnel and machine operators can detect machine faults in real-time.

6   Conclusion

This paper presents a machine learning-based fault detection system for textile machinery. We prepare a machinery fault data set from real experimentation on textile machinery. Fast Fourier analysis of the data indicates that the machinery shows a change in vibration frequency when during the occurrence of any fault. Furthermore, we develop different machine learning models that can detect machinery faults by training eight different machine learning algorithms. Among the different machine learning algorithms, the Decision Tree Classifier algorithm shows 98.9% F1 score. We measure these parameters through ten-fold cross-validation. The maintenance department in the textile industry can detect machine faults automatically with the help of our fault detection system which can reduce the chances of faulty fabric production. This can result in improving the production efficiency and safety of machinery.

In the future, we will test the impact of different sampling frequencies on the accuracy of machine-learning models. Furthermore, we plan to produce a more effective data set by varying more parameters in a textile machine. We will test our device for real-time fault detection in industry scenarios.

Acknowledgements. We would like to thank Bangladesh University of Textiles for funding this research. We would also like to acknowledge Saad Knitwear Limited for data collection purposes.

References

1. Ahmad, H.S.: Introduction to knitting. In: Structural Textile Design, pp. 185–196. CRC Press (2017)
2. Alamelu Manghai, T., Jegadeeshwaran, R.: Vibration based brake health monitoring using wavelet features: a machine learning approach. J. Vib. Control **25**(18), 2534–2550 (2019)
3. Aravanis, T.C., Sakellariou, J., Fassois, S.: A stochastic functional model based method for random vibration based robust fault detection under variable non-measurable operating conditions with application to railway vehicle suspensions. J. Sound Vib. **466**, 115006 (2020)
4. Bandara, P., Bandara, T., Ranatunga, T., Vimarshana, V., Sooriyaarachchi, S., De Silva, C.: Automated fabric defect detection. In: 2018 18th International Conference on Advances in ICT for Emerging Regions (ICTer), pp. 119–125. IEEE (2018)
5. Bhuiyan, M.H.R., Arafat, I.M., Rahaman, M., Toha, T.R., Alam, S.M.M.: Towards devising a vibration based machinery health monitoring system. Mater. Today Proc. **56**, 2490–2496 (2021)
6. Caggiano, A., Zhang, J., Alfieri, V., Caiazzo, F., Gao, R., Teti, R.: Machine learning-based image processing for on-line defect recognition in additive manufacturing. CIRP Ann. **68**(1), 451–454 (2019)
7. Delli, U., Chang, S.: Automated process monitoring in 3D printing using supervised machine learning. Procedia Manufact. **26**, 865–870 (2018)
8. Fouda, A.E.F.: Online quality control system in single jersey circular knitting machine dept. t. MEJ. Mansoura Eng. J. **45**(3), 6–10 (2020)
9. Han, S., Chen, Y., Ye, S.: Design and implementation of real time monitoring system of textile equipment based on MQTT. J. Phys. Conf. Ser. **1948**(1), 012024 (2021). https://doi.org/10.1088/1742-6596/1948/1/012024
10. Hanbay, K., Talu, M.F., Özgüven, Ö.F., Öztürk, D.: Real-time detection of knitting fabric defects using shearlet transform. Text. Apparel **29**(1), 1–10 (2019)
11. Hasan, M.Z., Haque, S., Khan, E.A.N., et al.: Buyer paying lower price of bangladeshi apparel: an empirical investigation on causes. Am. Sci. Res. J. Eng. Technol. Sci. (ASRJETS) **72**(1), 152–161 (2020)
12. Hu, G., Huang, J., Wang, Q., Li, J., Xu, Z., Huang, X.: Unsupervised fabric defect detection based on a deep convolutional generative adversarial network. Text. Res. J. **90**(3–4), 247–270 (2020)
13. Iftikhar, K., Anwar, S., Khan, M.T., Djawad, Y.A.: An intelligent automatic fault detection technique incorporating image processing and fuzzy logic. In: Journal of Physics: Conference Series, vol. 1244, p. 012035. IOP Publishing (2019)
14. Islam, M.S.: Ready-made garments exports earning and its contribution to economic growth in Bangladesh. GeoJournal **86**(3), 1301–1309 (2021)
15. Jia, L., Liang, J.: Fabric defect inspection based on isotropic lattice segmentation. J. Franklin Inst. **354**(13), 5694–5738 (2017)
16. Ku, P., Zhang, Z., Xu, G., Yang, D.: Design and analysis of finishing and detection device for knitting needle. In: 2021 4th International Conference on Advanced Electronic Materials, Computers and Software Engineering (AEMCSE), pp. 1254–1259. IEEE (2021)
17. Kure, N., Biradar, M.S., Bhangale, K.B.: Local neighborhood analysis for fabric defect detection. In: 2017 International Conference on Information, Communication, Instrumentation and Control (ICICIC), pp. 1–5. IEEE (2017)

18. Kushwah, K., Sahoo, S., Joshuva, A.: Health monitoring of wind turbine blades through vibration signal using machine learning techniques. In: Maji, A.K., Saha, G., Das, S., Basu, S., Tavares, J.M.R.S. (eds.) Proceedings of the International Conference on Computing and Communication Systems. LNNS, vol. 170, pp. 239–247. Springer, Singapore (2021). https://doi.org/10.1007/978-981-33-4084-8_22

19. Mauricio, A., Qi, J., Gryllias, K.: Vibration-based condition monitoring of wind turbine gearboxes based on cyclostationary analysis. J. Eng. Gas Turbines Power **141**(3) (2019)

20. Mohamad, T.H., Nazari, F., Nataraj, C.: A review of phase space topology methods for vibration-based fault diagnostics in nonlinear systems. J. Vibr. Eng. Technol. **8**(3), 393–401 (2020)

21. Nisha, F., Vasuki, P., Mansoor Roomi, M.: Fabric defect detection using sparse representation algorithm. J. Eng. 1–7 (2018)

22. Patange, A.D., Jegadeeshwaran, R., Dhobale, N.C.: Milling cutter condition monitoring using machine learning approach. IOP Conf. Ser. Mater. Sci. Eng. **624**(1), 012030 (2019). https://doi.org/10.1088/1757-899x/624/1/012030

23. Peeters, C., Antoni, J., Helsen, J.: Blind filters based on envelope spectrum sparsity indicators for bearing and gear vibration-based condition monitoring. Mech. Syst. Signal Process. **138**, 106556 (2020). https://doi.org/10.1016/j.ymssp.2019.106556. https://www.sciencedirect.com/science/article/pii/S0888327019307770

24. Senapaty, G., Rao, U.S.: Vibration based condition monitoring of rotating machinery. In: MATEC Web of Conferences, vol. 144, p. 01021. EDP Sciences (2018)

25. Sobie, C., Freitas, C., Nicolai, M.: Simulation-driven machine learning: bearing fault classification. Mech. Syst. Signal Process. **99**, 403–419 (2018)

26. technology way, O.: Adxl345 pdf, adxl345 description, adxl345 datasheets, adxl345 view alldatasheet (2021). https://pdf1.alldatasheet.com/datasheet-pdf/view/254714/AD/ADXL345.html. Accessed 20 Sept 2021

27. Yaghoubi Nasrabadi, V., Cheng, L., Van Paepegem, W., Kersemans, M.: Data preparation for training CNNs : application to vibration-based condition monitoring. In: 1st NeurIPS Data-Centric AI workshop (DCAI 2021), Proceedings, p. 5 (2021). https://datacentricai.org/neurips21/papers/103_CameraReady_Yaghoubi_DCAI_CR.pdf

28. Zhang, D., Gao, G., Li, C.: Fabric defect detection algorithm based on gabor filter and low-rank decomposition. In: Eighth International Conference on Digital Image Processing (ICDIP 2016), vol. 10033, p. 100330L. International Society for Optics and Photonics (2016)

29. Zhang, Z., et al.: Knitting needle fault detection system for hosiery machine based on laser detection and machine vision. Text. Res. J. **91**(1–2), 143–151 (2021)

30. Zhang, Z., et al.: Research on the knitting needle detection system of a hosiery machine based on machine vision. Text. Res. J. **90**(15–16), 1730–1740 (2020)

Easing Construction of Smart Agriculture Applications Using Low Code Development Tools

Isaac Nyabisa Oteyo[1,2]([✉]), Angel Luis Scull Pupo[1], Jesse Zaman[1], Stephen Kimani[2], Wolfgang De Meuter[1], and Elisa Gonzalez Boix[1]

[1] Software Languages Lab, Vrije Universiteit Brussel, Brussels, Belgium
{isaac.nyabisa.oteyo,angel.luis.scull.pupo,jesse.zaman,
wolfgang.de.meuter,elisa.gonzalez.boix}@vub.be
[2] School of Computing and Information Technology, Jomo Kenyatta University of Agriculture and Technology, Nairobi, Kenya
skimani@scit.jkuat.ac.ke

Abstract. Smart agriculture applications are a promising path to the future of modern farming. Building smart agriculture applications is a complex undertaking that requires considering different factors, such as the technology that can be used to implement the applications. These factors require advanced skills in software construction, such as handling the distributed setting for smart agriculture applications. As such, implementing smart agriculture applications requires engaging experienced developers with the skills to tackle the issues mentioned above. Low code development tools have risen that domain experts (e.g., agricultural extension workers that give advice to farmers) outside software engineering can use to construct software applications. The low code development tools provide visual programming environments that developers can use intuitively to construct applications. However, the existing low code development tools do not offer support for low infrastructure networking that sensors can use to communicate directly to mobile devices (e.g., smartphones and tablets), computation at the edge, and offline accessibility capabilities at the edge that are crucial for smart agriculture applications. In this paper, we present DisCoPar-K, a low code development tool that supports the properties mentioned above for implementing smart agriculture applications. We show how DisCoPar-K can improve the development of smart agriculture applications by implementing smart agriculture use cases on it.

Keywords: mobile applications · visual programming · smart agriculture · Internet of Things · cloud computing · edge computing

1 Introduction

Smart agriculture (SA) is a modern farming approach that is increasingly being exploited to improve processes, such as monitoring environmental conditions [5]. As a discipline, SA encompasses a set of technologies such as the Internet of Things, cloud computing,

S. Longfei and P. Bodhi (Eds.): MobiQuitous 2022, LNICST 492, pp. 21–43, 2023.
https://doi.org/10.1007/978-3-031-34776-4_2

and mobile applications that are integrated into smart agriculture applications (SAAs). Collectively, the SAAs can be applied to sensing environmental conditions, such as soil moisture and temperature [30]. The soil moisture and temperature conditions are critical parameters in the growth and development of crops right from the seeding and sprouting stage to maturity [35]. In fact, the sprouting of seeds determines the population of crops that reach maturity and, hence, the overall yield. As such, for agricultural extension workers and farmers to achieve optimal yields, it is important to keep track of the soil moisture and temperature conditions at the seeding and sprouting stage. By definition, agricultural extension workers advise and assist farmers to implement creative technologies geared toward improving yields [20]. As mentioned before, keeping track of soil moisture and temperature conditions can be done using sensors and SAAs. In this case, the sensors can be programmed to collect data and send it to the farmer's mobile phone in a timely fashion for decision-making. However, farm restrictions such as the physical space that must be covered to track the soil moisture and temperature conditions impose a constraint that forces the SAAs to be designed and implemented in a distributed setting. Designing and implementing SAAs in a distributed setting requires technological factors to be considered such as handling distribution and micro-controller programming. The technological factors require a combination of skills to implement the different parts of SAAs, e.g., distributed programming skills are required to handle the communication between the different components [6]. The SAAs rely on communication networks for the different parts to communicate with each other, something that can fail to happen when the networks become unavailable [19]. In such cases, data coming from the sensors can be lost, and this needs to be handled in the implementation. Lastly, micro-controller programming skills are required to specify how the application can receive data from sensors or process data near the source using sensors. This means that implementing all the different parts of SAAs can take considerable time.

Low code development tools (LCDTs) have risen as an alternative that domain experts outside software engineering (such as agricultural extension workers) can use to implement software applications [6, 22]. By definition, LCDTs are visual programming environments (VPEs) in which applications are constructed by dragging, dropping, and connecting visual components that represent different tasks in the application [22, 29]. To explain it in context, let's consider constructing *DiscoSense*, a sensing application for soil moisture and temperature conditions using LCDTs. The *DiscoSense* application requires connecting a soil moisture sensing component, a temperature sensing component, and a component to receive and display the data on the mobile phone. In addition, *DiscoSense* requires components that can process the data on the sensor (edge) and only send the aggregate values to the mobile phone. To avoid losing data when the network becomes unavailable, the application requires storing data on the sensor. The unavailable network can also affect the communication between the application and the server. As such, *DiscoSense* requires that the sensors collecting soil moisture and temperature data communicate directly to the mobile phone without going through a centralised server. The existing LCDTs partially support the above issues, such as environment sensing capabilities. In addition, the existing LCDTs are provided on the cloud through Platform-as-a-Service [22]. This can hinder the functioning of SAAs in areas that experience poor network coverage. To the best of our knowledge, none of the existing LCDTs offers support for: 1) low infrastructure networking for sensors to communicate directly to SAAs running on mobile devices, 2) components to support computation at the edge to process data near the source, and 3) components to support offline accessibility at the edge to store data on sensors when the network connection becomes unavailable. As such, none of the existing LCDTs can be used to implement *DiscoSense* or similar SAAs. For instance, DisCoPar [31–33], the LCDT that we consider in this work lacks components that can execute at the edge and directly communicate with applications running on smartphones or tablets without going through a centralised server.

In this paper, we extend DisCoPar [31–33] with an additional execution point to host components that can run on the edge. We implement components for environment sensing and performing computations at the edge that are domiciled in the new scope. We further advance the policies for offline accessibility on mobile devices to limit connecting a chain of successive offline accessibility components. In addition, we implement components for offline accessibility at the edge. In our implementations, we ensure that the components executing at the edge can communicate directly to those on mobile devices without going through a centralised server. This results in DisCoPar-Kilimo (DisCoPar-K), a low code development tool that we present in this paper. For validation, we show how DisCoPar-K can improve the development of SAAs by implementing smart agriculture use cases on it. From a theoretical perspective, we identify different properties that LCDTs should have to support implementing SAAs. We use the identified properties to compare different LCDTs that exist in the literature and motivate our work. To the best of our knowledge, our contribution is unique in the context of LCDTs. The rest of the paper is organised as follows. Section 2 presents the motivation and background. Section 3 describes DisCoPa-K together with the extensions added to support implementing SAAs. Section 4 describes the validation and discussions of the implemented use cases. Lastly, Sect. 5 presents the conclusions and gives directions for future work.

2   Motivation and Background

To motivate our approach, consider the scenario of corn seeding and sprouting, where the farmer's goal is to obtain the *maximum yield* from seeds planted. This is a representative scenario for SAAs derived from El-Sanatawy et al. [11], Sudozai et al. [26], and our interactions with extension workers and farmers in Kenya. To achieve the *maximum yield* goal, the crop must develop 'well' during all the 'cultivation' phases, i.e., planting, sprouting, developing, and maturity. Specifically, during the stage that encompasses seeding and sprouting of corn, maximum yield is ensured whenever 'optimal' sprouting is achieved. Optimal sprouting means that from the number of seeds planted, there is a threshold on the number of plants which does not affect the expected yield. To achieve such a threshold, farmers have to keep track of vital environmental conditions such as soil moisture and temperature that influence the sprouting of corn seeds [35]. The soil moisture gives an indication of the available water content to support the sprouting of corn seeds, i.e., inadequate soil moisture and extremely low or high temperatures negatively affect seed sprouting. As such, these conditions cannot be monitored in isolation.

Researchers have invented metrics that can give a general overview for soil moisture and temperature conditions, such as the *soil heat capacity* metric [35]. The soil heat capacity metric is important in explaining the interaction between soil moisture and temperature. As such, this metric can help farmers to react and take appropriate actions to ensure the optimal sprouting of corn seeds. Currently, the metric is measured using field observation approaches, such as calorimetric and force-restore methods [13]. The current practices can be improved by implementing the corn seeding and sprouting scenario as a smart agriculture application using LCDTs, since extension workers do not have a strong background in software programming. However, implementing the scenario requires LCDTs to support the following properties.

Environment sensing. The property is important to help in monitoring the prevailing soil moisture and temperature conditions. In the context of LCDTs, this property refers to whether LCDTs have in-built environment sensing capabilities for soil moisture and temperature conditions. In our scenario, the soil moisture and temperature conditions that are vital for corn seeding and sprouting cannot be read in isolation.

Computation at the edge. *Edge computation* is necessary to transform the data collected near the source into meaningful information. In our scenario, the computation that combines the soil moisture and temperature into the *soil heat capacity* metric can be performed at the edge. To minimise the number of requests sent to the server over communication networks, other computations, such as the average soil moisture and temperature, can be done at the edge before the aggregate values are sent to the mobile device.

Offline accessibility at the edge. In our scenario, we assume that the application for sensing the soil moisture and temperature conditions is programmed by the domain expert (agricultural extension worker) and used by the farmer. As mentioned before, the network connection may become unavailable and this can make the different parts of SAAs not communicate with each other. The 'availability' of the soil moisture and temperature data is key to making correct decisions about corn seeding and sprouting. Therefore, the microcontroller that is hosting sensors must be capable of *keeping all the data* that the sensors generate whenever the network becomes unavailable. It is assumed that farmers that are using the sensing application visit the farm at least once every day.

Low infrastructure networking. The *low infrastructure networking* property refers to whether different parts of a smart agriculture application constructed using LCDTs can communicate with each other without going through a centralised server as illustrated in Fig. 1. Relying on centralised cloudhosted servers can be a challenge in remote farms that experience unreliable internet connections [19].

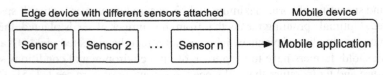

Fig. 1. Edge device featuring sensors communicating to a mobile application without a centralised cloud-hosted server.

In the next section, we use the above properties to perform a state-of-the-art (SOTA) analysis for LCDTs.

2.1 SOTA of LCDTs for Building SAAs

Table 1 shows a summary of the SOTA for different LCDTs. The LCDTs that were included in this summary were based on support for a web-based VPE. Secondly, we included LCDTs that are targeted for environmental sensing. All surveyed LCDTs provide support for web-based VPEs and environment sensing capabilities. However, in some tools like Node-RED, the sensing capability needs to be constructed into the target smart agriculture application. DisCoPar supports offline accessibility on mobile devices using in-database storage. None of the surveyed LCDTs supports low infrastructure networking, computation at the edge, and offline accessibility at the edge.

Table 1. Summary comparison of different low code development tools.

Tool	We-based VPE	Sensing capabilities	Offline accessibility	Edge computation	Low infrastructure networking
Mendix [15, 17]	✓	✓	✗	✗	✗
Blynk [12]	✓	✓	✗	✗	✗
AtmosphericIoT [3]	✓	✓	✗	✗	✗
Zenodys [34]	✓	✓	✗	✗	✗
Axonize [4]	✓	✓	✗	✗	✗
FRED [9]	✓	✓	✗	✗	✗
Node-RED [1]	✓	✓	✗	✗	✗
Simplifier [25]	✓	✓	✗	✗	✗
Salesforce [11, 23]	✓	✓	✗	✗	✗
D-NR [8]	✓	✓	✗	✗	✗
uFlow [27]	✓	✓	✗	✗	✗
DDFlow [18]	✓	✓	✗	✗	✗
WotKit Processor [7]	✓	✓	✗	✗	✗
glue.things [16]	✓	✓	✗	✗	✗
DisCoPar [31–33]	✓	✓	✓	✗	✗

From the LCDTs presented in Table 1, in DisCoPar: 1) computation tasks in applications are highly conceptualised into visual components for novice developers, and 2) the tool supports implementing web and mobile applications using drag-and-drop and point-and-click graphical user interface techniques. These techniques can be intuitive and useful to domain experts for constructing SAAs. Therefore, in this paper, we consider DisCoPar and extend it with components to support the properties that we previously identified for developing SAAs.

2.2 DisCoPar

DisCoPar embraces a flow-based programming approach in which an application is built out of different visual components, each representing a computation task [31–33]. The application is represented as a directed acyclic graph of n connected components. The example in Fig. 2 shows an application composed of three connected components (C1, C2, and C3) in one linear graph. Components execute on receiving data from external sources or upstream components. The computation results are sent out on the output ports (e.g., $C_1(out)$ and $C_2(out)$ in Fig. 2) to the downstream components. Upstream components precede the reference component backwards, while downstream components succeed the reference component forward. In Fig. 2, C1 is an upstream component to C2, while C3 is a downstream component to C2. Components can have zero or multiple input and output ports. In Fig. 2, components C1 and C2 have one output port each; C2 and C3 have one input port each. In terms of the task performed, the components in Fig. 2 can be classified into either *source* components (e.g., C1), *processor* components (e.g., C2) or *sink* (e.g., C3) components. As the name suggests, the *source* components generate data, while the *processor* components perform some processing and transformation of data flowing through the application graph. Some of the *sink* components can be used as viewing monitors to display data flowing through the application and build graphical user interfaces for applications.

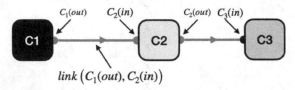

Fig. 2. Application flow graph featuring component ports and links.

Components are linked together via connections or arcs. DisCoPar's VPE only allows end-users to perform correct connections among data types on different components. In this regard, the composition mechanism is based on the supported data type, denoted by a distinct port colour. Therefore, given two components A and B, we can define $P_{input}(B)$ and $P_{output}(A)$ as the sets of input and output ports on components B and A, respectively. Outport $j \in P_{output}(A)$ and input port $k \in P_{input}(B)$ are compatible if they support the same data type such that they have the same port colour e.g., $c_1(out)$ and $c_2(in)$ in Fig. 2 or at least $k \in P_{input}(B)$ is coloured black e.g., $c_3(in)$ in Fig. 2, to accept any data. This implies that components A and B are compatible if $\exists j \in P_{output}(A)$ and $\exists k \in P_{input}(B)$ such that j and k are compatible. Component links have a colour coding that is inherited from the colour coding in the output port of the source component. In Fig. 2, $link(c_1(out), c_2(in))$ inherits the colour coding for port $c_1(out)$ in C1. Application designers can create connections between components in different scopes the same way they create connections between components in the same scope. Connections made between components residing in different devices are automatically handled by DisCoPar. For communication between components and graphs in different devices, DisCoPar uses web sockets (Socket.IO[1]) and RxJs[2].

Component Categories: DisCoPar applications run on mobile phones and communicate to a server backend or a web-based dashboard on the server. Depending on where the execution happens, components can be classified into three categories/scopes: mobile, server, and web components. The mobile scope contains components that execute on mobile devices (e.g., smartphones and tablets). The server scope contains components that execute on the server side for data processing. Lastly, the web scope contains components for web-based analysis and visualisation. Such components are used to build the dashboard for the server side. Some components can span multiple scopes, e.g., mobile and web scopes. Each scope houses respective components on the component menu represented as component categories, i.e., mobile, server, and dashboard.

3   DisCoPar-K

DisCoPar-K is an extension of DisCoPar to support environment sensing capabilities, computation at the edge, offline accessibility at the edge, and low infrastructure networking for SAAs. In this section, we describe the architectural overview and components that comprise DisCoPar-K.

Architectural Overview: Figure 3 shows the architecture of DisCoPar-K. The architecture consists of four different parts labelled 1, 2, 3, and 4 in Fig. 3, i.e., sensors at the edge, a mobile application, a server with a database, and a web dashboard for visualisation.

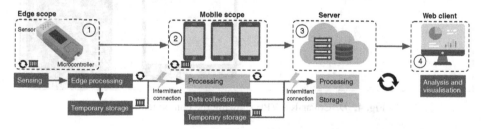

Fig. 3. Architectural overview of DisCoPar-K.

The work presented in this paper focuses on the parts labelled 1 (the edge scope) and 2 (the mobile scope) in Fig. 3. The edge scope hosts components that can execute on microcontrollers that have sensors attached to them. The sensors are used to gather data such as soil moisture and air temperature. The data collected is initially processed at the edge before being sent directly to mobile devices for further processing. The lightning strikes in Fig. 3 indicate intermittent network connections. When the network becomes

---

[1] https://socket.io/.

[2] https://rxjs.dev/.

unavailable, the collected data can be stored temporarily at the edge for transmission to mobile devices when the network becomes available. From mobile devices, the data can be sent to the server for storage and visualisation on a web dashboard. On mobile devices, the data can also be stored when the network becomes unavailable for transmission to the server when the network becomes available.

DisCoPar-K extensions: The extensions that comprise DisCoPar-K fall into the categories described below.

Visual Programming Environment: Components from the mobile, server and web scopes could not fully support implementing SAAs. As such, we extended DisCoPar with the edge scope as shown in the component menu in Fig. 4 (highlighted in yellow colour) to house components that support: 1) environment sensing, 2) computation at the edge and 3) offline accesibility at the edge. On the VPE, these components are distinguished by the blue colour. For example, in Fig. 4, the *ReadSoilMoisture* component is coloured blue and executes at the edge (i.e., sensors), while the *UnWrap* component is coloured black and executes on the mobile phone. Figure 4 shows the visual programming environment for DisCoPar-K with the added edge scope components.

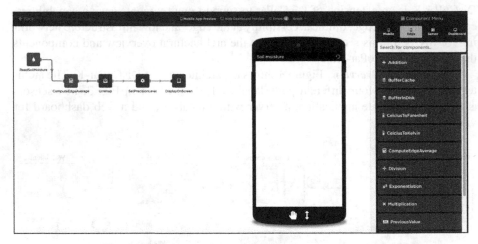

Fig. 4. DisCoPar-K's VPE showing the component menu.

On top of the existing components in DisCoPar, we added more components to meet different application requirements (goals) in the context of SA. Some of the requirements that were implemented into components include:

- *Keeping track on the number of connected devices:-* To accomplish this goal, we added the *ConnectedDevices* and *DataArrayToTable* components that function as follows. The *ConnectedDevices* component subscribes to an event to receive messages that contain the identity of each connected device. The received message is processed to remove duplicate entries, leaving only unique connections using the *DataArray-ToTable* component. The processed message is then converted into a dataset for display as a list using the *DisplayAsList* component. Each unique connection is counted to determine the number of connected devices that are displayed on the screen using the *DisplayOnScreen* component. In the *DataArrayToTable* component, each received message is stored in an array, and the array is then converted into a set to remove duplicates and return a new array with unique entries. Each element in the new array is converted into observation to meet the design requirements of DisCoPar-K. Each observation is then added to a global counter that keeps the total number of connected devices.

– *Accumulating data from different devices:-* To accomplish this goal, we added the *DeviceAccumulator* component that can accumulate data from several sensor devices. The component receives input data and stores it on a map using the device identifier as the key and the payload as the value. As a configuration setting, the component takes the number of connected devices from which to accumulate data. On its output port, the component sends only the values of data stored on the map and immediately resets the map to start accumulating new data.

– *Filtering data coming from sensors:-* We added the *UnWrap* and *UnWrapForSpecificDevice* components to accomplish this goal. The *UnWrap* component filters the payload from sensor data, while *UnWrapForSpecificDevice* component filters the payload for specific sensor devices. The *UnWrapForSpecificDevice* component takes as a configuration setting the identifier of the device to filter data for.

– *Generating and showing notifications:-* For this goal, we added the *SetThreshold* and *GenerateAndShowAlert* components. The *SetThreshold* component is configurable and takes the threshold or limit as a setting parameter. The set parameter is periodically sent out of the output port of the component. The *GenerateAndShowAlert* is configurable to specify the notification messages. For these two components to perform their tasks, we modified the existing *Compare* component to receive two inputs (the threshold from the *SetThreshold* component and some input data) and output a true/false value that can trigger the *GenerateAndShowAlert* component to generate and show notifications.

– *Sensing capabilities:-* To support sensing at the edge, we added the *ReadSoilMoisture*, *ReadTemperature*, and *ReadHumidity* components to read soil moisture, air temperature, and humidity, respectively. The three components directly receive input from the sensors.

– *Computing metrics at the edge:-* For computation at the edge, we added the following components: *SetConstant*, *Addition*, *Subtraction*, *Multiplication*, *Exponentiation*, and *ComputeEdgeAverage* components. The names of these components are indicative of the tasks that they perform.

Offline Accessibility Policies: We advance DisCoPar's offline accessibility both at the mobile and edge scope. DisCoPar-K implements policies to ensure that the offline accessibility components that execute on the mobile whenever used in an application graph can only be the last ones in the chain to connect to the server side. This means that an offline accessibility component on the mobile side cannot be connected to another mobile component or another offline accessibility component in a chain of successive components. For instance, in Fig. 5, the *InDatabaseBuffering* component that supports offline accessibility in the application can only be connected to the *ObservationDatabase* component that runs on the server side. In a similar way, while implementing edge applications, the buffering component on the edge should be the last one to connect to the mobile side downstream as shown in Fig. 6.

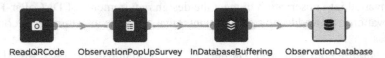

ReadQRCode   ObservationPopUpSurvey   InDatabaseBuffering   ObservationDatabase

Fig. 5. Application flow graph showing the *BufferObservation* connecting to *Observation-Database* component on the server-side.

Computation and Offline Accessibility at the Edge: In this work, we introduce edge components to perform computation at the edge. The edge components execute on the microcontroller on which sensors are attached. For instance, the *ReadSoilMoisture* component in Fig. 6 executes the *ReadSoilMoisture()* function which reads soil moisture from sensors.

At the edge, we implement a *BufferCache* component for buffering data in memory when the network becomes unavailable. The buffering in this component is based on the number of records. The buffer size can be specified as a configuration setting for the component. When the network becomes unavailable, sensor readings are stored until the buffer size is full. At this point, the oldest record is removed from memory to create room for new data. When the network becomes available, additional metadata is appended to the buffered data and then sent to the mobile application. The metadata contains the unique identifier for the sensor and the identifier of the connection link between the *BufferCache* component and the mobile component downstream, e.g., the link between the *BufferCache* and *UnWrap* components in Fig. 6.

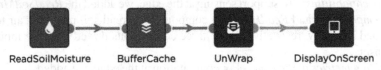

ReadSoilMoisture   BufferCache   UnWrap   DisplayOnScreen

Fig. 6. Application flow graph featuring the *BufferCache* component in use.

Low Infrastructure Networking: The notion of communicating directly to a server is abstracted to allow sensors to communicate directly to applications running on mobile devices, as illustrated in Fig. 7. The sensing environment runs the edge application created by the domain expert. The edge application runs on top of a lightweight JavaScript engine[3] and Arduino[4]. We use web sockets (Socket.IO[5]) to communicate events (observables) carrying an event name and a payload to the mobile device. All clients that are subscribed to the event can then receive the payload from that particular event. Data coming from the sensors is packaged to carry a unique identifier for the sensor device, the payload, and the identifier of the link (connection) for the last blue component connecting to the black components. The link is exported as part of the graph deployed to the edge from the main application graph.

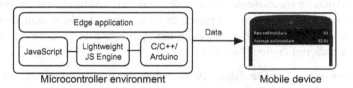

Fig. 7. Low infrastructure networking configuration.

Application Design and Deployment in DisCoPar-K: Figure 8 shows the workflow for designing applications in DisCoPar-K. Designing and validating the application is done on the VPE following the design choices for component composition and association. The entire application flow graph is exported and deployed to the mobile phone. For the edge, only the edge graph is exported and deployed to the microcontroller with sensors attached.

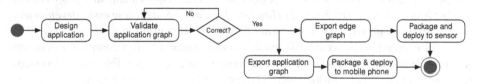

Fig. 8. Flow graph for application design and deployment in DisCoPar-K.

---

[3] https://duktape.org/.

[4] https://www.arduino.cc/en/software.

[5] https://socket.io/.

Exporting and Deploying the Edge Application: From an initial application graph, we build and deploy the edge application to the microcontroller with sensors attached. To build and export the edge application, we utilise the depth-first search method [28]. Using this method, we start from a root node and traverse the initial graph to generate the edge application. The root node is any blue (edge) component in the initial graph that has no predecessor component. We keep all root nodes in a list and process each item in the list. During processing, each neighbour of the root node is determined and visited. The visited nodes are kept in a list and their dependencies are determined. The dependencies are considered children of the visited nodes, kept in an ordered list. Using this information, we then build a segment of the initial application graph that is exported and deployed to the edge. For disjointed application graphs, we keep a list of visited nodes and iterate through all the items in the list. For each node in the list, we treat it as a root node and make a recursive call to all nodes that can be visited. For components that have a state, we export the state and pass it as an argument to the executed component function. On the microcontroller, the exported application is executed on top of the lightweight JavaScript engine (Fig. 7).

Runtime Environment at the Edge: At the edge, we use Arduino[6] and Duktape[7] to support edge applications. Duktape is a lightweight JavaScript engine that can run on microcontrollers. The engine permits integrating JavaScript programs with Arduino or C/C++ programs. This allows for deploying and executing JavaScript code on microcontrollers with sensors attached. We use the lightweight engine to allow implementation of the entire DisCoPar-K applications using one base language.

4   Validation and Discussion

To validate this work, we adopt a scenario-based approach and seek to answer the following questions: *1) How does DisCoPar-K fulfil the requirements and properties of the implemented scenarios?* and *2) How can DisCoPar-K as a low code development tool be used to improve the development of SAAs?* By definition, the scenario describes the set of interactions between different actors in a system and can comprise a concrete sequence of interaction steps (i.e., instance scenario) or a set of possible interaction steps (i.e., type scenario) [21]. More concretely, the validation scenario is conceptualised as a flow of computation tasks in the application [2]. In the scenario-based approach, the requirements of the scenario are validated against the expected behaviour of the application [2, 14, 21]. As such, we derived different scenarios that we use as case studies to validate this work. In the subsequent sections, we present each of the derived scenario and its implementation details.

---

[6] https://www.arduino.cc/en/software.
[7] https://duktape.org/.

4.1 Case Study 1: Monitoring Soil Moisture and Temperature

This case study was derived from the running example in Sect. 2 on corn seeding and sprouting. The goal of the use case is to ensure optimal sprouting of corn by keeping optimal soil moisture and temperature conditions. As such, this case study requires implementing the following requirements.

- Environment sensing to sense soil moisture and temperature.
- Computation at the edge to compute the averages of the data coming from sensors and soil heat capacity at the edge.
- Offline accessibility to buffer data at the edge when the network becomes unavailable.
- The microcontroller hosting the soil moisture and temperature sensors needs to send data directly to the mobile device (e.g., smartphone) without going through a centralised server.
- Track the global view of all soil moisture and temperature sensors installed on a farm. As such, the number of connected devices needs to be tracked.
- Accumulate soil moisture and temperature data from multiple sensors.
- Determine the maximum and minimum values for the accumulated soil moisture and temperature data.
- Compute the average of the accumulated soil moisture and temperature data.
- Track data for specific soil moisture and temperature sensors.
- Generate notifications based on specified limits and visualise average soil moisture over time.

The above requirements describe the expected behaviour of the implemented application. We compute the soil heat capacity (Q) using $Q = 4.2 \times 10^3 \times V \times (0.2 + W) \times \Delta T$, where V is the soil volume, W is the soil moisture, and ΔT is the change in temperature [35].

Fulfilling Key Properties for the Case Study: In this section, we describe how DisCoPar-K fulfils the requirements of case study 1.

1) *Environment sensing:* Figure 9 illustrates using the *ReadSoilMoisture* component to read and send soil moisture data. The data is sent to the *UnWrap* component that runs on the mobile device.

ReadSoilMoisture   UnWrap   DisplayOnScreen

Fig. 9. Component for sensing soil moisture and sending data to mobile devices.

2) *Computing average soil moisture at the edge:* Figure 10 illustrates using the *ComputeEdgeAverage* component to compute the running average for the soil moisture at the edge. The running average for soil moisture is computed since the data is sampled continuously as a stream. The *UnWrap* component unpacks the average soil moisture as the payload and sends it to the next component downstream.

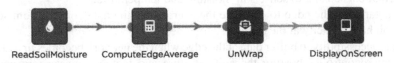

ReadSoilMoisture   ComputeEdgeAverage   UnWrap   DisplayOnScreen

Fig. 10. Flow graph featuring computing the average soil moisture at the edge.

3) *Offline accessibility at the edge:* Figure 11 illustrates using the *BufferCache* component for offline accessibility at the edge. The component supports in-memory data buffering based on the number of records. The buffer size defines the maximum number of records stored.

4) *Microcontrollers hosting sensors sending data directly to mobile devices:* In the applications presented in Fig. 9, Fig. 10, Fig. 11 and Fig. 12, the blue (edge) components communicate directly with the black (mobile) components without going through a centralised server.

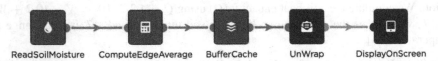

ReadSoilMoisture   ComputeEdgeAverage   BufferCache   UnWrap   DisplayOnScreen

Fig. 11. Flow graph featuring buffering data at the edge for offline accessibility.

5) *Generating and showing notifications:* In Fig. 12, we use the *SetThreshold* component to specify the limit for generating notifications. The threshold value is compared with the incoming average soil moisture data using the *Compare* component. This component receives two inputs, i.e., the threshold and the data value. The output from the component triggers generating and showing a notification to the *GenerateAndShowAlert* component downstream.

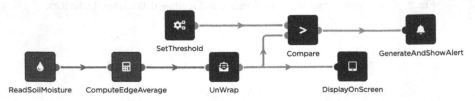

Fig. 12. Flow graph featuring setting thresholds and generating notifications.

6) *Tracking the global view and accumulating soil moisture and temperature data from multiple devices:* The application flow graph in Fig. 13 uses the *ConnectedDevices* component and the *DataArrayToTable* components to show the number of connected devices. The *DisplayOnScreen* component shows the number of connected devices on the screen, while the *DisplayAsList* shows the list of the connected components on the screen.

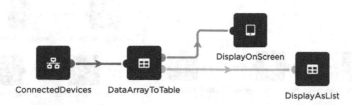

ConnectedDevices   DataArrayToTable   DisplayOnScreen   DisplayAsList

Fig. 13. Flow graph featuring showing the number of connected devices.

Figure 14 shows how to accumulate the average soil moisture data using the *DeviceAccumulator* component. The blue components run on the individual sensor devices, while the *DeviceAccumulator* runs on the mobile phone. The accumulated data is processed further to give more meaningful information, such as the global average for soil moisture.

ReadSoilMoisture   ComputeEdgeAverage   DeviceAccumulator   ComputeAverage   DisplayOnScreen

Fig. 14. Flow graph featuring accumulating data from multiple sensor devices.

7) *Tracking data for specific soil moisture and temperature sensors:* Data coming from multiple devices can be unpacked, such that data for specific devices can be inspected. In Fig. 15, we use the *UnWrapForSpecificDevice* component to unpack soil moisture for a specific device.

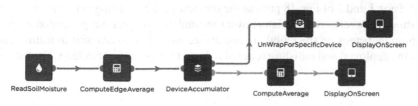

UnWrapForSpecificDevice   DisplayOnScreen

ReadSoilMoisture   ComputeEdgeAverage   DeviceAccumulator   ComputeAverage   DisplayOnScreen

Fig. 15. Flow graph featuring unwrapping data for specific devices.

8) *Determining the maximum and minimum value for soil moisture accumulated from several devices:* In Fig. 16, we use the *ComputeMaximum* and *ComputeMinimum* components to determine the maximum and minimum values for data received from multiple devices. The determined values are displayed on the mobile screen using the *DisplayOnScreen* components.

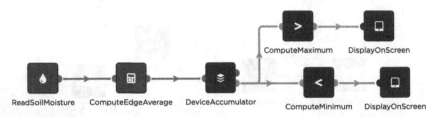

Fig. 16. Determining the maximum and minimum for data from multiple devices.

9) *Visualising average soil moisture over time:* In Fig. 17, we use the *PlotSoilMoisture-OverTime* component to visualise the average soil moisture over time. In addition to the average soil moisture, this component plots both the maximum and minimum thresholds. The maximum and minimum thresholds are set as constraints in the component configuration setting. The component receives, as input, the average soil moisture computed using the *ComputeAverage* component. The *ComputeAverage* component computes the average soil moisture for data accumulated from multiple devices using the *DeviceAccumulator* component.

Fig. 17. Flow graph featuring plotting the average soil moisture on a line chart.

Application Flow Graph and Preview of the Resulting Application: Figure 18 shows the overall application flow graph for monitoring soil moisture and temperature. The soil heat capacity is computed at the edge and the outcome is communicated to the mobile device. Parts 1 and 2 of Fig. 18 present the preview of the resulting application. The line chart shows the average soil moisture over time and the notifications generated displayed as pop-up messages on the mobile phone are generated at 57.5% soil moisture. Part 3 shows the deployed soil moisture (circled red) and temperature (circled white) sensors.

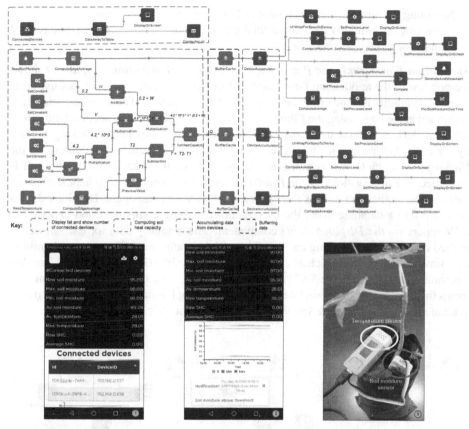

Fig. 18. Overall flow graph and preview of the mobile application for monitoring soil moisture and temperature.

4.2   Case Study 2: Monitoring Humidity and Data Collection

This use case is adapted from Serikul et al. [24]. In this use case, the goal of the farmer is to store paddy rice under optimal humidity conditions to maintain the quality of the rice and attract good prices in the market. The rice is packaged in paddy bags and stored in a warehouse after harvesting. At the warehouse, the paddy bags are stacked on top of each other. Previously, the humidity of the stored rice was randomly measured by inserting a digital humidity meter into selected paddy bags. Since in the warehouse the paddy bags are stacked on top of each other, it is difficult to measure the humidity in every bag. As such, this use case requires installing humidity sensors in random rice bags (e.g., per stack) as a representative of the entire warehouse. The humidity sensors collect data and send it to the farmer's mobile phone. The farmer uses the received humidity data to develop rice storage management plans. As such, this case study requires implementing the following requirements.

- Tracking average humidity data on a gauge chart.
- Tracking humidity data over time (e.g., on a line chart).

– Notifying the farmer when the humidity level goes beyond set limits.
– Collecting the humidity data into a database for storage and creating reports as CSV (comma-separated values) files.

Application Flow Graph and Preview of the Resulting Application: Figure 19 shows the preview of the application flow graph that meets the requirements of this use case. Tracking humidity is done using the *ReadHumidity* component. The average humidity is computed at the edge using the *ComputeAverage* component and its accumulation from different devices is done using the *DeviceAccumulator* component. Tracking humidity for individual paddy rice bags (i.e., individual humidity sensors) is done using the *UnWrapForSpecificDevice* component. Before sending the data to the database, it is converted into observations by the *DataToObservation* component. To handle network outages, the application utilises the *InDatabaseBuffering* component. Humidity data is collected into a database using the *ObservationDatabase* component and exported to CSV report via the *DisplayAsTable* component. The humidity data for each device is plotted on a gauge chart using the *PlotGaugeChart* component. The average humidity over time is plotted on a line chart via the *PlotHumidityOverTime* component. Humidity thresholds are set using the *SetThreshold* component. The *Compare* component performs the comparison of the set threshold and incoming humidity data. Lastly, alerts are generated using the *GenerateAndShowAlert* component.

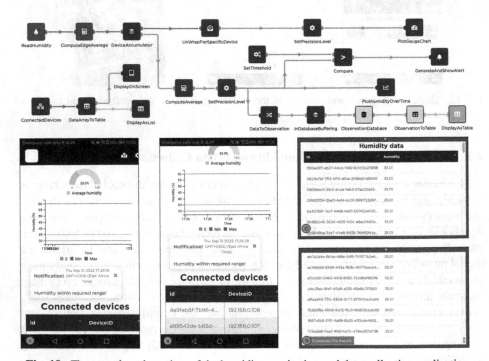

Fig. 19. Flow graph and preview of the humidity monitoring and data collection application.

Parts A and B of Fig. 19 show the preview of the resulting mobile application featuring the average humidity on a gauge chart and line chart. In addition, part B shows the generated notification and the list of connected devices. The list of connected devices is updated in real-time using the *ConnectedDevices* component to allow tracking when devices go off. Parts C and D show the humidity data displayed on a web dashboard. The data on the dashboard can be exported as a CSV report for further analysis by clicking the "Download CSV Report" button in part D. In comparison to the application presented in [24], our implementation adds 1) offline availability using the *InDatabaseBuffering* component to store humidity data when the network becomes unavailable, and 2) setting thresholds and generating notifications when the humidity goes beyond the required limit.

4.3 Case Study 3: Tracking Application Data

From our interaction with farmers in developing regions, they often collect plant specific data to monitor growth and development. For instance, at the sprouting stage, the farmers need to track the number of leaves per plant, the colour of the leaves and plant height. As such, the goal of this use case is to collect and track plant-specific data. Tracking the plant-specific data can be done using quick response codes as plant labels. Once the labels are scanned, a data entry survey is invoked that the farmers can use to directly input the data into the application. The data is sent from the application to the server from where it can be visualised on a dashboard. This use case requires implementing the following requirements.

– Scanning (reading) plant labels and invoking a data collection survey.
– Sending the data input into the application to a database and displaying it on a dashboard.
– Displaying collected data on a dashboard.
– Exporting the data stored in the database as a report in a CSV file for further analysis.

Application Flow Graph and Preview of the Resulting Application: The application shown in Fig. 20 fulfils the above requirements. Reading the plant labels is done using the *ReadQRCode* component. The *ObservationPopUpSurvey* component is used to generate the data collection survey. Part 1 of Fig. 20 shows the preview of the data collection survey on a mobile phone. The data collected is sent to the server for storage using the *ObservationDatabase* component and displayed on a web dashboard using the *DisplayAsTable* component, as shown in part 2 of Fig. 20. From the web dashboard, the data can be exported as a CSV file for further analysis.

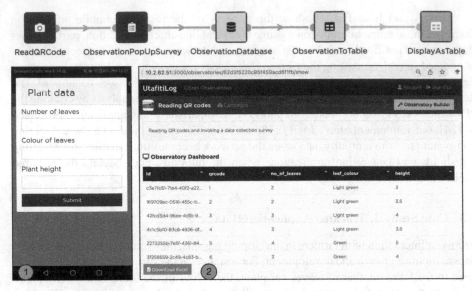

ReadQRCode   ObservationPopUpSurvey   ObservationDatabase   ObservationToTable   DisplayAsTable

Fig. 20. Preview for the data collection application with data on a dashboard.

4.4 Discussion

In this work, our validation sought to answer how DisCoPar-K fulfils the requirements and properties of the implemented scenarios and how it can be used to improve the development of SAAs.

Fulfilling the requirements and properties of the implemented scenarios: On this issue, DisCoPar-K offers components for sensing and monitoring environmental conditions (e.g., soil moisture, temperature and humidity). In addition, DisCoPar-K offers components for performing computations at the edge, buffering data at the edge when the network becomes unavailable, and supporting microcontrollers to communicate with mobile devices without a centralised server. Data received on the server side can be visualised on web dashboards.

Improving the development of SAAs: This issue is demonstrated in several ways. First, the visual components, drag-and-drop, point-and-click utilities, prebuilt UI components, and binding to data sources that DisCoPar-K provides can be used intuitively. Secondly, the pre-built components that DisCoPar-K provide hideaway issues like memory management and distribution, which can take considerable time to configure manually. As such, DisCoPar-K can speed up the application development process and make software programming more accessible to domain experts outside software engineering. This means that LCDTs in general can motivate small-scale and medium-scale farmers to adopt and use mobile computing technologies in their farming activities. Lastly, although the case studies presented in this work focus on sensing and data collection, the same methodology can be applied to other types of SAAs and other domains.

5   Conclusion and Future Work

Low code development tools provide visual programming environments with components that can be used to construct smart agriculture applications. The components abstract and transparently provide a software infrastructure for constructing smart agriculture applications. We believe that the visual components are easier to use, especially for non-experienced developers. However, to meet requirements for different domains, the low code development tools need to have the necessary pre-requisite components that can be used to implement different applications. These components provide application properties and support computational tasks that are specific and tailored to a specific domain. In a nutshell, this paper identifies properties in low code development tools to support implementing smart agriculture applications and presents DisCoPar-K, a low code development tool that supports low infrastructure networking, computation at the edge, and offline accessibility at the edge. Domain experts with less programming experience can use DisCoPar-K to implement smart agriculture applications. For future work, we aim to perform a heuristic-based evaluation of smart agriculture applications constructed using low code development tools.

Acknowledgement. This work is supported by the Legumes Centre for Food and Nutrition Security (LCEFoNS) programme which is funded by VLIR-UOS. The programme is a North–South Collaboration between the Katholieke Universiteit Leuven, Vrije Universiteit Brussel (both in Belgium) and Jomo Kenyatta University of Agriculture and Technology (Kenya).

References

1. Node-RED: Low-code programming for event-driven applications. https://nodered.org/. Accessed 30 Aug 2021
2. Arnold, D., Corriveau, J.P., Shi, W.: Scenario-based validation: beyond the user requirements notation. In: 2010 21st Australian Software Engineering Conference, pp. 75–84. IEEE (2010). https://doi.org/10.1109/ASWEC.2010.29
3. AtmosphericIoT: Simplify your IoT development with Atmosphere IoT Studio. https://atmosphereiot.com/studio/. Accessed 26 Aug 2021
4. Axonize: The smarter way to realize smart business potential. https://www.axonize.com. Accessed 31 Aug 2021
5. Babou, C.S.M., Sane, B.O., Diane, I., Niang, I.: Home edge computing architecture for smart and sustainable agriculture and breeding. In: Proceedings of the 2nd International Conference on Networking, Information Systems & Security. NISS19, ACM, New York, NY, USA (2019). https://doi.org/10.1145/3320326.3320377
6. Bexiga, M., Garbatov, S., Seco, J.A.C.: Closing the gap between designers and developers in a low code ecosystem. In: MODELS 2020, Association for Computing Machinery, New York, NY, USA (2020). https://doi.org/10.1145/3417990.3420195
7. Blackstock, M., Lea, R.: IoT mashups with the WoTKit. In: Proceedings of 2012 International Conference on the Internet of Things, IOT 2012, Wuxi, China, pp. 159–166 (2012). https://doi.org/10.1109/IOT.2012.6402318
8. Blackstock, M., Lea, R.: Toward a distributed data flow platform for the Web of Things (Distributed Node-RED). In: ACM International Conference Proceeding Series, pp. 34–39 (2014). https://doi.org/10.1145/2684432.2684439

9. Blackstock, M., Lea, R.: FRED: A hosted data flow platform for the IoT. In: Proceedings of the 1st International Workshop on Mashups of Things and APIs. MOTA 2016, Association for Computing Machinery, New York (2016). https://doi.org/10.1145/3007203.3007214

10. Choudharyor, N., Arya, V.: Salesforce IoT cloud platform. In: Singh Mer, K.K., Semwal, V.B., Bijalwan, V., Crespo, R.G. (eds.) Proceedings of Integrated Intelligence Enable Networks and Computing. Algorithms for Intelligent Systems, pp 301–309. Springer, Singapore (2021). https://doi.org/10.1007/978-981-33-6307-6_31

11. El-Sanatawy, A.M., El-Kholy, A.S.M., Ali, M.M.A., Awad, M.F., Mansour, E.: Maize seedling establishment, grain yield and crop water productivity response to seed priming and irrigation management in a mediterranean arid environment. Agronomy 11(4), 756 (2021). https://doi.org/10.3390/agronomy11040756

12. Ermi S.T., Rif'an, M.: Internet of Things (IoT): BLYNK framework for smart home. In: 3rd UNJ International Conference on Technical and Vocational Education and Training 2018, pp. 579–586 (2019). https://doi.org/10.18502/kss.v3i12.4128

13. Gao, Z., et al.: A novel approach to evaluate soil heat flux calculation: an analytical review of nine methods. J. Geophys. Res.: Atmos. 122(13), 6934–6949 (2017). https://doi.org/10.1002/2017JD027160

14. Gregoriades, A., Sutcliffe, A.: Scenario-based assessment of nonfunctional requirements. IEEE Trans. Softw. Eng. 31(5), 392–409 (2005). https://doi.org/10.1109/TSE.2005.59

15. Henkel, M., Stirna, J.: Pondering on the key functionality of model driven development tools: the case of mendix. In: Forbrig, P., Günther, H. (eds.) BIR 2010. LNBIP, vol. 64, pp. 146–160. Springer, Heidelberg (2010). https://doi.org/10.1007/978-3-642-16101-8_12

16. Kleinfeld, R., Steglich, S., Radziwonowicz, L., Doukas, C.: Glue.things: a mashup platform for wiring the internet of things with the internet of services. In: Proceedings of the 5th International Workshop on Web of Things, WoT 2014, pp. 16–21. Association for Computing Machinery, New York (2014). https://doi.org/10.1145/2684432.2684436

17. Michael, L., Field, D.: Mendix as a solution for present gaps in computer programming in higher education. In: Twenty-Fourth Americas Conference on Information Systems, pp. 1–5 (2018)

18. Noor, J., Sandha, S.S., Garcia, L., Srivastava, M.: DDFLOW visualized declarative programming for heterogeneous IoT networks on Heliot Testbed platform: demo abstract. In: Proceedings of the International Conference on Internet of Things Design and Implementation, IoTDI 2019, ACM, New York, NY, USA, pp. 287–288 (2019). https://doi.org/10.1145/3302505.3312598

19. O'Grady, M., Langton, D., O'Hare, G.: Edge computing: a tractable model for smart agriculture? Artif. Intell. Agric. 3, 42–51 (2019). https://doi.org/10.1016/j.aiia.2019.12.001

20. Ragasa, C.: Effectiveness of the lead farmer approach in agricultural extension service provision: Nationally representative panel data analysis in Malawi. Land Use Policy 99, 104966 (2020). https://doi.org/10.1016/j.landusepol.2020.104966

21. Ryser, J., Glinz, M.: A scenario-based approach to validating and testing software systems using statecharts. In: 12th International Conference on Software and Systems Engineering and their Applications (ICSSEA 2099). CNAM (1999). https://doi.org/10.5167/uzh-205008

22. Sahay, A., Di Ruscio, D., Pierantonio, A.: Understanding the role of model transformation compositions in low-code development platforms. In: Proceedings of the 23rd ACM/IEEE International Conference on Model Driven Engineering Languages and Systems: Companion Proceedings, MODELS 2020, Association for Computing Machinery, New York, NY, USA (2020). https://doi.org/10.1145/3417990.3420197

23. Salesforce: Discover low-code tools to reimagine workflows and increase productivity. https://www.salesforce.com/products/platform/low-code/. Accessed 26 Aug 2021

24. Serikul, P., Nakpong, N., Nakjuatong, N.: Smart farm monitoring via the Blynk IoT platform: case study: humidity monitoring and data recording. In: 2018 Sixteenth International Conference on ICT and Knowledge Engineering, pp. 70–75. IEEE (2018). https://doi.org/10.1109/ICTKE.2018.8612441
25. Simplifier: Enterprise Apps Made Simple. https://simplifier.io/en/. Accessed 27 Aug 2021
26. Sudozai, M.I., Tunio, S., Chachar, Q., Rajpar, I.: Seedling establishment and yield of maize under different seed priming periods and available soil moisture. Sarhad J. Agric. **29**, 515–528 (2013)
27. Szydlo, T., Brzoza-Woch, R., Sendorek, J., Windak, M., Gniady, C.: Flow-based programming for IoT leveraging fog computing. In: 2017 IEEE 26th International Conference on Enabling Technologies: Infrastructure for Collaborative Enterprises (WETICE), pp. 74–79 (2017). https://doi.org/10.1109/WETICE.2017.17
28. Tarjan, R.: Depth-first search and linear graph algorithms. SIAM J. Comput. **1**(2), 146–160 (1972). https://doi.org/10.1137/0201010
29. Waszkowski, R.: Low-code platform for automating business processes in manufacturing. IFAC-PapersOnLine **52**(10), 376–381 (2019). https://doi.org/10.1016/j.ifacol.2019.10.060,13thIFACWorkshoponIntelli-gentManufacturingSystemsIMS2019
30. Wolfert, S., Ge, L., Verdouw, C., Bogaardt, M.: Big data in smart farming: a review. Agric. Syst. **153**, 69–80 (2017). https://doi.org/10.1016/j.agsy.2017.01.023
31. Zaman, J.: DISCOPAR: A Visual Reactive Flow-Based Domain-Specific Language for Constructing Participatory Sensing Platforms. Ph.D. thesis, Vrije Universiteit Brussel (2018)
32. Zaman, J., Kambona, K., De Meuter, W.: DISCOPAR: A visual reactive programming language for generating cloud-based participatory sensing platforms, pp. 31–40. REBLS 2018, ACM, New York, NY, USA (2018). https://doi.org/10.1145/3281278.3281285
33. Zaman, J., Kambona, K., De Meuter, W.: A reusable & reconfigurable citizen observatory platform. Futur. Gener. Comput. Syst. **114**, 195–208 (2021). https://doi.org/10.1016/j.future.2020.07.028
34. Zenodys: A Fully Decentralised Data and Service Marketplace for Everyone. https://www.zenodys.com/wp-content/uploads/zenodys-ico-whitepaper.pdf. Accessed 30 Aug 2021
35. Zhang, Z., et al.: The change characteristics and interactions of soil moisture and temperature in the farmland in Wuchuan county, inner Mongolia China. Atmosphere **11**(5), 503 (2020). https://doi.org/10.3390/atmos11050503

R-MDP: A Game Theory Approach for Fault-Tolerant Data and Service Management in Crude Oil Pipelines Monitoring Systems

Safuriyawu Ahmed[✉], Frédéric Le Mouël, Nicolas Stouls, and Jilles S. Dibangoye

Univ Lyon, INSA Lyon, Inria, CITI, EA3720, 69621 Villeurbanne, France
`safuriyawu.ahmed@insa-lyon.fr`

Abstract. Failures in pipeline transportation of crude oil have numerous adverse effects, such as ecological degradation, environmental pollution and a decrease in revenue for the operators, to mention a few. Efficient data and service management can predict and prevent these failures, reducing the downtime of the pipeline infrastructure, among other benefits. Thus, we propose a two-stage approach to data and service management in Leakage Detection and Monitoring Systems (LDMS) for crude oil pipelines. It aims to maximise the accuracy of leakage detection and localisation in a fault-tolerant and energy-efficient manner. The problem is modelled as a Markov Decision Process (MDP) based on the historical incident data from the Nigerian National Petroleum Corporation (NNPC) pipeline networks. Results obtained guarantee detection in at least two deployed nodes with a minimum localisation accuracy of 90%. Additionally, we achieved approximately 77% and 26% reduction in energy consumption compared to a pessimistic strategy and a globalised heuristic approach, respectively.

Keywords: pipeline monitoring · iot · wsn · game theory · crude oil · data analytics

1 Introduction

The operations and processes across the oil and gas industry's three sectors (upstream, midstream, and downstream) present vast data. Although there are several efforts to gain insights into the data in the upstream and downstream sectors through big data analytics [1,2], the data in the midstream (transportation) sector is largely left unexploited. In this sector alone, every 150,000 miles of pipeline produces up to ten terabytes of data [3] through monitoring systems. Such data enable the timely detection and localisation of leakages in the pipeline and allow the deployment of services like predictive analysis, emergency service and others. The monitoring systems utilised include legacy Leak Detection

© ICST Institute for Computer Sciences, Social Informatics and Telecommunications Engineering 2023
Published by Springer Nature Switzerland AG 2023. All Rights Reserved
S. Longfei and P. Bodhi (Eds.): MobiQuitous 2022, LNICST 492, pp. 44–64, 2023.
https://doi.org/10.1007/978-3-031-34776-4_3

Monitoring Systems (LDMS) such as Supervisory Control And Data Acquisition (SCADA) and, more recently, Wireless Sensor Networks (WSN) and Internet of Things (IoT)-based systems.

Nowadays, data and service management has become paramount in the midstream sector due to ageing infrastructure, outdated technology, and incessant node vandalisation [4,5]. Its benefits include the reduction of the annual downtime of LDMS by 70% and the associated cost by 22% through timely failure detection and predictive maintenance [4]. Aliguliyev *et al.* and Hajirahimova, in their work [2,6], also highlight other benefits of data management and analytics in this context.

However, data and service management must be efficiently done as it affects various performance metrics in WSN and IoT-based LDMS. For example, despite enabling data processing through fog computing in these systems, their responsiveness, the energy consumption [7] and real-time management [8] in the form of network fluctuation, latency, communication failure, and node failures are nonetheless a challenge.

Therefore, this paper presents our work on efficient and robust data and service management in WSN and IoT-based LDMS. The objectives are:

1. To analyse the historical data related to pipeline failures in Nigerian National Petroleum Network (NNPC) pipelines.
2. To propose a Regionalised Markov Decision Process (R-MDP) for ensuring a similar level of performance across the NNPC pipeline network.
3. To determine strategies using the MDP on the pipeline network's defined regions for minimal total energy consumption.

We aim to achieve this by exploiting the fog computing paradigm for distributed data and service management through simultaneous data and service *placement, replication and migration.* This strategy is modelled as a Markov Decision Process management based on the historical incident data from the NNPC pipeline networks. Our technique is further divided into two stages: first, we determine the performance measure for each predefined pipeline region; then, we find the optimal value that minimises the energy consumption in the region considered.

The remainder of this work is structured as follows: In Sect. 2, we discuss related work, followed by our contribution in Sect. 3. In Sect. 4, we conclude the paper and present our future work.

2   Related Work

Cloud computing enabled advanced data analytics, optimisation and decision-making in IoT applications. However, the increased load for time-sensitive applications and real-time monitoring can significantly affect the system's performance. Fog computation and edge analytics addressed such limitations of centralised cloud computing [9] by its integration into the network design. This design significantly increases the scalability of the network by reducing latency and computational overhead at the cloud servers. In addition, maintenance or enhancement of system performance such as improved *fault tolerance* in real-time operations is realised. Other approaches have also been adopted to improve the overall system's performance.

Therefore, this section discusses several approaches to improved efficiency in WSN/IoT-based applications, real-time applications and fog-based infrastructures. In particular, we examine placement, communication strategies and game theories for optimisation in the following subsections.

2.1   Placements and Communication Strategies in Fog Architectures

Although fog-based infrastructures can reduce latency and computational overhead for real-time operations, misplacing data in the fog nodes can have a detrimental effect. Some of the applications of fog-based systems were demonstrated in [10], where it extends the data analytic capability of cloud computing in the context of smart cities using smart pipeline monitoring prototypes. Giordano *et al.* [11] also showed its application operating a platform that incorporates smart agents.

Paramount, however, are placement strategies on fog-enabled infrastructures aimed to reduce the overall network *latency* and increase the *fault tolerance* of the system. Naas *et al.* [12] proposed a runtime data placement algorithm in a fog-based architecture focused on the nature of the data, the holder node's behaviour and location. The results show that overall latency was reduced by 86% compared to cloud solutions and 60% to simple fog solutions. Eral *et al.* [13] worked on a replica placement algorithm using the size, location and priced storage as the constraints for reducing latency in edge networks. Their work yielded a 14% to 26% reduction -per tradeoffs- in latency compared to replicas' absence. Shao *et al.* in [14] also worked on placing data replicas for IoT workflows in both fog and cloud environments. Their work is based on an intelligent swam optimisation algorithm based on user groups, data reliability, and workflows. Results show improvement in comparison to other research.

In tandem with data placement, service placement plays a crucial role in the overall efficiency of a fog-enabled environment, i.e. generic or wrong placements could result in latency increment [15]. Hence, Velasquez *et al.* [15] defines an IoT service placement architecture fusing cloud and fog computing and constrained by the system's operating condition and latency requirements. They used a three-module (service repository, information collection, and service orchestrator) generic and scenario-agnostic placement algorithm. Services conforming to the state of the network and the user and server's location are placed in the fog nodes. Wang *et al.* [8] proposed an optimal data scheduling policy operating multiple channels based on a four-layer fog computing architecture. It comprises the device, data scheduler, Jstorm, and cloud layers. The Jstorm layer integrates geographically distributed fog nodes into several clusters. As such, generated big data is split into several blocks and transferred to different Jstorm clusters for processing. Simulation shows a 15% gain over other data scheduling policies.

Additionally, Elsayed *et al.* [16] worked on distributed fault tolerance of sensor node hardware WSNs. Experimental results proved their method performed better than the compared scheme by tolerating approximately 67% of the encountered failures. Yuvaraja *et al.* [17] also worked on fault tolerance in WSN by detecting and recovering node failures using a least disruptive topology repair mechanism.

Other considerations for efficient systems are the mechanisms of data transmission or flow between data producers (clients) and data consumers (agents). Commonly used are the publish-subscribe (PB) messaging paradigms between clients and agents [18]. Ioana *et al.* in their work [19] demonstrated the applicability of the PB systems in several complex scenarios, for example, the Open Platform Communication Unified Architecture protocol for Industry 4.0. Primarily, they exhibited how a multi-channel User Datagram Protocol (UDP) communication strategy for PB systems enables transmitting high-volume data like images in a time frame fitted for the industry. Aslam *et al.* [20] worked on adaptive methods to handle unknown subscriptions in a low-latency PB model for processing multimedia events. Their system achieved between 79% and 84% accuracy. Jafarpour *et al.* [21] focused on computing and transmission cost minimisation through content-subscribers-based requested formats.

2.2   System Optimisation Using Game Theory

Game theory is increasingly being used to improve application efficiency and optimise system performance. Garg *et al.*, in their work [22], evaluated three dynamic placements (greedy approximation, integer programming optimisation and learning-based algorithms) for maximal user equipment availability employing minimal infrastructure. A drone swarm application experiment indicates that all tested techniques met the latency requirement. Nevertheless, the learning-based algorithm performed better in terms of the minimal variation in solution providing a more stable deployment and thereby guaranteeing a reduction in infrastructural cost. Also, on placement optimisation, Ting *et al.* [23] presented an optimal provision of edge services such as storage, communication and computational resources. Using a trace-driven simulation, they carried out an analysis of the results obtained on optimal request scheduling (ORS as the baseline), greedy service placement with optimal request scheduling (GSP ORS) and greedy service placement with greedy request scheduling (GSP GRS). For joint service placement and resource scheduling, both GSP ORS and GSP GRS, including their linear programming relaxation, achieved optimal or near-optimal solutions.

Cai *et al.*, in their work [24], introduced a Reinforcement Learning Heuristic Optimisation (RLHO) framework aimed at the provision of better initial values for the algorithm. They conducted a comparative analysis between RLHO, simulated annealing and proximal policy optimisation. An experiment on a bin packing problem validated that RLHO outperformed pure reinforcement learning. Likewise, the following research based on game theory aims to improve pipeline monitoring systems.

Islam *et al.* [25] and Rezazdeh *et al.* [26] worked on third-party interference such as terrorist attacks on pipeline infrastructures. The former proposed a Stackelberg competition-based attacker-defender model to find the equilibrium between pipeline security and possible attacks. They proved that in an equilibrium state, the monitoring system achieves the best result by maintaining its strategy, assuming both the defender and attacker act rationally. On the other hand, the latter proposed two-player non-zero-sum modelling of the problem. They also assumed that both players acted rationally based on the chosen indices. Two methods were proposed to solve this problem: a local optimisation for comprehensive analysis of the effect of countermeasures on attacks and a global optimisation enabling the security personnel (defender) to provide a solution from the attacker's perspective. Rezazadeh *et al.* [27] worked on modelling a monitoring system for pipeline security using the Bayesian Stackelberg game. They proposed a scheduling policy based on time and distance discretisation. The proposed framework enables the ranking of security risks, allowing different patrol paths to be utilised.

While these works considered the efficient placement of data and services to reduce latency in fog-enabled architectures, they have not considered the robustness of their approach to failures. In addition, to the best of our knowledge, no work has considered a data-driven MDP for efficiently managing failures in crude oil pipelines. Thus, in our work, we take cognisance of failures, their nature and history to guarantee the monitoring system's availability and performance by optimising the placement strategies across a multi-layered architecture.

3   Data-Driven Resilient and Regionalised MDP (R-MDP)

This research implements fault-tolerant data and service management through distributed data and service *placement, replication and migration*. As a prerequisite, we propose a three-layer fog-based architecture shown in Fig. 1 that allows data and service placements closer to the users (sensors and gateways). The three layers comprise sensors at layer one, the gateways (fog nodes) at layer two and the cloud servers at layer three. The proposed architecture allows data sharing amongst predefined neighbourhood sensors at layer one, enabling the implementation of services such as detection and localisation of leakages at that layer as in our earlier works [28,29]. We also extend data placement to the fog layer to facilitate data processing, prioritisation, aggregation, replication, and migration services. Lastly, the cloud layer stores historical data for long-term services like predictive maintenance.

The sensor nodes produce various types of data made available through publication to which services can subscribe. As shown in Fig. 1, the data and services are divided into two sub-layers. The publish-subscribe paradigm is used as the sub-layer interaction model to improve efficiency further. The communication aspect is the same as in our previous works [28,29].

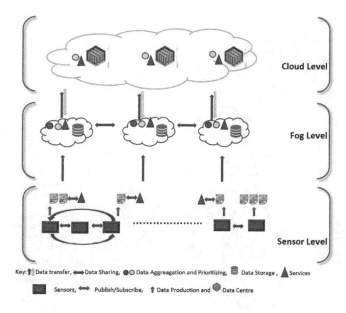

Fig. 1. Data and service placement

The following subsections elaborate on the problem definition and its modelling.

3.1 Background and Problem Definition

Failures in pipeline transportation of crude oil include erosion, corrosion, equipment failure, vandalisation, network failure, and others. Several pipeline monitoring systems focus on accurately detecting the leakages in the pipelines. However, the monitoring systems are also susceptible to third-party interference, which is one of the leading causes of failure in this mode of transporting crude oil. Consequently, this work aims to circumvent this problem through *efficient* data and service management for the *continuous detection* of leakages in the presence of failures in pipelines and deployed monitoring systems.

Our work is focused on a crude oil pipeline in Nigeria, specifically the NNPC pipeline network shown in Fig. 2. This pipeline network spans several thousand kilometres and is divided into five areas, i.e. PortHarcourt, Kaduna, Warri, Gombe and Mosimi, based on their geographical locations. Different kinds of failures characterise each area, each differing from another significantly. The factors contributing to this vast difference range from weather conditions to the pipeline area's proximity to the border; for instance, the Mosimi and PortHarcourt areas located close to the border experience the highest failure rates. A snippet of historical data, as shown in Fig. 3, presents the incident rate depicting the disparity in the number of incidents in each area.

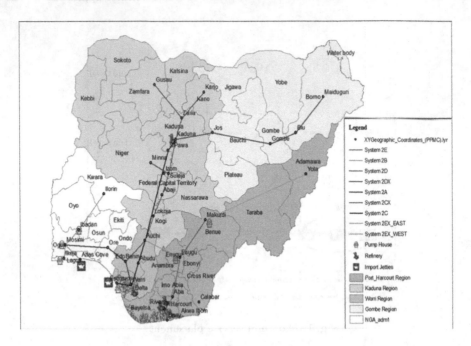

Fig. 2. NNPC pipeline network [30]

Thus, to model this problem, let us consider the two principal components we have discussed. On one hand, we have various *failure-causing elements* in pipeline transportation of crude oil. On the other hand, we have several *monitoring techniques* proposed as solutions to this problem.

Considering this information, we could model the problem as a non-cooperative two-player game with player 1 representing the failure-causing components and player 2, the monitoring system. Since our goal is to provide a fault-tolerant monitoring system, we could also apply the maximin strategy for player 2 (the monitoring system). The maximin strategy of a player is that strategy that maximises the player's worst-case payoff, i.e. the minimum amount of payoff guaranteed or the security level of the player [32]. For example, let us denote a player's security level as $\underline{Z_i}$; then, for player 2, the security level is defined in the following equation:

$$\underline{Z_2} = \max_{A_2} \min_{A_1} r_2(A_2, A_1) \tag{1}$$

Equation 1 above is used to find the policy that maximises player 2's security level through action(s)-A_2- and minimises the effect of action(s)-A_1- taken by player 1, i.e. the saddle point of the two players. With this approach, although pessimistic, we will guarantee leakage detection, whatever the failure is (i.e. the other player will not change its strategy based on the theory of Nash equilibrium).

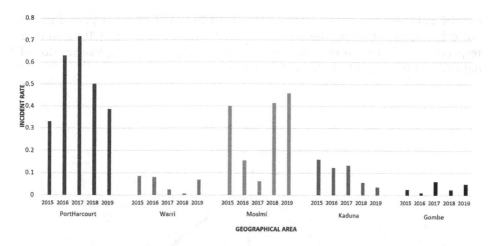

Fig. 3. 5 year pipeline incidents [31]

However, to consider our problem a two-player game, we must define the
actions set A and utilities r of at least one player. While we can easily quantify
the utility in the case of player 2, for example, as the number of leaks detected in
ratio to the total number of leaks- over a predefined period, it does not translate
to the same utility in the case of the other player. For player 1, most failure-
causing components like corrosion and erosion result from natural occurrences.
Thus, their effects cannot be considered utility for the player. Moreover, we are
more interested in the impact of player 1's action(s) on player 2 than its gain
for itself, if any. Thus, making it difficult to be modelled as a 2-players game.

However, we have an environment (NNPC pipeline network presented in
Fig. 2) with data that gives us information on the properties and the behaviour
of player 1. Hence, we model this problem as a game against nature, i.e. a
one-player game. In the subsequent subsection, we discuss, in more detail, this
modelling.

3.2 Environment Setting and Model Definition

Modelling the problem as a game against nature allows us to optimise the utilities
defined for our player (the monitoring system) solely in response to the failures
in our environment. While this can be applied as a global solution, the data
presented in Fig. 3 shows a large diversity in incident rates from one area to the
other. Thus, we propose a tailored solution for each area by broadly categorising
them into different *logical regions* defined as $R = \{r0, r1, r2\}$. The aim is to
optimise the performance of each region without the cost of a globalised solution.

Using an empirical study, we define a failure-rate-based threshold on which
the region of the area is determined. The area(s) with an incidents rate (IR)
of 0–5% is categorised as region $r0$ and represents the area(s) with the least
number of incidents. The area(s) with an average number of incidents from 6%

to 20% is in region $r1$. The area(s) with IR of 21% and above is placed in the critical region $r2$. Putting the areas into small, average and high ($r0, r1$, and $r2$ respectively) incident rates logical regions allows for practical implementation of data-driven strategies tailored to each region.

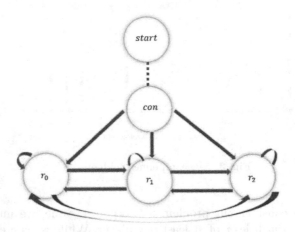

Fig. 4. State transition diagram

In addition, each area has a high probability of remaining in the same region for an extended period. For example, the PortHarcourt area is consistently in $r2$ while the Gombe and Kaduna areas are in the region $r0$ and $r1$ 80% of the time, only changing in the year 2017 and 2019, respectively. Mosimi and Warri represent areas with the most likely changes of approximately 40% of the timeline. Accordingly, the probability of each area transitioning from one region to another is low. Therefore, we depict such transition in a broad representation of each area's states as shown in Fig. 4. Each state will be discussed in more detail in the next subsection.

Following the definition of the regions, we aim to provide efficient and fault-tolerant data and service management using a *two-stage* approach. The first stage is to find the best detection policies (a learning agent behaviour) in terms of convergence and optimal detection accuracy using a data-based Markov Decision Process (MDP). We build the second stage on the results of the first stage to find the policy that minimises the processes' energy consumption. Thus, we propose our objective function summarised as follows:

$$\min_{(\pi^*, V^*)} V_e(\pi^*, V^*) \tag{2}$$

where π^* is the optimal policy, V^* is a value function following the policy π^*.

The value function obtained in each region allows us to measure and compare how good (reward and energy consumption) an applied policy is in that region. The performance measure is constrained by the number of nodes (at least two for fault tolerance in the monitoring system) that provide the accuracy within a bound, to be defined later. In the following subsections, we present the details of the two stages of the objective function.

3.3   The First Stage: Accuracy Optimisation

As discussed in Subsect. 3.2, we model our work as an MDP- a reinforcement learning formalisation in machine learning. Unlike other machine learning techniques, i.e. supervised learning (training a set of labelled data) and unsupervised learning (discovering structure in hidden collections of unlabelled data), reinforcement learning is used to learn dynamically through continuous *feedback* from its *interaction* in an environment to arrive at a *goal* [33].

Formalising the decision process in a stochastic environment using MDP is done by the tuple $< S, A, p, r >$, where S represents the sets of states, A the available actions, p the probability transition function, and r the reward function [32]. Another essential variable is the discount factor β for emphasising the importance of future rewards. Given these variables, an optimal policy that maximises a model's expected discounted cumulative reward can be determined using the well-known Bellman optimality equation. This cumulative reward helps us measure the goodness of a state, i.e. the maximum attainable reward in a state.

Generally, the Bellman equation following *an arbitrary policy* π is defined as follows:

$$\forall s : V^{\pi}(s) = \sum_{s'} p(s'|\pi(s), s)[(r(s, \pi(s)) + \beta V^{\pi}(s'))] \tag{3}$$

where $V^{\pi}(s)$ is the value in state s based on a policy π, $p(s'|\pi(s), s)$ is the probability of going from state s to s' with action following the policy, $(r(s, \pi(s))$ equals the immediate reward in state s, β is the discount factor for future rewards and $V^{\pi}(s')$ is the value in state s'.

To maximise the accumulated reward, an agent should follow *an optimal policy* -i.e. the policy that takes action with the maximum reward. This process is represented by the Bellman optimality equation as follows:

$$\forall s : V^{*}(s) = \max_{a} \sum_{s'} p(s'|s, a)[(r(s, a) + \beta V^{*}(s'))] \tag{4}$$

Note how the Bellman optimality equation (Eq. 4) differs from the Bellman equation (Eq. 3). In Eq. 4, the action a taken always returns the optimal reward, unlike the former with an arbitrary policy. The first part of Eq. 4 represented by $r(s, a)$ is the immediate reward, while the future reward for the second part is embedded in the iterative part $V^{*}(s')$. The hyperparameter β is a vital part of the equation for avoiding infinite cycles and allowing solutions to converge eventually. It also underscores the importance of future rewards, i.e. higher β value implies a more critical long-term reward and vice versa.

In the first part of our work, we use Bellman's optimality equation to evaluate different policies and to determine the policies that maximise the reward in terms of accurate leakage detection. Thus, we map the equation to the NNPC environment as follows:

The States S: We define a state as the conditions based on which the detection and localisation process is applied. So, S is represented as a set $S = \{start, con, r_0, r_1, r_2\}$, where $start$ and con are the initial states i.e., the state before any failure and the initialisation state, r_0, r_1, r_2 denotes the states during failure depending on the failure rate of the geographical area.

The Actions A: Actions are the mechanism of transitioning from one state to another. In our work, we define the set of actions as $A = \{s_t, c, s_a, r_{ds}, m_{ds}, rm_{ds}\}$. Each element in the set denotes process start, connection initialisation, service activation, replication of data and services, migration of data and services and replication and migration of data and services, respectively.

s_t (start-action): s_t, as the name implies, is a switch-on action which symbolises the beginning of the decision process.

c (connection initialisation): this action is used to realise the connectivity between nodes as defined in our previous work [29].

s_a (service activation): the s_a action denotes the activation of services in the nodes. Our work has two possible service deployment modes: service pre-deployment and optimised/dynamic service deployment. In the case of the former, the s_a action is used to reduce energy consumption by intermittently activating services as they are needed. It is, thus, applicable alongside other actions.

r_{ds} (data and service replication): r_{ds} denotes the replication of data and services. It represents the creation of copies of data as they are being produced or services in nearby nodes. In addition, it incorporates replication to the fog nodes instead of the limitation to sensor nodes in our earlier work. This extension to the fog nodes allows the implementation of other services, such as alarms, data prioritisation and filtration in the monitoring system. The amount of replication might change over time relative to changes in the experienced failure in the region.

m_{ds} (data and service migration): involves the migration of data and services. Although it is quite similar to r_{ds}, whereas r_{ds} is taken to counter failures, m_{ds} in addition to that is also used for specific needs. For example, we use this action to reassign services to other nodes in case of full storage. Increased latency between a service and its required data is another reason we migrate a service.

Both r_{ds} and m_{ds} have several, but different, communication requirements, as discussed in the following subsection.

rm_{ds} (data and service and replication/migration): this action allows the combination of replication and migration in a region where the failure rate is exceptionally high.

The States Transition Function p: The state transition function p utilises the information from the data presented in Fig. 3. It shows that some geographical areas are likely to transition from one region to another. Based on that, we determine the transition probability of each geographical area within the logical regions. In addition, Fig. 3 allows us to make a trend analysis on the failure pattern from one year to another and to specify the value and confidence level for future rewards using the hyperparameter β.

The Reward Function r: We define the reward function as $r \in [0, 100]$ per node for detection and localisation accuracy of leakages. For every action taken, the reward attainable is equivalent to the accuracy of leakage localisation. We also consider the number of nodes that falls within the allowance threshold for an acceptable accuracy level to represent the aspect of fault tolerance, as we will see later in the results section.

3.4   The Second Stage: Optimising the Energy Consumption

In the second stage of our work, the policy that minimises energy consumption for each region is selected based on the results obtained in the first stage. To determine the energy consumption of the policies, we first represent the environment described in Subsect. 3.1 as follows.

Let us define a set of nodes $N = \{n_1, n_2, ..., n_u\}$, where u equals the total number of sensor nodes and gateways. Each node $n_i \in N$ produces a set of data it also stores and is used by the services deployed in the system. If G is a matrix for the use of data by each service, then $g_{ij} = 1$ represents service in node n_i requiring data produced by node n_j. Hence, we propose h_{ij} to equate the number of hops between these nodes.

The modes of communication between sensor nodes and gateways is represented by $l_{ij} \in \{0, 1, 2\}$ where $l_{ij} = 0$ means no communication, $l_{ij} = 1$ a connection via LoRaWAN and $l_{ij} = 2$ a connection via 3G/4G communication networks. Each communication link varies in its capacity and will influence the kind of actions (or communication) between the nodes.

The service activation is a direct action depending only on the predefined neighbourhood connection, i.e. the implementation of state *con*.

To replicate, the communication between originating and destination nodes must be $l = 1$ for both data and services.

Migration of services necessitates higher bandwidth than data migration; therefore, their communication requirement is set as $l \in \{1, 2\}$ for data and service, respectively. For each action, the energy consumption is calculated using the following relation:

$$cost_{ij} = lc * h_{ij} \qquad (5)$$

where lc is the cost per packet, and per link of the service or data, h_{ij} is the number of hops between the origin and destination nodes. Note that service deployment mode results in changes to cost, i.e., the cost of service migrations is not included in the case of pre-deployed services. In such a scenario, the service activation action is used in place of the service migration action.

A good service placement is on nodes at most one hop away from the leakage point. Therefore, we can minimise energy consumption by reducing the distance (in the number of hops) between services and the needed data to run the service. We define the objective of the second stage as follows:

$$\min_{(\pi^*, V^*)} V_e(\pi^*, V^*) = \min_{(\pi^*, V^*)}$$

$$[\sum_{i=1}^{u} \sum_{j=1}^{u} cost_{ij} \cdot \sum_{s'} \phi^\pi(s')$$

$$\sum_s g_{ij}(s'|\pi(s), s) \cdot V^*(s')] \quad (6)$$

where $\phi^\pi(s') = p(s'|s, \pi)$ is the steady state defined by the probability of moving to the next state following a policy (π) in the current state, $cost_{ij}$ is the energy consumed defined in Eq. 5, $g_{ij}(s'|\pi(s), s)$ represents if data/service is resident in different nodes when we follow a policy from one state to another. This equation presents our objective function, i.e. to find and ensure convergence to the optimal reward with minimum energy consumption through the various placement strategies in the network nodes.

In the following section, we discuss the implementation of the objective function and the results.

4   Implementation and Results

The implementation of the model was carried out using the Gym library, an open-source toolkit for developing and approximating reinforcement learning algorithms. Furthermore, we simulated the pipeline environment shown in Fig. 2 using the NS3 network simulator. However, the realisation of the communication between OpenAI Gym and NS3 is based on the work conducted in [34] named ns3-gym. The ns3-gym enables seamless interaction between the NS3 network simulator and OpenAI Gym framework using an environment proxy in the Gym environment and an instantiated gateway in the network.

Figure 5 illustrates our implementation of the interface between the simulated pipeline network and OpenAI Gym in NS3. For comparative analysis, we used multiple agents on the gym side. Each agent interacts with a gateway through the dedicated proxy to implement the region placement strategies while carrying out the reinforcement learning using Algorithm 1.

We present the simulation parameters in Table 1. Other information exchanged between an agent and a gateway in each episode are (*i*) observation space, (*ii*) the action space, (*iii*) the reward and (*iv*) the game over conditions, defined in our work as follows:

The Observation Space: Failures, i.e. leakages, network or communication failures.

The Action Space: Actions include *start, connection, service activation, data and service replication* and *data and service migration*.

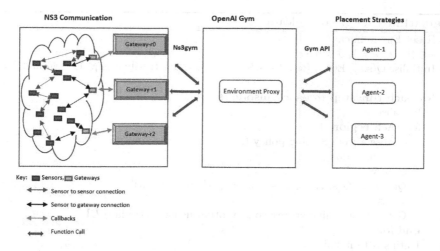

Fig. 5. Simulated pipeline network and OpenAI Gym interaction

Reward: The reward is based on the localisation accuracy of the leakage and the number of nodes that localises the leakages.

Game Over: A game is considered over at the end of the episodes.

Table 1. Simulation Parameters

Timestep	1000
Areas	5
Region	3
Proxy	1
Alpha	1
Beta	0.99
Number of episodes	1000
Reward per node	[0,100]
Error Type	Rate error model, list error model
epsilon	[0, 1]

The Q-learning algorithm is a well-known reinforcement learning algorithm for solving the Bellman Optimality Equation for MDPs by estimating the action-value function. It enables an early convergence to the optimal action-value function. Given the nature of the problem we are solving, we used the *epsilon*-greedy version of the Q-learning algorithm shown in Algorithm 1 and extracted from [33] to ensure a well-balanced exploration and exploitative steps.

Whereas the convergence to a global optimal value function is assured, the incident rate across the pipeline environment differs significantly, increasing the

---

Algorithm 1. ϵ−greedy Q-learning

1: Reset Environment
2: $\epsilon \in (0,1]$, $\alpha = 1$, $\beta = 0.99$
3: Initialise Q(s,a), E(s,a) for all s $\in S+$, a $\in$ A(s) arbitrarily except Q(terminal,.)=0

4: **for each timestep in each episode do**
5:      Initialise s
6:      **for each region do**
7:          Choose a from S using policy (ϵ−greedy) derived from Q
8:          Perform action a
9:          Observe r, s'
10:         $Q(s,a) \leftarrow Q(s,a) + \alpha[R + \beta max_a Q(s',a) - Q(s,a)]$
11:         s $\leftarrow$ s'
12:         Get corresponding energy consumption using 5 {Update E}
13:     **end for**
14:     Until s is terminal
15: **end for**
16: Reset Environment
17: For each region, choose the policy with the least energy consumption and optimal reward

---

overall cost, i.e. the energy consumption. Thus, we regionalised the environment to solve the MDP and determine the policy that minimises global energy consumption without affecting the optimal reward. In Algorithm 1, we begin by defining the region of each area in the NNPC pipeline network. We set the corresponding failure rate for each region for both failure types (rate and list error types). The state-action values are stored using a matrix - Q; then, we find the best policy that minimises the energy consumption by keeping track of the corresponding energy consumption using another matrix - E. We chose the optimal policy for each region at the end of all episodes.

In the subsequent subsections, we discuss the result obtained from the simulations.

4.1   Accuracy in Detection and Fault Tolerance

The *fault tolerance, accuracy* in each region (r0, r1 and r2) and the corresponding *obtainable reward* using the detection and localisation algorithm from our previous work [29] is evaluated in this subsection. To achieve this, we used two different types of communication failures, i.e. *Rate error type* and *List error type* in NS3. The Rate error type involves random packet drop, out-of-order delivery and delayed packet. In contrast, the list error type involves a pre-selected list of packet drops. We made a uniformly distributed selection for the list error type from all the packets shared among the nodes. Also, the simulation was carried out across several randomly selected leakage points. Obtained results are presented in Figs. 6, 7, 8, 9, 10 and 11. We limit this evaluation to error rates between the range of 0% to 20% as either detection or localisation beyond this range is impossible.

In addition, we present each evaluation -i.e. the fault tolerance, accuracy, and obtainable reward- with two figures each: the first figure represents all possible observations. In contrast, the second figure represents observations from High Performing Nodes (HPN), i.e. nodes with results greater than or equal to the target accuracy level of 90%. The set threshold defines the benchmark based on which we can ensure standardised performance. We choose this level of accuracy as the minimum level based on the requirements of the oil and gas operators for high localisation accuracy [35]. It also ensures that all regions have a standardised performance level.

Fault Tolerance. One of our detection and localising algorithm's strengths is removing single point of failure associated with centralised systems. To maintain this property, we ensure that there are at least two HPNs across all regions. Figures 6 and 7 show the number of nodes that can detect and localise leakages.

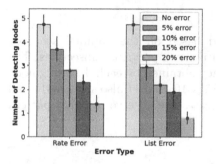
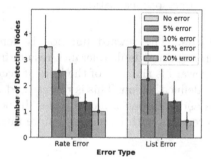

Fig. 6. Total number of nodes detecting leakage

Fig. 7. Total number of HPN

In Fig. 6, we capture the total number of nodes detecting and localising leakage without considering the accuracy level, while Fig. 7 shows only the HPN, i.e. with accuracy over 90%. Following the benchmark, we observe (from Fig. 7) that areas with 5% failure rate for both rate and list error types maintain the required number (at least two) of nodes for fault tolerance differing mostly in the variance. This variance is observed from nodes located at the extremities of the pipelines in the area(s), which can be addressed with increased node density in such location(s). However, other areas, i.e. with a failure rate above 5%, do not meet this requirement.

Accuracy. We examine how the accuracy level changes based on the failure rate. Results are presented in Figs. 8 and 9.

Figure 8 shows that the list error type provides a higher accuracy level than the rate error type, with both presenting similar trends in error. Nonetheless, when we consider results from HPN shown in Fig. 9, the rate error type presents

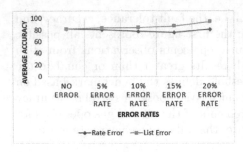

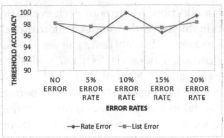

Fig. 8. Accuracy of leakage detection in all nodes

Fig. 9. Accuracy of leakage detection in HPN

much variance in changes in the accuracy of localisation compared to the list error type. Hence, we can conclude that while the lower error rates favour a higher number of nodes in leakage detection, it does not have such an impact on the accuracy of localisation.

Rewards. The reward function is defined based on the minimal accuracy requirement and fault-tolerance results from the two previous subsections. The total reward is the sum of the level of accuracy obtained by each detecting node in the defined region. This is represented in Figs. 10, and 11 also separated as all nodes and high-performance nodes. In both cases, we observe a similar pattern of decrements with increasing failure rate.

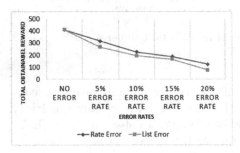

Fig. 10. Total obtainable reward across the error rates

Fig. 11. Total obtainable reward with HPN

Following the benchmarks discussed in Subsect. 4.1, we present the expected reward across all regions in Fig. 11. We expect to have two HPNs at all times for all failure rates, thus putting the target at the level shown in the figure.

4.2   Optimised Accuracy and Energy Consumption

This subsection discusses the rewards obtained based on our implemented algorithms (learning-based, heuristic and pessimistic).

We used a uniform-random policy and our proposed regionalised ϵ-greedy Q-learning (R-MDP) for the learning-based algorithms. The uniform-random policy has a uniform distribution over the space from which actions are taken. Given the objective function, the ϵ-greedy Q-learning algorithm lets the agent exploit (dependent on what the agent has learnt) and explore (take a random action with a probability of ϵ), thus evading local optimum in each region.

Also implemented is a heuristic approach based on weighted set cover service placement (WSC) from the work [36] to provide a baseline for comparison. The goal of the WSC in our context is also to maximise detection accuracy with minimum cost (i.e. energy consumption) in a globalised manner. The pessimistic approach deals with the worst-case scenario from the environmental data. Following is the performance evaluation of each algorithm.

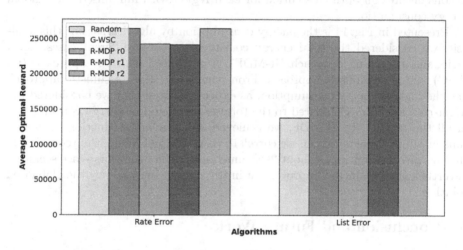

Fig. 12. Total reward by algorithm

Figure 12 reveals the optimal rewards following the three implemented algorithms. As expected, the random policy has the lowest total reward. Results from the ϵ-greedy algorithm for each region satisfy the optimality conditions defined in the objective function (Eq. 6). The WSC-based algorithm shows about a 6% increase in the obtained total value attributed to the dynamics of the environment.

To study the exploration effect, i.e. the value of ϵ on the results, we present the total energy consumption in Fig. 13. Results show less energy consumption for the average epsilon values less than 0.4 and much higher consumption as ϵ approaches the maximum average value of 1. We observe that the exploration's effect differs considerably for each region. For example, regions r0 and r2 perform much better with a near absolutely greedy policy. While the reward of r0 slightly varies as the exploration increases, the reward of r2 is inversely proportional to the epsilon value. However, region r1 presents optimal results with an epsilon

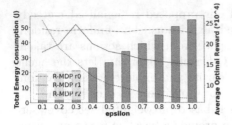

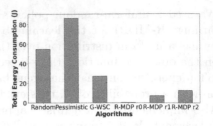

Fig. 13. Regional reward vs energy consumption

Fig. 14. Total energy consumption by algorithm

value of approximately 0.3. Thus, partitioning the environment into distinct regions ensures an optimal solution for each region with minimised total global energy consumption.

Presented in Fig. 14 is the energy consumption by algorithms. For this analysis, we considered the total energy consumed in three different cases, i.e. a regionalised learning approach (R-MDP), a globalised heuristic approach (G-WSC) and a pessimistic approach. From the result, the pessimistic approach has the highest energy consumption, as expected, given that we considered the worst-case scenario. Compared to the total energy (sum of energy consumption in all the regions) by R-MDP, we achieved about a 77% reduction in energy consumption. However, when we correlate R-MDP to G-WSC, the reduction in the energy consumption is about 26%, much lesser than the worst-case scenario, nevertheless, a significant improvement in the energy consumed by the globalised solution.

5   Conclusion and Future Work

This paper presented our work on fault-tolerant and energy-efficient data and service management modelled as an MDP. Our work is based on the NNPC pipeline network and the associated failures. We implemented a regionalised MDP that ensures optimal reward with a detection accuracy threshold above 90% in an energy-efficient manner. Results show that the total energy consumption is minimised by a significant reduction of nearly 77% compared to the pessimistic method and approximately 26% compared to a globalised heuristic technique. In future works, we will consider other forms of failures and constraints, such as latency issues, and dynamic topologies, such as mobile sensors/gateways - e.g. UAVs - for dynamic communication coverage.

Acknowledgment. This work was supported by the Petroleum Technology Development Fund (PTDF).

References

1. Mohammadpoor, M., Torabi, F.: Big data analytics in oil and gas industry: an emerging trend. Petroleum **6**(4), 321–328 (2018)

2. Aliguliyev, R., Imamverdiyev, Y.: Conceptual big data architecture for the oil and gas industry. Probl. Inf. Technol. **08**, 3–13 (2017)
3. Slaughter, A., Bean, G., Mittal, A.: Connected barrels: transforming oil and gas strategies with the Internet of Things. Deloitte Center for Energy Solutions, Technical report (2015)
4. Mittal, A., Slaughter, A., Zonneveld, P.: Bringing the digital revolution to midstream oil and gas. Deloitte Center for Energy Solutions, Technical report (2018)
5. Zonneveld, P., Slaughter, A., Mittal, A.: Protecting the connected barrels cybersecurity for upstream oil and gas. Deloitte Center for Energy Solutions, Technical report (2017)
6. Hajirahimova, M.: Opportunities and challenges big data in oil and gas industry. In: National Supercomputer Forum (NSKF-2015) (2015)
7. Song, J., He, H., Wang, Z., Yu, G., Pierson, J.-M.: Modulo based data placement algorithm for energy consumption optimization of mapreduce system. J. Grid Comput. **1**, 1–16 (2016)
8. Wang, W., Wu, G., Guo, Z., Qian, L., Ding, L., Yang, F.: Data scheduling and resource optimization for fog computing architecture in industrial IoT. In: Fahrnberger, G., Gopinathan, S., Parida, L. (eds.) ICDCIT 2019. LNCS, vol. 11319, pp. 141–149. Springer, Cham (2019). https://doi.org/10.1007/978-3-030-05366-6_11
9. Patel, P., Intizar Ali, M., Sheth, A.: On using the intelligent edge for IoT analytics. IEEE Intell. Syst. **32**(5), 64–69 (2017)
10. Tang, B., Chen, Z., Hefferman, G., Wei, T., He, H., Yang, Q.: A hierarchical distributed fog computing architecture for big data analysis in smart cities. In: Proceedings of ASE International Conference on Big Data (2015)
11. Giordano, A., Spezzano, G., Vinci, A.: Smart agents and fog computing for smart city applications. In: Alba, E., Chicano, F., Luque, G. (eds.) Smart-CT 2016. LNCS, vol. 9704, pp. 137–146. Springer, Cham (2016). https://doi.org/10.1007/978-3-319-39595-1_14
12. Naas, M.I., Parvedy, P.R., Boukhobza, J., Lemarchand, L.: iFogStor: an IoT data placement strategy for fog infrastructure. In: IEEE 1st International Conference on Fog and Edge Computing (ICFEC), pp. 97–104 (2017)
13. Aral, A., Ovatman, T.: A decentralized replica placement algorithm for edge computing. IEEE Trans. Netw. Serv. Manage. **15**(2), 516–529 (2018)
14. Shao, Y., Li, C., Tang, H.: A data replica placement strategy for IoT workflows in collaborative edge and cloud environments. Comput. Netw. **148**, 11 (2018)
15. Velasquez, K., Abreu, D.P., Curado, M., Monteiro, E.: Service placement for latency reduction in the internet of things. Ann. Telecommun. **72**, 105–115 (2017)
16. Elsayed, W.M., Sabbeh, S.F., Riad, A.M.: A distributed fault tolerance mechanism for self-maintenance of clusters in wireless sensor networks. Arab. J. Sci. Eng. **43**, 6891–6907 (2017)
17. Yuvaraja, M., Sabrigiriraj, M.: Fault detection and recovery scheme for routing and lifetime enhancement in WSN. Wireless Netw. **23**, 267–277 (2015)
18. Qian, S., Mao, W., Cao, J., Le Mouël, F., Li, M.: Adjusting matching algorithm to adapt to workload fluctuations in content-based publish/subscribe systems. In: Proceedings of the IEEE Conference on Computer Communications (INFOCOM 2019), Paris, France, pp. 1936–1944 (2019)
19. Ioana, A., Burlacu, C., Korodi, A.: Approaching OPC UA publish-subscribe in the context of UDP-based multi-channel communication and image transmission. Sensors **21**(4), 1296 (2021)

20. Aslam, A., Curry, E.: Investigating response time and accuracy in online classifier learning for multimedia publish-subscribe systems. Multimedia Tools Appl. **80**, 13021–13057 (2021)
21. Jafarpour, H., Hore, B., Mehrotra, S., Venkatasubramanian, N.: CCD: a distributed publish/subscribe framework for rich content formats. IEEE Trans. Parallel Distrib. Syst. **23**(5), 844–852 (2012)
22. Garg, D., Narendra, N.C., Tesfatsion, S.: Heuristic and reinforcement learning algorithms for dynamic service placement on mobile edge cloud. CoRR (2021)
23. He, T., Khamfroush, H., Wang, S., La Porta, T., Stein, S.: It's hard to share: joint service placement and request scheduling in edge clouds with sharable and non-sharable resources. In: 2018 IEEE 38th International Conference on Distributed Computing Systems (ICDCS), pp. 365–375 (2018)
24. Cai, Q., Hang, W., Mirhoseini, A., Tucker, G., Wang, J., Wei, W.: Reinforcement learning driven heuristic optimization. CoRR (2019)
25. Islam, M.S., Nix, R., Kantarcioglu, M.: A game theoretic approach for adversarial pipeline monitoring using wireless sensor networks. In: 2012 IEEE 13th International Conference on Information Reuse Integration (IRI), pp. 37–44 (2012)
26. Rezazadeh, A., Talarico, L., Reniers, G., Cozzani, V., Zhang, L.: Applying game theory for securing oil and gas pipelines against terrorism. Reliab. Eng. Syst. Saf. **191**, 106140 (2019)
27. Rezazadeh, A., Zhang, L., Reniers, G., Khakzad, N., Cozzani, V.: Optimal patrol scheduling of hazardous pipelines using game theory. Process Saf. Environ. Prot. **109**, 242–256 (2017)
28. Ahmed, S., Le Mouël, F., Stouls, N.: Resilient IoT-based monitoring system for crude oil pipelines. In: Proceedings of the 7th International Conference on Internet of Things: Systems, Management and Security (IOTSMS). IEEE (2020)
29. Ahmed, S., Le Mouël, F., Stouls, N., Lipeme Kouyi, G.: HyDiLLEch: a WSN-based distributed leak detection and localisation in crude oil pipelines. In: Barolli, L., Woungang, I., Enokido, T. (eds.) AINA 2021. LNNS, vol. 225, pp. 626–637. Springer, Cham (2021). https://doi.org/10.1007/978-3-030-75100-5_54
30. Ambituuni, A., Ochieng, E., Amezaga, J.M.: Optimizing the integrity of safety critical petroleum assets: a project conceptualization approach. IEEE Trans. Eng. Manage. **66**(2), 208–223 (2019)
31. NNPC: 2019 annual statistical bulletin. Nigerian National Petroleum Corporation, Technical report (2019)
32. Shoham, Y., Leyton-Brown, K.: Multiagent Systems Algorithmic, Game-Theoretic, and Logical Foundations. Cambridge University Press, Cambridge (2008)
33. Sutton, R.S., Barto, A.G.: Reinforcement Learning: An Introduction, 2nd edn, F. Bach, Ed. The MIT Press, Cambridge (2020)
34. Gawlowicz, P., Zubow, A.: ns-3 meets OpenAI Gym: the playground for machine learning in networking research. In: ACM International Conference on Modeling, Analysis and Simulation of Wireless and Mobile Systems (MSWiM) (2019)
35. Ostapkowicz, P.: Leak detection in liquid transmission pipelines using simplified pressure analysis techniques employing a minimum of standard and non-standard measuring devices. Eng. Struct. **113**, 194–205 (2016)
36. Garg, D., Narendra, N.C., Tesfatsion, S.: Heuristic and reinforcement learning algorithms for dynamic service placement on mobile edge cloud (2021)

UWB/IMU Fusion Localization Strategy Based on Continuity of Movement

Li Zhang[1](✉) ⓘ, Jinhui Bao[1] ⓘ, Jingao Xu[2] ⓘ, and Danyang Li[2] ⓘ

[1] HeFei University of Technology, Hefei 230000, China
lizhang@hfut.edu.cn
[2] Tsinghua University, Beijing 100000, China

Abstract. Commercial and industrial sectors are increasingly deploying inertial measurement unit (IMU) and ultrawideband (UWB) for motion control, automation, and positioning applications, such as intelligent manufacturing, smart homes and smartphones. However, it does not perform well in a multi-obstacle environment, such as the problem of locating workers in a multi-worker environment and finding cars in a large parking lot. This is because IMU can provide a low-cost and accurate inertial navigation solution in a short time, but its positioning error increases rapidly over time as a result of accumulated accelerometer measurement errors. On the other hand, even under line-of-sight (LOS) settings, UWB positioning and navigation accuracy is impacted by the real environment, resulting in unreliable leaps. Therefore, it is difficult to achieve high accuracy positioning using single positioning and navigation system in indoor environments. In this paper, a robust UWB and IMU fusion indoor localization system based on adaptive dynamic Kalman Filter (ADKF) algorithm has been proposed which relies on motion continuity and can be applied to indoor complex multipath environment. Specifically, in order to mitigate non-line-of-sight (NLOS) errors, one novel range-constrained weighted least square (RWLS) algorithm is presented. The experimental results show that both algorithms can mitigate NLOS errors effectively and reach a particular degree of robustness and ongoing tracking capability in integrated indoor positioning system (IPS).

Keywords: Kalman Filter (KF) · inertial measurement unit (IMU) · ultrawideband (UWB) · indoor positioning system (IPS)

1 Introduction

The accuracy of current navigation systems, such as the Global Positioning System (GPS) and the Global Navigation Satellite System (GLONASS), is high

Supported by the National Key Research and Development Program (2018YFB2100301); National Natural Science Foundation of China (61972131).

S. Longfei and P. Bodhi (Eds.): MobiQuitous 2022, LNICST 492, pp. 65–78, 2023.
https://doi.org/10.1007/978-3-031-34776-4_4

when used outdoors but very low when used indoors [1]. As a result, precise indoor localization and tracking have gained popularity and given rise to a number of applications, including augmented reality, intelligent advertising, and customer navigation. Recent publications of a wealth of research [2–10] demonstrate the growing interest in indoor location and tracking systems, which employ wireless signals, cameras, inertial measurement units (IMU), ultrawideband (UWB), etc.

IMU is the core of the inertial navigation system (INS) including a three-axis accelerometer and gyroscope [11]. The attitude information and motion characteristics of the object, such as acceleration, angular velocity and angle can be acquired by IMU [12]. The position of the carrier can be directly determined by mathematically integrating the acceleration without the use of a reference base station. Due to its low cost, minimal influence on the environment, and high accuracy in a short time, INS is frequently employed in moving target placement and navigation scenarios for aircraft, automobiles, pedestrians, and other moving targets; nevertheless, the error grows quickly with time [13]. Additionally, many indoor positioning systems use ultra-wideband (UWB) technology [14], constructing several non-visual distance processing techniques, such as the channel model [15], multipath component estimate [16], and theoretical lower band of positioning errors [17].

Utilizing nanosecond non-sinusoidal narrow pulse transmissions, UWB is a successful communication technology for position-sensing sensor networks [18]. Achieving centimeter-level range precision, UWB benefits from short pulse intervals, high time resolution, and robustness to the multipath effect [19,20]. Due to its high-frequency spectrum, UWB is only appropriate for a line-of-sight situation. When object occlusion occurs, the range accuracy of UWB is significantly decreased. As can be observed, employing simply IMU or UWB to obtain high accuracy in complicated indoor conditions is challenging.

To achieve high robustness and accuracy of the indoor localization system, this article focuses on the integration of IMU and UWB based on Kalman Filter technique. We propose a RWLS algorithm based on the distance constraint for UWB positioning and then an ADKF algorithm combining IMU and UWB based on motion continuity. Extensive experiments show that both algorithms can mitigate NLOS errors effectively and reach a particular degree of robustness and ongoing tracking capability in indoor complex and dynamic environments.

The main contributions are summarized as follows:

- We propose a RWLS algorithm based on the distance constraint, which can mitigate NLOS errors.
- A loosely coupled ADKF tracking algorithm is proposed to combine IMU and UWB, which can effectively reduce uncertain jumping caused by complex indoor environment.
- Extensive real-world experiments are performed to validate our algorithms. The experimental results show that our algorithms perform better in dynamic and complex indoor environments.

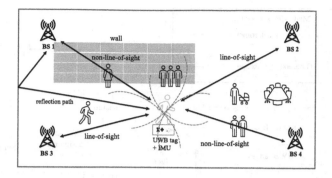

Fig. 1. Positioning in a complex indoor multipath environment.

2   Related Work

Complementary characteristics of IMU and UWB are considered to improve positioning accuracy. An improved PDR/UWB integrated system is proposed based on the variable noise variance (VNV) Kalman Filter algorithm to dynamically adjust the noise distribution through a non-line-of-sight evaluation function [21]. An integrated indoor positioning system (IPS) combining IMU and UWB is proposed through the extended Kalman Filter (EKF) and unscented Kalman Filter (UKF) to improve the robustness and accuracy [22]. The federated derivative cubature Kalman Filter (FDCKF) method is proposed by combining the traditional Kalman Filter and the cubature Kalman Filter then the observations of the UWB and the IMU can be effectively fused [23].

The algorithms proposed by predecessors can be applied to industrial robots, power plant positioning technology, judicial prisons, industrial warehouses and other relatively simple environments. However, in complex environments such as large parking lots and factories with a large number of workers, multi-path effect and non-line-of-sight effect will lead to poor location results.

3   Single Sensor Positioning Algorithm

In this section, we first introduce the IMU-based and UWB-based positioning algorithms, and propose a range-constrained weighted least square (RWLS) into UWB localization algorithm. The IMU sensor consists of a three-axis accelerometer and gyroscope. The UWB sensors consist of four base stations (BSs) with known positions and an unknown position tag.

3.1   Inertial Sensor Positioning Algorithm

The updating of the attitude matrix calculation in the strap-down INS (SINS) and the transformations of various coordinate systems have both received a lot of attention [24].

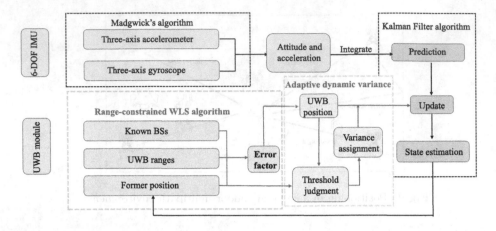

Fig. 2. System Overview.

It is crucial to use the suitable coordinate system in order to accurately characterize the tag's space motion state. Assume that the world coordinate system is $Ox_wy_wz_w$ and that $Ox_by_bz_b$ represents the body coordinate system, respectively. The attitude matrix of the carrier is the coordinate transformation matrix between the world coordinate system and the body coordinate system. The coordinates of the accelerometer and gyroscope in the system belong to the body coordinate system. While the world coordinate system is where the final results of acceleration, velocity, and position belong. Madgwick's algorithm [25] is considered to solve this problem of its low computational cost. Then the rotation matrix R can be obtained from the three-axis acceleration and gyroscope data. The acceleration in the body coordinate system, $\boldsymbol{a}^b$ is expressed in Eq. (1).

$$\boldsymbol{a}^b = \begin{bmatrix} a_x^b & a_y^b & a_z^b \end{bmatrix}^T \tag{1}$$

Thus, the acceleration in the world coordinate system, $\boldsymbol{a}^{w1}$, can be obtained by the coordinate transformation:

$$\boldsymbol{a}^{w1} = \begin{bmatrix} a_x^{w1} & a_y^{w1} & a_z^{w1} \end{bmatrix}^T = R\boldsymbol{a}^b. \tag{2}$$

After subtracting the gravitational acceleration, the acceleration is $\boldsymbol{a}^w$:

$$\boldsymbol{a}^w = \begin{bmatrix} a_x^w \\ a_y^w \\ a_z^w \end{bmatrix} = \begin{bmatrix} a_x^{w1} \\ a_y^{w1} \\ a_z^{w1} \end{bmatrix} - \begin{bmatrix} 0 \\ 0 \\ g \end{bmatrix}. \tag{3}$$

Let $\boldsymbol{v}^w(t_j)$ represents the velocity in the world coordinate system at the time t_j. Then, the velocity in the world coordinate system at the time t_{j+1}, $\boldsymbol{v}^w(t_{j+1})$, can be acquired by using the acceleration integral as shown below.:

$$\begin{bmatrix} v_x^w(t_{j+1}) \\ v_y^w(t_{j+1}) \\ v_z^w(t_{j+1}) \end{bmatrix} = \begin{bmatrix} v_x^w(t_j) \\ v_y^w(t_j) \\ v_z^w(t_j) \end{bmatrix} + \begin{bmatrix} a_x^w \\ a_y^w \\ a_z^w \end{bmatrix} \Delta t \tag{4}$$

Let $\boldsymbol{P}^w(t_j)$ represents the position in the world coordinate system at the time t_j, and then the position in the world coordinate system at the time t_{j+1}, $\boldsymbol{P}^w(t_{j+1})$, can be calculated as follows:

$$\begin{bmatrix} P_x^w(t_{j+1}) \\ P_y^w(t_{j+1}) \\ P_z^w(t_{j+1}) \end{bmatrix} = \begin{bmatrix} P_x^w(t_j) \\ P_y^w(t_j) \\ P_z^w(t_j) \end{bmatrix} + \begin{bmatrix} v_x^w \\ v_y^w \\ v_z^w \end{bmatrix} \Delta t + \frac{1}{2} \begin{bmatrix} a_x^w \\ a_y^w \\ a_z^w \end{bmatrix} \Delta t^2. \tag{5}$$

3.2   Ultra-wideband Positioning Algorithm

The ranging-based technique is typically used in the two-step UWB positioning approach. Measuring the distances between the unknown node and anchor nodes is the first step. The position of the unknown node is determined in the second phase by using distance information.

In our approach to range measuring, we employ the SDS-TWR optimization algorithm [26]. We use multilateration to establish the tag's position depending on the distance once the range measurements are finished. In particular, Fig. 1 illustrates a multilateration case in which the separations between the tag and four BSs are assessed. The tag should ideally be situated near the intersection of four circles centered on four BSs in the 2-D plane. Due to range error, particularly in the non-line-of-sight range, the intersection is typically not singular.

Suppose that the coordinates of unknown tag and the ith BS are (x, y) and (x_i, y_i), respectively. Then, the real distance between the unknown tag and the ith BS, d_i can be written as $\sqrt{(x_i - x)^2 + (y_i - y)^2}$. The distance between the mobile tag and the ith BS is d_i'. Therefore, the difference between the actual distance and measured distance is calculated by $\rho_i = d_i - d_i'$. We use the traditional LS approach to minimize the value of $\sum_{i=1}^{n} \rho_i^2$ to cope with the range noise. For each distance, the following equations are used to calculate the position of an unknown tag:

$$\begin{cases} d_1^2 = (x_1 - x)^2 + (y_1 - y)^2 \\ d_2^2 = (x_2 - x)^2 + (y_2 - y)^2 \\ \quad \vdots \\ d_n^2 = (x_n - x)^2 + (y_n - y)^2 \end{cases} \tag{6}$$

Let's remove the first equation from all the others to get

$$AX = b, \tag{7}$$

where

$$A = \begin{bmatrix} x_2 - x_1 & y_2 - y_1 \\ x_3 - x_1 & y_3 - y_1 \\ \vdots & \vdots \\ x_n - x_1 & y_n - y_1 \end{bmatrix}, X = \begin{bmatrix} x \\ y \end{bmatrix}$$

$$b = \frac{1}{2} \begin{bmatrix} x_2^2 + y_2^2 - d_2^2 - (x_1^2 + y_1^2 - d_1^2) \\ x_3^2 + y_3^2 - d_3^2 - (x_1^2 + y_1^2 - d_1^2) \\ \vdots \\ x_n^2 + y_n^2 - d_n^2 - (x_1^2 + y_1^2 - d_1^2) \end{bmatrix}.$$

(8)

Every range value in the LS approach has the same weight. The fact that the range error varies on each side makes it obvious that it is not very appropriate. The weighted least square (WLS) [22] approach was suggested by Daquan Feng et al. to address the issue. When the tag is nearer the BS during the ranging process, it is believed that the ranging error is lower. As a result, adopting a heavier weight for the smaller range value further reduces positioning error. The reciprocal of the ranging value d yields the weighting coefficient η as follows:

$$\eta = \begin{bmatrix} \frac{1}{d_2} & 0 & 0 & 0 \\ 0 & \frac{1}{d_3} & 0 & 0 \\ 0 & 0 & \ddots & 0 \\ 0 & 0 & 0 & \frac{1}{d_n} \end{bmatrix}.$$

(9)

Then, the WLS solution of X is calculated as follows:

$$X = \left(A^T \eta A\right)^{-1} A^T \eta b.$$

(10)

In actual environments, due to the complexity of space and the movement of pedestrians, the view that the closer the tag is to the BS, the smaller the ranging error may be untrue. Thus, we propose the range-constrained weighted least square (RWLS) algorithm based on the former position constraint to solve this problem. Due to the short sampling time of UWB, there is no obvious position change between two adjacent sampling points, which means continuity of movement. Assuming that $X_{t_{j-1}}$ is the former position, we introduce the ranging error factor $\Delta m_{i,j}$, which is the ranging error of the ith base station at the time t_j.

$$\Delta m_{i,j} = \left| \text{dis} \left(X_{t_{j-1}}, (x_i, y_i) \right) - d_{i,j} \right|,$$

(11)

where dis() represents the distance between two points and $d_{i,j}$ mean the measured distance from the tag to the ith BS at the time t_j. The error factor and $d_{i,j}$ is normalized as follows:

$$\Delta m_{i,j} = \frac{\Delta m_{i,j}}{\sum_{i=1}^{n} \Delta m_{i,j}}$$

$$d_{i,j} = \frac{d_{i,j}}{\sum_{i=1}^{n} d_{i,j}}.$$

(12)

We assign a higher weight for the smaller ranging error factor and smaller range d, the positioning accuracy will be further improved. Then we can get a new matrix of coefficients η_{new} as follows:

$$\eta_{\text{new}} = \begin{bmatrix} \frac{1}{\Delta m_{2,j} d_{2,j}} & 0 & 0 & 0 \\ 0 & \frac{1}{\Delta m_{3,j} d_{3,j}} & 0 & 0 \\ 0 & 0 & \ddots & 0 \\ 0 & 0 & 0 & \frac{1}{\Delta m_{n,j} d_{n,j}} \end{bmatrix}. \tag{13}$$

Finally, the positioning result at the time t_j is obtained:

$$X_{t_j} = \left(A^T \eta_{\text{new}} A\right)^{-1} A^T \eta_{\text{new}} b. \tag{14}$$

The complete RWLS algorithm is shown in **RWLS algorithm**.

RWLS algorithm

Input: $n, m, (x_i, y_i), X_{t_{j-1}}, d_{i,j}$
1: $n =$ numbers of BSs
  $m =$ numbers of UWB samples
2 : for j from 1 to m
3: **Initialization**
if $j = 1$:

$$\eta = \begin{bmatrix} \frac{1}{d_{2,1}} & 0 & 0 & 0 \\ 0 & \frac{1}{d_{3,1}} & 0 & 0 \\ 0 & 0 & \ddots & 0 \\ 0 & 0 & 0 & \frac{1}{d_{n,1}} \end{bmatrix}$$

  else:
4: **Calculate error factor**
for i from 1 to n :

$$\Delta m_{i,j} = \left| \text{dis}\left(X_{t_{j-1}}, (x_i, y_i)\right) - d_{i,j} \right|$$

5: **Normalized**
$$\Delta m_{i,j} = \frac{\Delta m_{i,j}}{\sum_{i=1}^{n} m_{i,j}} \quad d_{i,j} = \frac{d_{i,j}}{\sum_{i=1}^{n} d_{i,j}}$$
6: **New coefficient matrix**

$$\eta = \begin{bmatrix} \frac{1}{\Delta m_{2,j} d_{2,j}} & 0 & 0 & 0 \\ 0 & \frac{1}{\Delta m_{3,j} d_{3,j}} & 0 & 0 \\ 0 & 0 & \ddots & 0 \\ 0 & 0 & 0 & \frac{1}{\Delta m_{n,j} d_{n,j}} \end{bmatrix}$$

  end

7: **Position**

$$X_{t_j} = \left(A^T \eta A\right)^{-1} A^T \eta b$$

end

Output: P_{t_j}

---

4 Fusion Algorithm Based on UWB and IMU

It is known that the linear Kalman Filter can calculate the ideal carrier state in the linear Gaussian model, provided that the noise from the IMU and UWB sensors is independent of one another and that both abide by the Gaussian distribution with zero mean and variance σ^2. In this section, we propose an adaptive dynamic Kalman Filter (ADKF) algorithm based on the distance constraint. The design of an indoor positioning system based on the combination of IMU and UWB is shown in Fig. 2.

We first use UWB to provide the initial position X_0 by RWLS algorithm and initial velocity, $V_x = V_y = 0$. The state vector of the tag is $\hat{X}_{k-1}$ as follows:

$$\hat{X}_{k-1} = \begin{bmatrix} P_x \\ P_y \\ V_x \\ V_y \end{bmatrix}. \tag{15}$$

Assuming that the tag motion satisfies the uniformly accelerated motion model in a short time, we predict the state $\hat{X}_{k|k-1}$ by acceleration based on Madgwick's algorithm as follows:

$$\hat{X}_{k|k-1} = A\hat{X}_{k-1} + Bu$$
$$P_{k|k-1} = AP_{k-1}A^T + Q, \tag{16}$$

where

$$\mathbf{u} = \begin{bmatrix} a_x \\ a_y \end{bmatrix}, A = \begin{bmatrix} 1 & 0 & t & 0 \\ 0 & 1 & 0 & t \\ 0 & 0 & 1 & 0 \\ 0 & 0 & 0 & 1 \end{bmatrix}, B = \begin{bmatrix} t^2 & 0 \\ 0 & t^2 \\ t & 0 \\ 0 & t \end{bmatrix} \text{ and } Q \text{ is the process noise variance.}$$

Here t is sample interval. Then we calculate the UWB location results $Y_k = \begin{bmatrix} P_{x_{UWB}} \\ P_{y_{UWB}} \end{bmatrix}$ by the RWLS algorithm as observation. The relationship between the state vector and the observed values is as follows:

$$Y_k = H\hat{X}_k, \tag{17}$$

where $H = \begin{bmatrix} 1 & 0 & 0 & 0 \\ 0 & 1 & 0 & 0 \end{bmatrix}$.

The variety of indoor environments may lead to the occurrence of non-line-of-sight ranging. Since the tag motion changes very little in a short time, we consider introducing dynamic measurement variance adjustment based on the former position constraint. The distance between the current UWB position and the former optimal estimated position is defined as ε:

$$\varepsilon = \mathrm{dis}\left(Y_k, \hat{X}_{k-1}(0:2)\right), \tag{18}$$

where dis() represents the distance between two points. When the ranging error is larger, the UWB positioning deviation will be larger. Then a larger measurement noise variance should be assigned. We set an empirical threshold ΔX to judge the reliability of the current measurements to dynamically adjust observation noise variance as follows:

$$R = \begin{cases} R_0, \varepsilon \le \Delta X \\ \varepsilon \lambda R_0, \varepsilon > \Delta X, \end{cases} \tag{19}$$

where λ is the scale factor and R_0 is initial measurement noise variance. The corresponding Kalman gain is calculated according to the observation noise variance:

$$K_k = P_{k|k-1} H \left(H P_{k|k-1} H^T + R\right)^{-1}. \tag{20}$$

The state is updated with UWB location results as follows:

$$\hat{X}_k = \hat{X}_{k|k-1} + K_k \left(Y_k - \hat{X}_{k|k-1}\right). \tag{21}$$

The covariance matrix is updated as follows:

$$P_k = P_{k|k-1} - K_k P_{k|k-1}. \tag{22}$$

The complete algorithm is shown in **Adaptive Dynamic Kalman Filter algorithm**.

Adaptive Dynamic Kalman Filter algorithm

Input: $X_0, P_0, Y_k, R_0, Q, n, m, (x_i, y_i), d_{i,j}, \Delta X, \lambda$
initial position
1: $X_0 = \mathrm{RWLS}\left((x_i, y_i), d_{i,j}\right), \hat{X}_0 = \left[X_0^T\ 0\ 0\right]^T$
2: for $k = 1 : m$
3: $u = $ Madgwick's algorithm $(acc_t, gyro_t)$
4: **Predict**
5: $\hat{X}_{k|k-1} = A\hat{X}_{k-1} + Bu$
6: $P_{k|k-1} = AP_{k-1}A^T + Q$
7: $Y_k = \mathrm{RWLS}\left((x_i, y_i), d_{i,j}, \hat{X}_{k-1}\right)$
8: **Threshold judgment**
9: If dis $\left(Y_k, \hat{X}_{k-1}(0:2)\right) > \Delta X$
10:    $R = \mathrm{dis}\left(Y_k, \hat{X}_{k-1}(0:2)\right)\lambda R_0$

11: **else**
12:    $R = R_0$
13: **end**
14: **Update**
15: $K_k = P_{k|k-1} H \left(H P_{k|k-1} H^T + R \right)^{-1}$
16: $\hat{X}_k = \hat{X}_{k|k-1} + K_k \left(Y_k - \hat{X}_{k|k-1} \right)$
17: $P_k = P_{k|k-1} - K_k P_{k|k-1}$
18: **end**
Output: $\hat{X}_k$

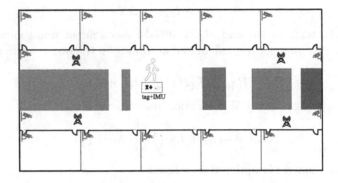

Fig. 3. The 17th floor plan of the laboratory building.

5   Implementations and Evaluations

In this section, we evaluate the performance of the proposed algorithms by experiments. Firstly, we compare the RWLS algorithm to other UWB localization algorithms (LS and WLS). Then, for the ADKF algorithm, we conduct the comparison experiment with traditional KF algorithm and the single UWB localization algorithms, and verify the practical effect of ADKF algorithm.

5.1   Experimental Setup

We evaluate our algorithms for different base station placements and multiple pedestrian movements resulting in LOS and NLOS situations. Hardware configuration has a 4-UWB anchor (MAX2000/DWM1000) and a 6-axis 1 UWB/MEMS-IMU (MPU6050) tag. Two scenarios are set up on the 17th floor of the laboratory building as shown in Fig. 3, namely scenario 1: no pedestrian movement (LOS), and scenario 2: multiple pedestrian (8–10 volunteers) movements (NLOS), which have lots of non-line-of-sight and reflection paths as shown in Fig. 1.

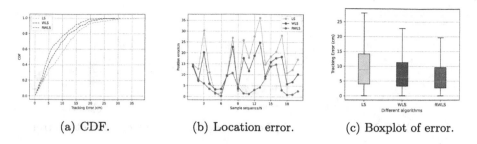

(a) CDF.   (b) Location error.   (c) Boxplot of error.

Fig. 4. RWLS algorithm evaluation in scenario 1.

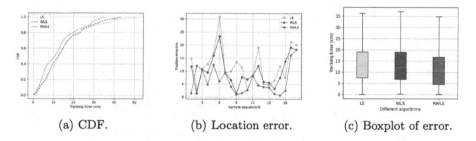

(a) CDF.   (b) Location error.   (c) Boxplot of error.

Fig. 5. RWLS algorithm evaluation in scenario 2.

5.2   RWLS Algorithm Evaluations

Figure 4 shows the experiment of RWLS, WLS and LS algorithms in scenario 1. In the LOS scenario, the maximum errors of RWLS, WLS and LS algorithms are 28.84 cm, 30.60 cm and 37.71 cm, respectively. The average errors of RWLS, WLS and LS algorithms are 6.25 cm, 7.83 cm and 9.67 cm respectively. The average positioning accuracy of RWLS is improved by about 35% compared with LS algorithm and improved by about 20% compared with WLS algorithm. RWLS algorithm is superior to WLS and LS as shown in the cumulative probability distribution function, error graph and boxplot. Figure 5 shows the experiment of RWLS, WLS and LS algorithms in scenario 2. In the NLOS scenario, the maximum errors of RWLS, WLS and LS algorithms are 34.82 cm, 43.71 cm and 51.70 cm, respectively. The average errors of RWLS, WLS and LS algorithms are 12.04 cm, 14.30 cm and 15.04 cm respectively. The average positioning accuracy of RWLS is improved by about 20% compared with LS algorithm and improved by about 16% compared with WLS algorithm. RWLS algorithm can alleviate non-line-of-sight error very well according to the cumulative probability distribution function, error graph and boxplot.

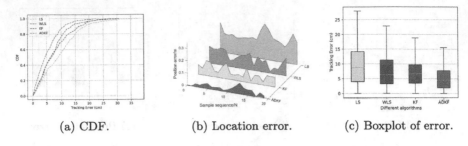

(a) CDF.   (b) Location error.   (c) Boxplot of error.

Fig. 6. ADKF algorithm evaluation in scenario 1.

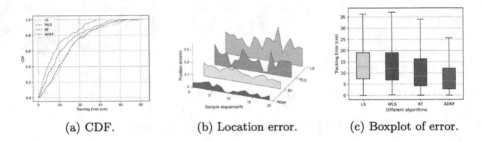

(a) CDF.   (b) Location error.   (c) Boxplot of error.

Fig. 7. ADKF algorithm evaluation in scenario 2.

5.3 ADKF Algorithm Evaluations

Figure 6 shows the experiment of ADKF, KF, WLS and LS algorithms in scenario 1. In the LOS scenario, the maximum errors of ADKF and KF algorithms are 22.73 cm and 30.84 cm. The average errors of ADKF and KF algorithms are 5.34 cm and 7.23 cm. Compared with the KF algorithm, the average positioning accuracy of ADKF is improved by about 26%. Further, compared with LS algorithm, ADKF algorithm effectively improves the positioning accuracy of 45%. Figure 7 shows the experiment of ADKF, KF, WLS and LS algorithms in scenario 2. In the NLOS scenario, the maximum errors of ADKF and KF algorithms are 28.76 cm and 48.98 cm. The average errors of ADKF and KF algorithms are 8.66 cm and 11.54 cm. Compared with KF algorithm, the average positioning accuracy of ADKF is improved by about 25%. Further, compared with the LS algorithm, the ADKF algorithm effectively improves the positioning accuracy of 42%. It implies that ADKF algorithm can well adapt to the dynamic changes of the environment and achieve a high positioning accuracy.

6 Conclusion

In this article, a range-constrained weighted least square (RWLS) algorithm and an adaptive dynamic Kalman Filter (ADKF) algorithm combining IMU and UWB based on continuity of movement are proposed. Experiments show that RWLS algorithm can alleviate the non-line-of-sight positioning error due to complex indoor environments. The state equation of the KF is calculated by the data from the IMU, whereas the observation equation of the KF is calculated by the data from the UWB. The ADKF algorithm, which can effectively reduce positioning data jitter, is introduced to improve positioning accuracy. It is based on several observation BSs and an IMU. The experimental results show that our proposed RWLS algorithm clearly improves the positioning accuracy by about 20% compared to LS algorithm. Further, compared with LS algorithm, our proposed ADKF algorithm effectively improves the positioning accuracy of 42%.

Acknowledgment. This work is supported by the National Key Research and Development Program (2018YFB2100301); National Natural Science Foundation of China (61972131).

References

1. Motte, H., Wyffels, J., Strycker, L.D., Goemaere, J.P.: Evaluating GPS data in indoor environments. Adv. Electr. Comput. Eng. **11**(3), 25–28 (2011)
2. Wu, C., Xu, J., Yang, Z., Lane, N.D., Yin, Z.: Gain without pain: accurate wifi-based localization using fingerprint spatial gradient. Proc. ACM Interact. Mob. Wearable Ubiquit. Technol. **1**(2), 1–19 (2017)
3. Wu, C., Yang, Z., Xiao, C., Yang, C., Liu, Y., Liu, M.: Static power of mobile devices: self-updating radio maps for wireless indoor localization. IEEE (2015)
4. Yang, Z., Wu, C., Liu, Y.: Locating in fingerprint space: wireless indoor localization with little human intervention. In: Proceedings of the 18th Annual International Conference on Mobile Computing and Networking, pp. 269–280 (2012)
5. Yang, X., Wang, J., Song, D., Feng, B., Ye, H.: A novel NLOS error compensation method based IMU for UWB indoor positioning system. IEEE Sens. J. **21**(9), 11203–11212 (2021)
6. Cao, Y., Dhekne, A., Ammar, M.: Itracku: tracking a pen-like instrument via UWB-IMU fusion. In: Proceedings of the 19th Annual International Conference on Mobile Systems, Applications, and Services, pp. 453–466 (2021)
7. Pirsiavash, H., Ramanan, D., Fowlkes, C.C.: Globally-optimal greedy algorithms for tracking a variable number of objects. In: 2011 IEEE Conference on Computer Vision and Pattern Recognition (CVPR) (2011)
8. Rai, A., Chintalapudi, K.K., Padmanabhan, V.N., Sen, R.: Zee: zero-effort crowdsourcing for indoor localization. Microsoft Research India; Microsoft Research India; Microsoft Research India; Indian Institute of Technology, Bombay (2012)
9. Sang, C.L., Adams, M., Hesse, M., Hormann, T., Ruckert, U.: A comparative study of UWB-based true-range positioning algorithms using experimental data. In: 2019 16th Workshop on Positioning, Navigation and Communications (WPNC) (2019)
10. Li, H., Qian, Z., Tian, C., Wang, X.: TILoc: improving the robustness and accuracy for fingerprint-based indoor localization. IEEE Internet Things J. **7**(4), 3053–3066 (2020)
11. Li, Y., He, Z., Gao, Z., Zhuang, Y., Shi, C., El-Sheimy, N.: Toward robust crowdsourcing-based localization: a fingerprinting accuracy indicator enhanced wireless/magnetic/inertial integration approach. IEEE Internet Things J. **6**(2), 3585–3600 (2018)

12. Zhuang, Y., Yang, J., Qi, L., Li, Y., Cao, Y., El-Sheimy, N.: A pervasive integration platform of low-cost mems sensors and wireless signals for indoor localization. IEEE Internet Things J. **5**(6), 4616–4631 (2017)
13. Ren, C., Liu, Q., Fu, T.: A novel self-calibration method for MIMU. IEEE Sens. J. **15**(10), 5416–5422 (2015)
14. Cao, Y., Yang, C., Li, R., Knoll, A., Beltrame, G.: Accurate position racking with a single UWB anchor. In: 2020 IEEE International Conference on Robotics and Automation (ICRA), pp. 2344–2350. IEEE (2020)
15. Chandra, A., et al.: Frequency-domain in-vehicle UWB channel modeling. IEEE Trans. Veh. Technol. **65**(6), 3929–3940 (2016)
16. Wang, S., Mao, G., Zhang, J.A.: Joint time-of-arrival estimation for coherent UWB ranging in multipath environment with multi-user interference. IEEE Trans. Signal Process. **67**(14), 3743–3755 (2019)
17. Abdulrahman, A., et al.: Ultra wideband indoor positioning technologies: analysis and recent advances. Sensors **16**(5), 1–36 (2016)
18. Marano, S., Gifford, W.M., Wymeersch, H., Win, M.Z.: NLOS identification and mitigation for localization based on UWB experimental data. IEEE J. Sel. Areas Commun. **28**(7), 1026–1035 (2010)
19. Lu, Y., Yi, J., He, L., Zhu, X., Liu, P.: A hybrid fusion algorithm for integrated INS/UWB navigation and its application in vehicle platoon formation control. In: Proceedings of the 2018 International Conference on Computer Science, Electronics and Communication Engineering (CSECE 2018), Sanya, China. Atlantis Press (2018)
20. Gunia, M., Protze, F., Joram, N., Ellinger, F.: Setting up an ultra-wideband positioning system using off-the-shelf components. In: Workshop on Positioning (2016)
21. Guo, S., Zhang, Y., Gui, X., Han, L.: An improved PDR/UWB integrated system for indoor navigation applications. IEEE Sens. J. **20**(14), 8046–8061 (2020)
22. Feng, D., Wang, C., He, C., Zhuang, Y., Xia, X.G.: Kalman filter based integration of IMU and UWB for high-accuracy indoor positioning and navigation. IEEE Internet Things J. **7**(4), 3133–3146 (2020)
23. He, C., Tang, C., Yu, C.: A federated derivative cubature Kalman filter for IMU-UWB indoor positioning. Sensors **20**(12), 3514 (2020)
24. Chang, L., Li, J., Chen, S.: Initial alignment by attitude estimation for strapdown inertial navigation systems. IEEE Trans. Instrum. Meas. **64**(3), 784–794 (2014)
25. Mahony, R., Hamel, T., Pflimlin, J.M.: Nonlinear complementary filters on the special orthogonal group. IEEE Trans. Autom. Control **53**(5), 1203–1218 (2008)
26. Wang, A., Song, Y.: Improved SDS-TWR ranging technology in UWB positioning. In: 2018 International Conference on Sensor Networks and Signal Processing (SNSP) (2018)

Security and Privacy

Anonymous Yet Alike: A Privacy-Preserving DeepProfile Clustering for Mobile Usage Patterns

Cheuk Yee Cheryl Leung[1], Basem Suleiman[1,2]([⊠])[iD],
Muhammad Johan Alibasa[3][iD], and Ghazi Al-Naymat[4][iD]

[1] School of Computer Science, University of Sydney, Sydney, Australia
{cheuk.y.leung,basem.suleiman}@sydney.edu.au
[2] School of Computer Science and Engineering, University of New South Wales,
Sydney, Australia
[3] School of Computing, Telkom University, Bandung, Indonesia
alibasa@telkomuniversity.ac.id
[4] Artificial Intelligence Research Center (AIRC), College of Engineering
and Information Technology, Ajman University, Ajman, UAE
g.alnaymat@ajman.ac.ae

Abstract. The ubiquity of mobile devices and unprecedented use of mobile apps have catalyzed the need for an intelligent understanding of user's digital and physical footprints. The complexity of their interconnected relationship has contributed to a sparsity of works on multi-contextual clustering of mobile users based on their digital and physical patterns. Moreover, with personalization the norm in users' lives and corporations collecting a multitude of sensitive data, it is increasingly important to profile users effectively while preserving their privacy. In this paper, we propose DeepProfile: a Multi-context Mobile Usage Patterns Framework for predicting contextually-aware clusters of mobile users and transition of clusters throughout time, based on their behaviors in three contexts - app usage, temporal and geo-spatial. Our DeepProfile framework preserves users' privacy as it intelligently clusters their mobile usage patterns and their transition behaviors while maintaining users' anonymity (i.e., without their gender, GPS location and high-level granularity application usage data). Our experimental results on a mobile app usage dataset show that the predicted user clusters have distinct characteristics in app usage, visited locations and behavioral characteristics over time. We found that on average, 18.6% to 23.6% of a cluster moves together to the next time segment, and other interesting insights such as over 90% of cluster transitions where users moved together, moved from a period of activity to inactivity at the same time.

Keywords: Deep learning · Clustering · Mobile usage · Behavioral patterns · Privacy

© ICST Institute for Computer Sciences, Social Informatics and Telecommunications Engineering 2023
Published by Springer Nature Switzerland AG 2023. All Rights Reserved
S. Longfei and P. Bodhi (Eds.): MobiQuitous 2022, LNICST 492, pp. 81–100, 2023.
https://doi.org/10.1007/978-3-031-34776-4_5

1   Introduction

Mobile phones are now ubiquitously embedded into people's daily lifestyles. As such, to better profile what lifestyle an individual leads and their behavioral patterns, it has become imperative to look at their actions in both the physical and digital sense. Despite this, there has been little academic research examining the intersection of the contexts of mobile app usage, mobility and behavioral patterns over time.

This level of user understanding is critical for personalization in the services used everyday - for instance, personalized content on Social Networking [16], targeted advertising [27] and many other applications. However, due to its nature, many corporations collect an abundance of sensitive data about their users. Consequently, privacy concerns are on the rise, posing a critical challenge in the ability to provide personalization without undermining user privacy [18]. This issue will only become more profound as the population of technologically adept and thus data-aware individuals grow. This is furthered by the difficulty of effectively mining patterns in users mobility, app usage patterns and their changing behavior without impeding on privacy, as location information is most easily detailed as a specific GPS location or longitude/latitude.

This complexity also exists in applications such as personalized content on social networking. For instance, Facebook gathers information such as your GPS location, what purchases you make, SMS log history and much more [5], in order to provide personalization in their News Feed, event suggestions and other features. Such data collection can have further impacts through other means, as seen in the Facebook data privacy scandal where the data analytics firm, Cambridge Analytica, harvested millions of Facebook users' personally identifiable profile information to influence election results [3].

In this study, we investigate the research question: how can we predict meaningful clusters of mobile users using multi-contextual information over time, in a way that maintains user privacy and allows for further analysis of behavioral transitions? To answer this question, we propose a novel DeepProfile framework for multi-context mobile usage clustering and transition patterns that enables the personalization of services while addressing the aforementioned challenges. Our DeepProfile framework enables effective profiling of users using only high-level data which is not composed of any granular details such as the user's gender or GPS location, with the assistance of unsupervised deep feature extraction to learn behavioral patterns. It can achieve personalization through user profiling in a way that provides a richer multi-contextual meaning to the resultant groups without using sensitive data.

The contributions of this paper are twofold: (1) a novel DeepProfile framework for multi-context mobile usage clustering and transition patterns, and (2) an extensive evaluation of our framework through a real-world dataset of 4.2 million app usage records from 871 unique users. To the best of our knowledge, we are the first to propose a framework that produces multi-contextual clusters of mobile users based on three contexts jointly: user mobile app usage, mobility and temporal behavior. Further, we believe that our proposed framework is the first designed to support effective analysis into mobile user cluster transitions throughout time. The framework includes a dynamic approach of time series segmentation that produces unique time segments based on the overall behavior of a dataset's population. Within the framework, we developed a deep feature extraction model that automatically extracts meaningful features over time. Finally, we extensively evaluated the framework by analyzing the clusters it produced and validating our framework's support for further examination into how users transition from cluster to cluster over time.

The rest of this paper is structured as follows. Section 2 discusses various studies related to our work. The details of our proposed approach, including our methods and algorithms, are introduced in Sect. 3. The experimental evaluation and result analysis are discussed in Sect. 4. A discussion of the results in the context of our research contributions is presented in Sect. 5. Finally, key conclusions and future work are described in Sect. 6.

2   Related Work

Many related works in the past decade used data mining on mobile app usage pattern to understand mobile user behaviors [4,14,15,20]. Common across these works is the lack of consideration for the inter-connected multi-contextual relationship between mobile apps usage, physical mobility and time. This observation was similarly made in works mining mobility patterns [1,8,17,23].

It is only in applications of predictive models where the multi-contextual aspects that influence user behavior are considered. For instance, to predict next app usage, Wang et al. [22] used a Bayesian mixture model to predict future app and location using information such as the specific visited places, their Point of Interest (PoI) distribution, and the categories of apps used. Xu et al. [24] took this further by also considering data from mobile sensors such as the accelerometer. Alternatively, Yu et al. [25] approached the app prediction task with limited information only, by just using PoI information of visited locations and app usage. Of interest is the work by Feng et al. [7] who used three distinct types of mobility data - call records, app data and social media data - and successfully showed a deep learning approach can effectively capture meaningful mobility patterns.

In the area of clustering and building user profiles of mobile users, past studies typically lacked multi-contextual consideration. For instance, Zhao et al. [28] clustered mobile users based on a vector of their overall app usage over four time periods on weekdays and weekends. Despite finding some interesting clusters, their results were limited to only a broad understanding of the different types of users. This is due to their aggregation of usage over large static time periods, and as such is unable to capture behavioral patterns in usage over time.

Conversely, Jones et al. [11] focused on a single behavioral characteristic only, by clustering users on their app re-visitation patterns. Their positive results amplify the notion that behavioral characteristics in terms of how users actually use their apps is critical in forming a better grasp of the individual. As such, if combined with other contextual information such as mobility patterns, could provide a much richer understanding of the different types of mobile users.

As such, we observe that most related studies tend to focus on single contexts - such as app usage alone, or mobility patterns alone. Moreover, these works typically do not consider user privacy in what kind of data is collected and used for these tasks.

3 Method: DeepProfile Framework

Our DeepProfile framework aims to produce multi-contextual deep clustering of mobile users. Particularly, the framework is designed to produce clusters of mobile users based on their app usage, mobility patterns, and behavioral patterns over a temporal context. Thus, we first present the modules that make up our novel DeepProfile framework and discuss their rationale, purpose and constitution. Afterwards, we detail the explorative analysis undertaken before reaching the final framework to help substantiate the proposed components.

3.1 DeepProfile Framework

Data gathered on mobile user's app usage and locations in past studies are typically highly granular, for instance, the users' longitude and latitude, the particular words typed by the users, or the users' demographic attributes. Such data collection led data privacy concerns, as such, our proposed DeepProfile framework tackles this privacy issue by centralizing its design to only use highly abstracted information. For instance, we use a distribution of the types of PoIs visited (e.g. Scenic Spot) instead of GPS location, and app category instead of specific app name. Our framework aims to produce rich and meaningful clusters of users with similar behavioral patterns in terms of their app usage, mobility, and temporal behavior. The proposed DeepProfile framework is shown in Fig. 1. In summary, the architecture of our framework is composed of five modules:

1. **Adaptive Time Segmentation Method** based on the overall activity behavior of users in the dataset to split the time series into meaningful segments.
2. **User Activity Partitioning** to transform data into usage dataframes for all active users in each time segment that will be used in the Deep Feature Extraction Model.
3. **Deep Feature Extraction Model** that is trained and validated to produce the Deep Feature Encoder.
4. **Deep Feature Encoder** which produces feature vectors that describe each active user's behavior in each time segment.
5. **Spatio-Temporal-App Usage Clustering** for each time segment.

3.2 Adaptive Time Segmentation Method

Mobile usage data is commonly recorded as a time-series thus time segmentation is critical to analyze it effectively. Each individual's behavior in mobile usage

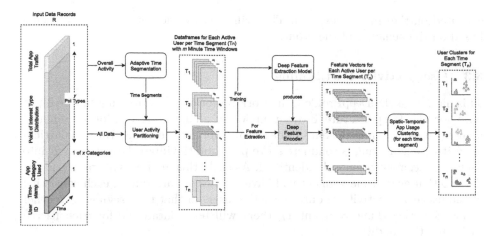

Fig. 1. DeepProfile: Proposed Framework Architecture

varies over time, and devices record the exact timestamp at which events or actions occur. Similar routine behaviors may occur at similar but still differing times everyday, particularly when considering multiple users. Whilst many past studies have utilized large static equal time segments [4,10,15,19], and others static unequal time segments [6,24,26,29], these methods fail to consider the broader cultural, geographic and socio-economic nuances that can affect the appropriateness of their static time segments. For instance, some countries may have a longer work week due to their corporate work culture.

In our DeepProfile framework, we use an adaptive change point algorithm which can detect change points in the behavior of a time series, which indicates the start of a new time segment. More specifically, we utilize the Pruned Exact Linear Time (PELT) algorithm [12]. PELT is an efficient change point detection algorithm that can achieve higher accuracy than other well-known methods such as Binary Segmentation [12]. Running the PELT algorithm on different datasets can produce a different set of change points which is unique based on the behavior of the users in the data provided. This is critical, as factors such as the cultural, geographical or socio-economic context of a population can have significant impacts on their general behavior.

The PELT algorithm is based on an Optimal Partitioning approach using Dynamic Programming by of Jackson et al. [9], but involves an extra pruning step to reduce computational cost within the dynamic program whilst unaffecting exactness [12].

In order to use this method, an appropriate penalty value must be determined. This is done by graphing an elbow plot which plots the number of change points identified against the penalty value used. The optimal value would be where the 'elbow' of the plot is, where change points induced by noise are no longer detected. Using the optimal penalty value, the PELT algorithm can be executed on the time series data. This will identify the optimal time segments based on the behavior of the input.

3.3   User Activity Partitioning

This module in the DeepProfile framework performs pre-processing on the input data for the Deep Feature Extraction Model. The data transformation here focuses on partitioning the data to be suitable for deep learning, thus no particular feature engineering is conducted. We partition the input data records R into each time segment previously identified. As such, this module will transform the data so that every time segment will have a series of dataframes, each consisting of the usage and activity of only the active users in that time segment. In other terms, for every Time Segment T_i, there will be a dataframe for each user u satisfying the condition:

$$| \{ r \in R \mid r_{\text{userId}} = u, T_i^{start} <= r_{\text{time stamp}} < T_i^{end} \} | > 0 \qquad (1)$$

where R is the entire input data of user activity records and r is a specific record in the input data.

As mobile usage data is typically recorded at the exact timestamp whenever events or actions occur, the time series results is irregularly spaced (or arbitrarily sampled). Therefore, this module transforms the data such that it is evenly sampled to be appropriately input into our Deep Feature Extraction Model. Each dataframe will be evenly sampled according to the time window m selected (e.g. if $m = 1$, each row of the dataframe would correspond to 1 min). The number of usage records per app category will be counted for each time window. Then, total app traffic is also summed up for each time window. For mobility information, we take the most occurring point of interest (PoI) distribution in each time window, to best reflect the key locations visited by the user.

Given the process of even sampling to a specified time window, shorter time segments will have less number of time windows. Therefore, all time segments will be padded with rows of zeroes to W, the number of time windows in the longest time segment. Therefore, each dataframe can be represented as

$$d_{\text{user, time segment}} \in \mathbb{R}^{W \times (x+y+1)} \qquad (2)$$

where W represents the number of time windows in the longest time segment, x represents the number of app categories, y represents the number of Point of Interest types and the final 1 is for the total app traffic for each time window. Thus $(x + y + 1)$ represents the total number of variables per time window.

3.4   Deep Feature Extraction Model

This module is a convolutional autoencoder consisting of two main components: the encoder and decoder. The autoencoder can effectively learn features as the encoder component comprises a bottleneck which creates a latent representation of the input in a smaller dimension. The decoder then attempts to reconstruct the original input from this smaller representation, thus requiring the encoder to capture and retain only the most meaningful features.

Each dataframe from the user activity partitioning is used as input to the convolutional autoencoder, thus the autoencoder handles inputs ($d_{\text{user, time segment}}$) of dimensions $W \times (x + y + 1)$. The first layer receives the input dataframe $d_{\text{user, time segment}}$. It is then passed into a series of 1D convolution, max pooling, and dropout layers.

3.5   Deep Feature Encoder

After the convolutional autoencoder is trained, the encoder component can be extracted out for use. The encoder is used to 'predict' feature vectors for all users in each time segment for clustering in the next module. The encoder can be represented as:

$$e : d_{\text{user, time segment}} \mapsto v \in \mathbb{R}^b \tag{3}$$

where b is the vector size of the bottleneck in the convolutional autoencoder (the final layer of the encoder component) and v is the resultant feature vector.

3.6   Spatio-Temporal-App Usage Clustering

In the Spatio-Temporal App Usage Clustering module, for each identified time segment, the following is executed. Firstly, for all active users in the time segment, we first input their dataframe ($d_{\text{user, time segment}}$) into the trained encoder e to extract its feature vector v. Once an encoded feature vector for the active users is produced, agglomerative hierarchical clustering is used to group similar users together. Users that did not have a single usage record in a time segment are automatically allocated to cluster '0'.

This clustering routine is conducted for each time segment. Subsequently, this means that every user is allocated into a cluster for every time segment. As such, this information can be then used for further analysis into the transition patterns of users and of clusters over time, as we demonstrate later in Sect. 4. The clustering results can also be used in algorithms for application areas such as advertising, in order to provide personalization that better maintains user privacy.

4   Experiments and Results

4.1   Dataset

Tsinghua App Usage Dataset [25] was used in our study, consisting of data collected from a mobile cellular network in Shanghai, China. The data spans a period of 7 days from 20 April 2016 to 26 April 2016, containing 4,171,950 records from 871 users and 9,851 base stations. Each record represents a data request on the mobile network by a user, and contains an anonymized user ID, timestamp, base station ID, used app ID and traffic. Data detailing the app category of each app, which were determined by Android Market and Google Play, and the number of Point of Interests (PoIs) in each PoI category for each base station is also provided.

4.2   Adaptive Time Segmentation

Our experiment splits the time according to the overall activity of the population in the dataset, since this will provide the clearest indication as to the general 'sections' of a day for their particular cultural, geographical, and social context. Since the Tsinghua App Usage Dataset consists of 1 week's data only, there were a few approaches we could take. Firstly, we could produce time segments for each day of the week individually. We could also average out weekday and weekend activity, and thus produce two sets of time segments. Finally, we could simply segment the entire week as one time series.

By examining the overall activity for the dataset per day, our first observation is that not all weekdays had similar activity patterns. Similarly, weekends were not seen to be much different from weekdays. As such, this means that we cannot simply average out activity for weekdays and then weekends, since there does not appear to be such a pattern in this dataset. In order to determine whether we should produce time segments for each day individually or for the entire week as one time series, we conducted experiments on both these approaches using the PELT algorithm. We use the Ruptures[1] [21] implementation.

Segmenting per Day. In order to determine the time segments based on the overall activity level for each day individually, we utilise a transformed version of the dataset that holds the number of app usage records per minute. We use the PELT algorithm to determine all change points in behavior, which act as the start/end of each time segment, to find all-time segments for each individual day. From producing the elbow plots for each day as described in Subsect. 3.2, the ideal Penalty Values were identified for Monday to Sunday as 3, 6, 3, 3, 4, 3, and 3.

Segmenting Entire Week. In this method, we segment the entire dataset time length as one time series, and also specify for the PELT algorithm to ensure that time segments are at least 60 min long. The identified Penalty Value for the PELT algorithm was 10. As shown in Fig. 2, segmenting our 1-week long dataset results in 44 time segments. In the figure, there is a vertical dotted gray line at the start of each day.

Conclusions. When examining the time segments from our second experiment using the entire week as one time series, we found that a new time segment often begin around 12:00AM but never exactly. Since these segments were identified

---

[1] https://centre-borelli.github.io/ruptures-docs/user-guide/detection/pelt/.

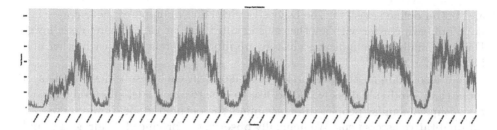

Fig. 2. Result Time Segments from our Adaptive Time Segmentation Method

from using the entire week as a single time series, these time segments reflect the natural change points of the overall activity behavior of the users. This is in contrast to the results from segmenting each day individually where a new time segment always starts at 12:00AM, as individuals are unlikely to always begin a new behavioral routine at exactly 12:00AM. Thus, we conclude that performing PELT change point detection to determine time segments on the entire week as one time series.

4.3 Deep Feature Extraction Model and Clustering

After performing adaptive time segmentation, we perform experiments on developing the Deep Feature Extraction component of our framework. We used Keras[2] to build the different Convolutional Autoencoders to evaluate for our Deep Feature Extraction Model. The models were trained on the training subset of data. The training to validation split was 80% : 20%. For all evaluated models, the number of epochs used to train is 25, with learning rate 0.001 using Adam optimization. These values were selected after empirical evaluation from experiments in training our model, by observing the validation and training losses to ensure a well-trained model without overfitting. In general, each model takes approximately 15 min to finish training on CPU. For our hierarchical clustering, we use the SciPy[3] implementation and for internal cluster validation metrics we use scikit-learn[4].

Evaluation Method. We conducted hierarchical clustering using the resultant feature vectors for each user in each time segment, which are the output from our Deep Feature Extraction Model and Encoder. To perform evaluation, we firstly use internal validation metrics of Calinski and Harabasz Score and Davies-Bouldin Score to observe the cluster quality of the resultant clusters produced using the different Deep Feature Extraction Models.

The Calinski and Harabasz Score is the ratio between the within-cluster dispersion and the between-cluster dispersion, thus a higher value indicates denser

---

[2] https://keras.io/.
[3] https://scipy.org/.
[4] https://scikit-learn.org/stable/index.html.

and better defined clusters. The Davies-Bouldin Score compares the average similarity of each cluster with another cluster most similar to it. Therefore, a lower Davies-Bouldin Score indicates clusters are more 'different' from each other and better separated.

We also examine the proportion of clusters in each result that consists of more than 1 individual, as we would like to ensure our model effectively discovers groups of similar people. In determining the optimal model however, we opt for qualitative assessment. We manually observe the produced dendrograms and resultant clusters to determine whether the groups formed have clearly identifiable behavioral characteristics and patterns. It is important that we use this qualitative assessment, as internal validation metrics cannot adequately measure the quality of the following critical features of our clustering. Users should show multi-contextual similarity, including what app categories they used, the behavioral characteristics of usage exhibited, and their mobility in terms of the types of locations visited, all considered over a temporal context. There are two components considered to qualitatively assess the cluster results.

1. **The ease of cluster description**: the clusters formed should be easily interpreted and described in terms of their content, showing aspects that clearly distinguish themselves from others. Clusters should be different from each other by at least 1 contextual aspect.
2. **How balanced the clusters are**: clusters should not be extremely unbalanced. No more than 25% of the resultant clusters can contain only 1 individual. Further, clusters should not necessarily be equal in size or be extremely large. A careful balance must be struck to ensure distinguishable and meaningful groups of users.

Given the expensive nature of the qualitative assessment, we conducted our evaluations on two time segments - one long time segment of Wednesday 7:35AM - 3:00PM (Time Segment 1), and one short time segment of Wednesday 3:00PM - 5:20PM (Time Segment 2). We performed ablation studies examining two main aspects: the impact of different time windows used for User Activity Partitioning and also different layer architecture in the convolutional autoencoder of our Deep Feature Extraction Model.

4.4   Evaluation Results

We first investigated the impact of different time windows for the User Activity Partitioning module (Subsect. 3.3) on the performance of the autoencoder-extracted features when clustering. The time window is used when evenly sampling our input data to form the rows of a user's dataframe for each time segment. The Base Convolutional Autoencoder used here is composed of an encoder with 4 sets of 1D Convolution, Max Pooling, and Dropout layers. The parameters of the 1D Convolution Layers are all set to filters = 16 and kernel size = 3. Following these sets, there is a flatten and dense layer to produce the feature vector. The decoder component is designed symmetrically to the encoder. We evaluate the impact of using 1 min, 5 min, 10 min and 15 min time windows.

Table 1. Ablation Study - Internal Metrics for Different Time Windows

Time Window	Time Segment	Calinski and Harabasz Score	Davies-Bouldin Score
1 min	Wed 7:35AM - 3:00PM	59.84838	0.38686
	Wed 3:00PM - 5:20PM	181.10552	0.40569
5 min	Wed 7:35AM - 3:00PM	97.31339	0.62215
	Wed 3:00PM - 5:20PM	653.044089	0.70322
10 min	Wed 7:35AM - 3:00PM	178.07984	0.87969
	Wed 3:00PM - 5:20PM	842.32609	0.65256
15 min	Wed 7:35AM - 3:00PM	483.40322	0.812233
	Wed 3:00PM - 5:20PM	2540.53143	0.61834

The results of our internal quality metrics evaluation on the produced clusters can be seen in Table 1. We saw that as the time windows increase, so does the Calinski and Harabasz Score, suggesting higher intra-cluster similarity. While we observe its highest value for the 15 min time window, we noted that this score was a significant spike. From a manual observation of the resultant clusters, the consequent aggregation from such a large time window reduced the model's ability to identify more detailed behavioral patterns, such as their frequency of app usage and other behavioral habits.

Moreover, we observed that moving from a time window of 10 min to 15 min did not provide any improvement on more balanced clustering - the proportion of clusters which had more than 1 user did not really increase ($84.745\% \rightarrow 87.692\%$ for Wed 7:35AM - 3:00PM, $75\% \rightarrow 78.571\%$ for Wed 3:00PM - 5:20PM). This is likely due to the low granularity of 15 min time windows. Given majority of our time segments are between 60–120 minutes, 15 min time windows means that each time segment would only have 4–8 timesteps. Since the convolution layers in our autoencoder itself slides across the timesteps to identify patterns over time, overly summarised data will undermine the benefits of our framework. As such, a 15 min time window is not appropriate.

Finally, when observing the resultant clustering using a 10 min window, we observed a good balance between focusing on the temporal aspect of users' app usage behavior and other factors such as the types of locations visited and app categories used. In contrast, 5 min time windows caused the model to focus too strongly on the temporal aspect of the users' app usage, causing the resultant clusters to only bear strong similarity in what time they used apps. In the 10-minute window, we observed a good compromise between the results from the 5 min time window and 15 min time window. Thus, we select the 10 min time window for our final best implemented model.

Similar to the previous ablation study, we also conducted experiments for various layer architecture in the convolutional autoencoder for our Deep Feature Extraction Model. The parameters of the models used, determined through our empirical evaluation, for this ablation study are shown in Table 2. After assessing the internal metrics and qualitative examinations of resultant clusters, the outcome of these additional experiments found the architecture of Model B to generate the best quality clusters.

Table 2. Definition of Models for Evaluation

Model	Layers	Convolution Layer Parameters
A	4 sets of:	All:
	1D Convolution, Max Pooling and Dropout Layers	filters = 16, kernel size = 3
B	4 sets of:	All: kernel size = 3
	1D Convolution, Max Pooling and Dropout Layers	First 2 sets: filters = 32
		Last 2 sets: filters = 64
C	3 sets of:	All: kernel size = 3
	1D Convolution, 1D Convolution, Max Pooling, Dropout	First 2 sets: filters = 32
		Last set: filters = 128

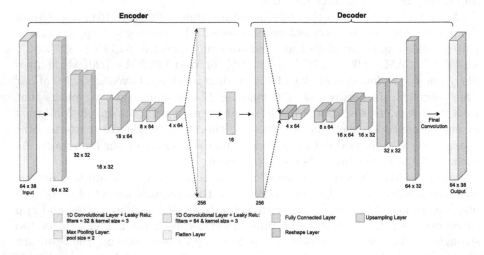

Fig. 3. Best Implemented Convolutional Autoencoder Model for Deep Feature Extraction

Best Model. As a result from our ablation studies, our best implemented model is using 10 min time windows using the layer architecture of Model B. This structure of the Deep Feature Extraction Model's Convolutional Autoencoder can be seen in Fig. 3.

4.5   Clustering Results from the Best Model

In this subsection, we provide examples for the cluster results produced by our implementation of the proposed framework and examine them to identify the nature of those users. The results provide evidence in our achievement of rich and meaningful clusters based on users' app usage, mobility, and temporal patterns. Our implementation of the proposed framework produced different clusters of users for each of the 44 time segments of the week's data. The two clusters we discuss in this paper are from Time Segment 1, Wednesday 7:35AM - 3:00 PM. Our framework produced a total of 64 clusters for this time segment.

Cluster 3. As seen in Fig. 4, Users in this cluster showed consistent usage of Utilities apps, recording around 100–150 instances of such usage in this time segment. Their behavioral characteristics are composed of consistent usage throughout these several hours, generally with frequent 'blocks' of usage . The locations these users visited tended to have several Business Affairs Point of Interests in the vicinity, with occurrences of Life Services, Residential, Government, Shopping and Restaurant PoIs (see Fig. 5) We can infer the locations these users visited reflect mixed-use development that blends residential, commercial, cultural, and institutional establishments into one space.

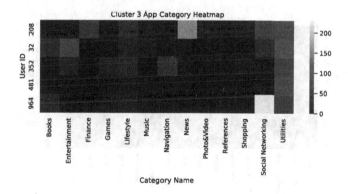

Fig. 4. Cluster 3 App Category Usage Heatmap, Wednesday 7:35AM - 3:00PM

Cluster 15. Users in this cluster were extremely heavy users of Social Networking apps - each user recorded over 1000 usage records in this category, with little of anything else (see Fig. 6).

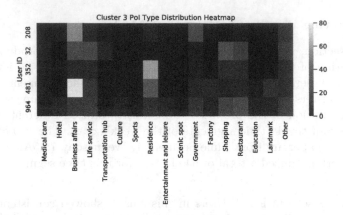

Fig. 5. Cluster 3 PoI Type Heatmap, Wednesday 7:35AM - 3:00PM

This is a significant contrast to the previous cluster that had approximately 200 usage records at most in any app category. The PoI distribution of Cluster 15's most visited locations included residential PoIs with some shopping and restaurants, as seen in Fig. 7. Their usage was also extremely consistent throughout the time period, with very heavy blocks of Social Networking use.

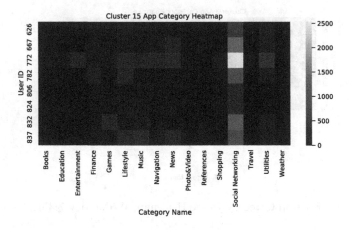

Fig. 6. Cluster 15 App Category Usage Heatmap, Wednesday 7:35AM - 3:00PM

The differences in the various contextual aspects of each cluster can significantly impact the optimal way to personalize for the users in each group. For instance, from our examination of each cluster's behavioral patterns in their app category usage through categorical Scatterplots over time, Cluster 15 demonstrated extremely heavy usage that was characterized by a pattern of high-frequency blocks of use throughout the entire time segment. If a firm wishes to provide mobile advertising to the users from this cluster, ads which exploit

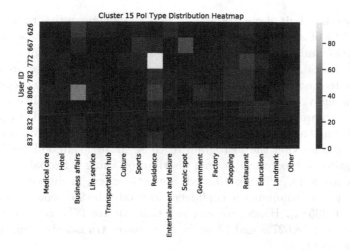

Fig. 7. Cluster 15 PoI Type Heatmap, Wednesday 7:35AM - 3:00PM

the technique of repetition can be optimal. This is contrast to the both sparse and significantly lighter usage of Cluster 3, which would be more motivated by ads that have a strong call to action. As such, the discovered clusters demonstrate the capturing of similar behavior across users' mobile app usage, visited locations, and behavioral patterns without utilizing more sensitive data.

4.6   Cluster Transitions Analysis

Using our best implemented deep feature extraction model, we clustered the users in all 44 time segments, as according to the method described in Subsect. 3.6. Any inactive users in each time segment are automatically assigned to cluster '0'. The number of clusters in each time segment is variable, since users were clustered for each time segment individually. This subsection details our analysis into how clusters transitioned from one time segment to the next . We analyze whether there are any transition patterns that certain clusters or individuals take part in. For instance, we check if there are specific clusters that all move together to the same cluster in the next time segment, or, are there individuals who perform the same cluster transitions for several time segments. By conducting this analysis and the previous examination of resultant clusters, we showed that our proposed framework can enable rich analysis into the behavioral characteristics and transitions of the produced clusters through time.

Transitions Between 2 Consecutive Time Segments. In order to examine the transitions of clusters between 2 consecutive time segments, we create a transition probability matrix for each transition. These matrices hold the likelihoods of someone in a specific cluster in one time segment, moving to another cluster in the next time segment. We found the median value to be 0.1052, indicating that in more than half of our transitions between 2 consecutive time segments, at least 10.52% of a cluster moves together to the next time segment. The mean value is 0.1987, indicating that on average, 19.87% of a cluster moves together to the next time segment, however further statistical testing is required to see if this is consistent across transitions between different pairs of time segments.

We then analyze the mean likelihoods of each transition. When computing the mean, we ignore transitions where the cluster is only comprised of 1 person, as 1 person moving to the next time segment would undoubtedly give a likelihood of 1.0. When observing the histogram of these mean likelihoods and plotting the data against a theoretical normal distribution using a Probability Plot, we found the data is normally distributed. Since the mean likelihoods is normally distributed, we can compute the confidence interval. The 95% confidence interval is (0.18627, 0.23584). Hence, we can say that we are 95% confident that on average, between 18.627% and 23.584% of a cluster transitions together to the next time segment.

We also observed specific cluster transitions where more than 40% of the cluster moved together to the next time segment and more than 2 people transitioned together. There were a total of 380 of such transitions, where the majority (344/380) are moving from an active cluster to cluster '0' (inactive), 18 transitions are moving from cluster '0' to cluster '0', and 18 transitions are moving from an active cluster to another active cluster. This suggests a strong tendency for clusters to move towards inactivity at the same time.

As an example, there is a cluster transition between Time Segment 23 (Saturday 10:05-17:30) and Time Segment 24 (Saturday 17:30-23:20), where 3 of 6 (50%) of users in cluster 87 moved together to cluster 9. The three users who transitioned together exhibited behavior of consistent app usage throughout Time Segment 23, with clear similarities in their Utilities and Social Networking usage. They then transitioned together to Cluster 9, where they all had app usage at only one point in time during this time segment. In terms of the PoI types at their visited locations, in Time Segment 23 all 3 users were mainly in a residential area, whilst in the next time segment, they moved to a more business-oriented area, with some shopping and restaurants.

5   Discussion

Our evaluation using real-world app usage dataset found the predicted clusters of individuals had similarities in several multi-contextual aspects - the app categories used, the behavior with which they used apps, the locations they visited in terms of what types of PoIs were in the vicinity, and the temporal characteristics of their mobility. The input data into our proposed framework was extremely high level. It did not consist of any granular information such as a user's ethnicity, age, gender, or GPS location. Despite this, the clusters predicted were still meaningful and distinguished from each other, with users in a cluster bearing multi-contextual similarities. Each cluster had distinct characteristics in their mobile app usage, mobility, and behavioral patterns over time.

This is in contrast to previous works, which tended to cluster users based on individual aspects only. For instance, some works [28] clustered users based only on their aggregated app usage over static time segments with aggregated data based on weekdays and weekends. As such, any rich insights into the behavioral characteristics they exhibited when using the apps or the temporal patterns undertaken could not be reflected. Some [11] took a granular approach, clustering users based only on their app re-visitation patterns. Again, this was based on aggregated data for each user and thus cannot provide insights into their temporal behavior. Other studies [2,13] clustered users based on their mobility patterns only, using specific GPS locations and undermining user privacy.

Finally, we provided an extensive analysis into the patterns of cluster transitions. We discovered several insights, such as how likely a cluster would transition together into the next time segment, along with the proportion of users who shared the same cluster transitions with another individual over several time segments. We found that on average, between 18.627% and 23.584% of a cluster typically transitions together to the next time segment. Moreover, over 90% of such cluster transitions where users moved together, moved from a period of activity to inactivity at the same time.

6   Conclusion and Future Work

In this work, we have presented DeepProfile: a multi-context mobile usage patterns framework that clusters users across time using multi contextual information without undermining user privacy. Our framework enables further analysis on the transition of users' behavior throughout time to discover insights into the behavioral patterns of different groups. Through our extensive evaluation of the framework, we found that the framework was able to produce rich and meaningful clusters that captured the several aspects of app usage, mobility and behavioral characteristics over time.

In the future, it could be interesting to explore the potential of a hybrid model that uses more than one Deep Feature Extraction Model for each type of contextual pattern. This could allow each feature extraction model to excel at learning patterns for the particular context it has been trained for. It could be also interesting to investigate modifications to the clustering method undertaken in this work to enable real-time clustering in an unsupervised manner, even while mobile data is being gathered.

References

1. Becker, R., et al.: Human mobility characterization from cellular network data. Commun. ACM. **56**(1), 74–82 (2013). https://doi.org/10.1145/2398356.2398375
2. Ben-Gal, I., Weinstock, S., Singer, G., Bambos, N.: Clustering users by their mobility behavioral patterns. ACM Trans. Knowl. Discov. Data **13**(4) (2019). https://doi.org/10.1145/3322126, https://doi-org.ezproxy.library.sydney.edu.au/10.1145/3322126
3. Cadwalladr, C., Graham-Harrison, E.: Revealed: 50 million Facebook profiles harvested for Cambridge analytica in major data breach. The Guardian (2018). https://www.theguardian.com/news/2018/mar/17/cambridge-analytica-facebook-influence-us-election
4. Do, T.M.T., Gatica-Perez, D.: By their apps you shall understand them: mining large-scale patterns of mobile phone usage. In: Proceedings of the 9th International Conference on Mobile and Ubiquitous Multimedia. MUM 2010, ACM, New York, NY, USA (2010). https://doi.org/10.1145/1899475.1899502, https://doi-org.ezproxy.library.sydney.edu.au/10.1145/1899475.1899502
5. Facebook: Data policy (2021). https://www.facebook.com/privacy/explanation
6. Farrahi, K., Gatica-Perez, D.: Probabilistic mining of socio-geographic routines from mobile phone data. IEEE J. Sel. Top. Signal Process. **4**(4), 746–755 (2010)
7. Feng, J., Li, Y., Zhang, C., Sun, F., Meng, F., Guo, A., Jin, D.: Deepmove: Predicting human mobility with attentional recurrent networks. In: Proceedings of the 2018 World Wide Web Conference. p. 1459–1468. WWW 2018, International World Wide Web Conferences Steering Committee, Republic and Canton of Geneva, CHE (2018). https://doi.org/10.1145/3178876.3186058
8. Herder, E., Siehndel, P.: Daily and weekly patterns in human mobility. In: UMAP Workshops, pp. 338–340. Citeseer (2012)
9. Jackson, B., et al.: An algorithm for optimal partitioning of data on an interval. IEEE Signal Process. Lett. **12**(2), 105–108 (2005). https://doi.org/10.1109/LSP.2001.838216
10. Jayarajah, K., Kauffman, R., Misra, A.: Exploring variety seeking behavior in mobile users. In: Proceedings of ACM International Joint Conference on Pervasive and Ubiquitous Computing: Adjunct Publication, pp. 385–390 (2014)
11. Jones, S.L., Ferreira, D., Hosio, S., Goncalves, J., Kostakos, V.: Revisitation analysis of smartphone app use. In: Proceedings of ACM International Joint Conference on Pervasive and Ubiquitous Computing, pp. 1197–1208. UbiComp 2015, ACM, New York, NY, USA (2015). https://doi.org/10.1145/2750858.2807542, https://doi-org.ezproxy.library.sydney.edu.au/10.1145/2750858.2807542
12. Killick, R., Fearnhead, P., Eckley, I.A.: Optimal detection of changepoints with a linear computational cost. J. Am. Stat. Assoc. **107**(500), 1590–1598 (2012)
13. Lu, E.H.C., Tseng, V.S., Yu, P.S.: Mining cluster-based temporal mobile sequential patterns in location-based service environments. IEEE Trans. Knowl. Data Eng. **23**(6), 914–927 (2011). https://doi.org/10.1109/TKDE.2010.155
14. Ma, H., Cao, H., Yang, Q., Chen, E., Tian, J.: A habit mining approach for discovering similar mobile users. In: Proceedings of the 21st International Conference on World Wide Web, pp. 231–240. WWW 2012, ACM, New York, NY, USA (2012). https://doi.org/10.1145/2187836.2187868, https://doi-org.ezproxy.library.sydney.edu.au/10.1145/2187836.2187868

15. Mukherji, A., Srinivasan, V., Welbourne, E.: Adding intelligence to your mobile device via on-device sequential pattern mining. In: Proceedings of the 2014 ACM International Joint Conference on Pervasive and Ubiquitous Computing: Adjunct Publication, pp. 1005–1014. UbiComp 2014 Adjunct, ACM, New York, NY, USA (2014). https://doi.org/10.1145/2638728.2641285, https://doi-org.ezproxy.library.sydney.edu.au/10.1145/2638728.2641285

16. Park, J.H.: The effects of personalization on user continuance in social networking sites. Inf. Process. Manage. **50**(3), 462–475 (2014). https://doi.org/10.1016/j.ipm.2014.02.002, https://www.sciencedirect.com/science/article/pii/S0306457314000120

17. Pavan, M., Mizzaro, S., Scagnetto, I.: Mining movement data to extract personal points of interest: a feature based approach. In: Lai, C., Giuliani, A., Semeraro, G. (eds.) Information Filtering and Retrieval. SCI, vol. 668, pp. 35–61. Springer, Cham (2017). https://doi.org/10.1007/978-3-319-46135-9_3

18. Rafieian, O., Yoganarasimhan, H.: Targeting and privacy in mobile advertising. Mark. Sci. **40**(2), 193–218 (2021)

19. Rawassizadeh, R., Momeni, E., Dobbins, C., Gharibshah, J., Pazzani, M.: Scalable daily human behavioral pattern mining from multivariate temporal data. IEEE Trans. Knowl. Data Eng. **28**(11), 3098–3112 (2016)

20. Srinivasan, V., Moghaddam, S., Mukherji, A., Rachuri, K.K., Xu, C., Tapia, E.M.: Mobileminer: mining your frequent patterns on your phone. In: Proceedings of ACM International Joint Conf. on Pervasive and Ubiquitous Computing, pp. 389–400. UbiComp 2014, ACM, New York, NY, USA (2014). https://doi.org/10.1145/2632048.2632052, https://doi-org.ezproxy.library.sydney.edu.au/10.1145/2632048.2632052

21. Truong, C., Oudre, L., Vayatis, N.: Selective review of offline change point detection methods. Signal Process. **167**, 107299 (2020). https://doi.org/10.1016/j.sigpro.2019.107299, https://www.sciencedirect.com/science/article/pii/S0165168419303494

22. Wang, H., et al.: Modeling spatio-temporal app usage for a large user population. Proc. ACM Interact. Mob. Wearable Ubiquitous Technol. **3**(1) (2019). https://doi.org/10.1145/3314414, https://doi-org.ezproxy.library.sydney.edu.au/10.1145/3314414

23. Xie, R., Ji, Y., Yue, Y., Zuo, X.: Mining individual mobility patterns from mobile phone data. In: Proceedings of International Workshop on Trajectory Data Mining and Analysis, pp. 37–44. ACM (2011). https://doi.org/10.1145/2030080.2030088, https://doi-org.ezproxy.library.sydney.edu.au/10.1145/2030080.2030088

24. Xu, Y., et al.: Preference, context and communities: a multi-faceted approach to predicting smartphone app usage patterns. In: Proceedings of the International Symposium on Wearable Computers, pp. 69–76. ISWC 2013, ACM, New York, NY, USA (2013). https://doi.org/10.1145/2493988.2494333, https://doi-org.ezproxy.library.sydney.edu.au/10.1145/2493988.2494333

25. Yu, D., Li, Y., Xu, F., Zhang, P., Kostakos, V.: Smartphone app usage prediction using points of interest. Proc. ACM Interact. Mob. Wearable Ubiquitous Technol. **1**(4) (2018). https://doi.org/10.1145/3161413, https://doi-org.ezproxy.library.sydney.edu.au/10.1145/3161413

26. Yu, K., Zhang, B., Zhu, H., Cao, H., Tian, J.: Towards personalized context-aware recommendation by mining context logs through topic models. In: Tan, P.N., Chawla, S., Ho, C.K., Bailey, J. (eds.) Advances in Knowledge Discovery and Data Mining, pp. 431–443. Springer, Berlin (2012). https://doi.org/10.1007/978-3-642-30217-6_36

27. Zhang, T., Cheng, X., Yuan, M., Xu, L., Cheng, C., Chao, K.: Mining target users for mobile advertising based on telecom big data. 2016 16th International Symposium on Communications and Information Technologies (ISCIT), pp. 296–301 (2016)

28. Zhao, S., et al.: Discovering different kinds of smartphone users through their application usage behaviors. In: Proceedings of ACM International Joint Conference on Pervasive and Ubiquitous Computing, pp. 498–509. UbiComp 2016, ACM, New York, NY, USA (2016). https://doi.org/10.1145/2971648.2971696, https://doi-org.ezproxy.library.sydney.edu.au/10.1145/2971648.2971696

29. Zhu, H., Chen, E., Xiong, H., Yu, K., Cao, H., Tian, J.: Mining mobile user preferences for personalized context-aware recommendation. ACM Trans. Intell. Syst. Technol. 5(4) (2014). https://doi.org/10.1145/2532515, https://doi-org.ezproxy.library.sydney.edu.au/10.1145/2532515

Best-Practice-Based Framework
for User-Centric Privacy-Preserving
Solutions in Smart Home Environments

Chathurangi Ishara Wickramasinghe[(✉)]

Georg-August-University Göttingen, Göttingen, Germany
`c.wickramasinghe@stud.uni-goettingen.de`

Abstract. The rapid technological progress causes smart environments, such as smart homes, cities, etc., to become more ubiquitous in our daily lives. Privacy issues arise when the smart objects in those smart environments collect and disclose sensitive data without users' consent. Therefore, existing works and the European General Data Protection Regulation (GDPR) are still calling for privacy-preserving solutions with more user involvement and automated decision-making. Existing works show research gaps regarding context-aware privacy-preference modellings. They do not present best-practice-based frameworks for user-centric privacy-preserving approaches allowing context-aware adapting of users' privacy and data disclosure preferences while considering their past activities. Hence, this paper proposes a best-practice-based framework for user-centric privacy-preserving solutions with automation options. The proposed approach supplies users data sharing recommendations with minimum human interference while considering (1) GDPR requirements, (2) context-sensitive factors and (3) users' past activities. The paper also outlines how the proposed framework can be integrated in an existing user-centric privacy-preserving approach in the future. In this way, the proposed approach can be integrated in the existing IoT architecture systems, which allow users to control the entire data collection, storage and disclosure process in smart home environments.

Keywords: Machine learning · Privacy preserving · Smart homes · Sensitivity · Data protection · Smart environments · Smart objects · Ubiquitous computing · Pervasive systems

1 Introduction

The technological progress in the context of pervasive systems leads to the fact that more and more smart objects are integrated into our personal spaces, such as in homes [11]. The integrated smart objects in such smart home environments are, for instance, smart bulbs, fridges, door locks, etc. [11]. Although these smart objects improve our lives, they also collect and disclose a vast amount of sensitive and non-sensitive data without users' consent [49,50]. Especially in smart home

S. Longfei and P. Bodhi (Eds.): MobiQuitous 2022, LNICST 492, pp. 101–120, 2023.
https://doi.org/10.1007/978-3-031-34776-4_6

environments, this privacy issue gains more importance because the integrated smart objects in smart homes collect data in a personal space [15]. In order to address the arising privacy issues in this context, several privacy-preserving solutions, including different machine learning and automated approaches, have been proposed, such as [3,22,23,26]. Note that most of them do not (1) allow the entire control over the data collection, storage and disclosure process [45] and also do not (2) supply users with data disclosure recommendations based on best practices, context-sensitive factors and users' past activities [25].

GDPR (Art. 4, 5, 9, 12, 15, 17, 19, 22 and 23) and existing works are still calling for privacy-preserving solutions with more user-centricity and possibility to consider context-aware user privacy preferences [1,25,38].

This paper proposes a best-practice-based framework for privacy-preserving in smart home environments to address these open issues. The proposed approach delivers user data disclosure recommendations while considering GDPR-based best practices, users' context-aware sensitive factors and their past activities. In order to allow users to control the entire data collection, storage and disclosure, the proposed framework is integrated within an existing user-centric privacy-preserving approach from [45]. The approach from [45] include four **User-Centric-Control-Points** (UCCPs), which can be integrated in existing IoT architecture systems. The four UCCPs from [45] include the following features:

- UCCP 1 - Data Object Tagging: Allows users to set their general sensitivity awareness by assigning themselves to one of the described profiles.
- UCCP 2 - Data Minimization and Aggregation: Allows users to minimize the collected data by the smart object sensors and set the aggregation period for the review regarding the collected data before data sharing.
- UCCP 3 - Data Sharing: Allows users to assess the sensitivity of the collected data types and associated privacy risks and advantages in the data disclosure context. Moreover, it also allows users to set their risk aversion or risk affinity.
- UCCP 4 - Data Access Limitations: Allows users to limit the data sharing while setting the data consumers and usage purposes of the shared data after considering the model's recommendations.

Further details regarding the integration of the proposed framework from this paper in the approach from [45] are described in Sect. 2. However, the implementation of the proposed approach is out of this manuscript. To sum up, the proposed approach in this paper contributes to the following points compared to previous work: (1) Providing users with best-practice-based and context-aware recommendations regarding data disclosure and (2) allowing them to consider users' privacy preferences from past activities with minimum human interference. Additionally, the integration of the proposed framework in [45] allows user-centric privacy-preserving in smart home environments.

This paper is structured as follows. Firstly, the derived best-practice-based framework and its integration in [45] are presented in Sect. 2 and its qualitative evaluation in Sect. 3. In Sect. 4, the proposed approach is discussed, and in

Sect. 5 the related work is presented. Closing remarks conclude this paper in Sect. 6, respectively.

2 The Framework for User-Centric Privacy-Preserving Approaches in Smart Homes

2.1 Proposed Framework

The Fig. 1 presents the proposed best-practice-based framework for user-centric privacy-preserving solutions. The proposed framework includes a supervised learning method, including the decision tree, which is an essential, efficient and significant way to find logical connections between learned and predicted items [46]. It also contains an active learning method, Support Vector Machines (SVM), which is a successful method for real-world learning [22,27]. Integrating the decision tree and SVM algorithm allows the proposed approach to run its technique in a less time-, cost-, and energy-consuming way [48]. This deployment allows the proposed approach to work in a privacy-preserved way since the data does not need to leave its smart home environment in order to be processed. In this way, data leakage can be prevented by applying the proposed approach. The proposed framework supplies users with data disclosure recommendations (1) based on GDPR-related best practices while (2) considering the impacts of users' past activities on their context-sensitive privacy preferences in those data disclosure recommendations. The integration of this best-practice-based framework in an existing user-centric privacy-preserving approach from [45] allows (1) users to control the entire data collection and disclosure process with minimum human interference and (2) the integration in existing IoT architecture systems. In the following, the necessary inputs, as well as the proposed framework, are described.

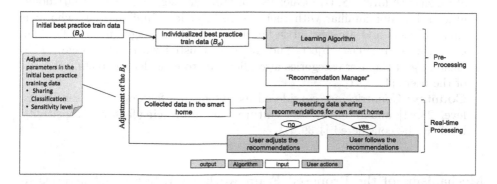

Fig. 1. Overview of the proposed best-practice-based automated framework

Initial Inputs for the Framework: In order to train the algorithm of the proposed framework to supply users with data disclosure recommendations, an initial best-practice train data (B_d) is derived and used for supervised learning. The B_d includes different information types, such as collected data type, smart object, user category, age, country, etc., which influence sensitivity perception and which then in turn influence users' privacy and data sharing attitude [6, 19,21,31,42]. The Table 1 presents an extract of the B_d, which is derived based on GDPR specifications, especially Art. 4, 5, 9, 12, 15, 17 and 19 [1,12,38] and literature review [4,17,28,31,39,41,45]. According to the GDPR demands and literature review the following information types are defined as most relevant variables of B_d and include the following definitions:

- **Data Type**: Collected data type by each smart home object [4,17,31,39,41, 45]
- **Smart Object**: Respective smart home object collecting the specific data type
- **Sensitivity Level**: Sensitivity Level of the respective collected data, according to GDPR demands [12]. The sensitivity level is set to 5 with "sensitive". In a later iteration, the proposed approach adjusts the sensitivity level of the corresponding data type based on users' past activities, which is described in the next section (scale: 1 = "non-sensitive" to 10 = "highly sensitive", with 5 = "sensitive")
- **Sharing Classification**: Sharing recommendations for the respective data collected based on the sensitive level derived from GDPR requirements [12] and literature analysis [45] (options: 0 = *do not share the data type* and 1 = *share the data type*). This variable can also be changed in a later iteration by the proposed approach according to users' preferences, which is also described in the next section
- **Age**: Age is considered as one of the influencing factors of sensitivity level [4,28,41] (groups: 1 = 18 - 30 years, 2 = 30 - 45 years and 3 = > 45 years)
- **User Category**: User category is considered as a further influencing factor of sensitivity level [28,41] (scale: 1 = unfamiliar users, who own smart home objects but not familiar with their usage, 2 = less familiar user, who own smart objects and are very little familiar with their usage and 3 = familiar user, who own smart objects and are very trusted with their usage). This clustering of the user categories also allows us to consider the technical skills of the users [4,39,41]
- **Country**: Countries are considered as influencing factors of the sensitivity level [28,41], and in this way, the culture as an influencing factor for sensitivity level can be considered [4,39,41]

Mechanisms of the Proposed Framework (A_f): In the first iteration to train the learning algorithm of A_f, the B_d is used so that the *Recommendation Manager* of A_f (see Fig. 1) can deliver data sharing recommendations while applying A_f in privacy-preserving approaches in the smart home context. This

Table 1. Extract of the initial best practice train data B_d [4,12,17,28,31,39,41,45]

Data Type	Smart Object	Sensitivity Level	Sharing Classification	Age	User Category	Country
Fingerprint	Smart door locks	5	0	3	1	Germany
Voice print	Smart speakers	5	0	2	1	UK
Medical history data	Smart wearable	5	0	2	3	Switzerland
Availability at home	Smart smoke detectors	5	0	3	2	Germany
Body images	Smart cameras	5	0	2	1	Austria

step is defined as "Pre-Processing" in Fig. 1 and in the first training iteration B_d and *individualized best practice train data* (B_{di}) contain the same data. After the first iteration, the automated solution can be applied in any smart home environment, defined as "Real-time Processing" in Fig. 1. The collected data types in that respective smart home environment are imported into the model in the second iteration. Based on the previous learning, the *Recommendation Manager* supplies users with data sharing recommendations. Based on the delivered recommendations, users have the opportunity to follow the recommendations or adjust them. In case, the users decide to adjust the recommendations, then two variables of B_d, **sharing classification** and **sensitivity level**, are adjusted and those adjustments are included in B_{di}[1]. The **sharing classification** is adopted according to users' settings, and the value can be changed between 1 and 0. The **sensitivity level** is adjusted according to the following scheme: In the first step, users are asked to set their perception regarding the dependencies between different collected data types in their smart home environment. The framework only asks users to indicate the dependencies for some of the collected data. In this step, the users will also be supplied with an "i" icon next to each collected data type, giving users some background information regarding the data type. An example for the supplied information ("i") regarding collected fingerprints or health data could be: "Biometrical data, such as fingerprints, voice prints, face IDs, describe specific characteristics of a natural human." or "Medical or health data, such as lifestyle data, wellness data, diagnoses, describe the way of corresponding human's lifestyle clearly." These details regarding "i" of corresponding data types are derived based on the data type clustering of previous surveys on data sensitivity, for instance [31,39,41]. An active learning method is used to derive the dependencies for the rest of the unassigned data based on users' indicated dependencies. As already mentioned, in this framework, the active learning method, SVM, is applied, which includes significant success in real-world learning functions for various reasons, such as the reduced need for labelling instances, good performance on unlabeled data [22,27]. When indicating the dependencies for a data sample, the users are also asked to set a *Weight Coefficient* between 0 (dependency is weak) to 1 (dependency is strong) for the indicated dependency. This *Weight Coefficient* is later used to adjust the sensi-

---

[1] From the second iteration the B_d and B_{di} do not contain the same data in case the users decide to adjust the data sharing recommendations.

tivity level of the dependent data types in case users decide to share one data type according to their preferences. One example in this context is presented in Fig. 2, and its results in Table 2. In this example, the user, Tim, owns four smart objects: (1) smart door locks collecting fingerprint and face ID, (2) smart speakers collecting voice print, (3) smart scale collecting weight and height data and (4) smart fridge collecting purchase data.

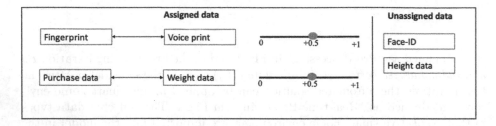

Fig. 2. Example scenario of Tim indicating the dependencies between collected data types

Table 2. Example scenario Tim: A possible result after assigning the data

Data Type	Dependency with other data types	Weight Coefficient for the Sensitivity Level	Assigned By
Fingerprint	Voice print	+ 0.5	user
Purchase Data	Weight data	+ 0.5	user
Fingerprint	Face ID	+ 0.5	framework
Weight Data	Height	+ 0.5	framework

Once the users decide to share an assigned data type, for example, fingerprint, twice in a row, which leads to the interpretation that the user does it deliberately, then the sensitivity level of the dependent data types, in Tim's scenario, voice print and face ID, will increase. In order to adjust the sensitivity level of the dependent data, in the proposed framework, the proportional-integral-derivative (PID) controller is used, a widely used control system in the industrial world and a variety of applications [7]. The technique of the PID controller includes the calculation of an error value $E(t)$, which is the difference between the expected set point SP and a measured process variable PV [7]. In the proposed framework, the PID controller is adapted as follows. The set point of a dependent data type SP_{dpn} is twice of *Weight Coefficient* of SP_{dpn} and PV_{dpn} is set to the corresponding *Weight Coefficient* of the dependent data type. In every iteration, the users decide to disclose a specific data type, the *Weight Coefficient* of the dependent data type will incrementally increase according to the set value of *Weight Coefficient* of the dependent data type (PV_{dpn}). In case the users decide to share a data type, the following calculation is performed:

$$E(t) = SP_{dpn} - PV_{dpn} \qquad (1)$$

In case $E(t) \geq 0$, the sensitivity level of the dependent data type increases by one. The maximum value of the sensitivity level is ten ("highly sensitive"), and the values of the sensitivity level can be increased to ten. When the users decide to disclose dependent data, which has already been increased in sensitivity level, they are explicitly asked whether they are sure about this decision because of the already shared data in the past. In case the users decide not to disclose an already disclosed data type twice in a row, which leads to the interpretation that the user does it deliberately, then the sensitivity level of the corresponding dependent data will be set back to the sensitivity level from B_d. Increasing the sensitivity level of a data type will always cause the sharing classification to be set to 0 if this is not the case. Integrating this mechanism helps to consider users' past activities and context-sensitive perceptions while supplying them with data disclosure recommendations according to their privacy preferences. Figure 3 presents the above-described process of the PID controller in the proposed framework.

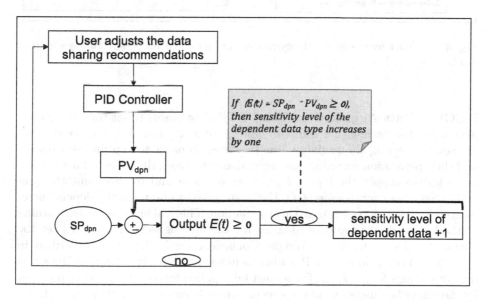

Fig. 3. Process of the adjusted PID controller in the proposed framework

2.2   Integration of the Proposed Framework in User-Centric Privacy-Preserving Approach

Integrating the described framework from the previous section in the user-centric privacy-preserving approach from [45] simplifies the original model for smart home environments. After the integration of the proposed framework in this paper, the modified user-centric privacy-preserving approach includes only two

User-Centric-Control-Points (UCCPs): (A) **UCCP 1: Data Aggregation** and (B) **UCCP 2: Data Sharing and Access Limitations.** The modified user-centric privacy-preserving approach is implemented in the Data Storage and Processing Node (*DSPN*) of the IoT device layer of the IoT system architecture, as recommended in [45]. Figure 4 illustrates the UCCPs of the modified model and their interrelationships.

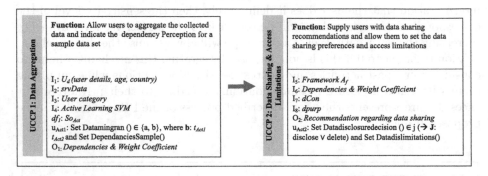

Fig. 4. Modified user-centric privacy-preserving approach for Smart Home Environments

UCCP 1: Data Aggregation: This UCCP allows users to set the aggregation period for their review *(Set Datamingran())*[2] from [45] and users are asked to set the settings during the **registration process**. In order to capture user details and their perception regarding the dependency between the collected data, users are asked to supply the inputs U_d[3], *User category* and to carry out the user action *Set DependanciesSample()*. Users are asked to indicate the dependencies for some of the collected data in this user action. This will help the active learning method I_4 to derive the dependencies for the unassigned data and deliver the output O_1: Dependencies & Weight Coefficient for UCCP 2, as described in Sect. 2.1. Furthermore, UCCP 1 also includes a further input I_2: srvData and default settings So_{Act}. I_2: srvData must be supplied by the smart object provider by the time when users install the specific smart home object in their smart home and include the collected data types by the smart home object service. The So_{Act} is set as in the original model[4] from [45].

---

[2] "The setting options regarding data aggregation allow end users to choose between two options. The two options are (1) the exact time of each action of the smart object for daily review (t_{Act1}) or (2) the time period users want to aggregate and review the collected data by their smart objects (t_{Act2}), for example, weekly, monthly. An example for t_{Act1} could be that the smart object owner is absent at 07:30 am on the 5th of February and present again at 8 pm in the living room. He gets up at 06:30 am and switches on his smart bulbs in two rooms, namely the bathroom and sleeping room. In contrast to this, an example for t_{Act2} could be that the smart object owner is available at home at various times per month and switches on his smart bulbs 200 times per month." [45].

[3] Examples for user details are age, country.

[4] "The default settings for So_{Act} regarding data aggregation layer is assigned to So_{Act1}, which means that the granularity of the data is set at the layer of sensors." [45].

UCCP 2: Data Sharing and Access Limitations: Complementary to UCCP 1, UCCP 2 supplies users data sharing recommendations while considering users' context-aware privacy preferences and past activities. Additionally, this UCCP also allows users to set their data sharing preferences and access limitations with the user actions, *Set Datadisclosuredecision ()* and *Set Datadislimitations()*. The UCCP 2 includes four inputs: (1) I_5: Framework A_f, (2) I_6: Dependencies & Weight Coefficient, (3) I_7: dCon[5] and (4) I_8: dpurp[6]. The proposed Framework (A_f) is integrated in this UCCP (I_5), as described in Sect. 2.1 and the O_1: Dependencies & Weight Coefficient from UCCP 1 is considered as the I_6. The data sharing recommendations are supplied during the **aggregation period**, and the users are also asked to carry out the user actions during this period. In case users decide not to follow the data sharing recommendations, supplied based on the A_f (O_2: Recommendation regarding data sharing), then the users are asked to set the *dCon* and *dpurp*. At this point the user preferences will be captured and used to update the two variables of B_d, **sharing classification** and **sensitivity level** according to the mechanisms of the A_f, as described in Sect. 2.1. In this UCCP, users can access the shared data with data consumers for different usage purposes. They can also disclose those already shared data with further data consumers for other usage purposes. The integration of the A_f in the approach from [45] allows supplying users with data sharing recommendations with minimum human interference while considering users' past activities and context-sensitive preferences. Moreover, integrating the proposed framework allows users to control the entire data collection, storage and disclosure process in smart home environments.

3   Evaluation

The proposed best-practice-based framework and its integration in an existing user-centric privacy-preserving approach address existing gaps, as mentioned in [25] as well as in the demands from GDPR, especially Art. 9, 12, 15, 17, 19 and 22 [1,12,38], and supply a solution regarding context-aware privacy-preference modelling. In the following sections, the evaluation of functional and non-functional requirements regarding the proposed framework is presented since, as mentioned at the beginning, the implementation of the framework is not a part of this manuscript.

3.1   Evaluation of Non-Functional Requirements

In this section, the non-functional requirements regarding the proposed framework are evaluated. The security-, privacy-, and performance-related non-functional requirements are derived based on existing literature [9,20] in the

---

[5] "*dCon* include third parties getting access to disclosed data, such as doctors, insurance company, government agencies, etc." [45].

[6] "... usage purposes informs end users for which purpose, such as personal health plan, statistical purposes, etc., the shared data are used by the *dCon*..." [45].

context of software and machine learning development. The considered non-functional requirements are: (1) performance, (2) maintainability, (3) legal, (4) portability, (5) deployability, (6) interoperability, (7) data integrity, (8) efficiency and capacity, (9) scalability, (10) availability. Since the real-world implementation of the proposed approach is not in the scope of the paper, the evaluation of non-functional requirements allows us to analyze the feasibility and the performance of the proposed framework.

Performance: According to [37], the user interfaces of software programs should be fast and deliver results within 250 ms. In order to address this performance issue in the proposed framework, several measurements are taken: (1) applied machine learning approaches and (2) technical equipment. Regarding the first point, two machine learning approaches are applied in the proposed approach: Decision tree and SVM. Decision trees are intuitive, more effortless, and not time-consuming in their implementation [48]. Furthermore, the decision trees include high flexibility and deliver high accuracy results regarding logical connections between learned and predicted items [48]. Additionally, SVM is considered as a powerful learning method allowing to achieve an efficient data classification with high accuracy [43] as well as to utilize less energy per second in comparison to other techniques, such as random forest, multi-layer perception, for instance, as outlined in a real-world IoT device experiment from [48]. Striking is that SVM includes complex training structures, which require more training time compared to other learning algorithms, as shown in the reference example from [48]. In the reference example [48], the training and inference speed of a data set with 100 instances (after data pre-cleansing) is tracked in seconds on an IoT device and outlines that training run time per instance is 0.75 s and inference run time per instance is 0.04 s. In the IoT and smart home context, where data sets contain millions of data, due to the second/minute measurement, it is useful to sample the valid training data set (after data cleansing according to [8,48]) while maintaining the representatives of the different values of various smart objects in own home environment [14] and considering user preferences regarding the aggregation period in order to allow less time-consuming learning for both applied algorithms, decision tree and SVM. Regarding the technical equipment, it is recommended to integrate a server element, for instance, an element with an i7 kernel and quad-core processor, in the technical component *DSPN* from [45] in order to integrate the both modified UCCPs with the learning algorithms of A_f in an energy-efficient and fast way. The real-world experiment [48] in the IoT context outlines based on different real-world data sets, such as energy efficiency data of different buildings, disease diagnostic data, etc., that running a classification algorithm on a computer element, such as a Personal Computer takes 0.017–0.029 s, compared to a Rasberry Pi model B integrated IoT device with 4.99–5.72 s run-time [48]. In their work [48], Yazici et al. considered the average time in their speed measurements after running each algorithm 20 times with each data set to deliver reliable speed measurements. This approach for the speed measurement can also be applied in the future real-life experiment of the proposed approach in this publication. Based on these previous observations, in order to achieve high accuracy in a real-life scenario of the proposed approach in this paper, the B_d should contain at least 100 instances with representative data sets. The model training for the classification based on SVM (with c hyperparameter between 0.1 and 1.0) and decision tree (with default hyperparameters) can be executed [32] after data pre-cleansing and -sampling on the *DSPN* from [45], which will cost about under 75 s. run time according to the previous reference example, such as [48]. Additionally, in the real-life experiment of the proposed approach, the SVM is considered in UCCP 1, carried out during the registration process. Its results will be presented later in the UCCP 2 during the aggregation period. In this way, sufficient time is available for the SVM to perform the elaborate training and produce the input for the UCCP 2 (I_6: Dependencies & Weight Coefficient). Furthermore, in a real-life experiment, the data cleansing and sampling methods are considered in the *DSPN* server element. They are already applied after the registration process before supplying users with data sharing recommendations in UCCP 2. In the real-world experiment, it could be possible to implement the *DSPN* server element in a smart home hub, such as Almond+, or Google OnHub, which ensures communication between the smart objects and allow their easy operations via a (mobile or web) application for smart home owners [5]. However, those existing smart home hubs must be expanded in terms of (privacy-preserving) functionality and hardware (non-functional requirements) in order to implement the modified user-centric privacy-preserving solution from Sect. 2.2. To sum up, implementing data pre-cleansing, -sampling, and the algorithms decision tree and SVM in the *DSPN* server element enables the proposed approach to address the performance issues and deliver the results, such as data sharing recommendations, to users within 250 ms on the corresponding user interface of the proposed privacy-preserving solution.

Maintainability: According to [30], maintainability includes the ease of customizing and modifying software to fix bugs, improve performance and make it adaptable. For the proposed modified user-centric privacy-preserving approach in this paper, no maintenance is needed after the initial installation of the approach. The updates for modification and customization are automatically installed during the nighttime not to influence the users and the use of the framework system.

Legal: The proposed automated approach with its algorithm is integrated into users' smart home environment at the *DSPN* in the IoT architecture system, as recommended in [45]. This implementation allows collecting and processing the collected data in a privacy-preserving way in users' environments according to the GDPR requirements from [12,38].

Portability: Users can have encrypted access to the data collected and processed in the *DSPN* of their smart environment via a mobile application. The main focus of the user-centric privacy-preserving approach is to supply users solutions with a minimum number of external accesses to allow control of the entire data collection, storage, and disclosure process [38,45]. According to Art.

20 of the GDPR [12], the proposed approach allows users to have an overview of the shared data with data consumers for different usage purposes, and it also allows users to supply additional data consumers with the already shared data.

Deployability: The proposed approach can be implemented using the Java-based open-source tool called WEKA 3[7]. This tool is recommended because it is portable and allows the integration of the framework with other Java-based user interfaces [2]. In addition, Java is also adaptable to different operating systems and devices [2]. Using WEKA 3 will allow the implementation of the entire proposed solution from Sect. 2.2 in the future.

Interoperability: According to [44], interoperability means that different software components can interact and cooperate despite different languages, user interfaces and platforms. The proposed approach is designed to integrate all types of smart home objects into the proposed user-centric privacy-preserving solution with the presented framework and to allow users control over the entire data collection, storage and disclosure process in their smart home environment with different smart home objects.

Data Integrity: The proposed framework and its integration into the existing framework from [45] allow the consideration and integration of all the collected data by users' smart home objects in their smart home environments. By integrating a server element with sufficient memory management in the *DSPN*, there will be hardly any technical limitations regarding the amount of data which can be stored.

Efficiency and Capacity: The proposed framework works in a less time-, cost- and energy-consuming and effective way because the proposed approach's machine learning algorithms are integrated in the server-based *DSPN* [48]. Additionally, considering the machine learning algorithms, decision tree and SVM in the proposed framework, integrated in the *DSPN*, help efficient data classification with high accuracy [43,48] in the IoT context. Furthermore, the consideration of the data cleansing and sampling methods in *DSPN* supports less time and efficient data processing [8,36].

Scalability: According to [10], scalability means when a system can perform tasks under growing work volumes and allows its enlargement. Integrating an efficient server element in the *DSPN* and the efficient and energy-saving integration of the machine learning algorithms allows the proposed framework to perform the corresponding tasks, such as supplying users with data sharing recommendations, in a growing environment of collected data. In case the initial supplied server capacity is insufficient, the server capacity of the *DSPN* can also be expanded accordingly by upgrading its capacity based on the supplied services of the corresponding provider.

Availability: According to [18], there are different levels of availability when it comes to the server and computer systems. The proposed framework recommends

---

[7] WEKA 3 is considered a very highly ranked top detection tool and data mining tool [35].

integrating at least a high-availability server element or better in the *DSPN*. Integrating such a system in the proposed framework could cause at most 5 min of service interruption per year [18]. If the integrated server element in *DSPN* is down, then it is conceivable to enable data access to the *DSPN* data on a private cloud, which is also installed in one's smart home environment and can be accessed by the smart home owner. This private cloud provides a backup of the *DSPN*.

To sum up, the evaluation outlines that considering the abovementioned requirements in the proposed framework allows fulfilling non-functional requirements from security-, privacy-, and performance-related categories.

3.2 Evaluation of Functional Requirements

This section evaluates the proposed solution with existing approaches, [3,22,23, 26], qualitatively in order to outline the added value of the proposed framework and to evaluate functional requirements. These works [3,22,23,26] are relevant works in this area and partially supply the basics for the proposed solution. While [22,23] propose standalone machine learning approaches allowing users to express their data sharing and data sensitivity preferences by labelling a sample of collected data, [26] presents a technique to present users derived conclusions based on collected data about users' daily routines and activities. Additionally, [3] presents an architecture allowing users to understand and control their smart home network. However, the detailed and qualitative evaluation of the previous solutions outlines that those approaches do not supply users with best-practice-based data sharing recommendations with minimum human interference while considering context-sensitive factors and users' preferences based on past activities. Furthermore, integrating the proposed framework in an existing user-centric privacy-preserving approach from [45] allows users to control the entire data collection, storage and disclosure process and integrate the proposed solution in existing IoT architecture systems.
The evaluation metrics are categorized into three clusters: (1) privacy-preserving features, (2) user-friendliness and (3) GDPR requirements for automated decision making (Art. 22). The metrics of each category are derived from [12,25,33, 38,45]. Table 3 presents the results of the qualitative evaluation.

4 Discussion and Limitations

4.1 Discussion

The proposed framework allows addressing (1) existing gaps from [25] and (2) demands from GDPR, especially Art. 9, 12, 15, 17, 19 and 22 [1,12,38], in context-aware privacy-preference modelling research. The proposed best-practice-based framework for user-centric privacy-preserving approaches in the smart home context supplies users with data sharing recommendations while considering (1) context-sensitive factors and (2) users' preferences based on users'

Table 3. Qualitative evaluation of the proposed solution: Each metric is evaluated by using the following rating scale: ○ = no possibility; ◑ = partially possible; and ● = possible.

Evaluation category	Metrics	Proposed Model	Model 2 from [22]	Model 3 from [23]	Model 4 from [26]	Model 5 from [3]
Privacy-preserving features	Allowing privacy-preserving data storage [45]	●	◑	◑	○	◑
	Allowing privacy-preserving and data protection of the users [25,45]	●	◑	◑	◑	○
	Limiting data access by limiting data consumers and usage purposes [33]	●	●	○	○	○
	Supplying best-practice-based data sharing recommendations [25]	●	○	○	○	○
	Considering context-sensitive factors while deriving data sharing recommendations [25,45]	●	○	○	◑	○
	Adjusting sensitivity of the data types according to already disclosed data [25]	●	○	○	○	○
User-friendliness	Minimum human interference (user inputs) [25,45]	●	◑	◑	◑	◑
	Consideration of users' data sharing preferences based on past activities [25]	●	○	○	○	○
GDPR (Art. 22) requirements for automated decision making	Users have the opportunity to intervene the automated processing [12,38]	●	◑	◑	◑	◑
	Automated approach includes suitable measurements to safeguard users' rights and privacy [12,38]	●	●	◑	◑	◑
	All the data types are considered in the automated approach [12,38]	●	◑	●	●	◑

past activities. The proposed framework with automation options, which can be integrated within an existing privacy-preserving approach with user-centricity from [45], allows users to control the entire data collection and disclosure process with minimum human interference. It also allows the integration of the proposed solution in existing IoT architecture systems. Addressing the mentioned gap in [25] and therefore including supervised and active machine learning methods allow supplying users with best-practice-based data sharing recommendations derived based on GDPR specifications according to Art. 4, 5, 9, 12, 15, 17 and 19 [12] while considering users' context-sensitive factors as well as past activities. Additionally, the related work from Sect. 5 with already proposed machine learning privacy-preserving solutions in this context do not include mechanisms which facilitate the process of preference specification based on users' past activities [13,25,29]. Furthermore, the analysis of previous works also outlines that other solutions must be introduced, which allow the presentation and control of the context-sensitive factors related to users' privacy preferences [25]. With the proposed approach in this paper, these research gaps are addressed, and it allows supplying data sharing recommendations based on GDPR-based best practices, which can be adjusted according to users' past activities and context-sensitive factors. In this way, the GDPR requirements in the context of user-centric privacy-preserving approaches and automated decision-making [12,25,38] are also addressed.

As mentioned, the included initial input B_d for the automated framework, A_f, is derived based on the GDPR specification in Art. 4, 5, 9, 12, 15, 17 and 19 [1,12,38]. Additionally, the users are asked to indicate the dependencies between the collected data types according to their perception. However, it must be investigated with user studies whether there is a user-friendly way to capture users' dependency perceptions in this respective context. Moreover, the initial input (B_d) must be validated and completed based on interviews with GDPR experts to cover all the cases. Furthermore, in the modified user centric privacy-preserving approach, the users are supplied with different inputs, such as $srvData$, $dCon$, $dpurp$, in the integrated user-centric privacy-preserving approach. These inputs must be validated with users within a user study to find out in which way these inputs can be adjusted and whether those inputs are sufficient for their decision-making process.

4.2   Limitations

The findings of this paper are mainly based on a literature review and previously derived approach from [45]. The proposed approach must be validated with user studies, and an additional real-world experiment to (1) validate the initial input, (2) find out a user-friendly way for deriving users' perceptions regarding data type dependencies and (3) investigate its acceptance and applicability, which will be addressed in the near future.

5   Related Work

Existing works can be clustered into two categories: (1) technical solutions for disclosure behaviour prediction in different contexts and (2) machine learning solutions in IoT and smart environments.

In the first category, solutions are presented, which supply users with disclosure recommendations based on predicting disclosure behaviour models. While [40] presents a machine learning mechanism to help users specify disclosure preferences in a location-sharing system, [16] proposes a privacy wizard in a social network context, which configures users' privacy settings based on machine learning mechanisms automatically after asking users different questions. Additionally, Knijnenburg and Jin outline in their work that users are willing to receive privacy recommendations by an assisted system and that the input for those recommendations will influence users' satisfaction positively [24]. In [47], Xie et al. present a prediction algorithm which allows users to configure privacy settings in location sharing context. In their work, Xie et al. also outline that the context and data consumers (audience) influence users' location privacy preferences, and the observations show that few users also share similar sharing preferences [47]. Moreover, Pallapa et al. present another context-aware privacy-preserving solution in the mobile context, which derive users' privacy preferences based on the interaction history between the users and apply those in new situations [34].

The second category includes machine learning solutions in IoT and smart environment contexts, which support users in the automatic configuration of privacy settings and supply users with recommendations for privacy settings. Several machine learning solutions are presented in the smart home context, such as [3, 22, 23, 26]. While [22] presents a machine learning-based framework allowing users to express their data sharing preferences by labelling some collected data in their smart home environments while considering the data consumers, usage purposes and information granularity, Keshavarz and Anwar propose in another work an active machine learning approach helping users to classify between sensitive and non-sensitive data according to users' privacy preferences [23]. Also, in this approach, Keshavarz and Anwar ask users to label some amount of data as sensitive or non-sensitive so that the model can learn users' privacy concerns and apply it while labelling the rest of the collected data [23]. Furthermore, Aïvodji et al. present in their work [3] an architecture called IOTFLA for data security and privacy in smart home environments. This approach allows users to improve the efficiency of the smart home systems, the understanding and control over the smart home networks [3]. Additionally, Kounoudes et al. present in their work [26] a data inference technique which derives conclusions about users' routines and activities based on the collected data to present those conclusions to the users and uses those conclusions to improve smart object services.

In comparison to all the above-mentioned previous works, the contribution of the proposed approach to this body of literature is three-fold: Best-practice-based framework supplying users data disclosure recommendations while considering (1) context-sensitive factors, (2) users' preferences in data sharing recommendations after learning from users' past activities and (3) its integration in an exiting solution allow users to control the entire data storage, collection and disclosure process with minimum human interference. Furthermore, the entire proposed approach in this paper allows addressing a few existing gaps in context-aware privacy-preference modelling with user focus, as mentioned in [25] and the demands from GDPR, especially Art. 9, 12, 15, 17, 19 and 22 [1,12,38].

6   Conclusions and Future Work

In this paper, a best-practice-based automated framework is proposed, which (1) supplies users with data sharing recommendations based on GDPR-related best practices and (2) allows to consider users' past activities, privacy preferences and context-sensitive factors. Integrating the proposed approach in an existing user-centric privacy-preserving approach allow users to control the entire data collection, storage and disclosure process with minimum human interference. Furthermore, this integration also allows us to implement the proposed automated approach in existing IoT architecture systems.

In order to investigate the performance and user acceptance, we plan (1) to implement the proposed approach in a real-world smart home environment and (2) to conduct user studies in the future.

Acknowledgments. We thank the anonymous reviewers for their feedback, and special thanks to Lindrit Kqiku, Alexandr Railean, Patrick Kühtreiber and Alexander Richter for the exchange and feedback.

References

1. GDPR Art. 9 Processing of Special Categories of Personal Data. https://gdpr-info.cu/art-9-gdpr/. Accessed May 2022
2. Aher, S.B., Lobo, L.: Data mining in educational system using Weka. In: International Conference on Emerging Technology Trends (ICETT), vol. 3, pp. 20–25 (2011)
3. Aïvodji, U.M., Gambs, S., Martin, A.: IOTFLA : a secured and privacy-preserving smart home architecture implementing federated learning: a secured and privacy-preserving smart home architecture implementing federated learning. In: Proceedings of 2019 IEEE Security and Privacy Workshops (SPW), pp. 175–180 (2019)
4. Al-Ameen, M.N., Tamanna, T., Nandy, S., Ahsan, M.M., Chandra, P., Ahmed, S.I.: We Don't Give a Second Thought Before Providing our Information: Understanding Users' Perceptions of Information Collection by Apps in Urban Bangladesh, pp. 32–43 (2020)
5. Awasthi, A., Read, H.O., Xynos, K., Sutherland, I.: Welcome PWN: almond smart home hub forensics. Digit. Investig. **26**, 38-S46 (2018)
6. Balapour, A., Nikkhah, H.R., Sabherwal, R.: Mobile application security: role of perceived privacy as the predictor of security perceptions. Int. J. Inf. Manage. **52**, 102063 (2020)
7. Bennett, S.: Development of the PID controller. IEEE Control Syst. Mag. **13**(6), 58–62 (1993)
8. Bermingham, M.L., et al.: Application of high-dimensional feature selection: evaluation for genomic prediction in man. Sci. Rep. **5**(1), 1–12 (2015)
9. Binkhonain, M., Zhao, L.: A review of machine learning algorithms for identification and classification of non-functional requirements. Expert Syst. Appl. X. **1**, 100001 (2019)
10. Bondi, A.B.: Characteristics of scalability and their impact on performance. In: Proceedings of the 2nd International Workshop on Software and Performance, pp. 195–203 (2000)

11. Carretero, J., García, J.D.: The internet of things: connecting the world. Personal Ubiquit. Comput. **18**(2), 445–447 (2014)
12. Consulting, I.: Art. 22 GDPR Automated Individual Decision-Making, Including Profiling.https://gdpr-info.eu/art-22-gdpr/. Accessed July 2022
13. Das, A., Degeling, M., Wang, X., Wang, J., Sadeh, N., Satyanarayanan, M.: Assisting users in a world full of cameras: a privacy-aware infrastructure for computer vision applications. In: 2017 IEEE Conference on Computer Vision and Pattern Recognition Workshops (CVPRW), pp. 1387–1396 (2017)
14. De Choudhury, M., Lin, Y.R., Sundaram, H., Candan, K.S., Xie, L., Kelliher, A.: How does the data sampling strategy impact the discovery of information diffusion in social media? In: Fourth International AAAI Conference on Weblogs and Social Media (2010)
15. Dutta, S., Chukkapalli, S.S.L., Sulgekar, M., Krithivasan, S., Das, P.K., Joshi, A.: Context sensitive access control in smart home environments. In: IEEE 6th Intl Conference on Big Data Security on Cloud (BigDataSecurity), IEEE Intl Conference on High Performance and Smart Computing (HPSC) and IEEE International Conference on Intelligent Data and Security (IDS), pp. 35–41 (2020)
16. Fang, L., LeFevre, K.: Privacy Wizards For Social Networking Sites. In: Proceedings of the 19th International Conference on World Wide Web, pp. 351–360 (2010)
17. Fietkiewicz, K., Ilhan, A.: Fitness tracking technologies: data privacy doesn't matter? The (Un)Concerns of users, former users, and non-users. In: Proceedings of the 53rd Hawaii International Conference on System Sciences, pp. 1–10 (2020)
18. Gray, J., Siewiorek, D.P.: High-availability computer systems. Computer **24**(9), 39–48 (1991)
19. Guhr, N., Werth, O., Blacha, P.P.H., Breitner, M.H.: Privacy concerns in the smart home context. SN Appl. Sci. **2**(2), 1–12 (2020)
20. Jahan, N., Ghani, T., Rasheduzzaman, M., Marzan, Y., Ridoy, S.H., Khan, M.M.: Design and feasibility analysis of nsugt a machine learning-based mobile application for education. In: 2021 IEEE 11th Annual Computing and Communication Workshop and Conference (CCWC), pp. 0926–0929. IEEE (2021)
21. Jozani, M., Ayaburi, E., Ko, M., Choo, K.K.R.: Privacy concerns and benefits of engagement with social media-enabled apps: a privacy calculus perspective. Comput. Human Behav. **107**, 106–260 (2020)
22. Keshavarz, M., Anwar, M.: Towards improving privacy control for smart homes: a privacy decision framework. In: 2018 16th Annual Conference on Privacy, Security and Trust (PST), pp. 1–3 (2018)
23. Keshavarz, M., Anwar, M.: The automatic detection of sensitive data in smart homes. In: International Conference on Human-Computer Interaction, pp. 404–416 (2019)
24. Knijnenburg, B., Jin, H.: The persuasive effect of privacy recommendations for location sharing services. SSRN Electron. J. 2399725 (2013)
25. Kounoudes, A.D., Kapitsaki, G.M.: A mapping of IoT user-centric privacy preserving approaches to the GDPR. Internet Things **11**, 100179 (2020)
26. Kounoudes, A.D., Kapitsaki, G.M., Katakis, I., Milis, M.: User-centred privacy inference detection for smart home devices. In: 2021 IEEE SmartWorld, Ubiquitous Intelligence & Computing, Advanced & Trusted Computing, Scalable Computing & Communications, Internet of People and Smart City Innovation (SmartWorld/SCALCOM/UIC/ATC/IOP/SCI), pp. 210–218 (2021)
27. Kremer, J., Steenstrup Pedersen, K., Igel, C.: Active learning with support vector machines. Wiley Interdiscipl. Rev. Data Mining Knowl. Disc. **4**(4), 313–326 (2014)

28. Kulyk, O., Reinheimer, B., Aldag, L., Mayer, P., Gerber, N., Volkamer, M.: Security and privacy awareness in smart environments-a cross-country investigation. In: International Conference on Financial Cryptography and Data Security, pp. 84–101 (2020)

29. Liu, B., et al.: Follow my recommendations: a personalized privacy assistant for mobile app permissions. In: Twelfth Symposium on Usable Privacy and Security (SOUPS 2016), pp. 27–41 (2016)

30. Malhotra, R., Chug, A.: Software maintainability prediction using machine learning algorithms. Softw. Eng. Int. J. (SeiJ). **2**(2) (2012)

31. Milne, G., Pettinico, G., Hajjat, F., Markos, E.: Information sensitivity typology: mapping the degree and type of risk consumers perceive in personal data sharing. J. Consum. Affairs **51**(1), 133–161 (2016)

32. Mohammed, R., Rawashdeh, J., Abdullah, M.: Machine learning with oversampling and undersampling techniques: overview study and experimental results. In: 2020 11th International Conference on Information and Communication Systems (ICICS), pp. 243–248. IEEE (2020)

33. Oetzel, M.C., Spiekermann, S.: A systematic methodology for privacy impact assessments: a design science approach. Eur. J. Inf. Syst. **23**(2), 126–150 (2014)

34. Pallapa, G., Das, S.K., Di Francesco, M., Aura, T.: Adaptive and context-aware privacy preservation exploiting user interactions in smart environments. Pervas. Mob. Comput. **12**, 232–243 (2014)

35. Peerspot: WEKA Review. https://www.peerspot.com/products/wcka-reviews. Accessed July 2022

36. Rahm, E., Do, H.H.: Data cleaning: problems and current approaches. IEEE Data Eng. Bull. **23**(4), 3–13 (2000)

37. Raskin, J.: The Human Interface: New Directions for Designing Interactive Systems. Addison-Wesley Professional (2000)

38. Regulation (EU): 2016/679 of the European Parliament and of the Council of 27 April 2016 on the Protection of Natural Persons with Regard to the Processing of Personal Data and on the Free Movement of Such Data, and Repealing Directive 95/46/EC (General Data Protection Regulation). Official Journal of the European Union L119/1, pp. 1–88 (2016)

39. Rumbold, J., Pierscionek, B.: What are data? A categorization of the data sensitivity spectrum. Big Data Res. **12**, 49–59 (2018)

40. Sadeh, N., et al.: Understanding and capturing people's privacy policies in a mobile social networking application. Pers. Ubiquit. Comput. **13**(6), 401–412 (2009)

41. Schomakers, E.M., Lidynia, C., Müllmann, D., Ziefle, M.: Internet users' perceptions of information sensitivity-insights from Germany. Int. J. Inf. Manage. **46**, 142–150 (2019)

42. Sheehan, K.B., Hoy, M.G.: Dimensions of privacy concern among online consumers. J. Publ. Policy Mark. **19**(1), 62–73 (2000)

43. Shen, M., Tang, X., Zhu, L., Du, X., Guizani, M.: Privacy-preserving support vector machine training over blockchain-based encrypted IoT data in smart cities. IEEE Internet Things J. **6**(5), 7702–7712 (2019)

44. Wegner, P.: Interoperability. ACM Comput. Surv. (CSUR) **28**(1), 285–287 (1996)

45. Wickramasinghe, C.I., Reinhardt, D.: A user-centric privacy-preserving approach to control data collection, storage, and disclosure in own smart home environments. In: International Conference on Mobile and Ubiquitous Systems: Computing, Networking, and Services, pp. 190–206 (2021)

46. Wu, H., Knijnenburg, B.P., Kobsa, A.: Improving the prediction of users' disclosure behavior by making them disclose more predictably? In: Symposium on Usable Privacy and Security (SOUPS) (2014)
47. Xie, J., Knijnenburg, B.P., Jin, H.: Location sharing privacy preference: analysis and personalized recommendation. In: Proceedings of the 19th international conference on Intelligent User Interfaces, pp. 189–198 (2014)
48. Yazici, M.T., Basurra, S., Gaber, M.M.: Edge machine learning: enabling smart internet of things applications. Big Data Cogn. Comput. **2**(3), 26 (2018)
49. Zeng, E., Mare, S., Roesner, F.: End user security and privacy concerns with smart homes. In: Proceedings of SOUPS 2013, Symposium on Usable Privacy and Security, pp. 65–80 (2017)
50. Zhou, W., Jia, Y., Peng, A., Zhang, Y., Liu, P.: The effect of IoT new features on security and privacy: new threats, existing solutions, and challenges yet to be solved. IEEE Internet Things J. **6**(2), 1606–1616 (2019)

FedGroup: A Federated Learning Approach for Anomaly Detection in IoT Environments

Yixuan Zhang[1], Basem Suleiman[1,2]([envelope]) [iD], and Muhammad Johan Alibasa[3] [iD]

[1] School of Computer Science, University of Sydney, Sydney, Australia
{nikki.zhang,basem.suleiman}@sydney.edu.au
[2] School of Computer Science and Engineering, University of New South Wales, Sydney, Australia
[3] School of Computing, Telkom University, Bandung, Indonesia
alibasa@telkomuniversity.ac.id

Abstract. The increasing adoption and use of IoT devices in smart home environments have raised concerns around the data security or privacy of smart home users. Several studies employed traditional machine learning to address the key security challenge, namely anomaly detection in IoT devices. Such models, however, require transmitting sensitive IoT data to a central model for training and validation which introduces security and performance concerns. In this paper, we propose a federated learning approach for detecting anomalies in IoT devices. We present our FedGroup model and algorithms that train and validate local models based on data from a group of IoT devices. FedGroup also updates the learning of the central model based on the learning changes that result from each group of IoT devices, rather than computing the average learning of each device. Our empirical evaluation of the real IoT dataset demonstrates the capability of our FedGroup model and anomaly detection accuracy as the same or better than federated and non-federated learning models. FedGroup is also more secure and performs well given all the IoT data are used to train and update the models locally.

Keywords: Internet of Things (IoT) · Anomaly Detection · Federated Learning · Machine Learning · Privacy · Smart Home

1 Introduction

With the advancement of the Internet technologies, it was predicted that the number of Internet of Things (IoT) devices in the smart home environment in 2020 would be 7 devices per person [1]. In smart home environments devices such as sensors, smartphones, and smart TVs are connected to the Internet so that they can be accessed and monitored remotely. To achieve this, data will be continuously sensed so that these IoT devices can perform certain functions. For

S. Longfei and P. Bodhi (Eds.): MobiQuitous 2022, LNICST 492, pp. 121–132, 2023.
https://doi.org/10.1007/978-3-031-34776-4_7

example, turning on the air conditioner when the temperature reaches a certain degree and switching off the TV when there is no one detected watching TV [2]. The significant growth of IoT devices in smart homes has also brought forward research interests in the very large amount of data that are collected and used to support different types of intelligent services for smart homes [3]. The collected data can be used to develop intelligent data-driven models for enhancing the user's experience of smart homes.

The connectivity of smart home devices to the Internet and continuous data sensing brought a number of key challenges to smart home users, including data privacy and malicious access and control of the sensitive IoT devices. The settings of IoT devices do not take users' privacy and security as a priority. Such IoT devices are often vulnerable to network attacks given it's connected to the Internet, and these attacks can be pervasive [4]. Such attacks may include access and transfer of data being sensed by these devices, remotely switching off security and monitoring cameras, and opening the doors remotely for unauthorised home residents. Recent research reported that around 59% of users are concerned about smart devices listening to them without permission and gathering data without their knowledge [5]. Therefore, it becomes crucial to maintain the highest levels of privacy and security while these IoT devices are used in smart homes. To address this challenge, a large amount of research work that employs AI-based approaches to detect anomalous behaviour in such IoT devices [6–9]. These approaches heavily focus on traditional machine learning models which also bring new challenges. Such machine learning approaches require transmitting all data sensed from all IoT devices to an external server to train and validate central anomaly detection models. This can be very expensive and could exhaust the bandwidth of the network. It also can expose the sensitive data collected from the IoT devices over the network which makes it vulnerable to cyber-attacks. The situation would not get better even with encrypting and decrypting the data as it could add performance overhead.

In this study, we address the anomaly detection problem on IoT devices by employing a federated learning approach. Federated learning allows the training of local models based on data sensed from a group of IoT devices within a smart home. The local models do not need to transmit the raw IoT data, but only model updates that result from local training. The model (parameter) updates are then shared with a central model which aggregates the values of the learning parameters and then sends them back to all local models, so they can update their learning. Although this federated learning approach addresses the above data security and performance overhead posed by traditional machine learning models, it has its unique challenges. In this paper, we address the research question: How to design local and central models that work in federated learning settings, given various IoT devices in smart homes?

Existing federated learning approaches suggest using the overall average to update the learning parameters shared by all local models. This might not be practical as it ignores the bias of the local models (each might have different data with or without anomalies). We propose a new federated learning model called FedGroup for anomaly detection in smart home environments. We present algorithms that detail the training process on data collected from a group of IoT devices and the process of updating learning parameters in the central model based on the learning results from each group of IoT devices. Our FedGroup addresses the bias resulting from averaging all updates from each device.

The main contributions of this paper are:

1. A new federated learning model and algorithms called FedGroup for anomaly detection on IoT devices. The FedGroup model computes the learning updates based on parameters from a group of IoT devices.
2. Empirical evaluation of FedGroup on real data collected from various IoT devices [6–9]. The evaluation also includes a performance analysis of the Fed-Group against federated learning and non-federated learning models.

The rest of this paper is organised as follows. Section 2 describes related work in the field of anomaly detection for IoTs. Section 3 presents the dataset used in this study and the FedGroup model and algorithms proposed in this paper. Experiments and Results are then presented in Sect. 4. Section 5 presents key conclusions and future work.

2 Literature Review

Various traditional machine learning and deep learning approaches have been utilised to identify attacks on IoT devices. One study by Stojkoska et al. (2017) [10] suggests that the cloud-centric of holistic IoT-based framework for smart home environments requires substantial data storage and processing infrastructure, and the current state is far from efficient. They highlighted that the new approaches should comprehend the issue of massive data management on the cloud. Furthermore, future studies also have to investigate different methods to ensure security since the cloud-based techniques pose an enormous risk of revealing personal information and data, which are considered as urgent issues.

Past research tended to focus on centralised anomaly detection in which the cloud collects data from various sources. This raises several issues including high communication load and data privacy. Federated Learning (FL) was proposed with the characteristic of lightweight communicating updates, and it was proven to successfully predict text input on mobile devices [11]. FL merges the updates from all the distributed devices thus the calculation on the cloud was significantly reduced, resulting in improved scalability and lightweight communication [12]. Another study [13] compared the IoT intrusion detection using different approaches, including centralised, on-device and FL. The efficiency of FL reached a similar accuracy to the centralised approach. Besides, the study suggests that FL outperformed the on-device approach as it could take advantage of the knowledge from others. FL answers significant drawbacks of centralised ML models that are expensive, computationally difficult, and have low scalability support.

Mohri et al. (2019) [14] indicated that different clients might be weighted differently by FL resulting in unfairness. Fairness in this context refers to both the training data and the training procedures. The study indicates that the uniform distribution is not the common distribution in many cases. Therefore, minimising the anticipated loss concerning the specific distribution is harmful and might lead to a mismatch with the target. Consequently, the study presented an agnostic FL framework in which the centralised model is optimised for any target distribution produced by a mixture of client distributions by utilising data-dependent Rademacher complexity. However, the optimisation of the single worst device is limited for a smart environment with numerous IoT devices. In separate research, Li et al. (2020) [15] concur that unfair distribution of model could bring disproportionate performance since overall accuracy is high but individual accuracy is uncertain. The generated model may be biased towards devices with massive data. Their study developed An enhanced model configured at a more granular scale to ensure equitable device distribution and maintain the same overall accuracy.

A study analysis [16] is crucial for understanding ensemble learning (EL) for network security, and anomaly detection can perform well in results. EL combines multiple learning models and achieves better prediction results. Furthermore, an ensemble of models has a stronger resilience in the face of training data uncertainty. The EL concept has similarity to how FL aggregate the training results. This opens up an opportunity to incorporate ensemble learning with FL.

As previously shown, many studies showed FL showed better performance than traditional ML and confirmed the high privacy level of FL. However, research identifying the attack using FL is still scarce and has not been explored in depth. Besides, there are issues, for instance, the bias of the distributed models is averaged to produce the final global model that will cause unfairness. The past studies neglected the reality that various local models have distinct functionality and structure. The research gaps in the smart home environments are that past research failed to address the similarity of network traffic flow data patterns of device models in the same category. The same type of IoT devices have similar vulnerability structures under similar attacks. Therefore, IoT devices within the same group should use similar parameters for anomaly detection. While it seems like a straightforward method to aggregate updates together, the bias in the training phase arises from the updating of participants' parameters that differ from one another and the selection of the average.

3   Methodology

Our study aims to build an anomaly detection to detect whether there are any attack attempts (Attack Detection). The first section Research Data displays the network traffic flow data, and attack data are the original input data. Then, the Research Method shows the details of designing models, and the Experiment and analysis provide the preparation and evaluation process.

3.1   IoT Datasets

Our dataset was obtained from the UNSW IoT analytics team, consisting of real-world attacks to assess the privacy and security dangers of IoT devices [6–

9]. The dataset was collected from 28 unique IoT devices in various categories and multiple non-IoT devices in the smart environment. There are 30 PACP files consisting of both attack and benign data in two separate stages. The dataset was split into two stages: the first stage is between 28/05/2018 and 17/06/2018, and the second stage is from 24/09/2018 to 26/10/2018. IoT devices are defined as devices linked to the Internet with application logic and executing TCP/IP connection. Ten IoT devices in this dataset contain benign and attack traffic datasets, whereas the others contain only benign data. The datasets used in our study can be found in Flow and Annotation data[1], the implementation of our algorithms and models, and supplementary results and materials can be accessed from the project repository[2]". Therefore, this research focuses on the selected ten IoT devices with wireless connection to the Internet in four categories listed in Table 1.

Table 1. IoT devices included in the dataset

IoT devices			
IoT Devices No	MAC Addresses	IoT devices	Category
IoT Device 0	00:16:6c:ab:6b:88	Samsung Smart Cam	Camera
IoT Device 1	00:17:88:2b:9a:25	Phillip Hue Lightbulb	Energy management
IoT Device 2	44:65:0d:56:cc:d3	Amazon Echo	Contollers/Hubs
IoT Device 3	50:c7:bf:00:56:39	TP-Link Plug	Energy management
IoT Device 4	70:ee:50:18:34:43	Netatmo Camera	Camera
IoT Device 5	74:c6:3b:29:d7:1d	iHome PowerPlug	Energy management
IoT Device 6	d0:73:d5:01:83:08	LiFX Bulb	Energy management
IoT Device 7	ec:1a:59:79:f4:89	Belkin Switch	Energy management
IoT Device 8	ec:1a:59:83:28:11	Belkin Motion Sensor	Energy management
IoT Device 9	F4:F5:D8:8F:0A:3C	Chromcast Ultra	Appliances

The network traffic flow data of the ten IoT devices are collected every minute, marked with activity, and recorded to the ten separate excel network traffic flow data files. The files contain "Timestamp", "NoOfFlows", and a significant number of attributes of patterns. Several features such as "InternetTcp", "InternetUdp", "LocalTcp", and "LocalUdp" are the contents of the following "From" and "To", and the contents after "Port" are port numbers (e.g., "From###Port###Packet"). Since the packet and byte are not closely connected and the sizes of the packets in this dataset vary, we decided to forecast attacks by including them. Based on the network traffic flow data, it is unknown which network flow is going to which IoT devices or coming from which IoT devices. The reasons are that different IoT devices use the same port number and use different port numbers simultaneously.

---

[1] https://iotanalytics.unsw.edu.au/attack-data.

[2] https://github.com/BasemSuleiman/IoT_Anomaly_Detection_Smart_Homes.

The UNSW IoT analytics team designed a set of attacks comparable to real-world attacks and are particular to several real-world consumer IoT devices. The tools were created in Python to find susceptible and vulnerable devices on the local network by running different tests against them. Then, the program performs targeted attacks on IoT devices that are susceptible. The attack condition includes the start and end time of the attacks, the impact of the attack, and attack types. When determining the normal behaviour or under the attacks, it relies on the rules "if (flowtime >= startTime × 1000 and endTime × 1000 >= flowtime, then attack = true". It is multiplied by 1000 since the times are recorded in different units: flow time in milliseconds while start time and end time are not.

3.2   Proposed Approach: FedGroup

FedAvg model accepts the initial model from the central server, training models on decentralised local device servers, and reports the best performance parameters to the central model [11]. For ML, there is only one step which is a client-to-server upload step. In contrast with Traditional Machine Learning, FedAvg sends code to data rather than send data to code. For FL-based learning, there are four steps in one iteration:

1. A server-to-client broadcast step
2. A local client update step
3. A client-to-server upload step
4. A server update step

While it is simple for FedAvg to summarise all the parameters from local servers and select the mean as the following round parameter, the main weakness is the failure to address the similarity of network traffic flow data patterns of the device models in the same category. Furthermore, the devices in smart homes are not assigned into different groups based on their similarity. The devices in the same groups should have similar functionalities and vulnerable risks. The bias in the training procedure was from the updates of device parameters that are different from each other and easily choose the average. Imaging the IoT devices in a smart home are mostly energy management applications such as plugs or blubs, the parameters of cloud server will bias to the energy management devices because the numbers of its are more remarkable than other groups.

Therefore, we present FedAvg with group masters called FedGroup that send parameters to the group master rather than the central server. The group masters have helped combine devices within the same group and aggregate parameters depending on the groups. In the central model, there are multiple group masters then send back the aggregated results to the corresponding participant local model, which is more efficient for the local model to focus on the information within the same group.

The product can be grouped into many categories based on features. The group can be defined based on the category of the IoT devices such as Camera or Energy management. Apart from that, the group can also be defined by other characteristics. If separate groups are based on features, for instance, the smart door product contains many features to open the door such as app control, fingerprint recognition, entering the password, scanning an intelligent card or simple using key unlock. If the smart door is under attack, the central model will tell which specific part is under attack.

The followings are the steps of FedGroup (Fig 1):

1. Every local model computes training network traffic flow data with all parameters and sends the parameters' best results to the central model;
2. Group master in the central model aggregates the parameters based on the group;
3. Group master sends back the aggregated results to devices in the corresponding group;
4. Local models update the models with the new parameters.

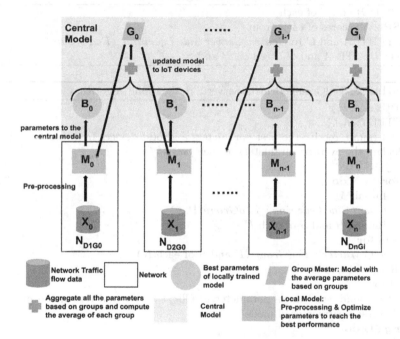

Fig. 1. The architecture of our proposed approach FedGroup

Definition: Using X_n to represent the network traffic flow data of the IoT devices and y_n to represent the prediction target. Network N_{DnGi}: N represents network, Dn means Device n and Gi represents Group i. The X_n and M_n are included in N_{DnGi}. During the training, setting the best score S, the best parameter B, the average score of the entire model C, and the average parameters of the entire model A. For each Model M, parameters $P = \{a, b, ...\}$ means parameters such as weights, n_estimator and so on with all possible parameters grid $p = \{a_0, a_1, ...\}, \{b_0, ...\}, ...$ such as n_estimator have parameters 1, 2 and so on. E represents the selected parameters grids in the local models after the update to the central model.

Algorithm 1. FedGroup: Client Side Learning Algorithm

1: INPUT: P, E
2: REQUIRE: X_n, y_n, M
3: OUTPUT: B and S to *Central Server Side Learning* : *FedAvg* with the related Group Master
4: SET: Local Model M
5: /* Fit possible parameters grids and return the best parameters and the best score*/
6: **for** $e \in E$ **do**
7:     Fit P in M with different grid e to train X_n and y_n
8:     Test the M to get the accuracy
9:     CALCULATE B and S
10: **end for**

Algorithm 2. FedGroup: Group Master Algorithm

1: INPUT: B and S of each d
2: DISPLAY: scores of each groups
3: OUTPUT: A and C to *Central Server Side Learning* : *FedGroup*
4: CALCULATE A and C based on B and S

Algorithm 3. FedGroup: Central Server Side Learning Algorithm

---
1: INPUT: M, P, p
2: OUTPUT: A, C
3: /* 1st round: receive the best parameters and best devices from every model, and calculate the average parameters of each group*/
4: **for** $g \in G$ **do**
5:     **for** $n \in N$ **do**
6:         Initial: M
7:         *Client Side Learning* : *FedGroup* (P, p)
8:         Return B and S of each N
9:     **end for**
10:     *Group Master* : *FedGroup* (B and S of each N)
11:     Return A and C
12: **end for**
13: /* 2nd round: send mean parameter to Client Server and return the mean score and average parameter of mode*/
14: **for** $g \in G$ **do**
15:     **for** $n \in N$ **do**
16:         *Client Side Learning* : *FedGroup* (P, A)
17:         Return B and S of each N
18:     **end for**
19:     *Group Master* : *FedGroup* (B and S of each N)
20:     Return A and C
21: **end for**

3.3   Experiment and Analysis

For network traffic flow data of the IoT devices, remove "NoOfFlow" because it counts the numbers of flow, which is highly correlated to all the other attributes. Due to the fact that different devices use the same port number and the same device use different port numbers, there are 253 attributes about bytes of port number and packages of the port number in total. When capturing the network behaviour of one device by milliseconds, various port numbers have not been used. In other words, the NaN data means there is no network behaviour for the corresponding port number. That is the reason we have missing data. To fill in the missing data, we assign the most likely value and the global constant to a particular value of 0. It signifies no network behaviour with zeros packet-level and zeroes byte-level network traffic flow data at that time point.

To predict whether it is an attack means that there are two options: attack or non-attack. Implementing Decision Tree, Logistic Regression and Ensemble Learning as local models on ML, FedAvg, and FedGroup as central models to attack detection. To avoid overfitting, StratifiedShuffleSplit split the dataset 80% training and 20% testing dataset. For training data, Stratified 5-Fold Cross-Validation randomly divides the entire data into five folds, fits four folds to the model, and validates the model using the remaining fold. Evaluate the 20% testing data to compute accuracy with an F1 score with a weighted average. To evaluate the model, the False Positive Rate (FPR) is used to calculate the probability of falsely rejecting the null hypothesis to measure the accuracy of the test.

4   Results

This study developed an anomaly detection system by using our proposed model, called FedGroup as described in the previous section. Table 2 provides the results summary from various models including Decision Tree, Logistic Regression and Ensemble Learning as the local model on traditional ML, FedAvg and Fed-Group to attack detection. EL can merge several models even if the individuals are weak, and we use it as an initial local training model. Using ML as an initial model for every IoT device is not always performed as expected because they are used to solve a specific question or a type of question. For example, logistic regression effectively classifies data into discrete classes by investigating the connection between a collection of labelled data. However, If the number of features is greater than the number of observations, Logistic Regression should not be utilised. Considering the various performances that sometimes perform good but sometimes perform not of machine learning models when solving a problem, ensemble learning joins various contributing models to seek better forecasts.

Firstly, anomaly detection can determine whether there is any attack attempt. The highest accuracy of 99.91% of attack detection was reached by the FedGroup model using Ensemble learning as the locally model to train. Secondly, FL-based learning models performed either similar or better than the traditional ML models. Considering the anomaly detection problem is a no binary

Table 2. The accuracy of FedGroup, FedAvg and traditional ML using different models

Algorithms		Attack Detection		
Local Model	Central Model	Accuracy	Running Times (seconds)	FPR
Decision Tree	Traditional ML	99.84%	8524	10.04%
Decision Tree	FedAvg	99.85%	154	9.57%
Decision Tree	FedGroup	99.87%	154	7.70%
Logistic regression	Traditional ML	99.76%	21376	24.48%
Logistic regression	FedAvg	99.77%	2912	20.28%
Logistic regression	FedGroup	99.77%	2999	20.18%
Ensemble learning	Traditional ML	99.85%	33940	9.60%
Ensemble learning	FedAvg	**99.91%**	2390	9.03%
Ensemble learning	FedGroup	**99.91%**	2143	9.43%

classification, while the StratifiedShuffleSplit is used to try to solve the problem of overfitting, the accuracy of all models is more than 99%. Therefore, FPR is a more reliable evaluation metric since higher FPR scores indicates higher ratio of negative events are incorrectly categorised as positive. As shown in Table 2, the FPRs of FL-based are less than the FPRs of the Traditional ML model indicating better performance with less overfitting issue.

The running time of FL-based is less than the traditional ML model where the client slide model spends $O(n)$ and central server takes $O(n^2)$. For example, using Ensemble learning as the local model and FedGroup as the Central Model spends 2143 s seconds which is around 1/16 of time spend on Traditional ML (33940 s) and 0.9 of time spend on FedAvg (2390 s seconds). As a result of lightweight communication, no central authority, and a decentralised learning model, FL uses the advantages of locally training data to reduce the running time. Besides, data safety is guaranteed without sending, communicating or sharing to other IoT devices or the Internet.

Each smart home has a large amount of IoT devices to make our life more efficient and easier. If we focus on the differences of FPRs that are larger than 1%, then FPRs of FedGroup are better than FPRs of FedAvg. Different IoT devices have different vulnerable functions and maybe under different attacks. Meanwhile, one similar attack may have similar functionality or patterns. When the central model learns attack types from the same category of IoT devices, FedGroup is useful to provide parameters of IoT devices within the same group. Besides combining all the smart environments to build smart cities or industries, FedGroup can learn all the attack detection and attack type detection based on group categorisation such as the traffic light group, subway group, and others.

5   Conclusion

In this paper, we introduce a new model called FedGroup model and algorithms which address the issue of IoT anomaly detection in the smart home environments. FedGroup allow training and detecting anomalies based on data collected from group of devices, and thus reduces the vulnerability of the IoT data transmitted and shared on a central server. We evaluate our FedGroup approach on real dataset collected from various IoT devices in smart-home settings to detect anomalous behaviour. Based on our experimental results, it can be concluded that the performance of FedGroup improved in terms of accuracy of anomaly detection compared to the traditional FedAvg. Furthermore, FedGroup can address the issue of fairness of the training procedure and can maintain data privacy, as the values of learning parameters need to be shared with the central model. Our results also demonstrated that Ensemble Learning as local models used in our FedGroup achieved the best accuracy, 99.91%.

While our finding has provided the comparison results of different models, more empirical studies on continuous real-time learning and alternative ways to ensure the fairness of federated learning need to be conducted to test further and refine our findings. Besides, expanding the model to other frameworks not limited to anomaly detection, finding the system cost and how the link instability of wireless networks affects the model updating are several opportunities for in future work.

References

1. Evans, D.: How the Next Evolution of the Internet Is Changing Everything. 11 (2011)
2. Robles, R.J., Kim, T.: Applications, systems and methods in smart home technology: a review. Int. J. Adv. Sci. Technol. **15**, 13 (2010)
3. Gubbi, J., Buyya, R., Marusic, S., Palaniswami, M.: Internet of things (IoT): a vision, architectural elements, and future directions. Futur. Gener. Comput. Syst. **29**(7), 1645–1660 (2013). https://doi.org/10.1016/j.future.2013.01.010
4. Abomhara, M., Køien, G.M.: Security and privacy in the Internet of Things: Current status and open issues. 8
5. 59 per cent of smart speaker users have privacy concerns - report—Mobile Marketing Magazine. Mobilemarketingmagazine.com. (2021). Accessed 23 Oct 2021. https://mobilemarketingmagazine.com/59-per-cent-of-smart-speaker-users-have-privacy-concerns-report
6. Habibi Gharakheili, H., Sivanathan, A., Hamza, A., Sivaraman, V.: Network-level security for the internet of things: opportunities and challenges. Computer **52**(8), 58–62 (2019). https://doi.org/10.1109/MC.2019.2917972
7. Hamza, A., Gharakheili, H.H., Benson, T.A., Sivaraman, V.: Detecting Volumetric Attacks on IoT devices via SDN-based monitoring of MUD activity. In: Proceedings of the 2019 ACM Symposium on SDN Research, pp. 36–48 (2019). https://doi.org/10.1145/3314148.3314352
8. Sivanathan, A., et al.: Classifying IoT devices in smart environments using network traffic characteristics. IEEE Trans. Mob. Comput. **18**(8), 1745–1759 (2019). https://doi.org/10.1109/TMC.2018.2866249
9. Sivaraman, V., Gharakheili, H.H., Fernandes, C., Clark, N., Karliychuk, T.: Smart IoT devices in the home: security and privacy implications. IEEE Technol. Soc. Mag. **37**(2), 71–79 (2018). https://doi.org/10.1109/MTS.2018.2826079

10. Stojkoska, B.L.R., Trivodaliev, K.V.: A review of internet of things for smart home: challenges and solutions. J. Clean. Prod. **140**, 1454–1464 (2017)
11. Yang, Q., Liu, Y., Chen, T., Tong, Y.: Federated Machine Learning: Concept and Applications. ArXiv:1902.04885 (2019). http://arxiv.org/abs/1902.04885
12. McMahan, B., Moore, E., Ramage, D., Hampson, S., Arcas, B.A.Y.: Communication-efficient learning of deep networks from decentralized data. Artificial Intelligence and Statistics, pp. 1273–1282 (2017). http://proceedings.mlr.press/v54/mcmahan17a.html
13. Rahman, S.A., Tout, H., Talhi, C., Mourad, A.: Internet of things intrusion detection: centralized, on-device, or federated learning? IEEE Netw. **34**(6), 310–317 (2020). https://doi.org/10.1109/MNET.011.2000286
14. Mohri, M., Sivek, G., Suresh, A.T.: Agnostic Federated Learning. 11 (2019)
15. Li, T., Sanjabi, M., Beirami, A., Smith, V.: Fair Resource Allocation in Federated Learning. ArXiv:1905.10497 [Cs, Stat] (2020). http://arxiv.org/abs/1905.10497
16. Vanerio, J., Casas, P.: Ensemble-learning approaches for network security and anomaly detection. In: Proceedings of the Workshop on Big Data Analytics and Machine Learning for Data Communication Networks, pp. 1–6 (2017).https://doi.org/10.1145/3098593.3098594

Privacy Protection Against Shoulder Surfing in Mobile Environments

David Darling, Yaling Liu, and Qinghua Li[✉]

University of Arkansas, Fayetteville, AR, USA
{dwdarlin,yl050,qinghual}@uark.edu

Abstract. Smartphones and other mobile devices have seen an unprecedented rise in use among consumers. These devices are widely used in public locations where traditional computers could hardly be accessed. Although such ubiquitous computing is desirable for users, the use of mobile devices in public locations has led to rising privacy concerns. Malicious individuals can easily glean personal data from a mobile device screen by visual eavesdropping without a user's knowledge. In this paper, we propose two schemes to identify and protect private user data displayed on mobile device screens in public environments. The first scheme considers generic mobile applications' complex user interfaces as an image, and uses a deep, convolutional object detection network to automatically identify sensitive content displayed by mobile applications. Such content is then blurred against shoulder surfing attacks. To allow users to identify custom fields in applications that they think should be hidden, we introduce methods for dynamic sample generation and model retraining that only need users to provide a small number of seed samples. The second scheme focuses on web applications due to the popularity of the web platform, and automates the detection and blurring of sensitive web fields through HTML (HyperText Markup Language) parsing and CSS (Cascading Style Sheets) style modification as showcased via a Chromium-based browser extension. Evaluations show the effectiveness of our schemes.

Keywords: privacy · mobile phones · web browsing · obfuscation · shoulder surfing attack

1 Introduction

Mobile devices such as smartphones and tablets have rapidly grown in popularity in recent years. These types of devices offer unparalleled convenience and ease of access for end users who increasingly need to be able to access applications and services on the go. Estimates of smartphone sales trends have shown that the market has rapidly grown since the early 2000s. In 2021 alone, smartphone manufacturers sold an estimated 1.43 billion devices [1]. This was an enormous increase over estimates in 2007 which placed sales at only 122 million units [2].

© ICST Institute for Computer Sciences, Social Informatics and Telecommunications Engineering 2023
Published by Springer Nature Switzerland AG 2023. All Rights Reserved
S. Longfei and P. Bodhi (Eds.): MobiQuitous 2022, LNICST 492, pp. 133–152, 2023.
https://doi.org/10.1007/978-3-031-34776-4_8

With this saturation of mobile devices among consumers, usage has likewise increased rapidly in public spaces.

Due to the convenience of having access to emails, text messages, and other applications, individuals frequently utilize devices in scenarios such as eating, riding a subway, or while walking where others behind or to the side of a user can easily see or visually eavesdrop the content on their device screens [3]. This clearly constitutes a privacy and security risk, as a majority of users are likely to access sensitive apps in public [4] such as text or productivity.

Although there exist privacy screen filters and protector products for mobile devices, they suffer from several drawbacks. They can only address visual eavesdropping attacks that come from the two sides of a user and are out of their view angles (60°C or 90°C for most screen filters/protectors), but attackers behind the user or within the view angle can still see the screen content (see illustration in Fig. 1). They are also known to cause darker screen all the time (since it is uneasy or inconvenient to remove the screen protector) which hurts use experience. Lastly, such filters/protectors cost a user a few dollars to tens of dollars, dependent on the brand and model.

To address the growing problem of visual eavesdropping, we explore software-based solutions for mitigation of visual eavesdropping in public places to allow users to still access their desired apps or websites while providing better protection for sensitive content. Specifically, we propose two schemes. The first scheme considers general mobile applications. To have an easily-deployable solution that does not rely on or make changes to an app's source code, we propose the idea of *user-interface-as-an-image* (UIaaI) to enable image processing and computer vision techniques to be applied to process live app UIs without being hurdled by the complexity of multi-layer UIs. A YOLO [5] style deep convolutional neural network (DCNN) is used to automatically detect sensitive content such as text messages in apps. To improve real-world usability and allow users to customize and dynamically adjust the model, we develop a method for dynamically retraining the sensitive content detection model based on user-specified sensitive content, without requiring too many seeding data samples from users. The second scheme provides an alternative protection method for web browser-based applications which are very popular among users, and provides accurate sensitive content field detection and protection. Specifically, we propose a novel HTML (HyperText Markup Language) parsing and CSS (Cascading Style Sheets) injection method to automatically detect and blur sensitive content on web pages, and implement a prototype system as a Chromium web browser extension that can protect web pages without requiring the pages to be modified by their developers.

The remainder of this paper is organized as follows. Section 2 provides an overview of related work. Section 3 describes the visual eavesdropping attack scenario. Sections 4 and 5 present the two proposed schemes and their evaluation results. Section 6 concludes the paper.

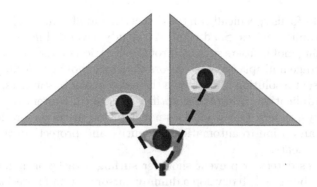

Fig. 1. Visualization of a potential attack scenario. The vulnerable "danger areas" relative to the user are shown in red with attacker gazes shown as black dashed lines. (Color figure online)

2   Related Work

Privacy protection in mobile and ubiquitous environments has been widely studied [6–10]. In the area of mitigating shoulder surfing attacks, much work has been done too. The majority of work relating to shoulder surfing attacks has focused on protecting phone password and authentication credentials. Kumar et al. [11] present a gaze-based password entry method for preventing shoulder surfing attacks by utilizing a user's gaze rather than their hands to enter password digits. Chakraborty and Mondal [12] present a honeypot-based scheme whereby if a shoulder surfer attempts to enter a credential containing a tag digit they would be detected. Yu et al. [13] propose an evolvable password protection scheme using images as keys rather than digit-based authentication. Zhang et al. [14] present an similar evolving password scheme using augmented reality displays to present an input field that is only visible to a specific user. Sun et al. [15] propose a graphical authentication scheme resistant to multiple attacks for password entry. Some works obscure other content types present on the screen. Zezschwitz et al. [16] distort photos on phones against unwanted observations. Eiband et al. [17] convert the font of text messages to the user's handwriting based on the assumption that people's handwriting is harder to read to strangers. Different from them, our work is not limited to any single type of content and attempts to mitigate attacks in more general cases.

Zhou et al. [18] present a scheme that can detect shoulder surfers, and respond by grey-scaling the screen, dimming the screen, limiting the visible area to a small view port that can be dragged, and replacing sensitive data with placeholders. These protective measures do not differentiate private content and non-private content, but our solutions only blur private content without affecting the usability of non-private content. Some works [19, 20] adopt eye tracking to display only the portion of the screen that is gazed by the users. Rendering only users' gaze area could potentially expose information that users are reading to attackers, which increases the risk of privacy leakage.

Some works focus specifically on the detection and alerting of shoulder surfing attacks for mobile devices. Saad et al. [21] study several different methods for actually alerting mobile users such as through vibration or visual indication. Lian et al. [22] leverage multiple types of sensors to detect shoulder surfing attacks. Ali et al. [23] present a solution that detects the existence of bystanders, and develop an Android application, iAlert, that notifies the user if content on the screen is readable by bystanders. Our work does not focus on methods for alerting users, but provides an option to automatically identify and protect private content in public environments.

Other works detect or prevent shoulder surfing attacks on non-mobile platforms. Watanabe et al. [24] develop a dummy cursor system for desktop or laptop platforms to hide the true cursor from attackers' views. Li et al. [25] present a shoulder surfing detection scheme for ATMs by tracking human bodies and faces. Brudy et al. [26] employ various sensors to detect shoulder surfing attackers and protect data for large public displays. Our work primarily focuses on mobile platforms due to their ubiquitous and uniquely susceptible nature.

3   Mobile Attack Scenario

In this work, we consider an attack scenario as any occasion where a mobile device user is located in a public space with other individuals. In this environment, the attacking party could be any person near enough to the user to recognize the content displayed on the device screen. Attackers can be located to the side or behind the user where the device screen is visible and not obstructed by the user's body. This work primarily aims to deal with these cases where the user is uniquely vulnerable to being spied on. Figure 1 provides a visual representation of a possible attack scenario. The attackers are featured behind and to the sides of the user in the blind spots highlighted in red.

4   User Interface as an Image (UIaaI) for Private Content Detection and Hiding

4.1   The Basic Idea

With modern mobile applications, there are often many complex layers of UI code to dynamically generate and present content to users in an accessible manner. Because of this, it may be difficult for many mobile app developers to add additional functionality for hiding private content dynamically. This could present an enormous commitment of time for large mobile apps with complex and nested user interface elements where it may be difficult to identify which content is currently visible and needs to be hidden from visual eavesdroppers.

To help mitigate this issue and provide a standardised methodology for dynamically hiding sensitive content on complex applications, we present *UI as an Image (UIaaI)*. The basic idea of this concept is that, computer vision techniques such as object detection and image filtering are highly applicable to the domain of private content detection, and could replace tedious and time consuming code conversion of existing applications. Under UIaaI, dynamically generated UI views are presented to the user entirely as a pre-rendered, interactive image rather than as direct views of the app UI. This approach offers several benefits, namely the technique for converting applications to utilize UIaaI is standardized for all applications no matter the underlying UI complexity, computer vision techniques can be applied directly to existing views of UI without the need to directly program any content-hiding logic, and complex private content can be automatically identified. Although utilizing images as displayed UI elements eliminates some interactivity, UIaaI can be used temporarily for situations where users are in public spaces. Apps can easily be switched back to their normal behavior once a user no longer has to worry about eavesdropping.

4.2 The Framework

In order to make UIaaI as universally adoptable as possible, we use a simple pipeline for providing conversion in apps. An application on iOS or Android that needs to implement dynamic content protection can follow the following general guidelines:

1. Implement a switchable mode which a user can activate content protection via a button or other UI element.
2. Once a user has switched to UIaaI mode, the application should pre-render its current UI view as a single image frame.
3. The pre-rendered UI view is displayed to the user on-screen.
4. A pass of content detection is performed over the image to identify any sensitive content that should be hidden.
5. A Gaussian blurring filter is utilized to dynamically hide any sensitive content. Note that other alternative blurring methods can be used here too.
6. Once a user has switched back to normal mode, the regular app display logic can be used again.

Utilizing this general guideline, even highly complex app UIs will not require complicated UI logic to enable dynamic hiding of sensitive content. The goal of this is to enable developers to easily make their applications shoulder surfing resistant and encourage adoption of content hiding to benefit end users. Additionally, being able to operate on pre-rendered images enables a variety of interesting computer vision techniques to be applied over the UI such as content swapping to hide content from view with dummy content. Most importantly, we propose that pre-rendered UI can be used to automatically detect private content with an object detection network.

The drawback to this design is a slight loss in user-interactivity. This is due to the fact that image-based views of complex UIs cannot directly emulate all of the visual actions that a traditional UI view is able to generate. For example, although a user's touch events and coordinates of the touch can be recorded and translated into the activation of a button or other element, the normal

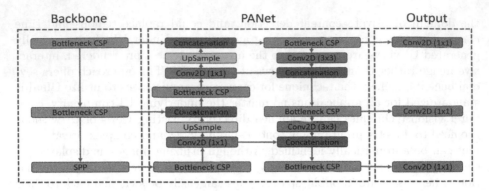

Fig. 2. Architectural overview of the private content detection network.

visualization of a button being depressed would require an additional series of pre-rendered views to be generated. Despite this, we maintain that for suitably large applications, the ease of enabling private content hiding through UIaaI outweighs this temporary lack of interactability.

4.3   Private Content Detection Network

In order to automate the detection of private content, we find that object detection networks such as YOLO [5] or EffecientDet [27], which have been used to great effect in fields of object tracking or generalized object detection, are uniquely useful in visually identifying user interface elements. This is due primarily to the fact that user interface elements generally share very similar visual attributes. For example, in an application which displays emails in an inbox, each email summary view will feature the same general attributes (a subject line, an icon representing whether the item has been read or not, and a brief excerpt from the email text). These similarities in visual appearance which are extremely common among UI elements should be learnable by an object detection network.

We implement an object detection network based on the YOLOv5 [28] architecture. This type of network features high inference speed and smaller model size relative to other state of the art networks. These features make it a prime candidate for inclusion onto mobile platforms. Figure 2 provides an overview of the implemented network architecture. The network relies on a feature extraction backbone built around cross-stage-partial (CSP) network layers [29] along with a spatial pyramid pooling (SPP) layer [30] for getting feature tensors of fixed output size irrespective of input image size. The feature aggregation or neck portion of the network is built around the path aggregation network (PANet) architecture [31] which has been used to great success in competing object detection networks. The final output layers are output from different downsampled feature spaces in the network. This is done to allow the network to identify spatially larger or smaller objects in an input image at different levels of granularity.

Resulting output vectors contain bounding box anchors, box width, box height, class prediction, and confidence interval information.

4.4 An Image Augmentation Method for User-Defined Content Retraining

We recognize that it is an impossible task to fully identify all forms of private content that a user might wish to be protected across many different mobile applications beforehand. Users may have a financial app which displays a summary of account balances which they would not want strangers in public to see for example. To this end, we propose a scheme for dynamic training sample generation. Under this scheme, users can manually identify a UI element they wish to automatically detect and hide within an app. Then many training image samples of the same element will be automatically generated using visual transformations. That way, the user does not have to manually generate many training samples. This is more user-friendly.

Flip Transformation. In order to simulate the different orientations that UI elements might take on a mobile phone, random horizontal and vertical flipping of pre-rendered views provides the model with variation in positioning that might be encountered in the wild as a user accesses their app.

Rotation Transformation. Similar to the flip transformation, the rotation transformation is proposed as a means to introduce more positional variation into a generated dataset. Rotations in 90° intervals are used, as mobile UIs almost never feature non-right angle rotations in the wild. The rotations combined with flip transformations are found to offer a great deal of positional variety even for very small numbers of original training samples.

Random Cropping and Tiling. To simulate the fact that many complex mobile UIs stack or layer UI elements together in the same views, we utilize randomized image cropping and tiling. This method is used to combine together different views of the same elements to force the model to learn to identify elements at any region of a pre-rendered UI view. Complementary slices of training images are used to form a full-sized training sample.

Figure 3 shows sample augmented images generated from a subset of the original text message dataset with only 10 images.

4.5 Private Content Blurring

Once private content is identified on a UI view, a new image is generated with areas containing private content rendered blurry. The obscured image is displayed on the phone screen as a means of defense against eavesdroppers.

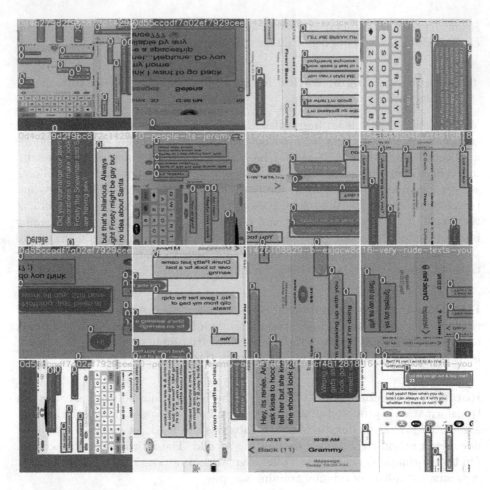

Fig. 3. Visualization of random transformations and augmentations applied over a subset of the full text message dataset.

To reduce the details and noise in the UI view image, we use OpenCV due to its large collection of low-pass filters. The blurring algorithms aim to remove high-frequency content present in an image, such as edges and noise, by convolving the image with low-pass filters. Some of the main blurring techniques provided by OpenCV are Averaging, Gaussian Blurring, Median Blurring and Bilateral Filtering [32]. Since our goal is to filter high frequencies and pass only low frequencies, we find Gaussian Blurring to be the optimal technique. Compared to other filters in OpenCV, Gaussian filters applies a smoother, blurrier effect on the edges.

The Gaussian filter from the OpenCV API takes a kernel size as an input to determine the amount of blurring to apply [33]. It allows a user to customize their needed blurriness level based on the device screen size and use habit.

Although Gaussian blurring is chosen in our implementation, it is worthy to note that our framework is compatible with any blurring algorithms that fit application needs.

4.6   Evaluation Results

Sensitive Content Detection. In order to evaluate the content detection network's ability to detect and classify different types of common UI elements that would contain private content in the real world, a dataset for text messages in the iOS Messages app was created for training the network. Text messages were selected as the UI element of choice in this case because they feature many visual similarities to other common private elements such as email summaries or phone call notifications. Text messages also have the potential to be challenging for an object detection network due to the large variation in size across different messages.

The created dataset contains 188 rendered text message conversations. The network was trained over 1000 epochs to determine how quickly it was able to converge. The resulting model was able to achieve 98.17% mean average precision at 0.5 intersection over union (mAP@0.5). The model was able to achieve this performance after 450 epochs of training. The results for this training are visualized in Fig. 4 along with precision and recall metrics. Sample forward pass predictions are visualized in Fig. 5. These results generally show that the model is highly capable of learning to distinguish UI elements even in a complex layout such as text message stacks.

Training takes 14 min and testing over an image takes about 10ms on an Nvidia Tesla T4.

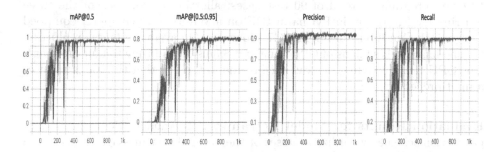

Fig. 4. Bounding box mean average precision (mAP), precision, and recall metrics over progressive training epochs. Note that charts are smoothed with original data shown as a shadow behind. The model is found to converge under all metrics after 450 epochs.

Gaussian Blurring. To achieve the proper amount of blurring effect and to give users more options, we define three blurring levels for the Gaussian filter, {LOW, MEDIUM, HIGH}. Figure 6 displays an example UI view image with Gaussian filters applied. Note that the blurriness levels shown in the figure are

classifications.png

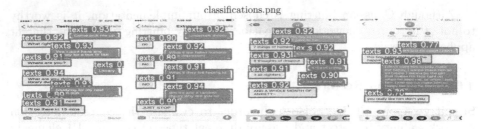

Fig. 5. Sample text detection output with confidence metric. The network is capable of accurately detecting text messages of varying sizes and positions.

Fig. 6. Gaussian blurring filters applied to private data detected on an UI image of the iOS Message App. The subsequent three images represent three levels of blurring: LOW, MEDIUM, and HIGH.

for illustration purposes; they might be different from what a user sees on a smartphone screen due to difference in image size. In practice, a user can adjust the blurring parameter for their needs.

We conduct an experiment to evaluate the execution time of the Gaussian Blurring program. A total of 90 test cases, allotting 30 for each of the three blurring levels, are run in PyCharm IDE on a Windows 10 computer equipped with a 11th Gen Intel Core i7-1165G7 processor. On average, Gaussian blurring for one image takes 9.9ms of CPU time and 8.3ms of wall time to blur an image. The CPU time exceeding the wall time is due to the fact that the computer uses a multiprocessor.

Evaluation Results for Model Retraining. To validate the training data generation scheme, we utilize a subset of the original text message dataset with only 10 images. These images were used to generate a new dataset of 150 augmented images (see samples in Fig. 3). The same model architecture as presented in Sect. 4.3. The model was able to nearly match the validation average precision of the model trained on the full dataset, reaching a mAP@0.5 of 95.65%. This level of accuracy demonstrates that it is possible to train a robust model for UI recognition with much fewer training samples than are traditionally required in object detection tasks. This is attributed primarily to the similarity in lighting conditions, visual properties, and shape of most UI views which are rarely so similar for more generalized recognition tasks. The results show that a user only needs to manually label a small number of data samples to train an accurate private UI detection model.

5 Private Content Detection and Hiding for Web Applications

Web users frequently access private services via web applications on mobile devices, which can give strangers the opportunity to acquire sensitive personal information. While the UIaaI approach applies to web browser applications too, in this section, we explore an alternative method dedicated to web applications, considering the unique characteristics of Web UIs.

To protect sensitive user input content in web pages, we develop an HTML parsing approach for detecting user input fields that might contain sensitive information and a CSS style modification approach for blurring sensitive field. In the following, we describe our approach based on a Chromium web browser extension that we implemented as a proof-of-concept. Our extension can be loaded in all Chromium-based browsers, including applications for mobile devices such as Safari on iOS and Kiwi on Android. In 2021, among the top five browsers making up the largest market shares worldwide, all but Firefox were chromium-based [34]. Thus, an extension targeting the Chromium-based browsers can benefit a majority of web users on mobile devices. It is worthy to note that our general approach of HTML parsing and CSS style modification can be adjusted and applied in other browsers too.

Our approach works as follows. Upon page loading, a content script runs on any URL (Uniform Resource Locator) that starts with a permitted scheme (http, https, file, or ftp, etc.). The sensitive data hiding process in the content script begins with the discovery of private information displayed on the web page. If sensitive data is identified, obfuscation techniques based on CSS style are applied to the page sections that contain the data. This logic is also configured to run dynamically to cover a wider range of browsing scenarios.

5.1 Background

Web pages in browsers are based on HTML. HTML uses tags to determine the format of the displayed content. The tags are used to describe headings, paragraphs, tables, link, etc. JavaScript code and CSS can also be embedded in a web page using these tags.

When a user enters a URL, the HTML code is fetched from the server and parsed by the browser. Parsing involves turning the data into tokens and building a DOM (Document Object Model) tree, which mirrors the relationships of the HTML tags. The root of the DOM tree is an $< html >$ element, and a parent node encompasses its child nodes.

Combined with the CSS rules, the DOM tree is then converted to a render tree where a set of computed styles is mapped to each visible node. During the reflow step, the sizes and locations of these nodes are calculated, and in the paint step they are converted to actual pixels on the screen. A page repaint could be caused by additional reflows as the page continues to load and as resources, such as images, get downloaded.

5.2   Identifying Sensitive Content

Private data on web pages, such as passwords, email addresses, phone numbers, and bank accounts, could frequently show up in log-in/sign-up forms and online transactions requiring credit card information. In addition, it is common for businesses to embed a single email address input field in their websites for subscriptions. In order to capture such sensitive content, our solution considers four generalized HTML patterns.

- The HTML $< form >$ elements that use POST as the HTTP method. For any $< form >$ that requires inputs of sensitive data such as passwords, the submitted data should not be exposed in the URL. Thus, these forms must use POST as their HTTP methods.
- An $< input >$ tag with a type attribute that specifies the input type. Among a list of values for the type attribute, 'email', 'password' and 'tel' (short for telephone) allow the $< input >$ element to contain private data. Therefore, these input fields need to be searched for individually if they are not wrapped up in a $< form >$ tag.
- An $< iframe >$ is used to embed another HTML document into the current website. Some web pages involving online payment enclose all the input fields (such as a credit card number field) in an $< iframe >$ for stronger security protection. According to the Same Origin Policy, if the embedded content comes from a different origin than the current window where the extension script runs, the content inserted in the $< iframe >$ tags cannot be accessed by the script. This extension checks whether the *allowpaymentrequest* attribute of a captured $< iframe >$ is set to true. If so, the $< iframe >$ must contain input fields that ask for input of credit-card-related information.
- Login buttons. Clicking these buttons changes the DOM tree. Sometimes, the change displays input fields for users to enter their usernames and passwords.

5.3   Dynamic Detection of Sensitive Content

Sensitive content detection needs to be performed dynamically when the loaded pages contain scripts or JavaScript events that generate private content.

Our web browser extension carries out content detection when a page is first loaded. The content script of the extension sets the *run_at* field to *document_idle* indicating that either *window.onload* event or *DOMContentLoaded* event has been called. However, in either case, there might still be scripts running as the event is triggered. Any additional node added into the DOM tree by these scripts cannot be captured in time because it does not exist in the tree when the content detection script is running.

To tackle this problem, we first explore the effectiveness of *window.requestAnimationFrame* which takes as an argument a callback function. The browser calls the callback whenever a page repaint occurs. This implementation catches all freshly inserted nodes. However, since page repainting occurs often to modify styling when a page is loaded, websites can suffer from severe performance deterioration. A better approach is to invoke the *setTimeout* function. The content detection and CSS style injection logic can be directly passed as a parameter callback to this function. This process is less costly, in terms of performance, because the callback can be delayed a few milliseconds before executing. This generally allows for enough time for all web page elements to load before attempting to detect sensitive content.

Another scenario where a content detection pass occurs is when any JavaScript event triggers a change in the DOM tree. This could occur when a user interacts with an element on a web page which activates a login field. To get around these interactive elements, a list of keywords is used: "login", "log in", "signin", "sign in", "sign up", "signup", "register", "join", "create new account", and "try it free". Any interactive element containing these keywords is attached with a click event listener to the element's event list.

5.4   Blurring Sensitive Content via Applying CSS Styles

Once sensitive content has been detected on a web page, the extension applies a set of CSS styles including color, text-shadow and font-weight for text and blurring for images to adjust their visual appearance, such that attackers will find it significantly more difficult to identify specific content like letters or numbers. The following algorithm applies the blurring CSS styles to sensitive content:

1. Apply styles to any captured HTML < *form* > elements that use POST methods. These could include forms such as payment information submissions.
2. If email input fields are the only captured elements, CSS styles are applied to these and the associated submit buttons or links. Buttons or links are identified as closest in the DOM tree rooted at the parent node of the email address input field. A recursive search of the parent tree is performed until

one is found. This step is vital for many online shopping websites, as they often contain email address input fields to allow easy subscriptions.

3. If the discovered content contains any HTML elements other than email address input fields, the CSS styles are simply applied to the entire page. In this scenario the DOM tree could contain iframes, password fields, or telephone fields.

5.5   Evaluation

Evaluation of Private Content Detection Accuracy. Our web browser extension for private content protection was tested on both Android and iOS devices. Kiwi Browser is a chromium-based browser available in the Play Store on Android 12, and it supports most chrome desktop extensions. With its built-in functionalities, we could easily load our extension in the browser. As for testing in Safari on iOS 15.4.1, extra steps were required in converting our source file to a Safari web extension using Xcode's command-line tool.

We looked at a series of 100 websites with the highest traffic ranked by RankRanger [35]. Except for four insecure and pornographic websites ytmp3.cc, xnxx.com, xvideos.com and pornhub.com, the other 96 websites were visited for testing, navigating a total of 483 pages which averages 5 pages per website. Throughout the process, two categories of test cases, namely false negative and false positive, are documented. False negative cases represent sensitive information failing to activate the extension app, and false positives indicate that blurring effects are applied to web pages that do not contain private data.

The results of Kiwi browser on Android and Safari on iOS prove to be consistent. Out of a total of 483 browsed pages, 24 (5.0%) pages are false negative and 18 (3.7%) are false positive. The main reasons that the extension fails to capture sensitive content stem from sign-up and log-in forms. For those that are triggered by JavaScript click events, some of the forms cannot be detected by the extension because the list of keywords we incorporated (see Section IV.C) does not cover all possible scenarios of web design. Additionally, some forms containing private data are not configured by a POST method, and some blanks that are not properly marked in the source code, such as an address input field on a McDonald's delivery service page. On the other hand, false positives are primarily due to the fact that some websites wrap up certain HTML elements, including search fields, 'Add to Cart' buttons or product options, with a POST-method $< form >$ element, which triggers the blurring effect application. We leave these issues to future work.

Blurring with CSS Style. Fig. 7 displays example web pages with obfuscating styling applied. In practice, a user can customize the blurriness level based on their needs.

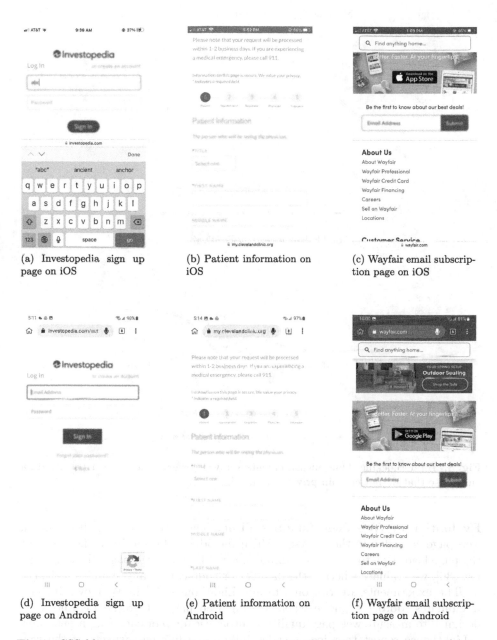

(a) Investopedia sign up page on iOS

(b) Patient information on iOS

(c) Wayfair email subscription page on iOS

(d) Investopedia sign up page on Android

(e) Patient information on Android

(f) Wayfair email subscription page on Android

Fig. 7. CSS blurring styles applied to the automatically detected user inputs. (a) to (c) are obfuscation results of three web pages on iOS, and (d) to (f) show results of the same web pages on Android. Note that the blurriness levels shown here are for illustration purposes; they might be different from what a user sees on a smartphone screen due to difference is image size. In practice, a user can customize the blurriness level based on their needs.

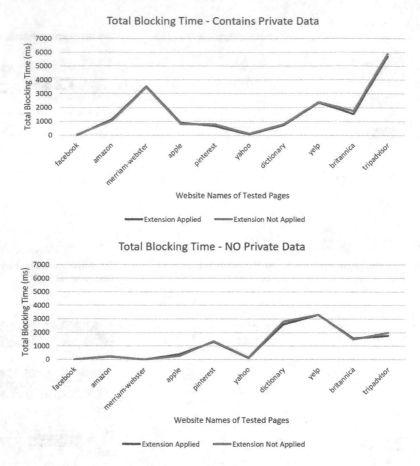

Fig. 8. Total Blocking Time measurements for web pages that contain private data and those that do not contain private data.

Evaluation of Web Page Loading Time. The extension is applied when a web page is loaded in the browser, which introduces JavaScript code to run at the page load. Due to the critical importance of keeping web pages' loading time low [36], we evaluate whether the JavaScript code causes any significant delay.

The experiments are run on Chrome Lighthouse [37] in Windows 10, and it emulates Moto G4 phone when loading web pages. Chrome Lighthouse is designed to measure web page qualities automatically. For each run, it generates a Lighthouse report that logs metrics indicating different aspects of the web page's performance.

To test web pages with the highest traffic, the top ten websites are selected from the same list used for evaluating content detection accuracy [35]. For each website, we picked two pages to run, one that contains private data and one that does not. To increase the accuracy of the experiments and lower the variance, five lighthouse tests are run on every page, and the averaged speed is calculated and exported as the final collected data.

Among the list of metrics, we choose Total Blocking Time [38] as the indicator for whether the extension delays users from browsing and interacting with the web page. Total Blocking Time records the duration of time before the page can respond to any user actions, such as scrolling down the page and clicking a button. The recording process begins when any part of the page content is rendered on the screen, and ends when the page becomes fully interactive. The results of the experiments are visualized in Fig. 8 with the orange line representing the Total Blocking Times of web pages when the extension is not applied, and the blue line illustrates the metric of the same web pages when the extension is run upon page load. For pages containing private content and those without private content, the orange line and the blue line generally overlap each other in both cases, which means that the extension does not increase the loading time and does not block users from their normal browsing experience. The reason is that the detection and blurring run fast, and they run as the web pages load content.

6 Conclusion and Future Work

In this work, we presented solutions for protecting private content on mobile device screens from visual eavesdroppers in public spaces. First, an automated private content protection scheme for generic applications was proposed. The scheme considers user interface as an image to simplify the detection of private content and achieved 98.17% mean average precision at 0.5 intersection over union. To allow users to more easily retrain the network to recognize custom identified content, we presented a series of training image transformations which allow for generation of new sample images from a small manually-labeled set. Upon the UI images containing private content, blurring is applied before they are displayed to the users. Then, we proposed an alternative approach for protecting content on web applications and a Chrome browser extension capable of automatically detecting and applying blurring to web page input fields which could contain private user information. We evaluated this extension on 96 high-traffic websites and found that the extension was able to perform well in most scenarios for both log in, sign up, and payment forms. These results demonstrate the potential for privacy protection against shoulder surfing attacks.

In future work, we will perform a user study to assess the effectiveness of privacy protection in the real world, and explore the tradeoff between privacy and usability by adjusting the blurriness level.

References

1. Gartner Says Global Smartphone Sales Grew 6% in 2021. https://www.gartner. com/en/newsroom/press-releases/2022-03-01-4q21-smartphone-market-share. Accessed 31 Aug 2022
2. Market Share: Smartphones, Worldwide, 4Q07 and 2007. https://www.gartner. com/en/documents/619509/market-share-smartphones-worldwide-4q07-and-2007. Accessed 31 Aug 2022
3. Saad, A., Liebers, J., Gruenefeld, U., Alt, F., Schneegass, S.: Understanding Bystanders' tendency to shoulder surf smartphones using 360-degree videos in virtual reality. In: Proceedings of the 23rd International Conference on Mobile Human-Computer Interaction (MobileHCI 2021), Article 35, pp. 1–8. Association for Computing Machinery. New York, NY, USA (2021). https://doi.org/10.1145/ 3447526.3472058
4. How Americans Use Their Cellphones in Public. https://www.pewresearch.org/ internet/2015/08/26/chapter-2-phone-use-in-public-areas/. Accessed 31 Aug 2022
5. Redmon, J., Farhadi, A.: YOLOv3: An Incremental Improvement (2018)
6. Darling, D., Li, A., Li, Q.: Automated bystander detection and anonymization in mobile photography. In: EAI International Conference on Security and Privacy in Communication Networks (SecureComm) (2020)
7. Darling, D., Li, A., Li, Q.: Feature-based model for automated identification of subjects and bystanders in photos. In: IEEE International Workshop on the Security, Privacy, and Digital Forensics of Mobile Systems and Networks (MobiSec) (2019)
8. Li, A., Darling, D., Li, Q.: PhotoSafer: content-based and context-aware private photo protection for smartphones. In: IEEE Symposium on Privacy-Aware Computing (PAC) (2018)
9. Li, A., Du, W., Li, Q.: PoliteCamera: respecting strangers' privacy in mobile photographing. In: International Conference on Security and Privacy in Communication Networks (SecureComm) (2018)
10. Li, A., Li, Q., Gao, W.: PrivacyCamera: privacy-aware photographing with mobile phones. In: IEEE International Conference on Sensing, Communication and Networking (SECON) (2016)
11. Kumar, M., Garfinkel, T., Boneh, D., Winograd, T.: Reducing shoulder-surfing by using gaze-based password entry. In Proceedings of the 3rd symposium on Usable privacy and security (SOUPS 2007), 13–19. Association for Computing Machinery, New York, NY, USA (2017). https://doi.org/10.1145/1280680.1280683
12. Chakraborty, N., Mondal, S.: Tag digit based honeypot to detect shoulder surfing attack. In: Mauri, J.L., Thampi, S.M., Rawat, D.B., Jin, D. (eds.) SSCC 2014. CCIS, vol. 467, pp. 101–110. Springer, Heidelberg (2014). https://doi.org/10.1007/ 978-3-662-44966-0_10
13. Yu, X., Wang, Z., Li, Y., Li, L., Zhu, W.T., Song, L.: EvoPass: evolvable graphical password against shoulder-surfing attacks. Comput. Secur. 179–198 (2017)
14. Zhang, R., Zhang, N., Du, C., Lou, W., Hou, Y.T., Kawamoto, Y.: AugAuth: shoulder-surfing resistant authentication for augmented reality. In: 2017 IEEE International Conference on Communications (ICC), pp. 1–6 (2017). https://doi. org/10.1109/ICC.2017.7997251
15. Sun, H.-M., Chen, S.-T., Yeh, J.-H., Cheng, C.-Y.: A shoulder surfing resistant graphical authentication system. IEEE Trans. Dependabl. Secur. Comput. 15(2), 180–193 (2018). https://doi.org/10.1109/TDSC.2016.2539942

16. Zezschwitz, E., Ebbinghaus, S., Hussmann, H., Luca, A.: You can't watch this! Privacy-respectful photo browsing on smartphones. In: Proceedings of the 2016 CHI Conference on Human Factors in Computing Systems (CHI 2016). Association for Computing Machinery, New York, NY, USA, 4320–4324 (2016). https://doi.org/10.1145/2858036.2858120

17. Eiband, M., Zezschwitz, E., Buschek, D., Hußmann, H.: My scrawl hides it all: protecting text messages against shoulder surfing with handwritten fonts. In Proceedings of the 2016 CHI Conference Extended Abstracts on Human Factors in Computing Systems (CHI EA 2016). Association for Computing Machinery, New York, NY, USA, 2041–2048 (2016). https://doi.org/10.1145/2851581.2892511

18. Zhou, H., et al.: Enhancing mobile content privacy with proxemics aware notifications and protection. In: Proceedings of the 2016 CHI Conference on Human Factors in Computing Systems (CHI 2016). Association for Computing Machinery, New York, NY, USA, 1362–1373 (2016). https://doi.org/10.1145/2858036.2858232

19. Khamis, M., Eiband, M., Zürn, M., Hussmann, H.: EyeSpot: leveraging gaze to protect private text content on mobile devices from shoulder surfing. Multimod. Technol. Interact. 2(3), 45 (2008). https://doi.org/10.3390/mti2030045

20. Ragozin, K., Pai, Y., Augereau, O., Kise, K., Kerdels, J., Kunze, K.: Private reader: using eye tracking to improve reading privacy in public spaces. In Proceedings of the 21st International Conference on Human-Computer Interaction with Mobile Devices and Services (MobileHCI 2019). Association for Computing Machinery, New York, NY, USA, Article 18, pp. 1–6 (2019). https://doi.org/10.1145/3338286.3340129

21. Saad, A., Chukwu, M., Schneegass, S.: Communicating shoulder surfing attacks to users. In: Proceedings of the 17th International Conference on Mobile and Ubiquitous Multimedia (MUM 2018), pp. 147–152. Association for Computing Machinery, New York, NY, USA (2018). https://doi.org/10.1145/3282894.3282919

22. Lian, S., Hu, W., Song, X., Liu, Z.: Smart privacy-preserving screen based on multiple sensor fusion. In IEEE Trans. Consum. Electron. 59(1), 136–143 (2013). https://doi.org/10.1109/TCE.2013.6490252

23. Ali, M.E., Anwar, A., Ahmed, I., Hashem, T., Kulik, L., Tanin, E.: Protecting mobile users from visual privacy attacks. In: Proceedings of the 2014 ACM International Joint Conference on Pervasive and Ubiquitous Computing: Adjunct Publication (UbiComp 2014 Adjunct), pp. 1–4. Association for Computing Machinery, New York, NY, USA (2014). https://doi.org/10.1145/2638728.2638788

24. Watanabe, K., Higuchi, F., Inami, M., Igarashi, T.: CursorCamouflage: multiple dummy cursors as a defense against shoulder surfing. In: SIGGRAPH Asia 2012 Emerging Technologies (2012)

25. Li, C., Liang, M., Xiao, K., Fong, S., Wang, Q., Song, W.: Human body and face detection based anti-shoulder attack system on ATM. In: Proceedings of the International Conference on Big Data and Internet of Thing (BDIOT2017), pp. 145–148. Association for Computing Machinery, New York, NY, USA (2017). https://doi.org/10.1145/3175684.3175706

26. Brudy, F., Ledo, D., Greenberg, S., Butz, A.: Is anyone looking? Mitigating shoulder surfing on public displays through awareness and protection. In: Proceedings of The International Symposium on Pervasive Displays (PerDis 2014), pp. 1–6. Association for Computing Machinery, New York, NY, USA (2014). https://doi.org/10.1145/2611009.2611028

27. Tan, M., Pang, R., Le, Q.V. : EfficientDet: Scalable and Efficient Object Detection (2020)

28. Jocher, G., e al.: ultralytics/yolov5: v5.0 - YOLOv5-P6 1280 models, AWS, Super-vise.ly and YouTube integrations (2021)
29. Wang, C. -Y., Mark Liao, H. -Y., Wu, Y. -H., Chen, P.-Y., Hsieh, J.-W., Yeh, I.-H.: CSPNet: a new backbone that can enhance learning capability of CNN. In: 2020 IEEE/CVF Conference on Computer Vision and Pattern Recognition Work-shops (CVPRW), pp. 1571–1580 (2020). https://doi.org/10.1109/CVPRW50498.2020.00203
30. He, K., Zhang, X., Ren, S., Sun, J.: Spatial pyramid pooling in deep convolutional networks for visual recognition. In: Fleet, D., Pajdla, T., Schiele, B., Tuytelaars, T. (eds.) ECCV 2014. LNCS, vol. 8691, pp. 346–361. Springer, Cham (2014). https://doi.org/10.1007/978-3-319-10578-9_23
31. Liu, S., Qi, L., Qin, H., Shi, J., Jia, J.: Path Aggregation Network for Instance Segmentation (2018)
32. OpenCV: Smoothing Images. https://docs.opencv.org/3.4/d4/d13/tutorial_py_filtering.html. Accessed 31 Aug 2022
33. OpenCV: Image Filtering. https://docs.opencv.org/4.x/d4/d86/group__imgproc__filter.html. Accessed 31 Aug 2022
34. Browser Market Share Worldwide -December 2021. https://gs.statcounter.come/browser-market-share. Accessed 31 Aug 2022
35. Top 100 Websites Ranking on the Web. https://rankranger.com/top-websites. Accessed 31 Aug 2022
36. Kivilohkare, G.: Optimizing the Critical Rendering Path for Decreased Website Loading Time. Åbo Akademi (2020)
37. Lighthouse - Chrome Developers. https://developer.chrome.com/docs/lighthouse/. Accessed 31 Aug 2022
38. Total Blocking Time - Chrome Developer. https://developer.chrome.com/docs/lighthouse/performance/lighthouse-total-blocking-time/. Accessed 31 Aug 2022

Human-Centric Sensing

A Shallow Convolution Network Based Contextual Attention for Human Activity Recognition

Chenyang Xu[1,2], Zhihong Mao[1], Feiyi Fan[2], Tian Qiu[1], Jianfei Shen[2,3(✉)], and Yang Gu[2]

[1] Intelligent Manufacturing Department, Wu Yi Unitersity, Jiangmen, Guangdong 529020, China
[2] Institute of Computing Technology, Chinese Academy of Sciences, Beijing100090, China
{fanfeiyi,shenjianfei,guyang}@ict.ac.cn
[3] Shandong Academy of Intelligent Computing Technology, Jinan 250102, Shandong, China

Abstract. Human activity recognition (HAR) is increasingly important in ubiquitous computing applications. Recently, attention mechanism are extensively used in sensor-based HAR tasks, which is capable of focusing the neural network on different parts of the time series data. Among attention-based methods, the self-attention mechanism performs well in the HAR field, which establish the correlation of key-query to fuse the local information with global information. But self attention fails to model the local contextual information between the keys. In this paper, we propose a contextual attention (COA) based HAR method, which utilize the local contextual information between keys to guide learning the global weight matrix. In COA mechanism, we use $k \times k$ kernel to encode input signal to local contextual keys to extract more contextual information between keys. By fusing local key and query to generate global weight matrix, we can establish the correlation between local features and global features. The values are multiplied by the weight matrix to get a global contextual key, which include global contextual information. We combine the local key and global key to enhance feature's expression ability. Extensive experiments on five public HAR datasets, namely UCI-HAR, PAMAP2, UNIMIB-SHAR, DSADS, and MHEALTH show that the COA-based model is superior to the state-of-the-art methods.

Keywords: Contextual Attention (COA) · Deep Learning · Human Activity Recognition

1 Introduction

Human avtivity recognition (HAR) system can recognize various activities, such as running, walking, etc. HAR systems are used in numerous application scenarios, including medication intake, health monitoring and fitness

© ICST Institute for Computer Sciences, Social Informatics and Telecommunications Engineering 2023
Published by Springer Nature Switzerland AG 2023. All Rights Reserved
S. Longfei and P. Bodhi (Eds.): MobiQuitous 2022, LNICST 492, pp. 155–171, 2023.
https://doi.org/10.1007/978-3-031-34776-4_9

tracker. For example, in health monitoring field, HAR is utilized to help people analyze human behaviors (e.g. fall detection and Parkinson's disease assessment). Recently, utilizing wearable device to predict human activities becomes popular [1].

In the previous study, numerous traditional methods such as Logistic Regression, Decision Trees, Random Forest, Extreme Learning Machine (ELM), and Naive Bayesian approaches [2,3] are extensively used in HAR area, which achieve remarkable performance. Despite the traditional machine learning (ML) method in HAR providing various benefits, they need to extract features from the raw signal data manually and are usually complicated as well as time-consuming. While shallow feature is not good at classifying complex activities. As a result, the effectiveness of traditional ML approaches for classification tasks is heavily reliant on the efficacy of feature engineering.

The emerging deep learning related methods, such as Convolutional Neural Network (CNN), Deep Belief Network (DBN), and Recurrent Neural Network (RNN), achieve enormous success in image segmentation, classification, object recognition, and natural language processing, etc. In HAR field, deep learning also achieves a great success, which overcomes the shortcoming of hand-crafted feature extraction approaches by using automated feature identification. We use the inertial measurement unit (IMU) in the wearable device to measure the values of the accelerometer, gyroscope, magnetometer. Then, the data is preprocessed, which needs to fill the missing values and resample the gyroscope, accelerometer, and magnetometer signal to adjust to a uniform sampling frequency. Finally, we concatenate the multiple channel signals. Then, we use sliding window technology to split the signal data of multiple channels to signal images. The existed approaches mostly split the sensor signal into fixed-size sequences and then classify the signal image using various machine learning methods.

With the popularity of self-attention mechanism, a HAR method based on self-attention mechanism is proposed [4], which extract useful information from sensor's signals by allocating their focus among signal features. The learned attention weights improve the ability to recognize target signals from background signals. However, self-attention mechanism mainly relies on the isolated pairwise query-key interaction to generate an attention matrix, as shown in Fig. 1(a), neglecting the rich contextual information between neighbour keys. For the signal feature of activity, as shown in Fig. 1(b), the change of the activity signal contains contextual information. Only considering the isolated key-query correlation can not extract enough features. Therefore, we need to consider the context features.

In this paper, we make use of the abundance of context features among input keys for a 2D sensor signal feature [5]. We propose a HAR method based on contextual attention (COA)(Figure 1(b)). The COA mechanism combines key context mining and self-attention learning over 2D signal feature into an unified architecture. In COA mechanism, we propose to build the COA in the following steps: (1) The $k \times k$ convolution is performed on all the neighbor keys to contextualize the local keys' representation. (2) The contextualized local keys and queries are concatenated by two successive 1×1 convolution operations to

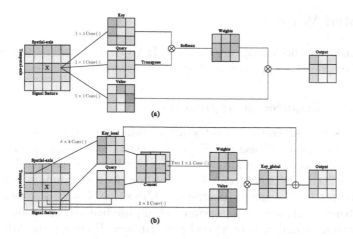

Fig. 1. Schematic comparison of (a) the traditional self-attention mechanism and (b) the proposed COA mechanism

generate global weight matrices. This process utilizes the reciprocal relationship between each query and all keys in self-attention to learn with the guidance of the local context information. (3) The learned attention weights matrix is employed to strengthen all the input values, forming global contextual information for the signal features. (4) We embed COA mechanism with CNN-HAR to enhance the ability of extracting contextual information. The contributions of our paper are summarized as follows.

- We propose a new COA mechanism for sensor-based HAR, which can make full use of input key's local contextual information to learn the global attention weights matrix. Then we multiply input values with attention weights matrix to obtain global keys.
- We employ two baseline networks (Resnet and 3-layers CNN), and add the COA mechanism to baseline network. We utilize large size kernel to capture local contextual information between keys. Then, we can employ local signal correlation to guide learning global feature correlation. The experiment result demonstrate that the local contextual features are significant.
- Extensive experiments on various benchmark datasets are carried out to demonstrate the higher performance of our proposed COA-HAR.

The following is a description of the paper's structure. We summarize HAR's related works in Sect. 2. The specifics of COA-HAR method are presented in Sect. 3. In Sect. 4, we detail experimental results obtained on five public HAR datasets, which are compared with the existing SOTAs. Moreover, several ablation studies about the COA-HAR method are provided. We describe conclusions in Sect. 5.

2 Related Works

This section gives a brief literature review of HAR field, including previous works on feature engineering approaches, deep learning approaches.

2.1 Feature Engineering Approaches

In previous study, several state-of-the-art classification methods are employed for HAR. Awais et al. [6] use the SVM as a classifier to bulid a sensors-based activity classification system for elderly people, which can accurately recognize four primary activities of everyday life, including sitting, standing, walking, and lying. Ignatov et al. [7] employ k-nearest neighbors (KNN) approach as a classifier in a IMU-based HAR scene. Akhavian et al. [8] use five ML methods to classify workers' activities, and achieve a good performance. However, the ML methods need a huge amount of hand-crafted training data, and the absence of training data might restrict its effectiveness. These widely used ML methods usually suffer from significant limitations in HAR, such as progress slowly in the training and inference procedure, and poor generalization performance. With the development of extreme learning machine (ELM), a single hidden layer feed-forward neural network benefits from a fast running speed and a high degree of generalization [3]. The problem with ELM is that the algorithm parameters affect recognition accuracy and the randomly generated weights make it instable.

2.2 Deep Learning Approaches

Deep learning methods are able to extract features from raw signals and generate accurate predictions. Many deep learning-based algorithms have been applied to HAR field, including CNN, LSTM, CNN-LSTM, and attention-based CNN.

CNN is used to identify human activities. We process the raw sensor signals into 2D signal images and then send the signal image to the CNN model. Huang et al. [9] propose a channel selection method: the Expected Channel Damage Matrix (ECDM) is used to identify the contribution of each channel, and the channel with a low contribution rate is recovered in the training stage. In addition, the channel with a high contribution rate is reassigned to the position of the recovered low contribution channel. Cui et al. [10] employ multi-scale CNN to make an end-to-end classifier for univariate time series data. Andrey et al. [11] propose a CNN-based method for IMU-based HAR, where CNN is employed to extract local features, and the global signal features is derived by using statistical features. However, CNN is only limited to extracting local temporal correlation and sensor channel correlation information, and can not establish long-range dependency in temporal dimension and cross channel correlation in sensor channel dimension.

Another extensively used member of the DL family is RNN. The HAR is a time-series classification task. It is critical to capture temporal dependencies in the signal data. RNN is well-suited for this task. Some researchers employ RNN to classify human activities. For example, Chen et al. [12] propose

LSTM-based feature extractor for human activity categorization. Ullah et al. [13] propose another LSTM-based model. Firstly, the signal from the gyroscope and accelerometer are normalised. Secondly, the normalised signal is given to a stacked LSTM network to obtain an output, which would be placed into a softmax layer afterwards. Yu et al. [14] propose bi-directional LSTM-based model for HAR. Although the RNN can extract long sequence signals, the uncorrelated signals [15] in the sensors will affect the RNN.

A hybrid of CNN and RNN is used in recent HAR research. Qian et al. [14] integrates CNN-RNN models into an integrated framework to automatically extract long-range temporal features, statistical features, and cross sensor channel features, then merge them into an integrated feature map for HAR. Zeng et al. [15] propose temporal and sensor attention with CNN-LSTM models for human activity recognition, which adaptively focus on essential signals. Ma et al. [16] propose AttnSense for human activity recognition. AttnSense introduces the framework of merging attention mechanism with CNN and Gated Recurrent Units (GRU) to capture the interdependence of sensor signals in both the sensor channel and temporal dimension, which demonstrates benefits in prioritized sensor selection and enhances the comprehensibility. In CNN-RNN methods, although the long-range features can be extracted by RNN. However, uncorrelated signals affect the RNN, and then affect the effect of the model.

More recent research on HAR field uses a combination of CNN and attention mechanisms. Ramanujam et al. [17] employ ConvLSTM network with self-attention mechanism to extract temporal and sensor channel features from sensor signal. But self-attention mechanism only uses isolated query-key pairs to extract feature correlation, which ignores the context information around key. Moreover, in self-attention mechanism, only global correlation is considered and local contextual correlation is ignored.

3   Methdology

This section introduces the COA mechanism in detail. We denote multiple raw sensor signals to a predetermined window size as $S = \{s_1, s_2, \ldots, s_n\}$, where $S \in \mathbf{R}^{m \times n}$, S is signal image given to network, m is the length of the time series, and n denotes the sensor channel dimension. Based on self-attention, we propose the contextual attention (COA), a novel attention mechanism, which has three main operations to learn signal's feature.

- Local key generation: The COA mechanism uses $k \times k$ convolution to contextualize keys to capture contextual information between keys.
- Global key generation: The COA mechanism combines local keys and querys to form weights matrix. Then, we use weights matrix mutiple values to form global keys to strengthen global information.
- Local key and global key combination: After the above steps, the local key and global key are obtained. We combine the local key and global key as the final attention weights.

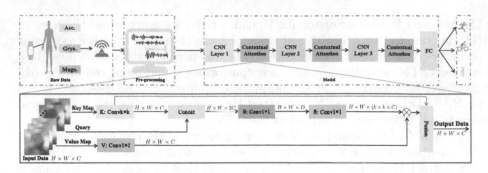

Fig. 2. Overview of Contextual Attention HAR Model Based on CNN

3.1 Rethinking Self-attention

In this part, let us rethinking the traditional self-attention [18]. The signal image is convolved to obtain a 2D feature map as $X^{C \times H \times W}$. Here C is the channel number, H is temporal axis of feature map, and W is sensor channel axis of feature map. We generate queries $Query = XW_{query}$, keys $Key = XW_{key}$, and values $Value = XW_{value}$ through X mutiple the embedding matrix $(W_{query}, W_{key}, W_{value})$ respectively. We can obtain each embedding matrix by 1×1 convolution. Then, the relation matrix $Mid \in \mathbb{R}^{C \times H \times W}$ between keys Key and queries $Query$ as is acquired as:

$$Mid = Key \otimes Query \tag{1}$$

where $\otimes$ is the operation of matrix multiplication, which calculates the pairwise correlation between each query. Mid represents the correlation information of each signal frame in the feature map.

After the above operation, we can obtain the attention matrix Att by normalizing the local matrix Mid with $Softmax$ activation function:

$$Att = Softmax(Mid) \tag{2}$$

The final output is obtained by multiplying the $Value$ with the Att weight matrix. The $Output$ can be written as:

$$Output = Value \otimes Att \tag{3}$$

These three transformations allow self-attention mechanism to aggregate local signal's temporal and sensor channel correlation, which helps the networks more accurately locate the objects of interest.

3.2 Contextual Attention Mechanism

The traditional self-attention mechanism establishes signal's temporal and sensor channel correlation. However, all correlation of query-key pairs in the traditional self-attention are learned on independent query-key pairs, which ignore the abundant contextual information between neighbor keys. The contextual information is significant to signal feature extraction in sensor signal, which extract local temporal and sensor channel correlation in signal context. In order to solve this problem, we propose a novel attention mechanism named Contextual Attention (COA), which can combine contextual information exploit with self-attention mechanism in a unified framework.

Specifically, given a 2D feature map $X \in \mathbb{R}^{C \times H \times W}$ as the input. We define the queries and values as $Query = X$ and $Value = XW_{value}$, respectively. Firstly, COA mechanism utilizes group convolution with $k \times k$ kernel size across all the neighbor keys in $k \times k$ signal feature in order to spatially contextualize each key representation. The contextualized keys $Key\_local \in \mathbb{R}^{C \times H \times W}$ represent the local neighbor keys' local contextual information, which capture local signal feature change. Secondly, we concatenate the Key_local and $Query$, which is followed by two convolution operations with 1×1 kernel size. So, we can make the local signal feature and global signal feature fuse. Here θ is a convolution operation activated by a $ReLU$ function, and δ contains only a convolution operation.

$$Att = \delta(\theta([Key\_local, Query])) \tag{4}$$

In each spatial position, the local attention matrix Att is generated by the $Query$ and the Key_local instead of the independent query-key pairs. This method improves the information mining ability of self-attention mechanism. Finally, We obtain the global feature map Key_global by aggregating values $Value$ with contextualized attention matrix Att.

$$Key\_global = Value \otimes Att \tag{5}$$

As described above, Key_global can capture the signal feature's global information. Therefore, we call the Key_global as the global contextual information of signal feature. The result of our COA mechanism $Output$ can be written as:

$$Output = Key\_local \oplus Key\_global \tag{6}$$

where $\oplus$ represents add operation.

3.3   COA Based HAR Method

As this paper aims to investigate a attention mechanism to augment the convolutional features for HAR networks, we take 3-layers CNN architecture as baseline network. Then, we embed the COA mechanism with CNN-HAR network to demonstrate the method's effectiveness. To demonstrate the effectiveness of the COA mechanism in other networks, we also use a 3-layer Resnet as the baseline network and embed the COA mechanism after the first layer. Each layer in Resnet has two convolution processes. Each shortcut connection contains a convolution operation. We give the specific implementation steps of COA and embed the COA mechanism into the CNN baseline network, as shown in Fig. 2. In Fig. 3, we give the two baseline models and the model with the embedded COA mechanism.

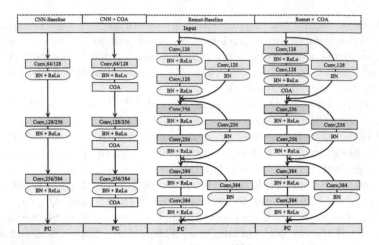

Fig. 3. Structure of 3-Layers Resnet and CNN (For UCIHAR dataset, the channel number of the first convolution layer is 64. For other datasets, the channel number is 128.)

4 Experiment

4.1 Datasets

In order to evaluate the effectiveness of the proposed method, we perform extensive experiments using five publicly available HAR datasets. The UCIHAR dataset [19], PAMAP2 dataset [20], UniMib-SHAR dataset [21], DSADS [22], and MHEALTH dataset [23] are employed as the five benchmark HAR datasets. The classification number, division proportion, and window size of the datasets are shown in Table 1, and the class description of five datasets is shown in Table 2.

Table 1. Briefly Description of The Operation for Each HAR Datasets

Operation	Dataset				
	UCIHAR	PAMAP2	UniMib-SHAR	DSADS	MHEALTH
Number of Classification	6	12	17	9	13
Ratio of Train-set	70%	80%	70%	70%	75%
Ratio of Test-set	30%	20%	30%	30%	25%
Sliding Window Size	128	512	151	*None*	100
Overlap Rates	50%	50%	50%	*None*	50

UCIHAR Dataset: The UCIHAR dataset is collected using the embedded accelerometer and gyroscope of the Samsung Galaxy S II smartphone at a sampling frequency 50 Hz. The dataset is obtained from 30 volunteers aged 19 to 48

Table 2. Class Description of UCIHAR, PAMAP2, UniMib-SHAR, DSADS and MHEALTH Datases

Dataset	The Class of Activity
UCIHAR	Walking, Walking_Upstairs, Walking_Downstairs, Sitting, Standing, Lying
PAMAP2	Lying, Sitting, Standing, Walking,Running, Cycling, Nordic Walking Descending Stairs, Vacuum Cleaning, Ironing, Rope Jumping, Ascending Stairs
UniMib-SHAR	StandingUpFS, StandingUpFL, Running, SittingDown, GoingUps, FallingBack, Syncope, Jumping, FallingLeft, GoingdownS, Walking, Falling with PS LyingDownS, FallingFrow, HittingObstacle, FallingRight, FallingBackSC
DSADS	Moving Around in an Elevator, Standing in an Elevator Still, Playing Basketball, Walking on a Treadmill with a Speed of 4 km/h (in Flat Position), Walking on a Treadmill with a Speed of 4 km/h (in 15 Deg Inclined Position), Exercising on a Stepper, Exercising on a Cross Trainer, Descending Stairs, Moving Around in an Elevator, Walking in a Parking Lot
MHEALTH	Standing Still, Sitting and Relaxing, Lying Down, Walking, Climbing Stairs, Waist Bends Forward, Frontal Elevation of Arms,Knees Bending, Cycling, Jogging, Running, Jump front & back, NULL

who wear a smartphone around their waist. The original signal data are preprocessed with a noise filter before being sliced according to the predetermined size of the sliding window. In this experiment, we utilize pre-processed data.

PAMAP2 Dataset: The PAMAP2 dataset is collected from nine volunteers. The volunteers performed 12 mandatory different activities including walking, cycling, rope jumping, etc. Multiple sensors including chest sensor, wrist sensor and ankle sensor are applied to record the data. T100 Hz sampling rate is downsampled to 33.3 Hz for further analysis. Sport intensity is estimated using a heart rate monitor with a sample rate 9 Hz.

UniMib-SHAR Dataset: The UniMib-SHAR dataset is collected by scholars from the University of Milano-Bicocca, which is intended to identify a variety of "falling" activities. Data is collected from 30 participants ranging in age from 18 to 60 years old using an Android smartphone. During the data collection process, all participants must wear smart phones in their left and right pockets. The sensor signals is sampled 50 Hz.

DSADS Dataset: The DSADS dataset collects 19 activities performed for five minutes by 8 participants. We used nine of these activities. The entire signal length for each participant's activity is five minutes. The participants are asked to complete the activities in their style. The activities occur at three campus locations: the Bilkent University Sports Hall, the Electrical and Electronics Engineering Building, and a flat outdoor area. The sensor signals is sampled 25 Hz.

Table 3. The Key Map Value of COA Mechanism

Layers	Dataset				
	UCIHAR	PAMAP2	UniMib-SHAR	DSADS	MHEALTH
COA1 After The 1st CNN Layer	$K=1$	$K=3$	$K=5$	$K=3$	$K=3$
COA2 After The 2nd CNN Layer	$K=1$	$K=3$	$K=5$	$K=5$	$K=5$
COA3 After The 3rd CNN Layer	$K=1$	$K=3$	$K=5$	$K=5$	$K=7$
COA1 After The 1st Resnet Layer	$K=1$	$K=5$	$K=3$	$K=5$	$K=3$

MHEALTH Dataset: The MHEALTH dataset contain recordings of body movements and vital signals from 10 participants with various characteristics. Each participants complete 12 exercises in an out-of-lab setting with no constraints. Three inertial measurement units (IMUs) are attached to the chest, right wrist, and left ankle of the participants, respectively. In addition, the IMU on the chest provides two-lead ECG readings. The sensor signals is sampled 50 Hz.

4.2   Experimental Platform

All the models are trained/tested on a single Nvidia RTX-3090 24GB GPU, Intel I5-10400 CPU, 32 GB memory. We use PyTorch deep learning library to implement all of the experiments (Table 4).

Table 4. Simple Description of The Neural Network Parameter

Dataset / Layers	conv	padding	stride	BN	ReLU	Dataset / Layers	conv	padding	stride	BN	ReLU
	UCI-HAR						PAMAP2				
layer1	(6,1)	(1,1)	(3,1)	✓	✓	layer1	(6,1)	(0,0)	(3,1)	✓	✓
layer2	(6,1)	(1,1)	(3,1)	✓	✓	layer2	(6,1)	(0,0)	(3,1)	✓	✓
layer3	(6,1)	(1,1)	(3,1)	✓	✓	layer3	(6,1)	(0,0)	(3,1)	✓	✓
batch_size	64					batch_size	8				
learning rate	0.001					learning rate	0.001				
	UniMib-SHAR						DSADS				
layer1	(6,1)	(1,0)	(3,1)	✓	✓	layer1	(3,3)	(2,0)	(1,1)	✓	✓
layer2	(6,1)	(1,0)	(3,1)	✓	✓	layer2	(3,3)	(2,0)	(1,1)	✓	✓
layer3	(6,2)	(1,0)	(3,1)	✓	✓	layer3	(3,3)	(2,0)	(1,1)	✓	✓
batch_size	128					batch_size	64				
learning rate	0.001					learning rate	0.001				

Dataset / Layers	MHEALTH				
	conv	padding	stride	BN	ReLU
layer1	(3,1)	(2,1)	(1,1)	✓	✓
layer2	(3,1)	(2,1)	(1,1)	✓	✓
layer3	(3,1)	(2,1)	(1,1)	✓	✓
batch_size	64				
learning rate	0.001				

4.3 Values of Hyperparameters Used in the Baseline

The details of network structure are shown in the Fig. 3 summarizes the values of the hyperparameters employed. The K value in the COA mechanism in every dataset is shown in Table 3. The default values are utilized for the other hyperparameters.

4.4 Comparison with Other Methods

Our method is compared with both baseline and state-of-the-art methods. The results are shown in the Table 5 and Fig. 4. Because feature-engineering-based machine learning approaches are difficult to be scaled, we compare COA-HAR model with deep learning-based methods in this study. We follow five HAR classification methods as a comparison, including Selective CNN (Huang et al. [9]), Shallow Convolutional (Zhang et al. [24]), DDNN (Qian et al. [25]), Local Loss CNN (Teng et al. [26]) and DanHAR (Gao et al. [27]). It can be seen from Table 5 that the COA method based on 3-Layers CNN proposed by us improve significantly in the four data sets compared with SOTA. Note that the results with * are directly cited from the references. Our method based on 3-layers CNN outperforms SOTA methods 1.16%, 0.23%, 0.50% on three datasets (PAMAP2, UniMib-SHAR, DSADS) respectively. And the COA method based on Resnet in UCIHAR, UniMib-SHAR, MHEALTH outperforms SOTA method 0.34%, 2.75%, 0.01%.

- Selective CNN [9]: a state-of-the-art Resnet-based model with 3 convolutional blocks. This method uses selective convolution to select the contribution of each channel through the ECDM matrix, replacing low-contribution channels with high-contribution channels. We reproduce the model by following the architecture described in the paper.
- Shallow Convolutional [24]: a state-of-the-art CNN-based model with 3 convolutional blocks and GCN block. This method uses GCN to capture the information between channels so that each channel is interconnected. We reproduce the model by following the architecture described in the paper.
- DDNN model [25]: a state-of-the-art LSTM and CNN model. This method uses LSTM to capture sensor channel and temporal features and CNN to capture the temporal and sensor channel connection. We reproduce the model by following the architecture described in the paper.
- Local Loss CNN [26]: a state-of-the-art CNN-based model with 3 convolutional blocks and local loss block. This method uses local loss block to optimize loss in the upstream part. We reproduce the model by following the architecture described in the paper.
- DanHAR model [27]: a state-of-the-art Resnet-based model with 3 convolutional blocks and temporal and sensor channel attention. This method uses Convolutional Block Attention Module (CBAM) [28] attention based Resnet for HAR. We reproduce the model by following the architecture described in the paper.

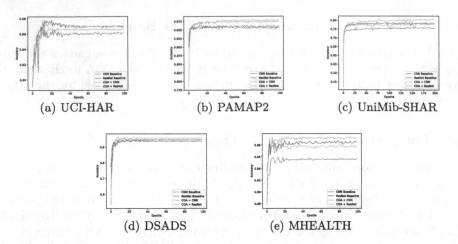

(a) UCI-HAR   (b) PAMAP2   (c) UniMib-SHAR

(d) DSADS   (e) MHEALTH

Fig. 4. Test Accuracy with Different Models on Five Datasets

4.5   Ablation Studies

In order to demonstrate the COA mechanism is critical, we execute a series of ablation experiments. As seen in Table 5, adding contextual information improves greatly the basic network. On the datasets UCIHAR, PAMAP2, UniMib-SHAR, DSADS and MHEALTH datasets, the 3-layer CNN with COA mechanism improve 0.53%, 0.73%, 2.18%, 1.96%, and 2.18% respectively. And in Resnet with COA mechanism, the accuracy improves 0.04%, 0.67%, 2.04%, 0.12% and 0.77% on UCIHAR, PAMAP2, UniMib-SHAR, DSADS, and MHEALTH respectively. These experiments show that the COA mechanism is necessary for HAR classification.

Table 5. mAcc(%) of Models on Various Datasets

Methods	Dataset				
	UCIHAR	PAMAP2	UniMib-SHAR	DSADS	MHEALTH
Resnet + COA	96.99	97.36	**80.35**	94.78	**99.19**
Resnet Baseline	96.95	96.00	78.31	94.66	98.42
CNN + COA	96.58	**97.80**	77.78	**95.81**	97.75
CNN Baseline	96.05	95.62	75.60	93.85	95.57
CNN + Self-Attention	96.20	93.56	76.71	95.31	96.73
Huang et al. [9]	96.40	95.67	77.55	94.44	98.76
Zhang et al. [24]	94.68	94.86	75.42	94.52	96.68
Qian et al. [25]	84.13	84.55	73.21	82.25	90.50
Teng et al. [26]	95.23	94.59	76.19	94.29	95.51
Gao et al. [27]	96.65	93.79	77.29	94.82	99.18
Xu et al.* [29]	–	–	80.02	–	–
Huang et al.* [30]	**97.35**	92.14	78.65	–	–

4.6   Visualizations

The COA-HAR approach may be seen as an additional stage of operation based on CNN that beats CNN and other SOTA classification methods in accuracy. The COA mechanism improves the accuracy of activity classification by extracting the local context signal features. Table 5 shows that the COA method based on 3-Layers CNN is superior to other SOTA methods in four datasets. As other HAR studies [24] [27], we use confusion matrix to illustrate the advantages of CNN in classification. The proposed model and the baseline CNN's confusion matrices on the UniMib-SHAR dataset for the HAR task are shown in Fig. 5(a) and Fig. 5(b). When comparing the COA-HAR method to the baseline CNN for two similar activities, "GoingUps" and "Walking", it is clear that the COA-HAR method has fewer misclassifications. For falls in different directions, take "Falling right" and "Falling back" as example. Although the activities are very similar, the classification accuracy is still improve.

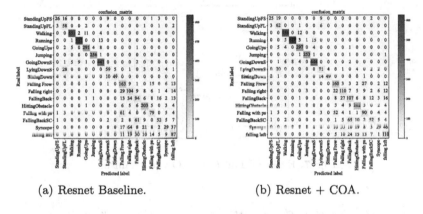

(a) Resnet Baseline.   (b) Resnet + COA.

Fig. 5. Confusion Matrices on UniMib-SHAR Dataset

4.7   Discussion

Where is the Best Position to Insert COA Mechanism? On the UCI-HAR dataset, we perform ablation experiments to evaluate the effect of COA block at various layers. As indicated in Fig. 6, the COA block should be added after the first, second, and third layers for maximum efficiency. It is due to the fact that high-level contextual information is encoded after the convolution process. The COA mechanism combined with multi-layer feature information can get better feature expression capability. As a result, adding COA mechanism at every convolution layer allows the network to acquire more meaningful information for activity recognition.

Can COA Mechanism Reduce the Depth of Network? According to our results in Table 5, especially on UCIHAR dataset, the 3-layers Resnet performance is similar to 3-layers CNN. As shown in Fig. 4(c), the 3-layer CNN with

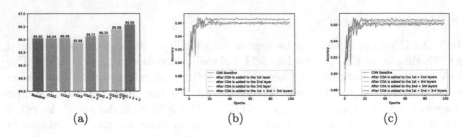

(a)   (b)   (c)

Fig. 6. Accuracy of COA Mechanism at Different Layers

COA mechanism is able to achieve a comparable or even better accuracy than the 3-layers Resnet. As a result, COA-HAR model may achieve similar classification precision than multi-layers model (Fig. 7).

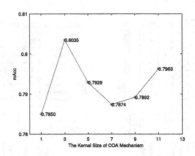

Fig. 7. Effect of The K in COA mechanism

How the Value of K Influence the Accuracy? According to our results on UniMib-SHAR dataset in Fig. 6, the result in Resnet is shown when the $K = 3$ the accuracy is the best. According to the dataset's characteristics, the activity signals are periodic or transient, such as "Running" or "Falling". Therefore, we infer that although the large K value can extract a larger range of contextual information, it will introduce irrelevant signal features (signals outside the period or after the activity occurs).

Does the COA-HAR Model is Robust? We find that the proposed COA-HAR method exhibits better robustness when compare with the other methods. In LSTM-CNN related methods, for instance, DDNN [25] is obviously inferior in UCIHAR and UniMib-SHAR, and Layer-wise CNN [26] is inferior in UniMib-SHAR. One reason could be that DDNN is a unified framework where the signal of different parts are learned together. The signal feature learned by LSTM might encode some noise in the data itself (such as irrelevant signal components) [15]. And because the size of the CNN convolution kernel is constrained, cross-channel information cannot be taken into account. In the Triple Cross-Domain related method [31], the accuracy is inferior in PAMAP2 dataset. The reason maybe that the sensor dimension, temporal dimension, and sensor channel dimension are captured by three attention branches, and they ignore the correlation between the dimensions. In conclusion, the COA-HAR model improved significantly compared with the baseline in multiple datasets. It performs well in four datasets, proving that our method is robust.

What is the Difference Between the COA Mechanism and Self-attention? As can be seen in Fig. 1, the COA mechanism fully considers the contextual information of signal features, which is significant for activity recognition. For periodic activity such as "Cycling", the HAR method based on self-attention only consider the isolated key-query correlation information. Therefore, the correlation between the signal at a certain time and the global signal can be considered, and the local contextual information within the periodic activity will be ignored. Unlike image data, sensor data is temporally correlated, and the sensor's channels are also correlated. The COA mechanism can correlate local context information and global information, which is very important for activity classification. It can be seen from the results in the Table 5 that the COA-HAR method is significantly improved compare with the HAR method based on self-attention, which proves the importance of contextual information in self-attention.

5 Conclusion

In this paper, we concentrate on exploring contextual information between the local signal feature and global signal feature for HAR problem with a CNN model. The COA-HAR method is proposed, which exploits the neighbour key's contextual information to guide self-attention to capture more correlation information of signal feature context. The COA mechanism first captures the local context among neighbor keys, then the COA mechanism is employed to guide self-attention to exploit the global context information. This method combines context exploiting and self-attention mechanism into an uniform framework, improving the capacity of signal feature recognition. Our experimental results show that the COA mechanism is critical for increasing the performance of CNN architectures.

Acknowledgments. This study is supported by the National Key Research & Development Program of China No. 2020YFC2007104, Natural Science Foundation of China (No.61902377), Youth Innovation Promotion Association CAS, Jinan S&T Bureau No. 2020GXRC030, the Funding for Introduced Innovative R&D Team Program of Jiangmen (Grant No.2018630100090019844), the Wuyi University Startup S&T research funding for senior talents 2019 (No. 504/5041700171).

References

1. Wang, Z., Jiang, M., Yaohua, H., Li, H.: An incremental learning method based on probabilistic neural networks and adjustable fuzzy clustering for human activity recognition by using wearable sensors. IEEE Trans. Inf Technol. Biomed. **16**(4), 691–699 (2012)
2. Woodford, B.J., Chandour, A.: An information retrieval-based approach to activity recognition in smart homes. In: Hakim, H., et al. (eds.) ICSOC 2020. Lecture Notes in Computer Science, vol. 12632, pp. 583–595. Springer, Cham (2020). https://doi.org/10.1007/978-3-030-76352-7_51
3. Donghui, W., Wang, Z., Chen, Y., Zhao, H.: Mixed-kernel based weighted extreme learning machine for inertial sensor based human activity recognition with imbalanced dataset. Neurocomputing **190**, 35–49 (2016)
4. Betancourt, C., Chen, W.H., Kuan, C.W.: Self-attention networks for human activity recognition using wearable devices. In: 2020 IEEE International Conference on Systems, Man, and Cybernetics (SMC), pp. 1194–1199. IEEE (2020)
5. Li, Y., Yao, T., Pan, Y., Mei, T.: Contextual transformer networks for visual recognition. In: IEEE Transactions on Pattern Analysis and Machine Intelligence (2022
6. Awais, M., Chiari, L., Ihlen, E.A.F., Helbostad, J.L., Palmerini, L.: Physical activity classification for elderly people in free-living conditions. IEEE J. Biomed. Health Inf. **23**(1), 197–207 (2018)
7. Ignatov, A.D., Strijov, V.V.: Human activity recognition using quasiperiodic time series collected from a single tri-axial accelerometer. Multimedia Tools Appl. **75**(12), 7257–7270 (2016)
8. Akhavian, R., Behzadan, A.H.: Smartphone-based construction workers' activity recognition and classification. Autom. Constr. **71**, 198–209 (2016)
9. Huang, W., Zhang, L., Teng, Q., Song, C., He, J.: The convolutional neural networks training with channel-selectivity for human activity recognition based on sensors. IEEE J. Biomed. Health Inf. **25**(10), 3834–3843 (2021)
10. Cui, Z., Chen, W., Chen, Y.: Multi-scale convolutional neural networks for time series classification. arXiv preprint arXiv:1603.06995 (2016)
11. Ignatov, A.: Real-time human activity recognition from accelerometer data using convolutional neural networks. Appl. Soft Comput. **62**, 915–922 (2018)
12. Chen, Y., Zhong, K., Zhang, J., Sun, Q., Zhao, X.: LSTM networks for mobile human activity recognition. In: 2016 International Conference on Artificial Intelligence: Technologies and Applications, pp. 50–53. Atlantis Press (2016)
13. Ullah, M., Ullah, H., Khan, S.D., Cheikh, F.A.: Stacked lstm network for human activity recognition using smartphone data. In: 2019 8th European Workshop on Visual Information Processing (EUVIP), pp. 175–180. IEEE (2019)
14. Yu, S., Qin, L.: Human activity recognition with smartphone inertial sensors using bidir-lstm networks. In: 2018 3rd International Conference on Mechanical, Control and Computer Engineering (ICMCCE), pp. 219–224. IEEE (2018)
15. Zeng, M., et al.: Understanding and improving recurrent networks for human activity recognition by continuous attention. In: Proceedings of the 2018 ACM International Symposium on Wearable Computers, pp. 56–63 (2018)
16. Ma, H., Li, W., Zhang, X., Gao, S., Lu, S.: Attnsense: Multi-level attention mechanism for multimodal human activity recognition. In: IJCAI, pp. 3109–3115 (2019)
17. Ramanujam, E., Perumal, T., Padmavathi, S.: Human activity recognition with smartphone and wearable sensors using deep learning techniques: A review. IEEE Sens. J. **21**(12), 13029–13040 (2021)

18. Zhao, H., Jia, J., Koltun, V.: Exploring self-attention for image recognition. In: Proceedings of the IEEE/CVF Conference on Computer Vision and Pattern Recognition, pp. 10076–10085 (2020)
19. Anguita, D., Ghio, A., Oneto, L., Parra, X., Reyes-Ortiz, J.L.: Human activity recognition on smartphones using a multiclass hardware-friendly support vector machine. In: Bravo, J., Hervas, R., Rodriguez, M. (eds.) IWAAL 2012. Lecture Notes in Computer Science, vol. 7657, pp. 216–223. Springer, Cham (2012)
20. Reiss, A., Stricker, D.: Introducing a new benchmarked dataset for activity monitoring. In: 2012 16th International Symposium on Wearable Computers, pp. 108–109. IEEE (2012)
21. Micucci, D., Mobilio, M., Napoletano, P.: Unimib shar: A dataset for human activity recognition using acceleration data from smartphones. Appl. Sci. **7**(10), 1101 (2017)
22. Altun, K., Barshan, B., Tunçel, O.: Comparative study on classifying human activities with miniature inertial and magnetic sensors. Pattern Recognit. **43**(10), 3605–3620 (2010)
23. Banos, O., et al.: mHealthDroid: a novel framework for agile development of mobile health applications. In: Pecchia, L., Chen, L.L., Nugent, C., Bravo, J. (eds.) IWAAL 2014. LNCS, vol. 8868, pp. 91–98. Springer, Cham (2014). https://doi.org/10.1007/978-3-319-13105-4_14
24. Huang, W., Zhang, L., Gao, W., Min, F., He, J.: Shallow convolutional neural networks for human activity recognition using wearable sensors. IEEE Trans. Instrum. Meas. **70**, 1–11 (2021)
25. Qian, H., Pan, S.J., Da, B., Miao, C.: A novel distribution-embedded neural network for sensor-based activity recognition. In: IJCAI, vol. 2019, pp. 5614–5620 (2019)
26. Teng, Q., Wang, K., Zhang, L., He, J.: The layer-wise training convolutional neural networks using local loss for sensor-based human activity recognition. IEEE Sens. J. **20**(13), 7265–7274 (2020)
27. Gao, W., Zhang, L., Teng, Q., He, J., Hao, W.: Danhar: dual attention network for multimodal human activity recognition using wearable sensors. Appl. Soft Comput. **111**, 107728 (2021)
28. Woo, S., Park, J., Lee, J.Y., Kweon, I.S.: Cbam: convolutional block attention module. In: Proceedings of the European Conference on Computer Vision (ECCV), pp. 3–19 (2018)
29. Shige, X., Zhang, L., Huang, W., Hao, W., Song, A.: Deformable convolutional networks for multimodal human activity recognition using wearable sensors. IEEE Trans. Instrum. Meas. **71**, 1–14 (2022)
30. Huang, W., Zhang, L., Wu, H., Min, F., Song, A.: Channel-equalization-HAR: a light-weight convolutional neural network for wearable sensor based human activity recognition. In: IEEE Transactions on Mobile Computing (2022)
31. Tang, Y., Zhang, L., Teng, Q., Min, F., Song, A.: Triple cross-domain attention on human activity recognition using wearable sensors. In: IEEE Transactions on Emerging Topics in Computational Intelligence (2022)

Does Cycling Reveal Insights About You? Investigation of User and Environmental Characteristics During Cycling

Luca Hernández Acosta[✉], Sebastian Rahe, and Delphine Reinhardt

Georg-August-Universität, Göttingen 37077, Germany
{hernandez,reinhardt}@cs.uni-goettingen.de

Abstract. Smartwatches are increasingly being used as fitness and health trackers. To provide such a service, these devices have to collect and process movement data gathered by built-in accelerometers and gyroscopes. Based on these data, existing studies leveraging smartphones have shown that it is possible to distinguish users when they (1) walk, (2) perform different hand gestures, or (3) pick up their phone from the table. However, to the best of our knowledge, the case of cycling has not been addressed yet. The goal of this paper is to close this gap by investigating whether it is possible to infer information about users wearing a smartwatch coupled with their smartphone when cycling, their bike type, seat height, gear, and the terrain. In addition, we explore whether it is possible to distinguish individual users based on their movement patterns that may lead to their (re)identification. To this end, we conducted a user study with 17 participants, equipped with a smartphone and a smartwatch, who had to ride along a bike road for two km. Among others, our results show that it is possible to infer the four characteristics bike type, gear, seat height, and terrain with accuracies of 93.05%, 92.23%, 95.76%, 94.24% respectively and distinguish participants with a probability of 99.01%.

Keywords: Behavior Analysis · Activity Recognition · Bike Identification · User Recognition

1 Introduction

The use of smart devices, such as smartwatches and smartphones, in our professional and private life is steadily increasing [1–3]. In addition to support easy communication and quick access to information on the Internet, these devices are also equipped with various sensors allowing for a myriad of applications. For example, they are gaining popularity in the areas of fitness and health tracking [4]. In order to provide such services, the applications collect and analyze data of the devices' users. Often, movement data are collected by built-in sensors, such as the accelerometer and gyroscope, for these purposes. These data

S. Longfei and P. Bodhi (Eds.): MobiQuitous 2022, LNICST 492, pp. 172–190, 2023.
https://doi.org/10.1007/978-3-031-34776-4_10

are then used for various tasks, such as counting daily steps, analyzing individual walking behavior and deriving additional health-related information [5], or to detect severe falling incidents [6]. Related work has also shown that the movement data can be used to recognize and distinguish different activities, such as walking, running, or cycling [7–9]. Even non-sports activities such as eating, drinking, or writing on a keyboard can be determined from these data [10, 11]. For walking, the data can even be used to distinguish and identify different users [12] by their gait. Kröger et al. give a detailed overview about potential inferences based on accelerometer data and show that besides activity and user recognition also personal information, such as the age or gender could be inferred [13]. However, cycling has not been considered yet. As a result, this raises the following research questions that we address in this paper:

- Which information about the cyclists can be derived from their movement data collected using their smartwatch and smartphone?
- Which information can be inferred about their bike (e.g., bike type, seat height, and gears)?
- Which information can be derived about the terrain?

To answer these questions, our contributions are as follows. First, we have built a data set consisting out of all combinations of the characteristics bike type, seat height, gear, and terrain. This data set is based on the sensor readings of one single person, resulting in a size of 1.1 gigabyte. Second, we conducted a user study with 17 participants (10 male, 7 female) between the ages of 19 and 64. In the study, they were equipped with a smartphone and a smartwatch and instructed to ride a predetermined bike road for two km. While the seat height could be adjusted depending on the participant, the type of bike remained the same for all participants. Inspired by existing studies on human gait recognition, we have processed the collected data and split it according to individual pedal rotations. The prepared data serves as basis for the training and testing of different machine learning models to explore whether characteristics about the participants, bikes, and/or terrain can be predicted and how unique cycling patterns are between participants. To this end, we have considered the following algorithms: Gaussian Naive Bayes (GNB), k-Nearest Neighbours (KNN), linear Support-Vector Classification (SVC), Decision Tree (DT), and Random Forest (RF). The results show that the best performances are obtained for the four characteristics bike type, gear, seat height, and terrain with accuracies of 93.05%, 92.23%, 95.76%, 94.24% respectively and distinguish participants with a probability of 99.01% all by utilizing the RF algorithm.

The remainder of this article is structured as follows. In Sect. 2, we discuss related studies that dealt with both activity and user recognition based on different activities and highlight our contributions. In Sect. 3, we are describing the methodology applied in our user study to collect our data. In Sect. 4, we describe the approach used for the analysis of the collected data, while we present our results in Sect. 5. In Sect. 6, we comment on the limitation of our study and future work, before making concluding remarks in Sect. 7.

2   Related Work

Related work can be split into the following two categories: (1) activity recognition and (2) user distinction.

In the field of activity recognition, both smartphones and smartwatches can be leveraged. Using smartphones and their accelerometers and gyroscopes, certain activities, such as walking, running, or cycling (e.g., [7–9,14–17]), can be recognized. Using smartwatches, additional activities such as eating, drinking, writing on a keyboard, and fitness activities can also be recognized (e.g., [10,11,18–20]).

Apart from activity recognition, movement data can also be used in order to identify users. Zou et al. show that using the collected accelerometer and gyroscope data from a smartphone in the field can be used to identify individual users based on their gait after training and evaluating the data with deep learning techniques [12]. The same applies for data that is collected by smartwatches. In a study performed by Andrew Johnston and Gary Weiss, the authors show that gait-based biometric identification is also possible with smartwatches [21]. Moreover, Häring et al. show that the pick up motion performed when picking up a smartphone from a desk could be used in order to support user authentication to the device, showing that the motion itself is highly depending on individual characteristics [22,23].

In contrast, we investigate to what extent it is possible to determine certain user characteristics based on data collected while cycling. Matkovic et al. show that is already possible to use the collected smartphone movement data in order to infer the respective bike type [24]. In a later study, they further include the detection of an e-scooter along with different bike types [25].

In comparison to the studies performed by Matkovic et al., we do not only explore bike type identification but also other characteristics, such as the gear, seat height, and the terrain, which to the best of our knowledge have not been investigated before. Moreover, we do not only rely on data collected by a smartphone like in other studies, but also consider data from smartwatches and investigate the usefulness of these data to identify the different characteristics. Last but not least, we also investigate whether it is possible to use the collected data to distinguish users based on their individual cycling patterns.

3   Data Collection

In this section, we describe the methodology used in our user study. We outline the devices used for data collection, where the devices are placed with our participants, how they are recruited, and the steps taken to comply with data protection.

3.1   Used Devices

Firstly, we have decided to use smartphone and smartwatch data to collect the movement data. Our decision is motivated by the fact that both devices are able to collect data at different positions on cyclists. While smartphones are often located in trousers' front/back pockets, a smartwatch is usually worn at the wrist. The smartwatch thus allows us to gather additional knowledge about users' movements and increases the probability to successfully infer additional characteristics about them and their context. The data collected by the smartwatch is transferred to the smartphone via a Bluetooth connection, where it is stored. We used a Google Pixel 4 and a Samsung Galaxy Watch (SM-R805F). Both configured to collect the considered sensor data 400 Hz 100 Hz, respectively. Pseudonyms were used to avoid the linking of the collected data to the participants.

3.2   Data Protection and Ethical Aspects

Before starting the study, we have distributed a consent form to the participants in order to inform them about both data collection and processing modalities following the *General Data Protection Regulation* (GDPR). Note that our study was submitted to the Data Protection Officer of our institution. A verification by the ethical board of our institution is however not mandatory in our field. Nevertheless, we have limited the efforts for the participants to the minimum. They have been informed that they could opt out at any time and that their data would be removed. On average, each participant took about 30 min to complete the study.

3.3   Recruitment

The participants were recruited within our social circle. Our recruitment strategy, however, does not impact our results due to absence of subjective questions in our study. The study took place between 14th of September 2021 and 14th of December 2021. Every participant executed the task once.

Table 1. Observed characteristics

Dimensions	Selected alternatives
Bike type	Road bike, Mountain bike, Gravel bike, E-bike
Gear	15th, 21st
Seat height	Low, Normal, High
Terrain	Dirt road, Bike road, Stone road, Asphalt road

3.4   Smartphone and Smartwatch Placement

In order to have the same conditions for all participants, the smartphone was located in the right front pocket of their trousers, upside down with the charging port at the top and the screen facing away from the body. Furthermore, the smartwatch was worn on their right wrist.

3.5   Scenario, Dimensions, and Parameter Variations

To answer our research questions, we aim at exploring whether the collected data can reveal information about five different dimensions: (1) the bike type, (2) seat height, (3) gear, (4) terrain, and (5) the participant. For the first four dimensions, we have selected different alternatives to define our ground truth as summarized in Table 1. For the bike type, this means a road bike, a mountain bike, a gravel bike, and an e-bike as displayed in Fig. 1. For all bikes, the seat height can be adjusted to low, normal, and high. We set the different seat heights by measuring the distance between the centre of the chain set and the top of the seat resulting in 60 cm for low, 85 cm for normal, and 95 cm for high. We further set the gears to the 15th or 21st gear for the different runs. We finally considered different terrains as depicted in Fig. 2: dirt road, bike road, stone road, and asphalt road. For analysis of the fifth dimension, i.e., possible differences between participants, all participants have ridden the same bike on the same road for two km, only the seat height has been adjusted depending on the participant. We have chosen these dimensions because we presume that they have a direct impact on the collected sensor data. Indeed, while bike type and seat height could affect the posture of the cyclist, gear could affect pedaling speed, and different terrains could create vibrations affecting the collected movement data.

(a) Road bike   (b) Mountain bike   (c) Gravel bike   (d) E-bike

Fig. 1. Bike types

4   Data Processing

In this section, we describe our approach to process the data collected according to the settings described in Sect. 3 in order to explore the different dimensions of interest.

(a) Dirt road   (b) Bike road   (c) Stone road   (d) Asphalt road

Fig. 2. Terrains

4.1 Preprocessing

We have first applied the following preprocessing step. Due to the high sampling rate 400 Hz, different readings share the same timestamp. We have hence first distributed all timestamps evenly across all recordings following this function:

Let the set $\{T_1, T_2, T_3, \ldots, T_n\}$ be the unrepaired timestamps. Then

$$T_{new}(x) = T_1 + x\frac{T_n - T_1}{n}$$

for $x = 1, 2, \ldots, n$ and where T_x is the xth recorded timestamp. $x \in \mathbb{N}$

4.2 Identification of Pedal Rotations

Like in gait recognition (see Sect. 2), we aim at first identifying repetitive patterns. While such patterns are defined by two consecutive steps in the case of gait recognition, we consider a single pedal rotation as a representation for the periodic repetitions during pedaling. In order to detect such a pedal rotation, we use the gyroscope data to identify the circular movement of the legs and therefore the identification of one complete pedal rotation.

In a first attempt to detect the bounds symbolizing the start and the end of a single pedal rotation, three options shown in Fig. 3 were possible: searching for (1) local maxima (see Fig. 3a), (2) minima (see Fig. 3b), or (3) turning points around the zero value whenever the value turns from negative to positive (see Fig. 3c). Among these options, we have selected the zero point approach, shown in Fig. 3c, because it turned out to be the most reliable approach to detect the bounds of a single pedal rotation.

One of the main problems that occurred in the process of identifying a pedal rotation was (1) that a non-pedal rotation is sometimes identified as a real pedal rotation (type I error; false positive) and on the other hand (2) some pedal rotations were not identified at all (type II error; false negative). When examining our participants' data, we notice that for some participants the turning point approach did not work as expected because the X-values oscillated above 0, leading to false positives. To make our approach more reliable in correctly identifying pedal rotations, we have further considered the Z values of the gyroscope data, which have a similar pattern as the X values. By doing so, the identification of false pedal rotations due to the oscillation of the X values around zero can be avoided. The principle behind this idea is that a new bound of a pedal rotation is only detected if both X and Z values are positive, if at least one negative value between X and Z was detected in the previous timestamp. The rotation is considered as complete when at least one timestamp exists where both X and Y values are negative.

Following this adjusted approach, we have eliminated all false positive pedal rotations and obtained fewer false negative detected pedal rotations leading to approximately 250 to 400 detected pedal rotations in rounds of 4 min cycling sessions. Even though we still have a few false negative pedal rotations this scenario is highly preferred as false positive pedal rotations might have a bad impact on the later classification of the characteristics.

4.3   Feature Extraction

After the successful identification of the individual pedal rotations, we now focus on feature extraction. Since all pedal rotations can differ in both length and number of sensor readings, we need to find an approach that makes all pedal rotations comparable. To solve this issue, we bin the sensor readings in a pedal rotation by separating the readings in fixed intervals. In more details, we use the start and end timestamps of a detected pedal rotation and calculate the respective timestamp for every sensor reading in the pedal rotation that matches our fixed interval following this function, where T_s is the first timestamp of a pedal rotation and T_e is the last timestamp of a pedal rotation:

$$T_x = T_s + x * \frac{T_e - T_s}{i - 1}$$

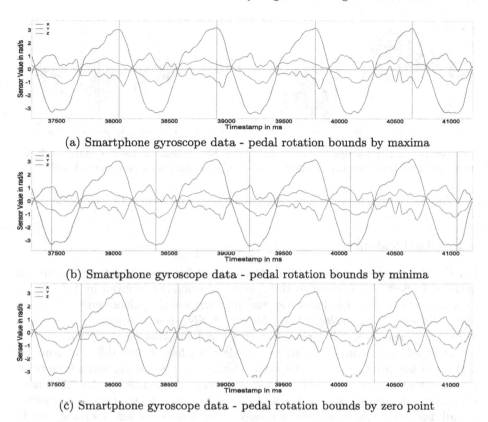

(a) Smartphone gyroscope data - pedal rotation bounds by maxima

(b) Smartphone gyroscope data - pedal rotation bounds by minima

(c) Smartphone gyroscope data - pedal rotation bounds by zero point

Fig. 3. Pedal rotation bounds detection methods

We next determine the sensor value for each calculated timestamp. If a sensor reading exists for this timestamp, we obviously use its value as the new value for our bin. Otherwise, we apply the following linear interpolation with T_a the timestamp before, T_b the timestamp after, V_a as the value at T_a and V_b as the value at T_b:

$$V_x = V_a + (V_b - V_a) * \frac{x - T_a}{T_a - T_b}$$

Figure 4 illustrates how such a binning process looks like for different intervals of 20 bins (see Fig. 4a) and 50 bins (see Fig. 4b). We hence follow this approach in order to normalise the values for each individual pedal rotation with varying lengths and number of readings.

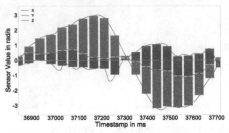
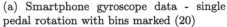
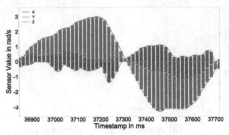

(a) Smartphone gyroscope data - single pedal rotation with bins marked (20)

(b) Smartphone gyroscope data - single pedal rotation with bins marked (50)

Fig. 4. Smartphone gyroscope data - single pedal rotation with bins marked

4.4   Classification

For the classification of the pedal rotations identified according to our approach detailed in Sect. 4 according to the specific characteristics given in Table 1, we explore and compare the following five machine learning algorithms: *Gaussian Naive Bayes* (GNB), *k-Nearest Neighbours* (KNN), *linear Support-Vector Classification* (linear SVC), *Decision Tree* (DT) and *Random Forest* (RF).

To avoid under- or overfitting our models, we have tested different configurations of our features. Since the binned sensor values are our most important features, we have investigated how the performance of the machine learning models changes depending on the size of our bins. In Fig. 5, we see that performance for all machine learning models increases as the number of bins increases, up to 25 bins. Just for the classification of the terrain and only for KNN we observe a dramatic decrease in the rate of correct classification, while the number of bins increases. Moreover, we notice that for the linear SVC performance degradation occurs once the number of bins exceeds 40. Based on these results, we have decided to select a number of 40 bins for further analysis.

Except for GNB, all other algorithms have hyper parameters that need to be tuned in order to reach the best performance. We have therefore run grid tests with cross-validation and obtained the following set of hyper parameters:

- KNN: number of neighbours = 6
- linear SVC: regularisation parameter = 1
- RF: maximum depth = 16; number of trees = 20
- DT: maximum depth = 5

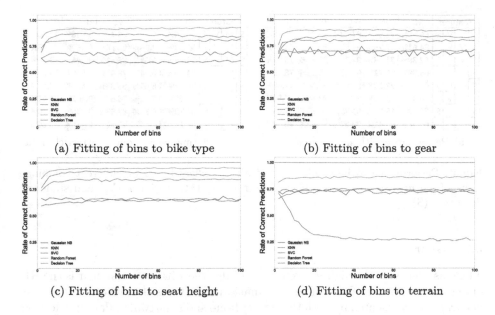

(a) Fitting of bins to bike type

(b) Fitting of bins to gear

(c) Fitting of bins to seat height

(d) Fitting of bins to terrain

Fig. 5. Fitting of bins to characteristics

Since the grid search for the optimal hyper parameters is quite computationally expensive, we do not exclude that additional fitting of these hyper parameters can lead to even more accurate models and thus to a classification with even a higher accuracy.

5 Results

To explore the best combination of features, we have run through all possibilities with smartphone and/or smartwatch data available. This means 24 possible combinations of the features minima/maxima, variance, and standard deviation. We discuss the corresponding results in what follows.

5.1 Bike Type

For the detection of the correct bike type, we find that the best classification can be made when considering the RF classifier, closely followed by linear SVC as shown in Fig. 6. A more detailed insight shows that the overall best performance can be achieved with the combination of all features maxima/minima, variance, and standard deviation. In this case, we achieve an accuracy of 93.05%, shown in Fig. 6a. In comparison, with the smartphone data only, the highest accuracy is equal to 91.48%, as depicted in Fig. 6b. Moreover, we observe that the road bike and the e-bike both with a precision of to 94% are the best classified types, while the gravel bike is worst with 90%. The mountain bike and the road bike are the two most likely bike types to be confused as shown in Fig. 7. Reasons for the F1-Score being higher than the accuracy is most probably due to the imbalanced nature of our dataset.

Features				GNB	KNN	SVC	RF	DT
S	M	V	S	66.99%	73.97%	91.47%	93.05%	75.28%
S	M	V	-	64.61%	72.26%	92.53%	92.93%	76.44%
S	M	-	S	62.88%	71.78%	92.26%	92.62%	75.62%
S	M	-	-	65.99%	69.22%	91.25%	92.11%	78.15%
S	-	V	S	66.47%	72.20%	89.64%	92.50%	77.05%
S	-	V	-	64.37%	73.33%	91.28%	92.59%	77.54%
S	-	-	S	66.47%	65.04%	91.77%	92.62%	77.08%
S	-	-	-	65.50%	65.41%	89.61%	90.52%	76.68%

(a) Performance with smartwatch data

Features				GNB	KNN	SVC	RF	DT
S	M	V	S	56.70%	88.14%	83.41%	90.36%	70.86%
S	M	V	-	55.43%	87.36%	84.66%	89.63%	71.68%
S	M	-	S	54.73%	86.48%	85.51%	91.48%	73.65%
S	M	-	-	54.40%	86.14%	78.47%	89.75%	73.23%
S	-	V	S	55.22%	86.66%	83.32%	89.96%	72.41%
S	-	V	-	57.06%	87.11%	78.53%	90.05%	74.41%
S	-	-	S	54.79%	84.32%	87.33%	89.36%	72.20%
S	-	-	-	54.12%	84.87%	75.50%	88.36%	70.86%

(b) Performance without smartwatch data

Fig. 6. Performance to infer bike type of all classifiers based on different combinations of features sensor data (S), maxima/minima (M), variance (V), and standard deviation (S)

5.2 Gear

The classifier with the highest accuracy to infer the 15th and 21st gear is the RF classifier, as shown in Fig. 8. The combination of features that results in the best accuracy is represented by both the smartphone and smartwatch data in addition with the maxima/minima and variance giving an accuracy of 92.23%, shown in Fig. 8a. In comparison with the smartphone data only, we only achieve an accuracy of 90.60%, depicted in Fig. 8b. In both cases the other observed classifiers are not able to achieve accuracies that are higher than 90%. Moreover, we observe that the precision and the recall are higher for the 15th gear, meaning that the RF classifier is slightly skewed towards predicting this gear as shown in Fig. 9.

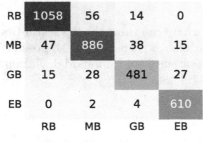

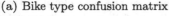

(a) Bike type confusion matrix

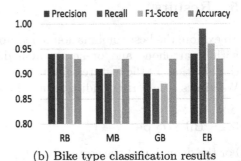

(b) Bike type classification results

Fig. 7. Confusion matrix and classification report for the bike types of road bike (RB), mountain bike (MB), gravel bike (GB), and e-bike (EB)

Features				GNB	KNN	SVC	RF	DT
S	M	V	S	61.41%	78.76%	82.69%	91.65%	83.05%
S	M	V	-	61.44%	78.48%	66.60%	92.23%	82.96%
S	M	-	S	62.33%	72.60%	83.42%	91.59%	83.79%
S	M	-	-	62.91%	73.03%	83.97%	90.46%	81.99%
S	-	V	S	62.42%	78.36%	59.92%	91.44%	82.05%
S	-	V	-	63.88%	78.67%	80.92%	91.34%	83.42%
S	-	-	S	62.33%	71.87%	83.75%	91.31%	83.66%
S	-	-	-	62.97%	72.23%	80.89%	90.12%	80.80%

Features				GNB	KNN	SVC	RF	DT
S	M	V	S	77.26%	86.66%	83.78%	89.78%	84.23%
S	M	V	-	75.59%	86.96%	79.14%	89.69%	82.23%
S	M	-	S	75.44%	84.87%	81.23%	90.60%	83.38%
S	M	-	-	74.59%	86.39%	82.08%	89.51%	80.87%
S	-	V	S	76.11%	85.60%	88.87%	89.66%	82.72%
S	-	V	-	74.62%	85.08%	82.02%	90.02%	82.87%
S	-	-	S	75.74%	83.78%	85.08%	90.48%	83.14%
S	-	-	-	73.32%	84.41%	65.16%	88.14%	80.56%

(a) Performance with smartwatch data   (b) Performance without smartwatch data

Fig. 8. Performance to infer gear of all classifiers based on different combinations of features sensor data (S), maxima/minima (M), variance (V), and standard deviation (S)

5.3 Seat Height

When observing the performance of all classifiers to infer the seat height, we see that the best results are achieved by the RF classifier, closely followed by linear SVC as shown in Fig. 10. We achieve a classification performance of 95.76% for the seat height by using the RF classifier with the feature combination of both smartphone and smartwatch data, maxima/minima, and standard deviation, as shown in Fig. 10a. By excluding the smartwatch data we notice that the classification results are still high and for some classifiers such as KNN and DT even higher than using smartphone and smartwatch data in combination, depicted in Fig. 10b. This shows, that the smartphone data are sufficient to classify the seat height, while the smartwatch data in some cases even reduced the classification performance. Moreover, we observe that normal and high seat settings sometimes are confused with each other, while low and high almost never get confused as shown in Fig. 11.

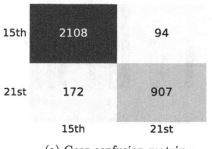

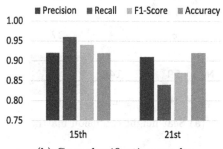

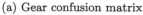

(a) Gear confusion matrix   (b) Gear classification results

Fig. 9. Confusion matrix and classification results for the gears of 15 and 21

Features				GNB	KNN	SVC	RF	DT
S	M	V	S	72.75%	70.86%	93.20%	95.03%	82.78%
S	M	V	-	70.77%	69.86%	92.38%	94.85%	83.42%
S	M	-	S	71.65%	67.02%	90.03%	95.76%	83.72%
S	M	-	-	72.63%	68.61%	92.47%	94.67%	83.69%
S	-	V	S	71.35%	70.89%	91.95%	94.57%	82.69%
S	-	V	-	72.48%	71.17%	93.45%	94.64%	82.41%
S	-	-	S	70.98%	65.53%	92.81%	95.00%	82.57%
S	-	-	-	72.75%	64.40%	93.17%	94.67%	81.93%

(a) Performance with smartwatch data

Features				GNB	KNN	SVC	RF	DT
S	M	V	S	69.13%	94.85%	91.78%	94.24%	82.38%
S	M	V	-	69.07%	94.24%	93.03%	95.21%	82.72%
S	M	-	S	69.41%	94.06%	94.33%	95.51%	83.51%
S	M	-	-	69.41%	94.03%	92.87%	95.15%	84.08%
S	-	V	S	69.44%	94.51%	94.00%	94.97%	82.87%
S	-	V	-	70.41%	94.00%	94.12%	95.33%	82.20%
S	-	-	S	68.28%	94.15%	93.30%	94.88%	82.38%
S	-	-	-	70.32%	94.39%	93.97%	94.51%	81.99%

(b) Performance without smartwatch data

Fig. 10. Performance to infer seat height of all classifiers based on different combinations of features sensor data (S), maxima/minima (M), variance (V), and standard deviation (S)

5.4   Terrain

For terrain detection, the RF classifier performed best, followed closely by the linear SVC, as shown in Fig. 12. To achieve the highest accuracy of 94.24%, a combination of all features: smartphone and smartwatch in addition with minima/maxima, variance, and standard deviation is needed, as depicted in Fig. 12a. By exploring the performances of all classifiers without the smartwatch data in Fig. 12b, we see that the accuracies dropped more significantly in contrast to the other dimensions such as the bike type, gear, and seat height when excluding the smartwatch data. This confirms that different terrains especially affect the steering behavior as well as the shaking of the handle bars. As expected, we also observe that bike road and asphalt terrains can get confused for each other as shown in Fig. 13.

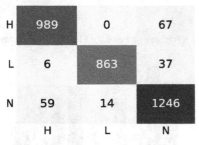

(a) Seat height confusion matrix

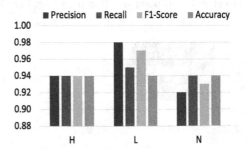

(b) Seat height classification results

Fig. 11. Confusion matrix and classification results for the seat heights of high (H), low (L), and normal (N)

Features				GNB	KNN	SVC	RF	DT
S	M	V	S	78.36%	88.05%	91.95%	94.24%	91.80%
S	M	V	-	78.27%	87.32%	89.91%	93.78%	90.98%
S	M	-	S	77.63%	49.80%	82.11%	93.90%	90.73%
S	M	-	-	78.67%	48.13%	84.36%	92.08%	87.56%
S	-	V	S	78.94%	88.08%	90.49%	93.75%	91.28%
S	-	V	-	78.21%	86.96%	85.71%	92.81%	90.61%
S	-	-	S	78.63%	38.86%	85.89%	92.81%	90.83%
S	-	-	-	76.96%	36.21%	70.13%	86.96%	72.42%

(a) Performance with smartwatch data

Features				GNB	KNN	SVC	RF	DT
S	M	V	S	46.51%	74.20%	81.96%	89.48%	80.99%
S	M	V	-	47.45%	74.80%	76.02%	88.48%	80.90%
S	M	-	S	48.48%	73.32%	81.78%	89.36%	81.20%
S	M	-	-	45.45%	72.47%	71.10%	85.81%	77.35%
S	-	V	S	44.09%	70.71%	80.23%	88.36%	80.29%
S	-	V	-	46.36%	71.98%	74.95%	86.11%	81.08%
S	-	-	S	45.09%	69.92%	54.67%	86.60%	81.20%
S	-	-	-	43.69%	68.37%	70.92%	81.84%	70.77%

(b) Performance without smartwatch data

Fig. 12. Performance to infer terrain of all classifiers based on different combinations of features sensor data (S), maxima/minima (M), variance (V), and standard deviation (S)

5.5 User Distinction

The classifier that worked out best to distinguish the participants of our user study is the RF classifier, closely followed by the linear SVC and GNB, as shown in Fig. 14. The highest accuracy of 99.01% resulted in a combination of the features smartphone and smartwatch data in addition with variance and standard deviation, depicted in Fig. 14a. When comparing those results with the performances that are achieved without the smartwatch data, shown in Fig. 14b, we see that the exclusion of the smartwatch data positively affected the KNN and linear SVC classifiers while it only slightly reduced the performance of the RF classifier. Therefore, we want to state that the smartwatch data does not drastically affect the performance to distinguish our participants and that the smartphone data alone is sufficient to distinguish our participants. The confusion matrix and the classification report respectively depicted in Fig. 15a and Fig. 15b show that there are no big confusions between the different participants.

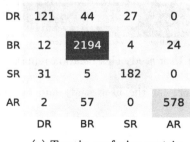

(a) Terrain confusion matrix

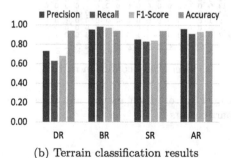

(b) Terrain classification results

Fig. 13. Confusion matrix and classification results for the terrains of dirt road (DR), bike road (BR), stone road (SR), and asphalt road (AR)

Features				GNB	KNN	SVC	RF	DT
S	M	V	S	96.31%	82.84%	95.32%	97.21%	79.15%
S	M	V	-	96.22%	79.80%	96.22%	98.11%	74.22%
S	M	-	S	96.06%	81.77%	96.63%	98.44%	80.13%
S	M	-	-	97.13%	81.61%	97.04%	98.60%	73.15%
S	-	V	S	95.40%	80.79%	95.48%	99.01%	64.86%
S	-	V	-	95.16%	81.61%	96.14%	98.60%	75.21%
S	-	-	S	96.72%	78.57%	95.73%	98.03%	66.34%
S	-	-	-	95.89%	80.62%	95.48%	98.52%	71.43%

(a) Performance with smartwatch data

Features				GNB	KNN	SVC	RF	DT
S	M	V	S	92.35%	97.31%	98.21%	98.05%	69.49%
S	M	V	-	92.03%	97.48%	98.05%	97.72%	66.48%
S	M	-	S	91.38%	98.54%	98.86%	98.05%	73.80%
S	M	-	-	91.46%	98.05%	98.05%	98.05%	70.06%
S	-	V	S	91.94%	98.37%	98.05%	98.37%	64.77%
S	-	V	-	90.40%	98.13%	98.45%	97.97%	69.73%
S	-	-	S	91.46%	97.48%	98.13%	97.64%	67.78%
S	-	-	-	91.29%	97.07%	98.45%	98.37%	73.80%

(b) Performance without smartwatch data

Fig. 14. Performance of all classifiers based on different combinations of features sensor data (S), maxima/minima (M), variance (V), and standard deviation (S)

In summary, we have shown that it is possible to infer characteristics such as the bike type, seat height, gear, and terrain when cycling by utilizing machine learning classifiers like RF and linear SVC. Besides the inference of those characteristics, we further show that our participants can be distinguished from each other by taking advantage of the data collected about our participants and training a RF classifier.

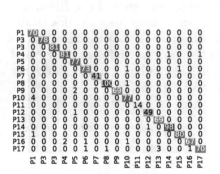

(a) User study confusion matrix

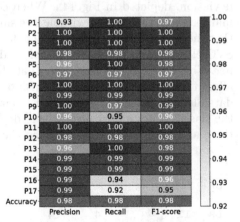

(b) User study classification report

Fig. 15. Confusion matrix and classification report for the user study and our 17 participants

6   Limitations and Outlook

Although we are able to correctly identify the characteristics discussed and also show that we are able to identify our participants based on the collected movement data, our results are based on a limited number of participants. As the number of people increases, the accuracy in identifying individual users might decrease. Moreover, our sample is not representative of the population. As a result, it would be interesting in the future to explore the feasibility to infer information, such as the age or the gender based on the unique cycling movements.

Moreover, it would be interesting to investigate the impact of the placement of the smartphone from the front pocket of the trouser to the back pocket, or other usual locations, such as a backpack [26].

In our study, we have also only explored different terrains without major decline or incline, which could be another interesting feature to observe in future studies.

Furthermore, we would like to note that we have not considered other factors, such as the weather or the way participants change directions with their bikes, which could be other interesting aspects for future studies.

While we have focused on showing the feasibility of inferring different types of information about our participants, their bike, and the terrain from movement data in this paper, we have left open, which solutions could be applied to prevent such inferences, while still allowing the underlying fitness applications to function.

An interesting direction to follow is how to communicate the resulting risks to their privacy and make transparent which data are collected. Works in this direction exist for smartwatches [2,27] or fitness trackers in general [28,29], but they are dedicated to other contexts and do not cover specifically our biking scenario. Similarly, the impact of applied privacy-preserving solutions on their data could be communicated to the cyclists like it is the case for the application of differential privacy on health data [30–32]

7 Conclusion

In this study, we have explored the potential of the movement data, generated by a smartphone and a smartwatch, to classify user as well as environmental characteristics when riding a bike. The four characteristics we observe are the bike type, gear, seat height, and terrain. Additionally, we examine on the potential to distinguish/identify users from each other solely on their unique cycling behavior. To this end, we first created a dataset based on movement data collected from a single person, representing all different combinations of the characteristics. Then, we conducted a user study with 17 participants who were equipped with a smartphone and a smartwatch and collected data while cycling for two km on the same road for all participants.

The results show that the RF classifier performed best among all classifiers that we have explored. Moreover, we were able to show that the smartwatch data can increase the performance accuracy for most characteristics. Especially for the detection of the terrain the smartwatch data increased the accuracy compared to the smartphone data alone. Our results show that we achieve prediction accuracies for our four characteristics bike type, gear, seat height, and terrain of 93.05%, 92.23%, 95.76%, 94.24% respectively. Also in the user study we were able to recognize a person from a crowd of 17 participants with a probability of 99.01%.

Overall, our results shed light on the performance of sensor readings collected by devices we use every day to predict user-specific and environmental characteristics. As a result, applications making use of these data can create fine-grained user profiles that users are often not aware of. We therefore recommend to design new user-friendly solutions, increase the transparency of the collected data, and allow users to make informed decisions about their privacy.

References

1. Richter, A., Kühtreiber, P., Reinhardt, D.: On the Impact of Information provided to Employees on their Intention to disclose Data collected by Smart Watches to their Employers. Association for Information Systems (AIS) (2022)
2. Richter, A., Kühtreiber, P., Reinhardt, D.: Enhanced privacy in smart workplaces: employees' preferences for transparency indicators and control interactions in the case of data collection with smart watches. In: Proceedings of the 37th International Conference on Information Security and Privacy Protection (IFIP SEC) (2022)
3. Hernández Acosta, L., Reinhardt, D.: A survey on privacy issues and solutions for voice-controlled digital assistants. Pervasive Mob. Comput. (PMC) **80**, 101523 (2021)
4. Siepmann, C., Kowalczuk, P.: Understanding continued smartwatch usage: the role of emotional as well as health and fitness factors. Electr. Markets (EM) **31**(4), 795–809 (2021)
5. Apple: Measuring Walking Quality Through iPhone Mobility Metrics (2021). https://www.apple.com/in/healthcare/docs/site/Measuring_Walking_Quality_Through_iPhone_Mobility_Metrics.pdf. Accessed 05 July 2022
6. Leiding, B., Bochem, A., Hernández Acosta, L.: Automated sensor-fusion based emergency rescue for remote and extreme sport activities. In: Proceedings of the 15th IEEE International Wireless Communications and Mobile Computing Conference (IWCMC) (2019)
7. Anjum, A., Ilyas, M.U.: Activity recognition using smartphone sensors. In: Proceedings of the 10th IEEE Consumer Communications and Networking Conference (CCNC) (2013)
8. Voicu, R.A., Dobre, C., Bajenaru, L., Ciobanu, R.I.: Human physical activity recognition using smartphone sensors. Sensors **19**(3), 458 (2019)
9. Kwapisz, J.R., Weiss, G.M., Moore, S.A.: Activity recognition using cell phone accelerometers. ACM SIGKDD Explor. Newsl. **12**(2), 74–82 (2011)
10. Weiss, G.M., Timko, J.L., Gallagher, C.M., Yoneda, K., Schreiber, A.J.: Smartwatch-based activity recognition: a machine learning approach. In: Proceedings of the 13th IEEE-EMBS International Conference on Biomedical and Health Informatics (BHI)
11. Balli, S., Sağbaş, E.A., Peker, M.: Human activity recognition from smart watch sensor data using a hybrid of principal component analysis and random forest algorithm. Meas. Control **52**(1–2), 37–45 (2019)
12. Zou, Q., Wang, Y., Wang, Q., Zhao, Y., Li, Q.: Deep learning-based gait recognition using smartphones in the wild. IEEE Trans. Inf. Forensics Secur. **15**, 3197–3212 (2020)

13. Kröger, J.L., Raschke, P., Bhuiyan, T.R.: Privacy implications of accelerometer data: a review of possible inferences. In: Proceedings of the 3rd International Conference on Cryptography, Security and Privacy, pp. 81–87 (2019)
14. Straczkiewicz, M., James, P., Onnela, J.P.: A systematic review of smartphone-based human activity recognition methods for health research. NPJ Digit. Med. **4**, 148 (2021)
15. Ramanujam, E., Perumal, T., Padmavathi, S.: Human activity recognition with smartphone and wearable sensors using deep learning techniques: a review. IEEE Sens. J. **21**(12), 13029–13040 (2021)
16. Mekruksavanich, S., Jitpattanakul, A.: LSTM networks using smartphone data for sensor-based human activity recognition in smart homes. Sensors **21**(5), 1636 (2021)
17. Sena, J., Barreto, J., Caetano, C., Cramer, G., Schwartz, W.R.: Human activity recognition based on smartphone and wearable sensors using multiscale DCNN ensemble. Neurocomputing **444**, 226–243 (2021)
18. Zimbelman, E.G., Keefe, R.F.: Development and validation of smartwatch-based activity recognition models for rigging crew workers on cable logging operations. PLoS ONE **16**(5), e0250624 (2021)
19. Mallol-Ragolta, A., Semertzidou, A., Pateraki, M., Schuller, B.: harAGE: a novel multimodal smartwatch-based dataset for human activity recognition. In: Proceedings of the 16th IEEE International Conference on Automatic Face and Gesture Recognition (FG) (2021)
20. Fatima, S.: Activity recognition in older adults with training data from younger adults: preliminary results on in vivo smartwatch sensor data. In: Proceedings of the 23rd International ACM SIGACCESS Conference on Computers and Accessibility (2021)
21. Johnston, A.H., Weiss, G.M.: Smartwatch-based biometric gait recognition. In: Proceedings of the 7th IEEE International Conference on Biometrics Theory, Applications and Systems (BTAS) (2015)
22. Lee, W.H., Liu, X., Shen, Y., Jin, H., Lee, R.B.: Secure pick up: implicit authentication when you start using the smartphone. In: Proceedings of the 22ND ACM on Symposium on Access Control Models and Technologies (2017)
23. Haring, M., Reinhardt, D., Omlor, Y.: Pick me up and i will tell you who you are: analyzing pick-up motions to authenticate users. In: Proceedings of the 16th IEEE International Conference on Pervasive Computing and Communications Workshops (PerCom Workshops) (2018)
24. Matkovic, V., Waltereit, M., Zdankin, P., Uphoff, M., Weis, T.: Bike type identification using smartphone sensors. In: Proceedings of the 19th ACM International Joint Conference on Pervasive and Ubiquitous Computing and Proceedings of the 2019 ACM International Symposium on Wearable Computers (2019)
25. Matkovic, V., Waltereit, M., Zdankin, P., Weis, T.: Towards bike type and e-scooter classification with smartphone sensors. In: Proceedings of the 17th EAI International Conference on Mobile and Ubiquitous Systems: Computing, Networking and Services (MobiQuitous) (2020)
26. Aboo, A.K.: Survey on human activity recognition using smartphone. AL-Rafidain J. Comput. Sci. Math. **15** (2021)
27. Shaw, P., Mikusz, M., Davies, N., Clinch, S.: Using smartwatches for privacy awareness in pervasive environments. In: Proceedings of the 18th International Workshop on Mobile Computing Systems and Applications (HotMobile) (2017)

28. Murmann, P., Beckerle, M., Fischer-Hübner, S., Reinhardt, D.: Reconciling the what, when and how of privacy notifications in fitness tracking scenarios. Pervasive Mob. Comput. **77**, 101480 (2021)
29. Velykoivanenko, L., Niksirat, K.S., Zufferey, N., Humbert, M., Huguenin, K., Cherubini, M.: Are those steps worth your privacy? fitness-tracker users' perceptions of privacy and utility. Proc. ACM Interact. Mob. Wearable Ubiquit. Technol. **5**(4), 1–41 (2021)
30. Murmann, P., Reinhardt, D., Fischer-Hübner, S.: To be, or not to be notified. In: Proceedings of the 34th IFIP International Conference on ICT Systems Security and Privacy Protection (2019)
31. Kühtreiber, P., Pak, V., Reinhardt, D.: Replication: the effect of differential privacy communication on german users' comprehension and data sharing attitudes. In: Proceedings of the 18th Symposium on Usable Privacy and Security (SOUPS) (2022)
32. Saifuzzaman, M., Ananna, T.N., Chowdhury, M.J.M., Ferdous, M.S., Chowdhury, F.: A systematic literature review on wearable health data publishing under differential privacy. Int. J. Inf. Secur. **21**(4), 847–872 (2022)

Feature Encoding by Location-Enhanced Word2Vec Embedding for Human Activity Recognition in Smart Homes

Junhao Zhao[1], Basem Suleiman[1,2]([✉]) [iD], and Muhammad Johan Alibasa[3] [iD]

[1] School of Computer Science, University of Sydney, Sydney, Australia
jzha5185@uni.sydney.edu.au, basem.suleiman@sydney.edu.au
[2] School of Computer Science and Engineering, University of New South Wales, Sydney, Australia
[3] School of Computing, Telkom University, Bandung, Indonesia
alibasa@telkomuniversity.ac.id

Abstract. Human Activity Recognition (HAR) in Smart Homes (SH) is the basis of providing automatic and comfortable living experience for occupants, especially for the elderly. Vision-based approaches could violate occupants' privacy and wearable sensors based approaches could be intrusive with their daily activities. In this study, we proposed an NLP-based feature encoding for HAR in smart homes by using the Word2Vec word embedding model and incorporating location information of occupants. We used the NLP approach to generate semantic and automatic features directly from the raw data that significantly reduced the workload of feature encoding. The results showed that both Word2Vec embedding and location-enhanced sequences can significantly improve the classification performance. Our best model which used both Word2Vec embedding and location-enhanced sequences achieved an accuracy of 81% and a weighted average F1 score of 77% on the test data with Sensor Event Windows (SEW) size of 25. This size is considered as a small SEW size which can be applied better to real-time classification due to the short latency.

Keywords: Human Activity Recognition · Smart Home · IoT · NLP · Feature Encoding

1 Introduction

With the development of the economy, the progress of medical care and the improvement of people's living standards, people's life expectancy is also getting longer than before. The World Health Organisation (WHO) reported that the elderly population (aged over 60) in the world is about to reach 2 billion by 2050 [19]. Although the smart home technology [16] is particularly attractive to young people, in recent years, an important application area of smart home is

S. Longfei and P. Bodhi (Eds.): MobiQuitous 2022, LNICST 492, pp. 191–202, 2023.
https://doi.org/10.1007/978-3-031-34776-4_11

to provide convenience for the life of the elderly such as health monitoring or ambient assisted living (AAL) [13]. The basis of such applications is so-called "Human Activity Recognition" (HAR) which requires smart home environments having the ability to represent context and characteristics of human activity.

There are two main categories of the system for HAR: vision-based and sensor-based. The sensor-based approach can further be divided into wearable sensors and ambient sensors. Vision-based systems use cameras to recognise human activity and environmental changes. However, there is generally some controversy surrounding this approach over privacy issues, especially "home" is considered a private place [3,11] Sensor-based systems solve this problem to some extent, because sensor data does not directly expose a person's life behaviour. Wearable HAR systems require users to wear smart devices like smart bands/watches with inertial measurement units to capture signals that are generated from different axes. Nevertheless, the use of body-worn devices may be uncomfortable and interfering with daily behaviour [2].

The ultimate goal of the HAR research field is to continuously improve recognition performance to the peak. Several studies [2,8,11] used different methods to incorporate features about occupants' location. By comparison, it can be concluded that after adding location information, the performance of the HAR recognition algorithm can be improved. Bouchabou et al. [4] was the first one to use word embedding for HAR. Due to the limitation of the dataset they used, it is impossible to capture the location features.

In summary, the contributions of this paper are:

1. improving activity recognition performance by using word embedding model with [13] as the baseline;
2. using NLP methods to further enhance the classification performance by introducing location information of user activities as inspired from the past studies [6,16,18];
3. using the combination of word embedding model and location-enhanced event generation method to achieve a model which uses SEW (sensor event window) size of 25 (a small SEW size);
4. processing the raw data directly to save effort on pre-processing data and feature selection compared to traditional methods.

In this study, we use the dataset that is obtained from ambient PIR motion sensors, door/temperature sensors and light switch sensors that are installed in a smart home environment. Such smart home environment architecture will make occupants feel "seamless" and unobtrusive. Compared with vision-based method, sensor-based methods do not enable monitoring of the actual activities of occupants, and these activities are out of the defined scope.

2   Related Works

To recognise human Activities of Daily Living (ADLs), traditional machine learning algorithms are used in the past studies. Avgoustinos et al. [2] compared the activity recognition performance among KNN, RF, LR and SVM. They used wrist-worn smart devices to capture 3-axis accelerometer data when participants perform different activities and further used BLE beacons to track participants' location. Their experiments showed that SVM outperformed other classifiers and was the most bootstrapped classifier by using beacon data. However, data collected from accelerometers were only applied to recognise ambulatory movements like running, walking, and failing. Diane J. Cook and Parisa Rashidi [6] experimented with SVM, HMM, CRF and NB on 3 different CASAS datasets and the SVM had the best performance across the 3 datasets (91.52% average accuracy across 3 datasets.). They further proposed the Activity Discovery (AD) algorithm to discover patterns of different activities which can assist Activity Recognition (AR) algorithms achieve better performance because the activity labels are not always annotated correctly in the raw dataset.

The traditional HAR always employs handcrafted feature extraction methods that require lots of pre-processing steps (feature selection, validation, etc.) and domain expert knowledge while deep learning methods can enable automatic feature extraction which is much more efficient. Munkhjargal Gochoo et al. [7] processed the raw data directly and generated an "Activity Image" for each sequence of sensor events and used 2D Convolutional Neural Networks (CNNs) for HAR whose best model achieved 0.951 F1 score for the eight activities. As an extension, Gochoo et al. [17] proposed a RGB activity image conversion method which achieved 95.2% accuracy on the sensor-based dataset. Their method mapped sensor events to the corresponding coordinates on the activity image as a pixel whose colour is dependent on the time of the event and the first two lines of the activity image refer to the two previous activities.

Enabling the NLP idea for HAR is a novel attempt in this area. Bouchabou et al. [4] used frequency-based encoding to encode sequences of events for automatic feature extraction and further used embedding layers in the Fully Convolutional Network (FCN) and LSTM model for gaining context knowledge. They used the Aruba dataset and treated each sensor event as a word so that it formed a "sentence" in each sliding window. Their experiments illustrated that gaining context knowledge can improve model performance and LSTM outperformed FCN. For further improvement, we can use embedding algorithms like Word2Vec for word embedding and sequence encoding because word embedding methods take into account the context of words in each sequence of events. In addition, as we discussed before, there are some studies that tried to bootstrap HAR algorithms by incorporating location information. Therefore, we can incorporate location "word" in each sequence of events for further improvement.

3   Proposed Methods

The problem is a classification task which classifies human activity in a smart home environment. There are k sensors $S = s_1, s_2, ..., s_k$ in the dataset that generate events $e_i \in E$. An event records the date, time, sensor id, room location, more detailed location, sensor value, sensor type and activity label when the sensor is activated. In this study, we focus on the sensor id, room location and sensor value so for each event we have $e_i = (s_i, L_i, v_i)$ where s_i is the sensor id,

L_i is the sensor location and v_i is sensor value. We use Sensor Event Windows (SEW) to segment the time series data so that each sequence of events will have a fixed length which equals the SEW size. Each sequence of events $Seq_i = (e_i, ..., e_k)$ is associated with one activity instance $a_i \in A$. The two timestamp indicators date and time are not taken into account because we consider that different occupants may have different habits for the same activity and the same activity may happen at any time during the day.

3.1   Data Pre-processing

In the raw dataset, each row represents one event. SEW segments the data into intervals with the same number of sensor events. Quigley et al. [14] illustrates that SEW is the second best sliding window approach and it can classify more activities than the Time Window which segments the data into intervals with the same time duration. The reason for using SEW is that we would like to use CNN which requires a fixed input size. By contrast, TW can generate different lengths for windows that have different counts of events.

NLP has many similarities with processing sequences of sensor events. Sensor events can be processed as the "words" and sequences of events can be processed as the "sentence" in natural language. Each "sentence" describes the features for each activity label. In addition, events in each sequence also have the contextualised relationship which also shows the parallel between NLP and sensor events processing. For each sensor event, we encode them by two approaches. The first approach is extracting the sensor ID and sensor value and combining them to be a "word". The second approach which is location bootstrapping, we further concatenate the sensor location into the word. For the location bootstrapping approach, the location information is recorded every other event. Each word is indexed when the vocabulary is being generated so that each word has an index (Fig. 1).

After index sequences are generated, SEW is used to generate sliding windows. In the literature, a SEW size 20–30 is always selected [1,3]. [4] experimented with even larger SEW sizes (50,75...) and their results showed that larger SEW sizes can improve the model's performance. Therefore, we select SEW sizes of 25, 50 and 75 to experiment. There are two different encoding approaches following the sliding windows generation step. For the frequency-based encoding approach, the length of each sequence is dependent on the size of the vocabulary. For the Word2Vec embedding approach, we need to pad the sequences whose length is less than the defined size of the SEW window to make sure they have the same length.

3.2   Our Model

Word2Vec can learn the similarities between words and capture a sense of word in the training corpus. There are 2 different training approaches for it. One is Continuous Bag of Words (CBOW) which predicts centre words from context words while another one is Skip-gram which predicts context words by a

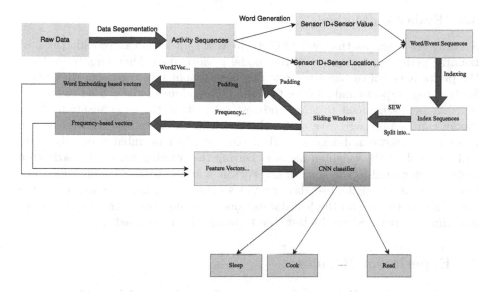

Fig. 1. Framework of the proposed method

given centre word. After generating the sequences of events and tokenizing each "word", the input for the Word2Vec model is ready. Skip-gram is selected for training the Word2Vec model because it works well with small datasets and can better represent less frequent words [12]. The word representation will be the inputs for CNN classifiers.

There could be some sequences with fewer events than the window size we decide. To make sure the length of every input stream is the same, value 0 is used for sequence padding. Our classifier is based on the Convolutional Neural Networks for sentence classification [10] and slightly modified during the experiment. The first layer of the CNN architecture is an Embedding layer which is used to extract the embedding matrix for mapping each word in the input sequence on its embedding vector. There are 3 1D convolutional layers. Each convolutional layer has a rectified linear unit activation which can help make the convergence faster. After the feature extraction, there is a Global Max Pooling layer followed by a flatten layer. Global Max Pooling (GMP) layer is frequently used for text classification tasks. One advantage of GMP is it can be used to reduce the dimensionality of feature maps and even replace Flattening or Dense layers [5]. Another advantage is there are not any parameters to be tuned for GMP. Before the output dense layer, there is one Batch Normalisation [9] layer and one dropout layer. Batch Normalisation can tackle the internal covariate shift problem so that it has a regularising effect. Dropout layer also solves the overfitting problems by randomly setting the outgoing edges of hidden units to 0 at each update of the training phase. The last layer is the output layer which is activated by softmax to perform the final classification.

3.3 Evaluation Method

A study [15] suggests that 80%/20% train/test split ratio can provide the best training performance and reveal the model performance. Therefore, to evaluate the performance of the classifier, the raw data is split into two parts where 80% for training purposes and 20% for testing. The random shuffle is used to prevent non-random assignment to train and test set so that the generalisation of the model can be improved. We adopt the following measurement metrics: recall, precision, F1-score and accuracy. To avoid the effect of unbalanced labels, we will also look at the weighted metrics. During the training phase, the early stop method integrated in the keras framework is adopted to avoid overfitting. The model's accuracy on the test data provides evidence for this method. Once the model's performance on the test dataset does not improve after n (n=10 in our experiment) epochs since the last, the training will be stopped.

4 Experiment Results

4.1 Comparison Between Frequency Encoding and Word2Vec Embedding Encoding

To validate the effect of Word2Vec embedding on the classifier, we need to control the SEW sizes and the approach of generating event sequences (Location-Enhanced vs None-Location). Based on Fig. 2a, 2c, 2e, it can be concluded that Word2Vec embedding can significantly improve the model's performance when we use the event sequences without location information. The two most affected indicators are macro average recall and macro average F1, which both have an increase equal to or more than 0.1 after using the Word2Vec word embedding model. To avoid the effect of imbalance labels on the evaluation metrics, the weighted average metrics should be focused on. Compared to the model using frequency encoding, the weighted average F1 scores increase by 0.1, 0.08 and 0.05 with SEW size 25, 50 and 75 respectively. As the SEW size increases, the gain brought by the Word2Vec model on the F1 score indicator decreases but the improvement was still significant. In terms of the accuracy, Word2Vec embedding can improve the accuracy by 0.08, 0.07, and 0.05 for SEW size 25, 50 and 75 respectively. Based on Fig. 2b, 2d, 2f, the 3 models that adopt the event sequences with location information, it can be concluded that Word2Vec embedding can still improve the model's performance. However, the magnitude of improvement is much smaller than that of the method which does not use location information. With regard to the accuracy, the Word2Vec embedding increases the accuracy by 0.01 for all the 3 models with different SEW sizes.

4.2 Comparison Between None-Location Models and Location-Enhanced Models

To validate the effect of Word2Vec embedding, we need to control the SEW size and the approach to encode the event sequences (Frequency encoding and

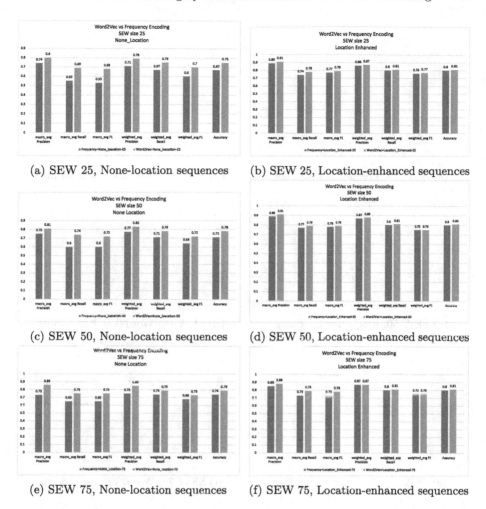

(a) SEW 25, None-location sequences   (b) SEW 25, Location-enhanced sequences

(c) SEW 50, None-location sequences   (d) SEW 50, Location-enhanced sequences

(e) SEW 75, None-location sequences   (f) SEW 75, Location-enhanced sequences

Fig. 2. Evaluation metrics comparison between Word2Vec approach and Frequency Encoding approach

Word2Vec embedding). Based on Fig. 3a, 3c, 3e, it can be concluded that using location information during the event sequence generating phase can significantly improve model's performance. Under the circumstance of frequency encoding for event sequences, location information can boost the weighted F1 score by 0.16, 0.11 and 0.07 for models with SEW size 25, 50 and 75 respectively. For the models with SEW size 25 and 50, most of the macro average metrics can achieve the improvement over 0.15. The magnitude of the improvement of the model with SEW size 75 is smaller than the other 2 models but the effect of the boost brought by location information is still significant. The accuracy is improved by 0.13, 0.09 and 0.06 for the models with SEW size 25, 50 and 75 respectively with the bootstrap of location information. Based on Fig. 3b, 3d, 3f, the conclusion

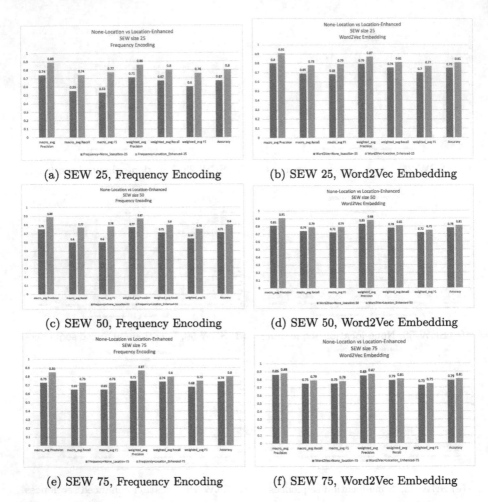

(a) SEW 25, Frequency Encoding   (b) SEW 25, Word2Vec Embedding

(c) SEW 50, Frequency Encoding   (d) SEW 50, Word2Vec Embedding

(e) SEW 75, Frequency Encoding   (f) SEW 75, Word2Vec Embedding

Fig. 3. Evaluation metrics comparison between None-Location approach and Location-Enhanced approach

is that under the circumstance of using Word2Vec embedding to encode event sequences, the location information can still significantly improve the model's classification performance. Compared with the None-Location aware model, the weighted average F1 score increases by 0.07, 0.03 and 0.02 for the models with SEW size 25, 50 and 75 respectively. Compared to the weighted average metrics, the magnitude of the improvement on macro average metrics is more significant. For all the three conditions, the accuracy is improved by 0.06, 0.03 and 0.02 with the help of location information for the models with SEW size 25, 50 and 75 respectively.

4.3   Comparison Between Different SEW Size

Based on Fig. 4a and 4b, the general trend is that with the increase of SEW, the model shows an upward trend in most metrics except the precision (Fig. 4a). Compared with the models with SEW size 25 and 50, the macro average precision of the model with SEW size 75 is reduced, but the magnitude is small. The weighted average precision also decreases for the model with SEW size 75 when it is compared with the model with SEW size 50. It can be concluded that increasing the SEW size can improve the overall performance for None-Location aware models, regardless of whether the model uses Word2Vec embeddings or frequency encoding for event sequences. However, a large SEW size could sometimes have a bad effect on some metrics. Figure 4c and 4d illustrate that, if we use Location-Enhanced method to generate event sequences, increasing the size of SEW cannot help to improve the classification performance. It can even decrease the performance, especially for the approach of using frequency encoding to encode sequences. Compared with SEW size 25 and 50, under the premise that the weighted average precision and recall are almost unchanged, the model with SEW size 75 significantly decreases the macro average precision and recall. The conclusion is that, once we use the Location-Enhanced approach for event sequence generation, small SEW size can also achieve good results and larger SEW size could sometimes have negative effect on the classifier performance.

4.4   Discussion

Based on the experiment result, both Word2Vec and location information model can increase the classifier's performance significantly. Compared to the model using frequency encoding to encode each event sequence, the model using Word2Vec can gain more semantics from context. Incorporating location information is another way to gain more semantics. For example, if an occupant triggers an environmental sensor installed in the kitchen, then we can at least determine that he/she must not be bathing, and other activities which certainly do not occur in the kitchen. Location information cannot help to distinguish those activities which occur in the same room but is beneficial for the classifier to distinguish those activities that happen in different rooms. The comparison between different SEW sizes shows that increasing the size of SEW can significantly increase the model performance for the models using the None-Location approach regardless of the encoding approach. Small SEW size is beneficial for real-time activity recognition because the delay is shorter. The analysis in the previous subsection illustrates that using larger SEW size has the potential to make the model unstable during the training phase.

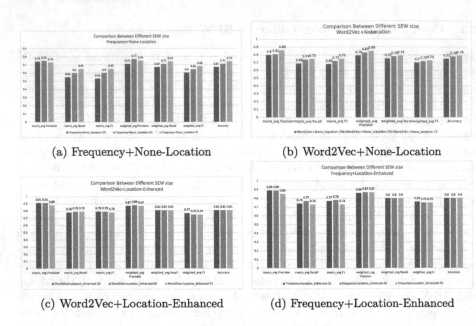

      (a) Frequency+None-Location   (b) Word2Vec+None-Location

    (c) Word2Vec+Location-Enhanced   (d) Frequency+Location-Enhanced

Fig. 4. Evaluation metrics comparison between different SEW sizes with a specific condition

5   Conclusion and Future Work

Our study extends the literature by using the Word2Vec embedding model for feature generation and location information to further bootstrap the classifier. Our results show that the best model can achieve a weighted average F1 score of 0.77 and an accuracy of 0.81 on the test dataset (16 predefined activity labels). Both Word2Vec embedding and Location-Enhanced approach can significantly improve the classification performance. The best model uses the Location-Enhanced approach to generate the event sequences and Word2Vec embedding for feature encoding with SEW size 25. It shows that even the small SEW size can achieve the best performance by using these two approaches together which is good for real-time activity recognition due to the shorter delay.

Vocabulary size and single representation for each word are the limitations of Word2Vec model. In addition, the comparison of different parameter combinations for Word2Vec has not been conducted. In the future, we can examine the effectiveness of contextualised embedding models such as ELMo and methods such as byte pair encoding (BPE) or WordPiece to split words into subwords to tackle the limitations of Word2Vec. Tuning the parameters of the Word2Vec model could also be one direction for performance improvement. The accuracy of the data recorded by the sensors also needs to be further verified. In the future, more detailed positions of sensors could be recorded during the collection process of sensor data which could help the classifier improve the ability to classify these activities that occur in the same room. Due to the time limitation, comparison with the state-of-the-art will also be conducted in the furture.

References

1. Aminikhanghahi, S., Cook, D.J.: Enhancing activity recognition using CPD-based activity segmentation. Pervasive Mob. Comput. **53**, 75–89 (2019)
2. Avgoustinos, F., William, O., Babak, T., George, L.: Location-enhanced activity recognition in indoor environments using off the shelf smart watch technology and BLE beacons. Sensors **17**(6), 1230 (2017)
3. Bouchabou, D., Nguyen, S.M., Lohr, C., Leduc, B., Kanellos, I.: A survey of human activity recognition in smart homes based on IoT sensors algorithms: taxonomies, challenges, and opportunities with deep learning. Sensors **21**(18), 6037 (2021)
4. Bouchabou, D., Nguyen, S.M., Lohr, C., LeDuc, B., Kanellos, I.: Fully convolutional network bootstrapped by word encoding and embedding for activity recognition in smart homes. In: Li, X., Wu, M., Chen, Z., Zhang, L. (eds.) DL-HAR 2021. CCIS, vol. 1370, pp. 111–125. Springer, Singapore (2021). https://doi.org/10.1007/978-981-16-0575-8_9
5. Christlein, V., Spranger, L., Seuret, M., Nicolaou, A., Maier, A.: Deep generalized max pooling. In: 2019 International Conference on Document Analysis and Recognition (ICDAR) (2019)
6. Cook, D.J., Krishnan, N.C., Rashidi, P.: Activity discovery and activity recognition: a new partnership. IEEE Trans. Syst. Man Cybern. Part B Cybern. Publ. IEEE Syst. Man Cybern. Soc. **43**(3), 820–828 (2013)
7. Gochoo, M., Tan, T.H., Liu, S.H., Jean, F.R., Alnajjar, F., Huang, S.C.: Unobtrusive activity recognition of elderly people living alone using anonymous binary sensors and DCNN. IEEE J. Biomed. Health Inf. **23**(2), 693–702 (2018)
8. Hardegger, M., Roggen, D., Calatroni, A., Troester, G.: S-smart: A unified bayesian framework for simultaneous semantic mapping, activity recognition, and tracking. ACM Trans. Intell. Syst. Technol. **7**(3), 1–28 (2016)
9. Ioffe, S., Szegedy, C.: Batch normalization: Accelerating deep network training by reducing internal covariate shift. In: International Conference on Machine Learning, pp. 448–456. PMLR (2015)
10. Kim, Y.: Convolutional neural networks for sentence classification. Eprint Arxiv (2014)
11. Lu, C.H., Fu, L.C.: Robust location-aware activity recognition using wireless sensor network in an attentive home. IEEE Trans. Autom. Sci. Eng. **6**(4), 598–609 (2009)
12. Mikolov, T., Chen, K., Corrado, G., Dean, J.: Efficient estimation of word representations in vector space. In: Bengio, Y., LeCun, Y. (eds.) 1st International Conference on Learning Representations (ICLR 2013), Scottsdale, Arizona, USA, 2–4 May 2013, Workshop Track Proceedings, pp. 1–12 (2013). http://arxiv.org/abs/1301.3781
13. Ni, Q., García Hernando, A., Pau, I.: The elderly's independent living in smart homes: a characterization of activities and sensing infrastructure survey to facilitate services development. Sensors **15**, 11312–11362 (2015). https://doi.org/10.3390/s150511312
14. Quigley, B., Donnelly, M., Moore, G., Galway, L.: A comparative analysis of windowing approaches in dense sensing environments. In: Proceedings, vol. 2, no. 19 (2018)
15. Rácz, A., Bajusz, D., Héberger, K.: Effect of dataset size and train/test split ratios in GSAR/GSPR multiclass classification. Molecules **26**(4), 1111 (2021)
16. Satpathy, L.: Smart housing: technology to aid aging in place-new opportunities and challenges (2006). https://scholarsjunction.msstate.edu/cgi/viewcontent.cgi?article=4966

17. Tan, T.-H.: Multi-resident activity recognition in a smart home using RGB activity image and DCNN. IEEE Sens. J. **18**(23), 9718–9727 (2018)
18. Tran, S.N., Zhang, Q., Smallbon, V., Karunanithi, M.: Multi-resident activity monitoring in smart homes: a case study. In: 2018 IEEE International Conference on Pervasive Computing and Communications Workshops (PerCom Workshops) (2018)
19. WHO: 10 facts on ageing and health (2017). https://www.who.int/news-room/fact-sheets/detail/10-facts-on-ageing-and-health

HoneyBreath: An Ambush Tactic Against Wireless Breath Inference

Qiuye He⬥, Edwin Yang⬥, Song Fang$^{(\boxtimes)}$⬥, and Shangqing Zhao⬥

University of Oklahoma, Norman, OK 73019, USA
songf@ou.edu

Abstract. Breathing rates can be used to verify the human presence and disclose a person's physiological status. Many studies have demonstrated success in applying channel state information (CSI) to infer breathing rates. Due to the invisibility of radio signals, the ubiquitous deployment of wireless infrastructures, and the elimination of the line-of-sight (LOS) requirement, such wireless inference techniques can surreptitiously work and violate user privacy. However, little research has been conducted specifically in mitigating misuse of those techniques. In this paper, we discover a new type of proactive countermeasures against all existing CSI-based vital signs inference techniques. Specifically, we set up ambush locations with carefully designed wireless signals, where eavesdroppers infer a fake breathing rate specified by the transmitter. The true breathing rate is thus protected. Experimental results on software-defined radio platforms show with the proposed defenses, the eavesdropper is no longer able to infer breathing rates accurately using CSI, and would be fooled by a fake one crafted by the transmitter instead.

Keywords: Breathing rate inference · Deceptive communication · Anti-eavesdropping · Channel state information

1 Introduction

Vital signs inference via wireless signals has drawn increasing attention because of the ubiquitous deployment of wireless infrastructures and the elimination of body contact with devices [1,3,10,28,29,36,38,41,56,57,62,64]. With such a technique, an eavesdropper can stealthily set up a wireless receiver on one side of the user to passively collect the signals emitted by a wireless Access Point (AP) which is on the other side of the user. The respiration-induced chest and stomach fluctuation may cause subtle disturbances in the received signals, which can be analyzed by the eavesdropper to learn sensitive vital signs.

The popularity of such techniques also brings privacy concerns as vital signs often contain sensitive information related to the state of personal essential body function [1,22,36,38,60]. Generally, the normal breathing rate for an adult at rest is 12 to 20 breaths per minute (bpm). Rapid, shallow breathing is often related to pulmonary diseases [11], hypertension or hyperthyroidism [7]; slow breathing may be caused by heart problems or drug overdose [20]; shortness of breath

S. Longfei and P. Bodhi (Eds.): MobiQuitous 2022, LNICST 492, pp. 203–226, 2023.
https://doi.org/10.1007/978-3-031-34776-4_12

can be a symptom of diseases such as asthma or pneumonia [53]; sleep apnea is often associated with cardiovascular diseases like stroke [22]. The disclosure of such health information can cause serious consequences such as employment discrimination based on health status [32], and a company's stock plummeting due to its CEO's health concerns [15,16]. Except for health information, there are also extensive research efforts that detect breathing for user presence identification [39,43,55,61], which can result in serious security issues. An adversary (e.g., a burglary) can infer whether users are at home or not by eavesdropping on wireless signals and then may target rooms without the user's presence to commit crimes to reduce the chance of getting caught.

Though research is booming in vital signs inference through wireless signals, there are few research efforts discussing corresponding countermeasures. Traditional anti-eavesdropping methods usually take the following two defenses: (1) *Cryptographic key based:* by encrypting transmitted messages between legitimate parties [48], an eavesdropper without the secret key cannot successfully decode the received message; and (2) *Friendly jamming based:* an ally jammer actively sends jamming signals (e.g., [26,47]) which interrupt the eavesdropping while the receiver can decode messages by canceling the impact of the inference signals. With either mechanism, the eavesdropper would capture encrypted or disrupted signals, which are often random and meaningless. Though the eavesdropper may not get the correct wireless signals, the unintelligibility of those signals indicates to her that her eavesdropping fails. She may thus make further efforts to break the wireless communication. For example, an eavesdropper may attempt to steal the secret key via social engineering methods (e.g., [31]) or side-channel attacks (e.g., [23]). Also, it has been shown that an attacker equipped with multiple antennas is able to separate the message from the jamming signals [50]. Due to the importance of health privacy, a more effective defense is thus much-needed to prevent wireless vital signs eavesdropping.

Orthogonal frequency-division multiplexing (OFDM) is widely used in modern wireless communication systems (e.g., 802.11a/g/n/ac/ad) with multiple subcarrier frequencies to encode a packet. The minute wireless signal disturbance caused by chest and stomach fluctuation can be captured by *received signal strength* (RSS) or *channel state information* (CSI). RSS only provides the average power in a received radio signal over the whole channel bandwidth, while CSI represents how the wireless channel impacts the radio signal that propagates through it (e.g., amplitude attenuation and phase shift). CSI offers fine-grained channel information, consisting of subcarrier-level information. As a result, CSI is more sensitive to breathing and has shown the best performance in inferring breathing rate compared with other wireless techniques [28].

What if we actively feed the eavesdropper with a meaningful but bogus breathing rate? When the eavesdropper is misled by the fake breathing rate, she would not take further methods to compromise the true one. In this paper, we thus develop a novel scheme against CSI-based vital signs inference techniques. Specifically, we set up an *ambush location*, choose a fake breathing rate, and convert it into a fake CSI. The transmitter then delivers the converted CSI to the ambush location by manipulating the transmitted wireless signals. As a

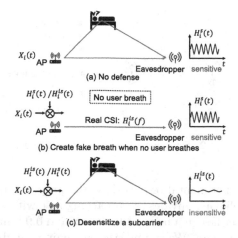

Fig. 1. Creating a fake (sensitive or insensitive) CSI.

result, the eavesdropper at the ambush location would infer the fake breathing rate with the estimated CSI.

Generally, as the reflected and line-of-sight (LOS) signals interfere constructively or destructively, a receiver may observe enhanced or weakened signals. Such effects may vary for different subcarriers, which can be categorized into two groups: sensitive and insensitive. With respiration-induced body movement, sensitive subcarriers enable the receiver to observe large amplitudes (or variances), while insensitive subcarriers rarely show correlated fluctuations. Thus, the breathing rate can be determined via observations of sensitive subcarriers.

We give an example to illustrate our idea. Without loss of generality, we utilize a single subcarrier for discussion. For OFDM systems, a transmitter sends a publicly known pseudo noise sequence $X_i(t)$, and the receiver estimates the channel frequency response $H_i(t)$ (i.e., subcarrier CSI) from the received, distorted copy $Y_i(t)$, i.e., $H_i(t) = \frac{Y_i(t)}{X_i(t)}$ [12,25]. If no defense is enforced, as shown in Fig. 1a, the eavesdropper (malicious receiver) can obtain the real CSI for the sensitive i^{th} subcarrier between itself and the AP, denoted with $H_i^s(t)$, which enables her to derive the breathing rate of the target user.

If there is no breathing activity, as shown in Fig. 1b, the ith subcarrier should be insensitive and the true CSI is denoted with $H_i^{is}(t)$. However, the AP multiples the signal $X_i(t)$ with a coefficient $H_i^s(t)/H_i^{is}(t)$, and sends the resultant signal, which also goes through the real wireless channel. Consequently, the received signal becomes $X_i(t) \cdot H_i^s(t)/H_i^{is}(t) \cdot H_i^{is}(t) = X_i(t)H_i^s(t)$, and thus the eavesdropper obtains an estimated subcarrier CSI $H_i^s(t)$ (sensitive), with which the breath rate specified by the transmitter can be extracted.

Now consider the scenario in Fig. 1c: the transmitter aims to hide the user's true breathing rate. Thus, it multiples the signal $X_i(t)$ with a coefficient $H_i^{is}(t)/H_i^s(t)$. As a result, the eavesdropper obtains $X_i(t) \cdot H_i^{is}(t)/H_i^s(t) \cdot H_i^s(t) = X_i(t)H_i^{is}(t)$. The calculated subcarrier CSI then becomes $H_i^{is}(t)$ (insensitive), causing failure of inferring the true breathing rate.

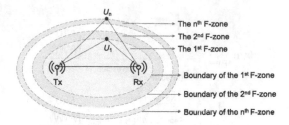

Fig. 2. Demonstration of Fresnel Zones.

Our real-world experimental results show the proposed defenses can fool an eavesdropper into believing any desired breathing rate with an error of less than 1.2 bpm when the user lies on a bed in a bedroom and 0.9 bpm when the user sits in a chair in an office room. We summarize our main contributions as follows:

- To the best of our knowledge, we are the first to propose a deceptive approach to defend against wireless vital signs inference attacks.
- By reverse engineering existing CSI-based breathing rate inference techniques, we design a customized scheme to convert a chosen breathing rate into a fake CSI. We also develop methods to enable the eavesdropper to estimate the fake CSI and thus attain the specified breathing rate.
- We implement real-world prototypes of both existing CSI-based breathing rate inference and the proposed defense schemes. We experiment on top of them to examine the impact of the defenses.

2 Preliminaries

In this section, we impart preliminary knowledge about the Fresnel Zone model and the general method used by existing work using CSI to infer breathing rates.

2.1 Fresnel Zone

In the context of wireless signal propagation, Fresnel Zones refer to concentric ellipses with the transmitter (Tx) and receiver (Rx) at two focal points, and denote regions of different wireless signal propagation strengths between the pair of communicators, as shown in Fig. 2. For a given radio wavelength λ, each ellipse can be constructed by ensuring

$$|\text{Tx}, U_n| + |\text{Rx}, U_n| - |\text{Tx}, \text{Rx}| = n\lambda/2, \tag{1}$$

where U_n is a point in the nth ellipse, and $|u, v|$ denotes the Euclidean distance between two points u and v. The innermost ellipse is the first Fresnel Zone, representing the region where the LOS signals can pass through. The nth (when $n \geq 2$) Fresnel Zone is the region between the $(n-1)^{\text{th}}$ and n^{th} ellipses.

The received signal at Rx is a linear combination of reflected and LOS signals. The distance difference ΔD (i.e., $n\lambda/2$) between the two paths generates a phase difference of $\frac{\Delta D}{\lambda} \cdot 2\pi = n\pi$ between the two signals. As the phase shift introduced by the reflection is π [56], the total phase difference $\Delta\phi$ between reflected and LOS signals equals $(n + 1)\pi$. Thus, if n is even, we obtain $\Delta\phi$ mod $2\pi = \pi$, causing the two signals to arrive at Rx to have opposite phases and destructively interfere with each other. In contrast, we have $\Delta\phi$ mod $2\pi = 0$ if n is odd, i.e., both signals have the same phase and constructively interfere with each other to form a boosted signal. The Fresnel Zone model can thus help reveal the signal change pattern (i.e., sensitive or insensitive) in each subcarrier (with different waveforms) caused by respiration-induced body movement [56].

2.2   CSI-Based Breathing Rate Inference

Existing CSI-based breathing rate inference schemes [28,36,56] usually utilize three steps to infer breathing rates, namely, CSI pre-processing, subcarrier selection, and breathing cycle extraction. The first phase removes outliers and noise from the CSI to improve its reliability. As discussed earlier, each subcarrier may be sensitive or insensitive to respiration due to the constructive or destructive interference effect of LOS and reflected signals. The second phase picks up sensitive subcarriers for breathing rate inference. A sensitive subcarrier often exhibits a sinusoidal-like periodic change pattern over time in the CSI amplitudes, which corresponds to periodic breathing. In the third phase, the peak-to-peak time interval of sinusoidal CSI amplitudes can be then extracted as the breathing cycle, with which, the breathing rate can be calculated.

3   Attack Model and Assumptions

We consider a general scenario, where an attacker only uses a wireless receiver to launch a breathing rate inference attack, as she has a preference to take advantage of an existing wireless transmitter to make the attack stealthier [36]. The transmitter (i.e., defender) is benign and aims to hide true breathing rates and inject fake ones into the eavesdropper.

We assume that the receiver (i.e., attacker) attempts to find a position that enables her to eavesdrop on the breathing rate, which is a common strategy [4]. We borrow the idea from a long-established military tactic – ambush: set up one or multiple ambush locations where an attacker may appear and be trapped. We further assume that the transmitter is able to obtain actual CSI between itself and an ambush location. This can be achieved by estimating the CSI from wireless signals emitted by a helper node placed at the ambush location.

4   Ambush Design

4.1   Overview

To lay an ambush, the transmitter first selects an ambush location and arbitrarily specifies a fake breathing rate to fool the attacker entering the ambush.

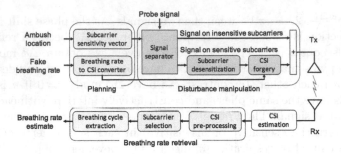

Fig. 3. Flow chart of the proposed ambush tactic.

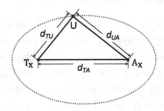

Fig. 4. Selecting an ambush location.

The locations where an eavesdropper may appear with the highest probabilities can be determined via eavesdropper tracking techniques (e.g., [9]) and ambush locations can be then deployed along the eavesdropper's possible route.

The transmitter then enters the *planning* phase, which consists of two parallel tasks: (1) determining sensitive subcarriers; and (2) converting a specified breathing rate into an artificial CSI. We utilize a binary decision variable α_i to indicate the sensitivity of the ith subcarrier, with 1 denoting sensitive while 0 showing insensitive. The sensitivities of all N subcarriers can be represented by a vector $\boldsymbol{\alpha} = [\alpha_1, \alpha_2, \cdots, \alpha_N]^T$. Since insensitive subcarriers do not contribute to the breathing rate inference, there is no need to manipulate their CSIs.

The next phase is *disturbance manipulation*. For signals on sensitive subcarriers, the transmitter aims to make the attacker estimate the converted CSI. As any transmitting signal has to go through the real wireless channel, the transmitter then applies a module of desensitizing subcarriers to remove the real impact of corresponding wireless sub-channels, and also crafts the artificial disturbance on these originally sensitive subcarriers for the attacker to observe. Finally, the transmitter combines the crafted signals on sensitive subcarriers with unchanged signals on insensitive subcarriers and transmits the aggregated signal out.

Consequently, the attacker infers breathing rate with estimated CSI by performing the general *breathing rate retrieval* process. Figure 3 shows the flow chart of the proposed ambush tactic.

4.2 Planning Phase

Obtaining Subcarrier Sensitivity. As shown in Fig. 4, T_x, U, and A_x denote the transmitter, the user, and an ambush location, respectively. A wireless signal sent by T_x travels on two paths, the LOS path and the reflection one. The distance difference Δd between the two paths is $\Delta d = d_{TU} + d_{UA} - d_{TA}$.

Let λ_i denote the wavelength of the ith subcarrier with frequency f_i, i.e., $\lambda_i = c/f_i$, where c is the speed of light. Correspondingly, the phase difference $\Delta\theta_i$ (between signals arrived at A_x through the two paths) equals the sum of the respective phase shifts caused by Δd and the reflection phenomenon, i.e., $\Delta\theta_i = \frac{2\pi\Delta d}{\lambda_i} + \pi$. We perform a modulus 2π operation on $\Delta\theta_i$ and obtain a phase difference $\Delta\theta_i'$ within the range of $[0, 2\pi)$, i.e., $\Delta\theta_i' = \Delta\theta_i \pmod{2\pi}$.

Based on the Fresnel Zone theory [56], if $\Delta\theta_i'$ is close to 0 or 2π, the ith subcarrier is sensitive, i.e., when $\Delta\theta_i' \in [0, \pi/2) \cup (3\pi/2, 2\pi)$, we obtain the binary decision variable $\alpha_i = 1$. On the other hand, if $\Delta\theta_i'$ approaches to π, this subcarrier becomes insensitive, i.e., $\alpha_i = 0$ for $\Delta\theta_i' \in [\pi/2, 3\pi/2]$. The relationship between α_i and $\Delta\theta_i'$ can be then denoted as $\alpha_i = \lfloor \frac{|\Delta\theta_i' - \pi|}{\pi/2} \rfloor$, where $\lfloor x \rfloor$ denotes the floor function, representing the largest integer less than or equal to x.

Converting Breathing Rate to CSI. Breathing rate to CSI conversion is the process of translating a selected breathing rate into a subcarrier CSI. It has been observed that periodic chest and stomach movement caused by respiration would make the amplitude of CSI on a sensitive subcarrier present a sinusoidal-like pattern over time [36,38,56]. We thus model the respiration-induced CSI amplitude stream on a sensitive subcarrier as a sinusoidal wave.

Let f_b denote the specified respiration frequency (Hz), so the corresponding breathing rate equals $60 \cdot f_b$ (bpm). We then convert it into a subcarrier CSI $W_b(t)$, which can be then denoted with $|W_b(t)|e^{j\varphi(t)}$, where $|W_b(t)|$ and $\varphi(t)$ represent amplitude and phase, respectively. Since the phase could be distorted due to an unknown time lag caused by the non-synchronized transmitter and receiver [46], most studies only use the amplitude to characterize the wireless channel [54] and extract breathing rate [36,38,56]. We also explore CSI amplitude and refer to it as just "CSI" in the following. In terms of $\varphi(t)$, it has no impact on breathing rate inference and we omit it for the sake of simplicity.

With the sinusoidal model, the CSI envelope at time t can be denoted by

$$|W_b(t)| = a \cdot sin(2\pi f_b t + \beta) + m + \mathcal{N}_0, \tag{2}$$

where a, β, m and $\mathcal{N}_0$ are the amplitude, initial phase, constant shift (which defines a mean level) of the sinusoidal wave, and the additive noise. In turn, with such a CSI envelope, the attacker can infer the breathing rate as $60 \cdot f_b$.

Formation of the Specified OFDM CSI: The specified CSI for an OFDM system with N subcarriers can be denoted with $\mathbf{W}(t) = [W_1(t), W_2(t), \cdots, W_N(t)]$. Let $\mathcal{S} = \{s_1, s_2, \ldots, s_K\}$ and $\bar{\mathcal{S}} = \{p_1, p_2, \ldots, p_{K'}\}$ denote the sets formed by the indexes of the sensitive and insensitive subcarriers, where $K + K' = N$. For $i \in \mathcal{S}$, we enable $W_i(t) = W_b(t)$; for $i \in \bar{\mathcal{S}}$, we have $W_i(t) = H_i(t)$ (i.e., no manipulation is required), where $H_i(t)$ is the original CSI of the ith subcarrier.

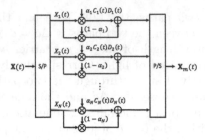

Fig. 5. An MAC process.

4.3 Disturbance Manipulation

The transmitter can utilize a multiply-accumulate (MAC) process to generate desired artificial disturbance, as shown in Fig. 5. Specifically, the public training sequence $\mathbf{X}(t)$ is encoded into N subcarrier signals by a serial-to-parallel (S/P) converter module, represented with $[X_1(t), X_2(t), \cdots, X_N(t)]^T$. We use $\mathbf{J}$ to represent an $N \times 1$ vector of all 1's. Thus, after the signal separator, the original N subcarrier signals will be divided into two groups: $\mathbf{S}(t) = \text{diag}(\boldsymbol{\alpha}) \cdot \mathbf{X}(t)$ and $\mathbf{IS}(t) = \text{diag}(\mathbf{J} - \boldsymbol{\alpha}) \cdot \mathbf{X}(t)$, denoting signals on sensitive and insensitive subcarriers, respectively, where $\text{diag}(\mathbf{V})$ denotes a square diagonal matrix with the elements of vector $\mathbf{V}$ on the main diagonal.

Signals on sensitive subcarriers would then go through two modules: subcarrier desensitization and CSI forgery. The former module with the coefficient vector $\mathbf{C}(t) = [C_1(t), C_2(t), \cdots, C_N(t)]$ aims to cancel the original channel impact, so that the real respiration-induced channel disturbance (i.e., the real breathing rate) can be hidden for the attacker. Accordingly, we have $C_i(t) = H_i^{-1}(t)$ if the ith subcarrier is sensitive, i.e., $i \in \mathcal{S}$, and set $C_i(t) = 0$ for $i \in \bar{\mathcal{S}}$. The latter module with a coefficient vector $\mathbf{D}(t) = [D_1(t), D_2(t), \cdots, D_N(t)]$ would add the effect of the artificial CSI for the attacker to estimate, where the forged subcarrier CSI $D_i(t) = W_i(t)$ if $i \in \mathcal{S}$ and we set $D_i(t) = 0$ for $i \in \bar{\mathcal{S}}$.

Finally, signals on originally sensitive and insensitive subcarriers are concatenated through a parallel-to-serial (P/S) converter module to form OFDM symbols to send via the realistic wireless channel. The resulting transmitting signal $\mathbf{X}_m(t)$ can be represented by

$$\mathbf{X}_m(t) = \text{diag}(\mathbf{D}(t)) \cdot \text{diag}(\mathbf{C}(t)) \cdot \mathbf{S}(t) + \mathbf{IS}(t). \tag{3}$$

Let $\mathbf{H}(t) = [H_1(t), \cdots, H_N(t)]^T$ denote the true OFDM CSI. The received signal at the attacker thus becomes $\mathbf{R}_m(t) = \text{diag}(\mathbf{X}_m(t)) \cdot \mathbf{H}(t)$, where we omit the noise term for the sake of simplicity. The attacker estimates CSI with the received signal and the public training sequence, i.e., $\mathbf{R}_m(t) = \text{diag}(\mathbf{X}(t)) \cdot \hat{\mathbf{H}}(t)$, where $\hat{\mathbf{H}}(t) = [\hat{H}_1(t), \cdots, \hat{H}_N(t)]^T$ represents the estimated CSI. Consequently, we have

$$\begin{aligned} \hat{H}_i(t) &= \alpha_i \cdot \frac{X_i(t) C_i(t) D_i(t)}{X_i(t)} \cdot H_i(t) + (1 - \alpha_i) \cdot H_i(t) \\ &= \alpha_i \cdot D_i(t) + (1 - \alpha_i) \cdot H_i(t) = W_i(t). \end{aligned} \tag{4}$$

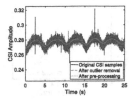
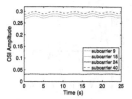

Fig. 6. CSI pre-processing.   **Fig. 7.** Subcarrier sensitivity.

This demonstrates that with the disturbance manipulation, when the ith subcarrier is sensitive, the transmitter is able to make the attacker obtain a fake subcarrier CSI $W_i(t)$ specified by itself in the planning phase. Meanwhile, if the ith subcarrier is insensitive, it is still observed as insensitive, i.e., the corresponding estimated subcarrier CSI equals the real value $H_i(t)$. This is because the transmitter does not manipulate signals on insensitive subcarriers.

4.4 Breathing Rate Retrieval

CSI Pre-processing. CSI pre-processing, consisting of outlier removal and noise reduction, aims to make the collected CSI reliable. The imperfect CSI can be caused by non-respiratory environmental change or hardware imperfections.

Hampel filter is a classical technique to remove outliers (i.e., samples that significantly differ from neighboring ones) in a given series [13,38]. As the collected CSI may have abrupt changes that are not caused by respiration, a Hampel filter is enforced to remove those outliers. It is observed that the CSI variations caused by the chest and stomach movement usually lie at the low end of the spectrum. Thus, we further adopt the moving average filter, which is optimal for reducing high-frequency noise while retaining a sharp step response [49]. Figure 6 illustrates an example of CSI pre-processing. It can be seen that the outliers and high-frequency noise are effectively removed.

Subcarrier Selection. Empirically, the CSI variance of a sensitive subcarrier is usually more than one order of magnitude larger than that of an insensitive subcarrier. This observation implies a threshold-based approach to distinguish the two types of subcarriers. Specifically, when there is no breathing activity, the average CSI variance σ^2 across all subcarriers can be measured, called *reference variance*, which will be then utilized as the threshold to determine the sensitivity of each subcarrier. Let v_i^2 denote the CSI variance for the ith subcarrier. If $\log_{10}(v_i^2/\sigma^2) < 1$ holds, we regard that the variance is caused by noise and the subcarrier is insensitive; otherwise, this subcarrier is sensitive. If CSI variances on all subcarriers have the same order with the reference variance, all subcarriers are insensitive (i.e., no breathing activity is detected).

Figure 7 plots the CSIs observed on 4 different subcarriers. In this example, we can see that subcarrier 24 has a quite flat CSI which rarely discloses any useful information about the breathing activity, while the CSIs of the remaining

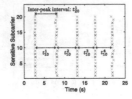

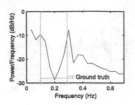

Fig. 8. Local peaks.   **Fig. 9.** Peaks in PSD.

subcarriers show evident periodical fluctuations. Accordingly, we can determine that subcarriers 9, 15, and 40 are sensitive, while subcarrier 24 is insensitive.

Breathing Cycle Identification. The CSI on a sensitive subcarrier often shows a sinusoidal pattern correlated with breathing activities. To obtain a breathing cycle, we can thus compute the inter-peak interval (i.e., the time between successive peaks) of the sinusoidal CSI.

Intuitively, the first derivative of a peak switches from positive to negative at the peak maximum, which can be used to localize the occurrence time of each peak. However, there may exist fake peaks caused by noise and consequently false zero-crossings. Motivated by the fact that a person usually cannot breathe beyond a certain frequency, a fake peak removal algorithm can be developed. Specifically, if the calculated interval between the current peak with the previous one is less than $60/R_{max}$ (seconds), where R_{max} (bpm) denotes the maximum possible breathing rate, this peak will be labeled as a fake one and then removed.

Figure 8 shows all detected local peaks on 20 sensitive subcarriers during 25 s. The breathing rate is calculated as 12.7 bpm for this example.

Inferring Multi-user Breathing Rates. For the multi-user scenario, we use the power spectral density (PSD) [36] to identify the frequencies with strong signal power in the frequency domain. Normally, each breathing signal from one person contributes to one evident peak in the obtained PSD [55]. The PSD on the ith sensitive subcarrier with L samples can be obtained by $PSD_i = 10 \log_{10} \frac{|FFT(H_i)|^2}{L}$, where H_i is the vector of CSI amplitude on the ith subcarrier.

When there are two users, the two strongest peaks in the PSD would indicate their breathing rates, as in an example shown in Fig. 9. The ground truths of two users' breathing rates are 6.0 and 17.3 bpm (corresponding to 0.10 ad 0.29 Hz); the estimated breathing rates based on the first two strongest peaks are 6.0 and 18.0 bpm (i.e., 0.10 and 0.30 Hz), showing that the estimation of two-user breathing rates is accurate.

4.5   From Point Ambush to Area Ambush

With more deployed ambush locations, the probability that an eavesdropper happens to be at any of them would be higher. Meanwhile, it helps to defend against multiple collaborative attackers, each of which searches for opportune eavesdropping locations.

Setting up Two Ambush Locations. The transmitter with two antennas can set up two ambush locations. Let $\mathbf{H}_{sr}(t)$ (s, $r \in \{1,2\}$) denote the overall CSI between the sth transmit antenna and the rth ambush location. The corresponding subcarrier sensitivity vector is represented by $\boldsymbol{\alpha}_{sr} = [\alpha_{sr}^1, \cdots, \alpha_{sr}^N]$, which can be pre-obtained with the method proposed in Sect. 4.2. At each ambush location, the received signal is the superposition of two signals, each from a different transmit antenna. If at least one of the two subcarriers between the respective transmit antenna and the rth ambush location is sensitive, we regard that this overall subcarrier between the transmitter and the rth ambush location is sensitive. Mathematically, let $\boldsymbol{\alpha}_r = [\alpha_r^1, \cdots, \alpha_r^N]$ denote the resultant subcarrier sensitivity vector of the transmitter for the rth ambush location, and $\alpha_r^i = \alpha_{1r}^i \vee \alpha_{2r}^i$. On the other hand, it may arouse suspicion of two colluding eavesdroppers if the breathing rates they infer separately are different. Thus, the transmitter should enable both ambush locations to observe the same breathing rate, i.e., the manipulated CSIs at corresponding sensitive subcarriers should be equal. If a subcarrier at either ambush location is sensitive, we then regard that the overall subcarrier between the transmitter and the two ambush locations is sensitive. Similarly, let $\boldsymbol{\alpha} = [\alpha^1, \cdots, \alpha^N]$ denote the subcarrier sensitivity vector of the transmitter for the two ambush locations, and $\alpha^i = \alpha_1^i \vee \alpha_2^i$.

Let $W(t)$ denote the fake CSI which is converted with a specified breathing rate. The transmitter aims to make the estimated CSI on sensitive subcarriers at each eavesdropper to be equal to $W(t)$.

As discussed in Sect. 4.3, the transmitting signals on sensitive subcarriers will be first desensitized and then multiply with the forged CSI before being sent out. In this scenario, let $H_{sr}^i(t)$ denote the CSI on i^{th} subcarrier between the sth transmit antenna and the rth ambush location. Thus, in terms of the coefficient vector $\mathbf{C}_s(t) = [C_s^1(t), \cdots, C_s^N(t)]$ for subcarrier desensitization at the sth transmit antenna, if $\alpha^i = 0$ (i.e., the ith subcarrier between the transmitter and the two ambush locations is insensitive), we set $C_s^i(t) = 0$, otherwise, we have $C_1^i(t) = \frac{H_{21}^i(t) - H_{22}^i(t)}{\zeta^i}$ and $C_2^i(t) = \frac{H_{12}^i(t) - H_{11}^i(t)}{\zeta^i}$, where $\zeta^i = H_{21}^i(t)H_{12}^i(t) - H_{22}^i(t)H_{11}^i(t)$. Also, the coefficient vector for the CSI forgery module at each transmit antenna is $\mathbf{D}(t) = [D_1(t), \cdots, D_N(t)]$, where we set $D_i(t) = 0$ if $\alpha^i = 0$ and have $D_i(t) = W(t)$ if $\alpha^i = 1$.

We rewrite Eq. 3 and the transmitting signal $\mathbf{X}_m(t) = [\mathbf{X}_1(t), \mathbf{X}_2(t)]^T$ after manipulation becomes

$$\mathbf{X}_m(t) = \begin{bmatrix} \text{diag}(\mathbf{D}(t)) \cdot \text{diag}(\mathbf{C}_1(t)) \cdot \mathbf{S}(t) + \mathbf{IS}(t) \\ \text{diag}(\mathbf{D}(t)) \cdot \text{diag}(\mathbf{C}_2(t)) \cdot \mathbf{S}(t) + \mathbf{IS}(t) \end{bmatrix}. \tag{5}$$

The transmitting signal $\mathbf{X}_m(t)$ would go through the realistic wireless channel. At the ambush location side, the received signal and the public training sequence will be then utilized to estimate CSI. Let $\hat{\mathbf{W}}_1(t)$ and $\hat{\mathbf{W}}_2(t)$ denote the estimated CSIs at the two ambush locations. We thus obtain

$$\hat{W}_r^i(t) = \alpha^i \cdot W(t) + (1 - \alpha^i) \cdot (H_{1r}^i(t) + H_{2r}^i(t)). \tag{6}$$

This implies the success of setting up two ambush locations simultaneously.

General Scheme for Area Ambush. The transmitter can deploy κ ambush locations with κ antennas. We consider colluding eavesdroppers and need to guarantee the breathing rate inferred by each eavesdropper at any ambush location stays the same.

The sensitivity of the ith subcarrier between the sth transmit antenna and the rth ambush location can be represented by α_{sr}^i ($s, r \in \{1, 2, \cdots, \kappa\}$). Meanwhile, let α_r^i denote the overall sensitivity of the ith subcarrier between the transmitter and the rth ambush location, i.e., $\alpha_r^i = \alpha_{1r}^i \vee \alpha_{2r}^i \cdots \vee \alpha_{\kappa r}^i$. Thus, in terms of the subcarrier sensitivity vector $\boldsymbol{\alpha}$ of the transmitter for all κ ambush locations, we have $\alpha^i = \alpha_1^i \vee \alpha_2^i \cdots \vee \alpha_\kappa^i$. Let $\mathbf{X}(t) = [\mathbf{X}_1(t), \cdots, \mathbf{X}_\kappa(t)]^T$ denote the manipulated signal sent by κ transmit antennas. The transmitter aims to make the estimated CSI at each ambush location be equal to the specified fake CSI, i.e., $\hat{\mathbf{W}}_r(t) = \mathbf{W}(t)$. Similarly, each transmit antenna utilizes the same coefficient vector $\mathbf{D}(t)$ for the CSI forgery module.

Accordingly, we can then solve the manipulated signal $\mathbf{X}_m(t)$, and rewrite Eq. 5 as

$$\mathbf{X}_m(t) = \begin{bmatrix} \mathrm{diag}(\mathbf{D}(t)) \cdot \mathrm{diag}(\mathbf{C}_1(t)) \cdot \mathbf{S}(t) + \mathbf{IS}(t) \\ \vdots \\ \mathrm{diag}(\mathbf{D}(t)) \cdot \mathrm{diag}(\mathbf{C}_\kappa(t)) \cdot \mathbf{S}(t) + \mathbf{IS}(t) \end{bmatrix}, \tag{7}$$

where $\mathbf{C}_s(t)$ is the coefficient vector for the subcarrier desensitization module at the sth transmit antenna.

Equation 7 has κ unknowns ($\mathbf{C}_1(t)$ to $\mathbf{C}_\kappa(t)$). As the number of transmit antennas equals the number of unknowns, the linear system formed by Eq. 7 has a unique solution. It demonstrates when the transmitter is able to set the coefficient vector for the subcarrier desensitization module at the sth transmit antenna with the computed $\mathbf{C}_s(t)$, the goal of deploying κ simultaneous ambush locations can be achieved.

4.6 Security Analysis

The proposed scheme is known by the eavesdropper. One concern is whether the eavesdropper can distinguish ambush locations or even indirectly compute the real CSI of sensitive subcarriers (to infer the true breathing rate).

Ambush Indistinguishability: With the Fresnel Zone principle, CSI-based breathing rate inference works at certain locations, while its performance may deteriorate greatly at other locations [10]. Thus, when the eavesdropper moves

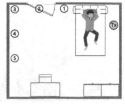
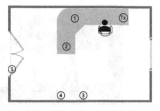

(a) Bedroom (User lies down).   (b) Office (User sits).

Fig. 10. Layout of the experimental environment.

out of the ambush location, though she cannot detect the breathing rate as when she is at the ambush location, she is still unable to distinguish this case from the normal one when the ambush scheme is not enforced. Such ambush indistinguishability leaves the eavesdropper in a dilemma: if she believes the inferred breathing rate, she will be deceived; instead, if she does not trust any inferred breathing rate, her ability to eavesdropping breathing rate is lost.

Indirect Calculation: To calculate the real CSI, an eavesdropper must compromise the phase of distribution manipulation. As shown in Sect. 4.3, suppose that the ith subcarrier is sensitive, the transmitting signal on this subcarrier can be represented as $X_i^m(t) = \alpha_i C_i(t) D_i(t) X_i(t) + (1 - \alpha_i) X_i(t)$. We utilize $M_i(t) = C_i(t) D_i(t)$ to denote the total impact of disturbance manipulation. Let R_i^e denote the signal received by the eavesdropper on the ith subcarrier, and $H_i^e(t)$ denote the corresponding real subcarrier CSI between the transmitter and eavesdropper. Thus, we have $R_i^e = X_i^m(t) H_i^e(t) = a_i M_i(t) X_i(t) H_i^e(t) + (1 - a_i) X_i(t) H_i^e(t)$.

To learn $M_i(t)$, the eavesdropper must learn both a_i and $H_i^e(t)$. However, this imposes a strong requirement for the eavesdropper. On one hand, without the knowledge of the accurate positions of the target user and the transmitter, the eavesdropper can hardly determine the subcarrier sensitivity except by guessing. On the other hand, the transmitter can always hide its real CSI between itself and the eavesdropper. Thus, $H_i^e(t)$ is not available. Consequently, the eavesdropper would fail to obtain $M_i(t)$ and cannot calculate the real CSIs of sensitive subcarriers for inferring the true breathing rate.

5   Experimental Evaluation

We implement CSI-based breathing rate inference and our proposed ambush schemes on top of Universal Software Radio Peripheral (USRP) X310s [19], which are equipped with SBX-120 daughterboards [18] and run GNU Radio [24] – an open-source software toolkit.

5.1   Evaluation Setup

The prototype system includes a transmitter Tx and an eavesdropper Eve (i.e., malicious receiver). Each node is a USRP X310. We recruited 5 participants

(a) Five-antenna transmitter with US-RPs.

(b) Ambush area.

Fig. 11. Setup for deploying an ambush area.

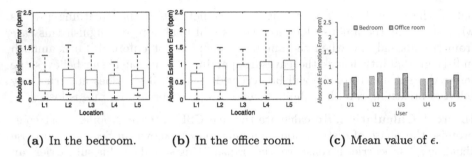

(a) In the bedroom.   (b) In the office room.   (c) Mean value of ϵ.

Fig. 12. Values of ϵ and ϵ at Eve when no defense is enforced.

and asked each to act as the target user of the inference attacks over three months.[1] Also, each wore a Masimo MightySat Fingertip Pulse Oximeter [40] with hospital-grade technology to obtain ground-truth breathing rate.

Testing Scenarios: We test two typical scenarios: (1) a bedroom, where the user lies on a bed; and (2) an office room, where the user sits in a chair. Figure 10 shows the ambush locations and the position of the transmitter. For each scenario, we place Eve at 5 different ambush locations to infer the user's breathing rate, and the transmitter launches the proposed ambush scheme.

To deploy a trap area, as shown in Fig. 11a, we use a 5-antenna transmitter, consisting of three USRP X310s, which are connected with a host computer through an Ethernet switch and synchronized with OctoClock-G [17]. As shown in Fig. 11b, five collaborative eavesdroppers are placed at 5 specified ambush points on the corridor outside of the office room: one in the center and the other four in the circle with a radius (i.e., antenna-antenna distance) of 0.75 m.

Metrics: Let $\hat{r}$ denote the estimated rate. We apply the following two metrics.

- *Absolute estimation error ϵ:* the difference between true and estimated breathing rates, i.e., $|r_{gt} - \hat{r}|$, where r_{gt} is the ground truth.
- *Absolute ambush error η:* the difference between estimated and specified breathing rates, i.e., $|r_a - \hat{r}|$, where r_a is the one specified by the transmitter.

---

[1] The study has been approved by our institution's IRB.

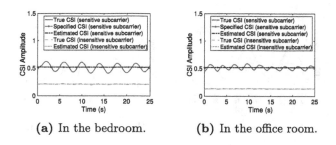

(a) In the bedroom.   (b) In the office room.

Fig. 13. Enabling Eve to obtain no breathing activity.

5.2   Breathing Rate Inference Attacks

We first verify the effectiveness of using CSI to infer breathing rates. As shown in Fig. 10, Eve is put at each ambush location in both of the two scenarios to estimate each participant's breathing rate, with 100 trials performed for every estimate. Figure 12 shows the obtained absolute estimation error when the proposed ambush scheme is not launched.

Figure 12a shows that the inference technique always achieves high accuracy with less than 1.6 bpm of error at all locations in the bedroom. The median absolute estimation error ranges from 0.4 to 0.6 bpm across all locations. Meanwhile, we see the value of ϵ on average is slightly larger at Location 2 than at other locations. This is because Location 2 is not in the LOS of the user and the resultant signal fading degrades the inference performance. We have similar observations from Fig. 12b. Figure 12c depicts the mean absolute estimation errors for different users (referred to as U1~U5). We can observe that the mean absolute estimation error is consistently low (i.e., below 0.8 bpm) across all users in both environments. Also, the average absolute estimation error for each user in the office room is larger than that in the bedroom. It can be explained by the fact that the user has less body movement irrelevant to breathing activity when lying on the bed than when sitting in the chair. These results demonstrate convincingly that an eavesdropper could utilize passively collected CSI to accurately infer a person's breathing rate in different scenarios.

5.3   Example Defenses

We examine three example defenses, in which we deploy the ambush location at Location 1 shown in Fig. 10a and Location 3 shown in Fig. 10b.

Example 1 - Making Breath Unobservable: We first show a defense method by hiding breathing rates, i.e., when Eve appears at the ambush location, she would obtain a breathing rate of 0 (i.e., no breathing activity is detected).

Figure 13 plots the real CSIs between the transmitter and the ambush location, the estimated CSIs at the ambush location, as well as the subcarrier CSI specified by the transmitter. In both environments, the transmitter can make Eve observe a CSI on a sensitive subcarrier significantly near to the specified

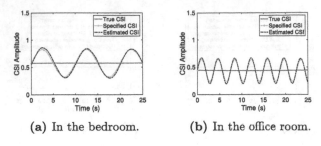

(a) In the bedroom.   (b) In the office room.

Fig. 14. Fabricating normal breath.

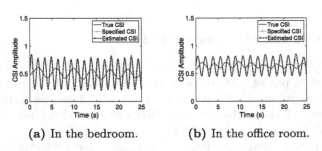

(a) In the bedroom.   (b) In the office room.

Fig. 15. Making Eve obtain abnormal breath.

one while both greatly deviate from the true one; with the estimated CSI, Eve obtains a breathing rate of 0 though the respective true breathing rates are 15.1 and 20.8 bpm. The absolute estimation errors in the bedroom and the office room are thus 15.1 and 20.8 bpm, while the corresponding absolute ambush errors are both 0. Besides, the CSI of the insensitive subcarrier keeps insensitive with the defense (we thus only focus on sensitive subcarriers in the later evaluation).

Example 2 - Fabricating Nonexistent Breath: We aim to make Eve obtain a fake breathing rate while there is no breathing activity in both scenarios. We specify a fake breathing rate of 6 (16) bpm for the bedroom (office) room.

As shown in Fig. 14, we see the true CSI is almost flat, as there is in fact no breathing activity, and the estimated CSI is quite consistent with the CSI specified by the transmitter. With the estimated CSI, Eve obtains a breathing rate of 6.4 bpm in the bedroom and 16.1 bpm in the office room. The absolute estimation errors in the two scenarios become 6.4 and 16.1 bpm, respectively; the respective absolute ambush errors are as small as 0.4 bpm and 0.1 bpm.

Example 3 - Falsifying Breath: We aim to hide a normal breathing rate by making Eve observe an abnormal one. We randomly specify an abnormal breathing rate of 40 bpm for the bedroom and 35 bpm for the office room.

Similar to the above examples, we observe from Fig. 15 that the estimated CSI is quite close to the specified CSI while it greatly differs from the true CSI in both environments. The estimated breathing rate of Eve in the bedroom becomes 40.2 bpm, instead of the true one (i.e., 19.9 bpm) derived from the Masimo

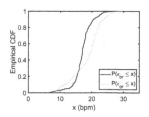 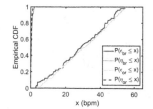 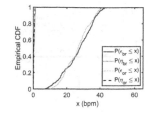

Fig. 16. CDFs of $P(\epsilon \leq x)$ for **D1**.

Fig. 17. CDFs of $P(\epsilon \leq x)$ and $P(\eta \leq x)$ for **D2**.

Fig. 18. CDFs of $P(\epsilon \leq x)$ and $P(\eta \leq x)$ for **D3**.

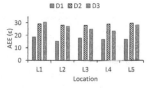 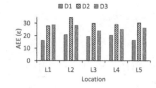

(a) In the bedroom.   (b) In the office room.

Fig. 19. Mean absolute estimation errors (AEE).

Oximeter. In the office room, Eve obtains a breathing rate of 35.2 bpm, instead of the ground truth (i.e., 17.0 bpm). Therefore, the absolute estimation errors for the bedroom and the office room are 20.3 bpm and 18.2 bpm, respectively, while the absolute ambush errors in these two scenarios are both just 0.2 bpm.

5.4 Overall Defense Impact

We examine the overall impact of the three defenses (numbered according to their respective cases): (1) a user is breathing while we aim to make Eve obtain no breathing activity; (2) no breathing activity occurs while we aim to make Eve obtain a fake breathing rate; (3) a user is breathing while we aim to make Eve obtain a different non-zero breathing rate. Eve estimates the breathing rate at every ambush location. For each estimate, we perform 100 trials.

D1: We test when the user has different breathing rates in the range of 6–27 bpm. For all trials, we find that Eve always obtains an estimated breathing rate of 0, indicating the consistent success of the defense. Let $P(\epsilon_{br} \leq x)$ and $P(\epsilon_{or} \leq x)$ denote the empirical cumulative distribution functions (CDFs) of the absolute estimation error ϵ_{br} for the bedroom and ϵ_{or} for the office room. Figure 16 shows that ϵ_{br} and ϵ_{or} lie in the ranges of [6.6, 26.5] and [7.5, 29.6] with probability 100%. Both demonstrate that Eve always has a significant error in the breathing rate estimation with the proposed defense.

D2: We randomly specify a fake breathing rate within the range of 3–55 bpm in each trial. Let $P(\eta_{br} \leq x)$ and $P(\eta_{or} \leq x)$ denote the CDFs of the absolute

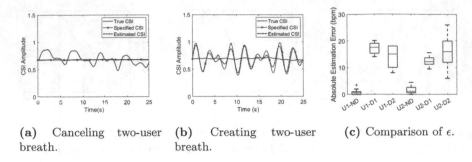

(a) Canceling two-user   (b) Creating two-user   (c) Comparison of ϵ.
breath.   breath.

Fig. 20. Extending defenses in two-user scenario.

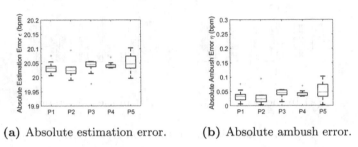

(a) Absolute estimation error.   (b) Absolute ambush error.

Fig. 21. Fabricating normal breath for a trap area.

ambush errors η_{br} for the bedroom and η_{or} for the office room. As shown in Fig. 17, we observe a small η and a high ϵ for both environments. For example, η_{br} is less than 1.5 bpm with a probability of 95.0%, while ϵ_{br} ranges from 3.0 to 54.8 bpm and is larger than 3.1 with a probability of 98.2%.

D3: Each participant has a normal breathing rate, and the transmitter chooses a bogus breathing rate randomly in an abnormal range (31–56 bpm). Figure 18 shows the CDFs of the corresponding ϵ and η. We can see that ϵ_{br} and ϵ_{or} are larger than 11 bpm with probabilities of 96.2% and 99.0%, respectively. Meanwhile, η_{br} is always less than 1.2 bpm, and η_{or} is always less than 0.9 bpm.

Figures 19a and 19b show the mean value of ϵ across all locations in both environments when the proposed defenses are employed. We observe that ϵ stays consistently high at all ambush locations for both environments. Compared with no defense, all defenses can significantly increase ϵ at Eve.

5.5   Two-User Scenario

First, we aim to make two persons' breathing unobservable (referred to as **D1**). We consider the scenario when two participants are in the office room simultaneously. As shown in Fig. 20a, the estimated CSI is quite close to the specified one while both deviate from the true CSI. Consequently, Eve obtains a breathing rate of 0 though the true breathing rates of the two users are 6.0 and 10.0 bpm, respectively. Second, we aim to make Eve observe two specified breathing rates (16 and 22 bpm) when there is no breathing activity (referred to as **D2**). As shown in Fig. 20b, though the true CSI is almost flat, indicating no person in the room, the estimated CSI and the specified one are alike, leading Eve to obtain two-person breathing rates of 16.0 and 22.1 bpm.

We repeat the above two experiments 40 times. For comparison, we also perform 40 attempts of inferring two-person breathing rates when no defense is applied (this case is denoted with **ND**). Figure 20c presents the absolute estimation errors (ϵ) for the cases with two real or fake users (U1 and U2). Without the defenses, the mean value of ϵ is quite small (around 0.8 bpm); while it is significantly increased (within the range of 12.6–17.2 bpm) with the proposed defenses (D1 and D2). Also, for D1, the mean values of the absolute ambush error η for the two users both equal about 0, while for D2, they are 0.1 and 0.4 bpm. These results convincingly show the proposed scheme can successfully mislead Eve with specified breathing rates for the two-user scenario.

5.6   Trap Area Evaluation

We aim to generate fake breath rates in the trap area consisting of five ambush points (referred to as P1~P5), as shown in Fig. 11b. We choose a breathing rate of 20 bpm when the target room has no breathing activity. We perform 10 trials of deploying a trap area.

Figure 21a shows that the absolute estimation errors at all ambush points are consistently large (close to 20 bpm). Figure 21b demonstrates that the absolute ambush errors at all ambush points are quite small, with the mean value ranging from 0.03 to 0.05 bpm across all ambush points. These results demonstrate that the proposed scheme can simultaneously deploy multiple ambush points to mislead collaborative eavesdroppers (or simply increase the probability to trap a single eavesdropper) with fake breathing rates.

6   Related Work

Generally, existing wireless breathing rate inference techniques fall into the following categories:

Ultra-Wideband (UWB) Radar Based: The expansion and contraction of the chest cavity may create changes in the multipath profile of the transmitting signal, which can be captured with UWB impulse responses for breathing rate estimation [28,45,52]. UWB transmissions, however, spread over a large frequency bandwidth [21]. Also, the receiver structure for UWB is highly complex [33].

Doppler Radar Based: Doppler radar systems have been proposed to achieve breathing detection [6,14,34,35,44]. According to the Doppler theory, a target with time-varying movement but zero net velocity will reflect the signal, whose phase is modulated in proportion to the displacement of the target [8]. A stationary person's chest and stomach can be thus regarded as a target. However, such Doppler radar based techniques suffer from the null point problem, which significantly degrades the measurement accuracy [27,35,63].

Frequency Modulated Continuous Wave (FMCW) Radar Based: An FMCW radar has also been utilized for breathing rate inference [3,5,51]. The breathing-induced body movement changes the signal reflection time. By analyzing such changes, the breathing rate can be extracted. However, high resolution (i.e., the minimum measurable change) requires a large swept bandwidth B as the resolution equals $\frac{C}{2B}$ [2], where C is the speed of light.

RSS-Based: The changes in received signal strength (RSS) on wireless links have been successful in estimating breathing rate [1,30,41,42]. For example, [1] puts a mobile device on the chest to collect RSS for inferring breathing rates. However, those methods are workable only when the target user stays close to the receiver. As an eavesdropper usually has a preference to be located far away to avoid being discovered, such RSS-based methods are not optimal.

CSI-Based: RSS represents coarse channel information while CSI represents fine-grained channel information, consisting of subcarrier-level information. As a result, CSI is more sensitive to detecting breathing activity and the CSI-based approaches are able to capture breathing from a distance. Accordingly, CSI-based breathing rate inference has drawn increasing attention [36–38,56,58,59,65]. In particular, a recent empirical study [28] reveals CSI provides the most robust estimates of breathing rate compared with UWB radar or RSS.

7   Conclusion

Wireless signal has demonstrated exceptional capability to detect breathing activity, which introduces a new threat to the security of personal health information. To address this issue, we design an ambush-based strategy by actively deploying ambush locations and feeding eavesdroppers who move to those ambush locations with fake breathing rates. This scheme enables the transmitter to encode the specified fake breathing rate into CSI, and then utilize disturbance manipulation to deliver it to the eavesdropper. We conduct an extensive real-world evaluation on the USRP X310 platform. Experimental results in different scenarios consistently demonstrate the effectiveness of the proposed defenses.

Acknowledgments. We would like to thank our anonymous reviewers for their insightful comments and feedback. This work was supported in part by NSF under Grants No. 1948547.

References

1. Abdelnasser, H., Harras, K.A., Youssef, M.: Ubibreathe: a ubiquitous non-invasive WiFi-based breathing estimator. In: Proceedings of ACM International Symposium on Mobile Ad Hoc Networking and Computing (MobiHoc), pp. 277–286 (2015)

2. Adib, F., Kabelac, Z., Katabi, D., Miller, R.C.: 3D tracking via body radio reflections. In: 11th USENIX Symposium on Networked Systems Design and Implementation (NSDI 2014), Seattle, WA, pp. 317–329. USENIX Association (2014)
3. Adib, F., Mao, H., Kabelac, Z., Katabi, D., Miller, R.C.: Smart homes that monitor breathing and heart rate. In: Proceedings of ACM Conference on Human Factors in Computing Systems (CHI), pp. 837–846 (2015)
4. Anand, N., Sung-Ju Lee, Knightly, E.W.: Strobe: actively securing wireless communications using zero-forcing beamforming. In: 2012 Proceedings IEEE INFOCOM, pp. 720–728 (2012)
5. Anitori, L., de Jong, A., Nennie, F.: FMCW radar for life-sign detection. In: 2009 IEEE Radar Conference, pp. 1–6 (2009)
6. Ascione, M., Buonanno, A., D'Urso, M., Angrisani, L., Schiano Lo Moriello, R.: A new measurement method based on music algorithm for through-the-wall detection of life signs. IEEE Trans. Instrum. Measur. **62**(1), 13–26 (2013)
7. Clark, B.J.: Treatment of heart failure in infants and children. Heart Disease **2**(5), 354–361 (2000)
8. Boric-Lubecke, O., Lubecke, V.M., Droitcour, A.D., Park, B.K., Singh, A.: Doppler Radar Physiological Sensing. Wiley Online Library (2016)
9. Chaman, A., Wang, J., Sun, J., Hassanieh, H., Roy Choudhury, R.: Ghostbuster: detecting the presence of hidden eavesdroppers. In: Proceedings of the 24th Annual International Conference on Mobile Computing and Networking, MobiCom 2018, pp. 337–351. Association for Computing Machinery, New York (2018)
10. Chen, L., et al.: Lungtrack: towards contactless and zero dead-zone respiration monitoring with commodity RFIDs. Proc. ACM Interact. Mob. Wearable Ubiquitous Technol. **3**(3), 79:1–79:22 (2019)
11. Cox, R.A., Torres, C.Z.: Acute heart failure in adults. P. R. Health Sci. J. **23**(4), 265–271 (2004)
12. Crepaldi, R., Jeongkeun Lee, Etkin, R., Sung-Ju Lee, Kravets, R.: CSI-SF: estimating wireless channel state using CSI sampling fusion. In: 2012 Proceedings of IEEE INFOCOM, pp. 154–162 (2012)
13. Davies, L., Gather, U.: The identification of multiple outliers. J. Am. Stat. Assoc. **88**(423), 782–792 (1993)
14. Droitcour, A.D., Boric-Lubecke, O., Kovacs, G.T.A.: Signal-to-noise ratio in doppler radar system for heart and respiratory rate measurements. IEEE Trans. Microw. Theory Tech. **57**(10), 2498–2507 (2009)
15. Duggan, W.: CSX stock plummets on CEO's health concerns. US News (2017). https://money.usnews.com/investing/stock-market-news/articles/2017-12-15/csx-corporation-stock-plummets-on-ceos-health-concerns
16. Ellyatt, H.: How CEO health can affect your wealth. CNBC (2012). https://www.cnbc.com/id/49115208
17. Ettus, M.: USRP users and developers guide (2005). www.olifantasia.com/gnuradio/usrp/files/usrp_guide.pdf
18. Ettus Research: SBX 400-4400 MHz Rx/Tx (2022). https://www.ettus.com/all-products/sbx120/
19. Ettus Research: USRP X310 (2022). https://www.ettus.com/all-products/x310-kit/
20. Fan, D., et al.: Breathing rhythm analysis in body centric networks. IEEE Access **6**, 32507–32513 (2018)
21. Federal Communications Commission and others: Revision of part 15 of the commission's rules regarding ultra-wideband transmission systems. First Report and Order, FCC 02-48 (2002)

22. Fekr, A.R., Janidarmian, M., Radecka, K., Zilic, Z.: Respiration disorders classification with informative features for m-health applications. IEEE J. Biomed. Health Inform. **20**(3), 733–747 (2016)
23. Genkin, D., Pachmanov, L., Pipman, I., Tromer, E.: Stealing keys from PCs using a radio: cheap electromagnetic attacks on windowed exponentiation. In: Güneysu, T., Handschuh, H. (eds.) CHES 2015. LNCS, vol. 9293, pp. 207–228. Springer, Heidelberg (2015). https://doi.org/10.1007/978-3-662-48324-4_11
24. GNU Radio project: GNU Radio - the free & open source radio ecosystem (2022). https://www.gnuradio.org
25. Goldsmith, A.: Wireless Communications. Cambridge University Press, New York (2005)
26. Gollakota, S., Katabi, D.: Physical layer wireless security made fast and channel independent. In: 2011 Proceedings of IEEE INFOCOM, pp. 1125–1133 (2011)
27. Gu, C.: Short-range noncontact sensors for healthcare and other emerging applications: a review. Sensors **16**(8), 1169 (2016)
28. Hillyard, P., et al.: Experience: cross-technology radio respiratory monitoring performance study. In: Proceedings of the 24th Annual International Conference on Mobile Computing and Networking, MobiCom 2018, pp. 487–496. Association for Computing Machinery, New York (2018)
29. Jia, W., Peng, H., Ruan, N., Tang, Z., Zhao, W.: WiFind: driver fatigue detection with fine-grained wi-fi signal features. IEEE Trans. Big Data **6**(2), 269–282 (2020)
30. Kaltiokallio, O., Yiğitler, H., Jäntti, R., Patwari, N.: Non-invasive respiration rate monitoring using a single COTS TX-RX pair. In: Proceedings of the 13th International Symposium on Information Processing in Sensor Networks (IPSN), pp. 59–69 (2014)
31. Krombholz, K., Hobel, H., Huber, M., Weippl, E.: Advanced social engineering attacks. J. Inf. Secur. Appl. **22**, 113–122 (2015). Special Issue on Security of Information and Networks
32. Lafky, D.B., Horan, T.A.: Personal health records: consumer attitudes toward privacy and security of their personal health information. Health Informatics J. **17**(1), 63–71 (2011)
33. Lampe, L., Witrisal, K.: Challenges and recent advances in IR-UWB system design. In: Proceedings of 2010 IEEE International Symposium on Circuits and Systems, pp. 3288–3291 (2010)
34. Li, C., Ling, J., Li, J., Lin, J.: Accurate doppler radar noncontact vital sign detection using the relax algorithm. IEEE Trans. Instrum. Meas. **59**(3), 687–695 (2010)
35. Li, C., Lubecke, V.M., Boric-Lubecke, O., Lin, J.: A review on recent advances in doppler radar sensors for noncontact healthcare monitoring. IEEE Trans. Microw. Theory Tech. **61**(5), 2046–2060 (2013)
36. Liu, J., Wang, Y., Chen, Y., Yang, J., Chen, X., Cheng, J.: Tracking vital signs during sleep leveraging off-the-shelf WiFi. In: Proceedings of ACM International Symposium on Mobile Ad Hoc Networking and Computing (MobiHoc), pp. 267–276 (2015)
37. Liu, X., Cao, J., Tang, S., Wen, J.: Wi-sleep: contactless sleep monitoring via WiFi signals. In: 2014 IEEE Real-Time Systems Symposium, pp. 346–355 (2014)
38. Liu, X., Cao, J., Tang, S., Wen, J., Guo, P.: Contactless respiration monitoring via off-the-shelf WiFi devices. IEEE Trans. Mob. Comput. **15**(10), 2466–2479 (2016)
39. Ma, Y., Zhou, G., Wang, S.: WiFi sensing with channel state information: a survey. ACM Comput. Surv. **52**(3), 1–36 (2019)

40. Masimo: MightySat fingertip pulse oximeter with bluetooth LE, RRp, & PVi (2021). https://www.masimopersonalhealth.com/products/mightysat-fingertip-pulse-oximeter-with-bluetooth-le-rrp-pvi

41. Patwari, N., Brewer, L., Tate, Q., Kaltiokallio, O., Bocca, M.: Breathfinding: a wireless network that monitors and locates breathing in a home. IEEE J. Sel. Top. Signal Process. **8**(1), 30–42 (2014)

42. Patwari, N., Wilson, J., Ananthanarayanan, S., Kasera, S.K., Westenskow, D.R.: Monitoring breathing via signal strength in wireless networks. IEEE Trans. Mob. Comput. **13**(8), 1774–1786 (2014)

43. Pradhan, S., Sun, W., Baig, G., Qiu, L.: Combating replay attacks against voice assistants. Proc. ACM Interact. Mob. Wearable Ubiquitous Technol. **3**(3), 1–26 (2019)

44. Rahman, T., et al.: Dopplesleep: a contactless unobtrusive sleep sensing system using short-range doppler radar. In: Proceedings of the 2015 ACM International Joint Conference on Pervasive and Ubiquitous Computing, UbiComp 2015, pp. 39–50. Association for Computing Machinery, New York (2015)

45. Salmi, J., Molisch, A.F.: Propagation parameter estimation, modeling and measurements for ultrawideband MIMO radar. IEEE Trans. Antennas Propag. **59**(11), 4257–4267 (2011)

46. Sen, S., Radunovic, B., Choudhury, R.R., Minka, T.: You are facing the Mona Lisa: spot localization using PHY layer information. In: Proceedings of the 10th International Conference on Mobile Systems, Applications, and Services, MobiSys 2012, pp. 183–196. Association for Computing Machinery, New York (2012)

47. Shen, W., Ning, P., He, X., Dai, H.: Ally friendly jamming: how to jam your enemy and maintain your own wireless connectivity at the same time. In: 2013 IEEE Symposium on Security and Privacy, pp. 174–188 (2013)

48. Shiu, Y.S., Chang, S.Y., Wu, H.C., Huang, S.C.H., Chen, H.H.: Physical layer security in wireless networks: a tutorial. IEEE Wirel. Commun. **18**(2), 66–74 (2011)

49. Smith, S.W., et al.: The Scientist and Engineer's Guide to Digital Signal Processing. California Technical Publishing, San Diego (1997)

50. Tippenhauer, N.O., Malisa, L., Ranganathan, A., Capkun, S.: On limitations of friendly jamming for confidentiality. In: Proceedings of the 2013 IEEE Symposium on Security and Privacy, SP 2013, USA, pp. 160–173. IEEE Computer Society (2013)

51. Van Loon, K., et al.: Wireless non-invasive continuous respiratory monitoring with FMCW radar: a clinical validation study. J. Clin. Monit. Comput. **30**(6), 797–805 (2016)

52. Venkatesh, S., Anderson, C.R., Rivera, N.V., Buehrer, R.M.: Implementation and analysis of respiration-rate estimation using impulse-based UWB. In: 2005 IEEE Military Communications Conference (MILCOM), vol. 5, pp. 3314–3320 (2005)

53. Wahls, S.A.: Causes and evaluation of chronic dyspnea. Am. Fam. Physician **86**(2), 173–82 (2012)

54. Wang, C., Liu, J., Chen, Y., Liu, H., Wang, Y.: Towards in-baggage suspicious object detection using commodity WiFi. In: 2018 IEEE Conference on Communications and Network Security (CNS), pp. 1–9 (2018)

55. Wang, F., Zhang, F., Wu, C., Wang, B., Liu, K.J.R.: Respiration tracking for people counting and recognition. IEEE Internet Things J. **7**(6), 5233–5245 (2020)

56. Wang, H., et al.: Human respiration detection with commodity WiFi devices: do user location and body orientation matter? In: Proceedings of the 2016 ACM International Joint Conference on Pervasive and Ubiquitous Computing (UbiComp), pp. 25–36 (2016)

57. Wang, X., Niu, K., Xiong, J., Qian, B., Yao, Z., Lou, T., Zhang, D.: Placement matters: understanding the effects of device placement for WiFi sensing. Proc. ACM Interact. Mob. Wearable Ubiquitous Technol. **6**(1), 1–25 (2022)

58. Wang, X., Yang, C., Mao, S.: Phasebeat: exploiting CSI phase data for vital sign monitoring with commodity WiFi devices. In: 2017 IEEE 37th International Conference on Distributed Computing Systems (ICDCS), pp. 1230–1239 (2017)

59. Wang, X., Yang, C., Mao, S.: Tensorbeat: tensor decomposition for monitoring multiperson breathing beats with commodity WiFi. ACM Trans. Intell. Syst. Technol. **9**(1), 1–27 (2017)

60. Whited, L., Graham, D.D.: Abnormal respirations. StatPearls, Treasure Island, FL, USA (2019). https://www.ncbi.nlm.nih.gov/books/NBK470309/

61. Wu, C., Yang, Z., Zhou, Z., Liu, X., Liu, Y., Cao, J.: Non-invasive detection of moving and stationary human with WiFi. IEEE J. Sel. Areas Commun. **33**(11), 2329–2342 (2015)

62. Yang, Y., Cao, J., Liu, X., Xing, K.: Multi-person sleeping respiration monitoring with cots WiFi devices. In: 2018 IEEE 15th International Conference on Mobile Ad Hoc and Sensor Systems (MASS), pp. 37–45 (2018)

63. Xiao, Y., Lin, J., Boric-Lubecke, O., Lubecke, V.M.: Frequency-tuning technique for remote detection of heartbeat and respiration using low-power double-sideband transmission in the ka-band. IEEE Trans. Microw. Theory Tech. **54**(5), 2023–2032 (2006)

64. Zeng, Y., Wu, D., Gao, R., Gu, T., Zhang, D.: Fullbreathe: full human respiration detection exploiting complementarity of CSI phase and amplitude of WiFi signals. Proc. ACM Interact. Mob. Wearable Ubiquitous Technol. **2**(3), 1–19 (2018)

65. Zhang, F., Zhang, D., Xiong, J., Wang, H., Niu, K., Jin, B., Wang, Y.: From Fresnel diffraction model to fine-grained human respiration sensing with commodity Wi-Fi devices. Proc. ACM Interact. Mob. Wearable Ubiquitous Technol. **2**(1) (2018)

LightSeg: An Online and Low-Latency Activity Segmentation Method for Wi-Fi Sensing

Liming Chen, Xiaolong Zheng[✉], Leiyang Xu, Liang Liu, and Huadong Ma

School of Computer Science, Beijing University of Posts and Telecommunications, Beijing, China

{chenliming1997,zhengxiaolong,xuleiyang,liangliu,mhd}@bupt.edu.cn

Abstract. WiFi based activity recognition mainly uses the changes of Channel State Information (CSI) to capture motion occurrence. Extracting correct segments that correspond to activities from CSI series is then a prerequisite for activity recognition. Researchers have designed various segmentation methods, including threshold-based and deep learning-based methods. However, threshold-based methods are highly empirical and the threshold is usually dependent on the application and environment. When dealing with mixed-grained activities, the predefined threshold will fail. On the other hand, deep learning-based methods are impractical for online systems with low-latency demand because of their high overhead. In this paper, we propose LightSeg, an online and low-latency segmentation method leveraging an activity granularity-aware threshold that quickly adjusts itself based on the granularity of the activity in the current detecting window. We propose a threshold post-decision mechanism that detects the end of a segment first and then decides the appropriate threshold based on the most recent activity. By this way, LightSeg automatically adapts to different activity granularity in practice. Compared to existing threshold-based methods, LightSeg greatly reduces the dependence on expertise to decide the threshold. Experimental results show that LightSeg improves the segmentation accuracy by up to 14% compared to the existing threshold-based method and reduces the data processing time by 97% compared to the deep learning-based method.

Keywords: WiFi sensing · CSI · Activity segmentation

1 Introduction

In recent years, wireless sensing has attracted more and more attention from both academy and industry. It leverages wireless signals such as WiFi, Bluetooth, RFID, and ZigBee, to sense the behaviors of a person or the states of

This work is supported in part by the National Natural Science Foundation of China (No. 61932013), the A3 Foresight Program of NSFC (No. 62061146002), and the Funds for Creative Research Groups of China (No. 61921003).

S. Longfei and P. Bodhi (Eds.): MobiQuitous 2022, LNICST 492, pp. 227–247, 2023.
https://doi.org/10.1007/978-3-031-34776-4_13

other objects, and then realize smart applications [17,19,24–26]. Since WiFi is ubiquitous and not affected by illumination, WiFi-based wireless sensing has been widely studied.

Since WiFi Channel State Information (CSI) contains finer-grained and more stable channel information [14] and can be extracted from commercial WiFi devices [20], it is commonly used in existing WiFi sensing applications. The complex-valued CSI contains amplitude and phase information. CSI phase is often interfered by uncertain disturbances such as carrier frequency offset (CFO) and sampling frequency offset (SFO) [21]. While the amplitude of CSI is the generally reliable and accessible metric for activity extraction and classification [21], thus CSI amplitude is a commonly used feature for WiFi sensing.

After obtaining CSI, two major stages are needed for WiFi sensing: activity segmentation and activity classification [2]. Accurate activity segmentation is a prerequisite of accurate activity classification. The most common activity segmentation method used in WiFi sensing is the threshold-based method. Existing works uses a predefined fixed threshold to extract activity [1,7,8,10,15]. These fixed-threshold methods have to set empirical parameters and select an appropriate denoising strategy to determine a good threshold. Some works take the environmental factors such as noise into account when determining the threshold [9,11,18,23]. They adjust the threshold automatically according to the noise level in the environment.

Most of the existing threshold-based segmentation methods only adjust the threshold based on noise but ignore the granularity of target activity. Different activities with different granularity can desire different and even contradictory thresholds. Fine-grained activities such as gestures require a small threshold in case missing the meaningful small CSI changes, but coarse-grained activities such as postures (falling, gait, etc.) desire a large threshold to exclude more noise. In practice, coarse-grained and fine-grained activities usually occur alternately and randomly. Then the threshold decided based on one granularity will extract incorrect CSI segments.

Take the application of elderly monitoring as an example. A target may walk to the living room, take a drink, and then sit down on a chair. The activity recognition system needs to continuously segment the coarse-grained activities (walking and sitting down) and the fine-grained activity (drinking). For existing methods, the predetermined threshold for activities of one granularity is not appropriate for the other, resulting in the decline of segmentation accuracy and affecting the accuracy of activity recognition. For example, for a pair of coarse-grained and fine-grained activities shown in Fig. 1, since the CSI changes caused by the coarse-grained activity are distinguishable from background CSI noise, a large threshold is appropriate, which can avoid the extracted activity containing unnecessary noise. But applying the large threshold to the fine-grained activities, meaningful CSI parts can be misjudged as noise and the extracted CSI segmentation can be incomplete, as shown in Fig. 1(a). On the contrary, if a small threshold appropriate for the fine-grained activity is applied to segment the coarse-grained activity, some unnecessary background noise might be included after activity extraction, as shown in Fig. 1(b).

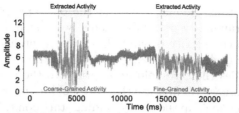

(a) Use threshold appropriate for the coarse-grained activity.

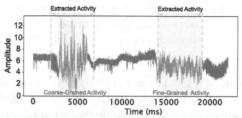

(b) Use threshold appropriate for the fine-grained activity.

Fig. 1. Illustration of inaccurate segmentation of existing threshold-based methods for mixed-grained activities. The gray parts are groundtruth. (Color figure online)

Existing threshold-based methods only set a threshold in an activity detection window according to activities with one granularity for a particular application. But before activity extraction, it is difficult to set an appropriate threshold for all kinds of activities without knowing their granularity, especially when there are multiple activities in one detection window. The lack of awareness of activity granularity is the fundamental reason why the existing threshold-based segmentation methods are not suitable for activities with mixed granularity.

A deep learning-based segmentation method [16] is proposed to segment activities with arbitrary granularity. Because the deep learning model can learn the activity granularity through training, the work has achieved remarkable results. However, the overhead (memory, latency, hardware requirements) of deep learning-based methods is much higher than threshold-based methods and even unaffordable to embedded WiFi devices. In practice, online activity recognition demands low latency but the deep learning-based segmentation will be time-consuming and hard to provide friendly WiFi sensing services.

A practical activity segmentation method for WiFi sensing should be able to segment multiple activities with different granularity in a detection window with low latency. To obtain such a method, several requirements should be satisfied: (1) low overhead and fast granularity perception, (2) environment independence, and (3) interference resistance. By satisfying these requirements, we propose LightSeg, a lightweight granularity-aware threshold-based activity segmentation method that can segment activities with different granularity with low latency to support online WiFi sensing applications. We adopt fast preprocessing policies and remove the redundant information of the CSI data first. Since the variation of CSI amplitude reflects the intensity of activities, then we use the moving variance in preprocessing module to obtain the one-dimensional preprocessed CSI series for fast granularity perception. Then we design a core segmentation algorithm with time complexity of only $O(N)$ that contains granularity-aware threshold decision and abnormal peak removal. Based on the estimated granularity, LightSeg decides the threshold appropriate to the target activity in the current detection window. We first use this threshold to determine the end point of an activity and then look up the corresponding start point. By this way, Light-Seg avoids using a predefined threshold and can adjust the threshold for each activity regardless of the environment influence. To avoid incorrect segmentation caused by interference, we propose an abnormal peak removal mechanism that uses a valid duration to distinguish activities and interference.

In summary, the main contributions are as follows:

- We propose an online and low-latency activity segmentation method for WiFi sensing. We design an activity granularity-aware threshold adjusting algorithm, which can solve the performance degradation of activity segmentation with mixed or unknown granularity.
- We solve several practical issues of LightSeg. We design the granularity perception method, granularity-based threshold adjustment, and abnormal peak removal to improve the segmentation performance in practical scenarios.
- Experimental results show that the segmentation accuracy of LightSeg is up to 14% higher than the state-of-the-art threshold-based method. Compared to the deep-learning based method, LightSeg achieves similar and even better accuracy but has much less overhead in terms of both computational latency and resources.

2   Related Work

Activity segmentation is a prerequisite of classification. Many works have been carried out on activity segmentation [6,13]. These segmentation methods can be categorized as threshold-based methods and deep learning-based methods.

2.1   Threshold-Based Activity Segmentation

Threshold-based activity segmentation methods use a threshold to identify the start and end points and extract the attached CSI segment as valid activity data [5], because the variation of CSI amplitude is detectable with the onset of activities. A fixed threshold is easy to implement but its performance depends on applications and environments. Virmani and Shahzad [8] found that principal component analysis (PCA) can effectively remove the noise in CSI streams. And then they use a fixed threshold on the second principal component of the CSI stream to identify the occurrence of activities. Wu et al. [15] proved that the general PCA could not meet scenarios of the signals through a wall. Hence, they introduced the opposite robust PCA and designed a normalized variance sliding window algorithm to process the first principal component for activity segmentation. Sheng et al. [7] presented a segmentation algorithm based on time series difference. The algorithm uses the mean absolute differences and the pre-set start threshold and end threshold to detect activities. Wang et al. [10] presented a two-stage segmentation algorithm to identify falling, they use a threshold-based sliding window method to identify whether the CSI waveforms are in a fluctuating state or a stable state. Then a backtracking window from the end point is used to detect the start point of a fall. Bu et al. [1] recognized the start and end of activities by calculating whether the variance in the window exceeded the empirical threshold, and presented a motion pause buffer algorithm to solve the wrong gesture segmentation caused by some short pauses in the gesture process.

To cope with dynamic noise, some segmentation methods adopt dynamic threshold. Feng et al. [3] divided the CSI stream in a detection window into several slots. Then the average difference between the sum of the largest half values and the sum of the smallest half values of CSI variance in each time slot is regarded as the threshold. Wang et al. [9] calculated the activity amplitude threshold based on the active and static CSI streams and updated the threshold based on newly collected CSI data to adapt to environmental changes. Yan et al. [18] presented an adaptive activity segmentation algorithm that updates the threshold based on CSI changes in the sliding window to balance the trade-off between performance and robustness. Wang et al. [11] used an Exponential Moving Average algorithm to update the noise level estimation and set the threshold three times as large as the noise level. Zhang et al. [23] presented kurtosis as the metric to evaluate power spectral density distribution (PSD). The detection threshold is set as three times as large as the PSD kurtosis when there is no movement. And an Exponential Moving Average algorithm is leveraged to update PSD kurtosis when there is no movement.

Both threshold-based segmentation studies focus on either fine-grained activities or coarse-grained activities and only adjust the threshold according to noise without consideration of the granularity of the target activity. Due to the unawareness of granularity of current activities in practice, the predefined threshold for specific activities can be inappropriate for other activities.

2.2 Deep Learning-Based Activity Segmentation

With the development of deep learning technique, researchers are applying deep learning to activity segmentation for WiFi sensing. Xiao et al. [16] proposed DeepSeg, a deep learning-based activity segmentation method. By using a large training dataset containing various activities with different granularity, the trained activity segmentation model can deal with the granularity unawareness problem.

However, the deep learning-based method is labor-intensive because it requires collecting a large amount of data with manually labeled ground-truth start and end points for each collected activity trace. What's worse, it requires huge computation and memory resources, which is hard to be affordable for embedded WiFi devices. Even if possible, the massive calculation of a deep learning model will be extremely time-consuming and lead to huge delay, hindering practical usages of online WiFi sensing application systems.

3   Design of LightSeg

In this section, we first present an overview of LightSeg and then introduce the design details of each module.

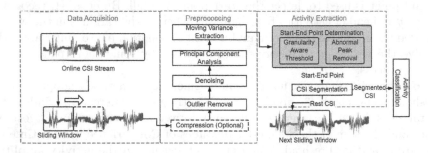

Fig. 2. Overview of LightSeg.

3.1   Overview

To realize online activity segmentation, we introduce a sliding window mechanism and ensure that all processing flows of activity segmentation are completed within the sliding window duration. As the overall workflow of LightSeg shown in Fig. 2, after obtaining a CSI stream online from a sliding window, Light-Seg uses the preprocessing module to process the CSI stream into sensing data easy to segment, including compression, amplitude limiting, DWT, PCA, and moving variance calculation. Then the activity extraction module uses our core algorithm to determine the start and end points of the activities. LightSeg first determines the end of an activity and then decides the threshold suitable for the current activity granularity to get the CSI segment. The resulting CSI segment containing the activity will be used for the following activity classification. To facilitate comparison, we reproduce the model of DeepSeg as the classifier. Users can also design or use other activity classification models. The remaining CSI samples after the decided end point in the current window will be spliced into the next sliding window to avoid incomplete activity extraction.

3.2   Data Acquisition

To facilitate the online WiFi application, the CSI data stream should be carefully handled since the very beginning from data acquisition.

Online CSI Stream. We develop a CSI real-time parser to handle the online CSI data streams. For each pair of transceivers, each received packet contains the CSI of 30 OFDM subcarriers. The parser will store the real part of the CSI (i.e., CSI amplitude) in the queue and wait for the sliding window to obtain the data. For multiple transceiver links (e.g. 3 pairs of transceivers in our implementation), instead of using all the links, we just select one of the links with good signal

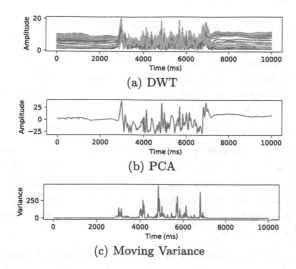

(a) DWT

(b) PCA

(c) Moving Variance

Fig. 3. Illustration of the preprocessing.

quality for activity segmentation and then obtain the segmented CSI data of multiple links.

Sliding Window. We use a sliding window to detect the target activities. Assume the length of a sliding window is $L_{sw} = L_{rest} + L_{new}$, where L_{rest} represents the remaining CSI in the previous sliding window and L_{new} represents the new CSI obtained from the queue in the current sliding window. When the queue length reaches L_{new}, the remaining CSI in the last segmentation will be combined with the CSI in the queue to form a new sliding window for segmentation, ensuring the integrity of the signal without overlapping. To prevent the length of the sliding window from being too long, resulting in substantial subsequent signal processing time, the rest length L_{rest} is limited and the rear of the remaining CSI signals will be retained if L_{rest} is larger than the limit. But if the limit of L_{rest} is too small, the unsegmented activity may be incomplete in the next sliding window; if it's too large, the processing time of the next sliding will increase. In our current implementation, we empirically set the limit to $1.5L_{new}$, which can avoid incomplete activities and minimize processing time.

Suppose the sampling rate of CSI is F_s, and the time of obtaining the new part of CSI equals L_{new}/F_s. For an online system, to avoid congestion caused by CSI in the queue that cannot be processed in time, the CSI of the current sliding window must be processed within L_{new}/F_s. In addition, sufficient time should be reserved for activity classification.

3.3   Preprocessing

The raw CSI data is extremely noisy and redundant. Extracting activities directly from CSI data is inaccurate and of high overhead. Hence, we design a four-step preprocessing module to remove noise and redundancy, and provide data easy to process for the following activity extraction module.

Outlier Removal. Amplitude limiting can filter out the impulse outlier caused by accidental factors, such as the opening and closing of power switches. Because CSI amplitude is positive and usually less than 30, we set the CSI amplitude exceeding the interval [0,35] to the maximum or minimum value of the interval to reduce the impact of outliers on subsequent calculations.

Denoising. Discrete Wavelet Transform (DWT) [6] can achieve an obvious denoising effect and well retain the original characteristics of the signal. We perform DWT denoising on the CSI of 30 subcarriers, as shown in Fig. 3(a). The segmentation features can be enhanced after DWT noise filtering. In addition, due to the fast computation of DWT, it is suitable for online systems with the requirements of low latency.

Principal Component Analysis (PCA). The 30 OFDM subcarriers of a single antenna pair have strong linear correlation [12], so they contain a large number of redundant information [22], which can be removed during segmentation to reduce computing overhead. PCA is a widely used mathematical dimension reduction method [6,23] to remove the redundancy, which converts a group of linearly related variables into a group of linearly uncorrelated variables, and the output variables are arranged from large to small according to the retention ratio of signal characteristics. We select the first principal component for the further preprocessing and denote it as P, as shown in Fig. 3(b).

Moving Variance Extraction. As shown in Fig. 3(b), the CSI changes during the activity are larger than that during the static part. Hence, we use a linear data processing method, moving variance to capture the difference. Moving variance calculates the variance of P in sliding windows with a length of L_{mv} and the result is denoted as V, as shown in Fig. 3(c). The moving variance corresponding to i-th window is denoted as v_i. From Fig. 3(c), we can find that the moving variance of the activity is much larger than that of the static part. In addition, coarse-grained activities will have a larger moving variance. Figure 4 shows the moving variance result of the set of mixed-grained activities shown in Fig. 1. The results demonstrate that we can use moving variance as an indicator to learn the activity granularity.

Compression. LightSeg has short processing time ($\sim 0.3s$ per activity) in commonly used hardware such as laptops. However, in real scenarios, users may need

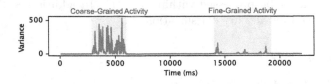

Fig. 4. Preprocessing results of mixed-grained activities.

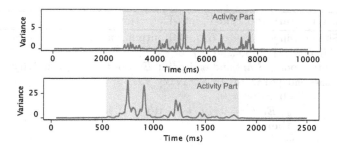

Fig. 5. Preprocessing results in different environments.

to deploy WiFi sensing to resource-limited hardware, which will increase the processing time of LightSeg and influence user experience. Reducing the sampling rate through data compression can significantly reduce the processing time, but it will sacrifice the segmentation accuracy instead. To balance the trade-off between efficiency and performance, a user can set the user-specified compression ratio. Since the low overhead of LightSeg, compression is only optional and not enabled by default. The compression method is the most commonly used equidistant sampling, which is consistent with DeepSeg.

Segmentation desires environment independence to be practical. Figure 5 shows the results V of activity "pushing" after above preprocessing in two different environments. It is obvious that results of the activity part in the two environment are very different. However, as long as the appropriate threshold is decided, the activity can be segmented because of the clear difference between the activity and the static part. Our threshold design is not predefined based on activity type or environment, it is adjusted based on each current activity. Hence, our method can be environment independent.

3.4 Activity Extraction

This module is designed to provide segmented CSI as the input for the classifier used for activity classification. The input size of the classifier is usually fixed, e.g., $200 \times 30 \times 3$. To retain the length feature of the activity, the length of all CSI segments is consistent. The segmented CSI can be fully retained or compressed according to the input size of the classifier. Suppose L_{output} is the output length of the activity extraction module, which is also the length of segmented CSI. It is usually larger than the length of the activity part, and the activity part will be placed in the middle of the segmented CSI.

To determine the position of the activity part, we design a lightweight algorithm described in Algorithm 1 to find the start and end points of the target activity. The inputs are the preprocessed CSI V, sliding window length L_{sw} and CSI output length L_{output}, and the outputs are the start and end points. The algorithm realizes granularity-aware threshold decision and abnormal peak removal. The former is used to perceive the granularity of the activity to segment, and the latter is used to resist interference.

Algorithm 1: Start and End Points Detection

Input: Sliding window length L_{sw}, CSI output length L_{output}, preprocessed
CSI $V = \{v_1, ...v_2, ..., v_{L_{sw}}\}$
Output: Start point $Start$ and end point End of the target activity
// find the end point of an activity first

1 $v_{max} = 0$, $End = 0$, $Start = 0$;
2 **for** $i = 0$; $i < L_{sw}$, $End == 0$; $i = i + 1$ **do**
3   **if** $v_i > v_{max}$ **then**
4        $v_{max} = v_i$;
5        $\delta = 4\% \cdot v_{max}$;
6   **else**
7   **if** $v_i < \delta$ **then**
8   **for** $a = i$; $a < i + L_{end}$, $\frac{number\ of\ v_a > \delta}{L_{end}} < 0.1$; $a = a + 1$ **do**
9   **if** $\frac{number\ of\ v_a < \delta}{L_{end}} > 0.9$ **then**
10                $End = i$;
11   break;
12          $i = a$;

// find the start point of the activity
13 **for** $i = End - L_{output}$; $i < End$, $Start == 0$; $i = i + 1$ **do**
14   **if** $v_i > \delta$ **then**
15   **for** $a = i$; $a < i + L_{end}$, $\frac{number\ of\ v_a < \delta}{L_{start}} < 0.5$; $a = a + 1$ **do**
16   **if** $\frac{number\ of\ v_a > \delta}{L_{start}} > 0.5$ **then**
17             $Start = i$;
18   break;
19       $i = a$;

20 **return** $Start$, End;

Granularity Aware Threshold Decision. For offline CSI stream processing, it is easy to control that only one activity exists in a sliding window or obtain the approximate location of a target activity. Then the threshold can be easily decided because only one activity is in the detection window. Based on the extensive experimental studies, we found that for a single activity in a detection window, setting the threshold to 4% of the maximum value of the target activity variance can accurately segment it. However, for online CSI streams, the time and number of activities occurrence are unpredictable, it is hard to ensure only one activity in each processing window (the sliding window). Then if more than one activities occur, the optimal threshold is hard to decide for all the activities, especially when they have different granularity.

To solve this problem, we propose a new threshold decision method, that is updating the maximum value online during the linear traversal of V, to obtain a granularity-aware threshold δ of the target activity. When the condition $v_i < \delta$ is continuously true for a certain number of samples, we find an end of an activity (line 9–11 in Algorithm 1). The number of samples is defined as the end window length L_{end} and the window is denoted as W_{end}. As shown in line 3–5 in Algorithm 1, the threshold δ keeps updating with the linear traversal of the current CSI steam. When the end of an activity is found, the corresponding threshold of this activity is decided. Then we can use this threshold to look for the start point.

Benefiting from linear traversal, the time complexity of our threshold decision is $O(N)$. Since V is positively related to activity granularity and the threshold is calculated from V, we can say our threshold has the ability to perceive and adapt to the granularity of the activity.

Abnormal Peak Removal. Due to pulse noise caused by environment changes or automatic gain control and even hardware errors of the WiFi transceivers, samples in the static part can be occasionally larger than the threshold δ, leading to incorrect detection of activities.

To cope with this problem, we propose abnormal peak removal that leverages the active duration correct the detection errors. We define the value of the static part above the threshold but with a duration obviously shorter than the duration of a normal activity as abnormal peak. From the concrete example in Fig. 6, we can find that the length of an abnormal peak is much shorter and its height is much smaller than the maximum value. Hence, we remove the peaks with a much short duration to calibrate the estimation of start and end points.

In the process of linear traversal of V, let current position i as the start of W_{end} and calculate the proportion of points smaller than δ in W_{end}. If the proportion exceeds a certain value, though some short-period peaks exist, i will be still regarded as the end of an activity. Otherwise, the activity does not end, W_{end} will be reset, and the start of the next W_{end} is the current position of the traversal. A similar operation is conducted when looking for the start point. By this way, we remove the abnormal peaks and obtain the correct start and end points of an activity. The result when using abnormal peak removal is shown in Fig. 6(b). Note that looking for the start point needs a back trace of the data

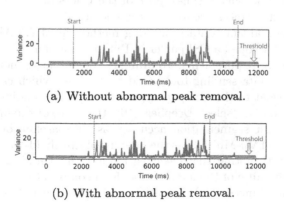

(a) Without abnormal peak removal.

(b) With abnormal peak removal.

Fig. 6. Segmentation results with and without abnormal peak removal.

but the traversal distance to find the start point is short. In general, the total distance of the twice traversal is less than L_{sw}.

In the algorithm, some parameters are determined empirically. L_{new} is set to the average length of normal activities, and adjustment within limits to it will not affect the segmentation performance. To ensure the integrity of the segmented CSI, we make L_{output} longer than the maximum length of the target activities. For different applications with different datasets, L_{new} and L_{output} can be different. But it should be noticed that all the system parameters are not affected by environment and activity granularity. The system parameters are general for different environments and activity granularity.

4   Evaluation

In this section, we first introduce the experiment settings and then present the experimental results comparing with baseline methods.

4.1   Experiment Settings

we evaluate LightSeg on the public dataset provided by DeepSeg [16], which contains both coarse-grained and fine-grained activities. The DeepSeg dataset [16] was collected in a meeting room. The transmitter is a commercial WiFi router with one antenna and the receiver is a laptop with Intel 5300 NIC and three antennas, which can provide CSI of 30 subcarriers from each pair of transmit-receive antennas. The dataset was provided by five users with different body shapes and ages, each of whom performed 10 activities 30 times each, including 5 coarse-grained activities (boxing, picking up, running, squatting and walking) and 5 fine-grained activities (hand swing, hand raising, pushing, drawing O and drawing X). The sampling rate of the collected data is 1000 packets/s. Based on these data, 150 activity sequence traces are used. In each CSI sequence, 10 activities were performed by a user, including a coarse-grained activity 5 times and a fine-grained activity 5 times. 80% of the traces are used as the training set and the rest 20% traces are used as the test set.

Based on the real-time data processing method in MATLAB developed by Lu et al. [4], we developed a CSI parser in Python that can run online according to the experimental requirements. To evaluate the online segmentation process, we develop a CSI data sending tool based on Python, which can send the CSI trace in DAT format to the CSI parser at a user-specific sending rate.

For comparison, we select DeepSeg [16], the state-of-the-art method that achieves the highest segmentation accuracy as the baseline of deep learning-based methods, and Wi-Multi [3] as the baseline of threshold-based segmentation methods. It's worth noting that DeepSeg reduces the sampling rate from 1000 to 50 packets/s because of the unaffordable high computation overhead. But for the threshold-based methods, Wi-Multi and LightSeg, there is no need to down sampling due to the much lower computation overhead.

We use the segmentation accuracy metric mentioned in DeepSeg to measure the performance of segmentation methods. For a given activity, the segmentation accuracy is equal to $|A \cap B|/max\{|A|, |B|\}$, where A represents the ground truth set of the start and end points of the activity, the start and end points of all activities are labeled and published by DeepSeg, and B represents the set of start and end points predicted by the segmentation method.

4.2   Performance of Activity Segmentation

We first compare LightSeg with DeepSeg and Wi-Multi and then evaluate its performance under different settings.

Comparison with DeepSeg. We first compare LightSeg with DeepSeg, which also aims at solving the granularity problem of activity segmentation for WiFi sensing. We compare their segmentation accuracy in three scenarios, (1) mixed-grained scenario where 5 coarse-grained and 5 fine-grained activities appear alternately, (2) coarse-grained scenario where only coarse-grained activities exist, and (3) fine-grained scenarios where only fine-grained activities exist. In all the scenarios, similar to the setting of DeepSeg, each activity sequence trace contains 10 activities. Then we use different methods to segment all the activities.

The average segmentation accuracy is shown in Fig. 7. We can find that in all the three scenarios, LightSeg achieves the best performance. The accuracy of LightSeg is 93%, 92.5%, and 93.6% in the mixed-grained, coarse-grained, and fine-grained scenarios, which is even slightly higher than DeepSeg. This is because LightSeg can perform segmentation on the high-rate CSI data but DeepSeg has to run on the down-sampling data, which inevitably causes inaccuracy. To validate this, we also conduct LightSeg on the data with the same sampling rate of DeepSeg and plot its results as the LightSeg with Compression in Fig. 7. We can find that when running on the compressed data, LightSeg has obvious performance degradation and its accuracy in three scenarios is 3.7% lower than DeepSeg in average. The result is as expected because with the same data, deep learning technique is much more powerful to extract segmentation

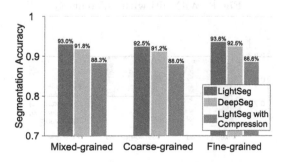

Fig. 7. Comparison with DeepSeg

features than the threshold. But thanks to the low overhead, threshold-based methods can use the high-rate CSI data to achieve better accuracy.

Comparison with Wi-Multi. We then compare LightSeg with Wi-Multi, the existing threshold-based method. Wi-Multi dynamically decides the threshold according to the parameter called sampling rate which must be preset according to the application scenario. Here, the so-called sampling rate in Wi-Multi means the ratio of the CSI sequence length to the slot length, i.e., the slot numbers in a detection window. It is different from the signal sampling rate. To avoid confusion, we use R_s to represent the sampling rate parameter in [3]. By default, Wi-Multi set R_s as 80. Given R_s, Wi-Multi can adjust the threshold according to the activities in the detection window. Hence, it still has the granularity problem. R_s has to be preset for different granularity scenarios, which is impossible for the online systems that cannot predict what activity is coming.

We vary R_s to investigate the accuracy of Wi-Multi under different granularity. The results are shown in Fig. 8. We can find that the segmentation accuracy in three scenarios reaches the peak at different R_s, which reveals that different granularity activities correspond to different optimal R_s. However, in practice, we cannot know which activities we are dealing with in the current detection window before classification. It is hard to preset or dynamically adjust R_s online. But LightSeg has no such problem because it leverages the granularity-aware threshold for the current activity.

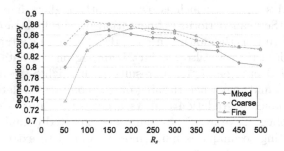

Fig. 8. Wi-Multi with different R_s

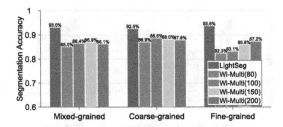

Fig. 9. Comparison with Wi-Multi

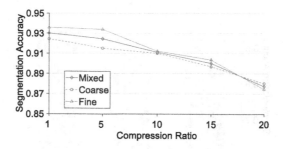

Fig. 10. LightSeg with different compression ratio

We compare the performance of Wi-Multi and LightSeg. Besides the default setting in [3], Wi-Multi(80), we also select several representative R_s for Wi-Multi according to the results in Fig. 8, including the mixed-grained optimal value 150, the coarse-grained optimal value 100, the fine-grained optimal value 200. The segmentation accuracy of LightSeg and Wi-Multi with different R_s is shown in Fig. 9. We can find that LightSeg has superior performance than Wi-Multi for all the three scenarios. Wi-Multi(80), the default setting, has the lowest accuracy, indicating the setting suitable for the dataset in [3] is no longer appropriate to the DeepSeg dataset. For mixed-grained, coarse-grained, fine-grained activities, Wi-Multi with the corresponding optimal setting has the best performance among the four settings, which is 86.9%, 88.5%, and 87.2% respectively for the three scenarios. Compared to the optimal result of Wi-Multi, LightSeg can still achieve 7.0%, 4.5%, and 7.3% higher accuracy. In practice, with a fixed preset R_s, LightSeg can obtain even better performance improvement.

Impact of Data Compression. We also investigate the impact of data compression on segmentation. When enabling compression, the CSI trace will be first down sampled and then performing segmentation. Figure 10 shows the accuracy degradation when increasing the compression ratio. When increasing the compression ratio from 1 to 20, the accuracy drops by 5% in average. When the compression ratio is 15, i.e., the sampling rate is 66 packets/s, LightSeg can still achieve the accuracy higher than 90%. Actually, due to the low overhead, LightSeg can directly use the data with the original sampling rate (1000 packets/s) and even higher rates.

Impact of the Selected Antenna. Unlike DeepSeg, which uses all receiving antennas as input, LightSeg selects one of the receiving antennas with good signal quality (Rx-1) for segmentation and avoids unnecessary computation. Figure 11 shows the segmentation accuracy of LightSeg when using Rx-1 and all antennas. Surprisingly, we find that using all antennas can even lower the accuracy. This is because there is an antenna providing low-quality CSI data that brings interference to the segmentation.

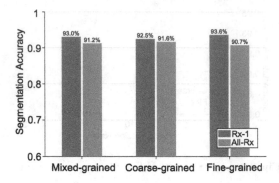

Fig. 11. LightSeg with Rx-1 or All-Rx

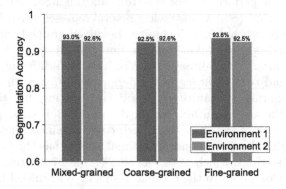

Fig. 12. Segmentation performance in different environments.

Environment Independence. To verify the environment independence of LightSeg, we collect a new dataset in a campus lab and evaluate the segmentation performance. Both the transmitter and receiver are industrial computers equipped with Intel 5300 NIC. The transmitter and receiver enable one and three antennas respectively. The sampling rate is 1000 packets/s. The dataset contains 1080 activity CSI traces provided by six users with different body shapes. Each user performs 9 activities 20 times each, including 4 coarse-grained daily activities (bending, falling, sitting and lying down) and 5 fine-grained gestures (pushing, sliding up, sliding up, sliding down, sliding left and sliding right).

Figure 12 presents the segmentation accuracy in two different environments, where Environment 1 represents the experimental environment of DeepSeg's dataset and Environment 2 represents the experimental environment of our dataset. For the results, we can clearly find that although the experimental environment is changed, LightSeg achieves similar performance for all the three activity granularity scenarios. The results demonstrate that LightSeg is environment independent.

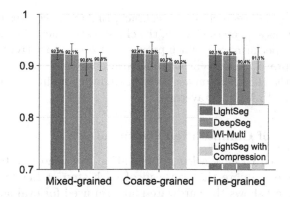

Fig. 13. Accuracy of activity classification

4.3 Performance of Activity Classification

We further evaluate the impact of segmentation on activity classification performance. We use the CNN-based deep learning model publicly provided by DeepSeg. The network structure of the CNN model used as the classifier is shown in Table 1 and the hyper-parameters of the classifier are consistent with the parameters used in DeepSeg. We use 80% of the CSI traces in DeepSeg dataset as the training set and the other 20% of the traces as the test set. We repeat the experiment ten times and plot the accuracy of four methods in Fig. 13, where the error bars indicate standard deviation.

Table 1. Network Architecture of CNN

NO	Operation	Configuration
1	Input	$200 \times 30 \times 3$ (CSI values)
2	Dropout	p = 0.2
3	Conv	Kernel = 3×3 FM = 96 WN lReLU
4	Conv	Kernel = 3×3 FM = 96 WN lReLU
5	Conv	Kernel = 3×3 Stride = 4×2 FM = 96 WN lReLU
6	Dropout	p = 0.5
7	Conv	Kernel = 3×3 FM = 192 WN lReLU
8	Conv	Kernel = 3×3 FM = 192 WN lReLU
9	Conv	Kernel = 3×3 Stride = 4×2 FM = 192 WN lReLU
10	Dropout	p = 0.5
11	Conv	Kernel = 3×3 FM = 192 WN lReLU
12	NiN	FM = 192 WN lReLU
13	NiN	FM = 192 WN lReLU
14	Pooling	FM = 192 Global Pooling
15	Dense	FM = 4 WN

Thanks to the high segmentation accuracy, LightSeg achieves the best classification accuracy, as expected. Overall, the classification accuracy is consistent to the segmentation performance, which proves that accurate activity segmentation indeed helps improve the classification accuracy. In three scenarios with different granularity, the classification accuracy of LightSeg is similar to DeepSeg, and 1.9% higher than Wi-Multi in average.

4.4   Evaluation of Computation Overhead

LightSeg is expected to have a low computation overhead due to our sophisticated designs. We evaluate the overhead of each step of LightSeg , compared to DeepSeg. Table 2 shows the hardware platform used for evaluation, including Raspberry Pi as the resource-limited hardware, a laptop as the normal WiFi device, and a high-performance server equipped with GPU resources.

Table 2. Hardware Information

	Raspberry Pi	Laptop	Server
Model	Raspberry Pi 4B	HUAWEI MateBook 14	DELL PowerEdge
CPU	Broadcom BCM2711	AMD Ryzen 4800H	Intel Xeon 6138
GPU	Null	Null	Nvidia GTX 2080Ti
Memory	4 GB	16 GB	256 GB
OS	Linux Debian 10	Windows 10	Linux Ubuntu 16.04

Table 3 shows the evaluation result of LightSeg. For the laptop using the original sampling rate (1000 packets/s), the average processing time of each activity is 0.3s, which is enough to meet the latency requirement of online activity segmentation. In addition, the maximum memory used is 193 MB, which is affordable for most common devices. For the Raspberry Pi using the original sampling rate, the total processing time is 3.48s, which is much larger. Hence, when applying WiFi sensing on a resource-limited device, we suggest using down-sampling data for segmentation. When using the rate of 50 packets/s, the total processing time is reduced to 0.2s and the used memory is about 100 MB. Although the sampling rate is reduced, the segmentation accuracy and classification accuracy still remain above 88% and 90% as shown in Fig. 7 and Fig. 13.

The input data of DeepSeg for each processing contains ten activities. We evaluate the average processing time of each activity and the memory used during the test phase of activity segmentation (excluding model training). Table 4 shows the results. The first two steps of DeepSeg run in MATLAB. Although MATLAB has a faster processing speed than Python, it uses more memory. For state inference, we run it on both the laptop and the server. The processing time is 73.92s and 23.35s when running on the laptop and the server. The average processing time for one activity is 9.976s when using CPU only and is 4.919s even when using GPU. But using GPU requires a much larger memory. Under the same hardware condition with the laptop, the average processing time of LightSeg is only 3% of that of DeepSeg.

Table 3. Computation overhead of LightSeg

Hardware	Laptop	Raspberry Pi	Raspberry Pi
Sampling Rate (packets/s)	1000	1000	50
Maximum Memory Used	193 MB	225 MB	103 MB
Preprocessing step	Processing Time (s)		
Outlier Removal	0.0031	0.0035	0.0007
DWT	0.2096	0.8695	0.0093
PCA	0.0403	1.3621	0.0237
Moving Variance	0.0016	0.0037	0.0022
Find End Point	0.0375	0.8292	0.0560
Find Start Point	0.0173	0.4183	0.0221
Total	0.3094	3.4862	0.1976

Table 4. Overhead of DeepSeg

Step	Hardware	Runtime Environment	Processing Time (s)	Memory	Graphics Memory
Preprocessing	Laptop	MATLAB	10.09	2901 MB	
Discretize CSI			15.62	2496.8 MB	
State Inference		Python	73.92	1449 MB	
	Server		23.35	3.803 GB	4474 MB
Extract Activity	Laptop		0.13	31.4 MB	
Total			99.76 (CPU) 49.19 (CPU+GPU)		
Average			9.976 (CPU) 4.919 (CPU+GPU)		

5 Conclusion

We present a low-latency activity segmentation method LightSeg for WiFi sensing, which can segment activities of different granularity online. We design a granularity aware threshold that can be quickly adjusted according to the activity granularity, which solves the performance degradation of mixed-grained activity segmentation. The algorithm has low complexity and high segmentation accuracy. We deploy LightSeg in hardware with different performance and evaluated the segmentation accuracy and overhead. Experimental results demonstrate the effectiveness and low overhead of LightSeg.

References

1. Bu, Q., Yang, G., Ming, X., Zhang, T., Feng, J., Zhang, J.: Deep transfer learning for gesture recognition with Wi Fi signals. Pers. Ubiquit. Comput., 1–12 (2020)
2. Chen, L., Chen, X., Ni, L., Peng, Y., Fang, D.: Human behavior recognition using Wi-Fi CSI: challenges and opportunities. IEEE Commun. Mag. **55**(10), 112–117 (2017)

3. Feng, C., Arshad, S., Zhou, S., Cao, D., Liu, Y.: Wi-multi: a three-phase system for multiple human activity recognition with commercial WiFi devices. IEEE Internet Things J. **6**(4), 7293–7304 (2019)
4. Lu, B., Zeng, Z., Wang, L., Peck, B., Qiao, D., Segal, M.: Confining Wi-Fi coverage: a crowdsourced method using physical layer information. In: Proceedings of IEEE SECON (2016)
5. Ma, Y., Zhou, G., Wang, S.: WiFi sensing with channel state information: a survey. ACM Comput. Surv. (CSUR) **52**(3), 1–36 (2019)
6. Palipana, S., Rojas, D., Agrawal, P., Pesch, D.: FallDefi: ubiquitous fall detection using commodity Wi-Fi devices. Proc. ACM Interact., Mob., Wearable Ubiquit. Technol. **1**(4), 1–25 (2018)
7. Sheng, B., Xiao, F., Sha, L., Sun, L.: Deep spatial-temporal model based cross-scene action recognition using commodity WiFi. IEEE Internet Things J. **7**(4), 3592–3601 (2020)
8. Virmani, A., Shahzad, M.: Position and orientation agnostic gesture recognition using WiFi. In: Proceedings of ACM MobiSys (2017)
9. Wang, F., Gong, W., Liu, J.: On spatial diversity in WiFi-based human activity recognition: a deep learning-based approach. IEEE Internet Things J. **6**(2), 2035–2047 (2018)
10. Wang, H., Zhang, D., Wang, Y., Ma, J., Wang, Y., Li, S.: RT-fall: a real-time and contactless fall detection system with commodity WiFi devices. IEEE Trans. Mob. Comput. **16**(2), 511–526 (2016)
11. Wang, W., Liu, A.X., Shahzad, M.: Gait recognition using WiFi signals. In: Proceedings of ACM UbiComp (2016)
12. Wang, W., Liu, A.X., Shahzad, M., Ling, K., Lu, S.: Understanding and modeling of WiFi signal based human activity recognition. In: Proceedings of ACM MobiCom (2015)
13. Wang, Z., Guo, B., Yu, Z., Zhou, X.: Wi-Fi CSI-based behavior recognition: from signals and actions to activities. IEEE Commun. Mag. **56**(5), 109–115 (2018)
14. Wu, D., Zhang, D., Xu, C., Wang, H., Li, X.: Device-free WiFi human sensing: from pattern-based to model-based approaches. IEEE Commun. Mag. **55**(10), 91–97 (2017)
15. Wu, X., Chu, Z., Yang, P., Xiang, C., Zheng, X., Huang, W.: TW-see: human activity recognition through the wall with commodity Wi-Fi devices. IEEE Trans. Veh. Technol. **68**(1), 306–319 (2018)
16. Xiao, C., Lei, Y., Ma, Y., Zhou, F., Qin, Z.: DeepSeg: Deep-learning-based activity segmentation framework for activity recognition using WiFi. IEEE Internet Things J. **8**(7), 5669–5681 (2020)
17. Xu, L., Zheng, X., Li, X., Zhang, Y., Liu, L., Ma, H.: WiCAM: imperceptible adversarial attack on deep learning based Wi-Fi sensing. In: Proceedings of IEEE SECON (2022)
18. Yan, H., Zhang, Y., Wang, Y., Xu, K.: WiAct: a passive WiFi-based human activity recognition system. IEEE Sens. J. **20**(1), 296–305 (2019)
19. Yang, K., Zheng, X., Xiong, J., Liu, L., Ma, H.: WiImg: pushing the limit of WiFi sensing with low transmission rates. In: Proceedings of IEEE SECON (2022)
20. Yang, Z., Zhou, Z., Liu, Y.: From RSSI to CSI: indoor localization via channel response. ACM Comput. Surv. (CSUR) **46**(2), 1–32 (2013)
21. Yousefi, S., Narui, H., Dayal, S., Ermon, S., Valaee, S.: A survey on behavior recognition using WiFi channel state information. IEEE Commun. Mag. **55**(10), 98–104 (2017)

22. Zhang, L., Liu, M., Lu, L., Gong, L.: Wi-Run: multi-runner step estimation using commodity Wi-Fi. In: Proceedings of IEEE SECON (2018)
23. Zhang, L., Wang, C., Ma, M., Zhang, D.: WiDIGR: direction-independent gait recognition system using commercial Wi-Fi devices. IEEE Internet Things J. **7**(2), 1178–1191 (2019)
24. Zhang, L., Zhang, Y., Zheng, X.: WiSign: ubiquitous American sign language recognition using commercial Wi-Fi devices. ACM Trans. Intell. Syst. Technol. (TIST) **11**(3), 1–24 (2020)
25. Zheng, X., Wang, J., Shangguan, L., Zhou, Z., Liu, Y.: Smokey: ubiquitous smoking detection with commercial WiFi infrastructures. In: Proceedings of IEEE INFOCOM (2016)
26. Zheng, X., Wang, J., Shangguan, L., Zhou, Z., Liu, Y.: Design and implementation of a CSI-based ubiquitous smoking detection system. IEEE/ACM Trans. Networking **25**(6), 3781–3793 (2017)

Revealing Mental Disorders Through Stylometric Features in Write-Ups

Tamanna Haque Nipa[✉] and A. B. M. Alim Al Islam

Department of Computer Science and Engineering, Bangladesh University of Engineering and Technology, Dhaka 1000, Bangladesh
`tamanna.haque8@gmail.com`, `alim_razi@cse.buet.ac.bd`

Abstract. Mental disorders present one of the leading causes of worldwide disability and have become a major social concern, as the symptoms behind mental disorders are almost hidden. Most of the conventional approaches used for diagnosing and identifying mental disorders rely on oral conversations (through interviews) having a limited focus on write-ups. Therefore, in this study, we attempt to explore identifying different types of mental disorders among people through their write-ups. To do so, we collect a total of 6893 posts and discussions that appeared in different problem-specific Internet forums and utilize them to identify different types of mental disorders. Leveraging appropriate machine learning algorithms over the collected write-ups, our study can categorize Depression, Schizophrenia, Suicidal Intention, Anxiety, Post Traumatic Stress Disorder (PTSD), Borderline Personality Disorder (BPD), and Eating Disorder (ED). To achieve a balanced dataset in the process of our study, we apply a combined sampling approach and achieve up to 89% accuracy in the identification task. We perform varied exploration tasks in our study covering 5-fold cross-validation, 5-times repetition on the used dataset, etc. We explain our findings in terms of precision, recall, specificity, and Matthews correlation coefficient to demonstrate the capability of our proposed approach in identifying mental disorders based on write-ups.

Keywords: Stylometric Marker · Imbalanced Dataset · Personal Pronoun

1 Introduction

The term "mental disorder" refers to illnesses characterized by abnormal thoughts, perceptions, emotions, behavior, relationships with others, and difficulties in dealings with daily grief and making healthy decisions [1]. This includes depression, bipolar disorder, schizophrenia, other psychoses, dementia, and developmental disorders such as autism. It needs proper attention, diagnosis, psychotherapy, medicines, and follow-up, as we do for physical problems. However, mental health issues are often ignored due to the stigma associated

© ICST Institute for Computer Sciences, Social Informatics and Telecommunications Engineering 2023
Published by Springer Nature Switzerland AG 2023. All Rights Reserved
S. Longfei and P. Bodhi (Eds.): MobiQuitous 2022, LNICST 492, pp. 248–265, 2023.
https://doi.org/10.1007/978-3-031-34776-4_14

with seeking help and fear of being perceived as a burden to society as well as the lack of provision of mental services, proper identification, social awareness, and human resources [1,2].

Different mental disorders are associated with different presentations. They are generally understood or predicted through our conversations and behaviors. One of the potential warning signs in this regard is talking or writing about hopeless feelings. Researchers have found that 50% to 75% of people with suicidal ideation gave a warning sign through sharing their thoughts with a friend or relative [3].

Nowadays, the widespread use of the Internet has allowed various communication platforms to flourish, where users can share their thoughts via posts or comments. To address the complex issue of diagnosing mental disorders through leveraging this reality, one vital technique can be exploiting the stylometric markers of an individual to reflect the person. Even some usual features of writing can link with abnormalities in mental states [4,5]. Research studies have already been conducted in this area. Still, the topic remains open, as the characteristics of human behavior depend on the surrounding conditions resulting in a yet-to-arrive of efficient approach for revealing mental disorders through stylometric features in write-ups.

To focus on this gap in the literature, we conduct a thorough study over a dataset of 6893 messages posted in 63 forums [6]. We identified seven different mental disorder groups and a control group through mining the text messages of normal and physically ill users. To deal with each user group separately from the rest, we applied binary categorization. As the nature of this dataset is imbalanced, we employed a combined sampling method (oversampling-under sampling) to get a better-balanced dataset. Then, we applied different classification models such as Logistic Regression (LR), K-Nearest Neighbor (KNN), and Support Vector Machine (SVM) successively together to reckon mental disorders from the personal pronouns used in the texts. Next, we utilized two ensemble models namely Random Forest (RF) and Stacking Classifier (SC) combining the baseline models for better prediction. We also investigated combining similar groups in a class. Among all the applied models and explorations, we achieved the best performance with Stacking Classifier while the Random Forest classifier also performed well. Our contributions made in this paper are summarized as follows.

- We proposed a new method of detecting different mental diseases from personal pronouns used in text data.
- We explored different approaches for feature extraction, machine learning-based model build-up, and evaluations over a benchmark dataset to demonstrate the efficiency of our proposed method.

The rest of this paper is organized as follows. Section 2 describes the previous work and Sect. 3 shows our method. Section 4 explains the training and testing processes. Section 5 and Sect. 6 provide the results and performance analysis. Section 7 concludes the paper by summarizing it with a recommended idea and notations to implement in the future.

2   Related Work

Existing studies show that many researchers have conducted their studies on author-ship attribution [7], authorship verification [8], authorship profiling [9], and classified text properties into five categories namely lexical, syntactic, structural, content-specific, and idiosyncratic [10,11]. Different text analyses considering lexical and syntactic features have been done based on word density [5,12], sentence length [13], frequency of nouns or pronouns [12], functional words [14], and part-of-speech n-grams [15,16]. Besides, structural attributes include attributes relating to text organization and layout [17]. Content-specific features follow word n-grams and depend on important keywords [17,18]. Idiosyncratic features show cultural differences in word formation such as incorrect spelling, misuse of words, and inaccurate verb forms [18,19].

Recent research studies have shown that pronouns can be used to identify gender [12]. It has been also demonstrated that Alzheimer's disease can be detected early through personal pronouns and sensory words [5,6]. For gender detection, 25,000 words have been aggregated across 30 selected articles by word frequency count based on a total of 29 personal pronouns and tested the possibility to be male or female. According to the study, 90% accuracy has been achieved using three personal pronouns namely my, her, and its. Another study has investigated the importance of stylometric markers for depression and Alzheimer's detection, which was based on 45 novels by Iris Murdoch and PD James covering a period from 1954 to 1995. RPAS visualization was applied based on richness, personal pronoun, activity power, and sensory adjectives and it was concluded that Alzheimer's can be detected from written text 12 years earlier.

Another investigation [6] has suggested that absolutist thinking is a vulnerable factor and related to suicidal ideation, borderline personality disorder, and an eating disorder. This study showed that suicidal ideation more relates to absolutist words than psychological distress through a statical analysis and a list of absolutist words was published. Besides, as investigated in [20], dark traits of human beings describe the causes of abuses and crimes, which can be measured by some words identified as negative or positive based on the Russian language.

Machine learning techniques with Natural Language Processing (NPL) can potentially offer new routes for learning mental health conditions and risk factors that have been surveyed in [21] and [22]. Another study presented a systematic review based on space disease diagnosis, psychological disorders, and classification techniques to address ADHD, Alzheimer's, Parkinson's, insomnia, schizophrenia, and mood disorder [23]. A similar review was done based on 565 relevant types of research from 2015 to 2020 [24]. Another research [25] applied unsupervised ML techniques based on 826,961 unique user posts during COVID-19 from 2018 to 2020 on 90 text-driven features. This study presented that BPD and PTSD are significantly associated with the suicidality cluster.

Some other studies reported a positive correlation between some specific words used, which frequently can help to figure out the intention of dying [14,26, 27]. Several surprising facts also observed that suicidal tendency increases due to the death of any famous person [14], both depression and suicidal ideation episodes contain 14 days [26], females and young adults aged from 15–24 years are the main victims of depression [26,27]. Besides, the study in [28] predicted the depression level of the writers based on a computational marker from the written text addressed by DASS-21 (Depression, Anxiety, and Stress Scale). This analysis covered 172 people and summarized that informal text is more suitable to detect depression. Additionally, an algorithm namely SAIPA was proposed using ML for predicting the future risk of suicide from 512,526 tweets followed by the countrywide death rate [29]. PSPO, a Chinese online suicide prevention system has been designed to detect people at risk through suicidal thoughts and behaviors. A total of 27,007 comments were analyzed and realized that suicide ideation is more related to future-oriented words than death-oriented words. All the reported classification accuracies varied around 56%–83% using different statistical measures, ML algorithms, and Deep Learning algorithms. Here, investigations confirmed that language plays an important role in life.

3   Our Proposed Methodology

We provided an overview of our solution in this section. As per our study process depicted in Fig. 1, we (1) collected written messages from different online group members related to their diseases or difficulties, (2) screened them for potential causes with proper data preprocessing, feature extraction, and data balancing method, (3) machine learning algorithms have applied to predict the disorders, and (4) finally we explored and compared the findings with a fitness assessment. This section is divided into different subsections that illustrate the workflow of the proposed experimental procedures in detail.

3.1   Data Collection and Arrangement

The dataset used in this study has been collected from https://figshare.com/ and the source of all the messages or posts are different English language-based internet forums [6,30]. For our study, we divided our study into two segments and rearranged the group formation according to our research aim. For the first portion, the test group is formed with any one group among the concerned mental illnesses and the control group consists of the rest of the mental diseases, general members, asthma, diabetes, cancer patient, students (young people), mums' group, elderly peoples with pension problem and people with job problems. This source dataset also consists of some members who have recovered from high depression and mentioned their improvements. However, this recovery group has not been included in our rearranged groups due to the possibility of noise and outliers. We kept the other groups remain the same. Therefore, this part of the analysis is based on 7 different datasets with different mental problem specifications. We have also cross-checked them with the excel file provided with the reference paper [6] and removed 350 indirect messages that address the problem of family members or friends.

For the second part of our study, we have prepared the four major classes combining the related groups to find out whether mental disorders can be separated from other classes or not. At this point, we have organized the analysis considering the mental disorder group vs. normal + physical health problem + recovery group, normal vs. mental disorder + physical health problem + recovery group, physical health problem vs. mental disorder + normal + recovery group, and recovery group vs mental disorder + physical health problem + normal group. Table 1 shows the number of messages that we consider for this experiment.

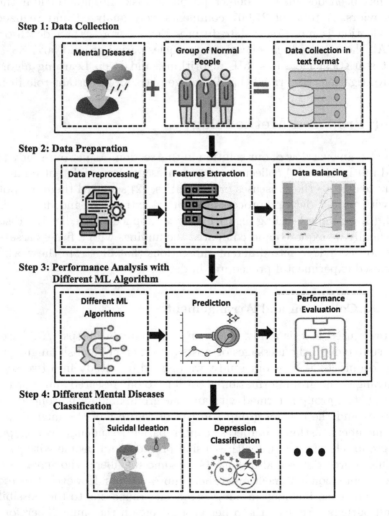

Fig. 1. Schematic diagram of our study to explore different mental diseases through Stylometric features in texts.

Four criteria have been maintained in the procedure of data collection: (a) all the messages must be in the English language (b) the minimum length of the post should be 100 words (b) the messages be directly represented by the members, and (c) the written text must be in continuous prose. Here only the first post of the members has been considered and for some cases, multiple posts have been combined into a single post as the signal post was very poor in length for consideration.

Table 1. Statistics of the dataset were collected from different internet forums [8].

Groups	No of messages	Sample percentage
Anxiety	596	8.6%
BPD	325	4.7%
Depression	531	7.7%
ED	546	8.0%
PTSD	535	7.7%
Schizophrenia	592	8.5%
Suicidal Ideation	366	5.3%
Normal (General, Mums, Pension, Student, Job Problem)	1373 (959, 157, 16, 132, 109)	20.0%
Physical Diseases (Asthma, Diabetes, Breast Cancer, Bowel Cancer, Lung Cancer, Prostate Cancer)	1461 (418, 590, 141, 96, 123, 93)	21.1%
Recovery	568	8.2%
Total	6893	100%

3.2   Data Preparation

After the arrangement of the groups, all the text files have been preprocessed for the avoidance of unwanted noise or redundancy. We have added the group type and index with each file. Each text file is presented as a tuple in the dataset with the index number.

Internet Acronyms Replacement. Non-standard words and phrases of language are mostly observed in the messages of internet users, such as U, GR8, MSG, B4, etc. These internet acronyms are used for easy interpretation by others and to save time in typing. It has become very important to detect, translate and replace the short form with the actual word or group of words. We have collected 2174 short forms of words from different websites [31,32]. While replacing them we found that the same acronyms can have multiple meanings. To avoid conflicts, we tried to pick the most potential one. For example, 'yr' can be 'your' or 'yeah right' or 'you'. In this case, we selected 'your' to substitute 'yr'.

Feature Extraction and Data Balancing. Our main effort is based on pronouns and used as an alternative to nouns to avoid repetition. English literature contains more than 100 pronouns which can be grouped into 10 categories: personal, possessive, reflexive, intensive, demonstrative, interrogative, relative, indefinite, reciprocal, and archaic. Among these, personal pronouns, progressive pronouns, reflexive pronouns, and intensive pronouns are used for a per-son or thing in a sentence specifically. Personal pronouns are words to highlight the people or things in our sentences which can be both subjective and objective. The personal pronouns for subjects are I, you, he, she, it, we, and they. For objects, personal pronouns are me, us, you, her, him, it, and them. A possessive pronoun (mine, ours, yours, hers, his, theirs) designates ownership and can substitute for noun phrases. Reflexive pronouns are pronouns that are used to show that the subject of the sentence is receiving the action of the verb (myself, yourself, himself, herself, itself, ourselves, themselves). Intensive Pronouns are pronouns that are used only to emphasize the subject. Intensive and reflexive pronouns are the same words; however, they act differently in the sentence. With these features, we also considered the possessive adjectives (my, our, your, her, his, their) as they resemble a pronoun [33]. A total of 29 words have been considered for the analysis.

According to our observation, all the groups are dissimilar to each other in respect of the total number of group members shown in Table 1. We have addressed 7 different mental problems to analyze every group separately from the others. We also considered 4 classes and explored every class separately from the other classes. Therefore, every test group and class is found highly imbalanced concerning others. To handle the issues of imbalance problem, we have applied SMOTEENN. Synthetic Minority Over-sampling Technique (SMOTE) and its variations were always found to be the better choice for oversampling. To avoid overfitting, we choose SMOTEENN, a hybridization of the oversampling and under-sampling process. It is a combination of SMOTE and, the Edited Nearest Neighbor (ENN) technique [34].

As a part of preprocessing, every sample has been normalized with the standard scaling procedure. Every instance of the concerned group or class is marked as 1 and other instances from the rest of the groups or classes are marked as 0. To keep the words in the messages, remain the same, we avoided the stemming process. Only the frequency of the identified words has been measured.

4   Evaluation Procedure

This section discusses the experimental techniques and classification models used for this research in detail. Aside from that, it has also shown the performance measures that have been used to evaluate the outcomes. Python 3.6 with scikit-learn is used as a machine learning tool. We have also investigated our prepared datasets using Weka 3.9.4 and chose the best-suggested algorithms for this processing.

4.1   Classification Methods

We employed the 3 most used Machine Learning algorithms: Logistic Regression (LR), K-Nearest Neighbors (KNN), and Support Vector Machine (SVM) to examine our experiments. The ratio of the training and testing data is 8:2. 5-fold cross-validation with 5 times repetition is used and the results are summarized by taking the mean of the outcomes. Further refinement is made by following the ensemble process, Stacking Classifier (SC), and Random Forest (RF) which shows a noteworthy upgrading.

4.2 Assessing Performances

Various assessing metrics are available in Machine Learning to analyze model performance. For the comparative performance analysis of our study, we have presented the consequence of the testing set using balanced accuracy, precision, recall, specificity, f1-score, and Matthews Correlation Coefficient (MCC). Instead of accuracy as a valuation tool, we used balanced accuracy as the dataset is imbalanced. We also included recall and specificity to illustrate how well a model can predict both majority and minority classes. Matthews correlation coefficient (MCC) is another powerful and informative measure that finds the correlation of true classes with the predicted labels. Likewise, the f1-score exhibits more significant performance measures than accuracy in the case of the imbalanced dataset considering precision and recall. Precision is the rate of correctly classified positive predictions made over all the positive predicted samples. Similarly, specificity measures the proportion of correctly identified negatives over the total negative prediction made by the model. However, recall measures the correctly identified positive samples from all actual positives. High precision with low recall indicates that very few results have been predicted and most of the predicted labels are correct. A model with low precision and high recall behave oppositely. High precision with high recall represents a better classification model [35, 36]. We have also shown the tradeoff between precision and recall using the precision-recall curve.

$$BalancedAccuracy = \frac{Sensitivity + Specificity}{2} \tag{1}$$

$$Recall or Sensitivity = \frac{TP}{TP + FN} \tag{2}$$

$$Precision = \frac{TP}{TP + FP} \tag{3}$$

$$Specificity = \frac{TN}{TN + FP} \tag{4}$$

$$F1 - score = \frac{2 * Precision * Recall}{Precision + Recall} \tag{5}$$

$$MCC = \frac{TP * TN - FP * FN}{\sqrt{(TP + FP)(TP + FN)(TN + FP)(TN + FN)}} \tag{6}$$

Here, TP, FP, TN, and FN represent true positive, false positive, true negative, and false negative respectively. Moreover, the experimental result has been
presented using the necessary graphical representation to compare different ML
models and assorted datasets. We have also applied the Chi-square test to identify the best combination of pronouns following the feature selection method for
better identification of mental disorders among all types of combined groups.

5   Experimental Results

In this section, we presented and compared the models used in our study on the
prepared datasets as mentioned before. First, we showed our testing to identify
Anxiety, BPD, Depression, ED, PTSD, Schizophrenia, and Suicidal ideation.
Next, we explored our experiment to differentiate among the classes of normal
people, recovery groups, people with mental disorders, and physically ill people.

5.1   Mental Disorder Detection and Performance Measure

First, we explore 5 machine learning algorithms and find the best fit for our
purpose. It is observed that both Stacking Classifier and Random Forest outper-
form on K-Nearest Neighbors, Support Vector Machine, and Logistic Regression
approach in all classification scenarios. While implementing Stacking Classifier,
we applied different model combinations and achieved the best result while the
base models were K-Nearest Neighbors, and the final estimator to combine the
predicted values of the base models was Logistic Regression. Stacking Classifier is slightly better than Random Forest concerning the performance metrics.
However, Random Forest performs much faster than Stacking Classifier. The performance measures of the assigned models for the identification of seven mental
disorder groups are listed in Table 2. It exhibits the mean values and standard
deviation of balanced accuracy, specificity, f1-score, and MCC representing all
the groups respectively.

Our first dataset is based on the samples labeled as Anxiety. Among the
implemented models, Stacking Classifier shows the best performance with highly
balanced accuracy, f1-score, and MCC (B.Ac. 86%, F1. 82%, MCC 73%). Precision and recall values are both found promising. However, precision is a little
higher in respect of its recall.

The second, third, and fourth datasets are based on BPD, Depression, and
ED. The similarity is found with Anxiety for BPD (B.Ac. 87%, F1. 84%, MCC
76%), Depression (B.Ac. 85%, F1. 80%, MCC 72%), and ED (B.Ac. 89%, F1.
87%, MCC 80%) detection using the Stacking Classifier model with higher precision and recall values. Random Forest and K-Nearest Neighbors are likewise
showing satisfactory performances. On the other hand, Support Vector Machine,
and Logistic Regression are found dis-satisfactory with lower evaluation metrics
compared to others.

The last three datasets are about PTSD (B.Ac. 59%–83%, F1. 77%–90%,
MCC. 25%–69%), Schizophrenia (B.Ac. 58%–83%, F1. 76%–90%, MCC. 20%–
69%), and Suicide Ideation (B.Ac. 69%–88%, F1. 78%–89%, MCC. 42%–78%)

Table 2. Class-wise different performance metrics (mean values) of ML models (SC = Stacking Classifier, RF = Random Forest, KNN = K-Nearest Neighbors, SVM = Support Vector Machine, LR = Logistic Regression, B.Ac. = Balanced Accuracy, MCC = Matthews Correlation Coefficient, F1 = F1-score, Pre. = Precision, Rec. = Recall, and Spe. = Specificity)

Group	Algo.	B.Ac.		MCC		F1		Spe.	
		AVG	STD	AVG	STD	AVG	STD	AVG	STD
Anxiety	LR	0.68	0.01	0.38	0.02	0.58	0.02	0.84	0.00
	RF	0.84	0.12	0.69	0.23	0.80	0.16	0.91	0.05
	SVM	0.80	0.13	0.61	0.24	0.74	0.17	0.91	0.05
	KNN	0.82	0.12	0.66	0.24	0.77	0.17	0.92	0.05
	SC	0.86	0.12	0.73	0.23	0.82	0.16	0.94	0.05
BPD	LR	0.66	0.01	0.33	0.01	0.57	0.01	0.82	0.01
	RF	0.86	0.14	0.72	0.28	0.82	0.18	0.91	0.07
	SVM	0.80	0.16	0.62	0.30	0.75	0.20	0.90	0.06
	KNN	0.83	0.15	0.68	0.29	0.79	0.20	0.92	0.07
	SC	0.87	0.14	0.76	0.27	0.84	0.19	0.94	0.07
Depression	LR	0.65	0.01	0.33	0.02	0.53	0.01	0.86	0.01
	RF	0.83	0.13	0.68	0.25	0.78	0.18	0.92	0.04
	SVM	0.78	0.15	0.58	0.28	0.69	0.23	0.92	0.04
	KNN	0.81	0.15	0.64	0.27	0.74	0.22	0.93	0.04
	SC	0.85	0.14	0.72	0.27	0.80	0.21	0.95	0.05
ED	LR	0.76	0.01	0.55	0.02	0.70	0.01	0.90	0.01
	RF	0.88	0.09	0.77	0.16	0.85	0.11	0.93	0.03
	SVM	0.85	0.10	0.71	0.17	0.81	0.12	0.93	0.03
	KNN	0.86	0.09	0.74	0.17	0.83	0.12	0.94	0.04
	SC	0.89	0.09	0.80	0.17	0.87	0.11	0.96	0.04
PTSD	LR	0.59	0.01	0.25	0.02	0.77	0.00	0.27	0.01
	RF	0.82	0.16	0.65	0.29	0.88	0.08	0.70	0.31
	SVM	0.75	0.18	0.53	0.33	0.85	0.09	0.55	0.37
	KNN	0.78	0.18	0.60	0.32	0.87	0.09	0.61	0.35
	SC	0.83	0.17	0.69	0.31	0.90	0.09	0.70	0.33
Schizophrenia	LR	0.58	0.01	0.20	0.02	0.76	0.00	0.28	0.02
	RF	0.80	0.16	0.62	0.30	0.88	0.09	0.69	0.30
	SVM	0.74	0.18	0.51	0.33	0.85	0.09	0.54	0.37
	KNN	0.77	0.18	0.58	0.33	0.87	0.09	0.60	0.35
	SC	0.83	0.17	0.68	0.32	0.90	0.09	0.69	0.34
Suicide	LR	0.69	0.01	0.42	0.02	0.78	0.01	0.54	0.02
	RF	0.86	0.12	0.74	0.23	0.90	0.09	0.80	0.19
	SVM	0.82	0.13	0.66	0.24	0.87	0.09	0.72	0.22
	KNN	0.84	0.13	0.71	0.24	0.89	0.09	0.76	0.20
	SC	0.88	0.12	0.78	0.23	0.92	0.09	0.82	0.20

respectively. Among the 5 ML models with five-fold cross-validation and five times repetition, Stacking Classifier has shown higher balance accuracy with a higher f1-score.

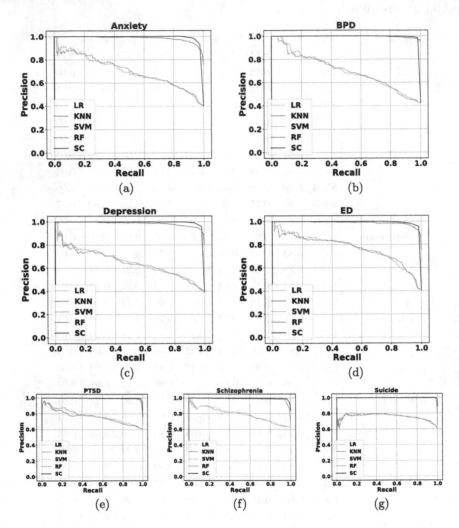

Fig. 2. Precision-recall curve for various mental disorder groups for different algorithms (a) Anxiety, (b) BPD (c) Depression (d) ED (e) PTSD, (f) Schizophrenia, and (g) Suicide Ideation

Figure 2 delineates a comparison among 5 ML algorithms using a precision-recall curve for the seven mental disorder groups. Our method has higher recall with higher precision in detecting specific mental problems from the other groups. The performance of the Stacking Classifier, Random Forest, and K-Nearest Neighbors for all the disorder detection showed significant achievement compared to Logistic Regression and Support Vector Machine. Both Stacking Classifier and Random Forest approach outperforms over baseline approach in all classification scenario. However, Stacking Classifier is slightly better than Random Forest in most cases, but Random Forest is much faster.

5.2 Class-Specific Performance Measure

In this study, we have also addressed specific class identification as groups in the same class can act similarly. We aim to differentiate people with mental suffering among a variety of people. We have mentioned above the class formation. Therefore, 5 ML algorithms are used for classification with these 4 mentioned classes. All the group statistics and the outcome of all models are revealed in Table 3.

Table 3. Class-wise different performance metrics (mean values) of ML models (SC = Stacking Classifier, RF = Random Forest, KNN = K-Nearest Neighbors, SVM = Support Vector Machine, LR = Logistic Regression, B.Ac. = Balanced Accuracy, MCC = Matthews Correlation Coefficient, F1 = F1-score, Pre. = Precision, Rec. = Recall, and Spe. = Specificity).

Groups	Mod	B.Ac	MCC	F1	Pre	Rec	Spe
Mental disorder vs. Normal +	LR	0.86	0.73	0.88	0.85	0.91	0.82
Physical health problem +	RF	0.88	0.75	0.88	0.88	0.88	0.87
Recovery group	SVM	0.87	0.74	0.88	0.87	0.89	0.85
	KNN	0.88	0.76	0.89	0.88	0.90	0.86
	SC	0.89	0.79	0.90	0.90	0.90	0.88
Normal vs. Recovery+	LR	0.77	0.57	0.71	0.81	0.64	0.90
Physical health problem+	RF	0.87	0.74	0.84	0.87	0.81	0.92
Mental disorder group	SVM	0.84	0.70	0.80	0.85	0.76	0.92
	KNN	0.86	0.73	0.82	0.88	0.78	0.93
	SC	0.88	0.78	0.86	0.90	0.82	0.94
Recovery vs. General+	LR	0.70	0.40	0.77	0.74	0.80	0.60
Physical health problem+	RF	0.85	0.71	0.89	0.88	0.89	0.81
Mental disorder group	SVM	0.81	0.63	0.86	0.84	0.89	0.74
	KNN	0.83	0.68	0.88	0.85	0.91	0.76
	SC	0.87	0.76	0.91	0.89	0.93	0.82
Physical health problem vs General+	LR	0.79	0.60	0.85	0.81	0.90	0.67
Mental disorder+	RF	0.86	0.73	0.90	0.88	0.92	0.80
Recovery group	SVM	0.84	0.70	0.89	0.86	0.92	0.76
	KNN	0.85	0.72	0.90	0.87	0.93	0.77
	SC	0.87	0.76	0.91	0.89	0.94	0.81

Findings are depicted in respect of the bar diagram representing balanced accuracy, precision, recall, specificity, f1-score, and MCC in Fig. 3. According to our observation, all the classes have good balanced accuracy and precision. Moreover, our method has shown a significant f1-score in detecting mental disorders (F1. 88–90%) and recovery groups (F1. 77–91%). It might be for high

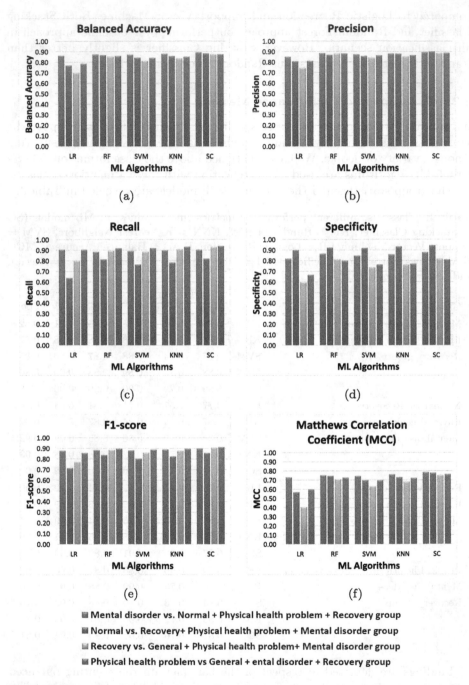

Fig. 3. Different performance metrics for comparison among the 4 classes with similar groups (a) Balanced Accuracy, (b) Precision (c) Recall (d) Specificity (e) F1-score, and (f) MCC

recall and precision indicating to be appropriate for mental problem classification. Specificity calculated for the physical health problem (Spe. 67–81%) and normal class (Spe. 92–94%) is much higher than the other classes which also indicates that opposite classes have been detected properly.

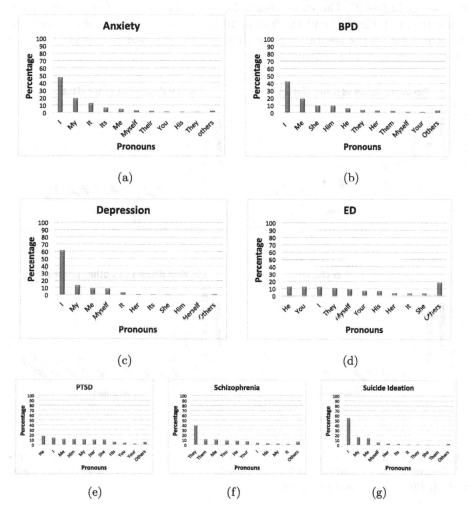

Fig. 4. Bar diagram for various mental disorder groups and 4 classes showing feature scoring for specific pronouns (a) Anxiety, (b) BPD (c) Depression (d) ED (e) PTSD, (f) Schizophrenia, and (g) Suicide Ideation

5.3   Performance for Specific Pronouns

We have tested the chi-squared feature selection method for 29 pronouns described before and observed some specific pronouns have significant scores compared to the other pronouns. The combination of pronouns is different for different groups. It is noticeable that every group and class has the pronoun 'I'. Surprisingly, both the mental disorder class and the normal class have 'I' with the highest score with almost 60% value. Similarity has been found for another two pronouns 'My' and 'Me' for Anxiety, BPD, Depression, and Suicide Ideation including 'I'. Therefore, combining several pronouns for disorder detection is required. Figure 4 and Fig. 5 show 10 pronouns with the largest score from the others for all the mental disorder groups and four classes respectively. The scores are presented in percentages.

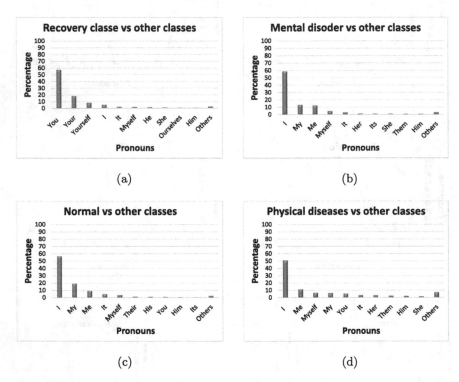

(a)   (b)

(c)   (d)

Fig. 5. Bar diagram for different classes showing feature scoring for specific pronouns (a) Recovery Class vs. others (b) Mental disorder vs. others (c) Normal class vs. others, and (d) Physical diseases vs. others

6   Discussion

Among the seven mental disorder groups, Suicide Ideation reported the highest score for correct prediction. PTSD and Schizophrenia also achieved higher scores respectively. Among the algorithms used to measure the implications, it is viewed that Stacking Classifier has performed better than the other algorithms with the highest balanced accuracy and high f1-scores. Random Forest and K-Nearest Neighbors are also investigated with better outputs. Similarly, a good result has been achieved for class-specific models' implementation and a sharp distance has been observed among the classes considering recall and f1-score. A surprising fact is found that the recovery group still has high similarity with the class mental disorder. Overall, this indicates that there are significant effects of functional words in screening mental diseases.

7   Conclusion

In this paper, we have developed ML-based models to differentiate between mental disease persons and normal individuals from their text messages written in English. Here, we have conducted our study over a benchmark dataset. We have rearranged the group and class formation in the dataset according to our requirements and ob-served the significance of pronouns in defining the status of individuals. Different types of pronouns show promising consequences for mental disease detection through presenting a simple, cost-effective, and less time-consuming approach for diagnosing. Here, as the benchmark dataset was highly imbalanced, the dataset presented a common limitation in data analysis. We have overcome the limitation through applying the necessary combined sampling methods.

To enhance this research further in the future, we need to expand our dataset through including more variety and using different classification processes. Besides, to perform our study more precisely in the future, we need to collect write-ups of clinically diagnosed and classified persons with proper pieces of evidence, experiences, and details that can enhance the diagnosis process. Still, with the success of prediction that can avert future discomforts and support people who are at risk, this study can be a big turn for the future.

Acknowledgement. The work has been conducted at and supported by the Bangladesh University of Engineering and Technology (BUET), Dhaka, Bangladesh.

References

1. World Health Organization. https://www.who.int/news-room/fact-sheets/detail/mental-disorders. Accessed 10 July 2022
2. Mental health: lessons learned in 2020 for 2021 and forward. https://blogs.worldbank.org/health/mental-health-lessons-learned-2020-2021-and-forward. Accessed 10 July 2022
3. Recognizing Suicidal Behavior. https://www.webmd.com/mental-health/recognizing-suicidal-behavior. Accessed 10 July 2022
4. How heavy use of social media is linked to mental illness. https://www.economist.com/graphic-detail/2018/05/18/how-heavy-use-of-social-media-is-linked-to-mental-illness. Accessed 10 July 2022
5. Kernot, D., Bossomaier, T., Bradbury, R.: The stylometric impacts of ageing and life events on identity. J. Quant. Linguist. **26**, 1–21 (2017)
6. Al-Mosaiwi, M., Johnstone, T.: In an absolute state: elevated use of absolutist words is a marker specific to anxiety, depression, and suicidal ideation. Clin. Psychol. Sci. **6**, 529–542 (2018)

7. Jockers, M.L., Witten, D.M.: A comparative study of machine-learning methods for authorship attribution. Literary Linguist. Comput. **25**(2), 215–223 (2010)
8. Halvani, O., Winter, C., Pflug, A.: Authorship verification for different languages, genres and topics. Digit. Investig. **16**, 33–43 (2016)
9. Mir, E., Novas, C., Seymour, M.: Social Media and Adolescents' and Young Adults' Mental Health. National Center for Health Research. http://www.center4research.org/social-media-affects-mental-health/. Accessed 10 July 2022
10. Roffo, G., Cristani, M., Bazzani, L., Minh, H.Q., Murino, V.: Trusting skype: learning the way people chat for fast user recognition and verification. In: IEEE International Conference on Computer Vision Workshops (ICCVW), Sydney, Australia, pp. 748–754 (2013)
11. Brocardo, M.L., Traore, I.: Continuous authentication using micro-messages. In: 12th Annual International Conference on Privacy, Security, and Trust, Toronto, Canada (2014)
12. Kernot, D.: Can three pronouns discriminate identity in writing? In: Sarker, R., Abbass, H.A., Dunstall, S., Kilby, P., Davis, R., Young, L. (eds.) Data and Decision Sciences in Action. LNMIE, pp. 397–411. Springer, Cham (2018). https://doi.org/10.1007/978-3-319-55914-8_29
13. López-Escobedo, F., Méndez-Cruz, C.F., Sierra, G., Solórzano-Soto, J.: Analysis of stylometric variables in long and short texts. In: International Conference on Corpus Linguistics (CILC 2013), pp. 604–611 (2013)
14. Burnap, P., Colombo, G., Amery, R., Hodorog, A., Scourfield, J.: Multi-class machine classification of suicide-related communication on Twitter. Online Soc. Netw. Media **2**, 32–44 (2017)
15. Argamon, S., Koppel, M., Avneri, G.: Routing documents according to style. In: Proceedings of the 1st International Workshop on Innovative Information (1998)
16. Baayen, H., Halteren, H.V., Tweedie, F.: Outside the cave of shadows: using syntactic an-notation to enhance authorship attribution. Literary Linguist. Comput. **2**, 110–120 (1996)
17. Hayne, S.C., Pollard, C.E., Rice, R.E.: Identification of comment authorship in anonymous group support systems. J. Manag. Inf. Syst. **20**, 301–329 (2003)
18. Koppel, M., Schler, J.: Exploiting stylistic idiosyncrasies for authorship attribution. In: Proceedings of the IJCAI Workshop on Computational Approaches to Style Analysis and Synthesis, pp. 69–72 (2003)
19. Abbasi, A., Chen, H.: Writeprints: a stylometric approach to identity-level identification and similarity detection in cyberspace. ACM Trans. Inf. Syst. **26**(7), 1–29 (2008)
20. Panicheva, P., Ledovaya, Y., Bogolyubova, O.: Morphological and semantic correlates of the dark triad personality traits in Russian Fackbook tests. In: Proceedings of the IEEE Artificial Intelligence and Natural Language Conference (AINL) Fruct Conference, Saint-Petersburg, Russia (2016)
21. Thieme, A., Belgrave, D., Doherty, G.: Machine learning in mental health: a systematic review of HCI literature to support the development of effective and implementable ML systems. ACM Trans. Comput.-Hum. Interact. **27**(5), 1–53 (2020)
22. Calvo, R.A., Milne, D.N., Hussain, S., Christensen, H.: Natural language processing in mental health application using non-clinical tests. Nat. Lang. Eng. **23**(5), 649–685 (2017)
23. Kaur, P., Sharma, M.: Diagnosis of human psychological disorders using supervised learning and nature-inspired counting techniques: a meta-analysis. J. Med. Syst. **43**(7), 1–30 (2019)

24. Kim, J., Lee, D., Park, E.: Machine learning for mental health in social media: biblio-metric study. J. Med. Internet Res. **23**(3), e24870 (2021)
25. Low, D.M., Rumker, L., Talkar, T., Torous, J., Cecchi, G., Ghosh, S.: Natural language processing reveals vulnerable mental health support groups and heightened health anxiety on reddit during COVID-19: an observational study. J. Med. Internet Res. **22**(10), e22635 (2020)
26. Nobles, A.L., Glenn, J.J., Kowsari, K., Teachman, B.A., Barnes, L.E.: Identification of imminent suicide risk among young adults using text messages. In: Proceedings of the 2018 CHI Conference on Human Factors in Computing Systems, pp. 413–435 (2018). https://doi.org/10.1145/3173574.3173987
27. Du, J., et al.: Extracting psychiatric stressors for suicide from social media using deep learning. BMC Med. Inform. Decis. Making **18**(43), 77–87 (2018)
28. Havigerová, J.M., Haviger, J., Kučera, D., Hoffmannová, P.: Text-based detection of the risk of depression. Front. Psychol. **10**, 513 (2019)
29. Roy, A., Nikolitch, K., McGinn, R., Jinah, S., Klement, W., Kaminsky, J.A.: A machine learning approach predicts future risk to suicidal ideation from social media data. NPJ Digit. Med. **3**(1), 78 (2020)
30. Supplemental Material (2022). https://doi.org/10.6084/m9.figshare.4743547.v1. Accessed 10 July 2022
31. More Than 2000 of The Most Common Text Abbreviations. https://dexatel.com/blog/text-abbreviations/. Accessed 10 July 2022
32. The Complete List of 1697 Common Text Abbreviations & Acronyms. https://www.webopedia.com/reference/text-abbreviations/. Accessed 10 July 2022
33. The Free Dictionary by Farlex. https://www.thefreedictionary.com/List-of-pronouns.html. Accessed 10 July 2022
34. Fernández, A., García, S., Galar, M., Prati, R.C., Krawczyk, B., Herrera, F.: Imbalanced classification for big data. In: Fernández, A., García, S., Galar, M., Prati, R.C., Krawczyk, B., Herrera, F. (eds.) Learning from Imbalanced Data Sets, pp. 327–349. Springer, Cham (2018). https://doi.org/10.1007/978-3-319-98074-4_13
35. Shamsudin, H., Yusof, U.K., Jayalakshmi, A., Khalid, M.N.A.: Combining oversampling and undersampling techniques for imbalanced classification: a comparative study using credit card fraudulent transaction dataset. In: 6th International Conference on Control & Automation (ICCA), pp. 803–808 (2020)
36. Precision-Recall. https://scikit-learn.org/stable/auto_examples/model_selection/plot_precision_recall. Accessed 10 July 2022

RoomE and WatchBLoc: A BLE and Smartwatch IMU Algorithm and Dataset for Room-Level Localisation in Privacy-Preserving Environments

Ada Alevizaki[(✉)] [iD] and Niki Trigoni [iD]

Department of Computer Science, University of Oxford, Oxford, UK
{antigoni.alevizaki,niki.trigoni}@cs.ox.ac.uk

Abstract. The increasing at-home way of living, which became essential due to the COVID-19 pandemic, yields significant interest in analysing human behaviour at home. Estimating a person's room-level position can provide essential information to improve situation awareness in smart human-environment interactions. Such information is constrained by two significant challenges: the cost of required infrastructure, and privacy concerns for the monitored household. In this paper, we advocate that ambient bluetooth signals, from IoT devices around the house, and inertial data from a smartwatch can be leveraged to provide room-level tracking information without additional infrastructure. We contribute a comprehensive dataset that combines real-world BLE RSSI data and smartwatch IMU data from two environments, which we use to achieve room-level indoor localisation. We propose an unsupervised, probabilistic framework that combines the two sensor modalities, to achieve robustness against different device placements and effectively track the user around rooms of the house, and examine how different configurations of IoT devices can affect the performance. Over time, through transition-events and stay-events, the model learns to infer the user's room position, as well as a semantic map of the rooms of the environment. Performance has been evaluated on the collected dataset. Our proposed approach boosts the localisation accuracy from 67.77% on average in standard BLE RSSI localisation, to 81.53%.

Keywords: indoor localisation · semantic mapping · smartwatch · ambient IoT device · BLE · IMU · probabilistic graphical models · HMM · dataset

1 Introduction

In recent years, people spend a considerable amount of their day in their home. An increased tendency towards self-employment, as well as businesses experimenting with new productivity schemes, have given more flexibility to people to work from home, a trend that has largely culminated to a necessity due to the COVID-19

© ICST Institute for Computer Sciences, Social Informatics and Telecommunications Engineering 2023
Published by Springer Nature Switzerland AG 2023. All Rights Reserved
S. Longfei and P. Bodhi (Eds.): MobiQuitous 2022, LNICST 492, pp. 266–289, 2023.
https://doi.org/10.1007/978-3-031-34776-4_15

pandemic. At the same time, the advances in medicine and the increase in life expectancy have resulted in the phenomenon of the ageing population; retired adults normally have many more years to live, but are often faced with age-related diseases that might keep them at home as they become more severe.

The increasing at-home way of living presents a unique opportunity to analyse human behaviour at home to improve situation awareness for Cyber Physical Systems (CPS) that function based on human-environment interactions. For example, smart homes could benefit from daily patterns to learn tasks, such as preheating a room that is frequented at a usual time. Similarly, older adults could be remotely supervised, and intervention could be called for should an abnormal incident be detected.

By investigating such scenarios, it becomes evident that human-environment interactions at home are largely correlated with semantic locations around the house and the mobility patterns of the user around different rooms. As such, inferring the position of a human inside their house as well as transition patterns across rooms can significantly improve situation awareness.

However, human positioning at home is far from trivial. Installation of bespoke infrastructure can be cumbersome and cost-prohibitive. Privacy concerns can also be raised, not only regarding the person monitored, but also for others that might be sharing the space. It is therefore important to identify methods that can exploit existing infrastructure to infer usage of the space and effectively capture mobility patterns, in a privacy-preserving way. Despite the surge of research activity in recent years in the area of human indoor positioning, these constraints rule out many methods that are very effective in different context.

Infrared (IF) positioning systems, for instance, though capable of providing very accurate position estimates, require installation of extensive infrastructure, making them cost-prohibitive for the home environment case [24]. Pedestrian Dead Reckoning (PDR) is an alternative that could minimise costs significantly, as it only requires cheap inertial sensors (accelerometer, gyroscope, magnetometer) that can also easily be attached on the person to be monitored and are widely available in everyday devices, such as smartphones and smartwatches; however, it requires very accurate knowledge of one's initial position, and it can also exhibit large errors due to drift [11]. This issue is exacerbated in smartwatches where there could be interference from multiple other non walk-related hand motions [11]. Other radio frequency (RF) localisation techniques have successfully been used in indoor public spaces (e.g., shopping malls), that are equipped with large wireless sensor networks (WSN/WLAN) with numerous access points (APs). These methods usually employ Wi-Fi APs or bluetooth low energy (BLE) beacons [37] together with smartphone inertial measurement unit (IMU) sensors [32], to achieve an accuracy with an estimated $2 - 10$ metres error [32]; errors beyond 4 m however would probably correspond to a completely different room in a house. Furthermore, they usually require extensive fingerprinting or crowdsourcing [36], which is not an option at home. Lastly, even though mobile phones are carried very often by their owners wherever they go, it is not common for people to carry the device at all times inside their house. Elderly people in particular, are often unfamiliar and resilient to use such technology. Device-free passive RF localisation, that does not require any sensors to be carried, could probably be effectively used to monitor people who live alone, but it will raise difficulties in more crowded houses, as there is no way to distinguish between movements of the occupants of the house (or visitors) if they are not carrying a tag, and requires careful training per house.

Furthermore, there are not many publicly available datasets that are suited to develop indoor positioning methods for the home scenario. In [18], the researchers collect geographical ground truth locations and BLE received signal strength indicators (RSSIs), but all data are collected in a single open space, with known device configurations and floorplan. Similarly, the UJIIndoorLoc-Mag database [27] provides semantic location data and smartphone IMU data, but is only constrained in snapshots of corridors, and not continuous movement across different rooms. The Miskolc IIS Hybrid IPS dataset [29] offers geographical ground truth location, BLE and Wi-Fi RSSIs, as well as magnetometer data from a smartphone, which constraints the viable positioning methods to those based on magnetic field (which usually require fingerprinting). The dataset collected with the Smart Home in a Box (SHIB) technology [17] is the most complete database, offering semantic location estimates and RSSIs from gateways and IMU data in a wrist wearable in a real home environment. Other datasets that offer smartwatch IMU recordings, e.g., [20,31], are not coupled with location information, as they are more suited to human activity recognition applications, than indoor localisation.

In this work we propose **RoomE**, a smartwatch-based method to achieve room-level localisation at home. Smartwatches are equipped with inertial sensors and Bluetooth radio, with which they can sense IoT devices in their vicinity. As these are seeing increasing use among the wider population, we assume this to be a practically infrastructure-free approach. We also introduce **WatchBLoc**, a new dataset of *smartwatch* IMU data and *BLE* RSSI, along with ground truth semantic *location* of the user, collected "in the wild" across two environments.

In summary, our main contributions are:

- We propose **RoomE**, a probabilistic algorithm that achieves semantic localisation and room identification, by sequentially fusing ambient location information with high-level mobility features derived from inertial data, no matter the IoT devices' placement in the environment.
- To our knowledge this paper introduces the first comprehensive dataset, **WatchBLoc**, comprising signals from BLE home devices and user-worn smartwatches allowing for the study of room-level localisation under a variety of conditions: users, IoT device layouts and home layouts.
- We investigate the challenges associated with the sensors we use in this study: i) how different placements of IoT devices around the house can affect the accuracy of room detection, and ii) the challenges associated with the use of motion data from smartwatches and the need for a simple yet robust approach to detecting candidate room change events.
- We evaluate our proposed approach on the new dataset across different floorplan layouts, IoT device placements and user motion patterns. We show that

our method mitigates the issue of high sensitivity of existing smartwatch room detection algorithms to the layout of ambient home devices. It increases the room detection accuracy compared to state of the art from 67.77% to 81.53% without making use of fingerprinting of the environment. It also provides the capability of inferring room transition probabilities without using floorplan information.

The remainder of the paper is organised as follows: Sect. 2 presents the newly introduced dataset and discusses challenges and lessons learnt in collecting as well as analysing the data for the indoor localisation scenario. Section 3 presents the architecture of our proposed indoor localisation system and illustrates how the different modules work together. Sections 4, 5 and 6 introduce the algorithmic details for each of the system's components, respectively, and evaluate their performance. Section 7 then discusses related state-of-the-art methods and the challenges each one faces. Finally, Sect. 8 concludes the paper and discusses limitations and future directions.

2   The Dataset: WatchBLoc

In this section we will present **WatchBLoc**, a new dataset that we collected to achieve indoor localisation for home environments using BLE RSSIs from ambient IoT signals and smartwatch IMUs.[1]

2.1   Dataset Description

We collected data from a number of participants recorded as they were freely performing their typical daily home activities. The data were recorded in two different environments: a *demo-home*, i.e., an office space that was set up to facilitate the experiment, and a *real-home*, i.e., a standard flat. The floorplans of the data collection environments are shown in Fig. 1. BLE beacons were placed in each room (including bathrooms, but excluding corridors), to simulate the existence of IoT devices that can normally be present in a house, like a BLE-connected TV or fridge. We assume that exactly one IoT device exists in each room of the house.

The *real-home* is an interesting case of a house to examine: it is a 2-bedroom/2-bathroom flat, with an open-plan kitchen-living room space. The bedroom denoted as study and the bathroom denoted as loo constitute an ensuite room. As such, even though there exist 6 different semantic locations (namely kitchen, living room, bedroom, bathroom, study and loo), these can be accounted as 5 or 4 distinct rooms: an open-plan kitchen/living room, a bedroom, a bathroom, and a study and loo, or a single ensuite space. We will discuss all 4 combinations in this work, denoted as *full*, *openplan*, *ensuite* and *merged*, respectively.

---

[1] The dataset is publicly available at: https://doi.org/10.5281/zenodo.7039554.

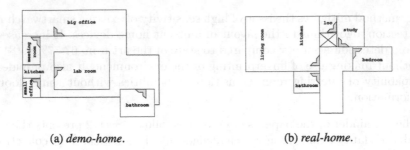

(a) *demo-home*.   (b) *real-home*.

Fig. 1. Data collection environment layouts. The floorplans of the two environments where we collected data for our dataset are presented. The *demo-home* consists of $N = 6$ rooms, arranged across a single floor. The *real-home* is a 2-bedroom/2-bathroom flat, with an open-plan kitchen-living room space. There are 6 distinct semantic locations, that however can be accounted as $N = 4$, $N = 5$ or $N = 6$ rooms, depending on whether we assume the open-plan kitchen and living room to constitute a single *openplan* room, the ensuite study and loo as a single *ensuite* room, or both.

The experiment was performed by 11 participants split across the two environments, yielding a total of 20 continuous recordings, each containing data for three beacon configurations as detailed below. Details on each of the recordings are listed in Table 1.

Table 1. Description of **WatchBLoc** dataset. A total of 11 users performed the experiment across two different environments. user1 performed the experiment in both the demo-home (for three distinct recording IDs, 1, 4 and 8) and the real-home (recIDs 13, 15, 17, 19). user11 performed the experiment in the real-home (recIDs 14, 16, 18, 20), and the rest of the users in the demo-home, yielding one recID each. Four versions of semantic layout for the *real-home* are considered: each semantic location is considered a separate room (*real-home:full*); an ensuite bathroom and bedroom are abstracted to a single ensuite room location in the *real-home:ensuite* case. An open-plan kitchen and living room existing in a space are abstracted to a single semantic room, kitchen/living room in *real-home:openplan*. Finally, both the ensuite and open-plan abstractions are considered in the *real-home:merged* case.

recID	environment	configurations	# rooms
1-12	*demo-home*	*centre, doors, far*	$N = 6$
13-14	*real-home:full*	*centre, doors, far*	$N = 6$
15-16	*real-home:ensuite*	*centre, doors, far*	$N = 5$
17-18	*real-home:openplan*	*centre, doors, far*	$N = 5$
19-20	*real-home:merged*	*centre, doors, far*	$N = 4$

We examined three possible IoT device configurations: placing beacons at the centre of each room (*centre*), at the entrances of each room (*doors*), and at locations around each room such that their pairwise distances are maximised (*far*). Combinations of the above device configurations might exist in real life, e.g., there might be a smart thermostat by one room's door and a smart speaker in the centre of another; we only discuss the aforementioned three configurations in this paper, but the dataset includes BLE RSSIs from all the above $3N$ locations simultaneously, allowing researchers to examine other combinations of device configurations should they wish.

Each of the recordings consists of BLE and IMU data, as perceived by a Sony Smartwatch 3, as well as ground truth semantic location of the user as detailed below:

1. BLE RSSIs from any BLEs in the vicinity of the user, at a frequency of 0.2 Hz,
2. Inertial data (accelerometer, gyroscope, magnetometer) of the smartwatch, at a frequency of 100 Hz.
3. Ground truth location of which room the user was in, logged by the user by tapping the smartwatch screen when changing rooms.

2.2   Challenges

The collection of this dataset has brought to light a few challenges associated with seamless, privacy preserving localisation of people. We will discuss some of these here, but will mention further difficulties encountered in the following sections, as they appear in the dataset's analysis and algorithm's evaluation.

The BLE RSSI data from different houses may vary significantly, even for houses that are of similar layout. Wireless signal strength can be affected by many factors, such as the existence of line-of-sight (LOS) between a BLE device and the smartwatch, attenuation at different levels depending on the construction of the walls' material [8], etc. As such, it is not always guaranteed that we will be hearing a BLE RSSI as we would expect in a space; sometimes RSSI from an IoT device that exists in an adjacent room may be stronger than the RSSI from an IoT device located in the space the user is in. Or, we might have missing data (i.e., not detecting certain beacons at all) even if we're continuously recording data; this can be the result of severe signal attenuation owing to the house's layout (e.g., walls), but also of the user's and other occupants' movements around the house [7], that might be creating additional obstructions to the LOS between device and smartwatch.

A few other challenges arise from the choice of the smartwatch as the sole sensing modality. To ensure long battery life, smartwatches may go to battery saving mode, e.g., when their screen is not touched for a long time; this can result to large segments of missing data, which can lead to uncertain positioning estimates for the corresponding periods of time. At the same time, the wrist attachment of the smartwatch means that the watch is recording inertial data that encode information not only due to the user moving across or within rooms, but also when any other activity is performed, as hand usage is entailed in most everyday activities [11]. This leads to a lot of additive "noise" and can significantly complicate distinguishing walking from other vigorous activities, such as brushing teeth or doing the dishes.

Ground truth collection whilst adhering to privacy concerns has also been a significant challenge during the design and data collection of this experiment. Initial attempts to data collection included ground truth collected in the form of hand-written notes from the user. This was impractical, as the exact timings of changing location and ground truth logs were almost impossible to align, and it was heavily relying on the participant to remember their exact course of actions. Camera-use was prohibited, as data collection included performing the experiment at participants' private houses and was thus considered a privacy breach by the Ethics Approval Committee. RF tags were also inappropriate to indicate ground truth location of the participant, as multiple people were using the data collection environments at the same time. Based on these issues, a logging application was developed and installed on the smartwatches, so that the participants could tap the appropriate semantic location on the smartwatch's screen every time they were moving to a new room. It is important to note that this approach can still have synchronisation issues, as it is almost impossible for the participant to tap their new location exactly at the moment of room-change. However, exploration of the data has shown that it is reasonable to assume that the lagging in the ground truth is no longer than approximately 5 seconds.

3   System Architecture: RoomE

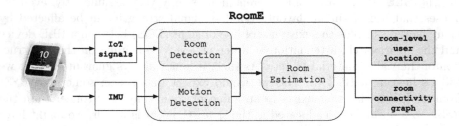

Fig. 2. System architecture

This section provides a high-level description of our system architecture and its three main algorithmic components, i.e., **Room Detection, Walking Detection** and **Room Estimation**, each of which will be detailed and evaluated in the following sections.

Our algorithm assumes a house with N rooms, each equipped with exactly one IoT device[2]. We also assume that we can infer a semantic label for the

---

[2] In practice this is not constraining in the presence of multiple IoT devices per room, as they can be aggregated into an e.g., 'max' or 'mean' BLE signal. Handling rooms with no BLE devices is more challenging and is an open topic for future work.

room that each IoT device is located in, through its identifiable name, e.g., an "IoT fridge" is located in "kitchen", etc. The inhabitant is in possession of a smartwatch, which can perceive these devices through their emitted signals. No information is available regarding the size of each room, their relative position in the house or the position of the IoT devices within the rooms.

The goal of our algorithm is to estimate the room-level location of the inhabitant as well as a semantic map of the environment, while they freely move around the house. This is achieved through **RoomE**'s three main components. These are depicted in Fig. 2 and outlined below:

1. **Room Detection**, giving initial estimates of the user's semantic location.
2. **Motion Detection**, to estimate potential room-transitions.
3. **Room Estimation**, to provide a definite, improved room-level user location and information on the house's layout.

The first two modules utilise the ambient IoT signals from the various IoT devices and the inertial data logged in the smartwatch, to derive initial estimates of the room-level semantic location and mobility of the user, respectively.

In the final module, we employ a probabilistic graphical model, which we train against the available data, to fuse the information extracted in the above modules in a probabilistic graph. Traversal of the graph in the inference phase provides refined room-level localisation for the user. The learnt model's parameters during the training phase are used to infer room-connectivity information, i.e., which rooms are accessible from others.

RoomE thus outputs a room-level location for the user at each timestamp, as well as an estimated semantic map of the house, in the form of a room-connectivity graph.

4 Room Detection

In this section we will discuss the details of the **Room Detection** module of our algorithm, and provide an analysis of the BLE RSSI data recorded in our dataset.

4.1 BLE Data Preprocessing

A basic preprocessing was used to prepare the BLE RSSI data from our collected dataset for the **Room Detection** module.

First, we segment each BLE RSSI signal in non-overlapping windows of length $5.12\,\text{s}$[3]. When multiple RSSI logs from the same device exist in a 5.12 s window, these are aggregated to a single RSSI value, the maximum among them. The timestamp t for the data in each window is thus now updated to be the end-time of the window. To deal with missing "no-signal" RSSI values, the BLE data

---

[3] The choice of the window size is related to the 0.2 Hz recording frequency of the BLE data, as well as an implementation detail in our approach for the **Motion Detection** module that eases time synchronisation of the two modalities.

are linearly interpolated, following the 5.12 s max-aggregation. Figure 3 shows an example of the behaviour of RSSIs from two different rooms in *real-home*, as well as the effect of the preprocessing on the final BLE data, which are used by the rest of the **Room Detection** module.

4.2   Algorithmic Details

For the **Room Detection** module, we employ a *maxRSSI* approach on the preprocessed BLE data, thus assuming that at any point, the user is nearest to the IoT device that emits the strongest RSSI and thus in the corresponding room in the house where the IoT device is placed.

Note that other algorithms that are able to infer semantic location from ambient IoT data could very well be used instead of *maxRSSI*. Our choice of *maxRSSI*, is based on the constraints that the home environment poses: we do not have any information about the dimensions of the rooms or the IoT devices' placements around the house; this makes the use of e.g., fingerprinting based algorithms less suitable for our problem. Even if we did have such information, we would need to re-calibrate the model in each house, as the signal propagation would be affected by the specific conditions of each environment.

maxRSSI is a simple approach that does not require prior training or calibrating, as it is only concerned with the strongest RSSI signal at each time. It has been considered accurate enough to generate the ground-truth location of users in human-robot interactions [21], as well as to identify the interactions of users with objects that have BLE beacons attached [13]. It also resembles

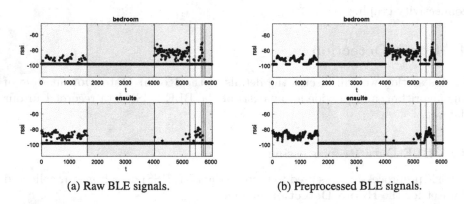

(a) Raw BLE signals.   (b) Preprocessed BLE signals.

Fig. 3. Example of raw and preprocessed BLE RSSIs across rooms. BLE RSSIs logged in two adjacent rooms, **bedroom** and **ensuite**, in the *real-home* environment of our dataset. The coloured areas denote the different ground truth room the user was in at each time, each colour corresponding to a separate room; pink and yellow in particular, correspond to ground truth bedroom and ensuite locations, respectively. We observe that in adjacent rooms, we can register RSSIs from multiple BLEs. Also, raw BLE RSSI recordings (left) can have missing data. Interpolation can help in smoothing intermittent no-signal phases (right).

the thought process behind log-linear path-loss radio propagation models, which are often employed to model the degrading effect of the distance between the transmitter and the receiver on the RSSI values:

$$r = r_0 - 10n \log_{10}(d),$$

where r is the RSSI at the distance d, r_0 is the received signal power of the receiver from a transmitter one meter away and n is the path loss exponent. As is obvious from the above, for $d_1 > d_2$ it holds that $r_1 < r_2$, i.e., the RSSI value decreases as the distance from the transmitter increases. As such, the maximum RSSI value will be obtain nearest to the transmitter.

As discussed in Sect. 4.1, the data passed to the *maxRSSI* algorithm are vectors of RSSIs, corresponding to the N RSSIs received from the N identified rooms in the house at each timestamp t (i.e., the end-time of the corresponding window):

$$vecRSSIs_t := [rssi_{r_1,t}, \ldots, rssi_{r_N,t}].$$

The room estimate r_t can then be computed as the room where the strongest signal device is located. For windows when, even after the preprocessing, no signal was received, we cannot have an accurate estimate for the user's location with the *maxRSSI*. As such, we assign these windows to an "unknown room":

$$r_t = \begin{cases} \text{unknown room,} & \text{if no RSSI from beacons,} \\ r_j, \; j = \text{argmax}\, vecRSSIs_t, & \text{otherwise.} \end{cases}$$

4.3 Evaluation

We evaluate the above *maxRSSI* approach, for the **Room Detection** module on the BLE RSSI data and the corresponding ground truth semantic location, as they were collected in our dataset.

Figure 4 demonstrates the performance of *maxRSSI* in room-level localisation for the two environments where we performed the experiment, and for the three beacon setups in the space, namely *centre*, *doors* and *far*.

A few interesting observations are in order: first, we verify that the device configuration within the space indeed matters. The performance of *maxRSSI* is largely variable between the various configurations for most users. For some users, performance might have less variability between configurations; our assumption is that this is related to which areas of the room each user covered when performing the experiment (recall that there was no prescribed path the users should follow). Second, it seems there might not be a global optimal configuration placement for all houses; we are only considering two environments in this paper and thus we cannot be conclusive, but the *centre* device configuration is dominant in the *demo-home*, in contrast with the *far* configuration which is the best performing in the *real-home*. Overall, the *maxRSSI* average accuracy is 67.77%.

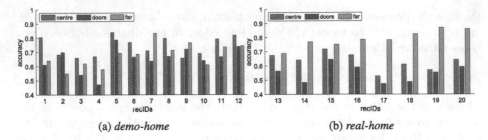

(a) *demo-home*   (b) *real-home*

Fig. 4. *maxRSSI* accuracies for all users and beacon configurations The accuracy of *maxRSSI* is calculated for three different device configurations (*centre, doors, far*) for each user. We observe significant variability in the *maxRSSI*'s accuracy depending on the configuration. Configurations behave similarly for all users in the same environment, i.e., configuration *centre* is best performing in the *demo-home* scenario (left), while *far* has the highest accuracy in the *real-home* scenario (right). We also observe a large variance across the users within a configuration set-up, even within the same environment, in particular for the *demo-home* case. Note that the axes start at 0.4 instead of 0, as *maxRSSI* exceeded this performance in all cases.

It is interesting to investigate whether we can attribute the low performance of *maxRSSI* to certain conditions. Figure 6a demonstrates the room-level locations estimated with *maxRSSI* for a case in the dataset where the *maxRSSI* approach is significantly low-performing: recID 19 − *centre* with just 57.03% accuracy. As is apparent, the recording includes long segments where no BLE RSSIs have been logged. It is also a case where two devices that are placed in separate rooms are sensed simultaneously, with the strongest RSSI value often heard from the adjacent room, and not the one that the user is in. We revisit this recording in Sect. 4, to demonstrate the improvements achieved in such a challenging case.

To conclude, with the **Room Detection** step, we have managed to exploit the IoT signals received in the smartwatch as the user is freely moving around the house, to infer estimates of their initial semantic locations. However, as we have seen, *maxRSSI*, can often have limited localisation accuracy, as it exploits the BLE data only and it thus unable to handle missing data or interferences from nearby rooms effectively. In the next section, we will see how we can make use of the additional mobility information provided by the smartwatch's IMU data, to eventually improve upon the results of *maxRSSI* in Sect. 4.

5   Motion Detection

The **Room Detection** step has provided initial room-level location estimates while the user is moving around the house, but has not taken into account any information about the mobility levels of the user in these rooms. The **Motion Detection** module aims to identify when the user is highly mobile, to help detect walking events that may hint room-transition, or idle events, which are correlated with the user not changing rooms.

5.1 IMU Data Preprocessing

A basic preprocessing was used to denoise, normalise and prepare the data for the **Motion Detection** module.

Similarly to the BLE data, we first perform linear interpolation to fill any missing values. Then, we perform moving median filtering, to achieve an initial reduction of noise, which is particularly present due to the sensor being on the user's wrist. A high-pass butterworth filter with cut-off frequency 0.3 Hz is then employed to remove the gravity vector from the acceleration data, and a low-pass butterworth filter with cut-off frequency 20 Hz (that corresponds to the range of frequencies of human activities) is used to further denoise the data [35]. The data are then bounded to $[-1, 1]$ and normalised to zero mean and unit standard deviation. The processed data can now be used from the **Motion Detection** module, as described below.

5.2 Algorithmic Details

For the **Motion Detection** module, we employ a simple *energyPeak* approach, based on the assumption that the overall energy of the acceleration signal recorded in the smartwatch should be higher during active phases, compared to idle phases.

There are many fitness-related smartwatch apps that aim to provide various information about mobility, including step counters or activity recognition apps, however these can be unreliable for the home environment case-study [6]. Smartwatches are known to effectively identify vigorous activities, such as switching between walking, cycling and running, but not so much activities performed at lower speeds [25] or combined with other domestic activities [6]. At the same time, smartwatch step counters commonly log many false-positive steps [23]; this might not be problematic for distances typically travelled outdoors, but it can be limiting when trying to estimate mobility within a house.

Regardless, for our scenario where floorplans of the house are also absent, a step-counter would have little benefit: as we are unaware of the size of the various rooms, as well as of their proximity, using a step counter as the mobility estimate would be inappropriate, as it would require assumptions about the number of steps that connect different rooms. It would also make it more difficult for the model to generalise across different houses.

Thus, we suggest that in order to have a system that easily applies to every environment and any type of smartwatch, and thus requires no calibration from the user, a much coarser mobility estimate would better suit our needs.

For our *energyPeak* approach, we first further filter the acceleration signal to the human walking frequencies, i.e., $[1.2, 2]$ Hz, to remove any redundant frequencies related to other activities. We then calculate the energy of the filtered signal through the Short-Time Fourier Transform (STFT) of the acceleration's magnitude, calculated in windows of $512 = 2^9$ samples, i.e., 5.12 s[4]. As we

---

[4] This ensures a synchronised 1-to-1 mapping between location and mobility estimates and explains the choice of 5.12 s window for the BLE RSSI data.

observed that high-energy contents gradually occur around ground truth transitions, we chose the envelope of the calculated energy as a final smoothed out energy estimate.

The motion estimates at time t are then chosen as the local peaks[5] of the normalised energy that are larger than the energy's average:

$$
m_t = \begin{cases} active, & \text{if } acc_{\text{energy,smooth}_t} \text{ is a peak and} \\ & acc_{\text{energy,smooth}_t} > \text{threshold}, \\ idle, & \text{otherwise}. \end{cases}
$$

5.3   Evaluation

Our contributing dataset does not log any information about the activities performed during the experiment. As such, we cannot verify whether the *energy-Peaks* we identified as walking events have been correctly classified as such. We can however verify how well our estimates capture ground truth room transitions. In a total of 555 transitions that occured across all the recordings in the dataset, our approach correctly identified 507 missing only 48, bringing the accuracy of *energyPeaks* for estimating room-transitions to 91.35%. A further 1388 timestamps were classified as walking events in a total of 45426 windows of not changing rooms; this is just 3.05% of the times the user stays within a room, which seems a valid behaviour of a user walking around a room while occupying it. In lack of ground truth activity data though, we cannot verify this any further.

To conclude, the suggested *energyPeaks* approach is simple and largely parameter free, yet effective at indicating room-transition events, albeit with some false-positives, as it cannot distinguish between movement during room changes, and casual walking within a room.

In the next section, we combine the outcomes of **Room Detection** and **Motion Detection** to provide a final, refined room-level user location.

6   Room Estimation

The **Room Detection** and **Motion Detection** modules have exploited the ambient IoT signals sensed from the smartwatch and its IMU to provide initial location estimates and estimates of walking events. In this step, we fuse this information together to improve upon the **Room Detection** module.

To fuse these two types of observations (r, m) - i.e., ambient location and mobility estimates - and thus derive refined room-level estimates, we take advantage of the inference capability of an appropriately defined Hidden Markov Model (HMM) with parameters $\theta \equiv (E_R, E_M, T, \pi)$, corresponding to the room emission probabilities E_R, the motion emission probabilities E_M, the state transition probabilities T, and the initial state vector probabilities π. We then refine our initial estimate by the parameters of the model that match our data for each house.

---

[5] Calculated with the MATLAB's findpeaks function.

6.1   Model Definition

We define the state space of our HMM using "one hot encoding" for the set of all possible N^2 room transitions. We choose this room-transitions-as-a-state representation, as our mobility estimate m is concerned with likely room transitions. As such, a state at timestamp t is defined as:

$$s_{k,t} := (r_{i,t-1} \rightarrow r_{j,t}), \text{where } i,j \in \{1,2,\ldots N\},$$
$$k := j + (i-1)N.$$

We also define the observation space using the sensor measurements obtained from the above modules, i.e., as the tuple $o_t := (r_t, m_t)$ at a given timestep. We assume that r and m are independent from each other.

To refer to a room-transition pair, and a combination of observations pair irrespective of time, we will use the following notation:

$$s_k \models (r_i \rightarrow r_j), \text{where } i,j \in \{1,2,\ldots,N\},$$
$$k := j + (i-1)N,$$

and

$$o \models (r,m), \text{where } r \in \{r_1, r_2, \ldots, r_N\},$$
$$m \in \{idle, active\},$$

assuming that a state is always defined across two consecutive room locations in time, and a pair of observations is only properly defined when these occur simultaneously.

The emission probabilities for each type of observation are detailed in the following paragraphs.

Room Emissions. We initialise the room emissions E_R based on the assumption that when we are moving to a new room, we would expect the strongest RSSI to be emitted from the IoT device that is located in the room we arrive in. This is inclusive of the case when we stay in the same room in two consecutive time windows, as this event is encoded as a transition from a room to itself in the states of the HMM. Note that we have N rooms, but we can also observe the 'unknown room'; we can thus have $N+1$ room observations.

The probability $p(r|s_k)$, i.e., the probability of observing room r when moving from r_i to r_j, is thus the following:

$$E_{r,k} = \begin{cases} 1 - \varepsilon_r, & \text{if } r_j \equiv r, \\ \varepsilon_r / N, & \text{otherwise.} \end{cases}$$

The above values are chosen to reflect our initial assumption that when moving into a new room, the beacon existing in this room will *almost surely* emit the strongest RSSI. The value ε_r is chosen to represent the uncertainty of the strongest RSSI being emitted from within the room of occupancy. For our experiment, we initialise $\varepsilon_r = 0.01$, to reflect the expected RSSI behaviour and for numerical stability.

Motion Emissions. The motion emission matrix must reflect that people are likely to be moving within a room without changing their semantic location, but not the opposite: it is impossible for a user to change their location without moving. As such, we define the probability of observing motion m when moving from r_i to r_j, i.e., $p(m|s_k)$, as:

$$
E_{m,k} = \begin{cases} \begin{cases} \varepsilon_{m,c}, & \text{if } m : idlc \\ 1 - \varepsilon_{m,c}, & \text{if } m : active. \end{cases} & \text{if } s_k = (r_i \rightarrow r_j), \ i \neq j, \\ \begin{cases} 1 - \varepsilon_{m,s}, & \text{if } m : idle \\ \varepsilon_{m,s}, & \text{if } m : active. \end{cases} & \text{otherwise.} \end{cases}
$$

The values $\varepsilon_{m,c}, \varepsilon_{m,s}$ are chosen to model our prior on the user's mobility. Depending on the application, and on our knowledge of the environment, these can be chosen to be either identical in all rooms, or to reflect the different mobility patterns in each room (e.g., we might expect higher mobility in a kitchen compared to a study). In this work, we assign $\varepsilon_{m,c} = 0.01$ to reflect the certainty of movement during room-changes. In reality, this probability is equal to 0; there is no way to move from one room to another in the absence of a walking event. However, we chose to allow a very low probability of $E_{idle,i \neq j} = 0.01$ to avoid numerical instabilities in the code. To initialise the states representing a "stay-in-the-same-room" transition, we assign $\varepsilon_{m,s} = 0.3$, as it is still possible to walk within a room without any intention of changing location. Research has shown that people are expected to be sitted at least 75% of their time when working [14], so we define the above probability loosely based on these statistics.

Initial State Vector. The initial state probabilities vector π is defined by assuming we start uniformly at random from any state representing a stay-in-same-room transition:

$$
\pi_k = \begin{cases} 1\,/\,\text{N}, & \text{if } s_k = (r_i \rightarrow r_i), \ i \in \{1, 2, \ldots, N\}, \\ 0, & \text{otherwise.} \end{cases}
$$

Transition Matrix. To define the state transition matrix T of the HMM, we first need to remember that each state represents a *room transition* from room r_i to room r_j, i.e., $s_k \models (r_i \rightarrow r_j)$. The transition matrix T of the HMM is thus defined subject to the constraint that the first part of the next state must agree with the last part of the current state. Any state-transition that adheres to this constraint has the same probability. Any other state-transition has zero probability:

$$
T_{fg} = \begin{cases} 1\,/\,\text{N}, & \text{if } s_f = (r_i \rightarrow r_j), \ s_g = (r_q \rightarrow r_p) \text{ and } j \equiv q, \\ 0, & \text{otherwise.} \end{cases}
$$

where $f, g \in \{1, 2, \ldots, N^2\}$ and $i, j, q, p \in \{1, 2, \ldots, N\}$.

6.2   Inference

Having initialised the parameters $\theta \equiv (E_R, E_M, T, \pi)$ of the model, we can infer the most likely sequence of underlying states of the model for our observations, using the Viterbi algorithm. The trail of the landing rooms of these states corresponds to our room-level location estimates.

In principle, if the initial parameters of the HMM are carefully chosen, the Viterbi path can give us already improved location estimates, compared to the single sensor modality estimates. This is the simple version of our method, which omits the learning step of the HMM; we denote this special case of **RoomE** as Room Inference (**RoomI**). Figure 5 (second group of boxplots) summarises the performance of **RoomI** for the three different device configurations; in comparison with the **Room Detection** results from *maxRSSI* (leftmost group of boxplots), **RoomI** demonstrates an improved performance, averaging to 80.46%.

Figure 6b revisits the recording we studied in Fig. 6a. **RoomI** effectively fuses the location data with the mobility data to account for the no-signal phases of *maxRSSI*, and significantly improves on the adjacent-rooms' noise. We will see how we can further improve this behaviour by learning the parameters of the HMM, to allow for a more informed final decision on semantic localisation.

6.3   Parameter Learning

RoomI, which essentially traverses the initialised graph of our model, can already provide significantly improved semantic location information. In this step we aim to improve the model's parameters, by learning the optimal values that best describe the observed data. Once we have the learnt model parameters, we can use the updated model to infer a refined estimate of the user's room-level position.

One key detail in our approach is that we do not need to learn the full set of the model's parameters. This can be justified by recalling that we want to use the mobility data m to *correct* the **Room Detection** estimates; we thus need the model to expect a motion event when in states that represent room-transitions but not room-stays. As such, we can keep our assumption regarding whether an idle event or an active event should ignite a room transition fixed over time. We also need our model to be able to work its way through 'unknown room' occurrences, by only trusting the *energyPeaks* estimates in such a case; thus, the 'unknown room' observation should maintain its low probability occurrence at all times.

We thus train the room emissions $E_{r,new}$, $r \neq$ 'unknown' and the state transitions T_{new}[6] only, with the Baum-Welch algorithm for expectation-maximisation (EM). The standard Baum-Welch algorithm is adapted as follows[7]:

For the E-step:

---

[6] Updating the state transitions might also be optional, as the transition matrix has been designed to only indicate allowed or not allowed transitions. However, learning this transition matrix can provide information about room connectivity.

[7] We refer the reader to the full set of Baum-Welch equations in [3].

- In the forward pass, the observed emissions can be modelled as the product of the corresponding elements of the two emission matrices, E_R, E_M, as these observations are independent:

$$\alpha_{t,k} = \sum_{f=1}^{N^2} \alpha_{t-1,f} T_{fk} E_{r_t,k} E_{m_t,k}, \ k \in \{1, 2, \ldots, N^2\},$$

$$r \in \{r_1, r_2, \ldots, r_N, \text{"unknown room"}\}, \ m \in \{idle, active\}.$$

where each forward probability $\alpha_{t,k}$ represents the joint probability of being in state $s_{k,t}$ at time t and observing the first t observations by time t, knowing the model parameters θ. It holds that $\alpha_{0,k} = \pi_k E_{r,k}(r_0) E_{m,k}(m_0), \ k \in \{1, 2, \ldots, N^2\}$.

- Similarly, the backward pass is defined as follows:

$$\beta_{t,f} = \sum_{f=1}^{N^2} T_{fk} \beta_{t+1,k} E_{r_{t+1},k} E_{m_{t+1},k}, \ k \in \{1, 2, \ldots N^2\},$$

$$r \in \{r_1, r_2, \ldots, r_N, \text{"unknown room"}\}, \ m \in \{idle, active\}.$$

with $\beta_{L-1,k} = 1, \ k \in \{1, 2, \ldots N^2\}$, L : the total number of timestamps.

- The probabilities $\gamma_{t,k}$ of being in state $s_{k,t}$ at time t and $\xi_{t,f,k}$ of being in state $s_{f,t}$ at time t and state $s_{k,t+1}$ at time $t+1$, are defined as standard, subject to the above modifications of $\alpha_{t,k}, \beta_{t,f}$.

For the M-step:

- As we have discussed, we only need to learn the room emission probabilities. As such, each element $E_{r,k_{new}}$ in the updated emission matrix is the normalised expected number of times in state s_k and observing r, i.e.:

$$E_{r,k_{new}} = \frac{\text{expected \# times in } s_k \text{ and observing } r}{\text{expected \# times in } s_k}, \ r \in \{r_1, r_2, \ldots, r_N\},$$

$$k \in \{1, 2, \ldots, N^2\}.$$

Note that the value for $r_i \equiv$ "unknown room" remains unchanged. We ensure that the full E_R matrix is always properly normalised, to ensure numerical stability and feasibility of the algorithm. The motion emission probabilities E_M also remain unchanged.

- To update the state-transitions, each element $T_{fg_{new}}$ in the updated transition matrix is the normalised expected number of transitions from s_f to s_g, i.e.:

$$T_{fg_{new}} = \frac{\text{expected \# transitions from } s_f \text{ to } s_g}{\text{expected \# transitions from } s_f}, \ f, g \in \{1, 2, \ldots, N^2\}.$$

Refined Room Estimation. Following the training of these parameters, we perform inference on the learnt model, thus obtaining the final room-level location estimates generated by our method. There are two modes of inference function our method can consider: *offline* and *real-time* inference. In the *offline* mode, the model computes the Viterbi path based on historical data (e.g., the full recording of the day), and then reports the full trail of estimated semantic locations of the user. In the *real-time* mode, the model computes the Viterbi using the L most recent observations ($L = 12$ in our case), and reports the current user location as the final room of the current Viterbi path estimate. Figure 5 summarises the performance of the *maxRSSI*, **RoomI** and **RoomE** estimates. **RoomE** achieves an average performance of 81.53%, an improvement of 20.3% on the *maxRSSI* estimates. **RoomE-RT**, denoting the *real-time* mode of our method, achieves an overall 77.6% localisation accuracy. As is apparent in the rightmost group of boxplots in Fig. 5, the *real-time* performance can be almost as good as the *offline* performance, depending on the device configuration. Figure 6c demonstrates the improvement of **RoomE** on the recording we examined in Fig. 6a and Fig. 6b.

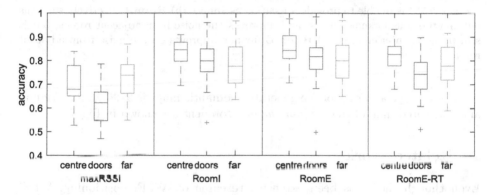

Fig. 5. Overall statistics The boxplots for the *centre*, *doors* and *far* configurations demonstrate the improved performance of **RoomI** compared to *maxRSSI* case, and the further improvement of **RoomE** against both **RoomI** and *maxRSSI*. The **RoomE-RT** section demonstrates the performance of **RoomE** in real-time. Note that the axes start at 0.4 instead of 0, as all methods exceeded this performance.

Semantic Map Estimation. With the learnt model, we can exploit the learnt state transition matrix to extract information about room connectivity, yielding a connectivity graph that resembles a semantic map of the house. To estimate the connectivity, we first estimate a room transition matrix from the state transition matrix, simply by averaging all the states that correspond to arrival in each room. We then calculate the semantic map as a normalised version of the room transition matrix, to remove the effect of how frequently each room is occupied: each line in the room-transition matrix is normalised, s.t. the probability of staying in the same room is 50%, and the probabilities of the remaining transitions sum up to the remaining 50%. In this way, we preserve the relative probabilities of transitioning to each room from a given starting point, but remove the information of how frequently each room is visited. This is the adjacency matrix of the possible room transitions, which can be compared to a ground truth adjacency matrix of the environment.

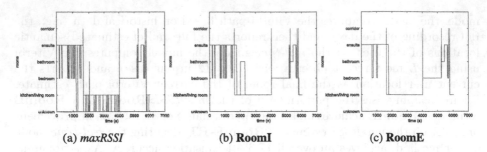

(a) *maxRSSI*   (b) **RoomI**   (c) **RoomE**

Fig. 6. Estimated vs ground truth locations for recID 19 : *centre*. (a) The *maxRSSI* fails to identify areas where the strongest signal comes from an adjacent room to the one the user is currently in. This is often the case for the adjacent `ensuite` and `bedroom` rooms of the *real-home*. For areas where there is no IoT device installed (e.g., corridors), or when no beacon is heard (e.g., in some parts of the *kitchen/living room*), the *maxRSSI* is unable to provide a location estimate. (b) **RoomI** effectively smooths out the previous unknown areas, and improves the noise from adjacent rooms, but is still prone to interferences. (c) **RoomE** further improves on the noise from adjacent rooms.

The average accuracy of the generated semantic maps is 97.85%. An original and estimated map of the *demo-home* environment are shown in Fig. 7

7   Related Work

Even though there has been extensive research on Wi-Fi positioning, Wi-Fi consumes significant power since the aim is to achieve signal propagation in long distances [34]. In indoor spaces however, this is not really required; with the

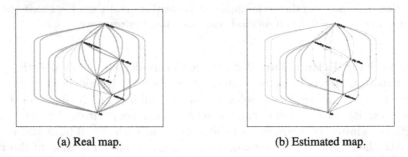

(a) Real map.   (b) Estimated map.

Fig. 7. Semantic maps. The ground truth connectivity graph of the *demo-home* environment is compared to an estimated connectivity graph generated with our method. The estimated map resembles the original map in terms of connectivity and probabilities of transition between rooms. Some information regarding the frequency of visiting each room (i.e., the room occupancy statistics for the user) is still encoded in the estimated connectivity graph, leading to some missing edges, e.g., from `bathroom` to `big office`. These however correspond to low-probability transitions in the original graph, and so do not cause a significant error in our estimation.

development of the low-power energy efficient BLE, work has been done towards examining the potential of BLE beacons as Wi-Fi substitutes [9,34], showing that BLE both better relates RSSI to distance and improves localisation, compared to Wi-Fi. A number of approaches to Wi-Fi and BLE indoor positioning have since emerged; fingerprinting methods have traditionally been a classic approach [12, 16,26,30,37]. Though most methods try to tackle various problems arising from the fingerprinting technique, e.g., the size of the fingerprint map, or the map's dependency to the device, most fingerprinting methods require a map of the environment [1] and a well-defined path-loss model [2], which usually are both unknown in a home environment.

Significant work has also been developed using smart devices, such as smartphones, tablets and smartwatches. These are equipped with a number of inertial sensors, (e.g., accelerometer, gyroscope, magnetometer), and they can also work as Wi-Fi or bluetooth signal receivers. They are also often carried on a person for the majority of the day, meaning they can provide significant information about mobility [16,33]. IMU data from smart devices though are usually very noisy, as the device may be held in many different ways. In this context, estimating the direction of movement in particular can prove of significant difficulty. To address this, [22] propose a 3-step algorithm, which projects the walking direction in two directions: the direction of interference and the direction of the earth's magnetic field. Similarly, [15] and [32] try to address the problems of both step detection and heading estimation, by breaking down the step identification to the basics of human gait analysis, and exploiting projections to global and local coordinate systems. Robust-PDR (R-PDR) [32] in particular introduces an orientation correction algorithm (RIOT) to address drift in the heading estimation, by estimating the gravity vector through the acceleration data. RIOT exploits mainly the gyroscope, and its inherent property to have low drift and high reliability over a short time window. Hence, the relative difference between two consecutive time windows can provide accurate estimates of orientation change. Towards the same goal, [5] introduce deep neural networks (DNN) to minimise drift from IMU measurements.

The above methods try to solve the indoor localisation point through a geographical viewpoint. In the home scenario however, knowing the exact path or number of steps taken is of little interest to most applications. Instead, knowledge of the user's semantic position is informative enough, and helps to further preserve privacy by e.g., removing the need for personal details such as the user's height or leg length that are required for accurate PDR (step detection and step length), or for exact floorplans of the house as required by the map-matching approaches. In the area of semantic localisation of users, [21] introduced an algorithm based on human-robot coexistence to estimate the user's room-level location based on smartphone human activity recognition (HAR) and human-robot colocations. Interestingly, the authors did not record ground truth location of the user externally; instead, they installed BLE beacons in the rooms of interest, and assigned as ground truth location the location corresponding to the beacon that emitted the maximum RSSI value at any given time. A very valuable approach from a human-only perspective, that is seamless and largely infrastructure-free is S-Smart [10]; this combines recognition of human activities with PDR to dynamically learn semantic positions of interest around the house, e.g., windows, doors, etc. It does require however a rather dense on-body sensor set-up, including a smartphone in the pocket, a wrist-worn IMU as well as a foot-mounted sensor, which are rather inconvenient for everyday use. On a similar note of using HAR to infer semantic locations around the house, the AtLAS system [19] fuses HAR and PDR from smartphone IMU data and Wi-Fi RSSIs to both locate landmarks in the environment and localise the user in it, but it requires Wi-Fi fingerprinting. In [28], the researchers, following the suggested approach of [4], are solely based on HAR estimated from smartwatch IMU data and BLE RSSIs from devices installed around the rooms of interest, but follow a supervised learning approach, to learn the correspondence between room-level locations and RSSI values.

RoomE can work around all the aforementioned usual problems of lack of environment maps, heading and distance drift due to noisy sensor data; the method learns the room-locations of the house over time in an unsupervised way, and is invariant to drift, as it does not seek to estimate exact trajectories. Instead, it utilises the energy levels of mobility instances and ambient signals to infer location and transitions, abstracting the notion of an exact trajectory to an accurate walk across nodes on a graph.

8   Conclusion

In this work we presented a comprehensive dataset, **WatchBLoc**, of ambient BLE and smartwatch IMU data for seamless room-level localisation. We discussed the challenges that occur in such positioning scenarios and demonstrated behaviours across different users, environments and device placements. We also introduced **RoomE**, a sensor fusion method acting on the above data to achieve privacy-preserving indoor localisation. Our method is less variable to device configuration compared to the state-of-the-art methods, and achieves accurate semantic localisation and mapping for the user at home.

There are still a few limitations in **RoomE**; we currently assume that every room in the house contains an IoT device that can be sensed through the smartwatch's IMU. In reality, there might be rooms in a house where no such device exists, as we do not yet truly live in fully-smart homes. Future work includes investigating how a minimal number of IoT devices can provide reliable localisation of the user both for rooms that are equipped with a device, but also for adjacent rooms that are not, extending our proposed approach to account for such scenarios.

References

1. Afyouni, I., Musleh, M., Basalamah, A., Tariq, Z.B.: Passive ble sensing for indoor pattern recognition and tracking. Procedia Comput. Sci. **191**, 223–229 (2021). https://doi.org/10.1016/j.procs.2021.07.028, www.sciencedirect.com/science/article/pii/S187705092101423X, the 18th International Conference on Mobile Systems and Pervasive Computing (MobiSPC), The 16th International Conference on Future Networks and Communications (FNC), The 11th International Conference on Sustainable Energy Information Technology
2. Bai, L., Ciravegna, F., Bond, R., Mulvenna, M.: A low cost indoor positioning system using bluetooth low energy. IEEE Access **8**, 136858–136871 (2020). https://doi.org/10.1109/ACCESS.2020.3012342
3. Bishop, C.M.: Pattern Recognition and Machine Learning (Information Science and Statistics). Springer, Berlin (2006)
4. Byrne, D., Kozlowski, M., Santos-Rodriguez, R., Piechocki, R., Craddock, I.: Residential wearable RSSI and accelerometer measurements with detailed location annotations. Sci. Data **5**(1), 180168 (2018). https://doi.org/10.1038/sdata.2018.168
5. Chen, C., Lu, X., Markham, A., Trigoni, N.: Ionet: Learning to cure the curse of drift in inertial odometry. CoRR abs/1802.02209 (2018), arxiv.org/abs/1802.02209
6. Chen, M.D., Kuo, C.C., Pellegrini, C.A., Hsu, M.J.: Accuracy of wristband activity monitors during ambulation and activities. Med. Sci. Sports Exerc. **48**(10), 1942–1949 (2016)
7. Christoe, M.J., Yuan, J., Michael, A., Kalantar-Zadeh, K.: Bluetooth signal attenuation analysis in human body tissue analogues. IEEE Access **9**, 85144–85150 (2021). https://doi.org/10.1109/ACCESS.2021.3087780
8. Faragher, R., Harle, R.: Location fingerprinting with bluetooth low energy beacons. IEEE J. Sel. Areas Commun. **33**(11), 2418–2428 (2015). https://doi.org/10.1109/JSAC.2015.2430281
9. Faragher, R., Harle, R.K.: An analysis of the accuracy of bluetooth low energy for indoor positioning applications (2014)
10. Hardegger, M., Roggen, D., Calatroni, A., Tröster, G.: S-smart: a unified bayesian framework for simultaneous semantic mapping, activity recognition, and tracking. ACM Trans. Intell. Syst. Technol. **7**(3) (2016). https://doi.org/10.1145/2824286
11. Hou, X., Bergmann, J.: Pedestrian dead reckoning with wearable sensors: a systematic review. IEEE Sens. J. **21**(1), 143–152 (2021). https://doi.org/10.1109/JSEN.2020.3014955
12. Jain, C., Sashank, G.V.S., N, V., Markkandan, S.: Low-cost BLE based indoor localization using RSSI fingerprinting and machine learning. In: 2021 Sixth International Conference on Wireless Communications, Signal Processing and Networking (WiSPNET), pp. 363–367 (2021). https://doi.org/10.1109/WiSPNET51692.2021.9419388
13. Jiménez, A., Seco, F., Peltola, P., Espinilla, M.: Location of persons using binary sensors and BLE beacons for ambient assitive living. In: 2018 International Conference on Indoor Positioning and Indoor Navigation (IPIN), pp. 206–212 (2018). https://doi.org/10.1109/IPIN.2018.8533714
14. Johansson, E., Mathiassen, S.E., Lund Rasmusse, C., Hallman, D.M.: Sitting, standing and moving during work and leisure among male and female office workers of different age: a compositional data analysis. BMC Public Health **20**(1), 826 (2020). https://doi.org/10.1186/s12889-020-08909-w

15. Kang, W., Han, Y.: Smartpdr: Smartphone-based pedestrian dead reckoning for indoor localization. IEEE Sens. J. **15**(5), 2906–2916 (2015). https://doi.org/10.1109/JSEN.2014.2382568

16. Lin, K., Chen, M., Deng, J., Hassan, M.M., Fortino, G.: Enhanced fingerprinting and trajectory prediction for IoT localization in smart buildings. IEEE Trans. Autom. Sci. Eng. **13**(3), 1294–1307 (2016). https://doi.org/10.1109/TASE.2016.2543242

17. McConville, R., Byrne, D., Craddock, I., Plechocki, R., Pope, J., Santos-Rodriguez, R.: A dataset for room level indoor localization using a smart home in a box. Data Brief **22**, 1044–1051 (2019). https://doi.org/10.1016/j.dib.2019.01.040, https://www.sciencedirect.com/science/article/pii/S2352340919300411

18. Mohammadi, M., Al-Fuqaha, A., Guizani, M., Oh, J.S.: Semi-supervised deep reinforcement learning in support of IoT and smart city services. IEEE Internet Things J. 1–12 (2017). https://doi.org/10.1109/JIOT.2017.2712560

19. Niu, X., Xie, L., Wang, J., Chen, H., Liu, D., Chen, R.: Atlas: an activity-based indoor localization and semantic labeling mechanism for residences. IEEE Internet Things J. **7**(10), 10606–10622 (2020). https://doi.org/10.1109/JIOT.2020.3004496

20. Roggen, D., et al.: Collecting complex activity datasets in highly rich networked sensor environments. In: 2010 Seventh International Conference on Networked Sensing Systems (INSS), pp. 233–240 (2010). https://doi.org/10.1109/INSS.2010.5573462

21. Rosa, S., Patanè, A., Lu, C.X., Trigoni, N.: Semantic place understanding for human-robot coexistence-toward intelligent workplaces. IEEE Trans. Hum.-Mach. Syst. **49**(2), 160–170 (2019). https://doi.org/10.1109/THMS.2018.2875079

22. Roy, N., Wang, H., Roy Choudhury, R.: I am a smartphone and i can tell my user's walking direction. In: Proceedings of the 12th Annual International Conference on Mobile Systems, Applications, and Services, pp. 329–342. MobiSys 2014, ACM, New York, NY, USA (2014). https://doi.org/10.1145/2594368.2594392, https://doi.org/10.1145/2594368.2594392

23. Saeb, S., Körding, K., Mohr, D.C.: Making activity recognition robust against deceptive behavior. PLOS ONE **10**(12), 1–12 (2015). https://doi.org/10.1371/journal.pone.0144795

24. Sakpere, W., Adeyeye-Oshin, M., Mlitwa, N.B.: A state-of-the-art survey of indoor positioning and navigation systems and technologies. South Afr. Comput. J. **29**, 145–197 (2017), www.scielo.org.za/scielo.php?script=sci_arttext&pid=S2313-78352017000300009&nrm=iso

25. Svarre, F.R., Jensen, M.M., Nielsen, J., Villumsen, M.: The validity of activity trackers is affected by walking speed: the criterion validity of garmin vivosmart(®) HR and StepWatch() 3 for measuring steps at various walking speeds under controlled conditions. PeerJ **8**, e9381 (2020)

26. Tegou, T., Kalamaras, I., Votis, K., Tzovaras, D.: A low-cost room-level indoor localization system with easy setup for medical applications. In: 2018 11th IFIP Wireless and Mobile Networking Conference (WMNC), pp. 1–7 (2018). https://doi.org/10.23919/WMNC.2018.8480912

27. Torres-Sospedra, J., Rambla, D., Montoliu, R., Belmonte, O., Huerta, J.: Ujiindoorloc-mag: a new database for magnetic field-based localization problems. In: 2015 International Conference on Indoor Positioning and Indoor Navigation (IPIN) pp. 1–10 (2015). https://doi.org/10.1109/IPIN.2015.7346763

28. Tsanousa, A., Xefteris, V.R., Meditskos, G., Vrochidis, S., Kompatsiaris, I.: Combining RSSI and accelerometer features for room-level localization. Sensors **21**(8) (2021). https://doi.org/10.3390/s21082723, www.mdpi.com/1424-8220/21/8/2723

29. Zsolt Tóth, J.T.: Miskolc IIS hybrid IPS: dataset for hybrid indoor positioning. In: 26st International Conference on Radioelektronika, pp. 408–412. IEEE (2016)
30. Wang, B., Zhou, S., Liu, W., Mo, Y.: Indoor localization based on curve fitting and location search using received signal strength. IEEE Trans. Ind. Electron. **62**(1), 572–582 (2015). https://doi.org/10.1109/TIE.2014.2327595
31. Weiss, G.M., Yoneda, K., Hayajneh, T.: Smartphone and smartwatch-based biometrics using activities of daily living. IEEE Access **7**, 133190–133202 (2019). https://doi.org/10.1109/ACCESS.2019.2940729
32. Xiao, Z., Wen, H., Markham, A., Trigoni, N.: Robust pedestrian dead reckoning (R-PDR) for arbitrary mobile device placement. In: 2014 International Conference on Indoor Positioning and Indoor Navigation (IPIN), pp. 187–196, October 2014. https://doi.org/10.1109/IPIN.2014.7275483
33. Yang, Z., Wu, C., Zhou, Z., Zhang, X., Wang, X., Liu, Y.: Mobility increases localizability: a survey on wireless indoor localization using inertial sensors. ACM Comput. Surv. **47**(3), 54:1–54:34 (2015). https://doi.org/10.1145/2676430, http://doi.acm.org/10.1145/2676430
34. Zhao, X., Xiao, Z., Markham, A., Trigoni, N., Ren, Y.: Does BTLE measure up against Wifi? a comparison of indoor location performance. In: European Wireless 2014; 20th European Wireless Conference, pp. 1–6, May 2014
35. Zhao, Y., Yang, R., Chevalier, G., Gong, M.: Deep residual bidir-lstm for human activity recognition using wearable sensors. CoRR abs/1708.08989 (2017), arxiv.org/abs/1708.08989
36. Zhou, B., Li, Q., Mao, Q., Tu, W.: A robust crowdsourcing-based indoor localization system. Sensors (Basel) **17**(4), 864 (2017)
37. Zou, H., Huang, B., Lu, X., Jiang, H., Xie, L.: Standardizing location fingerprints across heterogeneous mobile devices for indoor localization. In: 2016 IEEE Wireless Communications and Networking Conference, pp. 1–6, April 2016. https://doi.org/10.1109/WCNC.2016.7564800

Towards Cross Domain CSI Action Recognition Through One-Shot Bimodal Domain Adaptation

Bao Zhou, Rui Zhou[✉], Yue Luo, and Yu Cheng

University of Electronic Science and Technology of China, Chengdu, China
ruizhou@uestc.edu.cn

Abstract. Human action recognition based on WiFi Channel State Information (CSI) has attracted enormous attention in recent years. Although performing well under supervised learning, the recognition model suffers from significant performance degradation when applied in a new domain (e.g. a new environment, a different location, or a new user). To enable the recognition model robust to domains, researchers have proposed various methods, including semi-supervised domain adaptation, unsupervised domain adaptation, and domain generalization. Semi-supervised and unsupervised solutions still require a large number of partially-labeled or unlabeled samples in the new domain, while domain generalization solutions have difficulties in achieving acceptable accuracy. To mitigate these problems, we propose a one-shot bimodal domain adaptation method to achieve cross domain action recognition with much reduced effort. The method contains two key points. One is that it synthesizes virtual samples to augment the training datatset of the target domain, requiring only one sample per action in the target domain. The other is that it regards the amplitude and the phase as two consistent modals and fuses them to enhance the recognition accuracy. Virtual data synthesis is achieved by linear transformation with dynamic domain weights and the synthesis autoencoder. Bimodal fusion is achieved by the fusion autoencoder and feature concatenation under the criterion of consistency. Evaluations on daily activities achieved the average accuracy of 85.03% and 90.53% at target locations, 87.90% and 82.40% in target rooms. Evaluations on hand gestures achieved the average accuracy of 91.67% and 85.53% on target users, 83.04% and 88.01% in target rooms.

Keywords: Action recognition · Modal fusion · Data synthesis · Domain adaptation

1 Introduction

Action recognition is of great values in many aspects of our daily lives. Existing action recognition approaches are mainly based on visions and sensors. Vision-based solutions can achieve excellent recognition accuracy, but require Line of

© ICST Institute for Computer Sciences, Social Informatics and Telecommunications Engineering 2023
Published by Springer Nature Switzerland AG 2023. All Rights Reserved
S. Longfei and P. Bodhi (Eds.): MobiQuitous 2022, LNICST 492, pp. 290–309, 2023.
https://doi.org/10.1007/978-3-031-34776-4_16

Sight (LOS) and may incur privacy violations. Sensor-based solutions demand the users to carry dedicated devices, thus are inconvenient. As a non-intrusive and pervasive solution, WiFi-based action recognition has attracted increasing attention in recent years, due to the release of Channel State Information (CSI) tools [7,26]. A large number of studies on CSI-based action recognition have been launched since then [1,10], ranging from activity recognition, gesture recognition, to other miscellaneous applications. Most of these solutions exploit supervised learning to achieve high accuracy, requiring the training data and the testing data to follow the same distribution. This indicates that CSI-based action recognition under supervised learning only works well in unchanged domains. If the domain changes (e.g. user diversity, location variation, room change), the recognition accuracy will decline dramatically. To keep high performance in a new domain, a large number of new samples need to be collected in the new domain to retrain or fine-tune the original recognition model. This is impractical for real-world applications. To solve this problem, researchers have proposed various solutions, which may be semi-supervised domain adaptation, unsupervised domain adaptation, or domain generalization. Semi-supervised and unsupervised solutions still need to collect a large number of partially-labeled or unlabeled samples in the new domain, while domain generalization solutions have difficulties in achieving acceptable accuracy because it is difficult to capture the characteristics of the new domain without any real samples.

To minimize the effort of domain adaptation and meanwhile keep high accuracy, we propose a one-shot bimodal domain adaptation method, aiming to achieve cross domain CSI action recognition. Utilizing the source domain data and the only sample per action in the target domain, the method synthesizes a large number of virtual samples for the target domain. Virtual data synthesis is through linear transformation with dynamic domain weights and the virtual samples are made close to the target domain by the synthesis autoencoder. To further enhance the accuracy, the method fuses the amplitude and the phase under the criterion of consistency by the fusion autoencoder. The fused features of all the virtual samples are used to train the action classifier for the target domain. Evaluations proved that the proposed method could achieve one-shot domain adaptation for action recognition across users and locations as well as rooms. The contributions of the paper can be summarized as follows.

- Propose a data synthesis method based on linear transformation and the synthesis autoencoder. With one sample per action in the target domain and the samples in the source domains, the method can synthesize a large number of virtual samples for the target domain. The domain weights in the linear transformation are determined dynamically. The virtual samples are made close to the target domain by the synthesis autoencoder.
- Propose a bimodal fusion method based on Cosine Similarity and the fusion autoencoder, which fuses the amplitude and the phase under the criterion of consistency.
- With virtual data synthesis and bimodal fusion, the method achieves one-shot domain adaptation and hence action recognition across users and locations, with the accuracy of more than 85% in the target domains.

– For the task of cross room action recognition, the method achieves the accuracy of more than 82% in the target rooms with one-shot domain adaptation.

The rest of the paper is organized as follows. Section 2 reviews the related works. Section 3 provides the overview of the method. Section 4 elaborates on the methodology of one-shot bimodal domain adaptation, focusing on virtual data synthesis and bimodal fusion. Section 5 reports the evaluations on cross domain activity recognition and gesture recognition. Section 6 concludes the paper.

2   Related Works

Since the release of WiFi CSI tools [7, 26], studies on CSI-based action recognition have been boosting [1, 10]. These methods can be model-based or learning-based.

2.1   Model-Based Action Recognition

Model-based methods investigate wireless transmission theories and exploit signal processing techniques to achieve recognition, hence are agnostic to domains. But accurate modeling of WiFi propagation indoors is difficult. These methods usually require a relatively large number of transceivers and have limitations on their placement. Zhang et al. [29] correlated signal propagation with motions in the first Fresnel zone and linked amplitude variations with motions to detect activities. WiDrive [3] recognized in-car activities based on Doppler Frequency Shifts (DFS), employing Hidden Markov Model with Gaussian Mixture emissions Model (HMM-GMM) as the classifier, whose parameters were updated online to adapt to vehicles and drivers. Widar3.0 [32] derived the domain independent feature Body-coordinate Velocity Profile (BVP) from DFS and recognized gestures adaptive to environments, users, locations and orientations. AirDraw [9] achieved learning-free in-air handwriting by gesture tracking using CSI phase. It denoised raw CSI by the ratio between two adjacent antennas, separated reflected signals from noise by Principal Component Analysis (PCA), and corrected tracking by eliminating static components unrelated to hand motions. Niu et al. [16] analyzed DFS to quantify the relationship between signal frequencies and target locations, motion directions and speeds. They proposed movement fragments and relative motion direction changes as two features to recognize gestures across environments, users, locations and orientations.

2.2   Learning-Based Cross Domain Action Recognition

Learning-based methods have less limitations on the number and the placement of transceivers. They try to learn the relationship between CSI measurements and actions. But learning-based methods have dependance on the domains. To achieve cross domain recognition, researchers try to extract domain robust features or transfer knowledge from source to target domains.

Activity Recognition. To achieve location independent activity recognition, FALAR [27] reconstructed the amplitude data by Class Estimated Basis Space Singular Value Decomposition (CSVD) to discard most location information. EI [11] achieved environment and user independent activity recognition using amplitude based on adversarial networks, composed of a Convolutional Neural Network (CNN) feature extractor, an activity recognizer and a domain discriminator. CsiGAN [25] enabled activity recognition adaptive to users based on semi-supervised Generative Adversarial Network (GAN), leveraging limited unlabeled amplitude data to produce diverse fake samples to train a robust discriminator. WiLISensing [6] built a CNN model to recognize activities using amplitude and fine-tuned the model in new locations. Sheng et al. [18] achieved action recognition using amplitude by integrating CNN with Bi-directional Long Short Term Memory (BLSTM) and fine-tuned the model in new scenarios. HAR-MN-EF [20] achieved environment independent activity recognition by leveraging Matching Network with activity enhanced amplitude. Zhang et al. [31] recognized activities using amplitude images by a Dense-LSTM model. They synthesized variant activity data through CSI transformation to mitigate activity inconsistency and subject specific issues. Ma et al. [15] recognized activities across locations and users using amplitude, employing 2DCNN as the activity classifier, 1DCNN as the state machine, and reinforcement learning for neural architecture search.

Gesture Recognition. WiAG [22] achieved gesture recognition independent on locations and orientations as well as environmental dynamics, by generating virtual amplitude samples of gestures in the target domains through a translation function. CrossSense [30] enabled amplitude training samples to be collected once and used across sites, by employing an Artificial Neural Network (ANN) to train a roaming model that generated synthetic training samples of gestures or gaits for each target site. WiADG [35] and JADA [34] exploited unsupervised joint adversarial domain adaptation to realize gesture recognition based on phase difference, mapping the unlabeled target data and the labeled source data to a domain-invariant feature space. Yang et al. [28] enabled one-shot gesture recognition via a Siamese recurrent convolutional architecture based on phase difference, which used transferable pairwise loss to remove structured noise such as individual heterogeneity and various measurement conditions. To alleviate the effort of retraining in a new scenario or for a new user, Wang et al. [23] recognized gestures based on CSI images leveraging a deep similarity evaluation network. Also based on similarity evaluation, Ma et al. [14] achieved gesture recognition based on amplitude image that could recognize new types of gestures, or gestures performed by a new user or in a new scenario. Kang et al. [12] recognized gestures based on DFS through adversarial learning with feature disentanglement and an attention scheme, adaptive to environments, users, locations and orientations.

2.3 Multi-modal Action Recognition

Different information in CSI depicts the action from different dimensions, which can be combined to enhance the performance. WiFit [13] monitored body-weight exercises robust to environments and users, using amplitude, phase difference and Doppler velocity spectrum. TL-HAR [2] transformed amplitude and phase to images for multiple human activity recognition. MatNet-eCSI [21] employed Matching Network to perform one-shot learning to recognize activities in a new environment. They enhanced activity dependent information and eliminated activity unrelated information and fused amplitude and phase after enhancement. Shi et al. [19] authenticated users by recognizing their activities, using amplitude, relative amplitude and Short Time Fourier Transform (STFT) holograms. They employed an unsupervised domain discriminator to mitigate the impact of locations and environmental changes. FingerDraw [24] tracked finger drawings by exploiting the CSI-quotient model and the Fresnel zone model. It canceled out noise in amplitude and random offset in phase, and quantified the correlation between CSI dynamics and object displacements. DANGR [8] achieved gesture recognition by fusing amplitude and phase. They exploited GAN to augment the dataset and adopted Multi-kernel Maximum Mean Discrepancy (MK-MMD) to shrink the domain discrepancy. WiVi [33] recognized activities by combining vision and WiFi. It employed CNN to extract features from WiFi and a variant of C3D model for vision sensing. An ensemble neural network was constructed for decision. Bakalos et al. [4] detected abnormal activities based on BLSTM, fusing RGB imagery, thermographic imagery and CSI to capture the temporal inter-dependency.

2.4 The Difference

Compared with the prior works, our method is a universal solution for WiFi sensing tasks. Although we only evaluated on activity recognition and gesture recognition, the method can be extended to other CSI sensing tasks. Our method requires only one sample per class in the target domains, hence it achieves one-shot domain adaptation, requiring less effort than semi-supervised and unsupervised methods. Our method fuses amplitude and phase in feature extraction considering the consistency between them, hence enhances the recognition performance, achieving higher accuracy than domain generalization methods. Apart from user diversity and location variation, our method achieves acceptable accuracy for cross room action recognition, which is the most challenging issue in cross domain sensing.

3   Overview

The goal of our work is to recognize actions in new scenarios with the knowledge from the training scenarios. The training scenarios are known as the source domains, whereas the new scenarios, to which the recognition model is adapted, are known as the target domains. The source domains have adequate labeled data to train an accurate recognition model, while the target domains have very few samples, far from training a recognition model. Each scenario is regarded as a domain. Domain changes are caused by user diversity, location variation, room

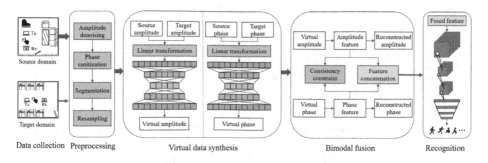

Fig. 1. Framework of the proposed method.

change and etc. Our aim is to achieve cross domain action recognition with little effort by means of one-shot domain adaptation, which requires only one sample per class in each target domain.

To achieve the aim, we propose the method framework as shown in Fig. 1, composed of data collection, preprocessing, virtual data synthesis, bimodal fusion and action recognition. The key components are virtual data synthesis and bimodal fusion. As there is only one sample per action in the target domain, the data synthesis component synthesizes a large number of virtual labeled samples for the target domain, leveraging linear transformation and the synthesis autoencoder. The bimodal fusion component extracts the consistent features from the amplitude and the phase under the constraint of Cosine Similarity via the fusion autoencoder, and concatenates the consistent features for the subsequent action classification. Before virtual data synthesis, the amplitude and the phase are retrieved from CSI, undergoing noise reduction in amplitude and shift removal in phase. After bimodal fusion, the concatenated features of the virtual samples are used to train the action classifier and recognize the actions in the target domain.

4   Methodology

4.1   Data Preprocessing

The amplitude and the phase retrieved from the raw CSI cannot be used directly for action recognition, as the amplitude contains noise and the phase contains shifts caused by Carrier Frequency Offset (CFO) and Sampling Frequency Offset (SFO). CFO is due to the unsynchronization of the central frequencies between the transmitter and the receiver, and SFO is due to the unsynchronized clocks. The data preprocessing goes through amplitude denoising, phase sanitization, data segmentation and data resampling. The raw amplitude sequences are denoised by a median filter, and the raw phase sequences are sanitized by a linear transformation method [17]. The denoised and sanitized data are segmented to retrieve the action part by mean square deviations. Finally the data are resampled to keep a consistent length by interval sampling.

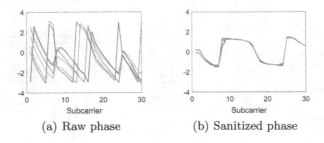

(a) Raw phase   (b) Sanitized phase

Fig. 2. Raw and sanitized phase.

As the raw phase values have significant errors due to CFO and SFO, we apply linear transformation to sanitize it [17]. The raw phase of the i-th subcarrier can be expressed as

$$\angle \hat{H}_i = \angle H_i - 2\pi \frac{m_i}{F} \Delta t + \beta + Z \tag{1}$$

where $\angle H_i$ is the true phase, m_i denotes the subcarrier index ranging from -28 to 28, F is the size of Fast Fourier Transform (FFT), Δt is the timing offset due to SFO, β is the unknown phase offset due to CFO, and Z is the measurement noise. Defining two terms k and b as

$$k = \frac{\angle \hat{H}_N - \angle \hat{H}_1}{m_N - m_1}, \quad b = \frac{1}{N} \sum_{i=1}^{N} \angle \hat{H}_i \tag{2}$$

where N is the number of subcarriers, Eq. (1) can be rewritten as

$$\angle \hat{H}_i = \angle H_i - k m_i - b \tag{3}$$

Apply Eq. (3) to the raw phase, we can obtain the sanitized phase. Figure 2 shows the raw and the sanitized phase, each curve representing a packet.

4.2 Virtual Data Synthesis

Suppose $D^s = \{(x_i^s, y_i^s) | i = 1, 2, \cdots, n^s\}$ represents the dataset of the source domains, where x_i^s is an action sample and y_i^s is the action label. Suppose $D^t = \{(x_i^t, y_i^t) | i = 1, 2, \cdots, n^t\}$ represents the datatset of the target domain, where x_i^t is an action sample and y_i^t is the action label. n^s and n^t are the numbers of samples in the source and the target domain, satisfying $n^t \ll n^s$. For one-shot domain adaptation, $n^t = C$, where C is the number of action types, i.e. each action has one sample in the target domain. As the target domain has only C samples, it is too few to train a classifier or fine-tune a pre-trained classifier. To achieve cross domain action recognition, we need to augment the dataset of the target domain. We synthesize virtual samples for the target domain, utilizing the real samples in the source domains and the only sample per action in the target domain. The method of virtual data synthesis is illustrated in Fig. 3.

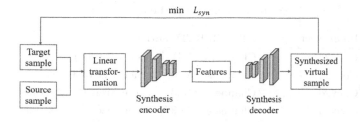

Fig. 3. Virtual data synthesis.

Linear Transformation. The CSI data are the superposition of the signals from all the paths. The static paths are reflected by the static objects, such as floor, ceiling and furniture, while the dynamic paths are reflected by the moving objects, i.e. the sensing targets. Therefore, the dynamic paths are related to the actions, whereas the static paths are environment related. As the synthesized data are for the target domain, they should contain both the action information and the target environment information. The action information mainly comes from the source domains and the target environment information comes from the target domain. Taking a sample from the source domains, denoted as $(x_i^s, y_i^s) \in D^s$, and taking a sample from the target domain, denoted as $(x_j^t, y_j^t) \in D^t$, satisfying $y_i^s = y_j^t$, we apply linear transformation on x_i^s and x_j^t to synthesize the virtual sample as

$$x_i^v = \alpha x_i^s + \beta x_j^t \tag{4}$$

where α and β are the domain weights, to balance the importance of the source domain and the target domain. The label of x_i^v is set as y_j^t.

Dynamic Domain Weights. In the synthesis of a virtual sample, the source domain sample and the target domain sample belong to the same action class, so they share the same action information but have different environment information. Through linear transformation, the common action information and both the environment information are contained in the synthesized sample. Since the synthesized samples are for the target domain, the target environment information should be retained while the source environment information should be removed. This can be achieved by setting the proper domain weights. When α decreases and β increases, x_i^v gets approaching the target domain sample x_j^t. Because different domains have different environmental characteristics, we propose to set the domain weights adaptively. We apply the synthesis autoencoder on the virtual sample x_i^v to determine the values of α and β. The synthesis autoencoder is a CNN, whose structure is shown in Table 1.

Target Domain Enhancement. In addition to the domain weights, the synthesis autoencoder tries to make the virtual data close to the target domain data. Using Mean Square Error (MSE) to calculate the distance between the

Table 1. Structure of the autoencoder

Input layer	(200×270) 2D matrix
Conv2d	Channels=(1,4), kernel size=(5,5), stride=2
Conv2d	Channels=(4,16), kernel size=(3,3), stride=2
Conv2d	Channels=(16,32), kernel size=(3,3), stride=2
Conv2d	Channels=(32,32), kernel size=(2,2), stride=1
ConvTranspose2d	Channels=(32,32), kernel size=(3,2), stride=1
ConvTranspose2d	Channels=(32,16), kernel size=(3,4), stride=2
ConvTranspose2d	Channels=(16,4), kernel size=(3,4), stride=2
ConvTranspose2d	Channels=(4,1), kernel size=(4,4), stride=2
Output layer	(200×270) 2D matrix

synthesized virtual data x_i^v and the target domain data x_i^t, the loss function of the synthesis autoencoder can be defined as

$$\min \quad L_{syn} = \frac{1}{n^s} \sum_{i=1}^{C} \sum_{j=1}^{n^c} (x_{ij}^v - x_i^t)^2 \tag{5}$$

where n^c is the number of samples in the source domains for an action. By training the synthesis autoencoder, the domain weights α and β can be set dynamically and the synthesized virtual samples contain the action information and the target environment information.

Figure 4 shows the virtual amplitude and the virtual phase synthesized from the real sample in the target domain with the action knowledge from the source domains. The virtual samples are similar to the target domain data, thus can be used to train the recognition model for the target domain.

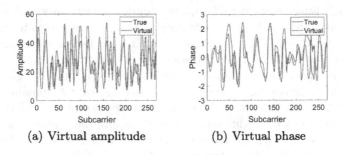

(a) Virtual amplitude   (b) Virtual phase

Fig. 4. Synthesized virtual samples

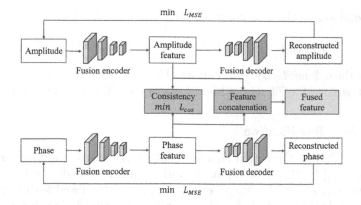

Fig. 5. Fusion of amplitude and phase.

4.3 Fusion of Amplitude and Phase

From CSI we can extract amplitude and phase. The two modals are affected by the actions simultaneously, hence have consistency. To learn the features more accurately, we propose to fuse the two modals in the feature level under the criterion of consistency, as illustrated in Fig. 5. The key in the structure is the fusion autoencoder, which is a CNN as shown in Table 1.

Suppose x^a denotes the amplitude sample and x^p denotes the phase sample. The fusion autoencoder is applied on them to extract the action features in each modal. We denote the features of x^a as $f^a = encoder(x^a)$ and the features of x^p as $f^p = encoder(x^p)$. Considering that x^a and x^p sense the same action simultaneously and have consistency in the feature space, we leverage Cosine Similarity to measure their consistency and minimize their cosine distance. The goal can be expressed as

$$\min \quad L_{cos} = 1 - cos(f^a, f^p)$$
$$= 1 - \frac{f^a \cdot f^p}{\parallel f^a \parallel \cdot \parallel f^p \parallel}$$
$$= 1 - \frac{\sum_{i=1}^{N} f_i^a f_i^p}{\sqrt{\sum_{i=1}^{N} (f_i^a)^2} \sqrt{\sum_{i=1}^{N} (f_i^p)^2}} \tag{6}$$

In addition to minimizing the distance between the amplitude and the phase, the extracted features should keep the original feature of each modal. Hence the reconstructions of x^a and x^p, denoted as $\bar{x}^a$ and $\bar{x}^p$, should be as close to the originals as possible, i.e.

$$\min \quad L_{MSE}(x^a, \bar{x}^a) = \frac{1}{N} \sum_{i=1}^{N} (x_i^a - \bar{x}_i^a)^2$$
$$\min \quad L_{MSE}(x^p, \bar{x}^p) = \frac{1}{N} \sum_{i=1}^{N} (x_i^p - \bar{x}_i^p)^2 \tag{7}$$

The total loss of the fusion autoencoder can be defined as

$$L_{fusion} = L_{cos} + \lambda L_{MSE}(x^a, \bar{x}^a) + \lambda L_{MSE}(x^p, \bar{x}^p) \tag{8}$$

where λ is the balance factor. The extracted features f^a and f^p are concatenated, expressed as $f = [f^a, f^p]$, as the fused feature for action classification.

4.4 Action Classification

We employ CNN as the action classifier, taking the fused feature of amplitude and phase $f = [f^a, f^p]$ as the input. f^a and f^p are the encoded features, having the dimensions of $22 \times 31 \times 32$. After concatenation, the fused feature f has the dimension of $22 \times 31 \times 64$. The action classifier contains 3 convolutional blocks followed by 3 fully connected layers, in which each convolutional block is composed of 1 convolutional layer and 1 max-pooling layer. ReLU is the activation function and cross entropy is the classification loss. The structure of the action classifier is shown in Table 2.

Table 2. Structure of the action classifier

Input layer	$(22 \times 31 \times 64)$ 3D matrix
Convolutional	Channels=(64,64), kernel size=(3,3), stride=1
Convolutional	Channels=(64,32), kernel size=(2,2), stride=1
Convolutional	Channels=(32,16), kernel size=(2,2), stride=1
FullyConnected	Nodes=1024
FullyConnected	Nodes=512
FullyConnected	Nodes=64
Output layer	Nodes=#actions

5 Evaluations

5.1 Experimental Setup and Datasets

To evaluate the proposed method, we conducted extensive experiments on activity recognition and gesture recognition. We deployed two laptops equipped with Intel WiFi Link 5300 as the transmitter and the receiver, each having 3 antennas. The sampling rate was 100 Hz for activity recognition and 1000 Hz for gesture recognition. As there were 9 antenna pairs and each had 30 subcarriers, each CSI packet contained 270 dimensions. After data preprocessing, each action sample had a time sequence of 200 packets with 270 dimensions.

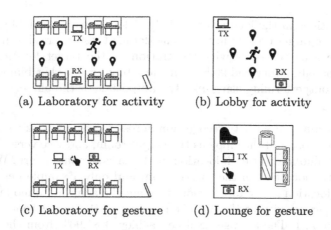

(a) Laboratory for activity   (b) Lobby for activity

(c) Laboratory for gesture   (d) Lounge for gesture

Fig. 6. Experimental scenarios and setup.

Activity Datasets. We set up two scenarios for activity recognition. One was a laboratory of size $6\,m \times 8\,m$ and the other was a lobby of size $5\,m \times 5\,m$. In the laboratory, as shown in Fig. 6(a), the transmitter and the receiver were placed on both sides of the aisle. The volunteer performed 4 activities (squatting down, standing up, walking and jumping) at 8 locations (as the location pins show in Fig. 6(a), adjacent locations are about one meter apart), and each activity was repeated 20 times per location. In the lobby, as shown in Fig. 6(b), the transmitter and the receiver were placed at two opposite corners of the room. The volunteer performed 6 activities (squatting down, standing up, walking, jumping, falling and climbing) at 5 locations (as the location pins show in Fig. 6(b), adjacent locations are about one meter apart), and each activity was repeated 20 times per location.

Gesture Datasets. We also collected data for gesture recognition in two scenarios: a laboratory of size $6\,m \times 8\,m$ and a lounge of size $5\,m \times 5\,m$. The transmitter and the receiver were placed in the aisle with $2\,m$ apart in the laboratory and $1.6\,m$ apart in the lounge, as shown in Fig. 6(c) and Fig. 6(d). Six volunteers, with different heights and weights, performed 6 gestures in both scenarios. The gestures were common letters {L, O, V, W, Z, S}, and each was repeated 20 times per person.

5.2 Experimental Results of Activity Recognition

Across Locations. In the laboratory, 7 locations were taken as the source domains and the left 1 as the target domain. In the lobby, 4 locations were taken as the source domains and the left 1 as the target domain. We used 20 samples per activity in each source domain and only 1 sample per activity in the target domain to train the adaptation model, and used 19 samples per activity in the target domain to test the adaptation model. The method was evaluated at the 8 locations in the laboratory and the 5 locations in the lobby, with each location as the target domain in turn. The detailed results are shown in Table 3. The average accuracy of activity recognition at the target locations reached 85.03% in the laboratory and 90.53% in the lobby for one-shot bimodal domain adaptation, outperforming using only the amplitude or the phase.

Across Rooms. For activity recognition across rooms, we took the laboratory as the source room and the lobby as the target room, and vice verse. The experiments were conducted at each location in the target room in turn. We used the data at all the locations in the source room and only 1 sample per activity at the current location in the target room to train the adaptation model, and used 19 samples per activity at the current location in the target room to test the adaptation model. The average accuracy achieved 87.90% from the laboratory to the lobby and 82.40% from the lobby to the laboratory, as shown in Table 5. The accuracy of bimodal fusion outperformed the amplitude or the phase alone.

5.3   Experimental Results of Gesture Recognition

Across Users. For gesture recognition in the laboratory and the lounge, we took 5 users as the source domains and the left 1 as the target domain. We used 20 samples per gesture in each source domain and only 1 sample per gesture in the target domain to train the adaptation model, and used 19 samples per gesture in the target domain to test the adaptation model. The method was evaluated on the 6 users in the laboratory and the lounge, with each user as the target domain in turn. As shown in Table 4, the average accuracy achieved 91.67% in the laboratory and 85.53% in the lounge for the target users using one-shot bimodal domain adaptation, outperforming using only the amplitude or the phase.

Across Rooms. For gesture recognition across rooms, we used the laboratory as the source room and took the lounge as the target room, and vice verse. The experiments were conducted on each user in the target room in turn. We used the data of 5 users in the source room and 1 sample per gesture of the left user in the target room to train the adaptation model, and used 19 samples per gesture of the target user in the target room to test the adaptation model. The average accuracy of cross room gesture recognition achieved 83.04% from the laboratory to the lounge and 88.01% from the lounge to the laboratory, as shown in Table 5. The accuracy of bimodal fusion outperformed the amplitude or the phase alone.

5.4   Comparison with Existing Works

We compared our method with the state of the art. We compared with the data augmentation method in Fido [5], which leveraged Variational Autoencoder (VAE) to synthesize virtual samples from the labeled samples. We compared

Table 3. Activity recognition at target locations (%)

Scenario	Source	Target	Amplitude	Phase	Bimodal
Lab	2-8	1	73.68	75.00	78.95
	1, 3-8	2	77.63	68.42	78.95
	1-2, 4-8	3	80.26	73.68	80.26
	1-3, 5-8	4	89.47	71.05	93.42
	1-4, 6-8	5	72.37	72.37	77.63
	1-5, 7-8	6	86.84	85.53	94.74
	1-6, 8	7	78.95	81.58	90.79
	1-7	8	77.63	75.00	85.53
		Average	**79.60**	**75.32**	**85.03**
Lobby	2-5	1	88.60	85.09	92.11
	1, 3-5	2	84.21	75.44	85.96
	1-2, 4-5	3	85.09	84.21	94.74
	1-3, 5	4	82.46	81.58	92.98
	1-4	5	81.58	78.07	86.84
		Average	**84.30**	**80.88**	**90.53**

Table 4. Gesture recognition on target users (%)

Scenario	Source	Target	Amplitude	Phase	Bimodal
Lab	2-6	1	85.09	79.82	90.35
	1, 3-6	2	88.60	78.95	90.35
	1-2, 4-6	3	92.11	88.60	97.37
	1-3, 5-6	4	83.33	78.07	85.96
	1-4, 6	5	86.84	78.95	92.11
	1-5	6	88.60	71.05	93.86
		Average	**87.43**	**79.24**	**91.67**
Lounge	2-6	1	75.44	69.30	77.19
	1, 3-6	2	81.58	75.44	85.09
	1-2, 4-6	3	91.23	86.84	95.61
	1-3, 5-6	4	79.82	71.93	83.33
	1-4, 6	5	82.46	80.70	85.09
	1-5	6	83.33	68.42	86.84
		Average	**82.31**	**75.44**	**85.53**

Table 5. Action recognition in target rooms (%)

Action	Source	Target	Amplitude	Phase	Bimodal
Activity	Lab	Lobby	83.16	79.21	**87.90**
	Lobby	Lab	76.48	73.03	**82.40**
Gesture	Lab	Lounge	79.53	71.49	**83.04**
	Lounge	Lab	83.77	75.73	**88.01**

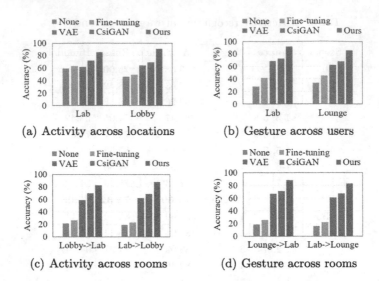

Fig. 7. Comparison with existing works.

with CsiGAN [25], which leveraged semi-supervised GAN for CSI-based activity recognition, using unlabeled samples to generate virtual samples to train a robust discriminator. We reimplemented the VAE-based data synthesis method in FiDo and reused the original implementation of CsiGAN. These methods were compared with no adaptation and fine-tuning as well. Using the same activity datasets and gesture datasets in Sect. 5.1, the results are shown in Fig. 7. Across locations and across users as well as across rooms in multiple scenarios, our method achieved the best performance in the target domains. The reasons are two-fold. Firstly, our method utilized one real sample per action in the target domain together with the real samples in the source domains to achieve domain adaptation, which could help capture the characteristics of the target domain more accurately. Secondly, our method enhanced the action features by fusing amplitude and phase, while FiDo and CSiGAN only made use of amplitude. We also compared our method with the existing works using only amplitude, and our method still achieved the best performance in the target domains.

5.5   Ablation Study

Effect of Dynamic Domain Weights. We apply linear transformation to synthesize virtual data, which assigns the weights to the source and the target domains, balancing their importance on data synthesis. As different domains have different characteristics, the domain weights should be set differently. Our method sets the domain weights adaptively through the synthesis autoencoder. To verify its effect, we compared it with fixed domain weights ($\alpha = 0.5$, $\beta = 0.5$). The comparison results are shown in Fig. 8(a) for activities and Fig. 8(b) for gestures. Dynamic domain weights outperformed fixed domain weights.

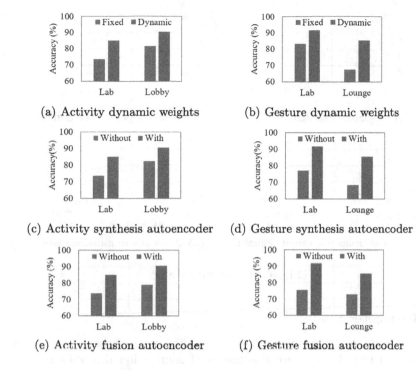

(a) Activity dynamic weights (b) Gesture dynamic weights

(c) Activity synthesis autoencoder (d) Gesture synthesis autoencoder

(e) Activity fusion autoencoder (f) Gesture fusion autoencoder

Fig. 8. The ablation study.

Effect of Synthesis Autoencoder. In addition to linear transformation, we leverage the synthesis autoencoder to reconstruct the virtual data and make them close to the target domain data, in order to enhance the target environment information. To verify the effect of the synthesis autoencoder, we compared it with not using the synthesis autoencoder. The comparison results are shown in Fig. 8(c) for activities and Fig. 8(d) for gestures. The synthesis autoencoder improved the accuracy by a large margin.

Effect of Fusion Autoencoder. The fusion autoencoder extracted the consistent features from different but consistent modals and meanwhile kept their original action features. To verify its effect, we compared it with not using the fusion autoencoder, which extracted the features from the amplitude and the phase and concatenated them. The comparison results are shown in Fig. 8(e) for activities and Fig. 8(f) for gestures. The fusion autoencoder improved the accuracy by a large margin. Without the fusion autoencoder, the features were extracted from the different modals separately, losing the consistency between them, causing the loss of useful information.

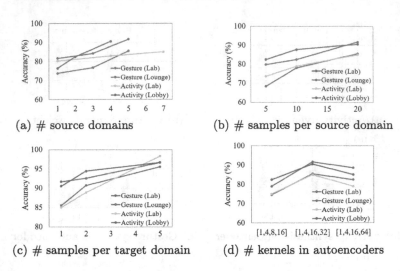

(a) # source domains   (b) # samples per source domain

(c) # samples per target domain   (d) # kernels in autoencoders

Fig. 9. The parameter study.

5.6   Parameter Study

Number of Source Domains. To evaluate the impact of the number of source domains, we tested on different numbers of source domains with one target domain. For activity recognition across locations in the laboratory, we took 1, 4, 7 locations as the source domains and a different location as the target domain. For activity recognition across locations in the lobby, we took 1, 2, 4 locations as the source domains and a different location as the target domain. For gesture recognition across users in the laboratory and in the lounge, we took 1, 3, 5 users as the source domains and 1 different user as the target domain. The recognition accuracies on the target domains are shown in Fig. 9(a). More source domains led to better performance, but incurred higher cost.

Number of Samples in Source Domains. We evaluated the impact of the number of samples per action in the source domains. For activity recognition across locations in the laboratory and the lobby and for gesture recognition across users in the laboratory and the lounge, we set the number of samples in each source domain as 5, 10, 20 per action and the target domain had 1 sample per action. The recognition accuracies on the target domains are shown in Fig. 9(b), indicating that the accuracy increased with the number of samples in the source domains, but requiring more effort.

Number of Samples in Target Domains. We also evaluated the impact of the number of samples per action in the target domain. For activity recognition across locations in the laboratory and the lobby and for gesture recognition across users in the laboratory and the lounge, we set the number of samples in the target domain as 1, 2, 5 per action, and the number of samples in each source

domain were 20 per action. The recognition accuracies on the target domain
are shown in Fig. 9(c). Although more samples achieved higher accuracy, they
incurred higher effort. One-shot adaptation achieved acceptable accuracy.

Number of Kernels in Autoencoders. The structure of the synthesis
autoencoder and the fusion autoencoder is important to domain adaptation.
We evaluated the performance of different numbers of convolution kernels in the
autoencoders. We compared 3 groups of kernel numbers, which were [1,4,8,16],
[1,4,16,32] and [1,4,16,64] for the encoders and inverse for the decoders. The
results on the target domain are shown in Fig. 9(e). [1,4,16,32] kernels achieved
the best performance, while [1,4,8,16] kernels could not extract the features effectively and [1,4,16,64] kernels caused overfitting.

6   Conclusions

To achieve cross domain CSI action recognition and sensing, we propose a one-
shot domain adaptation method based on virtual data synthesis and bimodal
fusion. The method synthesizes the virtual data for the target domains by a linear
transformation function and the synthesis autoencoder, which sets the domain
weights adaptively for different domains in linear transformation and makes the
virtual data close to the target domain data. To improve the recognition accuracy
with only one sample per action in the target domain, the method fuses the
amplitude and the phase by the fusion autoencoder, which extracts their action
features and keeps their consistency to the same actions. Real-world evaluations
of activity recognition and gesture recognition in multiple scenarios achieved
high accuracy across locations and users as well as rooms. The limitation of
the current method is that it still requires one sample per action in the target
domain. Zero-shot domain adaptation is our next step work.

References

1. Ahmed, H.F.T., Ahmad, H., Aravind, C.V.: Device free human gesture recognition
   using Wi-Fi CSI: a survey. Eng. Appl. Artif. Intell. **87**, 103281 (2020)
2. Arshad, S., Feng, C., Yu, R., Liu, Y.: Leveraging transfer learning in multiple
   human activity recognition using WiFi signal. In: IEEE 20th International Symposium on A World of Wireless, Mobile and Multimedia Networks (WoWMoM),
   pp. 1–10 (2019)
3. Bai, Y., Wang, Z., Zheng, K., Wang, X., Wang, J.: Widrive: adaptive wifi-based
   recognition of driver activity for real-time and safe takeover. In: 39th International Conference on Distributed Computing Systems (ICDCS), pp. 901–911. IEEE
   (2019)
4. Bakalos, N., Voulodimos, A., Doulamis, N., Doulamis, A., Papasotiriou, K., Bim-
   pas, M.: Fusing RGB and thermal imagery with channel state information for
   abnormal activity detection using multimodal bidirectional LSTM. In: Abie, H.,
   et al. (eds.) CPS4CIP 2020. LNCS, vol. 12618, pp. 77–86. Springer, Cham (2021).
   https://doi.org/10.1007/978-3-030-69781-5_6

5. Chen, X., Li, H., Zhou, C., Liu, X., Wu, D., Dudek, G.: Fido: ubiquitous fine-grained wifi-based localization for unlabelled users via domain adaptation. In: Proceedings of the Web Conference (WWW), pp. 23–33. ACM (2020)

6. Ding, X., Jiang, T., Li, Y., Xue, W., Zhong, Y.: Device-free location-independent human activity recognition using transfer learning based on CNN. In: ICC Workshops, pp. 1–6. IEEE (2020)

7. Halperin, D., Hu, W., Sheth, A., Wetherall, D.: Tool release: gathering 802.11n traces with channel state information. ACM SIGCOMM CCR **41**(1) (2011)

8. Han, Z., Guo, L., Lu, Z., Wen, X., Zheng, W.: Deep adaptation networks based gesture recognition using commodity WiFi. In: WCNC, pp. 1–7. IEEE (2020)

9. Han, Z., Lu, Z., Wen, X., Zhao, J., Guo, L., Liu, Y.: In-air handwriting by passive gesture tracking using commodity WiFi. IEEE Commun. Lett. **24**(11), 2652–2656 (2020)

10. He, Y., Chen, Y., Hu, Y., Zeng, B.: WiFi vision: sensing, recognition, and detection with commodity MIMO-OFDM WiFi. IEEE Internet Things J. **7**(9), 8296–8317 (2020)

11. Jiang, W., et al.: Towards environment independent device free human activity recognition. In: MobiCom, pp. 289–304. ACM (2018)

12. Kang, H., Zhang, Q., Huang, Q.: Context-aware wireless based cross domain gesture recognition. IEEE Internet Things J. **8**(17), 13503–13515 (2021)

13. Li, S., Li, X., Lv, Q., Tian, G., Zhang, D.: WiFit: ubiquitous bodyweight exercise monitoring with commodity wi-fi devices. In: 2018 IEEE SmartWorld, Ubiquitous Intelligence & Computing, Advanced & Trusted Computing, Scalable Computing & Communications, Cloud & Big Data Computing, Internet of People and Smart City Innovation, pp. 530–537. IEEE (2018)

14. Ma, X., Zhao, Y., Zhang, L., Gao, Q., Pan, M., Wang, J.: Practical device-free gesture recognition using WiFi signals based on Metalearning. IEEE Trans. Industr. Inf. **16**(1), 228–237 (2020)

15. Ma, Y., et al.: Location- and person-independent activity recognition with WiFi, deep neural networks, and reinforcement learning. ACM Trans. Internet Things **2**(1), 1–25 (2021)

16. Niu, K., Zhang, F., Wang, X., Lv, Q., Luo, H., Zhang, D.: Understanding WiFi signal frequency features for position-independent gesture sensing. IEEE Trans. Mob. Comput. **21**(11), 4156–4171 (2021)

17. Qian, K., Wu, C., Yang, Z., Liu, Y., Zhou, Z.: PADS: passive detection of moving targets with dynamic speed using PHY layer information. In: ICPADS, pp. 1–8 (2014)

18. Sheng, B., Xiao, F., Sha, L., Sun, L.: Deep spatial-temporal model based cross-scene action recognition using commodity WiFi. IEEE Internet Things J. **7**(4), 3592–3601 (2020)

19. Shi, C., Liu, J., Borodinov, N., Leao, B., Chen, Y.: Towards environment-independent behavior-based user authentication using WiFi. In: IEEE 17th International Conference on Mobile Ad Hoc and Sensor Systems (MASS), pp. 666–674 (2020)

20. Shi, Z., Zhang, J.A., Xu, R., Cheng, Q., Pearce, A.: Towards environment-independent human activity recognition using deep learning and enhanced CSI. In: GLOBECOM, pp. 1–6. IEEE (2020)

21. Shi, Z., Zhang, J.A., Xu, R.Y., Cheng, Q.: Environment-robust device-free human activity recognition with channel-state-information enhancement and one-shot learning. IEEE Trans. Mob. Comput. **21**(2), 540–554 (2022)

22. Virmani, A., Shahzad, M.: Position and orientation agnostic gesture recognition using WiFi. In: MobiSys, pp. 252–264. ACM (2017)

23. Wang, J., Gao, Q., Ma, X., Zhao, Y., Fang, Y.: Learning to sense: deep learning for wireless sensing with less training efforts. IEEE Wirel. Commun. **27**(3), 156–162 (2020)

24. Wu, D., et al.: FingerDraw: sub-wavelength level finger motion tracking with WiFi signals. Proc. ACM Interact. Mob. Wearable Ubiquitous Technol. (IMWUT) **4**(1), 1–27 (2020)

25. Xiao, C., Han, D., Ma, Y., Qin, Z.: CsiGAN: robust channel state information-based activity recognition with GANs. IEEE Internet Things J. **6**(6), 10191–10204 (2019)

26. Xie, Y., Li, Z., Li, M.: Precise power delay profiling with commodity WiFi. In: MobiCom, pp. 53–64. ACM (2015)

27. Yang, J., Zou, H., Jiang, H., Xie, L.: Fine-grained adaptive location-independent activity recognition using commodity WiFi. In: WCNC, pp. 1–6. IEEE (2018)

28. Yang, J., Zou, H., Zhou, Y., Xie, L.: Learning gestures from WiFi: a siamese recurrent convolutional architecture. IEEE Internet Things J. **6**(6), 10763–10772 (2019)

29. Zhang, F., et al.: Towards a diffraction-based sensing approach on human activity recognition. Proc. ACM Interact. Mob. Wearable Ubiquitous Technol. (IMWUT) **3**(1), 1–25 (2019)

30. Zhang, J., Tang, Z., Li, M., Fang, D., Nurmi, P., Wang, Z.: CrossSense: towards cross-site and large-scale WiFi sensing. In: MobiCom, pp. 305–320. ACM (2018)

31. Zhang, J., et al.: Data augmentation and dense-LSTM for human activity recognition using WiFi signal. IEEE Internet Things J. **8**(6), 4628–4641 (2021)

32. Zheng, Y., et al.: Zero-effort cross-domain gesture recognition with Wi-Fi. In: MobiSys, pp. 313–325. ACM (2019)

33. Zou, H., Yang, J., Das, H.P., Liu, H., Spanos, C.J.: WiFi and vision multimodal learning for accurate and robust device-free human activity recognition. In: IEEE/CVF Conference on Computer Vision and Pattern Recognition Workshops (CVPRW) (2019)

34. Zou, H., Yang, J., Zhou, Y., Spanos, C.J.: Joint adversarial domain adaptation for resilient WiFi-enabled device-free gesture recognition. In: 17th IEEE International Conference on Machine Learning and Applications (ICMLA), pp. 202–207 (2018)

35. Zou, H., Yang, J., Zhou, Y., Xie, L., Spanos, C.J.: Robust WiFi-enabled device-free gesture recognition via unsupervised adversarial domain adaptation. In: 27th International Conference on Computer Communication and Networks (ICCCN), pp. 1–8. IEEE (2018)

Drone Applications and Edge Computing

Sage: A Multiuser Cooperative Controller for Mobile Edge Systems

Nuno Coelho, Diogo Ribeiro, and Hervé Paulino$^{(\boxtimes)}$ iD

NOVA Laboratory for Computer Science and Informatics, Computer Science Department, NOVA School of Science and Technology, NOVA University Lisbon, Caparica, Portugal
{ng.coelho,dpi.ribeiro}@campus.fct.unl.pt, herve.paulino@fct.unl.pt

Abstract. Mobile devices have become ubiquitous, being used to perform all kinds of daily tasks, from surfing the web, reading e-mails, playing video games, reading and writing documents, and so on. As a result, the edges of the Internet have become resource-rich spaces with millions of devices. To contribute to the world of crowd-sourcing applications being developed for the edge, we propose a new category of applications that require participating users to cooperate among themselves, in order to achieve a common goal. To this end we propose SAGE, a distributed middleware for the real-time aggregation of events in the specific context of cooperative control. SAGE is a generic framework able to aggregate data received, from a small number to thousands of sources, into a stream of events to be handed out to the final application.

Keywords: Edge Computing · Mobile Computing · Cooperative Control · Real-Time Data Aggregation

1 Introduction

The massive concentration of devices at edge networks spawn rich environments in both human and machine resources. These new environments can be leveraged to create novel applications that require collaboration among the edge devices. Such collaboration can be achieved by creating crowd-sourced computing opportunities that require a human element, and also by solving the power and energy limitations inherent to mobile devices [7].

Several studies have already examined various social and technical aspects of user collaboration over an edge network. In [19], Vajk et al. demonstrated that the inclusion of sensors in mobile devices opened up the possibility to use them as controllers with a wide array of input possibilities. In [10], J. Leikas et al. studied the social behavior of users when interacting with a multi-user application, and perceived that the resulting social interactions are a strong motivation for using such applications.

This work was supported by FCT-MCTES via project DeDuCe (PTDC/CCI-COM/32166/2017) and NOVA LINCS (UIDB/04516/2020). We also wish to thank Samsung for supporting this work with state-of-the-art hardware.

S. Longfei and P. Bodhi (Eds.): MobiQuitous 2022, LNICST 492, pp. 313–333, 2023.
https://doi.org/10.1007/978-3-031-34776-4_17

In this context, we envision a new category of **collaborative control** applications that allow a large number of users in an edge network to cooperate towards a common objective. Users can form one or more groups and use their potentially mobile devices to participate in the application collectively.

Motivational Example. There are many application scenarios for cooperative control, from controlling characters or objects in computer games, to controlling real-world objects, such as stage lightning in a concert, to voting, among others. A real scenario builds from an activity that has been offered in past editions of our faculty's open day. It is an adaptation of the famous *Pong* [4] game that already makes use of cooperative control. The players are divided into two groups (placed in neighboring rooms) and cooperate with their group's members to control one of the game's paddles by showing or hiding green cardboards.

In our take of this adaptation, the players use their mobile phones to cooperatively control a paddle, being even able to sit in the same room.

Proposal. We propose SAGE, a distributed middleware to be deployed at edge networks with the task of continuously receiving and aggregating tenths to thousands of event flows into a single one, to be fed to a final application. With the goal of accommodating a large number of event sources, a SAGE deployment may comprise multiple aggregating servers that cooperate to compute the final event flow. Moreover, SAGE was thought for mobile environments, addressing issues such as dynamic discovery and connection, efficient network communication, and tolerance to churn. Lastly, SAGE is also a generic framework that enables programmers to tailor the system to the needs of their application by configuring several parameters, such as data rate, aggregation functions and action granularity.

To the best of our knowledge, there are several frameworks and protocols that perform data streaming and data aggregation in cloud and edge environments, but no previous work has addressed the specific challenges raised by the use of many sources to cooperatively control an asset. Therefore, the contributions of this paper are: 1. SAGE, a novel distributed system for the real-time aggregation of events in the specific context of cooperative control (Sect. 2). 2. The application of Sage to the context of cooperative gaming, with two games that require the users to collaborate to achieve the games' goals (Sect. 3). 3. A comprehensive experimental evaluation that addresses issues such as scalability, adaptability, tolerance to churn and energy consumption (Sect. 4).

2   Sage

SAGE is a distributed middleware that provides a generic framework for cooperative control. It enables users to cooperate among them by using their (potentially mobile) devices to perform collective operations. At its core, SAGE is a system for the real-time distributed aggregation of events directed to the specific context

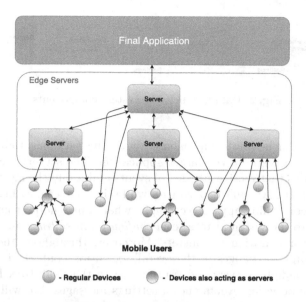

Fig. 1. System Architecture

of cooperative control. It collects and aggregates the event streams generated by the devices into a single stream to be handed out to the final application.

As displayed in Fig. 1, SAGE's architecture comprises three actors, physically distributed in an edge network: user devices, henceforth called **sources**, **servers** deployed in edge nodes connected by a LAN network and performing aggregations over incoming data, and the final **application** that receives the stream of aggregated results.

A source generates a flow of events representing actions performed by a user, such as pressing a button, choosing an option, tilting the device or moving it around. Users are assigned to groups to represent teams in a game, roles in multi-asset controlling system, and so and so forth. Source nodes have no mobility restrictions, meaning that they can move around and connect or disconnect from the system whenever they choose to. They are also independent from each other, not interacting directly among them, and thus not requiring any coordination.

The servers have the purpose of aggregating multiple streams of incoming events into a single one. If there is a need to accommodate a vast number of sources, several servers may be deployed, spawning an event aggregation tree. The sources become the leaves of this tree, being free to connect to any server. Obeying the tree structure, every node must connect to one and only one parent and the root server must connect to the application. Note that sources may connect to any server in the tree, not only to the leaves. Restricting the connection of the sources to leaf servers would result in an unbalanced system, in which mid-level servers would only process a small number of streams from their children servers, while the leaves would have to process the data generated by all sources. When necessary, user devices may also assume the role of a server, providing for the deployment of more flexible *ad hoc* structures.

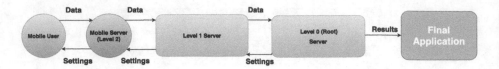

Fig. 2. Data flow between system components

SAGE was designed and implemented with the rationale that sources and servers may be agnostic to the target application. The servers are thus generic computing nodes that receive streams of events and apply the aggregation functions defined in the system's deployment, while the sources may be, for instance, generic game controlling apps. Accordingly, when a new node (source or server) first connects to the system it receives a *configuration settings* message with the application's configuration parameters. Moreover, throughout their execution, nodes may adapt to changes in the overall execution context. These adaption decisions are made by servers and transmitted to their sub-tree. Figure 2 illustrates the flow of action events and of settings messages. We will discuss both in the following sections.

2.1   Action Events and Configuration Settings

Sources generate events that represent an action performed by a user. These events always flow upwards in the SAGE tree and report a value bound to a particular action type performed by a particular group, *e.g.*: *moving a game paddle with vector value v by an element of group g*. To that end, an action event comprises several attributes that we now detail:

Source id - application-wide unique identifier that identifies the action's source node. Depending on the context, it may be either a Universally Unique IDentifier (UUID) or a uniformly distributed 32 bit random number.

Source type - may be a user device or a non-root server.

Group id - integer internally generated to represent an application-given group name. Only the group name is made known to the users (for instance, for them to choose the team they want to play on) but all communication makes use of the associated id.

Event id - application-wide event identifier.

Event value - value communicated in the event.

Event weight - number of sources that cooperated to produce the event's value: 1, in the case of a source; the number of sources that contributed to the aggregated value of the event, in the case of a server.

Group size - optional value that indicates the size of the group at the time of the action. It is useful for programming event-processing functions that take into account the size of the source population that could have contributed to the action versus the size of the one that actually did (the action's weight). Looking at the Pong motivational example (Sect. 1), moving to the left or to the right will depend on the relative weight of such events, as well as on the percentage of sources that actually moved. If most did not (neither left nor right), the decision has to be *not to move*.

Actions may be of two kinds: *discrete* or *continuous*. As its designation implies, the former classifies actions that take values in a discrete domain, such as pressing a button, while the latter classifies actions that take values in a continuous domain, such as tilting a device.

Due to their nature, continuous actions persist and evolve in time. To avoid having useless information repeatedly sent to the servers when there is no significant change in the action's value, we associate a *time-to-live* (TTL) and a *granularity* threshold to each action of this kind. The TTL is used to avoid sending the same event over and over, when a user is performing the same action for a while. A continuous action event is hence assumed to be valid in the system until its TTL expires or a new event of the same action type is generated by the same source. On the source's end, as soon as a different action of the same type is performed, a new event is issued. On the other hand, if the original action persists and the TTL expires, the event is resent and the TTL renewed. Besides greatly reducing network traffic, this approach also provides means for masking temporary disconnections by source nodes.

Regarding granularity, a change in an action's value, although yielding a value different from the previously reported, may not be relevant enough to generate a new event. To avoid generating events that are not distinct enough from the last one sent, we divide the action's domain in chunks of a given size (the *granularity*) and only consider as new values the ones that cross a chunk's boundary. An immediate application case is the use of a device's tilt to perform a paddle movement. The change in the device's inclination may not be relevant enough to generate a new action value.

As introduced in the beginning of Sect. 2, when a new node connects to the system it receives an *application configuration settings* message that includes the *parent*'s identifier; the description of the *actions* allowed, with id, type (discrete or continuous), TTL and granularity; the name and id of the *groups* to choose from (if allowed) or the *source's group*, if one was automatically assigned; the *transmission settings* that convey the application's requirements regarding the stream's rhythm (given as the period in milliseconds between events), and; the maximum number of clients allowed per server (if defined).

2.2 Action Event Processing

A node periodically transmits events to its parent, respecting the period defined in the settings message. For example, if the application specifies a transmission period of 200 ms, the root server will send aggregated action events to the application every 200 ms.

The number of events included in the aggregation depends on the number of groups, and on the number of actions defined per group. On the stream sent by the root server to the application, an aggregation comprises values for all continuous actions plus values for any discrete action that has been triggered during the interval. Continuing with the example above, if the application defines two teams and two actions per team, one continuous and one discrete, the root server produces a stream of aggregated events with a cadence of 200 ms. Each event aggregation must include a minimum of 2 events (the continuous actions) and may go up to 4 (the number of actions). Between the remaining nodes, the payload is reduced with the use of the aforementioned TTL and granularity mechanisms.

The nature and/or complexity of the aggregation algorithms, the volume of the incoming data (which may become too big for the server to process and aggregate in time) or network congestion (which may prevent the server from receiving enough data to process) may precipitate scenarios on which a server has no data to send when a transmission period expires. To ensure the desired output rate, SAGE adapts the transmission period of servers and sources to the conditions of the current execution context, namely to the volume of events produced and the ability of the servers to process them in time. When a server detects that it cannot keep the pace or it can actually process more data, it uses a *congestion control algorithm* to compute a new transmission period that it transmits to its children (more details in Sect. 2.6). The root server is the only node that does not receive adaptation messages, so its transmission period never changes. All the remainder nodes adapt their transmission settings whenever they are requested by their parents, and perform the task independently.

The adaptation process only considers continuous actions because discrete ones cannot be measured in a continuous time or space interval. It is, thus, not possible to predict when an event of such type is going to be issued.

2.3   Source Nodes

The architecture of a source node comprises several modules, of which we highlight four. The NetworkLayer is responsible for handling all communications with the server, sending the events generated by the node and receiving (and routing to the SystemController) all settings messages. The SensorLayer listens to all the configured device sensors, pre-processing the captured data and subsequently passing it to the SystemController for further processing. The UserInterface shows the application's information and detects all button pressings, which are also communicated to the SystemController. Lastly, the SystemController is the source's decision center. It processes the settings messages to adjust the node's configuration, namely the period between consecutive events, and processes the actions reported by the SensorLayer and the UserInterface to generate action events (respecting the actions' and the transmission settings).

2.4   Server Nodes

A server collects and processes the incoming streams and produces a single one that it transmits to its parent in the tree or to the application. Additionally, it also generates and sends adaptation requests to its children.

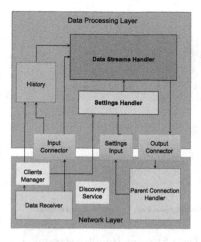

Fig. 3. Server architecture.

A server's architecture (displayed in Fig. 3) is composed of two layers: the Network Layer and the Data Processing Layer. In this paper we will briefly present the former and focus mainly on the latter.

Network Layer. The Network Layer is responsible for managing connections with clients and other servers, as well as receiving and sending data. It comprises four primary components: the Clients Manager manages the connectivity and communication with the server's children, the Data Receiver receives the action event streams, the Parent Connection Handler handles all communication with server's parent and the Discovery Service responds to server discovery requests.

Data Processing Layer. The core component of the Data Processing Layer is the Data Streams Handler, which makes use of a 6-stage Edgent [1] streaming topology to filter and aggregate the event streams. The Source stage simply routes the data received from the Network Layer to the following stages. The Group Split and the Action Split stages split a single input stream into multiple output streams. The first does it to produce a stream per group defined in the application's configuration settings and, the second, to produce a stream per action within a group (also for each action defined in the application's configuration settings). At the end of these 3 initial stages we have one stream per action per group. The Aggregation stage applies the aggregation function (a Java functor) defined for each pair (action, group), being the results merged into a single stream by the Union stage and routed to the Network Layer by the final Sink stage. Figure 4 illustrates the topology built to process streams in a scenario comprising two groups, 'A' and 'B', and two actions per each group, 'X' and 'Y'.

The input streams are discretized into batches that contain all the event values received (or collected from History) in the time window of the last out-

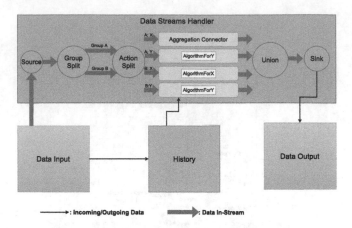

Fig. 4. Data Streams Handler streaming topology

going transmission period. The aggregation function is defined by extending the `Algorithm` abstract class and implementing its method `apply`:

```
abstract class Algorithm<In, Out> {
  abstract Pair<Out, Integer> apply(Collection<Pair<In, Integer>> data);
}
```

The method receives a collection of pairs, whose first element represents the value of the event, of type `In`, and the second element represents the event's weight. The result is a single pair of an output event type `Out` and its weight. If the return value is `null`, the framework assumes that no event is to be issued.

The class features other methods, such as `emit(Pair<T, Integer> data)`, `getPopulation()` and `oneValuePerSource(boolean value)`. The first enables the algorithm to generate more events than the one that is returned. The second returns the number of sources (of the given group) that are directly or indirectly connected to the server. As explained in Sect. 2.1, this information is elemental to develop algorithms that take the population's size (e.g. the number of players) in consideration when computing an aggregation. The third informs the framework to include all or just a single value per source in the data collection handed to the algorithm's `apply` method. The default is *multiple values*. If the *one value* option is chosen, only the most recently received value is kept.

Handling Continuous Actions. As introduced in Sect. 2.1, the value of a continuous action has a TTL that enables the server to deduce the action's current value from previously recorded data and, with that, reduce network traffic and mask temporary disconnections. For that, it makes use of the History module that stores the last events received per client for every continuous action (until the action's TTL expires). It thus keeps a relation between client identifiers, action identifiers and the last value received for each (client, action) entry.

When a child fails to transmit data for a continuous action in the interval defined by the sending period, the Aggregation stage detects the lack of data and, before applying the aggregation function, contacts the History module to retrieve it. History verifies if it contains a valid event (i.e. with a not expired TTL) to match the request. If so, it relays the event to the aggregation connector, otherwise it simply discards the event (if any).

Client Management. The History module also executes a periodic background task that removes any event that is no longer valid. To that end, the task collects the nodes that have had their events expired and asks the **Clients' Manager** module to verify if such nodes are still *alive* and, if not, remove them from the current source population.

2.5   Dynamic Server Discovery

For a node (source or server) to connect to a running SAGE deployment, it must find an existing server. For that purpose, the requesting node initially sends a discovery message to a predefined multicast group and waits for replies for a given time period t, with a read timeout of s seconds, with t and s configurable. The timeout assures that the servers that take more than s seconds to respond are not considered as candidates for connection.

Each server responds with its IP address and the number of connected clients, enabling the requesting node to choose the least occupied option. Currently, we are not considering processing power as a metric for server selection. We intend to address this issue in future work.

To dynamically balance the system, non-server nodes periodically run the discovery process to check if better options are currently available. If so, the node waits for a random period of time $\leq 5s$, and checks again. Whenever the conditions persist, the node simply disconnects from the current server and connects to the new one. Otherwise, if there is still a better server than the current but it is not the same as the one found before, the waiting process is restarted. The waiting period serves to avoid massive migrations when new servers arrive or reconnect to the system after temporary absence.

2.6   Adaptation

A SAGE deployment is expected to produce a stream of data with a regular rate, whose period is defined at deployment time. To meet this requirement, SAGE servers may disseminate configuration settings message to their sub-tree, causing their children to adjust their execution parameters and, if needed, disseminate a settings message of their own.

In a server, every settings message (either received or generated) is routed to a second Edgent topology to demand the **Parent Connection Handler** to change its sending period and/or to adapt the period of its sub-tree. To allow the system to stabilize, adaptation decisions may only be made every S seconds, with S being a value defined in the deployment settings (defaulted to 3).

A SAGE server is parameterizable w.r.t the period adaptation algorithm, which must implement the `PeriodAdapter` interface that defines two methods:

```
interface PeriodAdapter {
  int increase(int... lastPeriods);
  int decrease(int... lastPeriods);
}
```

The `increase` method is called whenever the network layer is unable to retrieve a value, for each continuous action defined per group, from the data processing layer (*i.e.* from the output connector of Fig. 4). Inversely, the `decrease` method is called whenever: (1) the transmission period is longer than the one defined by the application and (2) the network layer receives values for all continuous actions of all groups, n times in a row (for a given n value defined in the deployment settings, defaulted to 5). Both methods receive the last p values computed for the transmission period (with p also defined in the deployment settings, defaulted to 1) and must return the new value for the period.

Starting from a configured transmission period p, an adapted period may only take values in interval $[\frac{3}{4}*p, 10*p]$. Values smaller that the lower limit would force children nodes to send more values than required, ultimately wasting resources and compromising data fidelity. The upper limit prevents continuously increasing the period in abnormal scenarios, such as temporary network unavailability.

The Algorithms. We have implemented some algorithms based on techniques widely used in network congestion protocols, such as Additive Increase/Additive Decrease (AIAD), Additive Increase/Multiplicative Decrease (AIMD) and Cubic Increase/Multiplicative Decrease (CIMD) [9].

We also experimented with techniques used for the online adaptation of parallelism in parallel computing systems, namely we developed an algorithm inspired by *RUBIC* [12], which was originally designed for adjusting the parallelism level of transactional memory applications. *RUBIC* uses a combination of AIAD and CIMD. The frequency increase (period decrease) function begins with a cubic increase phase to quickly respond to change, proceeding then with subsequent linear increments, if necessary. The cubic function is defined as follows:

$$cubic(p) = \begin{cases} p + x , x < 0 \\ p - x , x \geq 0 \end{cases} \text{ for } x = \beta \times (\sqrt[3]{p * (\alpha/\beta)})^3$$

where p is the period before the adaptation process; α is the constant multiplication factor and β is a constant scaling factor that controls the period's reduction rate. Conversely, frequency decrease (period increase) begins softly with linear decreases and, if these persist, switches to the multiplicative factor (α).

3   Use Case: Cooperative Games

We developed an Android app for a game controller that allows the user to choose a team (if such is allowed), tilt its device left or right to move to the pretended direction and press buttons to emit actions, such as shooting or picking power-ups. The app is a SAGE source node that connects to a SAGE server and

```
1  ApplicationInfo pongInfo = ApplicationInfo.Builder.newBuilder()
2  .setAppName("Pong")
3  .setTransmissionPeriod(200)
4  .addGroups("Racket 1", "Racket 2")
5  .addToAllGroups(new ContinuousAction("Horizontal Movement", new MovementAlgorithm(), 350))
6  .build();
7  Sage.newServer(pongInfo).start();
```

Listing 1: The application information of Cooperative Pong

```
1  public Pair<Direction, Integer> apply(Collection<Pair<Direction, Integer>> data) {
2      int left = 0, right = 0, mid = 0;
3      for (var pair : data)
4          switch (pair.getKey()) {
5              case LEFT -> left += pair.getValue();
6              case MIDDLE -> mid += pair.getValue();
7              case RIGHT -> right += pair.getValue();
8          }
9      if (right == left || (mid >= left && mid>= right)) return Pair.of(MIDDLE, mid);
10     else if (right >= (left + mid)) return Pair.of(RIGHT, right);
11     else return Pair.of(LEFT, left);
12 }
```

Listing 2: Movement algorithm

generates a stream of actions events. The tilting is detected by adding the *game rotation vector* sensor [8] to the node's Sensor Layer and transforming its output into tilting degrees. We used this app as a controller in several games. Here we confine our discussion to the motivational example presented in Sect. 1 and the somewhat akin Arkanoid.

Cooperative Pong. The players only need to use the tilt functionality, tilting the devices in the direction they want the paddle to move. If they do not want to move the paddle, they need only to hold their devices in a horizontal position.

Listing 1 showcases the configuration of a server. The `ApplicationInfo` class provides for the definition of the application's settings. In this case, two groups (teams `Racket 1` and `Racket 2`) and a single action (`Horizontal Movement`) were defined. The action is continuous and was added to both groups (given that both teams have the same role). The aggregation algorithm (Listing 2) is a consensus algorithm that takes a collection of votes for moving left, right or not moving at all, and returns the direction with the most number of votes (V), paired with V. For example, if the winner is *left* with 100 votes, the result will be (LEFT, 100).

Cooperative Arkanoid. The second use case is the widely known *Arkanoid*, initially developed by the Taito Corporation [2]. This game has only one paddle, but users can pick up and activate power-ups. Following those specifications, we defined two actions: the paddle movement (as in Pong) and the power-up activation. The latter is a discrete action triggered by pressing one of the mobile controller's buttons. The aggregation algorithm is a two level algorithm. At the

Table 1. Specifications of the smartphones used in the test scenarios.

Device	Xiaomi Mi A1	Samsung S10+
CPU	Cortex-A53 Qualcomm Snapdragon 625 8 × 2GHz	Qualcomm SDM855 Snapdragon 855 1 × 2.84 GHz Kryo 485 & 3 × 2.41 GHz Kryo 485 & 4 × 1.78 GHz Kryo 485
RAM	4 GB	8 GB
Battery	3080 mAh	4100 mAh
Wi-Fi	WiFi (802.11 a/b/g/n/ac)	WiFi (802.11 a/b/g/n/ac)
OS	Android 10	Android 12

mid-level servers it returns the sum of all received values (discarding duplicates), and the corresponding weight. At the root server, it compares the weight of the action with the source population to check if, at least, half of the population pressed the button. If so, the action is relayed to the app, if not, it is discarded (the algorithm returns null).

4   Evaluation

In this section we evaluate SAGE to assert that it aggregates and delivers data efficiently under different conditions and workload assumptions. More specifically, our experiments aim to answer the following questions:

Q1. Scalability - How well does the SAGE scale with the increase of the number of sources?

Q2. Adaptation - What is the impact of the different adaptation algorithms in the system's performance?

Q3. Computational Complexity - How does the system perform when using aggregation algorithms with a significant processing overhead?

Q4. Churn - How well does a server handle the connection and disconnection of a large number of clients, while processing data?

Q5. Smartphones as Servers - How does the mobile device perform as a server?

Q6. Energy Consumption - How much energy is consumed by the mobile application when used as a simple client and as a mobile server?

Q7. Granularity - What is the impact of the defined granularity in a client's output rate?

Test Environments. We evaluated the behavior and performance of SAGE in two environments: **Real** - composed of physical source devices connected to a single stationary server. We used Android mobile devices (Table 1) running the controller app described in Sect. 3 and connected to the server via WiFi. **Emulated** - composed of one or more SAGE source node emulators, each running multiple nodes. We have used this emulation environment to evaluate other works

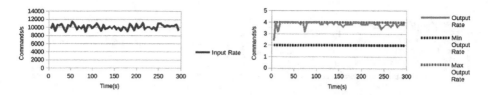

Fig. 5. Scalability: (servers: 1, sources: 7000, period: 1000)

such as [6,16,17]. In this particular setting, each emulator and server runs in a dedicated physical node of a computing cluster.

The *real* environment allowed us to evaluate and assert SAGE's usability in real-life applications and answer questions Q5 to Q7. The *emulated* environment allowed us to scale the number of sources to numbers that we could not do with the *real* test-bed and, with that, address questions Q1 to Q4.

Experiment Configuration. An experiment configuration in the emulated environment is specified by multiple parameters, namely: the number of servers, the number of sources, the transmission period and the adaptation algorithm. All experiments use a deployment configuration that features two teams, each one able to perform a continuous and a discrete action. Furthermore, all experiments had a duration of five minutes, with metrics being recorded every second.

Along this section we will use the term **failure** to designate an occasion on which the output rate does not meet the requested transmission period.

4.1 Scalability

Our first set of experiments aims to discover on how many clients a server can accommodate, while meeting the transmission period requested by the application. With the goal of stressing the system as much as possible, we disabled the adaptation process for these experiments. So, the base configuration for these experiments is (servers: 1, adaptation: none), with the number of sources and the transmission period varying among experiments.

For the first experiment, we set a transmission period of 1 s and the number of sources took values 1000, 2000, 4000, 5000, 6000 and 7000. The input and output rate of the server in all scenarios showed little variation, with the server comfortably dealing with the load. Figure 5 showcases the results for the 7000 client scenario.

To further stress the system, we reduced the period to 200 ms, *i.e.* a minimum of 10 events every second, and fluctuations in the input and output rates started to appear with more than 2000 sources. Although the large amount of input events (12 000 to 16 000 per second), the output rate still managed to stay relatively stable, only varying between 13 and 15 events per second. However, this was the first scenario on which we observed failures, which lasted for about 3 s. These failures became more frequent as the number of sources increased.

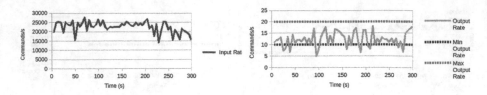

Fig. 6. Scalability: (servers: 1, sources: 5500, period: 200)

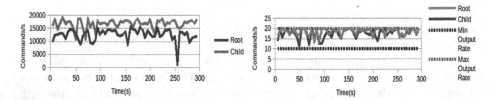

Fig. 7. Scalability: (servers: 2, sources: 5500, period: 200)

Figure 6 depicts the results for 5 500 clients, where it is visible that the server fails to meet the transmission period requirement.

The solution for such situations is to distribute the load among multiple servers. To assess SAGE's horizontal scaling, we repeated the last scenario with 2 servers; the results are presented in Fig. 7. Although some occasional variations in the input and output rates, the improvement of the system's performance is visible, with the output rate never falling below the desired minimum of 10 events per second. We further experimented with a transmission period of 50 ms only to confirm our findings. In these experiments the server starts to struggle with 4000 sources. So, as expected, the smaller the period, the fewer sources the servers can accommodate without compromising the expected output rate. Also, the use of more servers effectively shares the load. The dynamic server discovery and load balancing algorithm (Sect. 2.5) works very well in homogeneous networks, allowing the system to scale if $\frac{c}{S} \leq c_{limit}$, where c is the number of sources, s is the number of servers and c_{limit} is the upper limit for the number of clients per server. This limit depends on many variables, such as the number of clients and the complexity of the aggregation algorithms, but can be set in the deployment configuration. A server will not accept more connections than the limit imposed. As mentioned in Sect. 2.5, addressing heterogeneous networks is future work. Given the work in the field, it is more of a technical challenge than a research one.

4.2 Adaptation

Next, we analyze the impact of SAGE's period adaptation process, comparing the 3 algorithms implemented: AIMD, CIMD, and RUBIC. We are particularly interested in how the system reacts to sudden changes in the input and output

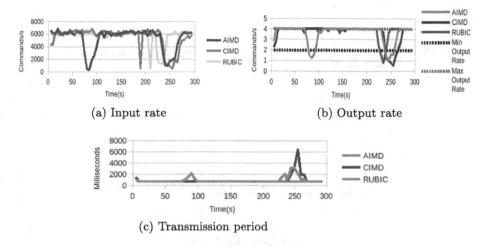

(a) Input rate

(b) Output rate

(c) Transmission period

Fig. 8. Adaptation: (servers: 1, sources: 4000, period: 1000)

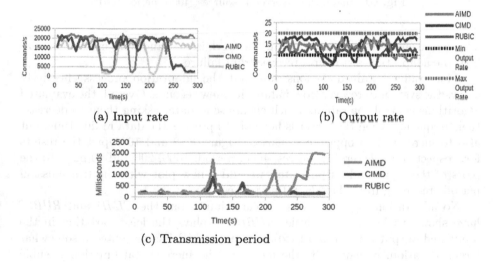

(a) Input rate

(b) Output rate

(c) Transmission period

Fig. 9. Adaptation: (servers: 1, sources: 4000, period: 200)

rates. Hence, the algorithms were parameterized with $\alpha = 0.7$, meaning that the incremental function of *CIMD* and the decremental function of *AIMD* change their interval aggressively[1], and with $\beta = 0.1$, to limit the incremental function of *CIMD* to the least possible.

For each algorithm we considered six scenarios: (servers: 1, sources: 500 or 4000, period: 1000, 200 or 50 ms). Additionally, at every second, sources have now a fixed probability of entering a pause period that may go from 1 to 4 s.

---

[1] The higher the α factor, the steepest is the *CIMD* increase and the *AIMD* decrease.

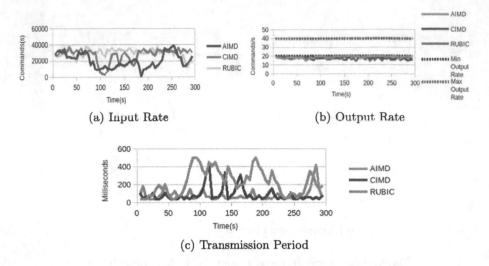

(a) Input Rate

(b) Output Rate

(c) Transmission Period

Fig. 10. Adaptation: (server 1, sources: 4000, period: 50)

This pause emulates periods of lag and network issues, and were used to analyze how the adaptation algorithms recover from failures.

The results obtained demonstrate that the adaptation process effectively allows the system to recover from failures in a few seconds. Overall, the evaluated algorithms control the rate at which clients send data, asking them to decrease their frequency when the server is not able to process the data in due time, but also to increase it in opposite scenarios. Figures 8, 9 and 10 depict the results for, respectively (servers: 1, sources: 4000, period: 1000, 200 and 50 ms). To the plots of the input and output rates, we add a new plot with the transmission periods resulting from the adaptation process.

No adaptation algorithm was a clear winner, but the *CIMD* and *RUBIC* have shown to be more versatile. *RUBIC* displays the least variation in the input and output rates in most experiments. *CIMD* has presented a somewhat larger variation, explained by the fact that the incremental function is cubic and the decremental function is multiplicative. Lastly, *AIMD* revealed to be an algorithm very sensitive to changes in the input and output rate, especially in scenarios with small periods and a low number of clients. In many moments the algorithm increased the interval consecutively and was not able to recover.

4.3   Computational Complexity

The next set of experiments aim to study the system's sensitivity to the computational complexity of the aggregation algorithms. To achieve this, we modified the previously used aggregation algorithms to include a loop that busy-waits for an indicated amount of time, denoted as the overhead, before the actual data processing. The base configuration is: (server: 1, sources: 500 and 4000, period: 1000, 200 and 50 ms, adaptation: RUBIC)

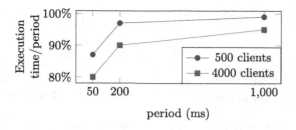

Fig. 11. Ratio between the algorithm execution time and period over which failures consistently happen.

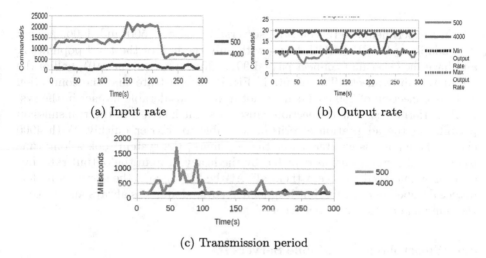

Fig. 12. Churn: (server: 1, sources: 500 and 4000, period: 200, adaptation: RUBIC). Half of the clients connect at 90 s and half disconnect at 210 s

For each scenario we increased the overhead until the system was not able to constantly keep the desired output rate. Figure 11 presents the results. For the lighter load of 500 clients, the server was able to keep the pace up until overheads of, respectively, 87%, 97% and 99% of the transmission period for periods of 50, 200 and 1000 ms. As expected, with more clients, the percentages decrease, in these cases to, respectively, 80%, 85% and 90%. Nonetheless, these results allow us to conclude that, in itself, the overall aggregation process is quite light, enabling the use of aggregation algorithms with execution times very close to the transmission period.

4.4   Churn

The next experiment aims to assess how a SAGE server responds to abrupt changes in its number of clients. This type of scenario may happen due to network-related causes, to system-related causes, such the failure or appearing of a server, or to changes in number of sources.

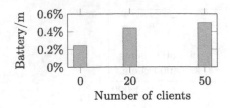

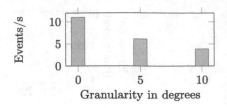

Fig. 13. Energy consumption of the mobile device, in battery % per minute

Fig. 14. Granularity: events sent with different granularity values for device tilting

Two experiments were defined: (servers: 1, sources: 500 and 4000, period: 200, adaption: RUBIC). Both begin with only the half of the total population, and have the other half connect passed 90 s. 120 s later (instant 210), half of the population disconnects. The results in Fig. 12 demonstrate that the connection and disconnection of 250 clients does not have a considerable impact in the system's performance. The connection caused a slight increase in the transmission period, but the adaptation algorithm was able to recover quickly. With 4000 clients the impact is greater. After the 90 s mark, the system took a long time to accept all connections, as depicted by the heavy drop in the output rate, but eventually managed to accept them all. At the 210 s mark, the system's performance dropped once again, but it quickly recovered and was always able to keep the minimum of 10 events per second.

4.5 Smartphones as Mobile Servers

The following experiment analyzed the performance of smartphones that work as aggregation servers, as well as standard clients. We expect mobile servers to serve tenths of clients not more. With this in mind, we set up two scenarios with the following configurations: (servers: 1, sources: 20 and 50, period: 50 ms, adaptation: RUBIC). Every source was running in the emulator and connected to the mobile server.

In both experiments, the mobile devices (of Table 1) were able to maintain a stable output rate of events. In the 20 source scenario, the servers received an average of 1108 events per second and output an average of 20 events per second. In the 50 source scenario, the device received an average of little more than 1115 events per second and output an average of 23 events per second. These results show that mobile devices can effectively act as mobile aggregation servers, whenever there is a need to reduce the load on the edge nodes or simply to have the system work in infrastructure-less environments.

4.6 Energy Consumption

We analyzed the energy consumption of a mobile device as a simple client and as a mobile server. The results for the Xiaomi Mi A1 device are displayed in

Fig. 13. We considered three scenarios: the device is used only as a source (0 clients), the device is also working as a mobile server with 20 and 50 clients.

The first conclusion to draw is that a commodity device may run our game controller app for many minutes, as the consumption per minute is around 0.2%. The addition of the server role has as greater impact, as can been observed in the 20 client bar. This slop is, however, much smaller when adding more clients. The impact comes mostly from the server engine itself than from the number of clients. To this contributes the fact that the *Arkanoid* deployment uses two simple aggregation algorithms. Computationally heavier algorithms may drain the battery much faster and should likely be entirely run by stationary servers.

4.7 Granularity

We performed tests to evaluate the impact of various granularity thresholds for the tilt of the device on the control of game characters. We are interested in the feedback of the users concerning playability and also on the number of events sent with each configuration. To that end, we invited several persons to experiment our version of the *Arkanoid* game using our game controller app. The granularity thresholds were set to $0°o$, $5°$ and $10°$.

There were significant differences in the average number of events sent per second for each threshold, as illustrated in Fig. 14, demonstrating that the mechanism has impact on network traffic and ultimately on the final results. The users reported that the $5°$ configuration was the one that provided the smoothest experience. This is the configuration that we are currently using with good game experience. However, it is essential to consider that different applications may require different thresholds, as the granularity value is inversely proportional to the number of events sent by the devices.

5 Related Work

Frameworks like Spark [21], Storm [18] and Flink [3] allow for the real-time aggregation of streamed data in cloud environments. There have also several proposals specifically designed for (or adapted to) edge and/or IoT environments. Prominent examples are Symbiosis [13], Azure Stream Analytics [11], SpanEdge [15], Amnis [20] and others, such as [5,14].

Most of these systems solve several of the challenges that we are addressing, namely the ones related to data aggregation of streamed data, such as discretizing data streams in time windows and aggregating data according to programmer-given algorithms. Some also address dynamic server discovery. However, none address the challenges raised by cooperative control, namely the adaptation to a rate imposed by an external entity, the use of historical data to mask temporary disconnections, the use of event value similarity to avoid sending the same data repeatedly.

6 Conclusions and Future Work

In this paper we presented SAGE, a novel distributed system for the real-time aggregation of events in the specific context of cooperative control. We have applied SAGE to the context of cooperative gaming with very good results, as it is being used to play games as cooperative Pong and cooperative Arkanoid.

A comprehensive evaluation allows us to conclude that SAGE may be used from a small number of sources to thousands. In our experiments, a server is able to withstand loads of hundredths to thousands, depending on the transmission period and on the complexity of the aggregation algorithms. Higher loads can be supported by horizontally scaling the system with more servers.

From the devices' point of view, the energy consumption of our game controlling app is quite low, allowing for the app to be used for several hours.

To work presented is novel in the field and opens opportunities for the development of new types of applications at the edge. Future work will focus mainly on such enterprise – the development of new cooperative control applications in different contexts – and on the improving of the system itself.

References

1. Apache Software Foundation Incubator: Apache Edgent Overview. https://edgent. apache.org/docs/home.html
2. ArcadeClassics.net: Arkanoid: Classic arcade game video, history and game play overview. https://arcadeclassics.net/80s-game-videos/arkanoid/
3. Carbone, P., Katsifodimos, A., Ewen, S., Markl, V., Haridi, S., Tzoumas, K.: Apache flink: stream and batch processing in a single engine. Bull. IEEE Comput. Soc. Tech. Committee Data Eng. **36**(4) (2015)
4. Centre for Computing History: Atari Pong. http://www.computinghistory.org.uk/det/4007/Atari-PONG
5. Dautov, R., Distefano, S.: Stream processing on clustered edge devices. IEEE Trans. Cloud Comput. **10**(2), 885–898 (2022)
6. Dias, J., Silva, J.A., Paulino, H.: Adaptive replica selection in mobile edge environments. In: Hara, T., Yamaguchi, H. (eds.) Mobile and Ubiquitous Systems: Computing, Networking and Services, vol. 419, pp. 243–263. Springer, Cham (2021). https://doi.org/10.1007/978-3-030-94822-1_14
7. Fernando, N., Loke, S.W., Rahayu, W.: Computing with nearby mobile devices: a work sharing algorithm for mobile edge-clouds. IEEE Trans. Cloud Comput. **7**(2), 329–343 (2016)
8. Google: Sensor types | android open source project. https://source.android.com/devices/sensors/sensor-types#game_rotation_vector
9. Ha, S., Rhee, I., Xu, L.: CUBIC: a new TCP-friendly high-speed TCP variant. ACM SIGOPS Oper. Syst. Rev. **42**(5), 64–74 (2008)
10. Leikas, J., Stromberg, H., Ikonen, V., Suomela, R., Heinila, J.: Multi-user mobile applications and a public display: novel ways for social interaction. In: Fourth Annual IEEE International Conference on Pervasive Computing and Communications (PERCOM 2006), pp. 5-pp. IEEE (2006)
11. Microsoft: Streaming Analytics - Data Analysis in Real Time. https://azure.microsoft.com/pt-pt/services/stream-analytics/

12. Mohtasham, A., Barreto, J.P.: RUBIC: online parallelism tuning for co-located transactional memory applications. In: Scheideler, C., Gilbert, S. (eds.) Proceedings of the 28th ACM Symposium on Parallelism in Algorithms and Architectures, SPAA 2016, Asilomar State Beach/Pacific Grove, CA, USA, 11–13 July 2016, pp. 99–108. ACM (2016)

13. Morales, J., Rosas, E., Hidalgo, N.: Symbiosis: sharing mobile resources for stream processing. In: IEEE Symposium on Computers and Communications, ISCC 2014, Funchal, Madeira, Portugal, 23–26 June 2014, pp. 1–6. IEEE Computer Society (2014)

14. Renart, E.G., Montes, J.D., Parashar, M.: Data-driven stream processing at the edge. In: 1st IEEE International Conference on Fog and Edge Computing, ICFEC 2017, Madrid, Spain, 14–15 May 2017, pp. 31–40. IEEE Computer Society (2017)

15. Sajjad, H.P., Danniswara, K., Al-Shishtawy, A., Vlassov, V.: Spanedge: towards unifying stream processing over central and near-the-edge data centers. In: IEEE/ACM Symposium on Edge Computing, SEC 2016, Washington, DC, USA, 27–28 October 2016, pp. 168–178. IEEE Computer Society (2016)

16. Sanches, P., Silva, J.A., Teófilo, A., Paulino, H.: Data-centric distributed computing on networks of mobile devices. In: Malawski, M., Rzadca, K. (eds.) Euro-Par 2020. LNCS, vol. 12247, pp. 296–311. Springer, Cham (2020). https://doi.org/10.1007/978-3-030-57675-2_19

17. Silva, J.A., Cerqueira, F., Paulino, H., Lourenço, J.M., Leitão, J., Preguiça, N.M.: It's about thyme: on the design and implementation of a time-aware reactive storage system for pervasive edge computing environments. Future Gener. Comput. Syst. **118**, 14–36 (2021)

18. Toshniwal, A., et al.: Storm@twitter. In: Dyreson, C.E., Li, F., Özsu, M.T. (eds.) International Conference on Management of Data, SIGMOD 2014, Snowbird, UT, USA, 22–27 June 2014, pp. 147–156. ACM (2014)

19. Vajk, T., Coulton, P., Bamford, W., Edwards, R.: Using a mobile phone as a "wii-like" controller for playing games on a large public display. Int. J. Comput. Games Technol. **2008** (2008)

20. Xu, J., Palanisamy, B., Wang, Q., Ludwig, H., Gopisetty, S.: Amnis: Optimized stream processing for edge computing. J. Parallel Distributed Comput. **160**, 49–64 (2022)

21. Zaharia, M., et al.: Apache spark: a unified engine for big data processing. Commun. ACM **59**(11), 56–65 (2016)

Multi-MEC Cooperation Based VR Video Transmission and Cache Using K-Shortest Paths Optimization

Jingwen Xia, Luyao Chen, Yong Tang$^{(\boxtimes)}$, Ting Yang, and Wenyong Wang

University of Electronic Science and Technology of China, Chengdu, China
worldgulit@uestc.edu.cn

Abstract. In recent network architectures, multi-MEC cooperative caching has been introduced to reduce the transmission latency of VR videos, in which MEC servers' computing and caching capability are utilized to optimize the transmission process. However, many solutions that use the computing capability of MEC servers ignore the additional arithmetic power consumed by the codec process, thus making them infeasible. Besides, the minimum cache unit is usually the entire VR video, which makes caching inefficient.

To address these challenges, we split VR videos into tile files for caching based on the current popular network architecture and provide a reliable transmission mechanism and an effective caching strategy. Since the number of different tile files N is too large, the current cooperative caching algorithms do not cope with such large-scale input data. We further analyze the problem and propose an optimized k-shortest paths (OKSP) algorithm with an upper bound time complexity of $O((K \cdot M + N) \cdot M \cdot \log N))$, and suitable for shortest paths with restricted number of edges, where K is the total number of tiles that all M MEC servers can cache in the collaboration domain. And we prove the OKSP algorithm can compute the caching scheme with the lowest average latency in any case, which means the solution given is the exact solution. The simulation results show that the OKSP algorithm has excellent speed for solving large-scale data and consistently outperforms other caching algorithms in the experiments.

Keywords: 360° virtual reality video · Virtual reality · Mobile edge computing · K-shortest paths

1 Introduction

Virtual Reality (VR) is emerging as a killer use case of 5G wireless networks. Users can watch VR videos with mobile devices such as VR glasses to obtain an immersive experience. The VR video mentioned in this paper refers to the panoramic video of horizontal 360° × vertical 180°.

Supported by the Sichuan Provincial Science and Technology Department Project (No. 2021YFHO171).

S. Longfei and P. Bodhi (Eds.): MobiQuitous 2022, LNICST 492, pp. 334–355, 2023.
https://doi.org/10.1007/978-3-031-34776-4_18

The transmission problem of VR video has attracted extensive attention in academia and industry [13]. Under the premise of ensuring a good viewing experience, the bit rate required for VR video is much higher than that of traditional video. If users fetch all the VR videos they need from the data center, the bandwidth consumption of the 5G network backhaul link will increase dramatically. Besides, an immersive VR experience requires the network to provide ultra-low transmission latency (less than 20 ms) to avoid user discomfort [29]. However, under the traditional network architecture, the traffic in the core network and the Internet changes dynamically, which will cause fluctuations in the network load, resulting in unpredictable performance degradation of watching VR videos.

The mobile edge computing (MEC) proposed in the 5G network technology can greatly alleviate the above problem [15]. The MEC server is introduced in the traditional network architecture and deployed near the base station where the user accesses. The MEC server caches the current popular videos, thus significantly mitigating the request latency of mobile VR devices. However, compared with data centers, the resources of a single MEC server is very insufficient [23]. To fully utilize the limited storage space to meet more user requests, it is an inevitable trend to collaborate with multiple MEC servers in close geographical proximity and share their storage space.

The computing capability of the MEC server can also be utilized for VR video transmission. Before further analysis, we need to know the process of VR video from production to rendering [20], which includes (1) *shooting and stitching*: capturing video by multi-camera array, then projecting the captured video frames into the spherical space and then stitching to get the panoramic video; (2) *mapping and encoding*: mapping and projecting the panoramic video image into the 2D plane (e.g., using equirectangular projection technique) to get the 2D plane image, and then encode the video using universal video encoder; (3) *transmission*: transmitting the encoded video to the VR device through the network; (4) *rendering*: the VR device decodes the VR video, and projects the 2D video frames into the spherical space and then displays them on the screen.

Many papers [4,13,18,29] have studied offloading the rendering task in (4) to the MEC server, and later transmitting the rendered video to the VR device, to reduce the overall latency. However, there are many problems with this optimization.

The operation involved in step (4) is simply applying a series of trigonometric functions to the coordinates of each point in the 2D video frame. Constant time complexity can be considered for an operation on a particular pixel point [22], so the rendering process does not take much time. After offloading the rendering task to the MEC server, the VR video needs to be decoded before rendering. The decoding operation will take extra time. Because the MEC server may be equipped with a GPU dedicated to processing video, it will reduce the rendering time. However, after rendering, the VR video size equals the original uncompressed video size, which depends on the compression ratio (could be as high as 1000:1 in H.265 encoding [28]). Without compression, transmitting a video with such a high bitrate is impractical. But if the MEC server compresses the rendered video, the time consumed by additional codecs is even higher than the rendering time saved, leaving aside the loss of picture quality. Overall, using the computing capability of the MEC server to handle the rendering task does not improve the user viewing VR video experience but makes the problem more and more complicated.

But the computational capability of the MEC server can be utilized for compute-intensive tasks such as predicting user head motion to reduce the amount of data transfer. When a user watches a 360° VR video, the field of view (FoV) usually accounts for only about 12.5% of the panoramic field of view (90°× 90°/360 °× 180° [12]). In other words, if the entire VR video is transmitted, most of the frame area is not visible to the user during viewing. To reduce the problem of large bandwidth consumption and high latency caused by the transmission of 360° surround images, most existing transmission schemes [10,17,21] transmit only the high bit rate of the image within the user's FoV. The specific operation is that in the VR video production process (2), the panoramic video after equirectangular projection is spatially and equidistantly divided into $x \times y$ independently codable and decodable whole-length tile video files [4], whose duration is equal to that of the original video. Due to the users' gaze shifting while watching the video, the request rate of whole-length tile video fluctuates with time and maybe low at certain times [19]. If the whole-length tile video file is the minimum cache unit, the MEC server's cache efficiency is low, so it can be split into equal-sized tile videos in time, which we call tile files or tiles.

If the request only occurs when the VR device detects the need to render a particular tile file, it will result in a very short tolerant latency (e.g., less than 20 ms), and the user experience will be poor. The split operation will be useless if the whole frame is cached. Thus, it is necessary to predict and cache the tile files that users may watch in advance, which requires the prediction of the users' head motion trajectory in the coming period. Related research [27] shows that various head motion prediction models have been proposed to predict short-term head trajectory changes with high accuracy in recent years. In the tile-based prediction model presented in the literature [5], prediction accuracy can reach 84.22% when the prediction period is set to 1s.

Even though the existing prediction model has high accuracy, there are still cases in which the required video frame is not requested in advance when the VR device is ready to render. In this case, if the entire tile file belonging to the missing video frame is requested, it is easy to time out and causes the user to feel the local screen lag. To solve this problem, servers can extract the currently missing tile frames for transmission instead of transmitting the entire tile files. However, only transmitting the missing frames presents a problem. Because in the mainstream video encoding [6] includes 3 types of frames: I (Intra-coded), P (Predictive), B (Bi-predictive). I frames include complete image data. P or B frames contain information about the changes between the previous and subsequent I or P frames (which is used to create the resulting image). So if the missing frame is a P or B frame, it cannot be directly decoded on the VR device. As a result, a feasible remediation method on the server-side is to reconstruct the missing frame, compress it into an I frame, and then respond to the VR device.

In summary, head motion prediction and remediation to deal with prediction failure can be offloaded to the MEC server, allowing the VR device to focus on video decoding and displaying. Based on the optimization points analyzed above, we aim to build an efficient mobile VR video transmission framework with a multi-MEC cooperative caching mechanism. Our contributions are summarized as follows:

- We describe a multi-MEC cooperative network architecture and provide a reliable transmission mechanism.
- For the large-scale tile caching problem, we analyze the caching profit of tiles under the cooperative architecture and equivalently rebuild the tile caching problem into the k-shortest problem.
- Due to the high time complexity of the original k-shortest paths algorithm [30] in this paper's application scenario, we propose an optimized k-shortest paths (OKSP) algorithm. And upper bound time complexity of the OKSP algorithm is $O((K \cdot M + N) \cdot M \cdot logN))$, where K is the total number of tiles that all M MEC servers can cache in the collaboration domain, and N is the number of different tile files. We also prove the solution of the OKSP algorithm is the exact solution.

The remainder of this paper is organized as follows. Section 2 reviews the relevant work. Section 3 presents the system architecture and transmission mechanism. Section 4 analyzes the cache profit and shows the specific optimization details of the OKSP algorithm. Section 5 discusses the simulation results. Section 6 concludes this paper.

2 Related Work

In recent years, some papers have utilized the characteristics of VR video in their transmission network architecture, since the user can only view a portion of the panoramic video at any given moment, transmitting the user's current FoV results in significant savings in bandwidth consumption. As a result, [7] proposes a tile-based scheme to transmit VR videos. [5] further improves the quality of user experience by deriving a user's head motion trajectory model based on real data training. [5,7] focus on the prediction of head motion when users watch VR videos, describing the details of the prediction model and giving experimental results. The linear regression method is adopted for trajectory tracking in [14,24]. The authors in [23] propose a method for determining tile resolution based on user head movements and network conditions. A 360° video streaming scheme is proposed in [14] to maximize user experience by predicting the user's viewport and prefetch video segments that will be viewed soon.

Some studies adopt different bitrate transmission for the inner and outer regions of FoV to reduce the data transmission volume. Ghosh et al. [9] assume the FoV is known exactly beforehand before fetching the invisible portion at the lowest resolution and determining the visible portion's resolution using bandwidth prediction. A heuristic method [26] is proposed for allocating video resolution by assigning different weights to different regions inside and outside the current FoV. [25,34] calculate the popularity of the current FoV to predict the popularity of FoV for a while in the future, among which [25] proposes a novel algorithm for assigning bitrate based on viewpoints.

Also, some papers use the aid of MEC technology in VR video transmission. [4,29] propose a MEC-based network architecture to deliver mobile VR videos. In [29], a FoV-based caching architecture is proposed to save bandwidth consumption and meet the low latency requirement of VR videos. [4] proposes a MEC-based architecture for 360° VR video delivery and actively exploits the predictable nature of user FoV to cache VR videos. However, both studies work only with a single MEC server and do not consider the potential of multi-MEC cooperation.

Hou et al. [11], Ndikumana et al. [23] and Wang et al. [32] notice the advantages of multi-MEC cooperation. Wang et al. [32] propose a zone-based cooperative content caching and delivery scheme and develops a heuristic cooperative content caching strategy. Hou et al. [11] also propose a service architecture based on multi-MEC cooperation and a cooperative caching strategy based on migration learning under the service architecture. Ndikumana et al. [23] propose a joint computation, caching, communication, and control optimized caching strategy based on a multi-MEC cooperative architecture. However, these studies all concentrate on general video content and do not exploit the features of VR video.

Using multi-MEC cooperative transmission, some studies exploit VR's characteristics. Ge et al. [8] propose a multipath cooperative routing scheme to facilitate transmission of 360-degree MVRV among edge data centers, base stations, and users. A mobile edge computing system [33] is proposed which utilizes the computing and caching resources of mobile VR devices to reduce communication-resource consumption. To enable high-quality VR streaming, Chakareski et al. [3] integrate scalable layered 360 video tiling, viewport-adaptive rate allocation, optimal resource allocation, and edge caching.

3 System Architecture

3.1 Network Architecture

The network architecture based on multi-MEC cooperation is shown in Fig. 1. The network architecture consists of three parts: a remote content server (e.g., cloud server) located in a data center, a 5G core network, and a MEC collaboration domain. We assume the cloud server has a massive storage space on which all the encoded tile files are stored. Since the coverage area of a base station is relatively tiny (≤ 500 m [31]), multiple base stations are usually deployed in a living/commercial area, so these base stations are close geographically. A MEC collaboration domain can be artificially created by dividing MEC servers near these base stations in order to share computing and caching resources.

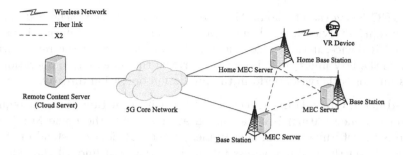

Fig. 1. Network architecture diagram.

Assume that there are M MEC servers in a collaboration domain, which is denoted as {MEC server 1, ..., MEC server M}. Each MEC server maintains a resource access table, which records the tile files it cached. The base station directly connected to the VR device are called home base station and the MEC server deployed near home base station are called home MEC server.

3.2   Transmission Process

As discussed in previous, it would be necessary for VR devices to prefetch the tiles that will be used in the future period. Various head motion prediction models have recently been proposed to predict short-term trajectory changes with high accuracy [27]. Therefore, the prediction task must continuously predict during the user's viewing process. The prediction work requires a certain amount of computation, and offloading it to the home MEC server can relieve the load on the processor of the VR device. While the VR device focuses only on decoding and displaying VR videos, the home MEC server is responsible for continuously predicting the user's short-term head motion trajectory and transmitting the tile files that may be involved based on the predictions.

However, due to the prediction bias, the VR device may find that the tile file is not requested in advance when rendering the VR video. In this case, the VR device must immediately request the currently missing tile video frames. The user's current viewing information can be sent to the home MEC server each time the VR device refreshes the screen to detect the prediction misses early and remedy the situation.

In this paper, the VR device and the home MEC server each perform the following transmission process.

For VR Devices. When the user starts watching the video, the VR device establishes a long connection with its home MEC server. The current playback status is detected every screen rendering interval Δt_{fps} time. If the video playback is finished, the interaction process end and the VR device disconnects from its home MEC server. Otherwise, perform the screen rendering operation; simultaneously, the user's current FoV and the video playback time t_v are sent to its home MEC server.

For MEC Servers. The home MEC server will record the cache status of the users within its service area, when the MEC server receives an information packet from a VR device, it can judge whether the user is missing the render frames based on the FoV and t_v of this packet. Perform the remediation operation first if it is missing; otherwise, perform the prediction operation directly.

Remediation Operation. As mentioned in the introduction, since the request's tolerance latency (20 ms) is rather harsh at this point, the home MEC server responds by returning the missing frames of the VR device instead of the tile files. Based on the resource access table, the server will find all the generated missing video frames in this rendering process and sends them back to the VR device, and then perform prediction operation.

Prediction Operation. The home MEC server adds the user's current FoV to the user's trajectory and runs the prediction model to predict the user's trajectory for the next period $(t, t + \Delta t]$ and the tile files involved in this trajectory. After that, the server will find all the tile files that the device is not cached and sends them back to the VR device. Since a tile file contains multiple frames, some may be earlier than t_v, which means they will never be watched, so unless necessary, we only send the frames later than t_v.

The exceptions are due to the video compression method. P and B frames cannot be directly decoded on the VR device, so we need to look forward to the nearest I frame position and send from that position. Considering the size of a single tile file is small, all frames later than t_v are sent together even if they may not be rendered in the future.

4   Cache Strategy

To design an ideal caching algorithm, we will analyze the latency involved in each possible request path, establish a profit model for the amount of latency reduction, and finally propose an algorithm for the k edge-disjoint shortest paths problem with a constraint on the edge number of shortest paths. The algorithm will eventually give the highest profit caching scheme.

4.1   Delay Analysis

When computing the caching scheme, assume that N different tiles have been requested in the entire MEC collaboration domain, and the tiles are denoted as $\{tile_1, ..., tile_N\}$. A $request_r$ about $tile_n$ from a VR device will have a data size of sz_r, a bandwidth of Bu_r between the user and MEC server, a bandwidth of B_m between MEC servers, and a bandwidth of B_{dc} between MEC servers and the cloud server. Both request and response packets on the MEC servers will experience queuing before they are processed and sent. We assume that all MEC servers in the collaboration domain are moderately loaded when running, so the queuing delay would not be too long. The T_{q_1} is used to represent the upper limit of delay time of waiting to be processed after the request arrives at the receive buffer of the MEC server, and T_{q_2} is used to represent the upper limit of queuing delay before the response data is sent. All request goes through one or two communication processes as follows.

VR Device $\leftrightarrow$ Home MEC Server. There is only one hop between the VR device and its home MEC server. Since radio waves travel at the speed of light, and the distance between them is usually less than 1 km, propagation delays can be negligible. The delay of this case is

$$ch(sz_r, Bu_r) = \frac{sz_r}{Bu_r} + T_{q1} + T_{q2}. \tag{1}$$

Home MEC Server $\leftrightarrow$ Other MEC Server. Base stations in the collaborative domain communicate via the X2 interface [23], and the underlying physical link is optical fiber, a one-hop wired link. It is not more than 10 km between the MEC servers, so propagation delay can also be negligible. MEC servers in the collaborative domain have similar network configurations, so the communication bandwidth between any two servers is the same. The delay of this case is

$$cmm(sz_r) = \frac{sz_r}{B_m} + T_{q1} + T_{q2}. \tag{2}$$

Any MEC Server $\leftrightarrow$ Data Center. As the network conditions from the home MEC server to the remote data center are complex, including multi-hop links and network fluctuations due to line instability, it is impossible to calculate the delay accurately. In order to determine the time it takes packets to pass through these links, we use the communication delay $T_{m \leftrightarrow dc}$, which fluctuates within a range. The delay of this case is

$$cc(sz_r) = \frac{sz_r}{B_{dc}} + 2 \cdot T_{m \leftrightarrow dc}. \tag{3}$$

As shown above, the system of equations can be used to estimate the time delay of both prefetch and remediation requests. However, remediation requests will incur processing latency for extracting the frames required for compression from the missing tile file. Because the closest I frame information is on-demand, remediation can only be performed on the MEC server with the missing tile file. The processing delay is independent of the cache strategy. As a result, we do not consider that the processing delay can be reduced.

Afterwards, we discuss how the cache distribution of each tile file affects the request delay. Let the requests about $tile_n$ on MEC server m be $R_{m,n}$. We find that once any replica of $tile_n$ is in the collaboration domain, it generates a global profit

$$v_n^{glo} = \sum_{m=1}^{M} \sum_{r \in R_{n,m}} cc(sz_r) - cmm(sz_r), \tag{4}$$

Because once a replica exists within the collaboration domain, the path of all requests to $tile_n$ shifts and the request endpoint changes from the cloud server to the MEC server within the collaboration domain. This global profit can only be accrued once. Also, The $tile_n$ cache on a special MEC server m generates a local profit

$$v_{n,m}^{loc} = \sum_{r \in R_{n,m}} cmm(sz_r), \tag{5}$$

Since all $tile_n$ requests within the service area of MEC server m are handled directly, inter-MEC server communications are eliminated.

4.2   Abstraction Method

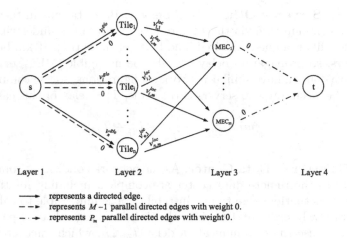

Fig. 2. The illustration on reformulating cache problem to k-shortest paths problem.

After we split all original VR videos into equal size tile files, Let S denote the size of a tile file, and $P_m = \frac{C_m}{S}$ denote the maximum number of tile files stored in MEC server m, where C_m is the storage capacity of the MEC server m. In our specific case, the cache distributed problem can be reformulated as the graph structure $G = (V, E)$ with a single source and a single sink illustrated in Fig. 2, which is a directed acyclic graph (DAG).

Nodes with depth d are called layer-d nodes for convenience. In the DAG G, there are only four layers. Layer-1 is the source node s, layer-2 is the tile nodes corresponding to each tile file, layer-3 is the MEC nodes corresponding to the MEC servers in the collaboration domain, and layer-4 is the sink node t.

If there is only one directed edge from node i to node j, it will be represented as $e_{i,j}^t$, and if there is more than one, $e_{i,j}^t$ will be used to represent the tth parallel directed edges. Edge weights are expressed as $c(e_{i,j}^t)$. The details of the G will be described below.

$s \rightarrow$**Tile Nodes.** In the collaboration domain, each tile file will store at most M replicas. Therefore, there are M parallel directed edges $\{e_{s,i}^1, ..., e_{s,i}^M\}$ from node s to tile node i. Since the global profit can only be accumulated once, $c(e_{s,i}^1) = v_i^{glo}$, and $c(e_{s,i}^2), ..., c(e_{s,i}^M)$ should be 0.

Tile Nodes → MEC Nodes. For any layer-3 MEC node j, its optional storage object includes all tile files, so for any layer-2 tile node i, there is a directed edge $e_{i,j}$, and $c(e_{i,j}) = v_{i,j}^{loc}$.

MEC Nodes → t. To limit MEC's storage capacity, for any layer-3 MEC node j, there are M parallel directed edges $\{e_{j,t}^1, ..., e_{j,t}^M\}$ from j to t with 0 weight.

Any path between source node s and sink node t in G represents a caching operation in the original problem, selecting a simple directed path $< s, i, j, t >$ is equivalent to storing tile file i on MEC server j. After negating the weights of all edges, the original problem is reformulated as a k *shortest edge-disjoint paths* problem, which has been extensively studied in the literature on network optimization [1].

Let $K = \sum_{m=1}^{M} P_m$, which indicates the maximum number of tile files the collaboration domain can store. Our goal became to find the K paths $\{p_1, ..., p_K\}$ from source node s to sink node t, such that the total cost of the paths is minimum, and the problem can be solved using the k-shortest paths (KSP) algorithm [30].

Algorithm 1 gives a pseudocode summary of the original KSP algorithm, and a brief workflow of KSP algorithm can be described as (1) construct the graph G as mentioned above; (2) compute the shortest path p from s to t; (3) in G, reverse the direction of all edges in p, and negating their weights; (4) repeat step (2)(3) $k - 1$ times.

In l^{th} iteration, an augmenting path ap_l with be calculated by shortest path algorithm, let $AP_l = \{ap_1, ..., ap_l\}$ be the set of all l augmenting paths computed up to iteration l, and the negative edges of G will form the shortest paths set $P_l = \{p_1, ..., p_l\}$. In particular, after every iteration, there are no negative cycles in the graph G, which is proved in [30].

4.3 Model Analysis

Table 1. Notation Definition

Symbol	Description
N	Number of different tile files
M	Number of MEC servers in the collaboration domain
P_m	The MEC server m can store a maximum of P_m tile files
K	The collaboration domain can store a maximum of K tile files
$e_{i,j}^t$	The tth parallel directed edge from node i to node j
$c(e_{i,j}^t)$	The weight of edge $e_{i,j}^t$

The worst-case complexity of Algorithm 1 is $O(K \cdot M \cdot N)$, which means the original KSP algorithm can not handle the situation where N becomes larger. Below, we demonstrate how some optimizations can significantly reduce the algorithm's time complexity. We find that the layer-3 nodes are significantly fewer than layer-2 nodes ($M \ll N$), and we can optimize the KSP algorithm from this point. Eventually, we propose the *optimized k-shortest paths* (OSKP) algorithm (Table 1).

Theorem 1. *In G, there exists a shortest path set $AP_K^* = \{ap_1, ..., ap_K\}$; for any path $ap \in AP_K^*$, every node in ap will only appear once, except for the tile nodes in layer-2.*

Proof. Since there are no negative cycles in G at each iteration, and removing non-negative cycles does not increase the path length, we can run the KSP algorithm to get a set AP_K, then remove cycles in the paths that do not satisfy the requirement repeatedly until all paths in AP_K are meet the requirements.

Theorem 2. *In the augmenting pathfinding process, if the path's endpoint is at layer-3 node j, then the condition to transfer via layer-2 node i to another layer-3 node k is that MEC server j stores $tile_i$ and MEC server k does not.*

We refer to the process in Theorem 2 as a *transfer*, it results in a *transfer loss* of $v_{i,j}^{loc} - v_{i,k}^{loc}$, and we denote i as a *transit node*.

Theorem 3. *For any $ap \in AP_K^*$, the edge number of ap does not exceed $2 \cdot M + 1$.*

Proof. Path ap will reach a layer-3 node after the first two edges (node s does not appear twice), and then it will *transfer* between layer-3 nodes or reach sink node t. As each MEC node in ap does not appear twice, initially one layer-3 node has been visited, and the number of visited layer-3 nodes increases by one after each *transfer*. With M layer-3 nodes, the *transfer* time does not exceed $M - 1$, and the edge number after each *transfer* increases by 2. As a result, the edge number in the ap does not exceed $2 \cdot M + 1$ (the *transfer* does not increase the depth, and ap need 3 edges to reach the sink node t).

Using the above theorem, we propose the OKSP algorithm, which is equivalent to KSP algorithm, but has lower time complexity in our model. As the number of tiles N in the scenario of this paper is much larger than the number of MEC servers M, the following analysis assumes that $N > M$.

Optimization 1. Use ordered arrays to maintain the shortest distance from the source node s to every layer-3 node.

Assume in the augmenting pathfinding process, the path's endpoint is s, and it needs to go forward two edges ($s \rightarrow i \rightarrow j$) to reach MEC node j. There are $2 \cdot N$ possible paths, and if we check every tile node, the time complexity is $O(N)$. However, the path will eventually select the two edges with the highest profits (minimum sum of edge weights).

It doesn't matter which the first two edges are chosen. The path's endpoint always becomes node j, node j becomes a visited MEC node, and edge set $\{e_{from,to}^k | from = s \ or \ to = j\}$ can no longer be chosen. In this case, it's better to pick the two edges that will generate the maximum profit.

Initially, we add all $2 \cdot N$ possible paths from node s to each MEC node j into the array $PathArray_j$ and sort their profits in descending order.

During the pathfinding process, whenever a transfer from node s to MEC node j occurs, we simply take the path with the highest profit from the $PathArray_j$ and dynamically remove infeasible solutions at each iteration. For details, see *Initialize-Possible-Paths* and *Maintain-Path-Array* in Algorithm 2.

Optimization 2. Use priority queues to maintain the shortest distance between the layer-3 nodes.

Assume in the augmenting pathfinding process, the path's endpoint is MEC node j, and ready to *transfer* to MEC node k. Multiple transit nodes may be available for *transit*, and the time complexity will be $O(N)$ if all tile nodes need to be checked. But it can be proved that the path will eventually choose the *transit node* with the minimum *transfer loss*.

Because no matter which *transit node* is selected, the path'endpoint always becomes MEC node k, MEC node k becomes a visited MEC node, and edge set $\{e^k_{from,to}|from = j \ or \ to = k\}$ can no longer be chosen. In this case, it's better to pick the *transit node* that will cause the minimum *transfer loss*.

The priority queue $LossQueue_{j,k}$ can be used to dynamically maintain all feasible *transit nodes* of MEC server j to transfer to MEC server k. For details, see *Maintain-Loss-Queues* in Algorithm 2.

After the above optimization, the tile nodes of layer-2 are hidden, and the original graph G can be transformed into a new graph G' with the number of nodes $M + 2$ in Fig. 3.

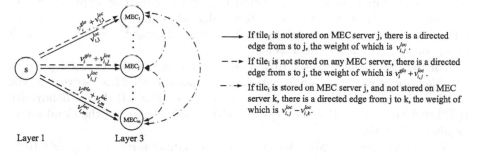

Fig. 3. The illustration on optimizing the k-shortest problem. Note that the graph shows the possible cases of tile$_i$ profits in the collaborative domain.

Theorem 4. *The total length of k shortest paths calculated by the OKSP algorithm is equal to the KSP algorithms.*

Proof. Assume that the augmenting path ap_l obtained by G' in l^{th} iteration is $(s \rightarrow MEC_1 \rightarrow ... \rightarrow MEC_j \rightarrow ...t)$. From Optimization 1 and 2, we know that $s \rightarrow MEC_1$ will greedily choose the path with the maximum profit, and $MEC_j \rightarrow MEC_{j+1}$ will choose the transit node with the minimum *transfer loss*, and the algorithm covers all available options when maintaining *PathArray* and *LossQueue*, and the length of all shortest paths equals the length of all augmenting paths. Therefore, Theorem 4 holds.

The following is an analysis of time complexity. The primary time consumption of the OKSP algorithm is as follows. (1) Calculating the augmenting path. There are K iterations, each time using the Dijkstra algorithm. The time complexity is $O(K \cdot M^2)$. (2) Maintaining MECPathArray. PathArray needs to sort the profits of all possible cache choices for each MEC node, and the time complexity is $O(M \cdot N \cdot \log N)$. (3) Maintaining MECLossQueue. Since the edge number of augmenting path obtained from each iteration will not exceed $O(M)$, the add operation will not exceed $O(K \cdot M^2)$ times. The time complexity of a priority queue add operation is $O(\log N)$; the remove operation times will not exceed the add operation and can be omitted.

Therefore, the total time complexity is $O((K \cdot M + N) \cdot M \cdot \log N)$. For random input, the edge number of augmenting path of each iteration is much smaller than M, and the run time will be faster than expected.

In the MEC collaboration domain, the collaboration system periodically runs the OKSP algorithm, selecting the least loaded MEC server in the collaboration domain to compute the caching scheme and distributing it to the other MEC servers. As soon as other MEC servers receive the cache scheme, they will request the tile files they do not have and need to cache.

5   Experiment

In order to evaluate the OKSP algorithm's low complexity and applicability to large-scale input data, we conducted numerical simulation experiments. In addition, we demonstrate that the OKSP algorithm can compute the caching scheme with the lowest average request latency in all cases by comparing it with other cooperative caching algorithms.

For the parameters, we set their values based on the fundamental physical situation and concerning similar studies. We assume all MEC servers in the collaboration domain have the same storage space. The VR device bandwidth is [50,100] Mbps, the MEC server bandwidth is 500 Mbps, and the cloud server bandwidth is 1 Gbps.

The tile file size is 10 MB. Assume that a remediation request requests 10%–20% of a tile's size, and a prefetch request requests 50%–100% of a tile's size. As in most studies [2,32], we assume the popularity of tiles follows a Zipf distribution and the shape parameter α of the Zipf distribution is 1.5. Generally, the greater the shape parameter α, the more concentrated the popular content. We assume the queuing delay T_{q1} during communication is 1 ms and T_{q2} is 2 ms. The packet transmission delay $T_{m \leftrightarrow dc}$ on the link between the VR device and the cloud server is [50,100] ms.

In the collaboration domain, a cache hit results in a lower request latency than a cloud response. The request latency reduction is called request latency optimization. And all request latency optimizations for the same tile equal the tile's caching profit. By reducing request latency, we aim to improve users' experience. Thus, we use the average request latency (ARL) optimization in the collaboration domain as a metric for evaluating the algorithm. We compare the OKSP algorithm with the following caching algorithms.

– *Distributed*: Each MEC server in the collaboration domain has completely different tiles to achieve as many tiles as possible in the collaboration domain. The time complexity of the Distribution algorithm is $O(M \cdot N \cdot logN)$.
– *Self-Top*: Each MEC server in the collaboration domain caches the most popular tiles within its service area. The time complexity of the Self-Top algorithm is $O(M \cdot N \cdot logN)$.
– *MixCo*: In MixCo [32], the storage space of each MEC server is divided into sub-zone dedicated storage space and zone-shared storage space. In the implementation of MixCo, after each dedicated space is allocated to a MEC server, an algorithm with time complexity $O(M \cdot N)$ is performed to calculate the average request latency in the current storage state of the collaboration domain. The worst time complexity of the MixCo algorithm is $O(L \cdot M^2 \cdot N)$.

In the above time complexity representation, L is the maximum number of tiles cached by a single MEC server, M is the number of MEC servers, and N is the total number of different tiles.

5.1 Run Time

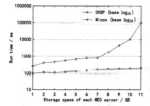
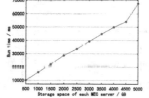
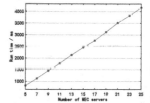

Fig. 4. Run time comparison of the OKSP and Mixco algorithms for different storage space

Fig. 5. Run time of the OKSP algorithm for different storage space

Fig. 6. Run time of the OKSP algorithm for different number of MEC servers

In this section, we will evaluate the speed of our OKSP algorithm. From the time complexity representation, the Self-Top and Distributed algorithms are faster than the OKSP algorithm. Thus, we do not take them into account. We perform a speed comparison experiment of the OKSP and MixCo algorithms.

This experiment fixes the number of tiles and MEC servers at 10,000 and 10, respectively, and adjusts the storage space of MEC servers. The results are shown in Fig. 4. Run time for the OKSP algorithm tends to increase linearly with increasing storage space, whereas the run time for the Mixco algorithm tends to grow exponentially. Due to more storage space available on MEC servers, MixCo generates multiple dedicated space partitioning iterations with time complexity $O(M \cdot N)$, which hinders algorithm performance. Therefore, applying the MixCo algorithm in a practical large-scale data environment is unrealistic.

To probe the speed limit of the OKSP algorithm, we further increase the data size. We fix the number of tiles and the number of MEC servers as 500,000 and 10, respectively, and increase the storage space of each MEC server. Figure 5 shows the results. The speed of OKSP increases linearly as storage space increases, which is consistent with the effect of storage space on its speed intuitively based on time complexity.

In addition, we continued to experiment with the effect of MEC servers numbers variation on OKSP speed, and the results are shown in Fig. 6. 200,000 tiles and 2TB of storage space on each MEC server are fixed in this experiment. Due to the small order of magnitude of the MEC servers, the results indicate linear effects on OKSP speed. Generally, the OKSP algorithm is suitable for large-scale data problems.

5.2   Performance Comparison

In the following experiments, we specifically study the effects of the MEC storage space, the number of tiles and the shape parameter α of Zipf distribution on the performance of the above four caching algorithms. The MixCo algorithm does not apply to large-scale data, so we first test the performance of the four algorithms with smaller-scale data, then remove the MixCo algorithm and test the remaining three algorithms with large-scale data. The following results are the average of three simulation runs.

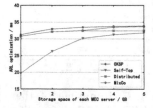 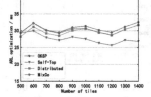 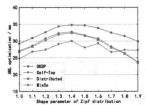

Fig. 7. Performance comparison for different storage space

Fig. 8. Performance comparison for different number of tiles

Fig. 9. Performance comparison for different shape parameter α

First, we compare the ARL optimization when the storage space of the MEC server varies. We fix the number of MEC servers and the number of tiles as 5 and 1500, respectively. We increase the storage space of the MEC server from 1 GB to 5 GB. Figure 7 shows the results. The ARL optimization of all caching algorithms increases as storage space increases. Because by increasing the storage space, more tiles can be cached in the MEC collaboration domain, preventing more requests from being sent to the cloud.

Figure 8 depicts the ARL optimization for the different numbers of tiles. This experiment assumes the MEC server space is 2 GB and the MEC server number is 5. Due to the scattering of popular tiles and the different popular tiles on each MEC server, the Self-Top algorithm performs poorly.

Figure 9 shows the effect of the shape parameter α on ARL optimization. We fix the number of MEC servers is 5, MEC server storage space is 2 GB, and the number of tiles is 1000. In Fig. 9, we can observe that the ARL optimization of the four algorithms increases at the beginning as α increases. However, the ARL optimization of the four algorithms decreases as α improves further. Because as α increases, the popular tiles become more concentrated. That is to say, a small number of tiles occupy most of the request traffic. Thus, the collaboration domain caching of these tiles can bring good profit. As we continue to increase α, despite the overall latency savings, the number of requests per tile increases, eventually showing a decrease in the ARL optimization.

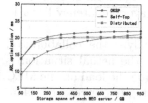 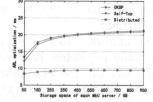 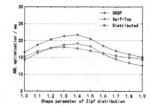

Fig. 10. Performance comparison of the OKSP, Self-Top and Distributed algorithms for different MEC server storage space (popular tiles are similar on each MEC server)

Fig. 11. Performance comparison of the OKSP, Self-Top and Distributed algorithms for different MEC server storage space (popular tiles are different on each MEC server)

Fig. 12. Performance comparison of the OKSP, Self-Top and Distributed algorithms for different shape parameter α

Finally, we test the ARL optimization of the remaining three algorithms on larger-scale data without Mixco. Figure 10 and Fig. 11 depict the ARL optimization under MEC server storage space variation. Assume there are 10 MEC servers and 500,000 tiles. In Fig. 10, each MEC server's popularity is similar, while in Fig. 11, each MEC server's popularity is entirely random. Under different popularity distribution scenarios, the Self-Top and Distributed algorithms perform very differently. In contrast, the popularity distribution does not limit the performance of the OKSP algorithm, and it can keep steady regardless of whether the popular tiles are scattered or concentrated.

ARL optimization under α variation is shown in Fig. 12. We assume the number of MEC servers is 10, MEC server storage space is 500 GB, and the number of tiles is 500,000. In Fig. 12, the results present a phenomenon similar to the experiment under small-scale data (in Fig. 9). In general, the OKSP algorithm consistently performs better than the other algorithms.

6 Conclusion

This paper provides a reliable transmission mechanism and an effective caching strategy under the current popular multi-MEC cooperative network architecture. We leverage MEC servers' computing and caching capabilities to improve users' viewing experience quality. For computing, we propose to let MEC servers handle prediction and remediation when predictions fail, while VR devices focus only on decoding and playing VR videos. For caching, VR videos are split into tile files, which improves cache hit rates.

To solve the order-of-magnitude huge tile caching problem, we first analyze the caching profit of tiles and then formulate the problem in graph theory as k-shortest paths problem. Then, we propose an OKSP algorithm to solve the reformulated problem quickly, which has an upper time complexity of $O((K \cdot M + N) \cdot M \cdot logN))$ and is suitable for shortest paths with restricted number of edges. Finally, we evaluate the proposed OKSP algorithm through run time and performance comparisons. Results show the OKSP algorithm is high-speed for solving large-scale data in our situation and has an average latency lower in any case than other caching schemes.

As part of the model formulating process, we analyze the collaboration domain load in the average queueing delay. However, the actual situation is more complex. Introducing a reasonable model to describe the load on the MEC server and refining the model in this paper is the next step in our research plan.

A   Appendix - KSP Algorithm

In this appendix, Algorithm 1 gives a pseudocode summary of the original k-shortest paths algorithm [30], Algorithm 2 gives a pseudocode of the optimized k-shortest paths algorithm. In Algorithm 2, there will be edges with negative weight in the graph after many iterations, we use the tips in the Johnson's algorithm [16] to re-weight all edges and make them all positive, then apply the Dijkstra algorithm to compute the shortest path trees at each iteration. We refer the interested reader to [30] for further details.

Algorithm 1: Original-K-Shortest-Paths

---

1 **Function** *Reverse(G, p)*
   /* Reverse the direction of all edges in p,
   and negating their weights.   */
2   **for** $e_{i,j}^t \in p$ **do**
3   Add $e_{j,i}^t$ in G
4          $c(e_{j,i}^t) = -c(e_{i,j}^t)$ Remove $e_{i,j}^t$ from G
5   **return** G

6 **Function** *Original-K-Shortest-Paths*
7   Construct the initial graph G described in 4.2
8   **for** $l \leftarrow 1$ *to* K **do**
9          $AugmentingPath_l \leftarrow Shortest\text{-}Path\text{-}Algorithm(G, s, t)$
10   **if** $AugmentingPath_l$ *not exists* **then**
11   Break
12         $G \leftarrow \text{Reverse}(G, AugmentingPath_l)$
13     $P \leftarrow$ find the shortest paths in G based on the negative edges
14   **return** P

Algorithm 2: Optimized-K-Shortest-Path Part-1

---

1 **Function** *Initialize-Possible-Paths*
2   **for** $j \leftarrow 1$ *to* M **do**
3   **for** $i \leftarrow 1$ *to* N **do**
            /* Two kinds of profits of tile$_i$ store in MEC server j. */
4   Add $(v_{i,j}^{loc} + v_i^{glo}, i)$ to $PathArray_j$
5   Add $(v_{i,j}^{loc}, i)$ to $PathArray_j$
6   Sort $PathArray_j$ in descending order

7 **Function** *Maintain-Path-Array*
8   **for** $j \leftarrow 1$ *to* M **do**
        /* Remove infeasible paths from $PathArray$.   */
9   **while** $PathArray_j$ *is not empty* **do**
10             $(profit, i) \leftarrow$ the maximum profit element in $PathArray_j$
11   **if** $tile_i$ *is stored in the collaboration domain* **then**
                /* Check if the global profit of tile$_i$ has been
                accrued.   */
12   **if** $profit > v_{i,j}^{loc}$ *or* $tile_i$ *is stored in MEC server* j **then**
13   Remove $(profit, i)$ from $PathArray_j$
14   Continue
15   Break

16 **Function** *Setup-Graph(G')*
    /* Because the shortest path algorithm, negating the weights of
    all edges   */
17   Initialize All nodes in G' are unreachable to each other **for** $j \leftarrow 1$ *to* M **do**
18   **if** $PathArray_j$ *is not empty* **then**
19             $(profit, i) \leftarrow$ the maximum profit element in $PathArray_j$
20             $c(e_{s,j}) \leftarrow -profit$
21   **if** *MEC server* j *has storage space left* **then**
22             $c(e_{j,t}) \leftarrow 0$
23   **for** $k \leftarrow 1$ *to* k *and* $k \neq j$ **do**
24   **if** $LossQueue_{j,k}$ *is not empty* **then**
25                 $(loss, i) \leftarrow$ the minimum loss element in $LossQueue_j, k$
26                 $c(e_{j,k}) \leftarrow -loss$

---

16 Function *Maintain-Loss-Queues(spath, CacheTable)*

      /* The edges of *spath* are denoted as $(j \rightarrow k, i)$, indicating that MEC node j is transferred to node k via $tile_i$; In particular, the first edge of spath $(s \rightarrow sj, si)$ indicates that the MEC server sj newly store the tile si, which is not transferred from another MEC; the last edge $(tj \rightarrow t, null)$ does not contain the transferred tile; and the remaining edges are considered *transferred edges*.   */

17   Mark MEC server sj is caching $tile_{si}$ in *CacheTable*

18   The number of copies of $tile_{si}$ cached in the collaboration domain $+= 1$

19   The remaining storage space of MEC server $tj \mathrel{-}= 1$

      /* Adding the new transfer nodes.   */

20   **for** $(remove \rightarrow add, i) \in transferred\ edges$ **do**

21   Mark MEC server add is caching $tile_i$ in *CacheTable*

22   Mark MEC server $remove$ no longer cache $tile_i$ in *CacheTable*

23   **for** $j \leftarrow 1$ to M **do**

24   **if** $j \neq add$ **and** *MEC j does not cache $tile_i$* **then**

25   Add $(v_{i,add}^{loc} - v_{i,k}^{loc}, j)$ to $LossQueue_{add,j}$

26   **if** $j \neq remove$ **and** *MEC j is caching $tile_i$* **then**

27   Add $(v_{i,j}^{loc} - v_{i,remove}^{loc}, j)$ to $LossQueue_{j,remove}$

      /* Remove infeasible transfer nodes.   */

28   **for** $j \leftarrow 1$ to M **do**

29   **for** $k \leftarrow 1$ to k **and** $k \neq j$ **do**

30   **while** $LossQueue_{j,k}$ *is not empty* **do**

31 $(loss, i) \leftarrow$ the minimum loss element in $LossQueue_j, k$

32   **if** *MEC server j does not cache $tile_i$* **or** *MEC server k is caching $tile_i$* **then**

33   Remove $(loss, i)$ from $LossQueue_j, k$

34   Continue

35   Break

36 Function *Optimized-K-Shortest-Paths*

37   CacheTable $\leftarrow$ a hash table for recording cache status

38   Construct G' containing M MEC nodes, s node, and t node

39   Initialize-Possible-Paths()

40   Setup-Graph(G')

41 $p_1 \leftarrow$ *Flody-Algorithm*(G', s, t)

42   Re-Weight-All-Edges(the shortest path trees node s) **for** $l \leftarrow 1$ to K **do**

43   Setup-Graph(G')

44 $p_l \leftarrow$ *Dijkstra-Algorithm*(G', s, t)

45   **if** p_l *not exists* **then**

46   Break

47   Re-Weight-All-Edges(the shortest path trees node s)

            MaintainLossQueues$(p_l,$ CacheTable$)$

48   **return** CacheTable

References

1. Berclaz, J., Fleuret, F., Turetken, E., Fua, P.: Multiple object tracking using K-shortest paths optimization. IEEE Trans. Pattern Anal. Mach. Intell. **33**(9), 1806–1819 (2011)
2. Borst, S., Gupta, V., Walid, A.: Distributed caching algorithms for content distribution networks. In: 2010 Proceedings IEEE INFOCOM, pp. 1–9 (2010). ISSN 0743-166X
3. Chakareski, J.: VR/AR immersive communication: caching, edge computing, and transmission trade-offs. In: Proceedings of the Workshop on Virtual Reality and Augmented Reality Network, VR/AR Network 2017, pp. 36–41. Association for Computing Machinery, New York (2017)
4. Cheng, Q., Shan, H., Zhuang, W., Yu, L., Zhang, Z., Quek, T.Q.: Design and analysis of MEC-and proactive caching-based 360° mobile VR video streaming. IEEE Trans. Multimedia **24**, 1529–1544 (2021)
5. Fan, C.L., Lee, J., Lo, W.C., Huang, C.Y., Chen, K.T., Hsu, C.H.: Fixation prediction for 360° video streaming in head-mounted virtual reality. In: Proceedings of the 27th Workshop on Network and Operating Systems Support for Digital Audio and Video, NOSSDAV 2017, pp. 67–72. Association for Computing Machinery, New York (2017)
6. Filippov, A., Norkin, A., Alvarez, J.R.: Video Codec Requirements and Evaluation Methodology. Request for Comments RFC 8761, Internet Engineering Task Force (2020). https://doi.org/10.17487/RFC8761. https://datatracker.ietf.org/doc/rfc8761
7. Gaddam, V.R., Riegler, M., Eg, R., Griwodz, C., Halvorsen, P.: Tiling in interactive panoramic video: approaches and evaluation. IEEE Trans. Multimedia **18**(9), 1819–1831 (2016)
8. Ge, X., Pan, L., Li, Q., Mao, G., Tu, S.: Multipath cooperative communications networks for augmented and virtual reality transmission. IEEE Trans. Multimedia **19**(10), 2345–2358 (2017)
9. Ghosh, A., Aggarwal, V., Qian, F.: A rate adaptation algorithm for tile-based 360-degree video streaming. arXiv preprint arXiv:1704.08215 (2017)
10. Guntur, R., Ooi, W.T.: On tile assignment for region-of-interest video streaming in a wireless LAN. In: Proceedings of the 22nd International Workshop on Network and Operating System Support for Digital Audio and Video, pp. 59–64 (2012)
11. Hou, T., Feng, G., Qin, S., Jiang, W.: Proactive content caching by exploiting transfer learning for mobile edge computing. Int. J. Commun. Syst. **31**(11), e3706 (2018)
12. Hou, X., Dey, S., Zhang, J., Budagavi, M.: Predictive adaptive streaming to enable mobile 360-degree and VR experiences. IEEE Trans. Multimedia **23**, 716–731 (2021)
13. Hsu, C.H.: MEC-assisted FoV-aware and QoE-driven adaptive 360 video streaming for virtual reality. In: 2020 16th International Conference on Mobility, Sensing and Networking (MSN), pp. 291–298. IEEE (2020)
14. Hu, H., Xu, Z., Zhang, X., Guo, Z.: Optimal viewport-adaptive 360-degree video streaming against random head movement. In: ICC 2019–2019 IEEE International Conference on Communications (ICC), pp. 1–6. IEEE (2019)
15. Jedari, B., Premsankar, G., Illahi, G., Di Francesco, M., Mehrabi, A., Ylä-Jääski, A.: Video caching, analytics, and delivery at the wireless edge: a survey and future directions. IEEE Commun. Surv. Tutor. **23**(1), 431–471 (2020)

16. Johnson, D.B.: Efficient algorithms for shortest paths in sparse networks. J. ACM (JACM) **24**(1), 1–13 (1977)
17. Kimata, H., Ochi, D., Kameda, A., Noto, H., Fukazawa, K., Kojima, A.: Mobile and multi-device interactive panorama video distribution system. In: The 1st IEEE Global Conference on Consumer Electronics 2012, pp. 574–578. IEEE (2012)
18. Liu, Y., Liu, J., Argyriou, A., Wang, L., Xu, Z.: Rendering-aware VR video caching over multi-cell MEC networks. IEEE Trans. Veh. Technol. **70**(3), 2728–2742 (2021)
19. Mahzari, A., Taghavi Nasrabadi, A., Samiei, A., Prakash, R.: FoV-aware edge caching for adaptive 360° video streaming. In: Proceedings of the 26th ACM International Conference on Multimedia, MM 2018, pp. 173–181. Association for Computing Machinery, New York (2018)
20. Mangiante, S., Klas, G., Navon, A., GuanHua, Z., Ran, J., Silva, M.D.: VR is on the edge: how to deliver 360 videos in mobile networks. In: Proceedings of the Workshop on Virtual Reality and Augmented Reality Network, pp. 30–35 (2017)
21. Mavlankar, A., Girod, B.: Video streaming with interactive pan/tilt/zoom. In: Mrak, M., Grgic, M., Kunt, M. (eds.) High-Quality Visual Experience, pp. 431–455. Springer, Heidelberg (2010). https://doi.org/10.1007/978-3-642-12802-8_19
22. Moon, P., Spencer, D.: Spherical coordinates (r, θ, ψ). In: Field Theory Handbook, Including Coordinate Systems, Differential Equations, and Their Solutions, pp. 24–27. Springer, Heidelberg (1988)
23. Ndikumana, A., Tran, N.H., Ho, T.M., Han, Z., Saad, W., Niyato, D., Hong, C.S.: Joint communication, computation, caching, and control in big data multi-access edge computing. IEEE Trans. Mob. Comput. **19**(6), 1359–1374 (2019)
24. Nguyen, D.V., Tran, H.T., Pham, A.T., Thang, T.C.: An optimal tile-based approach for viewport-adaptive 360-degree video streaming. IEEE J. Emerg. Sel. Top. Circuits Syst. **9**(1), 29–42 (2019)
25. Ozcinar, C., Cabrera, J., Smolic, A.: Omnidirectional video streaming using visual attention-driven dynamic tiling for VR. In: 2018 IEEE Visual Communications and Image Processing (VCIP), pp. 1–4. IEEE (2018)
26. Ozcinar, C., De Abreu, A., Smolic, A.: Viewport-aware adaptive 360 video streaming using tiles for virtual reality. In: 2017 IEEE International Conference on Image Processing (ICIP), pp. 2174–2178. IEEE (2017)
27. Rondón, M.F.R., Sassatelli, L., Aparicio-Pardo, R., Precioso, F.: A unified evaluation framework for head motion prediction methods in 360° videos. In: Proceedings of the 11th ACM Multimedia Systems Conference, MMSys 2020, pp. 279–284. Association for Computing Machinery, New York (2020)
28. Sullivan, G.J., Ohm, J.R.: Meeting Report of 13th JCT-VC Meeting (2013). https://phenix.it-sudparis.eu/jct/doc_end_user/current_document.php?id=7746
29. Sun, Y., Chen, Z., Tao, M., Liu, H.: Communications, caching, and computing for mobile virtual reality: modeling and tradeoff. IEEE Trans. Commun. **67**(11), 7573–7586 (2019)
30. Suurballe, J.W.: Disjoint paths in a network. Networks **4**(2), 125–145 (1974)
31. Verizon: How far does 5G reach? (2020). https://www.verizon.com/about/news/how-far-does-5g-reach
32. Wang, N., Shen, G., Bose, S.K., Shao, W.: Zone-based cooperative content caching and delivery for radio access network with mobile edge computing. IEEE Access **7**, 4031–4044 (2019)

33. Yang, X., et al.: Communication-constrained mobile edge computing systems for wireless virtual reality: scheduling and tradeoff. IEEE Access **6**, 16665–16677 (2018)
34. Zhang, Y., Jiang, X., Wang, Y., Lei, K.: Cache and delivery of VR video over named data networking. In: IEEE INFOCOM 2018-IEEE Conference on Computer Communications Workshops (INFOCOM WKSHPS), pp. 280–285. IEEE (2018)

Drone Base Stations Transmission Power Control and Localization

Salim Janji$^{(\boxtimes)}$ and Adrian Kliks

Institute of Radiocommunications, Poznan University of Technology, Poznań, Poland
salim.janji@doctorate.put.poznan.pl

Abstract. We target the problem of deploying drone base stations (DBSs) to serve a set of users with known locations after dividing it into two problems: users clustering along with 2D localization of drones, and transmission power control. For clustering, we propose an algorithm inspired by the expectation-maximization (EM) algorithm that boosts link reliability. As for transmission power control, we utilize the Monte Carlo tree search (MCTS) algorithm. Furthermore, we show that the resulting mechanism can also adapt to user changes without rebuilding the search tree, and it also intrinsically avoids collision between DBSs. Also, our simulations show that our proposed algorithm improves the link reliability and system energy efficiency substantially in comparison to another mechanism mentioned in the literature. The results show that controlling the power of DBSs does not only reduce power consumption but also improves the users' links quality. Finally, we show the improvement in system performance relative to the baseline method where DBSs are randomly distributed and users are changing their location according to the random waypoint mobility model.

Keywords: Ad hoc networks · Interference management · Drone base stations · Users clustering

1 Introduction

Drone base stations (DBS) are considered as promising solutions for the barriers faced by future wireless networks [1]. In areas where fixed infrastructure with high capacity is not always needed, DBSs can provide on-demand cost-effective coverage when such a capacity is required [2]. For example, they can also offload traffic from base stations in areas with crowded events or flash mobs [3]. Moreover, in cases where a fixed infrastructure is unavailable in isolated or disaster-struck areas, a number of DBSs can provide adequate connectivity for the required duration [4]. Compared to ground base stations, a DBS can establish Line-of-Sight (LOS) communication links to the users with reduced path loss, and it can continuously adapt its location to improve the performance of the communication system. Finally, due to their altitude, DBSs can leverage the use of free space optical (FSO) communications in the backhaul layer which can achieve higher data rates, longer transmission range, and less interference [5].

S. Longfei and P. Bodhi (Eds.): MobiQuitous 2022, LNICST 492, pp. 356–377, 2023.
https://doi.org/10.1007/978-3-031-34776-4_19

However, the use of DBSs also has its limitations. Multiple DBSs can cause severe co-channel interference when operating close to each other. Another issue is the limited onboard energy which restricts the transmission power, capacity, and deployment period of the DBS. Determining the location of the DBS should take into consideration the aforementioned factors. In this paper, we deal with the problem of 2D localization and transmission power control of DBSs while optimizing for users' signal-to-interference-plus-noise ratio (SINR) and satisfying the drones capacity constraint.

Our contributions are summarized as follows:

- Given the settings of drones' transmission powers, we find the 2D location for each DBS such that the path loss is minimized along with reducing interference between clusters served by different DBSs. We do so by proposing a novel algorithm derived from the standard expectation-maximization clustering algorithm (EM). We call it SINR-EM.
- We find the settings of drones' transmission powers such that the number of served users achieving a minimum signal-to-interference-plus-noise ratio (SINR), after applying SINR-EM, is maximized while satisfying the drones capacity constraint. This problem is modeled as a game tree in which the solution is found using Monte Carlo tree search. We call our algorithm Transmission Power Monte Carlo Tree Search (TP-MCTS). We also show that TP-MCTS can learn from its previous tree history for building a new tree whenever the deployment parameters of DBSs are to be updated.
- By simulations we show that our proposed algorithm performs substantially better in terms of link reliability and energy efficiency when compared to another algorithm that uses particle swarm optimization (PSO) [6].
- While utilizing the random waypoint mobility model (RWP) [7] we simulate our proposed algorithm against the baseline scenario in which DBSs are randomly distributed in a given area and show that our algorithm can adapt to the changes in users' locations.
- Finally, we discuss the insights that our results provide into the trade-off between the number of DBSs deployed, their transmission power settings, system performance in terms of efficiency, and the users' quality of service.

The rest of the paper is structured as follows. Section 2 gives an overview of related work in the literature. Section 3 presents the system model including the scenario considered, channel model, and the performance indicators that are to be achieved or maximized. Section 4 begins by introducing the standard EM algorithm then we introduce our proposed SINR-EM solution along with illustrating the effect of the threshold parameter which we introduced. Monte Carlo Tree Search is then introduced in Sect. 5, followed by an illustration of our version which is adapted to the problem in hand to which we also present a complete algorithmic description. Furthermore, Sect. 6 presents the simulation results for two scenarios: TP-MCTS against the PSO solution [6] for a static distribution of dense users; and TP-MCTS against the random deployment of DBSs in a given area for moving users. Finally, Sect. 7 concludes the paper.

2   Related Work

UAVs applications in wireless networks were the focus of extensive research in recent years [1,2,8–10]. In the matter of a single DBS deployment, the authors in [11] formulated a circle placement and smallest enclosing circle problems such that the transmit power is minimized while maximizing coverage. Similarly in [12], the scenario considers users with different signal-to-noise ratio (SNR) requirements where the goal is again to maximize their coverage. In [13] the optimal altitude for the DBS is derived for optimal coverage. On the other hand, in [14] a grid search algorithm was proposed to maximize the number of served users and sum-rates as far as the backhaul capacity permits.

Moreover, the problem of deploying multiple DBSs introduces further complexity and numerous solutions were proposed of which we mention a few. In [15], the authors proposed deploying DBSs sequentially along a spiral path to minimize the required number of DBSs and cover users. In [16], the authors proposed Q-learning and deep Q-learning (DQL) algorithms for the deployment of a single DBS and multiple DBSs respectively such that the fairness in coverage is maximized along with reward penalties for collision avoidance and interference minimization between different DBSs. Similarly, the authors in [17] designed the state representation, action, and reward for training a deep Q-network using prioritized replay which eventually determines the locations of DBSs such that user coverage is maximized using an obstacle-aware channel model while disregarding interference between DBSs. Furthermore, Liu et al. in [18] utilize Deep Deterministic Policy Gradient (DDPG) to train actor-critic networks such that the movement of DBSs is determined in continuous space and the individual coverage, coverage fairness, and energy consumption are optimized. A subset of UAVs serve as gateways through satellite links, and a penalty is applied whenever a DBS is far from any gateway and is therefore offline. However, instead of considering ground users, the algorithm considers points of interest and interference between DBSs is not taken into account. In [19], the authors consider a street graph model where only outdoor users are considered and represented by their densities along the graph edges and vertices. Moreover, they formulate an unconstrained optimization problem whose objective is a combination of three functions: the first calculates the total coverage achieved by DBSs, while the other two are heuristic functions that introduce a penalty based on the interference between DBSs and the distance to the nearest charging pole. As explained, the problem can be solved distributively whereas each DBS moves only when its local objective function can be improved.

Besides the specified differences, all of the aforementioned works with a focus on multiple DBSs deployments do not consider the capacity of DBSs which will, in reality, be limited due to bandwidth or backhaul constraints. Furthermore, the mobility of users is also neglected whereas we show that our proposed solution is able to continuously adapt to the changes in the users' distribution without restarting the state. Moreover, instead of considering the coverage in terms of SNR we directly target the optimize the signal-to-interference-plus-noise ratio (SINR) which takes into account the interference between DBSs and plays an

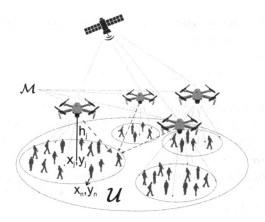

Fig. 1. The considered scenario in which users with known locations are served by a set of DBSs.

important role in the achieved link quality. We do so because we consider that the available number of DBSs is sufficient to provide coverage to the considered area and optimize the location and transmission power of DBSs. The authors of the work in [6] to which we compare our results make similar assumptions and use particle swarm optimization (PSO) to determine the 3D locations of DBSs.

3   System Model

The considered scenario is shown in Fig. 1 in which a set $\mathcal{U}$ of U users are served by the set $\mathcal{M}$ containing M drones. Such scenarios can include temporary events or crowded areas that are not covered by fixed infrastructure (e.g., due to destruction). For simulations, two users distribution models are considered. The first is a static distribution with different uniform densities in different regions similarly to [6], and the second utilizes RWP [7] to model the movement of users. A 3D Cartesian coordinates system is used such that the location of each drone is given by $\mathbf{m}_j = (x_j, y_j, h_j)$ where $j \in \{1, 2, .., M\}$. Similarly, the 2D location of each user is given by $\boldsymbol{u}_n = (x_n, y_n)$ where $n \in \{1, 2, .., U\}$. The users are assumed to be at ground level height ($h_n = 0$) and the drone height, h_j, is given above ground level (AGL). Furthermore, we assume that each drone j is transmitting at a controllable power of $P_{T_j} \leq P_{\max}$, where $P_{\max}$ is the maximum transmission power of the DBS. Finally, we assume that the DBSs are backhaul-connected via satellite links [15].

3.1   Channel Model

The distance between DBS j and user n is calculated as

$$d_{j,n} = \sqrt{(x_j - x_n)^2 + (y_j - y_n)^2 + h_j^2}. \tag{1}$$

As presented in [13], the probability of a LOS connection between the j-th DBS and n-th user can be given by

$$Pr_{\text{LOS}_{j,n}} = \frac{1}{1 + \alpha \times e^{-\beta(\omega - \alpha)}}, \tag{2}$$

where α and β are environment-dependent variables that can be set according to the environment type (i.e., suburban, dense urban, highrise urban, etc.), and $\omega = \arctan(\frac{h_j}{d_{j,n}})$. Accordingly, the probability of a non-line-of-sight connection can be obtained from (2) as $Pr_{\text{NLOS}_{j,n}} = 1 - Pr_{\text{LOS}_{j,n}}$. Furthermore, the path loss is a combination two components: a free-space path loss component, and an average path loss that depends on link type (LOS or NLOS). The path loss is therefore represented as

$$L^{\text{[dB]}} = 20 \log \left(\frac{4\pi f_c d}{c} \right) + \eta_{path}, \tag{3}$$

where f_c is the carrier frequency, c is the speed of light, d is the distance, and η_{path} is the average loss depending on the link type. The expected path loss between a DBS j and user u can therefore be given as

$$L_{j,n}^{\text{[dB]}} = 20 \log \left(\frac{4\pi f_c d_{j,n}}{c} \right) + Pr_{\text{LOS}_{j,n}} \times \eta_{\text{LOS}} + Pr_{\text{NLOS}_{j,n}} \times \eta_{\text{NLOS}}, \tag{4}$$

whereas $\eta_{\text{LOS}} < \eta_{\text{NLOS}}$. Given the total bandwidth of a DBS B_D and the allocated bandwidth to the user $B_n \le B_D$, the received power for user n can be obtained by

$$PR_{j,n} = \frac{B_n P_{T_j} 10^{\frac{-L_{j,n}}{10}}}{B_D}. \tag{5}$$

Using (5), the received signal-to-noise ratio (SNR) is given by

$$\text{SNR}_{j,n} = \frac{PR_{j,n}}{\sigma_0^2}, \tag{6}$$

where σ_0^2 is the receiver noise power. The signal-to-interference-plus-noise ratio (SINR) is therefore given on the user side as

$$\Gamma(j, n) = \frac{PR_{j,n}}{\sigma_0^2 + \sum_{i \ne j}^{M} PR_{i,n}}. \tag{7}$$

3.2   Problem Formulation

In the considered scenario it is assumed that the transmission power of each drone can be varied up to the maximum limit specified by $P_{\max}$. Also, the 2D location of each drone is denoted by $\mathbf{m}_j = (x_j, y_j)$ where the height h_j is omitted and assumed to be constant with a value of h. To balance the load, we assume that each DBS can serve up to a maximum number of $U_{\max}$ users that are given a bandwidth share of $B_n = \frac{B_D}{U_{\max}}$.

A considered figure of merit is the system energy efficiency, ζ, which can be derived as the total bit rate divided by the total transmission power of the drones as follows

$$\zeta = \frac{R_{\text{total}}}{P_{\text{total}}}. \tag{8}$$

Using Shannon's capacity formula, the total bit rate in Kbps is

$$R_{\text{total}} = \frac{1}{1000} \sum_{j=1}^{M} \sum_{n=1}^{U} W(j,n) B_n \, \log_2(1 + \Gamma(j,n)), \tag{9}$$

where

$$W(j,n) = \begin{cases} 1 & \text{if } j = \underset{j'}{\text{argmax}} \; \Gamma(j',n) \\ 0 & \text{otherwise} \end{cases} \tag{10}$$

maps the association of user n to drone j which provides the highest SINR value. The total transmitted power in Watts is given by

$$P_{\text{total}} = \sum_{j=1}^{M} P_{T_j}. \tag{11}$$

Another performance metric is the number of served users achieving an SINR value greater than or equal to a predefined threshold Γ_{Th},

$$N_j = \sum_{n=1}^{U} W(j,n) H \left(\Gamma(j,n) - \Gamma_{Th} \right), \tag{12}$$

where $H(x)$ is the Heaviside step function. Taking into consideration the capacity constraint of $U_{\max}$, the total number of users served with an SINR requirement or Γ_{Th} is

$$N_{\text{SU}} = \sum_{j=1}^{M} N_{Sj}, \tag{13}$$

where

$$N_{Sj} = \begin{cases} N_j, & \text{if } N_j \leq U_{\max} \\ U_{\max}, & \text{otherwise.} \end{cases} \tag{14}$$

Let $N_{th} = \Phi U$ be the minimum required number of served users achieving an SINR value greater than or equal to Γ_{Th} where Φ is the desired percentage of served users (or link reliability), then the problem is formulated as

$$\max_{P_{T_j}, \mathbf{m}_j} \zeta \tag{15a}$$

$$\text{s.t.} \quad N_{\text{SU}} \geq N_{th} \tag{15b}$$

$$0 \leq P_{T_j} \leq P_{\max} \tag{15c}$$

The formulation in (15) aims to maximize the system energy efficiency after ensuring that the minimum required number of users are served with an SINR value satisfying Γ_{Th} which is ensured by the constraint in (15b). Both the location of the j-th drone and its power can be varied whereas the latter is constrained to be less than $P_{\max}$ as dictated by the second constraint in (15c).

4 Expectation-Maximization Algorithm

4.1 Standard EM

EM algorithm usually utilizes Gaussian Mixture Models (GMMs) that model the set of sample points as being drawn from a "mixture" of Gaussian distributions [20]. A GMM gives the probability of a sample point being drawn from the mixture and it can be defined as:

$$\pi(\boldsymbol{u}; \theta) = \sum_{j=1}^{M} P(j) N(\boldsymbol{u}; \boldsymbol{\mu}_j, \boldsymbol{\Sigma}_j), \tag{16}$$

where the parameters $\theta = \{P, \boldsymbol{\mu}, \boldsymbol{\Sigma}\}$ include mixing proportions P, means of Gaussian components $\boldsymbol{\mu}$, and covariance matrices $\boldsymbol{\Sigma}$, and $N(\boldsymbol{u}; \boldsymbol{\mu}_j, \boldsymbol{\Sigma}_j)$ gives the probability of sample point $\boldsymbol{u}$ taken from the j-th Gaussian distribution.

The EM algorithm learns the parameters θ given a set of sample points, $\mathcal{U}$, and the number of mixtures, M. In this paper, the notation for the number of Gaussian components, M, and the set of sample points, $\mathcal{U}$, is consistent with the mapping of these parameters to the total number of drones and the set of 2D locations of users respectively. Moreover, each mean, $\boldsymbol{\mu}_j$, corresponds to the 2D location of drone j. At each iteration the algorithm performs two steps:

1. Estimation step (E-step). Evaluate the posterior assignment probabilities given by:

$$p^{(l)}(j|n) = p(j|\boldsymbol{u}_n, \theta^{(l)}) = \frac{P^{(l)}(j) N\left(\boldsymbol{u}_n; \boldsymbol{\mu}_j^{(l)}, \boldsymbol{\Sigma}_j^{(l)}\right)}{\pi(\boldsymbol{u}_n; \theta^{(l)})}, \tag{17}$$

where (l) denotes iteration number, and $\boldsymbol{u}_n = \begin{bmatrix} x_n \\ y_n \end{bmatrix}$ is the sample $n \in \{1, .., U\}$, where U is the total number of samples.

2. Maximization step (M-step). Update parameters according to:

$$P^{(l+1)}(j) = \frac{\hat{n}(j)}{U}, \quad \text{where } \hat{n}(j) = \sum_{n=1}^{U} p^{(l)}(j|t). \tag{18a}$$

$$\boldsymbol{\mu}_j^{(l+1)} = \frac{1}{\hat{n}(j)} \sum_{n=1}^{U} p^{(l)}(j|n) \boldsymbol{u}_n. \tag{18b}$$

$$\boldsymbol{\Sigma}_j^{(l+1)} = \frac{1}{\hat{n}} \sum_{n=1}^{U} p^{(l)}(j|n) \left(\boldsymbol{u}_n - \boldsymbol{\mu}_j^{(l+1)}\right) \left(\boldsymbol{u}_n - \boldsymbol{\mu}_j^{(l+1)}\right)^T. \tag{18c}$$

The E-step obtains the posterior probabilities, $p^{(l)}(j|n)$, that denote the probability of having the sample observed $(\boldsymbol{u}_n)$ being drawn from the j-th Gaussian component. In the M-step, the parameters of each component j are updated to increase the total likelihood of the GMM. It is worth noting that the EM algorithm is guaranteed to converge to a local optimal solution [20].

4.2 EM-Based Clustering Algorithm

We propose a new clustering algorithm inspired by EM. Since we are interested in obtaining the 2D locations of DBSs we only consider the estimation step given by (17) and the mean update given by (18b). In particular, we modify (17) such that we replace the posterior probabilities $p(j|n)$ by weights that are proportional to the achieved SINR $\Gamma(j, n)$. The proposed solution aims to:

1. Directly incorporate the transmission power of DBSs into the posterior probabilities calculations and mean updates. The result is that a higher transmission power for DBS j entails a cluster with a larger area (i.e., for any $\boldsymbol{u}_n$ within that area, $p(j|n) > p(k|n)$ for every $k \neq j$). By building such a relationship we can then delegate the task of choosing the best transmission power settings to TP-MCTS.
2. Allow each $\boldsymbol{u}_n$ to contribute to the mean update of cluster j with a value of $p(j|n)$ proportional to the SINR received from that cluster (i.e., DBS) relatively to the other clusters. Furthermore, completely prevent users from contributing to the mean updates of clusters that will not serve them.

Proposal 1: The posterior probabilities obtained in (17) are replaced by probabilities that directly map the achieved SINR given by (7). Specifically, the vector of new probabilities for each user is obtained by

$$\boldsymbol{q}'^{(l)}(\cdot|n) = s(\boldsymbol{\Gamma}_n^{(l)}), \tag{19}$$

where different entries in this vector are associated with different DBSs and $\boldsymbol{\Gamma}_n^{(l)}$ is the vector of achieved SINR values (see (7)) for user n with each DBS. That is,

$$\boldsymbol{\Gamma}_n^{(l)} = \left[\Gamma(1, n)^{(l)}, \Gamma(2, n)^{(l)}, .., \Gamma(M, n)^{(l)}\right]^T, \tag{20}$$

and $s(\boldsymbol{z})_j$ is the Softmax function defined as

$$s(\boldsymbol{z})_j = \frac{e^{C z_j}}{\sum_{j'=1}^{M} e^{C z_{j'}}}, \tag{21}$$

where C is an arbitrary scaling constant. Using (19) for determining the posterior probabilities instead of (17) means that each user contributes to the parameters update of each DBS, j, with a magnitude proportional to how likely it is for the user to be served by this particular drone and not the others. The probability or magnitude of association between drone j and user n is directly proportional to the achieved SINR given by (7) relatively to the achieved SINR by other drones.

Proposal 2: We define a dynamic SINR threshold below which $q(j|n)$ will be set to zero if $\Gamma(j,n) < \Gamma_{\mathrm{th}_n}^{(l)}$. This threshold is defined as

$$\Gamma_{\mathrm{th}_n}^{(l)} = \max\left\{\boldsymbol{\Gamma}_n^{(l)}\right\} - S_{\mathrm{th}}, \tag{22}$$

where the first term on the right-hand side denotes the highest achieved SINR between all drones in dB, and S_{th} is the SINR dropout value that determines how fast the users are decoupled from non-serving drones. After obtaining the SINR threshold value from (22), the decoupling mask is defined as

$$\boldsymbol{M}_n^{(l)} = \left[H\left(\Gamma(1,n)^{(l)} - \Gamma_{\mathrm{th}_n}^{(l)}\right), .., H\left(\Gamma(M,n)^{(l)} - \Gamma_{\mathrm{th}_n}^{(l)}\right)\right]. \tag{23}$$

Finally, the normalized masked probabilities can be obtained using

$$\boldsymbol{q}^{(l)}(\cdot|n) = \frac{\boldsymbol{M}_n^{(l)T} \odot \boldsymbol{q}'^{(l)}(\cdot|n)}{||\boldsymbol{M}_n^{(l)T} \odot \boldsymbol{q}'^{(l)}(\cdot|n)||}, \tag{24}$$

where $\odot$ denotes the dot product operation and $||\cdot||$ denotes the L2 norm of a vector. The numerator discards DBSs with SINR below the threshold and the denominator normalizes the results so that their summation is equal to one.

At every iteration after obtaining the probabilities defined in (24) the 2D locations of the DBSs can be updated using (18b) but with using $q^{(l)}(j|n)$ instead of $p^{(l)}(j|n)$. The pseudocode for SINR-based EM algorithm is shown in Algorithm 1 where the clusters locations are initialized using a set of unique initial locations μ_{init}. Furthermore, the convergence is determined whenever an iteration results in a mean update less than some predefined threshold ϵ for all clusters.

Algorithm 1. SINR-Based EM Algorithm.

Input: $\mathcal{U}$, M, $\boldsymbol{P}_T$
Output: $\boldsymbol{\mu} = [\boldsymbol{\mu}_1, \boldsymbol{\mu}_2, .., \boldsymbol{\mu}_M]$
   initialisation: $\boldsymbol{\mu} = \boldsymbol{\mu}_{\mathrm{init}}$
repeat
      Calculate SINR-based probabilities using (24)
      Obtain new DBSs 2D locations using (18b)
until convergence

4.3   On Outliers and the Choice of S_{th}

S_{th} can be chosen such that DBSs will not be placed in sub-optimal locations where outliers might exist. By introducing $S_{\mathrm{th}} > \epsilon$ for some $\epsilon > 0$ we allow the points that do not belong to the subset of outliers to *attract* cluster j to some extent. Figure 2 illustrates the difference in results obtained from SINR-EM for the cases of $S_{\mathrm{th}} = 0$, $S_{\mathrm{th}} > 0$, and $S_{\mathrm{th}} = \infty$ for a given users distribution. On the other hand, increasing S_{th} indefinitely allows more users that are not served

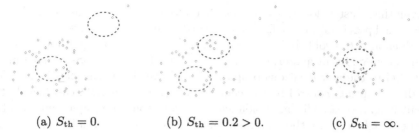

(a) $S_{\text{th}} = 0$.   (b) $S_{\text{th}} = 0.2 > 0$.   (c) $S_{\text{th}} = \infty$.

Fig. 2. Comparison of SINR-EM resulting clusters overlap for different values of S_{th}.

by a cluster j to contribute to the mean update of (18b) of j, and therefore results in an increased overlap between different clusters which in turn degrades the overall achieved link quality of the users due to interference (see Fig. 2c).

4.4   On Collision Between DBSs

Collision avoidance is an important aspect to consider in multi-UAV applications and it has received substantial attention in literature [8]. In the case of SINR-EM, and since all DBSs are flying at the same height, a collision can be modeled as the event when the 2D distance between any two DBSs is below a certain threshold. However, we know that by introducing the dynamic SINR threshold inside SINR-EM (see (22)) the clusters served by different DBSs are disjointed in the sense that users served by one DBS do not contribute to the location update of other DBSs as previously discussed.

Lemma 1. *For any two points u_n and u_t and given any two DBSs j and k, if $\Gamma(j,n) > \Gamma(k,n)$ and $d_{k,t} > d_{j,n}$ then $\Gamma(j,t) > \Gamma(k,t)$.*

Proof. Since the heights of the DBSs are all equal and fixed, and $\eta_{\text{LOS}} < \eta_{\text{NLOS}}$ then $\Gamma(j,n)$ monotonically decreases as $d_{j,n}$ decreases for any P_{T_j}. This can be directly deduced from (2), (3), and (7).

Theorem 1. *Assuming $U >> M$, and at any SINR-EM iteration l, and for any two clusters j and k, $k \neq j$, after obtaining the sets of points associated with each cluster defined as $\mathcal{U}_j^{(l)} = \{u_n : q^{(l)}(j|n) > q^{(l)}(k|n)\}$ and $\mathcal{U}_k^{(l)} = \{u_n : q^{(l)}(k|n) > q^{(l)}(j|n)\}$, there exists an ϵ such that for any $S_{\text{th}} \leq \epsilon$ the location update of (18b) will not result in $u_j = u_k$ in any further iteration.*

Proof. As a consequence of Lemma 1, and regardless of any other DBS, the 2D space is split into two regions $R_1 \supseteq \mathcal{U}_j^{(l)}$ and $R_2 \supseteq \mathcal{U}_k^{(l)}$. Furthermore, we can always find $S_{\text{th}} = \epsilon$ such that a subset of points in $\mathcal{U}_j^{(l)}$ discards cluster k by applying the mask in (22). Therefore, given that the mean result in (18b) is the weighted average of the locations, then we are certain that $u_j^{(l+1)} \neq u_k^{(l+1)}$ when not all the points are included in the mean update of each cluster because of the 2D spatial distribution of the points in $\mathcal{U}_j^{(l)}$ and $\mathcal{U}_k^{(l)}$ and the proof is complete.

Given that clusters locations are initialized to distinct locations given by μ_{init} as mentioned previously, then Theorem 1 states that we can always choose S_{th} to be small enough to avoid the case where SINR-EM results in equal locations for different clusters. In this paper, we ignore the case where two DBSs collide during their travel to the new locations proposed by TP-MCTS as this can be avoided through appropriate control by the central unit (e.g., each DBS can travel at a different height, or a collision avoidance algorithm could be implemented [21]). In Subsect. 6.2 we verify the aforementioned deductions by simulation.

5   Monte Carlo Tree Search

Monte Carlo Tree Search (MCTS) is a tree search algorithm. It tries to find optimal decisions in a given domain through sampling the decision space and building a search tree according to the results [22]. In its simplest form, MCTS incrementally builds an asymmetric tree where each node defines a unique decision at a given state. At each iteration the algorithm begins at the root node and progresses to a specific node through a series of selections that conform to a certain policy which balances between exploration of new states and exploitation of previous results. Next, the selected node is expanded by adding a child node to the tree. Starting from this child node a simulation (or playout) is run until a terminal state is reached. In the context of games this can be a *win* or *loss*. Finally, the result is back-propagated from the terminal state through its ancestors to the root node by updating the states of those nodes [22].

5.1   Transmission Power MCTS

An adapted MCTS algorithm is proposed to determine each DBS transmission power. The algorithm is denoted as Transmission Power Monte Carlo Tree Search (TP-MCTS). In TP-MCTS each node is uniquely defined by a set of transmission power settings for all DBSs. Starting from an initial setting of maximum power for all DBSs (i.e., $P_T = [P_{T_1} = P_{max}, .., P_{T_M} = P_{max}]$) a root node is defined. A child node is created by decreasing the transmission power of one DBS by a predefined step of P_Δ (e.g., $P_T = [P_{max}, P_{max} - P_\Delta, .., P_{max}]$). For each selected node, SINR-EM is performed given the specified transmission powers, and two figures of merit are obtained as a result: the first is the number of served users, $N_{SU,node}$, given by (13); and the second is the achieved energy efficiency, ζ_{node}, given by (8). Both are used to obtain the score (reward) of each node. Let $N_{th} = \Phi U$ be the minimum required number of served users achieving an SINR value greater than or equal to Γ_{th}, where Φ is the desired percentage of served users (or link reliability). Then, the score of each node in the i-th iteration is obtained as

$$S_{node}^i = \begin{cases} \frac{N_{SU,node}^i}{U} & \text{if } N_{SU,node}^i < N_{th}. \\ \Phi + \frac{\zeta_{node}^i}{B_n} & \text{otherwise.} \end{cases} \qquad (25)$$

If N_{th} is achieved, then the score would also include a value proportional to the achieved energy efficiency, independently of the assigned bandwidth, in order to search for solutions that further optimize the system's energy efficiency since the score guides the tree search as will be explained later below.

Figures 3a to 3d illustrate an example of TP-MCTS for four iterations. Each node is defined by the set of specified transmission powers below it, and its state contains the score and number of visits. Note that the number of visits is incremented only when a child of that node is visited through it, not when it is selected. For the sake of demonstration, we assume that the root node initially has a score of 0.6 obtained from the deployment results of SINR-EM with the initial maximum transmission power settings. The algorithm proceeds as follows:

– **Iteration 1**: The child node which reduces the transmission power of the first drone is selected (the selection criterion will be presented later). After performing SINR-EM, a result of 0.65 is achieved which is higher than the node's sole ancestor (i.e., the root) score so a *win* has occurred and the result is back-propagated upwards.
– **Iteration 2**: The root node score is updated with the resulting *win* from its child. When a *win* occurs, all of the winning node ancestors' scores are updated after receiving the score (see (25)) achieved by the winning child. The new scores are calculated according to the cumulative average

$$S_{node}^{i+1} = S_{node}^i + \left(\frac{S_{win}^i - S^i}{V_{node}^i + 1} \right), \tag{26}$$

where V_{node}^i is the visits count and S_{win}^i is the winning child node's score. The next selected node reduces the transmission power of DBS M and results in a score lower than its highest ancestor score (the root in this case) and therefore a *loss* occurs. The score is not back-propagated in the case of *loss*.
– **Iteration 3**: The child node with the reduced transmission power for the first DBS is selected again. Given that this node was selected before then it is not considered a *win* and therefore the algorithm continues. That is, a *win* or *loss* occur only when a node selected for the first time. Next, a further child node is created by again reducing the transmission power of the first drone ($j = 1$), and SINR-EM results in a score of 0.65. Since this score is equal to the highest ancestor score (0.65 belonging to the parent in this case) then again no *win* or *loss* occur. Finally, another child node is selected which reduces the transmission power of the second drone ($j = 2$) and the obtained score is 0.7, which is higher than 0.65, and therefore a *win* has occurred and the result is back propagated. The optimal state (shaded) is the one that has so far achieved the highest score during creation.
– **Iteration 4**: Assuming that the losing node of the second iteration is selected again, we observe that no loss occurs. Next, a further child node is created by an additional decrease of the last DBS power ($j = M$) and the achieved score is 0.58. Although the score is higher than its parent node, a loss occurs because the highest ancestor score is 0.644 belonging to the root node which is higher than the score achieved by this child.

In TP-MCTS the selection, expansion, and simulation steps of the standard MCTS are lumped together, and at each iteration, the algorithm progresses by

(a) iteration 1: first win occurred after reducing P_{T_1}.

(b) iteration 2: reducing P_{T_M} results in a loss.

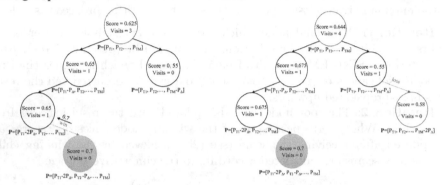

(c) iteration 3: reducing P_{T_2} after reducing P_{T_1} for the second time caused a win.

(d) iteration 4: the second loss occurred after reducing P_{T_M} again.

Fig. 3. MCTS example. Note how the ancestors scores are updated after each iteration.

selecting child nodes until reaching a terminal node which is selected for the first time such that it terminates with a *win* or *loss* if the achieved score of the considered node is higher or lower respectively than the highest score in the traversed nodes. The score is back-propagated only in the case of *win*.

5.2 Selection Criterion

To select the next node, the scores of all possible child nodes are taken into consideration, while the missing scores of the nodes that are not yet created are substituted by the parent score (i.e. current). We select the child node with the maximum upper confidence bound (UCB) value given by [23]

$$\text{UCB}_{child} = S_{child} + K\sqrt{\frac{\ln(visits_{parent})}{visits_{child} + 1}}, \tag{27}$$

where K is an arbitrary constant controlling the level of exploration.

Algorithm 2 shows the object-oriented programming (OOP) pseudocode for TP-MCTS which is implemented recursively. Each node is an object (line 7) which can be simulated by invoking the SIMULATE method (line 12). Each child receives its ancestor's highest score to check for a *win* or *loss* after performing SINR-EM with the given transmission power $\boldsymbol{P}_T$ and set of users $\mathcal{U}$. Starting with the *root* node, and for a given number of max iterations (*iteration*$_{\max}$), the SIMULATE method is invoked. On the first call to each node's SIMULATE method, we obtain the score after performing SINR-EM and we compare it to the global highest score to keep track of the optimal simulated state (line 16). Then we instantiate each possible child of the current node by decreasing the transmission power of a uniquely selected drone and the score of each child is initiated to the parent achieved score as mentioned previously. Then, we compare the achieved score to the highest ancestor score, $S_{ancestor}$, which is the highest score between the nodes on the path from the parent of the current node to the root. In the case of a *win* (line 26) we return the achieved score; in the case of a *loss* we return 0. If it is not the first simulation of the node or no *win* or *loss* occurred we proceed by selecting a child of the current node according to the UCB policy (see (27)) and invoking its SIMULATE method. Whenever a positive score resulting from a win is back-propagated from the child simulation the parent node updates its score according to (26).

5.3   Time-Based Updates

Assuming that DBSs are deployed to serve non-stationary users, the mobility of drones can be utilized to adapt to the movement of users and periodically update the locations of DBSs so that the overall performance of the system is improved. Instead of initializing the TP-MCTS tree at each update interval and performing a substantial number of iterations to approach the optimal solution, we can make use of the experience embedded in the current tree structure. To proceed further we make the following assumption: after a duration of t_{update}, the new optimal solution lies in the vicinity of the previously found solution. That is if t_{update} is small enough relative to the speed of movement of users, then the existing branches weights (scores) can still be utilized to guide the search to the next optimal solution, and last winning node can possibly serve as a good starting point for the next search. Accordingly, after each t_{update} we reset the *simulated* attribute of each node so that when a previously simulated node is selected, EM-SINR will be performed again for the current users' distribution and the node's score is updated accordingly. The *visits* count is also reset for all nodes. Furthermore, consider that the previously winning node is given by $node_{\text{win}}$, then after simulating this node and the *root* node again we compare

---

Algorithm 2. Transmission Power Monte Carlo Tree Search.

Input: $\mathcal{U}$, M, $P_{\max}$, P_Δ,
Output: P_T, $\boldsymbol{\mu} = [\mu_1, \mu_2, .., \mu_M]$
 1: $root \leftarrow \text{NODE}([P_{\max}, .., P_{\max}], 0)$
 2: $S_{max} \leftarrow 0$
 3: $P_{best} \leftarrow [P_{\max}, .., P_{\max}]$
 4: **for** $iteration < iteration_{max}$ **do**
 5:      $root.\text{SIMULATE}(0, \mathcal{U})$
 6: **end for**

```
7:  object NODE(P_T, S_parent)
8:      visits ← 0
9:      simulated ← false
10:     childs ← { }
11:     S ← S_parent
12:     function SIMULATE(S_ancestor, U)
13:         if simulated = false then
14:             perform SINR-EM (see Algorithm 1).
15:             S = obtain node score according to (25).
16:             if S > S_max then
17:                 S_max ← S
18:                 P_best ← P_T
19:             end if
20:             for i ← 1, M do
21:                 P_{T_child} ← P_T
22:                 P_{T_child,i} ← P_{T_child,i} − P_Δ
23:                 childs ← {childs, NODE(P_{T_child}, S)}
24:             end for
25:             simulated ← true
26:             if S > S_ancestor then return S          ▷ win occurred
27:             else if S < S_ancestor then return 0      ▷ loss occurred
28:             end if
29:         end if
30:         visits ← visits + 1
31:         child ← child with highest UCB value obtained according to (27)
32:         result ← child.SIMULATE(max{S, S_parent}, U)
33:         if result > 0 then update score according to (26)    ▷ update if win
34:         end if
35:         return result
36:     end function
37: end object
```

the achieved scores and select the node with the highest score as the current root to search from. We call this *best root selection* (BRS) (see Algorithm 3).

6 Simulation and Discussions

In this work we perform two sets of simulations each against a different baseline method and with different environment settings:

1. **Scenario 1:** Through extensive simulations, we compare the results achieved by TP-MCTS to the results of a popular PSO-based solution mentioned in [6] for uniformly distributed users.
2. **Scenario 2:** Using the random way-point mobility model (RWP) [7], we simulate TP-MCTS against the baseline settings in which DBSs are randomly distributed. On the other hand, TP-MCTS updates the location of drones every t_{update} seconds in accordance with Subsect. 5.3.

Algorithm 3. TP-MCTS with best root selection.
___
Input: $\mathcal{U}$, M, $P_{\max}$, P_Δ,
Output: P_T, $\mu = [\mu_1, \mu_2, .., \mu_M]$
1: Perform TP-MCTS as defined in Algorithm 2.
2: At every $t = Nt_{\text{update}}$ s.t. $N \in \{1, 2, 3..\}$
3:     Set *visits* $\leftarrow 0$, *simulated* $\leftarrow$ *false* for all nodes.
4:     $node_{\text{win}} \leftarrow$ the node with highest score so far.
5:     $root$.SIMULATE$(0, \mathcal{U})$
6:     $node_{\text{win}}$.SIMULATE$(0, \mathcal{U})$
7:     **if** $node_{\text{win}}.score > root.score$ **then**
8:         **for** $iteration < iteration_{\max}$ **do**
9:             $node_{\text{win}}$.SIMULATE$(0, \mathcal{U})$
10:        **end for**
11:    **else**
12:        **for** $iteration < iteration_{max}$ **do**
13:            $root$.SIMULATE$(0, \mathcal{U})$
14:        **end for**
15:    **end if**
___

In both cases, we discuss the results and deduce insights into the trade-off between different deployment parameters such as transmission power settings, users' quality of service, number of DBSs, and the achieved energy efficiency. Also, in both cases, given the required rate, R, for users and the capacity of DBS, $C_{\text{BS}} = B_D \times \gamma$ where γ is the system average spectral efficiency, the maximum number of users per DBS can be obtained as

$$U_{max} = \left\lfloor \frac{C_{\text{BS}}}{R} \right\rfloor. \tag{28}$$

6.1 Scenario 1 (PSO)

Simulation Settings (PSO). In this work we compare the results of the aforementioned PSO solution to our TP-MCTS algorithm assuming an area of 1 km × 1 km with 500 users. We simulate using different numbers of serving DBSs, beginning with the minimum number estimated by dividing the total number of users by the maximum number of users per DBS obtained in (28). Also, we vary the SINR requirement of Γ_{th}. The maximum number of iterations is limited to $I = 200$. Table 1 lists the simulation parameters. The PSO-related parameters are listed in Table 1(c) using the same notations as in [6]. ϕ (also called the inertia weight) is set as a linearly decreasing weight (LDW) [24] obtained as $\phi = \phi_{\max} - \frac{\phi_{\max} - \phi_{\min}}{I} i$, where i is the current iteration count, and ϕ_1 and ϕ_2 are randomly drawn uniformly from the specified ranges.

Table 1. (a) System parameters, (b) TP-MCTS parameters, (C) PSO parameters.

(a)

Parameter	Value
Number of users U	500
Path loss parameters α, β, η_{LOS}, and η_{NLOS}	9.61, 0.16, 1 dB, and 20 dB
Carrier frequency f_c and drone bandwidth B_D	2 GHz and 20 MHz
Noise power σ_0^2, required rate R, and spectral efficiency γ	-110 dBm, 1 Mbps, and 2 bps/Hz
Link reliability Φ and SINR threshold Γ_{th}	0.95 and -2/ 0 dB

(b)

Parameter	Value
Softmax scale C and dropout SINR difference S_{th}	4 and 0.5
Drone height h and exploration constant K	70 and 0.01
Power step P_Δ and maximum power P_{max}	100 mW and 500 mW

(c)

Parameter	Value
ϕ_{min}, ϕ_{max}, c_1, and c_2	0.9, 0.95, 0.095, and 0.15
ϕ_1 and ϕ_2	$\in [0.8\ 1.8]$

Number of Served Users (N_{SU}). Figure 4 shows the value of N_{SU} per iteration achieved by each algorithm for different numbers of serving DBSs, M, and two different conditions of Γ_{th}. In Fig. 4a it can be observed that for $M = 14$ and $M = 15$ the PSO solution was, on average, not able to provide the required $N_{th} = 475$ (indicated by the straight line). On the other hand, it appears that clustering users using EM-SINR without power control did already satisfy the requirement and TP-MCTS changes the transmission power of DBSs in such way that N_{SU} is rather decreased while optimizing for the achieved energy efficiency ζ (see (25)). Additionally, Fig. 4b plots the results given $\Gamma_{th} = 0$ dB. Evidently, the PSO algorithm was far from finding a solution that satisfies the requirements whereas TP-MCTS was able to find a solution for $M = 14$, and EM-SINR had already satisfied the requirements in the cases of $M = 15$ and $M = 16$.

Energy Efficiency (ζ). For $\Gamma_{th} = -2$ dB, Fig. 5a shows that TP-MCTS is able to substantially improve the energy efficiency by around 575%. Furthermore, increasing the number of DBSs from $M = 14$ to $M = 16$ decreases the total required transmission power which is expected when cells are more dense. We observe that a higher number of DBSs initially results in degraded system performance in terms of ζ but later improves further than the cases with less DBSs as TP-MCTS optimizes the transmission powers.

Transmission Power (P_T). The average transmission power for all DBSs per iteration is plotted in Fig. 6. For the case when $\Gamma_{th} = -2$ dB, TP-MCTS seem to substantially decrease the transmission power of all DBS to almost 100 mW. This improves the interference levels between DBSs as can be deduced from

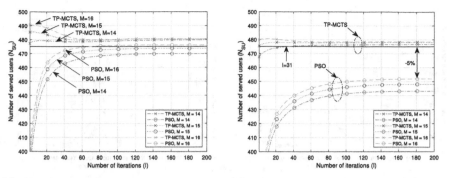

(a) N_{SU} per iteration for $\Gamma_{th} = -2$ dB,(b) N_{SU} per iteration for $\Gamma_{th} = 0$ dB, $N_{th} = N_{th} = 475$ (solid line).   475 (solid line).

Fig. 4. TP-MCTS vs. PSO by N_{SU}. TP-MCTS always achieves the required Γ_{th} and substantially outperforms the PSO solution.

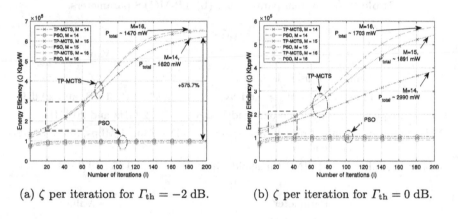

(a) ζ per iteration for $\Gamma_{th} = -2$ dB.   (b) ζ per iteration for $\Gamma_{th} = 0$ dB.

Fig. 5. TP-MCTS vs. PSO by ζ.

previous plots. By examining the results when $M = 16$, we observe that after a substantial number of iterations the average power per DBS is below 100 mW. Since $P_\Delta = 100$ mW (see Table 1) this indicates that TP-MCTS results in completely turning off a DBS by setting its transmission power to zero.

6.2   Scenario 2 (RWP)

Simulation Settings. We simulated the proposed TP-MCTS solution for a moving set of users generated according to the RWP model [7] against the base-line scenario where DBSs are distributed randomly. 200 moving users were considered in an area of 0.5×0.5 Km^2 that are served using 5 or 6 DBSs. TP-MCTS is run every $t_{update} = 5$ seconds for 20 iterations (see Subsect. 5.3). 1000 trials are run and the duration of each simulation trial is 120 seconds (i.e., 120 s of network functioning in real life). Table 2 lists the simulation parameters.

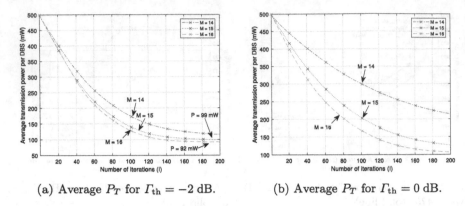

(a) Average P_T for $\Gamma_{\text{th}} = -2$ dB.   (b) Average P_T for $\Gamma_{\text{th}} = 0$ dB.

Fig. 6. Average transmission power per DBS. Increasing the number of DBSs allows less transmission power per DBS.

Table 2. (a) System parameters, (b) TP-MCTS parameters.

(a)

Parameter	Value
Number of users U	200
Path loss parameters α, β, η_{LOS}, and η_{NLOS}	9.61, 0.16, 1 dB, and 20 dB
Carrier frequency f_c and drone bandwidth B_D	2 GHz and 20 MHz
Noise power σ_0^2, required rate R, and spectral efficiency γ	-110 dBm, 1 Mbps, and 2 bps/Hz
Link reliability Φ and SINR threshold Γ_{th}	0.95 and 0 dB

(b)

Parameter	Value
Softmax scale C and dropout SINR difference S_{th}	4 and 0.5
Drone height h and exploration constant K	70 and 0.01
Power step P_Δ and maximum power $P_{\max}$	100 mW and 500 mW
t_{update} and number of iterations	5 s and 20

Number of Served Users (N_{SU}). Figure 7a shows the achieved N_{SU} for 5 and 6 serving DBSs. The random approach achieves a constant performance on average whereas TP-MCTS performance seems to decay between update intervals, and increases up to a maximum value after every update. TP-MCTS seems to also preserve a steady performance which means that the tree is indeed able to adapt to the new users' locations and find new solutions. Figure 7b shows the average achieved ζ for 5 and 6 serving DBSs along with using the random distribution approach versus TP-MCTS. Clearly, when adding an extra DBS the achieved energy efficiency decreases, but in TP-MCTS it can be intelligently deployed to improve the performance of the system. Figure 7c plots ζ per second obtained using TP-MCTS with and without best root selection. The improvement resulting from using BRS is evident. The lack of such improvement in the case of no BRS is expected for a low iterations number of 20 since the tree search would never reach deep states that sufficiently reduce the transmission powers of DBSs.

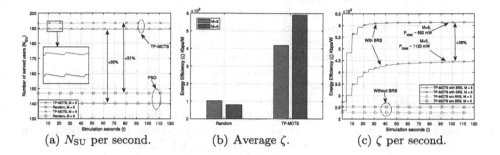

(a) N_{SU} per second.   (b) Average ζ.   (c) ζ per second.

Fig. 7. Results for the second simulation scenario.

Collision Avoidance. In support of the arguments mentioned in Subsect. 4.4 we measured the minimum distance that occurred between any DBSs during all trials. In the case of $M = 5$, the minimum distance recorded was 119.5 m, whereas for $M = 6$ the minimum distance was 107 m (see Fig. 8).

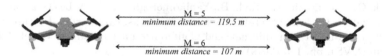

Fig. 8. Minimum distance between any two DBSs during simulation.

7 Conclusions

We showed that TP-MCTS outperformed the other baseline methods in terms of link reliability and energy efficiency. TP-MCTS is flexible and can optimize for whatever goals we set by defining the score appropriately. For example, the score given by (25) can be modified to include the system spectral efficiency instead of ζ depending on the design requirements. Also, simulations showed that TP-MCTS can remove redundant DBSs by setting their transmission power to zero. Furthermore, our results proved that intelligent densification of cells can improve the system performance if properly managed. Finally, we showed that TP-MCTS can utilize its tree history to guide the search towards more promising nodes.

References

1. Mozaffari, M., Saad, W., Bennis, M., Nam, Y.-H., Debbah, M.: A tutorial on UAVs for wireless networks: applications, challenges, and open problems. IEEE Commun. Surv. Tutor. **21**(3), 2334–2360 (2019)
2. Zeng, Y., Zhang, R., Lim, T.J.: Wireless communications with unmanned aerial vehicles: opportunities and challenges. IEEE Commun. Mag. **54**(5), 36–42 (2016)
3. Osseiran, A., et al.: Scenarios for 5G mobile and wireless communications: the vision of the metis project. IEEE Commun. Mag. **52**(5), 26–35 (2014)
4. Liu, X., Ansari, N.: Resource allocation in UAV-assisted M2M communications for disaster rescue. IEEE Wirel. Commun. Lett. **8**(2), 580–583 (2019)
5. Gu, Z., Zhang, J., Sun, X., Ji, Y.: Optimizing networked flying platform deployment and access point association in FSO-based fronthaul networks. IEEE Wirel. Commun. Lett. **9**(8), 1221–1225 (2020)
6. Kalantari, E., Yanikomeroglu, H., Yongacoglu, A.: On the number and 3D placement of drone base stations in wireless cellular networks. In: 2016 IEEE 84th Vehicular Technology Conference (VTC-Fall), pp. 1–6 (2016)
7. Bettstetter, C., Resta, G., Santi, P.: The node distribution of the random waypoint mobility model for wireless ad hoc networks. IEEE Trans. Mob. Comput. **2**(3), 257–269 (2003)
8. Hayat, S., Yanmaz, E., Muzaffar, R.: Survey on unmanned aerial vehicle networks for civil applications: a communications viewpoint. IEEE Commun. Surv. Tutor. **18**(4), 2624–2661 (2016)
9. Fotouhi, A., Qiang, H., Ding, M., Hassan, M., Giordano, L.G., Garcia-Rodriguez, A., Yuan, J.: Survey on UAV cellular communications: practical aspects, standardization advancements, regulation, and security challenges. IEEE Commun. Surv. Tutor. **21**(4), 3417–3442 (2019)
10. Cicek, C.T., Gultekin, H., Tavli, B., Yanikomeroglu, H.: UAV base station location optimization for next generation wireless networks: overview and future research directions. In: 2019 1st International Conference on Unmanned Vehicle Systems-Oman (UVS), pp. 1–6 (2019)
11. Alzenad, M., El-Keyi, A., Lagum, F., Yanikomeroglu, H.: 3-D placement of an unmanned aerial vehicle base station (UAV-BS) for energy-efficient maximal coverage. IEEE Wirel. Commun. Lett. **6**(4), 434–437 (2017)
12. Alzenad, M., El-Keyi, A., Yanikomeroglu, H.: 3-D placement of an unmanned aerial vehicle base station for maximum coverage of users with different QoS requirements. IEEE Wirel. Commun. Lett. **7**(1), 38–41 (2018)
13. Al-Hourani, A., Kandeepan, S., Lardner, S.: Optimal lap altitude for maximum coverage. IEEE Wirel. Commun. Lett. **3**(6), 569–572 (2014)
14. Kalantari, E., Shakir, M.Z., Yanikomeroglu, H., Yongacoglu, A.: Backhaul-aware robust 3D drone placement in 5G+ wireless networks. In: IEEE International Conference on Communications Workshops (ICC Workshops) 2017, pp. 109–114 (2017)
15. Lyu, J., Zeng, Y., Zhang, R., Lim, T.J.: Placement optimization of UAV-mounted mobile base stations. IEEE Commun. Lett. **21**(3), 604–607 (2017)
16. Abeywickrama, H.V., He, Y., Dutkiewicz, E., Jayawickrama, B.A., Mueck, M.: A reinforcement learning approach for fair user coverage using UAV mounted base stations under energy constraints. IEEE Open J. Veh. Technol. **1**, 67–81 (2020)
17. Qiu, J., Lyu, J., Fu, L.: Placement optimization of aerial base stations with deep reinforcement learning. In: ICC 2020–2020 IEEE International Conference on Communications (ICC), pp. 1–6 (2020)

18. Liu, C.H., Chen, Z., Tang, J., Xu, J., Piao, C.: Energy-efficient UAV control for effective and fair communication coverage: a deep reinforcement learning approach. IEEE J. Sel. Areas Commun. **36**(9), 2059–2070 (2018)

19. Huang, H., Savkin, A.V.: A method for optimized deployment of unmanned aerial vehicles for maximum coverage and minimum interference in cellular networks. IEEE Trans. Industr. Inf. **15**(5), 2638–2647 (2019)

20. Singh, R., Jaakkola, T., Mohammad, A.: 6.867 machine learning (2006). MIT OpenCourseWare. https://ocw.mit.edu

21. Abeywickrama, H.V., Jayawickrama, B.A., He, Y., Dutkiewicz, E.: Algorithm for energy efficient inter-UAV collision avoidance. In: 2017 17th International Symposium on Communications and Information Technologies (ISCIT), pp. 1–5 (2017)

22. Browne, C.B., et al.: A survey of Monte Carlo tree search methods. IEEE Trans. Comput. Intell. AI Games **4**(1), 1–43 (2012)

23. Auer, P.: Using upper confidence bounds for online learning. In: Proceedings 41st Annual Symposium on Foundations of Computer Science, pp. 270–279 (2000)

24. He, Y., Ma, W., Zhang, J.: The parameters selection of PSO algorithm influencing on performance of fault diagnosis. In: MATEC Web of Conferences, vol. 63, p. 02019 (2016)

Joint Edge Resource Allocation and Path Planning for Drones with Energy Constraints

Giorgos Polychronis[(✉)] and Spyros Lalis

University of Thessaly, Volos, Greece
{gpolychronis,lalis}@uth.gr

Abstract. Several applications use drones as mobile sensors which can fly directly over the points of interest with minimal human intervention. In some cases, the data that is captured at a given point has to be processed before moving to the next one. Even though, in the spirit of edge computing, such computations can be offloaded to nearby servers, this becomes challenging when edge servers have limited resources and drones have limited operational autonomy. In this paper, we propose an algorithm that jointly plans the paths for the drones and allocates the available edge resources between drones in a fair way, while respecting such constraints. We evaluate our algorithm through a wide range of experiments and find that it can significantly reduce the mission times with no offloadings, by up to almost 28% while performing close to the ideal case where offloading is always possible.

Keywords: Drones · Resource allocation · Computation offloading · Path planning · Edge computing

1 Introduction

Aerial unmanned vehicles, also referred to as drones, have become a valuable tool for many different applications. In particular polycopter drones are very popular thanks to their agility and ability to fly/hover, takeoff and land vertically, making it possible to gather data via their onboard sensors in a flexible way.

In this work, we focus on applications where the drone has to visit specific points of interest, take measurements using its onboard sensors, and perform some computation on the data. We assume that each computation must be performed in situ, before moving to the next point of interest. For instance, it may be desirable to take some special action depending on the result of the computation. For heavyweight computations, the overall mission time can be reduced,

This research has been co-financed by the European Union and Greek national funds through the Operational Program Competitiveness, Entrepreneurship and Innovation, under the call RESEARCH - CREATE - INNOVATE, project PV-Auto-Scout, code T1EDK-02435.

S. Longfei and P. Bodhi (Eds.): MobiQuitous 2022, LNICST 492, pp. 378–399, 2023.
https://doi.org/10.1007/978-3-031-34776-4_20

significantly, by exploiting edge servers located near the points of interest. However, this may not always be possible if several drones wish to use the same servers at the same time, in which case it is important to allocate the available server resources among the competing drones in a fair way.

Another challenge, which affects such resource allocation decisions, is the typically limited operational autonomy of small drones that run on batteries. In the general case, this is not sufficient to conduct large missions, especially ones that may involve time-consuming processing as discussed above. Therefore, drones need to perform one or more intermediate stops to switch batteries before they can proceed to execute the rest of the mission.

We tackle the problem in a holistic way, by jointly building paths that can be safely followed by the drones despite their energy constraints and fairly allocating the available edge resources so that the mission time of each drone is fairly reduced with respect to others. The main contributions of our work are: (i) we capture the above problem in a formal way; (ii) we propose an algorithm that builds paths under energy constraints while at the same time making a fair allocation of the edge resources among drones so that they evenly reduce their mission time; (iii) we evaluate the performance and robustness of the proposed algorithm for different battery switching delays and degrees of autonomy, showing that it can reduce the mission times with no offloadings, by up to almost 28% while performing close to the ideal case where offloading is always possible.

The rest of the paper is structured as follows. Section 2 discusses related work. Section 3 provides a formal description of the system model and problem. Section 4 presents the proposed algorithm, which is evaluated in Sect. 5. Finally Sect. 6 concludes the paper.

2 Related Work

Various works explore the efficient offloading of a task from nodes to more powerful computing infrastructures. In [7], the authors deal with the problem where a drone has to stop at predefined waypoints and perform heavyweight computations. To reduce the mission time, instead of performing the computation onboard, the drone opportunistically offloads its computations when it is in range of an edge server and the expected computation time is better than the local one. Another work that studies dynamic offloading decisions is [9], where a drone-based system is used for tracking moving objects. The authors try to minimize the response time by deciding whether to offload a computation or execute it on the drone locally. The authors of [5], propose a scheme for deciding the offloading of computations at the edge or the cloud. In [17], the main idea is to offload tasks that require intensive computations to the cloud, and communication-heavy tasks to the fog. In both cases, tasks are prioritized following an earliest deadline first (EDF) policy. The authors of [6] propose an algorithm for offloading decisions and resource allocation for multiple UAVs. Their goal is to minimize the average service latency.

As a key difference with the above, our work jointly addresses computation offloading and path planning. Also, we allocate the edge resources among drones to evenly reduce their mission time, instead of (just) minimizing service latency.

In many works, drones are used as edge nodes that serve mobile users. Such a problem is studied in [19] where a UAV is used as a base station for providing video content to multiple users. The objective is to plan the trajectory of the drone and the associated resource allocation to provide the required QoS and minimize the drone's operation time. In [18] the authors investigate a problem where mobile IoT devices offload their computation to a UAV. The goal is to make decisions about the offloading, resource allocation and UAV trajectory, so that the overall energy needed for the IoT devices to complete their tasks is minimized. Both works follow a similar algorithmic approach, which is to split the problem in smaller sub-problems that are solved iteratively until the value of the optimization criterion converges. In [20], a UAV is used by multiple mobile devices to offload their tasks, with the goal to minimize the average weighted energy consumption of the UAV and the mobile devices, by optimizing the trajectory of the UAV, the allocations of computation resources and the offloading decisions. [2] investigates a similar problem, for a UAV that is used to serve vehicles in a highway. The authors of [3] study the use of multiple drones for serving IoT devices. In this case, the problem is to optimize the number of drones, their association with specific locations so as to best serve the devices and the drone paths.

Unlike the above works that consider drones as mobile servers, in our case the drones are the clients that need to offload their tasks to stationary edge servers. From a high-level algorithmic perspective, we employ a similar approach to some of these efforts. Namely, our algorithm also separates the path optimization and the resource allocation dimension and deals with each problem separately, while optimizing the joint solution in an iterative way.

There is a large body of work targeting different path planning problems for drones, also considering their energy constraints. We briefly discuss some indicative efforts. In [4], multiple drones are controlled by different ground stations in order to perform a set of tasks under certain constraints, such as fuel tank capacity and maximum number of drones served per ground station, while optimizing various objectives, like the total fuel consumption, the number of drones used and the total travel distance and mission time. The authors of [13] consider drones carrying supplies to different locations after a disaster incident. Apart from the energy constraints, drones have payload limitations and must return to depot stations to reload. The goal is to minimize the total distance, time or cost of the routes while supplying the target locations giving priority to the ones with the greater needs. A dynamic pickup and delivery problem is studied in [10] for drones that can switch batteries at depot stations, with the objective to produce safe flight plans that minimize delivery time and unnecessary aerial movement.

Similar to the above works, we propose a path-planning heuristic for drones with energy constraints. However, the main difference is that we do this in tandem with resource allocation at the edge so that drones can exploit the available servers in order to perform the required computations faster and perhaps even save some intermediate depot visits, leading to a reduced mission time.

Another well studied topic are mobile wireless sensor networks (WSNs). In these scenarios, the aspect of mobility concerns the sinks and/or sensors of the WSN [16]. The case of mobile sinks is more similar to our problem, especially regarding the planning of their movement inside or around the sensor network. A survey of such work is given in [8]. The main difference between mobile WSNs and our work is the key objective. Mobile WSNs typically focus in prolonging the lifetime of the system, improving the coverage or reducing the data delivery latency. In contrast, our work focuses on the exploitation of edge computing to accelerate processing and minimize the mission time in a fair way for all drones.

3   System Model and Problem Formulation

3.1   Drones, Paths and Flight Model

Let there be M drones, $d_m, 1 \leq m \leq M$. Each drone is assigned an independent mission, in which it must visit a set of waypoints $\mathcal{V}_m$. These waypoints represent points of interest where the drone has to perform some sensing and then process the collected data on the spot, e.g., to take further action if a problem is detected.

To visit the points of interest assigned to it, each drone d_m follows a path P_m, which is encoded as a sequence $P_m[i], 1 \leq i \leq \text{len}(P_m)$. The path must include all points of interest exactly once, $\exists! i : 1 \leq i \leq \text{len}(P_m) : P_m[i] = p, \forall p \in \mathcal{V}_m$. Also, each drone d_m initially starts its mission by taking off from a depot dep_m, and ends its mission by returning and landing at dep_m. We encode this in the drone's path by letting $P_m[1] = P_m[\text{len}(P_m)] = dep_m$. Without loss of generality, we assume the depot does not coincide with a point of interest, i.e., $dep_m \notin \mathcal{V}_m$. As will be discussed in the sequel, a drone may perform additional depot visits in order to switch batteries. Such intermediate depot visits, also referred to as depot detours, are explicitly encoded in the drone's path by inserting the depot as an intermediate waypoint.

Our flight model assumes polycopter drones, which have vertical take-off and landing capability, can fly between waypoints in a straight line, and can hover over a given position. Let $flyhT_m^{i,i+1}$ be the time that is needed for d_m to fly horizontally between $P_m[i]$ and $P_m[i+1]$. Further, let $takeoffT_m$ be the time needed for d_m to take-off from dep_m and reach the flight altitude for the mission at hand, and let $landT_m$ be the time needed to vertically land back at dep_m. These extra overheads are taken into account to derive the total flight delay between two successive waypoints in the drone's path, as follows:

$$flyT_m^{i,i+1} = \begin{cases} flyhT_m^{i,i+1}, & \text{if} P_m[i], P_m[i+1] \neq dep_m \\ flyhT_m^{i,i+1} + takeoffT_m, & \text{if} P_m[i] = dep_m \\ flyhT_m^{i,i+1} + landT_m, & \text{if} P_m[i+1] = dep_m \end{cases} \tag{1}$$

Note that the case where $P_m[i] = P_m[i+1] = dep_m$ is not handled above. This would mean that the drone takes-off from the depot only to immediately land back there, which cannot hold in a properly formed flight plan.

3.2   Sensing and Computation

At each point of interest, the drone takes some measurements via its onboard sensors, and then processes this data. We assume that each drone performs the same type of sensing and data processing at all points of interest. However, different drones may perform different types of sensing and data processing. Also, we assume that data processing needs to be performed in situ, while the drone is positioned over the point of interest, before moving to the next waypoint.

Let $senseT_m$ be the time that is needed for d_m to perform the required sensing. Also, let $comp_m$ be the type of computation that needs to be performed on this data, taking $data_m^{in}$ amount of data as input and returning $data_m^{out}$ amount of data as a result. Notably, the type of computation determines the amount of resources res_m^{req} needed to run the computation on a computing platform.

Onboard Computation. Each drone d_m has an onboard computer with hardware platform hw_m, which can be used to perform $comp_m$ locally. In order for the drone to be truly autonomous, its onboard platform has sufficient available resources to run the computation in question, $res_m^{avl} \geq res_m^{req}$. In this case, we assume that (local) data movement for $data_m^{in}$ and $data_m^{out}$ takes a negligible amount of time. Thus the total computation delay when processing is performed locally on the drone is $compT_m = procT(comp_m, hw_m)$.

Computation Offloading. As another option, the drone can offload its computation to a nearby server located at the edge in order to accelerate processing and reduce the mission time. We assume that each edge server is suitably prepared to provide such a computation as a service. For instance, the respective software can be packaged and shipped to the servers in the form of micro-VMs or containers, before the drones start their missions.

Let there be K edge servers, $s_k, 1 \leq k \leq K$, at different locations in the wider area where the drones operate. Each server s_k may have a different hardware platform hw_k with available computing resources res_k^{avl}. Also, each server is accessible via a dedicated local wireless network with bandwidth bw_k and communication range $range_k$. When drone d_m visits a point of interest $P_m[i]$ which is in range of server s_k, it can offload its computation $comp_m$ to it. Then, the computation delay for the drone is

$$compT(m, k) = procT(comp_m, hw_k) + \frac{data_m^{in} + data_m^{out}}{bw_k} \tag{2}$$

taking into account the time needed to perform the computation on the server and transfer the respective input and output over the network. For convenience, let $compT(m, 0) = compT_m$ (the server identifier 0 means "no offloading").

Let $S_m[i]$ encode the offloading for d_m during its mission. More specifically, $S_m[i] = k$ if the drone shall offload $comp_m$ to s_k at $P_m[i]$, else $S_m[i] = 0$ if the drone shall perform the computation locally. Also, $S_m[i] = 0$ for $P_m[i] = dep_m$ as the drone does not perform any computation at the depot station.

Note that the drone may not be able to *immediately* offload its computation to $S_m[i]$ as soon as it completes sensing at $P_m[i]$. The reason is that server's resources may be used by other drones at that time. It is, however, possible for the drone to wait for the server to become available, and then proceed with the offloading process as usual. Let the extra waiting time for this be $W_m[i] \geq 0$. We let $W_m[i] = 0$ for all waypoints where $S_m[i] = 0$ and the drone does not use any server for offloading.

Based on the above, the time spent by the drone in order to perform the necessary sensing and computation at each point of interest $P_m[i] \in V_m$, is

$$pT_m^i = senseT_m + W_m[i] + compT(m, S_m[i]) \tag{3}$$

Server Resource Usage Constraint. Let matrix U encode the planned usage of the server infrastructure, where $U[k][m][t] = 1$ if s_k allocates resources to run the service for $comp_m$ at time t, else $U[k][m][t] = 0$. Note that the total amount of resources allocated on a server due to offloading cannot exceed its overall resource capacity:

$$res_k^{avl} \geq \sum_{m=1}^{M} U[k][m][t] \times res_m^{req}, \forall k, t \tag{4}$$

We assume that the resources res_m^{req} associated with the service for performing $comp_m$, remain allocated only while the service is actually being used by a drone. More specifically, if d_m starts offloading its computation to s_k at time t_{start}, it will consume resources during the entire duration of the computation including the required input/output data transfers, $U[k][m][t] = 1, t_{start} \leq t \leq t_{start} + compT(m, k)$. Notably, we assume that an edge server cannot further offload a computation to another edge server or the cloud.

3.3 Energy Model

We assume battery-operated drones (however, our model can be equally applied to drones with an engine and a fuel tank). Let E_m^{max} be the maximum energy storage capacity of d_m's battery. Obviously, bigger values of E_m^{max} translate to larger autonomy, allowing the drone to operate for a longer amount of time before it needs to land.

Let the energy that is consumed by d_m to fly between two waypoints $P[i]$ and $P[i+1]$ be a linear function of flight time, $flyE_m^{i,i+1} = \beta_m \times flyT_m^{i,i+1}$. In the same spirit, the energy consumed by the drone to hover above $P[i]$ is a linear function of the time spent at that point in order to perform the required sensing and computing task, $pE_m^i = \gamma_m \times pT_m^i$. We consider the energy spent for onboard computation or the communication with a server to be negligible compared to the energy spent for hovering. Also, for polycopter drones flying at moderate speeds, we assume that $\beta_m \approx \gamma_m$, i.e., the energy spent for flying is comparable to the energy spent for hovering.

Safety Constraint. Let $remE_m^i$ denote the remaining energy of d_m at $P_m[i]$, after sensing and processing. Initially, $remE_m^1 = E_m^{max}$ as every drone starts from its depot with full batteries. The remaining energy at the next point in the drone's path is equal to the energy that was available at the previous point less the energy spent to fly to the next waypoint and the energy spent there (to hover while performing the required sensing and processing):

$$remE_m^{i+1} = remE_m^i - flyE_m^{i,i+1} - pE_m^{i+1} \tag{5}$$

Note that it is crucial to build flight paths and make offloading decisions so that the bellow equation holds:

$$remE_m^i > 0, \forall i, m \tag{6}$$

This constraint states that at no point during the execution of the mission should a drone deplete its batteries. Such an event would lead to an emergency landing, which is not only undesirable from a purely operational perspective but may also lead to material damages or even injuries, depending on the area of operation.

Depot Detours. To satisfy the above constraint, drones with limited autonomy or long missions may have to perform intermediate depot visits (detours) in order to switch batteries so that they can proceed with the rest of their mission. Let $depT_m$ denote the time it takes for d_m to switch batteries once it has landed at its depot dep_m. Taking this into account, we extend Eq. 3 to redefine the time spent at each point in the drone's path as

$$pT_m^i = \begin{cases} senseT_m + W_m[i] + compT(m, S_m[i]), & \text{if } P_m[i] \neq dep_m \\ depT_m, & \text{if } P_m[i] = dep_m \wedge 1 < i < len(P_m) \\ 0, & \text{otherwise} \end{cases} \tag{7}$$

The first case captures the time spent at points of interest (all waypoints that do not represent a depot visit), as per Eq. 3. The second case captures the time spent at a depot to switch the drone's batteries before it can continue its mission. If, however, the drone is at its depot in the beginning and end of its path, the third case applies, setting the time spent at the depot to 0. This is because each drone starts its mission with fully charged batteries and the mission is considered to be completed the moment the drone lands at its depot for the last time (the battery switch time after the mission's completion does count in the actual mission time).

In the same vein, we re-define the energy spent at each point in the path as

$$pE_m^i = \begin{cases} \gamma_m \times pT_m^i, & \text{if } P_m[i] \neq dep_m \\ -E_m^{max} + remE_m^{i-1} - flyE_m^{i-1,i}, & \text{if } P_m[i] = dep_m \wedge remE_m^{i-1} - flyE_m^{i-1,i} > 0 \\ 0, & \text{otherwise} \end{cases} \tag{8}$$

The first case applies to all points of interest, as already discussed above. The battery switching at the depot is captured by the second case, which sets the energy spent to a *negative* value so that the remaining energy of the drone $remE_m^i$ after a successful depot visit is equal to E_m^{max} as per Eq. 5. Note, however, that this artificial correction is allowed only if the drone has sufficient energy to reach the depot in the first place, as ensured by the second term of the condition for this case. Else, the third case of the above equation applies, which sets the energy spent at the depot to 0 so that $remE_m^i \leq 0$ as per Eq. 5, indicating that the drone will deplete its batteries before reaching the depot. As already stressed, this should never be the case in a properly planned mission.

3.4 Problem

Given the above, the time needed for d_m to complete its entire mission can be captured as:

$$mT_m = \sum_{i=1}^{len(P_m)-1} flyT_m^{i,i+1} + pT_m^{i+1} \tag{9}$$

Our goal is to exploit the available edge server infrastructure in order to reduce the mission time of all drones. More specifically, the problem we tackle in this work is the following:

Given drones $d_m, 1 \leq m \leq M$ with assigned points of interest $\mathcal{V}_m$ where they have to perform some sensing and data processing, and stationary servers $s_k, 1 \leq k \leq K$ located in the mission area, which can be used for offloading the drones' computations, produce paths P_m and offloading plans S_m that minimize mT_m (as per Eq. 9) *in a fair way for all drones*, while ensuring that the constraints of Eq. 4 and Eq. 6 are satisfied.

We capture the fairness objective by using as a reference the makespan of a default path P_m^{def} that does not involve any computation offloading. The corresponding mission time mT_m^{def} can be computed as per Eq. 9 for a special "empty" offloading schedule S^{def} where $S_m^{def}[i] = 0, 1 \leq i \leq len(P_m^{def})$. Based on this reference, we set as the optimization target

$$\text{maximize } min_{m=1}^{M}(\frac{mT_m^{def} - mT_m}{mT_m^{def}}) \tag{10}$$

In other words, we wish to maximize, across all drones, the relative reduction of their mission time, using the available server infrastructure for offloading. The rationale is for all concurrently running missions to benefit from the shared server resources in an even way.

We assume that the drone's maximum battery capacity E_m^{max} is sufficient so that d_m can move from its depot dep_m (starting with full batteries) to any point of interest $P_m[i]$ and back to dep_m even if the computation at that point is performed locally on the drone. This is to ensure that the problem always has a feasible solution irrespective of the points of interest assigned to each drone and the degree of contention among drones for the shared server resources.

4   Algorithm

Since the classic vehicle routing problem (VRP) is NP-hard, the above (more complex) problem is also NP-hard. Therefore, obtaining an exact solution for large instances of the problem would be too time consuming, even for an offline algorithm.

4.1   Overview

To tackle the above problem in reasonable time, we propose an energy-aware path planning and offload scheduling heuristic (EPPOS). The heuristic works in the spirit of a variable neighborhood search (VNS) algorithm [12], gradually improving the best solution found so far by exploring neighbouring solutions through random search. In our case, the solution consists of (a) the paths to be followed by the drones and (b) the schedule for offloading their computations to nearby edge servers. In turn, the offloading schedule is produced based on the expected computation time at each point of interest in the drone's path, and the so-called candidate selection order in which the drones are examined to find the next best possible offloading option. The latter is encoded as a sequence of drone identifiers, e.g. $[1, 2, 3.., 1, 2, 3..]$ means that the algorithm will first plan the next offloading option for drone d_1, then for d_2, then for d_3 etc. Note that the same identifier may appear more than once in this sequence, each such occurrence dictating when the algorithm will plan the next offload for that drone with respect to others.

4.2   Description

The high-level logic of the heuristic is given in Algorithm 1 while the main auxiliary functions are described in Algorithm 2. The algorithm takes as input the set of drones $\mathcal{D}$, an initial path P_m^{init} for each drone d_m (computed using an off-the-shelf TSP algorithm without considering energy constraints or computation offloading options), and the number of iterations of the optimization loop.

As a first step, it computes the default path P_m^{def} for each d_m by adjusting P_m^{init} so that it becomes fully safe assuming that all computations will be performed locally on the drone. More specifically, intermediate depot visits (detours) are inserted in the path to ensure that every hop can be performed based on the drone's battery level at each point, as per Eq. 6. Further, for each drone d_m, the expected time spent at each point of interest $pT_m^{exp}[i]$ is set equal to the sensing time $senseT_m$ plus the average computation time over all servers in range of $P_m[i]$ and the local computation at d_m (assuming that each option is equally probable and that d_m will not have to wait before starting the computation for that point of interest). As a last initialization step, the candidate selection order is set to a randomly chosen round-robin order.

Then the algorithm iteratively improves the paths and offloading schedule. Each iteration starts by resetting the path P_m of each d_m to P_m^{init} and adjusting these paths based on the expected times pT_m^{exp} spent at each point of interest, via function ADJUSTPATHS(). More specifically, if the expected remaining energy of d_m does not suffice to reach all points of interest, its path P_m is considered unsafe and one or more intermediate depot visits (detours) are inserted at the proper points in order to switch batteries. This is done by finding the next waypoint in the path that cannot be reached because the drone will have exhausted its battery, and then checking the previous waypoints in the path (up to the last depot visit) to insert a detour between two waypoints so as to minimize the extra

---

Algorithm 1. Energy-aware path planning and offload scheduling (EPPOS)

---

function MAIN($\mathcal{D}, P^{init}, iterations$)
    for each $d_m \in \mathcal{D}$ **do**
        $P_m^{def} \leftarrow$ calcSafePath(P_m^{init})
        for each $P_m[i] \neq dep_m$ **do**
            $pT_m^{exp}[i] \leftarrow senseT_m + \text{avg}(compT(m,k)), \forall s_k$ in range of $P_m[i]$ and $k = 0$
        end for
    end for
    $order \leftarrow rndRoundRobinOrder(\mathcal{D})$
    $bestMinReduction \leftarrow -1$

    for $iterations$ **do**
        $P \leftarrow$ ADJUSTPATHS($\mathcal{D}, P^{init}, pT^{exp}$)
        $P, S, W, U, reductions \leftarrow$ SCHEDULEOFFLOADING($\mathcal{D}, P, pT^{exp}, order$)
        $minReduction \leftarrow \min(reductions)$
        if $minReduction > bestMinReduction$ **then**
            $bestMinReduction \leftarrow minReduction$
            $bestP, bestS, bestW, bestU \leftarrow P, S, W, U$
            $bestOrder, bestpT^{exp} \leftarrow order, pT^{exp}$
        end if
        $order \leftarrow$ SHAKEORDER($bestOrder, reductions$)
        $pT^{exp} \leftarrow$ ADAPTEXPTIMES($bestpT^{exp}$)
    end for
end function

function ADJUSTPATHS($\mathcal{D}, P, pT^{exp}$)
    for each $d_m \in \mathcal{D}$ **do**
        if isUnsafe(d_m, P_m, pT_m^{exp}) **then**
            insertDepotDetours(P_m)
            trySwapReverseSubPaths(P_m)   ▷ if this reduces contention
        else
            tryReversePath(P_m)   ▷ if this reduces contention
        end if
    end for
    return P
end function

Algorithm 2. Auxiliary functions

---

function SCHEDULEOFFLOADING($\mathcal{D}, P, pT^{exp}, order$)
 for each $d_m \in \mathcal{D}$ **do**
  $pos_m, remE_m^1 \leftarrow 1, E_m^{max}$ $\triangleright$ start from $P_m[1] = dep_m$ with full batteries
  $S_m[i] = 0, W_m[i] = 0, 1 \leq i \leq len(P_m)$ $\triangleright$ no offloading / waiting times yet
  $U[k][m][t] \leftarrow 0, \forall k, t$ $\triangleright$ no server reservations yet
 end for
 while $order \neq \emptyset$ **do**
  $d_m \leftarrow$ pickNxtDrone($order$)
  $pos_m, P_m, k, t^{arr}, waitT \leftarrow$ fndNxtOffload($pos_m, P_m, pT^{exp}, S, W, U$)
  if $pos_m \neq len(P_m)$ **then** $\triangleright$ offload option found
   $S_m[pos_m], W_m[pos_m] \leftarrow k, waitT$
   $U[k][m][t] \leftarrow 1, \forall t, t^{arr} + waitT \leq t \leq t^{arr} + waitT + compT(m, k)$
  else $\triangleright$ arrived at the end of the path
   $order \leftarrow$ rmvAllEntries($order, d_m$)
   $reductions_m \leftarrow \frac{mT_m^{def} - mT_m}{mT_m^{def}}$ $\triangleright$ reduction as per Equations 9 and 10
  end if
 end while
 return $P, S, W, U, reductions$
end function

function SHAKEORDER($order, reductions$)
 $moves \leftarrow$ pickRndRange($moves^{low}, moves^{high}$)
 $bestD \leftarrow$ sortDiscendingReductions($reductions, \mathcal{D}$)
 $worstD \leftarrow$ sortAscendingReductions($reductions, \mathcal{D}$)
 for m **from** 1 **to** $moves$ **do**
  $first\_occ \leftarrow$ pickRndRange($first\_occ^{low}, first\_occ^{high}$)
  $order \leftarrow$ moveFirstEntriesToTail($order, bestD[m], first\_occ$)
  $last\_occ \leftarrow$ pickRndRange($last\_occ^{low}, last\_occ^{high}$)
  $order \leftarrow$ moveLastEntriesToHead($order, worstD[m], last\_occ$)
 end for
 if pickRndBinary($prob_{swap}$) = $true$ **then**
  $swaps \leftarrow$ pickRndRange($swaps^{low}, swaps^{high}$)
  for $swaps$ **do**
   $m_1, m_2 \leftarrow$ pickRndPair($order$)
   $order \leftarrow$ swapEntries($order, m_1, m_2$)
  end for
 end if
 return $order$
end function

function ADAPTEXPTIMES($bestpT^{exp}$)
 if pickRndBinary($prob_{pTcng}$) = $true$ **then**
  $pTchng \leftarrow$ pickRndRange[$pTchng^{low}, pTchng^{high}$]
  $pT_m^{exp}[i] \leftarrow bestpT_m^{exp}[i] \times pTchng$ $\triangleright \forall P_m[i] \neq dep_m$ in range of a server
 else
  $pT_m^{exp}[i] \leftarrow bestpT_m^{exp}[i]$ $\triangleright \forall P_m[i] \neq dep_m$ in range of a server
 end if
 return pT^{exp}
end function

---

flight delay. As a result of such detours, P_m is effectively split in smaller subpaths separated by depot visits. In this case, the algorithm considers swapping the order of these subpaths as well as reversing the order in which the different points of interest are visited within each subpath, to reduce the expected contention for the available server resources. More precisely, the contention at each waypoint $P_m[i]$ is estimated by dividing the number of drones expected to arrive at points of interest covered by the servers that are in range of $P_m[i]$ (where the arrival time falls within the time window where offloading is still beneficial despite the potential waiting time due to server overload), with the number of servers that cover $P_m[i]$. High contention at a point of interest means that the drone has lower probability to successfully offload its computation to some server. To avoid performing an exhaustive search for this, we only consider a limited (up to a fixed maximum) number of swap/reversal samples, which are randomly selected in each iteration. Else, if P_m is safe (no depot detour is added), the algorithm simply considers a reversal of the entire path in order to reduce contention.

These path adjustments are illustrated in Fig. 1. Note that these adjustments are applied to the P_m only if they reduce the average contention along that path.

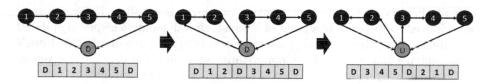

Fig. 1. Path adjustment example. The initial main path $[p_1, p_2, p_3, p_4, p_5]$ (left) is considered unsafe and as a consequence a depot detour is inserted between point of interest p_2 and p_3, resulting in two subpaths $[p_1, p_2]$ and $[p_3, p_4, p_5]$ (center). In addition, to minimize contention, the two resulting subpaths are swapped and the subpath $[p_1, p_2]$ is reversed and becomes $[p_2, p_1]$ (right).

After the paths are reset and adjusted, a new offloading schedule is produced via the SCHEDULEOFFLOADING() function. This starts from a fresh state where all servers are unoccupied at all times and no computation offloading is planned for any drone. Then, drones are considered according to the candidate selection order, and for each one the next computation offload is planned. This is done via the $fndNxtOffload()$ function, which finds the next best safe offloading option in the drone's path (not shown for brevity). Notably, this function transparently handles the case where, as a side-effect of offloading decisions taken in previous steps, the actual time spent by d_m at some point of interest $P_m[i]$ may turn out to be different that what was expected, $pT_m[i] \neq pT_m^{exp}[i]$. If such individual or accumulated deviations render P_m infeasible, an intermediate depot detour is inserted in P_m in the drone's path to ensure the safety constraint as per Eq. 6 and the search for the next best offloading option is repeated. In any case, the function returns a possibly updated path and the offloading suggestion at the next possible point of interest, along with the respective server and waiting time

Table 1. Parameters guiding the random search of the EPPOS.

Parameter	Description
$moves^{low/high}$	Bounds for the random pick of the number of best and worst candidates to be moved to the tail and head of the candidate order/selection list, respectively.
$first\_occ^{low/high}$	Bounds for the random pick of the number of occurrences of the best candidate to be moved to the tail of the order list.
$last\_occ^{low/high}$	Bounds for the random pick of the number of occurrences of the worst candidate to be moved to the head of the order list.
$prob_{swap}$	Probability to swap entries in the order list.
$swaps^{low/high}$	Bounds for the random pick of the number of swaps to be performed in the order list.
$prob_{pTchng}$	Probability for changing $bestpT^{exp}$ to be used as input for the next iteration
$pTchng^{low/high}$	Bounds for the random pick of the change factor for $bestpT^{exp}$.

so that the server capacity constraint as per Eq. 4 is satisfied. If the returned point indeed corresponds to a point of interest, the offloading schedule is updated accordingly. Else, the returned point corresponds to the last point in the drone's path implying that no offloading opportunity was found for d_m, all occurrences of the drone are removed from the ordered candidate selection list.

When the SCHEDULEOFFLOADING() function returns, it is checked whether the newly produced paths and offloading schedule improves the optimization criterion vs the best solution found so far (achieves a higher worst relative reduction of the mission time across all drones). If so, the new paths and schedule, along with the corresponding candidate selection order and expected time spent by each drone at each point of interest, are stored as the best solution.

Finally, before entering the next iteration, the best candidate selection order and best expected times at each point are modified via the SHAKEORDER() and ADAPTEXPTIMES() function, respectively. These functions randomly change these crucial parameters in search for a better solution, and are briefly discussed in the following. Table 1 lists the parameters that guide this random search.

Function SHAKEORDER() changes the best selection order found so far to build a new selection order in which the drones will be considered for offloading in the next iteration. This is done in two different ways. On the one hand, it picks *moves* drones that achieved the highest relative reduction of their mission times and for each one moves its *first_occ* first occurrences in the order list to the tail of the list. Also, it picks the same number of drones that achieved the lowest relative reduction of their mission times and for each one moves its *last_occ* last occurrences in the order list to the head of the list. On the other hand, with probability $prob_{swap}$, it swaps the order of two randomly chosen list entries. This is repeated for *swaps* times. Figure 2 illustrates simplified scenarios for those operations. The rationale of the first transformation is to strike a better balance by promoting the drones with the worst mission time improvement so that they are considered earlier for offloading in the next iteration, while demoting the drones with the best improvement. The second transformation is a simple random mutation.

(a) Move the first occurrence of the drone with the highest relative reduction of the mission time, let d_2, to the tail of the list, and move the last occurrence of the drone with the lowest relative reduction, let d_3, to the head of the list.

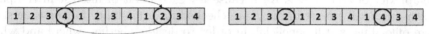

(b) Throw a binary dice which gives *true* with probability $prob_{swap}$. If *true*, pick two random occurrences in the list, e.g., the first occurrence of d_4 and the last occurrence of d_2, and swap them.

Fig. 2. Shake operations (mutations) on the order/candidate selection list (for *moves* = 1, *first_occ* = 1, *last_occ* = 1, *swaps* = 1).

Function ADAPTEXPTIMES() adapts the expected time that will be spent by the drones at each point of interest, based on the values that were used to find the best solution so far. More specifically, with probability $prob_{pTchng}$, the expected times at each point of interest for the next iterations are set to $bestpT_m^{exp}[i]$ adapted by a factor $pTchng$, else they are set equal to $bestpT_m^{exp}[i]$. The underlying rationale for this adaptation is to compensate for the fact that these estimates are based on rough approximations for the time that will be spent at each point of interest to perform the computation. Note that all the above variables (*moves*, *first_occ*, *last_occ*, *swaps*, *pTchng*) are randomly picked from respective intervals that are specified via the bounds given in Table 1.

4.3 Complexity

The runtime complexity of the EPPOS heuristic is determined by the number of iterations and the complexity of the procedures that are executed in each iteration, briefly discussed below. For brevity we let $V = \sum_{m=1}^{M} |\mathcal{V}_m|$ denote the total number of visits to points of interest to be performed by the drones. Also, let $D = \frac{\sum_{m=1}^{M} max_{s_k \text{ in range of } \mathcal{V}_m} (compT_m - compT(m,k))}{M}$ be the maximum difference between the local computation time of a drone and the computation time at the fastest server in range of a point of interest, averaged over all drones. Note that

D corresponds to the average number of checks needed to determine whether a drone can offload its computation to a server at an acceptable waiting time so that this is still beneficial compared to performing the computation locally.

The complexity of the path adjustment procedure (ADJUSTPATHS function) is $O(V) + O(M \times V \times D \times K)$, for the insertion of depot detours and the consideration of path reversal/swaps, respectively. In the former case, the path of each drone needs to be traversed linearly (with limited backwards checks that do not increase the complexity). In the latter case, for each drone, a fixed number of subpath reversal/swap combinations are checked for contention against the path of every other drone. In turn, the contention check at each point of interest is done for all servers in range and for the time slots where computation offloading remains beneficial. Resource allocation (SCHEDULEOFFLOADING function) has a complexity of $O(V \times D \times K)$ because for each point of interest in the path of each drone, all servers in range are checked for availability for the time slots where offloading is still beneficial, in order to decide whether, where and when to offload the computation of the drone. The random adaptation of the expected time spent by each drone at each point of interest (ADAPTEXPTIMES function) has a complexity of $O(V)$. Finally, the complexity of the random rearrangement of the candidate selection list (SHAKEORDER function) is $O(V)$ as the total number of performed mutations (regulated through the random variables $moves$, $first_{occ}$, $last_{occ}$ and $swaps$) cannot be larger than V.

It follows that the aggregate complexity of an iteration is $O(M \times V \times D \times K)$. Even though this is not negligible, it is relatively lightweight compared to an exhaustive check of all possible drone path and offloading combinations, allowing the algorithm to scale for larger instances of the problem.

5   Evaluation

We evaluate the EPPOS algorithm through simulation experiments. The goal of our evaluation is to demonstrate the performance, robustness and fairness of EPPOS for a wide range of scenarios, in particular regarding the battery switching time at the depot station and the operational autonomy of the drone.

Although we have the capability to experiment with real drones, such tests in the field come with numerous limitations. In particular, various flight restrictions but also changing weather conditions make it very hard, if not practically impossible, to conduct a large number of experiments with long-running missions over a wider area so that the different results can be compared with each other in fair way. This is why we resort to simulations. However, for both the drone and the server we use realistic parameter settings, based on the real hardware platforms we use in our field experiments.

5.1 Topology and Missions

The missions are conducted inside a rectangular area, with 441 different locations arranged in a 21 × 21 grid, as shown in Fig. 3a. The nodes of the grid serve as potential locations of interest of a mission. Neighboring vertical and horizontal nodes are 20 m apart. The depot stations of all drones are located at the center of the grid.

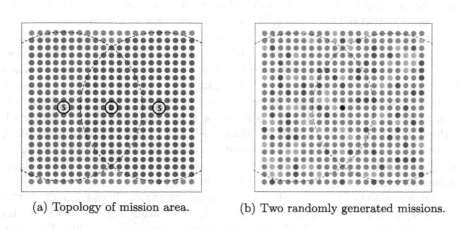

(a) Topology of mission area.   (b) Two randomly generated missions.

Fig. 3. Mission area for the experiments.

We assume two servers in the area of operation, near the yellow nodes marked with an S. Each server has a WiFi interface with a range of 200 m at constant throughput of 52 Mbps (this was measured via the NS3 [15] for TCP/IP communication over high gain antennas). The dashed lines and coloured areas mark the regions from where each server can be used for offloading: red for the server on the left; green for the server on the right; brown points are covered by both servers. The gray nodes are out of range for both servers.

We perform our experiments for randomly generated missions in the above topology, by randomly picking for each drone from 60 up to 80 points of interest (each drone is assigned a different random mission). Two indicative randomly generated missions are shown in Fig. 3b. The blue and orange nodes denote the points of interest for the first and second mission, respectively, while the brown nodes are common for both missions. These points of interest are fed into a typical TSP algorithm to produce the initial paths (P^{init}) for the drones, which, in turn, are handed over to the EPPOS algorithm in order to produce the optimized drone paths and offloading plan to the shared edge infrastructure.

5.2 Drone and Server Model Parameters

In the experiments presented in this paper, we assume drones with the same flight characteristics and onboard computing platform. As an indicative embedded computing platform, featured in the drone we use for our field experiments, we consider an RPi 4 model B with 2 GB of RAM running a headless Ubuntu server 20.04. The RPi also has a WiFi interface through which it can communicate with the edge servers.

At each point of interest, the drone takes a picture using its onboard camera and processes the image in order to detect certain objects of interest. The sensing delay (image capture) is set to 1 s (as measured on the RPi) while the image captured is roughly 465 KB. Object detection is done using YOLO [14]. The local computation delay on the RPi was measured at roughly 10 s.

For the horizontal movement of the drone, we assume steady acceleration 0.8 m/s^2 when departing from a waypoint until the drone reaches the operational speed of 4 m/s, and steady deceleration 1.6 m/s^2 as the drone approaches and stops at the next waypoint. So, for example, the distance of 20 m between two neighbouring points in the above topology (Fig. 3a), is covered in about 9 s. Also, we assume that the drone needs 5 s for a vertical take-off from the depot to the operational flight altitude of 10 m, and 20 s to perform vertical landing at the depot. These times were confirmed using our drone running the ArduPilot [1] autopilot stack onboard as well as via the ArduPilot software-in-the-loop configuration, which produced similar results.

The autonomy of the drone is the total amount of time it can remain in the air based on its battery capacity, including the time needed to take-off from the depot, fly from one point of interest to the next, hover over a point of interest to perform the required sensing and data processing, and to land at the depot. As already discussed in the previous section, drones always leave the depot with their batteries fully charged. We assume that drones consume the same amount of energy when hovering, flying, taking-off and landing. This assumption is quite realistic for small drones given that the above flight model includes moderate acceleration/deceleration values.

As an edge server platform we use a laptop with an i7-8550U CPU running a VM with 4 cores and 4 GB of RAM. The object detection service used for offloading runs inside the VM as a container using Docker [11]. The total computation delay including container loading and the time that is needed to transmit the request with the image and the detection results over WiFi, is measured at about 2 s. The number of drones that can be served concurrently by each such server is set to 1, because we observed a significant increase in the processing time when two or more services run concurrently in the VM.

5.3   Settings for EPPOS Parameters

The settings for the parameters of the random search heuristic of EPPOS are given in Table 2. We arrived at those values empirically, after a number of exploratory runs. With these settings, the algorithm converges quickly to a good solution. More specifically, in practically all the exploratory runs, convergence was reached long before 400 iterations – additional iterations had a negligible effect on the quality of the solution yielding marginal or no improvement. Thus, in the experiments presented here, we set the *iterations* parameter to 400.

Table 2. Settings for the parameters guiding the random search of EPPOS.

Parameter	value
$moves^{low}$, $moves^{high}$	1, $\frac{M}{3}$
$first\_occ^{low}$, $first\_occ^{high}$	1, 5
$last\_occ^{low}$, $last\_occ^{high}$	1, 5
$prob_{swap}$	0.1
$swaps^{low}$, $swaps^{high}$	$\frac{M}{2}$, M
$prob_{pTchng}$	0.6
$pTchng^{low}$, $pTchng^{high}$	0.7, 1.3

We note that the time that is needed to perform these iterations is acceptable for an offline algorithm, roughly 1 min. This time was measured on a commodity laptop running Windows10, with i7-8550U CPU and 8 GB of RAM, with an implementation of the EPPOS algorithm in Python3.

5.4   Presentation of Results

In the sequel, we report the results of experiments that are performed for 20 drones operating concurrently in the mission area, where we vary (i) the battery switching time at the depot and (ii) the autonomy of the drones.

As a reference for the results produced by EPPOS, we use a deterministic algorithm that optimizes the initial paths (P^{init}) under the assumption that each drone can immediately offload its computation, with zero waiting time, to one of the servers that are in range of the respective points of interest. This algorithm works in a similar way to the part of the ADJUSTPATHS() function (see Algorithm 1) where intermediate depot detours are added to make the path safe, without the path reversal logic. Note, however, that since the algorithm assumes perfect offloading, the result corresponds to a *potentially infeasible* lower bound for the mission time (and upper bound for the maximum relative reduction vs the default mission time), for the ideal case where there is no contention between the drones that operate concurrently in the mission area.

For each experiment scenario, we report the outcome of 5 different sets of randomly generated missions (every set consists of 20 missions, one mission per drone). Given that the EPPOS algorithm is itself randomized, we run it five times for each mission set and report the median. The results are presented via two barplots placed next to each other (one bar per drone, one row per mission set). In the left plot, the bars show the mission time achieved by EPPOS vs the default and ideal mission time for each drone (left Y-axis). We also indicate the number of depot detours that are introduced for each drone (right Y-axis). In the right plot, we show the relative reduction for EPPOS as well as for the ideal case assuming no contention vs the default mission time. The percentage on top of the plot indicates the worst relative reduction that is achieved by EPPOS over all drones (the optimization objective).

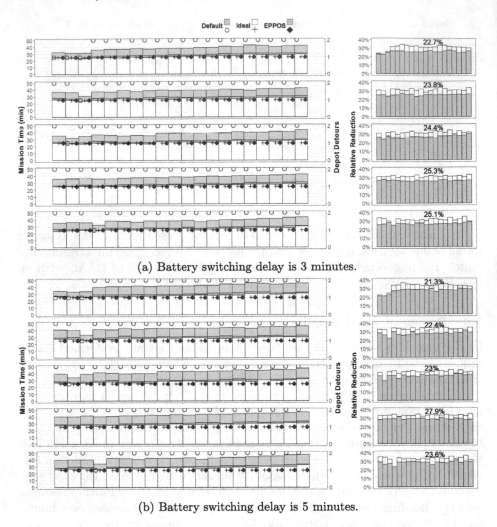

(a) Battery switching delay is 3 minutes.

(b) Battery switching delay is 5 minutes.

Fig. 4. Different battery switching delays (autonomy is 15 min).

5.5   Experiments for Different Battery Switching Delays

In a first set of experiments we study the performance of the EPPOS algorithm for battery switching delays of 3 min and 5 min, for an autonomy of 15 min. The results are shown in Fig. 4. Averaged over all five randomly generated path sets, the worst relative reduction of the mission time across all drones is 24.3% and 23.6% for a battery switching delay of 3 and 5 min, respectively. Compared to the ideal case of zero contention, the results of EPPOS are worse by merely 0.89% and 0.75%.

The difference between EPPOS and the ideal case becomes less significant for an increasing battery switching delay. The reason is twofold. Firstly, larger

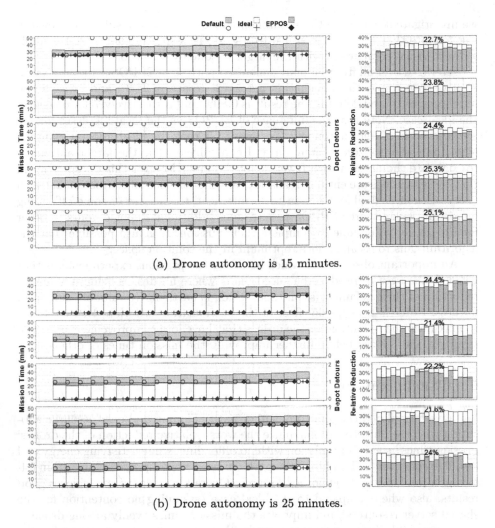

(a) Drone autonomy is 15 minutes.

(b) Drone autonomy is 25 minutes.

Fig. 5. Different degrees of autonomy (battery switching delay is 3 min).

battery switching delays reduce contention as every drone that makes a depot detour spends more time at the depot and as a result stays out of competition for the shared edge resources for a longer period. Secondly, when the battery switching delay is large and a depot detour is unavoidable in order for a drone to safely complete its mission, the time that can be saved thanks to offloading becomes less significant for the total mission time.

5.6 Experiments for Different Degrees of Autonomy

In a second set of experiments, we keep the battery switching delay to 3 min and vary the autonomy of the drones. In addition to the autonomy of 15 min, we investigate scenarios with an autonomy of 25 min. The results are shown in Fig. 5. Note that Fig. 5a is identical to Fig. 4a; it is shown again here to enable a direct visual comparison with the larger autonomy scenario.

Averaged over all five randomly generated path sets, EPPOS achieves a worst relative reduction of the mission time across all drones, of 24.3% and 22.7% for an autonomy of 15 and 25 min. The result is 0.89% and respectively 7% worse than the ideal case. Note that the difference of EPPOS vs the ideal increases for the scenario with a larger autonomy. The reason is that the ideal mission planning algorithm assumes zero contention and can fully exploit the larger autonomy to complete the mission with fewer depot detours. However this does not mean that theses savings are entirely realistic given that the actual contention between drones is non negligible. This, in turn, may lead to the loss of some offloading opportunities and force EPPOS to introduce additional depot detours in order for the drones to be able to complete their mission. It is also possible that the algorithm fails to escape a local optimum in the solution space.

An important observation, which holds for the previous experiments, is that EPPOS manages to produce balanced plans where all drones achieve a similar reduction of their default mission time, which is particularly valuable in light of fairness. Note that, as a side-effect of the optimization criterion, EPPOS tends to maximize the reduction for the drones that have lower improvement potential (shortest white bars) before further improving the mission times of others.

6   Conclusion

We have formulated the joint problem of path planning and edge resource allocation with the objective to maximize the worst relative reduction of the drones' mission times vs a default mission with no offloading, while satisfying energy and resource constraints. To address the problem, we have proposed an algorithm following a randomized neighborhood search. Overall, the algorithm achieves good results, also when compared to the ideal case (assuming no contention for the shared server resources) and improves the mission times evenly among drones.

As a possible direction for future work, it could be interesting to transform the problem into an equivalent formulation of a more abstract optimization problem, such as an integer programming (IP) problem, and compare the results of the proposed algorithm with standard solutions that have been proposed for the latter. The problem could also be extended to consider offloading among edge servers via a backbone network as well as between the drone and the cloud via a direct 4/5G mobile network link.

References

1. Ardupilot web site. https://ardupilot.org
2. Al-Hilo, A., Samir, M., Assi, C., Sharafeddine, S., Ebrahimi, D.: UAV-assisted content delivery in intelligent transportation systems-joint trajectory planning and cache management. IEEE Trans. Intell. Transp. Syst. **22**(8), 5155–5167 (2020)

3. Asim, M., Mashwani, W.K., Belhaouari, S.B., Hassan, S.: A novel genetic trajectory planning algorithm with variable population size for multi-UAV-assisted mobile edge computing system. IEEE Access **9**, 125569–125579 (2021)
4. Atencia, C.R., Del Ser, J., Camacho, D.: Weighted strategies to guide a multi-objective evolutionary algorithm for multi-UAV mission planning. Swarm Evol. Comput. **44**, 480–495 (2019)
5. Chemodanov, D., Qu, C., Opeoluwa, O., Wang, S., Calyam, P.: Policy-based function-centric computation offloading for real-time drone video analytics. In: 2019 IEEE International Symposium on Local and Metropolitan Area Networks (LANMAN), pp. 1–6. IEEE (2019)
6. Chen, J., Chen, S., Luo, S., Wang, Q., Cao, B., Li, X.: An intelligent task offloading algorithm (iTOA) for UAV edge computing network. Digit. Commun. Netw. **6**(4), 433–443 (2020)
7. Kasidakis, T., Polychronis, G., Koutsoubelias, M., Lalis, S.: Reducing the mission time of drone applications through location-aware edge computing. In: IEEE International Conference on Fog and Edge Computing (ICFEC), pp. 45–52 (2021)
8. Khan, A.W., Abdullah, A.H., Anisi, M.H., Bangash, J.I.: A comprehensive study of data collection schemes using mobile sinks in wireless sensor networks. Sensors **14**(2), 2510–2548 (2014)
9. Kim, B., Min, H., Heo, J., Jung, J.: Dynamic computation offloading scheme for drone-based surveillance systems. Sensors **18**(9), 2982 (2018)
10. Liu, Y.: An optimization-driven dynamic vehicle routing algorithm for on-demand meal delivery using drones. Comput. Oper. Res. **111**, 1–20 (2019)
11. Merkel, D., et al.: Docker: lightweight Linux containers for consistent development and deployment. Linux J. **2014**(239), 2 (2014)
12. Mladenović, N., Hansen, P.: Variable neighborhood search. Comput. Oper. Res. **24**(11), 1097–1100 (1997)
13. Rabta, B., Wankmüller, C., Reiner, G.: A drone fleet model for last mile distribution in disaster relief operations. Int. J. Disaster Risk Reduction **28**, 107–112 (2018)
14. Redmon, J., Farhadi, A.: YOLOv3: an incremental improvement. arXiv preprint arXiv:1804.02767 (2018)
15. Riley, G.F., Henderson, T.R.: The *ns*-3 network simulator. In: Wehrle, K., Güneş, M., Gross, J. (eds.) Modeling and Tools for Network Simulation, pp. 15–34. Springer, Heidelberg (2010). https://doi.org/10.1007/978-3-642-12331-3_2
16. Sabor, N., Sasaki, S., Abo-Zahhad, M., Ahmed, S.M.: A comprehensive survey on hierarchical-based routing protocols for mobile wireless sensor networks: review, taxonomy, and future directions. Wirel. Commun. Mob. Comput. **2017**, 23, Article ID 2818542 (2017). https://doi.org/10.1155/2017/2818542
17. Stavrinides, G.L., Karatza, H.D.: A hybrid approach to scheduling real-time IoT workflows in fog and cloud environments. Multimed. Tools Appl. **78**(17), 24639–24655 (2019). https://doi.org/10.1007/s11042-018-7051-9
18. Xiong, J., Guo, H., Liu, J.: Task offloading in UAV-aided edge computing: bit allocation and trajectory optimization. IEEE Commun. Lett. **23**(3), 538–541 (2019)
19. Zhan, C., Hu, H., Sui, X., Liu, Z., Wang, J., Wang, H.: Joint resource allocation and 3D aerial trajectory design for video streaming in UAV communication systems. IEEE Trans. Circ. Syst. Video Technol. **31**(8), 3227–3241 (2020)
20. Zhang, J., et al.: Stochastic computation offloading and trajectory scheduling for UAV-assisted mobile edge computing. IEEE Internet Things J. **6**(2), 3688–3699 (2018)

Wireless Networks

Range and Capacity of LoRa 2.4 GHz

Reyhane Falanji, Martin Heusse, and Andrzej Duda[✉]

Univ. Grenoble Alpes, CNRS, Grenoble INP, LIG, 38000 Grenoble, France
{reyhane.falanji,martin.heusse,andrzej.duda}@univ-grenoble-alpes.fr

Abstract. LoRa 2.4 GHz is a new variant of LoRa networks that uses the 2.4 GHz ISM band, different from the standard 868 MHz LoRa version. The LoRa physical layer takes advantage of a Chirp Spreading Spectrum (CSS) modulation with robust signals for transmission over long distances. While the standard LoRa in the 868 MHz band covers a range of 5–10 km, the actual capacity and range of LoRa 2.4 GHz are still not fully investigated. A shorter range is expected with the higher carrier frequency and an increased bandwidth. However, the wider bandwidth allows for the transmission of larger frames and a shorter airtime.

In this study, we evaluate the coverage range and capacity of LoRa 2.4 GHz through precise simulations, taking into account a path loss model tailored for urban environments and frequencies over 2 GHz. We also take into account the effect of Rician or Rayleigh fading, as well as collisions in low and high load traffic conditions. The results show a maximum range of 1.13 km and capacity around 360 nodes for low traffic and for the case in which each node in the network benefits from a minimum 60% Packet Delivery Ratio (PDR). This range drops to 1 km when the target PDR increases to 90%, accommodating 310 nodes. Under the assumption of Rayleigh fading and for the target PDR of 60% and heavy load, the range attains 557 m with capacity of 880 nodes, and it drops to 265 m for the 90% target PDR.

Keywords: LoRa 2.4 GHz · LoRaWAN · Packet Delivery Ratio · Range · Capacity · Simulations

1 Introduction

In this paper, we consider the problem of evaluating the range and capacity of LoRa 2.4 GHz networks. This new variant specifies a physical layer based on Chirp Spread Spectrum (CSS) for IoT communications in the 2.4 GHz ISM band [1]. LoRa 2.4 GHz networks are similar to the standard LoRa defined in the sub GHz band: they use the same CSS modulation with the notion of the Spreading Factor (SF) and take advantage of the LoRaWAN MAC layer with the same frame structure and the unslotted ALOHA access method. The main difference with the standard LoRa is the use of a different frequency band with an increased data rate up to 254 kb/s for SF5, a larger 1625 KHz KHz bandwidth, and the MAC payload size up to 248 B (SF5–SF10). The use of the 2.4 GHz band makes the coverage range smaller with the higher carrier frequency and an

S. Longfei and P. Bodhi (Eds.): MobiQuitous 2022, LNICST 492, pp. 403–421, 2023.
https://doi.org/10.1007/978-3-031-34776-4_21

increased bandwidth, which becomes of the order of 1.1 km compared to 5–10 km of the standard LoRa variant. However, the wider bandwidth allows for the transmission of frames of larger sizes and a shorter airtime.

The objective of this paper is to analyze the performance of LoRa 2.4 GHz networks in terms of the Packet Delivery Ratio (PDR), coverage, and capacity depending on different parameters such as SF, the environment type (channel characteristics), and the number of devices in a cell.

There are only a few studies of the LoRa 2.4 GHz performance [2–8]. They show that the coverage is smaller than the standard LoRa and the performance highly depends on the environment. Previous work analyzed the range and performance only depending on channel conditions (path loss and fading) and they did not take into account the influence of device contention and collisions. With an increasing number of devices, collisions are more likely to happen so they mostly limit the capacity of the network. Thus, in this study, we focus on both aspects: we use models to simulate collisions and take into account the channel propagation behavior with a path loss model tailored for urban environments and frequencies over 2 GHz as well as with Rician or Rayleigh fading to provide a more precise evaluation of the LoRa 2.4 GHz range and capacity.

In summary, we bring the following contributions:

- we develop and use a simulator written in Python to evaluate PDR in different cases,
- we present a set of results: i) first, to calibrate the simulation results, we compare them with reported measurements in an aquatic outdoor environment over a lake (the case of no collisions), ii) then, we valuate the performance of LoRa 2.4 GHz for the case of the SNR boundaries and maximal load due to the duty-cycle limitations of LoRa 868 MHz, and finally, iii) we perform extensive simulations for various levels of load, different target values of PDR, and fading models to evaluate the performance of LoRa 2.4 GHz.

The results show a maximum range of 1.13 km and capacity around 360 nodes for low traffic and for the case in which each node in the network benefits from a minimum 60% Packet Delivery Ratio (PDR). This range drops to 1 km when the target PDR increases to 90%, accommodating 310 nodes. Under the assumption of Rayleigh fading and for the target PDR of 60% and heavy load, the range attains 557 m with capacity of 880 nodes, and it drops to 265 m for the 90% target PDR.

Our study shows that LoRa 2.4 GHz can effectively support application traffic with higher intensity than the standard LoRa over a range of around 1 km depending on the target PDR and communication environments thus making LoRa 2.4 GHz a new kind of a "long-range Wi-Fi" network for supporting applications even beyond IoT.

The paper starts with a background on the LoRa 2.4 GHz characteristics (Sect. 2), we then discuss related work on LoRa modeling and measurements (Sect. 3), and describe the simulator (Sect. 4). Finally, we present a set of simulation results (Sect. 5).

Table 1. LoRa 868 MHz vs. 2.4 GHz

Transceiver	SX1278	SX1280
Frequency	868 MHz	2.4 GHz
Duty Cycle (EU)	1%	–
Max. Trans. Power	14 dBm	12.5 dBm
Max. Receiver Sensitivity	−148 dBm	−130 dBm (BW = 203 kHz)
	−148 dBm	−120 dBm (BW = 1625 kHz)

Table 2. Sensitivity and SNR limits.

SF	Sensitivity (dBm)	SNR$_{\text{limit}}$ (dB)
5	−99	7
6	−103	3
7	−106	0
8	−109	−3
9	−111	−5
10	−114	−8
11	−117	−11
12	−120	−14

2   Background on LoRa 2.4 GHz

The standard LoRa devices operate in the sub-GHz ISM band (the 868 MHz band in Europe and the 915 MHz band in the US). The new LoRa variant takes advantage of the 2.4 ISM GHz band with a higher data rate and wider available bandwidth. The physical layer of LoRa has the following parameters [1]:

Bandwidth (BW) corresponds to the range of the frequency sweep done in CSS. It may have the following values: 203, 406, 812, and 1625 kHz within the band of 2.4–2.5 GHz.

Spreading Factor (SF) characterizes the number of bits carried by a chirp: SF bits are mapped to one of 2^{SF} possible frequency shifts in a chirp. SF varies between 5 and 12, with SF12 resulting in the best sensitivity and range, at the cost of the lowest data rate and worst energy consumption. Decreasing SF by 1 unit roughly doubles the transmission rate and divides by 2 the transmission duration as well as energy consumption.

Coding Rate (CR) – the rate of Forward Error Correction (FEC) that improves the packet error rate in presence of noise and interference. A lower coding rate results in better robustness, but increases the transmission time and energy consumption. The possible values are: 4/5, 4/6, 4/7, and 4/8.

Transmission Power (P) varies between −18 and 12.5 dBm.

Table 1 compares the main features of the two LoRa variants.

Receiver sensitivity (RS) determines to what extent the receiver can receive and demodulate the received signal, considering the existence of noise and collisions. RS depends on many factors, including the temperature, bandwidth, and

Table 3. Data rates for LoRa 2.4 GHz

BW (kHz)	Data rate DRj for SFj (kb/s)							
	SF5	SF6	SF7	SF8	SF9	SF10	SF11	SF12
203	32	19	11	6	4	2	1	0.6
406	63	38	22	13	7	4	2	1
812	127	76	44	25	14	8	4	2
1625	254	152	89	51	29	16	9	5

Table 4. LoRa 2.4 GHz parameters for 1625 kHz bandwidth [9]

SF	Max MAC payload (B)	Airtime (ms)
5	248	10.28
6	248	17.41
7	248	29.95
8	248	52.81
9	248	94.60
10	248	170.29
11	123	201.96
12	59	202.27

the noise figure (NF) and is given by (Table 4):

$$RS = -174 + 10 \log_{10} BW + NF + SNR_{limit}. \tag{1}$$

Table 2 presents the values of RS for bandwidth of 1625 kHz and the Signal to Noise Ratio (SNR) limits for different spreading factors. Table 3 presents the available data rates for given bandwidth, for each SF. As expected, the data rate increases for larger bandwidth, but decreases as SF increases.

Regional duty cycle regulations restrict LoRa devices operating in sub-GHz frequency bands. The duty cycle depends on the frequency band: LoRa devices have to limit their occupation of each frequency band to 1% of time with 3 to 5 frequency channels in each band of 868 MHz in Europe. These duty cycle restrictions do not apply to the 2.4 GHz ISM band so devices may generate traffic with higher intensity. However, higher load may also lead to increased contention and worse performance when too many devices compete for the channel.

3   Related Work

3.1   Performance of the Standard LoRa

Many studies investigated the capacity of the standard LoRa networks either in a simulation setup [10–12], on real test beds [13–16], with mathematical/numerical analysis [17–20] or with hybrid methods [21–23]. They are not directly applicable to LoRa 2.4 GHz due to differences in their characteristics (i.e., duty cycle restrictions, SF ranges, etc.). Some simulations used models that might not be precise or proper for LoRa 2.4 GHz, for instance, path loss propagation is mainly modeled as an exponential function, which does not reflect the realistic path loss behavior with sufficient accuracy.

3.2 Performance of LoRa 2.4 GHz

There are only a few studies of the LoRa 2.4 GHz performance.

Zhang et al. measured PDR in device-to-device communication experiments (no collisions) over a lake (mainly obstacle-free environment) achieving a 100% PDR over a range of 2.2 km (NLOS) to 2.7 km (LOS) for SF12 [2].

Polak et al. analyzed coexistence between Wi-Fi and LoRa 2.4 GHz to show high robustness of LoRa against interference [3]. Their results also reveal that LoRa robustness highly depends not only on the used LoRa system parameters, but also on the interferer properties and the assumed coexistence scenarios. To improve the coexistence of LoRa and Wi-Fi, Chen et al. proposed LoFi, a method for detecting weak signals [4].

Janssen et al. investigated the maximal theoretical communication range of LoRa 2.4 GHz in three different scenarios: free space, indoor, and urban path loss [5]. For the free-space channel model, a maximal theoretical range is 133 km while the same model results in the range of 921 km for the standard LoRa (roughly 7 times more). The authors estimated the maximal communication range in an urban environment of 443 m for SF12 and 203 KHz bandwidth.

Schappacher et al. have designed a LoRaWAN architecture that uses Time Slotted Channel Hopping (TSCH). They evaluate the communication range of LoRa 2.4 GHz with the designed architecture based on an indoor scenario. They measure the success rate by considering different frequencies, bandwidth, and SF. Measurements from this study show that the existence of walls can drastically reduce the delivery rate. However, with a lower bandwidth, a higher success rate can be achieved [6].

Wolf et al. explored the use of LoRa 2.4 GHz for two-way Time-of-Flight ranging with the Semtech SX1280 chip [7]. In this context, the authors concluded that two-way ranging exchanges fail for ranges greater than 500 m. In LOS conditions (straight road at the distance of 550 m), the ranging errors were inferior to 40 m in 50% of cases involving moving devices. Another study on the ranging capabilities of the SX1280 transceiver [8] reveals that the maximum reliable distance to measure with the chip is 1.7 km (with 100 requests per exchange). This study also shows that a higher SF is not necessarily a better setup and parameters such as bandwidth and SF should be set according to the distance.

Note that previous work analyzes the range and performance only depending on channel conditions (path loss and fading) and they do not take into account the influence of device contention and collisions. With an increasing number of devices, collisions are more likely to happen so they mostly limit the capacity of the network. Thus, in this study, we focus on both aspects: we use models to simulate collisions and take into account the channel propagation behavior to provide a more precise evaluation of the LoRa 2.4 GHz range and capacity.

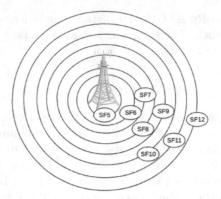

Fig. 1. Annuli of SF allocation around the gateway (the SF boundaries are equidistant in the figure, which is not the case in reality).

4   Simulator of LoRa 2.4 GHz

We have developed a discrete event simulator in Python for a single LoRa frequency channel used by a large number of nodes.[1] Compared to existing simulators such as NS-3, each experiment simulating a complete network with a large number of devices (e.g., hundreds of nodes) over 24 h takes a few minutes only. In contrast, the same scenario would take considerably longer times with existing simulators. Moreover, the simulator implements an advanced collision model that detects signal decoding of interfering packets. To the best of our knowledge, no existing simulator of LoRa 2.4 GHz covers the requirements of our study.

In this simulator, we assume that devices are homogeneously scattered with spatial density ρ and they wake up to send data at intervals determined by applications, a usual assumption of IoT applications. Although devices may send packets at constant intervals, the sources are not synchronized, and they switch channel randomly so the superposition of traffic in a single channel coming from a large number of devices tends to a homogeneous Poisson process. We denote its intensity λ that depends on the data generation intensity of IoT applications and the number of frequency channels over which it is distributed.

For an increasing distance to the gateway, a device needs to change SF to maintain the desired level of PDR: further from the gateway, nodes need to use larger SF to increase the probability of frame reception. We can thus define SF boundaries around the gateway in form of concentric annuli in which devices share the same value of SF and the same frequency channel (see Fig. 1) [21]. The number of nodes in a given SF zone is a function of the radii defining a given annulus around the gateway and the node density. The simulator assumes that

---

[1] https://gricad-gitlab.univ-grenoble-alpes.fr/Drakkar-LIG/lora-2g4-simulator.git.

all devices in a given SF zone use the same SFj (so each transmission has the same airtime and data rate DRj) and they contend for the same channel.

The simulator takes into account various channel propagation models, Rayleigh and Rician fading, the capture effect, as well as co-SF interference.

4.1   Channel Propagation Model

The simulator implements the ECC-33 model developed by Electronic Communication Committee [24]. It extends the earlier Okumura-Hata model [25,26] created based on the propagation experiment in Tokyo. However, it is only suitable for propagation of signals operating in frequencies from 150 to 1500 MHz. The ECC-33 model modified the assumptions of Okumura-Hata to adapt it for signals in 2 GHz bands, so corresponding to LoRa 2.4 GHz. The model defines the following path loss:

$$L_{ecc} = A_{fs} + A_{bm} - G_b - G_r, \tag{2}$$

where A_{fs}, A_{bm}, G_b, and G_r are the free space attenuation, the basic median path loss, base station height gain factor and receiver height gain factor, respectively, defined as follows:

$$A_{fs} = 92.4 + 20 \log d + 20 \log f, \tag{3}$$

$$A_{bm} = 20.41 + 9.83 \log d + 7.89 \log f + 9.56 (\log f)^2, \tag{4}$$

$$G_b = \log(\frac{h_b}{200})(13.958 + 5.8 log(d))^2, \tag{5}$$

$$G_r = (42.57 + 13.7 \log f)(\log h_r - 0.585), \tag{6}$$

where f is the frequency in GHz, d is the distance between the gateway and the LoRa transceiver in km, h_b is the gateway antenna height in meters, and h_r is the transceiver antenna height in meters.

Equation 6 corresponds to a medium city environment. In case of large cities, the following equation for G_r applies:

$$G_r = 0.759 h_r - 1.862 \tag{7}$$

4.2   Fading Models

The simulator takes into account Rayleigh fading [16,21] that may greatly influence the packet reception for transmissions over long distances. The model assumes that a signal will randomly loose its strength or fade according to a

Table 5. Simulation parameters

Parameter	Value
Packet arrival intensity λ	1/12.33, 1/2 min^{-1}
Payload size	59 B
Node density ρ	90, 900 nodes/km^2
Frequency	2.4 GHz
Bandwidth	406, 1625 kHz
Path loss model	ECC-33
Fading	Rician ($K = 100$), Rayleigh
Simulation interval	24 h
Gateway antenna height	17 m
Node antenna height	6 m
Transmission power	12.5 dBm

Rayleigh distribution—a multiplicative random variable with an exponential distribution of unit mean affects the received signal power.

We also consider Rician fading for comparisons with measurements. The simulation generates samples from a complex random variable $|X + jY|$, where X, Y are Gaussian random variables with non-zero mean and standard deviation that depend on a given K factor.

The Rayleigh and Rician fading model are used in combination with the ECC model.

4.3 Collision Model

The reference design of the LoRa 2.4 GHz gateway uses multiple transceivers—four SX1280 transceivers: three dedicated to reception and one to transmission allowing simultaneous reception over three LoRa modulated channels operating on a single, programmable spreading factor [27].

To consider collisions, the simulator uses a variation of the model of the standard LoRa [21] with the assumption that the timing of frame reception does not matter and successful frame reception is conditioned by having a (conservative) margin of 6 dB against interference. During frame reception, the simulator computes the sum of the power of the interfering transmissions and, if it is more than the power of the present transmission minus a power capture margin of 6 dB, the simulator considers the frame as lost.

For the sake of simplicity, the simulator assumes that the interference from transmissions with other SFs is negligible as they are quasi-orthogonal [28,29]: except for rare near-far conditions, the gateway can receive simultaneous transmissions using different values of SF.

4.4 Simulation Setup

Table 5 summarizes the values of parameters for the simulation. We assume that packet arrival times are distributed according to a random exponential time

Table 6. Experimental results [2] vs. simulations for 406 kHz bandwidth and 16 B payload.

	Measured PDR	Range
Experimental	100%	2200 m
Simulation (no Rayleigh)	98%	2050 m
Simulation (Rician, $K = 100$)	98%	1840 m
Simulation (Rayleigh)	98%	431 m

(Poisson distribution of arrivals) with parameter λ. This assumption is justified if a large number of devices generate packets even if the intervals between packets are constant, a typical behavior of sensing devices. The simulator assumes 59 B for the size of the MAC payload (SF5 to SF12).

All simulation results appearing below are the average of 100 runs, each of which corresponds to 5 days of traffic. The confidence intervals are less than one percentage point so they are not marked on the graphs.

5   Simulation Results

In this section, we present the simulation results for different cases and scenarios.

5.1   Validation: Comparison with Reported Measurements

At the beginning, we compare the simulation results with the measurements done by Zhang et al. [2] in an outdoor environment over a lake. They measured PDR between two end-devices (no contention) over three distances: 1600 m, 2200 m, and 2700 m in different conditions of LOS, obstructed LOS, and NLOS. Even if the authors consider some cases as NLOS, devices are placed at the border of a lake, so that the environment rather corresponds to LOS or slightly obstructed LOS conditions. They used SX1280 modules with omnidirectional antennas (3 dBi) and the following parameters: transmission power of 12.5 dBm, bandwidth of 406 kHz, CR of 4/5, preamble length of 8 symbols, SF6 to SF12, and payload of 16 B.

An interesting case to compare with is the measurement over 2200 m that gives 100% PDR for SF12 and lower values of PDR for lower SFs, so it corresponds to a kind of a range limit. The LOS conditions were also satisfied for the case of 2700 m but we do not know if this distance is a range limit, because 100% PDR could have also be achieved for longer distances.

To compare with the measurements, we assume only one device per SF annulus in the simulation so there is no collision. Table 6 compares the simulation results with the measurements.

The simulations give the results close to 2200 m when assuming the case of no Rayleigh and Rician path loss. Actually in the measurement experiments [2],

Table 7. SNR-based SF boundaries for the 1625 kHz bandwidth

PDR$_{target}$	SF5	SF6	SF7	SF8	SF9	SF10	SF11	SF12
70%	0.096	0.156	0.226	0.306	0.371	0.481	**0.636**	0.816

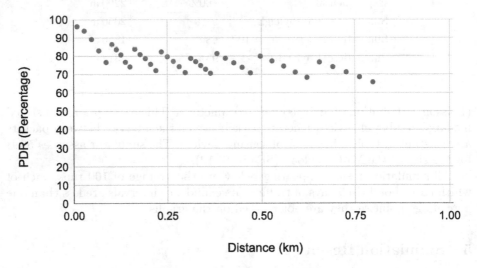

Fig. 2. Case of the SNR boundaries and maximal load as for the standard LoRa: cell radius of 0.636 km, node density ρ of 90 nodes per km^2, Rayleigh fading. Around 180 nodes within 0.8 km of the gateway, using up to SF12 receive a PDR of at least 65%. Traffic intensity limited by the 1% duty cycle in the standard LoRa (1/12.33 min^{-1}).

although the scenario is presented as a NLOS case, the experimental environment corresponds to LOS conditions that are better represented with the Rician model. We can observe that taking into account Rayleigh fading results in a much shorter range.

In the rest of the evaluations, we use the Rician model representative of the measured environment and a model with Rayleigh fading that corresponds to a case of a dense urban environment.

5.2 Case of SNR Boundaries and Maximal Load in the Standard LoRa

In this section, we evaluate the performance of LoRa 2.4 GHz for the case of the SNR boundaries and maximal load analyzed for the standard LoRa [21] (Sect. 6.1). We use the most optimistic bandwidth of LoRa 2.4 GHz, which is 1625 kHz and the maximum payload of 59 B at the MAC layer. The simulations assume the same traffic load as used in the analysis of the standard LoRa cell capacity: all devices have the same interpacket generation interval that gives the 1% duty cycle for SF12 [21]: 1/12.33 min^{-1}. So, we address the following

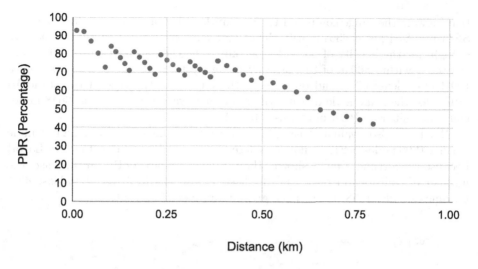

Fig. 3. Case of the SNR boundaries and maximal load as for the standard LoRa: cell radius of 0.636 km, node density ρ of 900 nodes per km^2, Rayleigh fading. Around 880 nodes within 0.558 km of the gateway, using up to SF11, receive a PDR of at least 60%. Traffic intensity limited by the 1% duty cycle in the standard LoRa ($1/12.33\,\text{min}^{-1}$).

question: what would be the effect of upgrading standard LoRa devices to LoRa 2.4 GHz for the same application traffic?

For the standard LoRa [21], the SF boundaries were determined using an analytical model with a probability function of PDR—the SF boundary corresponds to the case for which the probability of successful packet delivery reaches a given target PDR (e.g., 60%). The *target PDR* corresponds to the minimum value that we want obtain in all annuli of a cell—we use two representative values: 90% or 60%. The target PDR of 90% may be sufficient enough for some data collecting applications. With 60% PDR, applications may obtain reliable data delivery by using some transmission redundancy in the form of inter-frame Error Correction Codes or transmission repetitions [13].

Computing SF boundaries is not possible in the same way as for the standard LoRa, so we determine them by running the simulator first for a small number of nodes (no collisions) and we use the target PDR of 70% corresponding to PDR of 60% with a margin of 10% (see Table 7). Then, we run simulations with a given number of nodes determined by the node density of 90 or 900 nodes per km^2. For 900 nodes per km^2 and the interpacket interval of $1/12.33\,\text{min}^{-1}$, collisions may happen so PDR may go down to 60%.

Figures 2 and 3 present the results for LoRa 2.4 GHz under the assumption of Rayleigh fading because this model was assumed for the analysis of the standard LoRa [21]. The fact of using the wider bandwidth of 1625 kHz in the 2.4 GHz band lowers the range compared to the standard LoRa—the boundary between SF11 and SF12 is at 636 m. Still, the capacity in terms of the number of devices is high: for the density of 90 nodes per km^2, the cell can have up to 180 nodes scattered within 800 m of the gateway using up to SF12 and benefiting from a PDR of at least 60%, and often more than that. In the case of the standard LoRa, for the same node density, the boundary was at 3.59 km and 3648 nodes could benefit from PDR of at least 60% [21].

We have also evaluated the capacity of LoRa 2.4 GHz for a higher node density (900 nodes per km^2, not considered in the analysis of the standard LoRa) because the airtime is much shorter than in the standard LoRa. In this case, the number of collisions increases so the distance for getting PDR of at least 60% becomes smaller (558 m) but for a greater number of nodes (880).

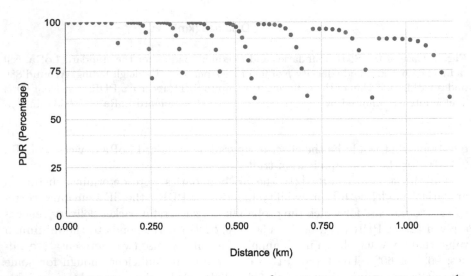

Fig. 4. Low load (density ρ of 90 nodes per km^2, traffic intensity of $1/12.33\,\mathrm{min}^{-1}$), SF boundaries for target PDR of 60%, Rician fading. Cell capacity around 360 nodes.

5.3   Analysis of LoRa 2.4 GHz Capacity

In this section, we provide the results from running simulations of a LoRa 2.4 GHz cell for various traffic intensities ($1/2$ and $1/12.33\,\mathrm{min}^{-1}$) and for various node densities (90 and 900 nodes per km^2). For these results, we determine the SF boundaries between SF annuli for a given simulation setup in an iterative way to match the target PDR.

The process starts with the initialization of the nodes in the first zone of SF5. Beginning with the zero distance from the gateway, we extend the border further away with a fixed step size. Based on the selected node density ρ and the area of the zone delimited by the current border, we compute the number

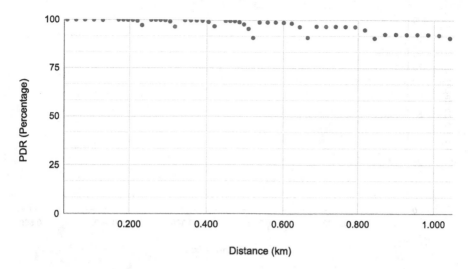

Fig. 5. Low load (density ρ of 90 nodes per km^2, traffic intensity of $1/12.33\,\mathrm{min}^{-1}$), SF boundaries for target PDR of 90%, Rician fading. Cell capacity around 310 nodes.

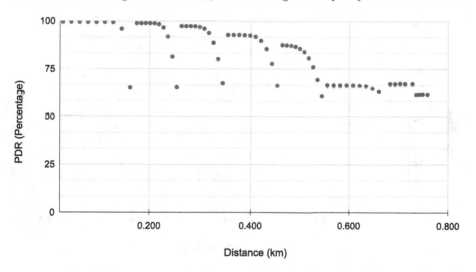

Fig. 6. High load (density ρ of 900 nodes per km^2, traffic intensity of $1/2\,\mathrm{min}^{-1}$), SF boundaries for target PDR of 60%, Rician fading. Cell capacity around 1620 nodes.

of nodes and place them at random distances within the area. The simulator generates packet transmissions at random instants and runs the discrete-event simulation to obtain the PDR of each node: it considers the transmission of the packet with the closest scheduled transmission time, keeps track of other possibly concurrent packet transmissions, and determines if there are collisions based on the timings and the power of transmissions. The number of successfully received packets gives us the PDR of each device in this zone.

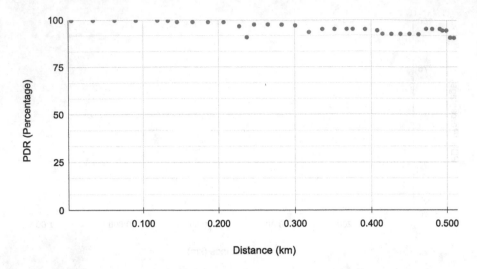

Fig. 7. High load (density ρ of 900 nodes per km^2, traffic intensity of $1/2\,\text{min}^{-1}$), SF boundaries for target PDR of 90%, Rician fading. Cell capacity around 735 nodes.

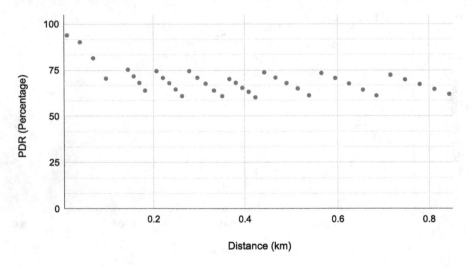

Fig. 8. Low load (density ρ of 90 nodes per km^2, traffic intensity of $1/12.33\,\text{min}^{-1}$), SF boundaries for target PDR of 60%, Rayleigh fading. Cell capacity around 200 nodes.

If the minimum PDR of all nodes in the SF5 zone is still above the target PDR, we extend the border one step further and repeat the simulation to obtain the PDR of all nodes once again. When we reach the target PDR, the distance corresponds to the SF boundary. At this distance, the area of the next SF begins (SF6). We repeat this process for each SF up to SF12.

Figures 4, 5, 6 and 7 present PDR and capacity of a LoRa 2.4 GHz cell for different settings of load and target PDR under the assumption of Rician fading.

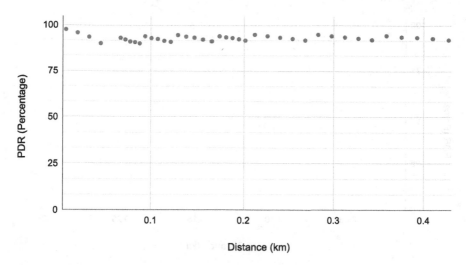

Fig. 9. Low load (density ρ of 90 nodes per km^2, traffic intensity of $1/12.33\,\mathrm{min}^{-1}$), SF boundaries for target PDR of 90%, Rayleigh fading. Cell capacity around 50 nodes.

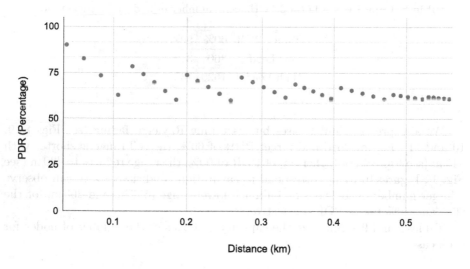

Fig. 10. High load (density ρ of 900 nodes per km^2, traffic intensity of $1/2\,\mathrm{min}^{-1}$), SF boundaries for target PDR of 60%, Rayleigh fading. Cell capacity around 880 nodes.

We can observe that for low load (density ρ of 90 nodes per km^2, traffic intensity of $1/12.33\,\mathrm{min}^{-1}$) and relaxed PDR condition of 60%, the cell range is fairly long with 1.13 km (see Fig. 4). When we require the higher PDR of 90%, the range reduces to 1 km. Figures 6 to 7 present saturation conditions (high load—density ρ of 900 nodes per km^2, traffic intensity of $1/2\,\mathrm{min}^{-1}$), with an increased impact of collisions and a much lower range (758 m, and 510 m, for 60% and 90% target PDR, respectively).

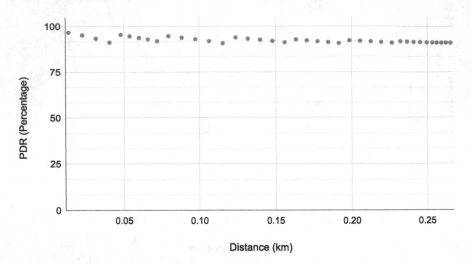

Fig. 11. High load (density ρ of 900 nodes per km², traffic intensity of $1/2\,\text{min}^{-1}$), SF boundaries for target PDR of 90%, Rayleigh fading. Cell capacity around 200 nodes.

Table 8. Capacity of a LoRa 2.4 GHz cell (number of nodes) for Rician fading

Target PDR	60%	90%
Low Load	360	310
High Load	1620	735

We also present similar cases but assuming Rayleigh fading (see Figs. 8, 9, 10 and 11). For low load and target PDR of 60%, the cell range is shorter with 845 m (see Fig. 8). For higher target PDR of 90%, the range reduces to 430 m (see Fig. 9). Figures 10 to 11 correspond to saturation conditions so we can observe a larger number of collisions and a much lower range (557 m, and 265 m, for the 60% and 90% target PDR, respectively).

Tables 8 and 9 summarize the capacity in terms of the number of nodes for each case.

Table 9. Capacity of a LoRa 2.4 GHz cell (number of nodes) for Rayleigh fading

Target PDR	60%	90%
Low Load	200	50
High Load	880	200

6   Conclusion

In this paper, we have evaluated the capacity of a LoRaWAN network operating in the 2.4 GHz band. We have developed a discrete event simulator in Python that integrates a propagation model within an urban environment in GHz bands (ECC) with Rayleigh or Rician fading. It also models collisions and capture phenomena in a precise way.

To calibrate the simulation results, we have compared them with reported measurements for a specific case of an aquatic outdoor environment over a lake. Our simulator gives the results of the same order of magnitude.

We have then evaluated the performance of LoRa 2.4 GHz for the case of the SNR boundaries and the maximal application traffic determined by the 1% duty cycle of the standard LoRa. The range of the LoRa 2.4 GHz cell becomes much smaller—the boundary between SF11 and SF12 is at 636 m. The capacity in terms of the number of devices depends on the load: for low load, the cell can have up to 180 nodes using up to SF12 benefiting from a PDR of at least 60% in a disc of 800 m radius. For a higher node density, the number of collisions increases so the distance for getting PDR of at least 60% is smaller (558 m) but for a greater number of nodes (880).

Finally, we provide simulation results for LoRa 2.4 GHz in case of different traffic intensities (1/2 and 1/12.33 min^{-1}), various node densities (90 or 900 per km^2), the target PDR of 60% and 90%, and the fading model of Rician or Rayleigh. The results show that LoRa 2.4 GHz performance highly depends on channel load and the target PDR: the cell range can be fairly long (1.13 km) with capacity of 360 nodes benefiting from PDR of 60% for low load under the assumption of Rician fading. When load increases, the range becomes shorter (758 m) with a capacity of 1620 nodes. Adopting the assumption of Rayleigh fading, which may correspond to a dense urban environment, results in a further decrease of the range and capacity.

In the future, we aim at experimental validation of the simulator to improve its capacity to emulate the realistic channel behavior in different environments.

Acknowledgments. This work has been partially supported by the French Ministry of Research projects PERSYVAL-Lab under contract ANR-11-LABX-0025-01 and DiNS under contract ANR-19-CE25-0009-01.

References

1. Semtech: SX1280/SX1281 Long Range, Low Power, 2.4 GHz Transceiver with Ranging Capability, DS.SX1280-1.W.APP (2020)
2. Zhang, Z., Cao, S., Wang, Y.: A long-range 2.4 GHz network system and scheduling scheme for aquatic environmental monitoring. Electronics **8**(8), 909 (2019)
3. Polak, L., Milos, J.: Performance analysis of LoRa in the 2.4 GHz ISM band: coexistence issues with Wi-Fi. Telecommun. Syst. **74**(3), 299–309 (2020). https://doi.org/10.1007/s11235-020-00658-w

4. Chen, G., Dong, W., Lv, J.: LoFi: enabling 2.4 GHz LoRa and Wi-Fi coexistence by detecting extremely weak signals. In: IEEE INFOCOM 2021-IEEE Conference on Computer Communications. IEEE (2021)

5. Janssen, T., et al.: LoRa 2.4 GHz communication link and range. Sensors **20**(16), 4366 (2020)

6. Schappacher, M., Dant, A., Sikora, A.: Implementation and validation of LoRa-based systems in the 2.4 GHz band. In: 2021 IEEE 4th International Conference on Advanced Information and Communication Technologies (AICT). IEEE (2021)

7. Wolf, F., et al.: Benchmarking of narrowband LPWA physical layer ranging technologies. In: 2019 16th Workshop on Positioning, Navigation, and Communications (WPNC). IEEE (2019)

8. Andersen, F., et al.: Ranging capabilities of LoRa 2.4 GHz. In: 2020 IEEE 6th World Forum on Internet of Things (WF-IoT). IEEE (2020)

9. Semtech   (2021).   https://lora-developers.semtech.com/documentation/tech-papers-and-guides-/physical-layer-proposal-2.4ghz

10. Van den Abeele, F., et al.: Scalability analysis of large-scale LoRaWAN networks in NS-3. IEEE Internet Things J. **4**(6), 2186–2198 (2017)

11. Bor, M., et al.: Do LoRa low-power wide-area networks scale? In: Proceedings of the 19th ACM International Conference on Modeling, Analysis and Simulation of Wireless and Mobile Systems (2016)

12. Varsier, N., Schwoerer, J.: Capacity limits of LoRaWAN technology for smart metering applications. In: 2017 IEEE International Conference on Communications (ICC). IEEE (2017)

13. Coutaud, U., Heusse, M., Tourancheau, B.: High reliability in LoRaWAN. In: IEEE 31st Annual International Symposium on Personal, Indoor and Mobile Radio Communications. IEEE (2020)

14. Coutaud, U., Heusse, M., Tourancheau, B.: LoRa channel characterization for flexible and high reliability adaptive data rate in multiple gateways networks. Computers **10**(4), 44 (2021)

15. El Chall, R., Lahoud, S., El Helou, M.: LoRaWAN network: radio propagation models and performance evaluation in various environments in Lebanon. IEEE Internet Things J. **6**(2), 2366–2378 (2019)

16. Attia, T., et al.: Experimental characterization of LoRaWAN link quality. In: 2019 IEEE Global Communications Conference (GLOBECOM). IEEE (2019)

17. Georgiou, O., Raza, U.: Low power wide area network analysis: can LoRa scale? IEEE Wirel. Commun. Lett. **6**(2), 162–165 (2017)

18. Mikhaylov, K., Petaejaejaervi, J., Haenninen, T.: Analysis of capacity and scalability of the LoRa low power wide area network technology. In: European Wireless 2016; 22th European Wireless Conference. VDE (2016)

19. Sørensen, R., et al.: Analysis of latency and MAC-layer performance for class a LoRaWAN. IEEE Wirel. Commun. Lett. **6**(5), 566–569 (2017)

20. Duda, A., Heusse, M.: Spatial issues in modeling LoRaWAN capacity. In: Proceedings of the 22nd International ACM Conference on Modeling, Analysis and Simulation of Wireless and Mobile Systems (2019)

21. Heusse, M., et al.: Capacity of a LoRaWAN cell. In: Proceedings of the 23rd International ACM Conference on Modeling, Analysis and Simulation of Wireless and Mobile Systems (2020)

22. Yousuf, A., et al.: Throughput, coverage, and scalability of LoRa LPWAN for the Internet of Things. In: 2018 IEEE/ACM 26th International Symposium on Quality of Service (IWQoS). IEEE (2018)

23. Attia, T., et al.: Message in message for improved LoRaWAN capacity. In: 30th IEEE International Conference on Computer Communications and Networks, ICCCN 2021 (2021)
24. Electronic Communication Committee (ECC) within the European Conference of Postal and Telecommunications Administration (CEPT): The analysis of the coexistence of FWA cells in the 3.4–3.8 GHz band. ECC report 33 (2003)
25. Okumura, Y.: Field strength and its variability in VHF and UHF land-mobile radio service. Rev. Electr. Commun. Lab. 16, 825–873 (1968)
26. Hata, M.: Empirical formula for propagation loss in land mobile radio services. IEEE Trans. Veh. Technol. 29(3), 317–325 (1980)
27. Semtech: LoRa 2.4 GHz 3 channels single SF reference design performance report (2020)
28. Goursaud, C., Gorce, J.-M.: Dedicated networks for IoT: PHY/MAC state of the art and challenges. EAI Endorsed Trans. Internet Things (2015)
29. Mahmood, A., et al.: Scalability analysis of a LoRa network under imperfect orthogonality. IEEE Trans. Ind. Inf. 15(3), 1425–1436 (2018)

Reception of Terrestrial DAB+ and FM Radio with a Mobile Device: A Subjective Quality Evaluation

Przemyslaw Falkowski-Gilski[✉] ⓘ

Faculty of Electronics, Telecommunications and Informatics, Gdansk University of Technology, Narutowicza 11/12, 80-233 Gdansk, Poland
przemyslaw.falkowski@eti.pg.edu.pl

Abstract. Nowadays, terrestrial broadcasting enables to receive content anytime and everywhere. People can obtain information both with a portable or desktop receiver, which include pocket-sized devices as well as high-end Hi-Fi equipment, not to mention car audio systems. Numerous manufacturers include FM-compatible chipsets in a variety of user equipment (UE), including mobile phones. However, digital radio signal processing modules, such as, i.e., Digital Audio Broadcasting plus (DAB+), are not that popular. Currently, only one smartphone available on the market offers such possibilities This paper examines the reception quality of terrestrial digital DAB+ and analog FM radio with the use of a mobile device. The study was carried out on a number of broadcasts simulcasted in both standards, and involved a group of 30 listeners aged between 20–25 years old. Next, results were compared with subjective scores obtained using a high-end desktop radio receiver. The aim of this work is to determine whether small size mobile UE can offer high-quality reception, and whether a smartphone can compete with a traditional indoor receiver. Results of carried out studies may aid and inspire devices manufacturers as well as content and service providers, speeding up the whole digitization process.

Keywords: Coding · Compression · Mobile Devices · Signal Processing · Quality Evaluation

1 Introduction

Terrestrial radio transmission accompanies us every day during numerous activities. Whether we are traveling to work or during vacations, we like to stay informed about, e.g., traffic and weather conditions. We also like to listen to music during every day routines or just to relax ourselves. The market offers numerous radio receivers, compatible with, e.g., analog FM, Digital Radio Broadcasting plus (DAB+), Internet streaming services, not to mention numerous wireless interfaces like Bluetooth, that enable us to connect headsets, etc. [1]. However, most people are interested particularly in portable devices, such as the smartphone [2]. Almost every device running on Android or iOS has a build-in chipset

© ICST Institute for Computer Sciences, Social Informatics and Telecommunications Engineering 2023
Published by Springer Nature Switzerland AG 2023. All Rights Reserved
S. Longfei and P. Bodhi (Eds.): MobiQuitous 2022, LNICST 492, pp. 422–430, 2023.
https://doi.org/10.1007/978-3-031-34776-4_22

responsible for processing analog radio signals. Therefore, it is quite intriguing why manufacturers do not offer compatibility with a variety of digital terrestrial services. Among them, DAB+ is the most widely-spread standard for transmission of digital radio [3, 4]. Yet, only one mobile device is capable of processing and presenting this type of content. This paper is focused on a study, considering the reception of terrestrial FM and DAB+ radio with a smartphone. Its main aim is to determine whether such user equipment (UE) can compete with the quality offered by more pricy high-quality desktop devices. That is why this subjective evaluation was carried out. Previous investigations considering the advancements in the broadcast industry as well as the radio digitization process are well-summarized in [5].

2 Digital Radio Market

In [6], the author focuses on the considerable scale and pace of change in broadcast radio over the first two decades of the twenty-first century, an on-going process showing little sign of abating. Developments in digital broadcasting, the increasing consumption of audio via Internet protocol (IP) and the arrival of the smart speaker are all major factors impacting the future of radio broadcasting. No longer a stand-alone medium, this paper argues that the future of broadcast radio rests on the way in which it addresses the various challenges and opportunities offered by its use of new technologies and multiple platforms. Change is not simply being driven by technological and regulatory developments within the industry. Equally importantly, change is also being driven by external factors and by wider societal pressures. Today, radio faces greater levels of challenge and competition than at any time in its long history.

Public service broadcasting (PSB) is generally characterized by a remit to provide high-quality news, educational content, cultural enrichment and entertainment as free public goods with as broad a public reach as possible, while also filling critical gaps in the media ecosystem. However, in the current digital environment, the ability to reach audiences is increasingly intermediated by online platforms managed by powerful technology companies who do not necessarily share the same objectives or values as PSBs. In [7], interviews were conducted with PSB executives and managers working on digital products and strategy in the U.K. and U.S., to examine the challenges and tensions PSB entities face in the context of growing commercial platform power and the strategies emerging in response, such as investing in new platforms and digital infras-tructures rooted in traditional public service values. The study also discusses differences in capacities to respond to platform power between the decentralized U.S. PSB system and centralized U.K. system. Finally, the study discusses some theoretical and practi-cal implications, and suggests ways PSB services might survive and thrive with robust fidelity to democratic needs.

The aim of this work [8] was to perform an analysis of the current state of various digital broadcasting systems around the world and the switchover trends from the ana-log to digital domain, as recommended by the International Telecommunication Union (ITU). As shown, the main cause is not only the lack of unoccupied frequency resources, but also the society's growing demands for up-to-date information and content.

Another paper [9] focuses on breakdowns experienced in the media field due to technology and digitization. As shown, concepts such as speed, mobility, screen, connectivity and interaction are rapidly finding application in digital media environments. When viewed from this perspective, it is seen that many new media production areas with technology references have emerged. One of these new areas are digital radios. With the traditional analog broadcasting being replaced by digital over time, it has become much more efficient to deliver content in the virtual environment. From now on, broadcasts are no longer a media tool that is listened to, but also a communication environment that can be watched and interacted with. Thanks to the web technology that transforms the radio into a watchable platform, it is seen that the content reaches the listener and the audience through the screens. For this reason, it can be said that the area of influence of radio broadcasting has expanded and radio broadcasting has taken a much more active position in the media sector.

As the lines between production, distribution, and platform technologies blur, and as the digital transformation moves to the cloud, the European Broadcasting Union (EBU) Technical Committee's work becomes more important than ever, as members seek the scale and sophistication that typifies global super aggregator offerings. EBU's focus is on delivering the products and facilitating the exchanges that underpin the strategic elements in these transitions by federating the members' interests [10]. Yet still, work could be done in order to familiarize users with the possibilities digital radio can offer.

3   About the Study

3.1   Multiplex Configuration

The tested DAB+ multiplex consisted of 9 services transmitting audio content, with bitrates ranging from 64 to 128 kbps. Among them, some delivered mostly speech signals, while other broadcasted typically music signals, whereas some provided mixed speech-music signals, depending on the profile of a particular radio station. The relation between type of broadcasted audio content and bitrate of respective radio programs is discussed in [11].

Generally speaking, the HE-AAC v1 variant of the coding algorithm is utilized in case of the lower bitrates, whereas the AAC-LC variant is used when processing audio content at higher bitrates. The description of each evaluated radio program in this particular experiment is described in Table 1.

As observed, some broadcasts are simulcasted in analog FM radio (6 out of 9). Each services was evaluated in a subjective study with two receivers, namely a mobile as well as desktop device.

Table 1. Configuration of the tested DAB+ multiplex.

No	Profile	Codec	Bitrate [kbps]	Simulcasted in FM
1	Talk 1	AAC-LC	112	Yes
2	Arts	AAC-LC	128	Yes
3	Talk 2	AAC-LC	112	Yes
4	Pop Music	AAC-LC	128	Yes
5	Informative EN	AAC-LC	64	No
6	Informative PL	HE-AAC v1	64	Yes
7	Classical Music	AAC-LC	128	No
8	Children	HE-AAC v1	72	No
9	Regional	AAC-LC	112	Yes

3.2 Tested Devices

The tested devices included a mobile UE, namely the LG Stylus 2 [12], which quite surprisingly is still the only smartphone with DAB+ reception compatibility available on the market. Although it was released in Q1 2016, the newer generation of the Stylus line did not offer such features. The principle technical specification of this device is described in Table 2.

Table 2. Principal technical specification of the LG Stylus 2 smartphone.

Feature	Description
CPU	4-core, 1.20 GHz
RAM	2 GB
Supported terrestrial radio standards	FM, DAB+
Audio output	3.5 mm jack
Storage	16 GB (build-in), microSD-card slot (external)
Communication	Bluetooth, Wi-Fi, 2 G, 3 G, 4 G
Operating system	Android 6.0 Marshmallow

Whereas, the principal technical specification of the desktop radio receiver, namely TechniSat DigitRadio 350 IR [13], is described in Table 3.

As shown, the desktop receiver is a hybrid device, enabling to handle both terrestrial FM and DAB+ radio, as well as other various audio sources. After a careful examination, no data were available considering the type of integrated chipset in case of each receiver, responsible for handling terrestrial radio signals. Nevertheless, both were subjected to the same testing procedure.

Table 3. Principal technical specification of the TechniSat DigitRadio 350 IR receiver.

Feature	Description
Supported terrestrial radio standards	FM, DAB+
Audio output	3.5 mm jack,
Storage	USB (external)
Communication	Wi-Fi, Ethernet, USB

3.3 Testing Procedure

Tests were carried out in turns, one participant after another, according to [14]. The group of listeners involved 30 individuals aged between 20–25 years old. At first, they evaluated the DAB+ radio programs, presented in a randomized manner, and then switched to the simulcasted FM radio program. Of course no one was informed about the name nor bitrate (in case of DAB+) of the currently assessed broadcast. Each DAB+ and FM program was presented over a period of approx. 20 s, separated by a 5 s interval necessary to write down the scores.

Listeners started their evaluation with a mobile UE, and then repeated the whole procedure with the desktop receiver. Each one took a 5–10 min break before moving from one device to the other. Neither of them had hearing impairments.

The quality evaluation took place in an indoor environment, with both devices set to fixed locations next to each other. The subjective study was carried out using Beyerdynamic Custom One Pro headphones. Each individual was allowed to set the volume level according to his or her preferences during the training phase. The tests were performed over a period of one week.

4   Results

Results of the subjective quality evaluation study, in a 5-step variant of the Mean Opinion Score (MOS) scale from 1 (bad quality) to 5 (excellent quality), carried out on both mobile and desktop devices, considering a group of 30 individuals, are shown in Figs. 1, 2, 3 and 4. The scores obtained for all 9 DAB+ radio broadcasts are shown in Fig. 1.

It can be summarized that each radio program, except for Informative EN on a desktop device, received an overall score of above 4.0. Additionally, the difference between respective broadcasts was quite small. Figure 2 shows the Subjective Difference Grade (SDG) concerning scores obtained for DAB+ radio on both devices, based on data presented in Fig. 1. Quite surprisingly, listeners tend to favor the mobile UE.

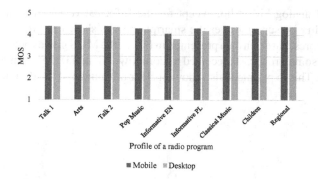

Fig. 1. Subjective quality evaluation of DAB+ radio programs.

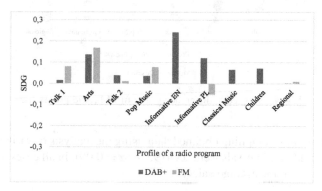

Fig. 2. Subjective difference grade of DAB+ radio programs.

Results considering the reception quality of FM radio, are shown in Fig. 3.

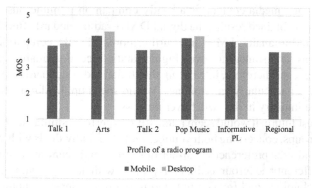

Fig. 3. Subjective quality evaluation of FM radio programs.

In case of analog FM radio, except for the Informative PL program, the desktop device proved to be superior over the smartphone. As shown in Fig. 4, describing the SDG of FM scores, based on data presented in Fig. 3, the MOS grades were simply higher. Additionally, some broadcasts received a score lower than 4.0 (between acceptable and good quality). This experiment also shows a clear advantage of the digital standard over the analog.

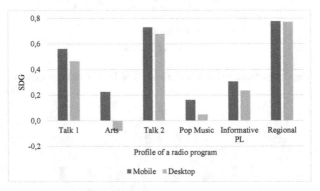

Fig. 4. Subjective difference grade of FM radio programs.

When statistically compiling obtained data using the analysis of variance (ANOVA) method, the confidence intervals were set to 95% ($\alpha = 0.05$). In all cases, the dispersion was less than 10% of the average values.

5   Conclusions

As shown, a portable light-weight device offers comparable reception quality to a heavier desktop one. The modern-day smartphone, with its possibilities of receiving, processing and presenting rich media content, is a handy companion in numerous activities [15–17]. According to obtained results, the digital DAB+ radio standard offers higher quality content compared to analog FM radio. Furthermore, a DAB+ compatible smartphone offers as good as, and sometimes even higher, audio reception quality than traditional household receivers. Therefore, integrating the digital radio standard into a wider range of consumer UE, particularly smartphones, would speed up the digitization process, as well as help the industry in the switchover process.

In the nearest future, it would seem interesting to perform similar studies considering different age groups, concerning both younger and older individuals with varying quality expectations and user preferences. Furthermore, it would seem interesting to evaluate people with different backgrounds, including those with audio-visual impairments, that are keen on technology and frequently listen to radio broadcasts. Another aspect is the design of the user interface itself, regardless whether talking about a physical receiver device or a mobile application.

As we know, digital terrestrial radio offers much more possibilities that the mere transmission of audio signals in the form of speech and music content. Therefore, efforts could be made in order to determine the potential of possible advertisements that could raise the overall income of broadcasters. This would certainly speed up the digitization process and the switchover from the analog to digital domain. Additional source of inspiration that may encourage future study directions, focused on the digital radio market and related fields in numerous countries around the world, may be found in [18–26].

References

1. WorldDAB: https://www.worlddab.org/. Accessed 13 July 2022
2. Falkowski-Gilski, P.: On the consumption of multimedia content using mobile devices: a year to year user case study. Arch. Acoust. **45**(2), 321–328 (2020)
3. Hoeg, W., Lauterbach, T.: Digital Audio Broadcasting: Principles and Applications of DAB, DAB+ and DMB, 3rd edn. John Wiley & Sons, Chichester (2009)
4. Oziewicz, M.: Digital radio DAB+, 1st edn. Springer, Cham (2022)
5. Falkowski-Gilski, P.: Digital transformation of terrestrial radio: an analysis of simulcasted broadcasts in FM and DAB+ for a smart and successful switchover. Appl. Sci. **11**(23), 11114 (2021)
6. Halett, L.: Broadcast radio: technology, challenges and opportunities in the twenty-first century. Interact.: Stud. Commun. Cult. **12**(1), 17–37 (2021)
7. Martin, E. N.: Can public service broadcasting survive Silicon Valley? Synthesizing leadership perspectives at the BBC, PBS, NPR, CPB and local U.S. stations. Technol. Soc. **64**, 101451 (2021)
8. dos Santos, V.M.J.: The current state and trends of the development of digital tele-radio broadcasting systems in the world. Synchroinfo J. **1**, 17–23 (2021)
9. Mayda, M.: Design empathy on digital radio platforms. OPUS – J. Soc. Res. **19**(48), 588–602 (2022)
10. Parnall, J.: European broadcasting union (EBU) update 2022. SMPTE Motion Imaging J. **131**(8), 82–87 (2022)
11. Zyka, K.: The influence of the bitrate level on the subjective sound quality perception of the concatenated non-entropic audio coding algorithms in the digital broadcasting chain. Radioengineering **29**, 672–682 (2020)
12. LG Newsroom: https://www.lgnewsroom.com/2016/03/lg-stylus-2-first-smartphone-to-sup port-dab/. Accessed 13 July 2022
13. TechniSat DigitRadio 350: https://www.technisat.com/en_XX/Productsheet/352-775/?pro duct=10328&createpdf. Accessed 13 July 2022
14. ITU Recommendation S.1284: General methods for the subjective assessment of sound quality (2003)
15. Falkowski-Gilski, P., Uhl, T.: Current trends in consumption of multimedia content using online streaming platforms: a user-centric survey. Comput. Sci. Rev. **37**, 100268 (2020)
16. Zhu, W., Wang, X., Gao, W.: Multimedia intelligence: when multimedia meets artificial intelligence. IEEE Trans. Multimedia **22**(7), 1823–1835 (2020)
17. Dao, N.N., Tran, A.T., Tu, N.H., Thanh, T.T., Bao, V.N.Q., Cho, S.: A contemporary survey on live video streaming from a computation-driven perspective. ACM Comput. Surv. 2022 (2022)
18. Stroink, D., Edwards, E.: Radio and audio in 2020. J. Radio Audio Media **28**(2), 344–354 (2021)
19. Bonet, M., Fernández-Quijada, D.: Sounds without borders: exploring the cross-national expansion of commercial European radio groups. Eur. J. Commun. **36**(6), 610–625 (2021)

20. Cusumano, M.A., Gawer, A., Yoffie, D.B.: Can self-regulation save digital platforms? Ind. Corp. Chang. **30**(5), 1259–1285 (2021)
21. Day, R.: A snapshot of Irish radio 2021. Interact.: Stud. Commun. Cult. **12**(1), 65–78 (2021)
22. McEwan, R., Mollgaard, M.: "Dollars and Listeners": revisiting the great New Zealand radio experiment of market deregulation. J. Radio Audio Media **28**(1), 162–181 (2021)
23. Nemcova Tejkalova, A., Gheorghiev, O., Supa, M., Nainova, V.: Children and the radio: who should listen to whom? Journal. Pract. **2021**, 1–19 (2021)
24. Laor, T.: Radio on demand: new habits of consuming radio content. Global Media Commun. **18**(1), 25–48 (2022)
25. Lv, J., Tao, Y.: Development and performance evaluation of digital technology and radio and television integration based on big data model. J. Sens. **2022**, 1843753 (2022)
26. Malmstedt, J.: Rhythms of silence: digital audio analysis of Swedish radio broadcasting, 1980–1989. J. Cult. Analytics **7**(1), 108–138 (2022)

Federated Learning-Based Interference Modeling for Vehicular Dynamic Spectrum Access

Marcin Hoffmann[(✉)], Pawel Kryszkiewicz, and Adrian Kliks

Institute of Radiocommunications, Poznań University of Technology, Polanka 3,
61-131 Poznań, Poland
marcin.hoffmann@put.poznan.pl

Abstract. A platoon-based driving is a technology allowing vehicles to
follow each other at close distances to, e.g., save fuel. However, it requires
reliable wireless communications to adjust their speeds. Recent studies
have shown that the frequency band dedicated for vehicle-to-vehicle communications can be too busy for intra-platoon communications. Thus it
is reasonable to use additional spectrum resources, of low occupancy, i.e.,
secondary spectrum channels. The challenge is to model the interference
in those channels to enable proper channel selection. In this paper, we
propose a two-layered Radio Environment Map (REM) that aims at providing platoons with accurate location-dependent interference models by
using the Federated Learning approach. Each platoon is equipped with
a Local REM that is updated on the basis of raw interference samples
and previous interference model stored in the Global REM. The model
in global REM is obtained by merging models reported by platoons. The
nodes exchange only parameters of interference models, reducing the
required control channel capacity. Moreover, in the proposed architecture platoon can utilize Local REM to predict channel occupancy, even
when the connection to the Global REM is temporarily unavailable. The
proposed system is validated via computer simulations considering non-
trivial interference patterns.

Keywords: Federated Learning · Radio Environment Map ·
Vehicle-to-Vehicle Communications · Vehicular Dynamic Spectrum
Access · Interference Modeling

1 Introduction

A platoon-based driving [7, 29, 33] is a technology allowing vehicles to follow each
other at short distances, i.e., of a few meters [40]. There are several significant
benefits originating from this innovative approach. First, due to short inter-car

The work has been realized within project no. 2018/29/B/ST7/01241 funded by the
National Science Centre in Poland.

© ICST Institute for Computer Sciences, Social Informatics and Telecommunications Engineering 2023
Published by Springer Nature Switzerland AG 2023. All Rights Reserved
S. Longfei and P. Bodhi (Eds.): MobiQuitous 2022, LNICST 492, pp. 431–454, 2023.
https://doi.org/10.1007/978-3-031-34776-4_23

distances, the road capacity can be improved by placing more vehicles on the road [41]. Second, vehicles following each other benefit from better aerodynamic conditions. This further implies fuel savings, and reduction of emitted pollution [10]. Most important, those gains from the platoon-based driving pattern are achieved with no need for additional road infrastructure, e.g., expensive and time-consuming building of additional road lanes. One, typically first, vehicle in the platoon is a so-called platoon leader. Depending on the concept, it can be either an autonomous vehicle or a vehicle with a human driver [18,36]. In most cases, the platoon leader is responsible for the platoon behavior, and other vehicles not only adjust their speed to the platoon leader but also follow its maneuvers, e.g., line change. However, it is a non-trivial task, especially, when the platoon leader is forced to sudden breaking. Research has shown that for the purpose of safe driving while maintaining short inter-vehicle distances, it is not enough to rely on the onboard sensors or cameras [45]. Additionally, reliable wireless communication must be established between the vehicles within the platoon to exchange control information, e.g., messages related to speed adjustment [39]. There are several protocols already defined that are aimed at wireless communications between vehicles (known as a vehicle-to-vehicle scheme, V2V), between vehicles and network infrastructure (called vehicle-to-infrastructure communications, V2I), and between vehicles and pedestrians (named vehicle-to-pedestrians V2P) [2]. These are collectively referred to as vehicles-to-everything (named widely V2X). In general, the idea of V2X communications can be realized either in a centralized way with the use of cellular technology (i.e., Cellular-V2X, C-V2X [1,20]), or in a distributed fashion by means of, e.g., Dedicated-Short-Range-Communication (DSRC) [22]. The DSRC solution can utilize 802.11p and Wireless Access in Vehicular Environment (WAVE) standards, in physical, and medium access layers, respectively [3]. Although there are dedicated frequency bands for both DSRC and C-V2X, these might not be sufficient when road traffic is high. Some research has shown that with a growing number of vehicles utilizing DSRC interference in this part of the spectrum will drastically grow, decreasing the reliability of the wireless communications [8,34]. Similar results were observed for C-V2X [43]. The low reliability is caused by the fact that under the high level of interference the DSRC and C-V2X-dedicated frequency bands will not be able to ensure the capacity of the wireless channel required by the platoon. This would further imply a need to increase the inter-vehicle spaces within the platoon to prevent potential intra-platoon crashes causing e.g., lower fuel savings. This contradicts the overall concept of a platoon-based driving pattern discussed above.

Therefore, it seems reasonable to look for alternative frequency bands where intra-platoon communication can be offloaded. Although almost all frequency bands are assigned to some wireless systems, the majority of these spectral resources are underutilized [24]. However, the frequency availability can vary with location or time. A platoon can potentially use a frequency band if it is not used at a given time in a given location. This requires detecting the radio activities of the so-called primary users (PUs), who are licensed to transmit in a particular frequency band. If PUs activity is not detected in this frequency band, this part of the spectrum can be opportunistically used by other systems. This approach is known in the literature as a Dynamic Spectrum Access (DSA) [49], and when it relates to V2X communications, the Vehicle DSA (VDSA) scenario is then considered [12]. In our work, we concentrate on the latter scheme.

Detection of the PU's signal presence may be done by means of the so-called spectrum sensing (such as energy detection). However, stand-alone spectrum sensing has limited performance. In addition, knowledge about the radio environment is out-dates fast as a result of vehicle movement in VDSA. An entity that can be used to retain and aggregate knowledge about the radio environment is a database called a Radio Environment Map (REM) [47]. The REM stores, updates, and process location-dependent information about the present PU's signal, which from the perspective of the unlicensed, so-called secondary user (SU) may be treated as interference. Such processing of historical data about interference possibly from many devices provides more insight into the availability of secondary spectrum channels. Moreover, please note that REMs may save also information about other ongoing SU transmissions.

The main challenge while utilizing a REM for VDSA is accurate modeling of interference caused by PU's signals along the route of the vehicle. In this context, the state-of-the-art models of interference utilized by REM are very simple, i.e., they characterize observed PU's signal power in a given location by its first-order statistics - the mean received power of unwanted signal [25, 27, 42]. Such a simple approach was reliable enough when DSA was applied to the terrestrial television band, as the transmitted digital terrestrial television (DTT) signals are stable over frequency and time. However, in the general case, especially when unlicensed bands are considered, the PUs can utilize various algorithms for medium access controls and different transmission schemes. In such situations, more sophisticated models must be used to deal with complex interference distributions. This observation fits well with the considered VDSA scheme, where the observed unwanted signal distributions vary as a function of the road (location) and time. The creation of stable and precise models of unwanted signals may be time-consuming, and in practice, only a limited number of interference samples can be collected at one time. Thus, proper mechanisms for updating interference models in REM must be proposed. These mechanisms should be designed so as to enable the simultaneous contribution of several data sources, e.g., multiple platoons.

In this paper, to deal with potentially complex distributions of interference generated by PUs, a Gaussian Mixture Model (GMM) [35] will be used. GMM can model a Probability Density Function (PDF) of interference samples power, as a weighted sum of Gaussian distribution PDFs. Based on the model a wireless channel capacity can be calculated and the optimal frequency obtained using the algorithm proposed by us in [21]. However, that paper did not deal with a merger of knowledge from many sources. As the GMM model of interference varies in space, we proposed to store GMM-location pairs in the REM. Moreover, we propose a two-layer architecture of REM dedicated for VDSA, consisting of a Global, and a Local REM respectively. In our approach platoons can download the estimated GMM from Global REM to its Local REM, and update Local

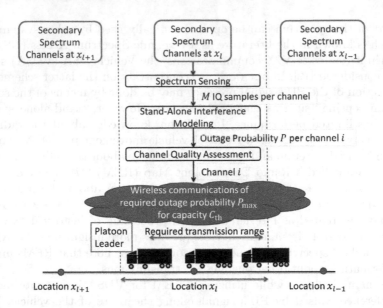

Fig. 1. Illustration of the stand-alone system model.

REM during ride based on local spectrum sensing. Later on, the locally updated GMM models from potentially many platoons are sent back to the Global REM to be merged into a single model therein. Such an architecture is enabled via Federated Learning (FL) [26,28]. We confirm the effectiveness of this scheme via computer simulations and compare it against local sensing. The local interference modeling, without REM utilization, provides much worse insight into the distribution of interference for the platoon. Moreover, we show that the more platoons contribute to the update of Global REM the higher accuracy interference models can be obtained.

The paper is organized as follows: In Sect. 2 a stand-alone system model is described, i.e., without REM. The proposed two-layered REM architecture together with formulas for an update of both local and global models is presented in Sect. 3. The simulation setup is described in Sect. 4. The results are discussed in Sect. 5. Finally, the conclusions are formulated in Sect. 6.

2   Stand-Alone System Model

Let us consider the generic case, where platoons offload a portion of their traffic from congested CV2X/DSRC bands to other frequency ranges, already occupied by the PU. All U platoons apply the VDSA scheme trying to select the best frequency channels from all $\mathcal{I}$ candidate channels of bandwidth B. However, no additional edge intelligence, e.g., REM is used. A single platoon of index u is formulated by N_u vehicles, as depicted in Fig. 1. At a given time instance a platoon u is located at position $\mathbf{x}_l$ being a vector of geographical coordinates related to platoon location expressed in arbitrary chosen coordinates system e.g., earth-centered earth-fixed (ECEF). The behavior of the platoon, including maintaining proper inter-vehicle distances and management of intra-platoon communications, is realized by the first vehicle, which acts as a platoon leader. It sends proper management information to the remaining $N_u - 1$ vehicles using wireless communications. To benefit from the platoon-based driving pattern, vehicles must drive at a very short distance. This implies wireless communication to meet high requirements on QoS. In our scenario, VDSA is assumed, so each platoon is looking for the secondary spectrum channel that would meet the platoon communication requirements. The selection of i-th frequency channel out of setting $\mathcal{I}$, consists of several steps (Fig. 1), mainly spectrum sensing, interference modeling, and channel quality assessment These steps are described below from the perspective of a single platoon, yet all U platoons are performing them independently.

2.1   Capture of Samples

The first step is to capture power samples from secondary spectrum channels available at location $\mathbf{x}_l$. We assume that every vehicle in the platoon can be potentially involved in this process. Thus samples can be simultaneously collected from several secondary spectrum channels. In each channel, a batch of M in-phase and quadrature (IQ) received signal samples is collected in total.

2.2   Channel Quality Assessment

Although in Fig. 1 *Interference Modeling* stands for the second step, it will be easier to understand the whole idea when the Channel Quality Assessment (CQA) would be described first. Moreover, some mechanisms used in interference modeling are related to the proposed CQA method.

First, when discussing the CQA, the challenge is to choose the proper evaluation metric. From the perspective of overall communications reliability, one of the most important aspects is to monitor the latency [14]. However, it is not straightforward to estimate it, as latency highly depends on the utilized radio access technology and medium access protocol. Both are in general not known when considering secondary spectrum channels, especially when many systems of different radio access technologies may operate. Moreover, according to the state-of-the-art models to assess latency, the knowledge of the arrival rate distribution of the incoming packets is necessary [48]. Its estimation is also case-dependent. On the other hand, a well-established metric is the Shannon capacity of a wireless channel being the upper bound estimate of the real system throughput. This metric is irrespective of the properties of the particular communication system, e.g., medium access control, and modulation schemes. Thus, in this paper, we follow this approach to assess channel quality.

We compute the capacity of channel i of bandwidth B as a sum over N_f narrow sub-channels, which is motivated by the following observations. First, in the secondary spectrum, there may be potentially many interference sources of various frequency-dependent transmission characteristics, e.g., some of them may be narrow-band, and some wide-band. Second, in most of the contemporary communication protocols dedicated to V2V the multicarrier modulation scheme (Orthogonal-Frequency-Division-Multiplexing, OFDM) is applied, e.g., in IEEE 802.11p or CV2X using LTE or 5G networks. We consider the communication between the platoon leader and the last vehicle, as it is the most challenging because of the highest path loss. In consequence, at location $\mathbf{x}_l$ the Shannon capacity of the secondary spectrum channel i, between the two most distant vehicles within the platoon is given by:

$$c^{(i,\mathbf{x}_l)} = \frac{B}{N_f} \sum_{f \in \mathcal{F}} \log_2 \left(1 + \frac{P_{\text{tx}}^{(i,\mathbf{x}_l)} \cdot H(i, \mathbf{x}_l)}{\sigma_n^2 + I_f^{(i,\mathbf{x}_l)}} \right),$$

(1)

where $\mathcal{F}$ is a set of usable sub-channels (indexed by f), $H(i, \mathbf{x}_l)$ is a large scale channel gain (including transmit and receive antenna gains) at location $\mathbf{x}_l$ between the platoon leader and the last car. Next, $P_{\text{tx}}^{(i,\mathbf{x}_l)}$ is the transmitter power per sub-channel, σ_n^2 is the noise power over one sub-channel f, and $I_f^{(i,\mathbf{x}_l)}$ stands for the interference power on sub-carrier f. According to the field measurements, communication between vehicles following each other in the close distance, i.e., below 60 m, is expected to be mainly under Line-Of-Sight (LOS) conditions for roof-top antennas [32]. This observation can be applied to the communication between the platoon leader, and the last vehicle in a platoon consisting of a few vehicles, e.g. 3–4. As a result we expect channel to be relatively stable and flat. On the other hand interference in secondary spectrum potentially comes from the variety of sources having different transmission schemes. Therefore, our main focus is on the interference impact on the channel capacity.

While interference varies randomly, the capacity also becomes the random variable. From the perspective of the intra-platoon communication it is crucial to determine how likely is that channel capacity $c^{(i,\mathbf{x}_l)}$ falls below the acceptable level C_{th}, i.e., to derive the outage probability $\mathcal{P}(c^{(i,\mathbf{x}_l)} < C_{\text{th}})$. Having (1) as a starting point, in our previous work, we proposed to utilize Shannon capacity simplification proper for low Signal to Noise Ratio (SNR), in order to obtain the formula for the computation of the outage probability on the basis of interference distribution, and remaining transmission parameters, e.g., bandwidth, transmission power [21]:

$$\mathcal{P}\left(\chi^{(i,\mathbf{x}_l)} < \ln \frac{\ln 2 \cdot C_{\text{th}} \cdot N_f}{B \cdot P_{\text{tx}}^{(i,\mathbf{x}_l)} \cdot H(i, \mathbf{x}_l)} \right),$$

(2)

where $\chi^{(i,\mathbf{x}_l)}$ is a random variable logarithm of aggregated interference and noise given by:

$$\chi^{(i,\mathbf{x}_l)} = \ln \left(\sum_{f \in \mathcal{F}} \frac{1}{I_f^{(i,\mathbf{x}_l)} + \sigma_n^2} \right).$$

(3)

With the use of the above equations quality of the available secondary spectrum, channels can be assessed, and the platoon leader can make the decision on the transmission channel to be in use. The detailed mathematical reasoning aimed at transformation of (1) into the (2) can be found in [21].

2.3   Interference Modeling

After the introduction of the CQA metric given by (2), it can be observed that this metric requires an accurate model of interference term $\chi^{(i,\mathbf{x}_l)}$. The secondary spectrum channels can be occupied by many interference sources of different emission powers, diverse radio access technologies, various modulations, and not identical bandwidths. As a result the interference term $\chi^{(i,\mathbf{x}_l)}$ can follow a non-trivial, multi-modal distribution. It has been shown that such multi-modal distributions can be efficiently modeled with the use of the so-called Gaussian Mixture Model (GMM) [6]. The idea behind the GMM is to represent an arbitrary Probability Density Function (PDF), as a properly weighted sum of J Gaussian distribution PDFs. In the considered case $\chi^{(i,\mathbf{x}_l)}$ is a one-dimensional random variable, thus GMM would be given by:

$$p(\chi^{(i,\mathbf{x}_l)}) = \sum_{j=1}^{J} \pi_j \mathcal{N}(\chi^{(i,\mathbf{x}_l)}|\mu_j,\sigma_j), \tag{4}$$

where $p(\chi^{(i,\mathbf{x}_l)})$ denotes the distribution of $\chi^{(i,\mathbf{x}_l)}$, π_j is the j-th mixture component weight, i.e., the probability that $\chi^{(i,\mathbf{x}_l)}$ comes from the j-th mixture component. Next, $\mathcal{N}(\chi^{(i,\mathbf{x}_l)}|\mu_j,\sigma_j)$ is the conditional Gaussian distribution of $\chi^{(i,\mathbf{x}_l)}$, i.e., Gaussian distribution of $\chi^{(i,\mathbf{x}_l)}$, under assumption that it comes from the j-th mixture component with mean μ_j and standard deviation σ_j. To obtain parameters of a random distribution it is common to use a closed-form maximum likelihood estimator, i.e., closed form expressions are computed through maximization of the likelihood function. Unfortunately, in the case of GMM the log-likelihood function is a sum over the exponential functions, and no closed-form estimator exists [6]. Instead an iterative algorithm named Expectation Maximization (EM) is widely in use [15].

In this work the EM algorithm will be used to compute the parameters of GMM on the basis of $N_s = \frac{M}{N_f}$ samples of interference term $\chi^{(i,\mathbf{x}_l)}$. These samples are obtained from M IQ samples captured each time any of the U platoons visits location $\mathbf{x}_l$. The M IQ samples are first divided into N_s non-overlapping segments, each of N_f samples. For each of these segments a Discrete Fourier Transform of size N_f is applied. Next, the power samples are computed within each sub-channel. Finally, by applying (3) a single value of $\chi^{(i,\mathbf{x}_l)}$ is obtained for each of these segments. These N_s samples of variable $\chi^{(i,\mathbf{x}_l)}$ constitutes an input to the EM algorithm. In the stand-alone approach discussed in this section, the platoon u can rely only on the temporarily computed GMM to obtain the least occupied secondary spectrum channel i. In other words, the platoon senses the channel i for the assumed period (obtaining N_s samples of interference term $\chi^{(i,\mathbf{x}_l)}$), and generates the GMM interference model following the traditional EM approach. Once it is done, it decides on the spectrum occupancy and prospective capacity as described in Sect. 2.2. We will refer to this schema as *Stand-Alone Interference Modeling* (SAIM) throughout the rest of this paper, as it models the spectral usage characteristic without additional information provided by other entities, e.g., REM. We treat it as a reference solution.

The SAIM approach has a significant drawback. The GMM model is computed only on the basis of a limited number of locally collected samples. To make the generated GMM reliable, the simplest approach would be to set N_s to a large value. However, the primary goal of wireless communications within the platoon is to maintain safety on the road, especially when the inter-car distances are very short. Thus, it would be inefficient for the platoon to spend too much time on sensing, and thus N_s is expected to be low, creating a risk of inaccurate interference modeling through the GMM. In the following section (Sect. 3) we show how to overcome this issue by equipping the network infrastructure with REM modules utilizing a Federated Learning algorithm in order to enable continuous improvement of interference distribution models.

3   REM and Federated Learning for Interference Modeling

In order to overcome the drawbacks of the SAIM approach we propose to utilize historical knowledge gathered about the interference observed in the location x_l for better spectrum utilization estimation. We also propose the application of the federated learning approach for improving the interference modeling by exchanging interference awareness between all interested platoons.

3.1   REM for Interference Modeling

From the perspective of spectrum management and the best channel selection, the REM may be treated as an intelligent database containing location-dependent information about various signal sources (both, wanted and of interference type) observed in the wireless communication system [47]. The users can communicate with REM via a side link to e.g. obtain information about the interference related to their positions or provide REM with their own measurement data. The entries in the database may have various forms, from raw measurements to some averaged figures of merit such as averaged received power in the band of interest. Although such REM databases may be applied to any frequency band and to any application, in the context of DSA the terrestrial television band was often in focus [23,37,38]. In this frequency band, the interference is usually homogeneous, i.e., it has a stable average level over time and at a given location. In such a case, the interference can be easily modeled by the average power of the observed signal. However, as already mentioned, this idea can be extended to build a REM database capable of modeling more complicated distributions, e.g., with interference power varying in time and frequency. Mainly, instead of average power, the parameters of GMMs related to the secondary spectrum channels $\mathcal{I}$ can be stored for each location x_l. This structure of the

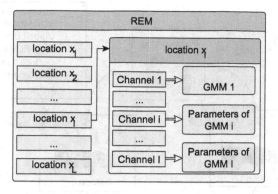

Fig. 2. The structure of data in REM.

data in REM is depicted in Fig. 2. One can observe that each location is associated with the dictionary of tuples: channel and related GMM model parameters. From the architectural perspective, we propose a two-layered scheme, as depicted in Fig. 3, where Global REM and Local REMs are shown. Global REM is a part of the network infrastructure (belonging to, e.g., mobile network operator). It stores the global interference models, distributes them to the Local REMs, i.e., platoons, and is capable to combine them together in order to update its own global interference model. In turn, the Local REM is deployed and managed (updated) at each platoon u. Thus, in our case, in the first step, the Local REM will be populated by the data downloaded from the Global REM. Next, these entries will be updated locally every time the platoon captures new N_s samples of interference term $\chi^{(i,\mathbf{x}_l)}$. Once processed locally, they will be used for updating the global REM, when the link to it is available. The idea behind the two-layered REM architecture aims at increasing the reliability of the system. While every platoon has its own Local REM, it can still use the interference models even when the side link to the Global REM is temporarily unavailable. Local REM is being updated on the basis of the raw samples, associated with the local environment, so it can reflect the current situation in the network and update the received model accordingly. As mentioned above, Local REM may also contribute to updating the Global REM models by sending back local observations or trained parameters. However, as the Local REM contains the whole GMM model it is enough to send only the model parameters to the Global REM instead of raw measurements. This results in significant traffic load reduction, i.e., order of tens parameters per GMM model vs hundreds of captured raw samples that have to be sent over the side link. Such an approach is inspired by the popular federated learning scheme [30,44,46], where the trained model details are exchanged between the central and surrounding nodes in order to better train the model and better reflect the local environment observed by each node. The procedure of secondary spectrum channel selection which utilizes interference

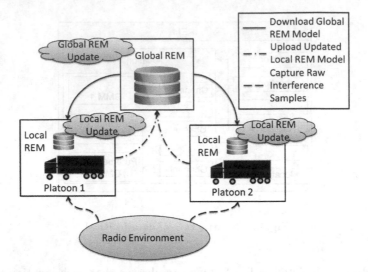

Fig. 3. Two-Layer REM architecture with FL cycle marked.

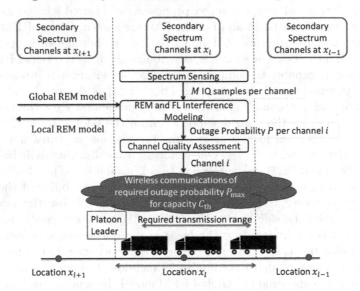

Fig. 4. Illustration of the REM and FL-based system model.

modeling based on REM and FL is summarized in Fig. 4. It can be seen that it is an extension of the state-of-the-art SAIM approach presented in Sect. 2.

3.2   Local REM Update

Let us denote the set of GMM parameters in Local REM related to the channel i, location $\mathbf{x}_l$, and platoon u as $g_u(\mathbf{x}_l, i)$. These GMM parameters are obtained from the total number of samples equal to $N_{r,u}(\mathbf{x}_l, i)$. Every time when the location $\mathbf{x}_l$ is visited by the platoon u, only N_s new samples of interference term $\chi^{(i,\mathbf{x}_l)}$ per each secondary spectrum channel i can be captured. These new samples are used to update the parameters of Local REM model $g_u(\mathbf{x}_l, i)$. The update procedure starts from computation of a temporal GMM model of J components from those new N_s samples. The set of parameters of this temporal GMM model is denoted as $\tilde{g}_u(\mathbf{x}_l, i)$. The same number of GMM components J for both $g_u(\mathbf{x}_l, i)$, and $\tilde{g}_u(\mathbf{x}_l, i)$. In general, J can be established every time a new temporal GMM model of parameters set $\tilde{g}_u(\mathbf{x}_l, i)$ is built, by creating several models and comparing them against each other in terms of the chosen metric, e.g., Akaike Information Criterion (AIC), which is the function of model log-likelihood, and the number of parameters [5]. To reduce the number of GMM parameters to be sent between Local and Global REM we decided to use the shared-covariance variant of GMM, where a single variance is computed and shared among all J components.

The parameters set of GMM model from Local REM $g_u(\mathbf{x}_l, i)$ consists of: shared variance $\sigma_u^2(\mathbf{x}_l, i)$, vector of means $\boldsymbol{\mu}_u(\mathbf{x}_l, i) = \{\mu_{u,j}(\mathbf{x}_l, i)\}_{j=1}^J$, vector of components proportions $\boldsymbol{\pi}_u(\mathbf{x}_l, i) = \{\pi_{u,j}(\mathbf{x}_l, i)\}_{j=1}^J$. The parameters set of temporal GMM model $\tilde{g}_u(\mathbf{x}_l, i)$ computed from the new N_s samples of interference term $\chi^{(i,\mathbf{x}_l)}$ is created by: $\tilde{\sigma}_u^2(\mathbf{x}_l, i)$, $\tilde{\boldsymbol{\mu}}_u(\mathbf{x}_l, i) = \{\tilde{\mu}_{u,j}(\mathbf{x}_l, i)\}_{j=1}^J$, $\tilde{\boldsymbol{\pi}}_u(\mathbf{x}_l, i) = \{\tilde{\pi}_{u,j}(\mathbf{x}_l, i)\}_{j=1}^J$. For implementation purpose of combining together corresponding pairs of Local REM model parameters $g_u(\mathbf{x}_l, i)$ and temporal GMM model parameters $\tilde{g}_u(\mathbf{x}_l, i)$ we recommend to sort the vectors $\boldsymbol{\mu}_u(\mathbf{x}_l, i)$, $\boldsymbol{\pi}_u(\mathbf{x}_l, i)$, according to the $\boldsymbol{\mu}_u(\mathbf{x}_l, i)$ values, and vectors $\tilde{\boldsymbol{\mu}}_u(\mathbf{x}_l, i)$, $\tilde{\boldsymbol{\pi}}_u(\mathbf{x}_l, i)$ according to the $\tilde{\boldsymbol{\mu}}_u(\mathbf{x}_l, i)$.

Now the parameters of the Local REM model $g_u(\mathbf{x}_l, i)$ are updated utilizing modified formula of incremental GMM learning [11]:

$$\sigma_u(\mathbf{x}_l, i) \leftarrow \frac{N_{\text{th},u}(\mathbf{x}_l, i) \cdot \sigma_u(\mathbf{x}_l, i) + N_s \cdot \tilde{\sigma}_u(\mathbf{x}_l, i)}{N_{\text{th},u}(\mathbf{x}_l, i) + N_s},$$

$$\mu_{u,j}(\mathbf{x}_l, i) \leftarrow \frac{N_{\text{th},u}(\mathbf{x}_l, i) \cdot \mu_{u,j}(\mathbf{x}_l, i) + N_s \cdot \tilde{\mu}_{u,j}(\mathbf{x}_l, i)}{N_{\text{th},u}(\mathbf{x}_l, i) + N_s},$$

$$\pi_{u,j}(\mathbf{x}_l, i) \leftarrow \frac{N_{\text{th},u}(\mathbf{x}_l, i) \cdot \pi_{u,j}(\mathbf{x}_l, i) + N_s \cdot \tilde{\pi}_{u,j}(\mathbf{x}_l, i)}{N_{\text{th},u}(\mathbf{x}_l, i) + N_s},$$

$$N_{r,u}(\mathbf{x}_l, i) \leftarrow N_{r,u}(\mathbf{x}_l, i) + N_s,$$

(5)

where $N_{\text{th},u}(\mathbf{x}_l, i) = \min\{N_{r,u}(\mathbf{x}_l, i), k \cdot N_s\}$, and k is a positive integer. The N_{th} parameter is defined so as to ensure that model can potentially follow the environment changes, it can be think of as a learning rate, i.e., how much impact on the model new data have. The larger the k is the less impact the parameters of temporal GMM model $\tilde{g}_u(\mathbf{x}_l, i)$ have on the update of Local REM model parameters $g_u(\mathbf{x}_l, i)$. In the case when at a given platoon location $\mathbf{x}_l$ there is no information about interference model in REM, the values of GMM model parameters in Local REM are assumed to be initialized with set of temporal GMM model parameters $\tilde{g}_u(\mathbf{x}_l, i)$.

3.3 Global REM Update

In general, we can expect that multiple platoons can follow the same or partially overlapping route. A platoon u will update its Local REM, following the procedure described in Sect. 3.2. Suppose there are U platoons that updated their Local REMS and send updated models back to the Global REM. The question arises of how to combine the U models from Local REMs into the Global REM model. One could notice that this concept fits well into the idea of FL, where multiple clients train their local models, which are sent to server and processed to update the global model [4]. Thus, in order to update the Global REM, We have decided to implement the state-of-the-art FL algorithm named FedAvg [31]. The FedAvg formula for updating the Global REM is defined as a weighted average of the parameters from the Local REMs. The detail update rule of GMM model parameters in Global REM related to channel i, and location $\mathbf{x}_l$ is presented below:

$$
\sigma_g(\mathbf{x}_l, i) \leftarrow \frac{\sum_{u=1}^{U} N_{\text{th},u}(\mathbf{x}_l, i) \cdot \sigma_u(\mathbf{x}_l, i)}{\sum_{u=1}^{U} N_{\text{th},u}(\mathbf{x}_l, i)}
$$

$$
\mu_{g,j}(\mathbf{x}_l, i) \leftarrow \frac{\sum_{u=1}^{U} N_{\text{th},u}(\mathbf{x}_l, i) \cdot \mu_{u,j}(\mathbf{x}_l, i)}{\sum_{u=1}^{U} N_{\text{th},u}(\mathbf{x}_l, i)} \tag{6}
$$

$$
\pi_{g,j}(\mathbf{x}_l, i) \leftarrow \frac{\sum_{u=1}^{U} N_{\text{th},u}(\mathbf{x}_l, i) \cdot \pi_{u,j}(\mathbf{x}_l, i)}{\sum_{u=1}^{U} N_{\text{th},u}(\mathbf{x}_l, i)},
$$

where $\sigma_g(\mathbf{x}_l, i)$ is the standard deviation shared among all GMM components, $\mu_{g,j}(\mathbf{x}_l, i)$ is the mean of j-th GMM component, and $\pi_{u,j}(\mathbf{x}_l, i)$ is the proportion of j-th GMM component.

3.4 Federated Learning Cycle

The procedure of Local REM update described in Sect. 3.2, together with the procedure of Global REM update described in Sect. 3.3 would follow each other in a cyclic manner in order to learn Global REM with interference distributions. This constitutes an FL cycle, that according to the principles defined in [4], can be specified as shown in Algorithm 1. This FL cycle can be visible also in the proposed two-layer REM architecture in Fig. 3.

4   Simulation Scenario

Training of the GMM models requires a lot of data to be processed, especially when multiple platoons are considered. To guarantee the reliability of the model, a dedicated and detailed simulation environment has been built in order to generate interference samples along with the consecutive platoon locations. We consider three non-overlapping Wireless Local Area Network (WLAN) channels having 2.412 GHz, 2.437 GHz, and 2.462 GHz center frequencies, respectively. At the same time, they formulate a set of available secondary spectrum channels $\mathcal{I}$,

Algorithm 1. FL Cycle for Update of Global REM

1: Distribute parameters of Global REM model among U platoons in the location $\mathbf{x}_l$
2: **for each** platoon $u \in U$ **do**
3:     **for each** channel $i \in \mathcal{I}$ **do**
4:         Capture M new IQ interference samples
5:         Obtain N_s samples of interference term $\chi^{(i,\mathbf{x}_l)}$
6:         Compute set of temporal GMM model
           parameters $\tilde{g}_u(\mathbf{x}_l, i)$ from N_s aggregated
           interference samples using EM algorithm
7:         Update parameters of Local REM model
           $g_u(\mathbf{x}_l, i)$ with the use of eq. (5)
8:     **end for**
9: **end for**
10: Send sets of Local REM's models parameters $g_u(\mathbf{x}_l, i)$ from U platoons to Global REM
11: Update Global REM following the eq. (6)

---

for which we model the interference using the proposed algorithms. Choice of this frequency band (i.e. ISM band) is motivated by the fact that there are many devices of potentially various medium access control algorithms, and modulations transmitting therein. As a result, non-trivial interference distributions are expected to be observed, which makes the modeling process challenging. The set of platoon locations $\mathbf{x}_l$ together with the deployment of interfering access points is depicted in Fig. 5. We are considering a 1 km long fragment of the route, which is split into 30 equally spaced segments (platoon locations) $\mathbf{x}_l$. Moreover, there are in total 11 wireless access points deployed along the considered platoon route. They generate interference over 3 different radio channels that correspond to orange, purple, and yellow triangles, respectively.

Every time a platoon u visit location $\mathbf{x}_l$, a batch of N_s new aggregated interference samples is calculated according to (3). We assume bandwidth $B = 10$ MHz, number of sub-channels $N_f = 64$, and number of used sub-channels $|\mathcal{F}| = 48$ with spacing set to 156.3 kHz, as defined in the 802.11p specification [3]. To generate interference from the access point a four-state model of spectrum occupancy is used [19]. In this model idle state between acknowledgment message and transmission of new data, the block is modeled by an exponential distribution of traffic rate parameter $\lambda = 0.0054$ ms^{-1}. The remaining busy states including the transmission of data and acknowledgment message last jointly 0.81 ms under the assumption of 512-byte packet size. To compute the large-scale fading coefficient of the radio channel between an access point and a platoon, a two-slope model proper for vehicular communications is used [13]. The small-scale variations of the radio channel are generated using Rayleigh distribution, and power-delay profile proper for the scenario where the platoon route is crossing an urban area [17]. Finally, the Gaussian-distributed thermal noise of power proper for the temperature of 20 °C is considered.

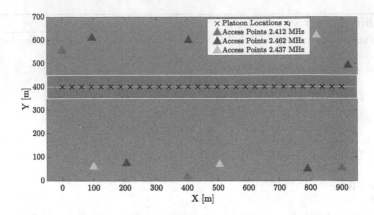

Fig. 5. Simulation scenario with platoon locations (black "x"), and access points locations (orange, purple, and yellow triangles respectively) (Color figure online)

Table 1. Parameters of Simulation Scenario

Parameter	Value
number of vehicles in a platoon N_u	3
platoon-leader to N_u-th vehicle distance	50 m
distance traveled by the platoon	1 km
number of the platoon location	30
number of access points	11
secondary spectrum channels $\mathcal{I}$	2.412, 2.437, 2.462 GHz
secondary channel bandwidth B	10 MHz
transmitted power per sub-carrier P_{tx}	3.19 dBm
desired capacity C_{th}	3 Mbit/s
number of sub-channels N_f	64
number of usable sub-channels $|\mathcal{F}|$	48
traffic rate parameter λ	0.0054 ms^{-1}

The considered location can be simultaneously visited by the $U \geq 1$ platoons. In each platoon, the distance between the platoon-leader and the last N_u-th vehicle is equal to 50 m. It corresponds to a 3-truck platoon. It is the minimum number of vehicles that are required to capture interference samples from all sets of three secondary spectrum channels $\mathcal{I}$. Transmitted power per subcarrier P_{tx} value is the maximum allowed in the 2.4 GHz band [16] and set to 3.19 dBm, including antenna gains. Finally, 3 Mbit/s is set to be the desired capacity C_{th}. It is the lowest supported bitrate in 802.11p, claimed to be used for emergency messages [9].

The simulation parameters are summarized in Table. 1.

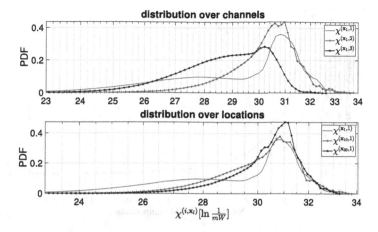

Fig. 6. Distribution of the aggregated interference $\chi^{(\mathbf{x}_l,i)}$ over different channels and platoon locations

5   Results

In this Section the evaluation of the algorithms proposed in Sect. 2, and Sect. 3 is performed using the simulation environment described in Sect. 4.

5.1   Baseline Model

At the first stage, we have analyzed an interference distribution $\chi^{(i,\mathbf{x}_l)}$ on the basis of large batch of captured samples, i.e., $M = 39321600$ IQ samples, that corresponds to the $N_s = 614400$ samples of aggregated interference. This reflects a scenario where all data captured by the platoons were reported to REM, and once the statistically large number of samples has been collected, the proper GMM models can be computed. To prove our claim that interference can follow non-trivial, multi-modal distributions, there are representative examples of probability density functions related to $\chi^{(i,\mathbf{x}_l)}$ distributions depicted in Fig. 6. As it can bee observed, the distributions are complex, and they are varying over locations, and between channels. On the basis of these results, GMM models have been created for every secondary spectrum channel in each of the 30 platoon locations. They will serve as baseline models for evaluation of the proposed algorithms: SAIM, and based on REM and FL. Set of parameters of these GMM models are denoted as $g_B(\mathbf{x}_l, i)$. In order to determine the number of components J for the GMMs, we have built baseline models of $J \leq 15$ components on the basis of 90 data sets, i.e., 30 locations and 3 frequencies. The $g_B(\mathbf{x}_l, i)$ models are evaluated in terms of their AIC. The average AIC is depicted in Fig. 7. It can be seen that after the number of GMM components is above $J = 7$ the AIC remains stable, and the observed AIC improvement is very small. Thus, we decided to fix this number, i.e., $J = 7$ in the following simulations. Clearly, in practice, the value of J has to be adjusted to each situation, based on observed

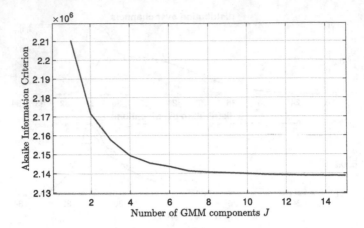

Fig. 7. Average AIC related to the GMM models of J components. There are 90 training data sets considered.

and sensed interference sources, and based on the length of the considered road fragment.

5.2 Single Platoon Scenario

We first evaluate the accuracy of the proposed method of interference modeling in the scenario where the number of the platoons that simultaneously travel the considered route is set to one, i.e., $U = 1$. In this scenario, our main aim is to evaluate the algorithm of the Local REM update as described in Sect. 3.2. In one simulation run, the platoon travels the same route 25 times, i.e., Local REM is updated 25 times at each location $\mathbf{x}_l$. To smooth the results, up to 50 simulation runs are performed. There are two parameters to be evaluated: the number of captured aggregated interference samples N_s, and the learning rate $N_{\text{th},u}(\mathbf{x}_l, i)$ driven by the parameter k, as defined by (5). First, k is arbitrary set to 5, and the impact of the number of captured aggregated interference samples N_s on the Local REM update is under consideration. The Root-Mean-Square-Error (RMSE) computed between the outage probability estimated with the use of updated Local REM and the baseline model is depicted in Fig. 8. It can be seen that after about 15 updates of Local REM, i.e., after the platoon traveled the considered route 15 times, all results tend to stabilize, and no further improvement of the RMSE could be observed. However, the level of stabilization depends on the number of captured aggregated interference samples N_s. For the lowest $N_s = 1024$ RMSE is approximately equal to 0.007, while for the $N_s = 4096$ is about 0.0055, that is over 20% improvement with N_s increase. Obviously, it can be further improved by increasing N_s, but the cost to be paid is less time for the intra-platoon communications. On the other hand, the initial analysis not presented here shows that decreasing the N_s leads to computational instability while estimating the set of GMM model parameters $\tilde{g}_u(\mathbf{x}_l, i)$.

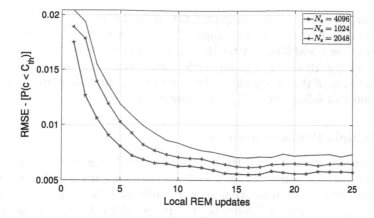

Fig. 8. RMSE computed between the outage probability estimated with the use of updated Local REM and the baseline model, for $k = 5$. Results are averaged over 50 simulations.

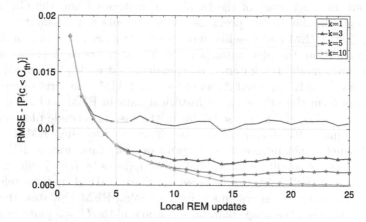

Fig. 9. RMSE computed between the outage probability estimated with the use of Local REM and the baseline model, for $k = 5$. Results are averaged over 50 simulations.

Later on, we have investigated the impact of the parameter k defining the learning rate on the Local REM updates. This time the number of collected aggregated interference samples N_s is set to the 4096. The related RMSE between the outage probability computed with the use of Local REM and baseline model, respectively, is depicted in Fig. 9.

It can be seen that the higher the parameter k, the better the RMSE. However, one should note that in the considered case interference being produced by each of the access points is a stationary random process. In the practical systems, it might not be true, thus it is reasonable not to choose very big k allowing adaptation to the changing radio conditions, e.g., turn-off of an access point. Moreover, it can be seen that when $k = 1$, results are unstable. It is because in this case newly computed GMM model possibly of low accuracy because of a limited number of samples N_s, has the same weight as the GMM model stored in Local REM. After the stabilization of the results, RMSE values obtained for $k = 10$ are approximately 5 times better than those for $k = 1$. The final conclusion is that k should be large enough to provide stable results, but small enough to follow the radio environment changes.

5.3   Multiple Platoons Scenario

Having the algorithm of Local REM updates evaluated now is the time to move to the general case where $U \geq 1$ platoons can capture interference samples simultaneously at a given location $\mathbf{x}_l$, and participate in the process of improving the Global REM model, following the proposed FL-based approach. In this scenario, U platoons travel through the set of locations 15 times. This procedure is repeated 50 times in order to average the results. Now, we set number of aggregated interference samples N_s to 4096, and the k parameter to 5. Our focus is put on the impact of the number of platoons U on the Global REM improvement. Similar to the previous plots, the outage probability computed with the Global REM and baseline models are compared in terms of RMSE in Fig. 10. In addition, the plot contains a result that refers to the scenario where the interference model is computed independently at each platoon only on the basis of the currently captured N_s samples, i.e., SAIM. The first observation is that benefits from the utilization of historical data in REM and FL are significantly compared to the SAIM scenario. In the case of a single platoon, $U = 1$ RMSE after many REM updates is about 3 times lower than RMSE obtained for SAIM which is not improving as a result of lack of memory in REM. Moreover, in the case of simultaneous Global REM updates by $U = 7$ platoons, a 4.5 fold reduction of the RMSE can be observed after 25 REM updates referring to the SAIM. Comparing the systems utilizing Global REM Updates, the biggest difference is between the single platoon scenario and the $U = 3$ platoon scenario, i.e., about 27% after 25 REM updates. While increasing further the number of simultaneously sensing platoons only a very little improvement can be observed, e.g., comparing between $U = 5$ and $U = 7$ the improvement is at the level of about 3%.

5.4   Channel Selection

It is important to take into account that the proposed algorithm of interference modeling realized with the use of a REM and FL is not the target itself. It is a tool to enable the selection of a proper secondary spectrum channel, as described in Sect. 2. On the basis of the interference models stored in REMs, platoons can decide which channels should be chosen along their route, e.g., on the basis of Dijkstra's algorithm, as discussed in [21]. In this paper, the simplest approach is evaluated, where a platoon chooses a wireless channel characterized by the

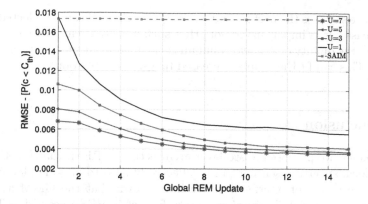

Fig. 10. RMSE computed between the outage probability estimated with the use of Global REM and the baseline model, for $N_s = 4096$, $k = 5$, and the varying number of platoons U. Additionally, the results of the SAIM scheme are included. Results are averaged over 50 simulations.

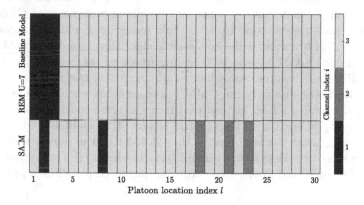

Fig. 11. Index i of channel offering the lowest outage probability in the consecutive platoon locations $\mathbf{x}_l$ computed on the basis of baseline, Global REM, and *Spectrum Sensing* interference model.

lowest outage probability. In Fig. 11 there is an index of channel offering the lowest outage probability in the consecutive platoon locations computed on the basis of the baseline model, the model utilizing REM (with Local and Global REM updates), and SAIM. We assume that the Global REM that is used is built from data captured by the $U = 7$ platoons during 15 route travels, and the considered parameters are: $N_s = 4096$, and $k = 5$. It can be seen that the channels marked as the best on the basis of the interference model from REM cover up with the ones computed using the baseline model in all cases, which is highly expected and proves the correctness of the proposed method. On the other hand, results based on SAIM correctly indicate the best radio channels only in 24 out of 30 platoon locations. It means that on the basis of only currently available interference samples the best secondary spectrum channel can be selected only in 80 % of cases. It is important to note that such a mistake can have a significant impact on the quality of wireless communications between vehicles formulating a platoon. This can further imply decreased fuel saves or platoon crash in extreme case.

6   Conclusion

In this paper, we proposed a two-layer architecture of REM, that together with FL and local spectrum sensing can be effectively used to provide platoons with an accurate model of interference. We have shown that the GMM accurately models the non-trivial distributions of interference in VDSA scenarios. Through the extensive computer simulations studies, we came to conclusion that historical data from REM can much improve the accuracy of interference models used by the platoon to predict radio channel occupancy in relation to the state-of-the-art SAIM approach. Moreover, it has been observed, that due to utilization of the FL multiple platoons can contribute to the improvement of Global REM interference models even more. Up to 4.5 fold reduction in channel capacity estimate RMSE was observed while comparing algorithm based on REM and FL against standard SAIM approach. It is important to notice that the proposed two-layer REM architecture have low requirements on the capacity of control channel. This is because only the GMM parameters are exchanged between the Local and the Global REM, instead of direct spectrum sensing results. Finally, equipping every platoon with Local REM ensures that channel capacity can be predicted even, when the side link to the Global REM is temporarily unavailable. What increases the system's reliability. In the future the measurement campaign can be conducted in order to verify the proposed algorithms in real-world scenario.

References

1. 3GPP: LTE; 5G; Overall description of radio access network (RAN) aspects for Vehicle-to-everything (V2X) based on LTE and NR. Technical Report (TR) 37.985, 3rd Generation Partnership Project (3GPP) (07 2020), version 16.0.0
2. Abboud, K., Omar, H.A., Zhuang, W.: Interworking of DSRC and cellular network technologies for v2x communications: a survey. IEEE Trans. Veh. Technol. **65**(12), 9457–9470 (2016). https://doi.org/10.1109/TVT.2016.2591558
3. Abdelgader, A.M., Lenan, W.: The physical layer of the IEEE 802.11p WAVE communication standard: the specifications and challenges, San Franscisco (2014)
4. Abdulrahman, S., Tout, H., Ould-Slimane, H., Mourad, A., Talhi, C., Guizani, M.: A survey on federated learning: the journey from centralized to distributed on-site learning and beyond. IEEE Internet Things J. **8**(7), 5476–5497 (2021). https://doi.org/10.1109/JIOT.2020.3030072
5. Akaike, H.: A new look at the statistical model identification. IEEE Trans. Autom. Control **19**(6), 716–723 (1974). https://doi.org/10.1109/TAC.1974.1100705

6. Bishop, C.M.: Pattern Recognition and Machine Learning (Information Science and Statistics). Springer-Verlag, Berlin (2006)
7. Bonnet, C., Fritz, H.: Fuel consumption reduction in a platoon: experimental results with two electronically coupled trucks at close spacing. In: Future Transportation Technology Conference Exposition. SAE International, August 2000. https://doi.org/10.4271/2000-01-3056
8. Böhm, A., Jonsson, M., Uhlemann, E.: Performance comparison of a platooning application using the IEEE 802.11p MAC on the control channel and a centralized MAC on a service channel. In: IEEE 9th International Conference on Wireless and Mobile Computing, Networking and Communications (WiMob), pp. 545–552 (2013). https://doi.org/10.1109/WiMOB.2013.6673411
9. Campolo, C., Molinaro, A., Vinel, A., Zhang, Y.: Modeling event-driven safety messages delivery in IEEE 802.11p WAVE vehicular networks. IEEE Commun. Lett. **17**(12), 2392–2395 (2013). https://doi.org/10.1109/LCOMM.2013.102913.131863
10. Chan, E.: Overview of the SARTRE platooning project: technology leadership brief. In: SAE Convergence 2012. SAE International, October 2012. https://doi.org/10.4271/2012-01-9019
11. Chen, C., Zhang, N., Shi, S., Mu, D.: An efficient method for incremental learning of GMM using CUDA. In: 2012 International Conference on Computer Science and Service System, pp. 2141–2144 (2012). https://doi.org/10.1109/CSSS.2012.532
12. Chen, S.: Vehicular dynamic spectrum access: using cognitive radio for automobile networks. Ph.D. thesis, Worcester Polytechnic Institute, Worcester (2012)
13. Cheng, L., Henty, B.E., Stancil, D.D., Bai, F., Mudalige, P.: Mobile vehicle to-vehicle narrow-band channel measurement and characterization of the 5.9 Ghz dedicated short range communication (DSRC) frequency band. IEEE J. on Sel. Areas Commun. **25**(8), 1501–1516 (2007). https://doi.org/10.1109/JSAC.2007.071002
14. de Oliveira Souza, F., Torres, L.A.B., Mozelli, L.A., Neto, A.A.: Stability and formation error of homogeneous vehicular platoons with communication time delays. IEEE Trans. Intell. Transp. Syst. **21**(10), 4338–4349 (2020). https://doi.org/10.1109/TITS.2019.2939777
15. Dempster, A.P., Laird, N.M., Rubin, D.B.: Maximum likelihood from incomplete data via the EM algorithm. J. Roy. Stat. Soc. B (Methodol.) **39**(1), 1–38 (1977). http://www.jstor.org/stable/2984875
16. Vangeel, E.: Wideband transmission systems; Data transmission equipment operating in the 2,4 GHz band; Harmonised Standard for access to radio spectrum HS Wideband transmission systems 2,4 GHz. Standard EN 300 328, ETSI, Sophia Antipolis Cedex, France (2019). https://www.etsi.org/deliver/etsi-en/300300-300399/300328/02.02.02-60/en-300328v020202p.pdf
17. ETSI: Intelligent Transport Systems (ITS); Access Layer; Part 1: Channel Models for the 5,9 GHz frequency band). TR 103 257-1 V1.1.1, European Telecommunications Standards Institute, May 2019
18. Fernandes, P., Nunes, U.: Platooning with IVC-enabled autonomous vehicles: strategies to mitigate communication delays, improve safety and traffic flow. IEEE Trans. Intell. Transp. Syst. **13**(1), 91–106 (2012). https://doi.org/10.1109/TITS.2011.2179936
19. Geirhofer, S., Tong, L., Sadler, B.M.: A measurement-based model for dynamic spectrum access in wlan channels. In: MILCOM 2006–2006 IEEE Military Communications Conference, pp. 1–7 (2006). https://doi.org/10.1109/MILCOM.2006.302405

20. Harounabadi, M., Soleymani, D.M., Bhadauria, S., Leyh, M., Roth-Mandutz, E.: V2x in 3GPP standardization: NR sidelink in release-16 and beyond. IEEE Commun. Stand. Mag. **5**(1), 12–21 (2021). https://doi.org/10.1109/MCOMSTD.001. 2000070

21. Hoffmann, M., Kryszkiewicz, P., Kliks, A.: Frequency selection for platoon communications in secondary spectrum using radio environment maps. IEEE Trans. Intell. Transp. Syst. **23**(3), 2637–2650 (2022). https://doi.org/10.1109/TITS.2021. 3136681

22. IEEE: IEEE standard for information technology- local and metropolitan area networks- specific requirements- part 11: Wireless lan medium access control (mac) and physical layer (phy) specifications amendment 6: Wireless access in vehicular environments. IEEE Std 802.11p-2010 (Amendment to IEEE Std 802.11-2007 as amended by IEEE Std 802.11k-2008, IEEE Std 802.11r-2008, IEEE Std 802.11y-2008, IEEE Std 802.11n-2009, and IEEE Std 802.11w-2009) pp. 1–51 (2010). https://doi.org/10.1109/IEEESTD.2010.5514475

23. Katagiri, K., Sato, K., Fujii, T.: Crowdsourcing-assisted radio environment database for V2V communication. Sensors **18**(4) (2018). https://doi.org/10.3390/s18041183, https://www.mdpi.com/1424-8220/18/4/1183

24. Kliks, A., Kryszkiewicz, P., Perez-Romero, J., Umbert, A., Casadevall, F.: Spectrum occupancy in big cities - comparative study - measurement campaigns in Barcelona and Poznan. In: ISWCS 2013; The Tenth International Symposium on Wireless Communication Systems, pp. 1–5 (2013)

25. Kliks, A., Kryszkiewicz, P., Umbert, A., PéRez-Romero, J., Casadevall, F., Kulacz, L.: Application of radio environment maps for dynamic broadband access in TV bands in urban areas. IEEE Access **5**, 19842–19863 (2017). https://doi.org/10. 1109/ACCESS.2017.2751138

26. Konečný, J., McMahan, H.B., Ramage, D., Richtárik, P.: Federated optimization: distributed machine learning for on-device intelligence. CoRR abs/1610.02527 (2016). arxiv: 1610.02527

27. Yin, L., Li, J., Yin, S., Li, S.: Cognitive spectrum handoff game in the TV white space with radio environment map. In: 2012 IEEE 14th International Conference on Communication Technology, pp. 369–373 (2012). https://doi.org/10.1109/ICCT. 2012.6511245

28. Liu, S., Yu, G., Chen, X., Bennis, M.: Joint user association and resource allocation for wireless hierarchical federated learning with IID and Non-IID data. IEEE Trans. Wireless Commun. **21**(10) (2022). https://doi.org/10.1109/TWC.2022.3162595

29. Maiti, S., Winter, S., Kulik, L.: A conceptualization of vehicle platoons and platoon operations. Transp. Res. Part C: Emerg. Technol. **80**, 1–19 (2017). https://doi. org/10.1016/j.trc.2017.04.005, https://www.sciencedirect.com/science/article/pii/ S0968090X17301110

30. McMahan, H.B., Moore, E., Ramage, D., Hampson, S., Aguera y Arcas, B.: Communication-efficient learning of deep networks from decentralized data. In: Singh, A and Zhu, J (ed.) Artificial Intelligence And Statistics, vol 54. Proceedings of Machine Learning Research, vol. 54, pp. 1273–1282. Microtome Publishing, 31 GIBBS ST, Brookline, MA 02446 USA (2017), 20th International Conference on Artificial Intelligence and Statistics (AISTATS), Fort Lauderdale, FL, APR 20–22 (2017)

31. McMahan, H.B., Moore, E., Ramage, D., Hampson, S., y Arcas, B.A.: Communication-efficient learning of deep networks from decentralized data (2017)

32. Nilsson, M.G., Gustafson, C., Abbas, T., Tufvesson, F.: A measurement-based multilink shadowing model for V2V network simulations of highway scenarios. IEEE Trans. Veh. Technol. **66**(10), 8632–8643 (2017). https://doi.org/10.1109/TVT.2017.2709258

33. Qin, Y., Wang, H., Ran, B.: Stability analysis of connected and automated vehicles to reduce fuel consumption and emissions. J. Transp. Eng. Part A: Syst. **144**(11), 04018068 (2018). https://doi.org/10.1061/JTEPBS.0000196

34. Reddy G.R.R.R.: An Empirical study on MAC layer in IEEE 802.11p/WAVE based Vehicular Ad hoc networks. Procedia Comput. Sci. **143**, 720–727 (2018). https://doi.org/10.1016/j.procs.2018.10.443, http://www.sciencedirect.com/science/article/pii/S1877050918321410, 8th International Conference on Advances in Computing & Communications (ICACC-2018)

35. Reynolds, D.A.: Gaussian mixture models. (eds.) Encyclopedia of Biometrics, pp. 659–663. Springer, Boston (2009). https://doi.org/10.1007/978-0-387-73003-5_196

36. Robinson, T., Chan, E., Coelingh, E.: Operating platoons on public motorways: an introduction to the SARTRE platooning programme. In: 17th World Congress on Intelligent Transport Systems, vol. 1, p. 12 (2010)

37. Sroka, P., Kryszkiewicz, P., Kliks, A.: Radio environment maps for dynamic frequency selection in V2X communications. In: 2020 IEEE 91st Vehicular Technology Conference (VTC2020-Spring), pp. 1–6 (2020). https://doi.org/10.1109/VTC2020-Spring48590.2020.9128655

38. Sybis, M., Kryszkiewicz, P., Sroka, P.: On the context-aware, dynamic spectrum access for robust intraplatoon communications. In: Mobile Information Systems 2018 (2018). https://doi.org/10.1155/2018/3483298

39. Thunberg, J., Lyamin, N., Sjöberg, K., Vinel, A.: Vehicle-to-vehicle communications for platooning: safety analysis. IEEE Networking Letters **1**(4), 168–172 (2019). https://doi.org/10.1109/LNET.2019.2929026

40. Tsugawa, S., Kato, S.: Energy its: another application of vehicular communications. IEEE Commun. Mag. **48**(11), 120–126 (2010). https://doi.org/10.1109/MCOM.2010.5621978

41. van Arem, B., van Driel, C.J.G., Visser, R.: The impact of cooperative adaptive cruise control on traffic-flow characteristics. IEEE Trans. Intell. Transp. Syst. **7**(4), 429–436 (2006)

42. van de Beek1, J., et al.: Desmet, M.: REM-enabled opportunistic LTE in the TV band. In: 2012 IEEE International Symposium on Dynamic Spectrum Access Networks, pp. 272–273 (2012). https://doi.org/10.1109/DYSPAN.2012.6478140

43. Wang, P., Di, B., Zhang, H., Bian, K., Song, L.: Cellular V2X communications in unlicensed spectrum: harmonious coexistence with VANET in 5G systems. IEEE Trans. Wireless Commun. **17**(8), 5212–5224 (2018). https://doi.org/10.1109/TWC.2018.2839183

44. Wang, S., Tuor, T., Salonidis, T., Leung, K.K., Makaya, C., He, T., Chan, K.: Adaptive federated learning in resource constrained edge computing systems. IEEE J. Sel. Areas Commun. **37**(6), 1205–1221 (2019). https://doi.org/10.1109/JSAC.2019.2904348

45. Xu, L., Wang, L.Y., Yin, G., Zhang, H.: Communication information structures and contents for enhanced safety of highway vehicle platoons. IEEE Trans. Veh. Technol. **63**(9), 4206–4220 (2014)

46. Yang, Q., Liu, Y., Chen, T., Tong, Y.: Federated machine learning: Concept and applications. ACM Trans. Intell. Syst. Technol. **10**(2) (2019). https://doi.org/10.1145/3298981

47. Yilmaz, H.B., Tugcu, T., Alagöz, F., Bayhan, S.: Radio environment map as enabler for practical cognitive radio networks. IEEE Commun. Mag. **51**(12), 162–169 (2013). https://doi.org/10.1109/MCOM.2013.6685772
48. Zeng, T., Semiari, O., Saad, W., Bennis, M.: Joint communication and control for wireless autonomous vehicular platoon systems. IEEE Trans. Commun. **67**(11), 7907–7922 (2019). https://doi.org/10.1109/TCOMM.2019.2931583
49. Zhao, Q., Sadler, B.M.: A survey of dynamic spectrum access. IEEE Signal Process. Mag. **24**(3), 79–89 (2007). https://doi.org/10.1109/MSP.2007.361604

A Study of Extensive LoRaWAN Downlink Communication in a Mobility Scenario

Mads Smed Enggaard Thomassen[1], Kasper Stenholt Winkler[1],
Davide Magrin[2], and Michele Albano[1]([⊠]) [iD]

[1] Department of Computer Science, Aalborg University, Aalborg, Denmark
{mthoma18,kwinkl18}@student.aau.dk, mialb@cs.aau.dk
[2] Department of Computer Engineering, University of Naples Federico I, Naples, Italy
davide.magrin@unina.it

Abstract. Low Power Wide-Area Networks (LPWANs) are gaining a lot
of attention in use cases related to the Internet of Things . Most LPWAN
communication technologies are asymmetric and have inherently better uplink communication, thus can implement ubiquitous monitoring
and data collection efficiently. On the other hand, there is a growing
demand for a sizable downlink channel. This work aims at providing a
framework to study the feasibility of extensive downlink communication
in LoRaWAN with moving End Devices (EDs). Starting from a real-
world implementation of a Firmware Update Over the Air application,
we experiment with two simple strategies to reduce packet loss when EDs
move from within range gateway to another. Then, we extend the ns-3
LoRaWAN module to scale up the study by means of simulation. Such
tests show that the chosen strategy and the deployment of the gateways
have a strong impact on packet loss and on the time needed to complete
the transmission of the data to the EDs. The code of the ns-3 module is
available at https://github.com/madsthom/lorawan.

Keywords: LoRa · experimental · simulation · FUOTA

1 Introduction

Low power wide-area network (LPWAN) technologies offer long-range communication capabilities that consume little energy, at the cost of limited bandwidth.
LPWAN is gaining prominence for use cases based on battery-powered Internet
of Things (IoT) devices, for which the End Device (ED) count is predicted to
grow rapidly [11].

LoRaWAN is a Media Access Control (MAC) and networking layer built on
top of the LoRa [20] physical layer. The technology has gained momentum in
recent years because of its low-cost EDs, the long lifetime of the devices' battery,
its reliability based on its ability to send confirmed messages, and its adaptive
data rate protocol [4] that allows to optimize the data rate depending on the
condition of the network.

S. Longfei and P. Bodhi (Eds.): MobiQuitous 2022, LNICST 492, pp. 455–468, 2023.
https://doi.org/10.1007/978-3-031-34776-4_24

As most LPWAN communication technologies, LoRaWAN is asymmetric by design, and provides more support to the uplink channel, since it considers that most use cases focus on collecting data from the physical world. Occasionally, however, downlink communication might also be needed, for instance, to support setting transmission parameters at the EDs or when confirmed traffic is needed by the application. To this aim, LoRaWAN supports three different communication modes, one of them being Class C, which prioritizes downlink communication, and allows the EDs to switch between communication modes when the need arises. Multicast sessions are also supported by the specification, enabling the network to broadcast a single message to multiple EDs listening on the same channel. This functionality can, for instance, be used to support the Firmware Update Over The Air (FUOTA)[1] use case, where large amounts of data need to be delivered to the EDs over LoRaWAN.

This paper investigates the feasibility of extensive downlink communication with moving EDs in LoRaWAN. However, we acknowledge that mainstream network simulators lack Class C simulation capabilities and non Line of Sight (nLoS) scenarios require a validation step employing real device implementations since channel propagation is more complicated when the presence of buildings and other obstacles is taken into account. Thus, this work contributes to the state-of-the-art by means of:

- developing a ns-3 module to simulate communication for LoRaWAN Class C devices;
- identifying a suitable propagation loss model for nLoS LoRaWAN based on measurements from a physical reference application;
- showcase the implemented ns-3 module by proposing and evaluating two simple strategies, by means of both a testbed and simulations, to optimize the communication strategy of LoRaWAN with respect to the scenario at hand.

The structure of the paper is as follows; in Sect. 2 background information is laid out. In Sect. 3 the purpose and the aim of this work are explained. Section 4 presents the reference physical implementation. Furthermore, in Sect. 5 the simulation results of Class C LoRaWAN are described. Finally, in Sect. 6 conclusions are drawn and future work is proposed.

2   Background Information

This section provides an overview of the LoRaWAN technology, of the network simulator 3 (ns-3), which is the tool we used to perform our simulations, and of work related to LoRaWAN extensive downlink communication.

2.1   An Overview of LoRaWAN

The growing demand for IoT-type connectivity [11] recently paved the way for various LPWAN communication technologies. Use cases usually focus on

---

[1] Firmware Over The Air means that an update is supplied wirelessly to the End Devices.

collecting small amount of data over large deployments, and in that sense LPWAN is a great match for ubiquitous sensing. In fact, LPWAN provides the ability to send small messages over a long distance without consuming a large amount of energy.

Among the plethora of LPWAN technologies that hit the market in the past few years, LoRaWAN [16] is arguably the most widely adopted, and the one that is pushing the LPWAN paradigm forward the most [10]. Uplink focused LPWAN technologies such as, SigFox [21] and NB-IoT [17] are the most used in IoT applications, where the EDs benefit from having a long battery life.

LoRaWAN operates on the unlicensed ISM bands between 137 and 1020 MHz, and claims a range of up to five kilometers in urban areas and up to 15 km in line of sight scenarios [20]. In Europe, the LoRaWAN protocol has duty cycle restrictions that apply to all functioning modes and must be complied with. Because of the specification's frequency layout in relation to the available regulatory sub-bands, in LoRaWAN such restrictions translate to 1% Duty Cycle for uplink communication, and 10% Duty Cycle for downlink.

One of the most important operational parameters exposed by the underlying LoRa modulation is that of the Spreading Factor (SF), which decides the "spreading" of the signal over the available frequency band. If multiple packets are transmitted simultaneously and on the same frequency but with different SF, all packets can be typically demodulated correctly (provided some restrictions on the reciprocal powers are met) [9]. Lower values of SF (with 7 being the minimum) mean that the communication happen at shorter range but packet will be transmitted at a higher data rate, while higher values (with 12 being the maximum) determine a longer range but longer on-air time to transmit the same amount of data.

LoRaWAN EDs can be configured to operate according to three different communication modes called Class A, Class B and Class C. **Class A** is primarily for uplink messages and requires the least amount of power to operate, furthermore, it is mandatory for all EDs to implement it. Devices can receive in fact downlink messages can be received only after the ED sends an uplink message. **Class B** is a beaconing mode, and compared to Class A it has a lower latency due to pre-scheduled transmission windows (ping slots), but it consumes more power. When operating under **Class C**, the EDs keep their interface on at all times, to receive packets without an uplink transmission. This mode consumes the most power of the three configurations and it is intended to be used for a short time only, with the ED going back to other modes as soon as possible. One of the most prominent use cases for Class C is to update the software/firmware of the ED.

When operating in Class A, whenever the ED sends an uplink message, it must open two receive windows, **RX1** that operates on the same frequency as the uplink message itself, and **RX2** that operates on a configured fixed frequency. The timing in which these windows are opened is configurable but normally the RX1 window opens after a one-second delay and the RX2 window opens after a two seconds delay after the uplink transmission is completed. The LoRaWAN

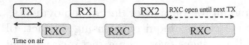

Fig. 1. Class C receive windows

specification [16] states that an ED in Class C must open extra receive windows RXC, meaning that the ED should listen to incoming RX signals whenever it is not transmitting, whose parameters are the same as RX2. The behaviour of Class C devices is shown in Fig. 1, and Class A devices operate in the same manner, except for the absence of RXC.

Targeting multiple EDs with the same packet transmission can be accomplished using **multicast**, which is a way to avoid transmitting the same packet multiple times and is possible for both Class B and C. Using multicast requires creating a multicast group of EDs and having that group perform a clock synchronization to match the timing on every ED, for example to respect the downlink slots of Class B. The tolerance regarding the timing for multicast commands to work properly is approximately one second [3].

Implementing a LoRaWAN architecture (see Fig. 2) requires a setup including at least a **network server**, a **gateway (GW)**, an ED, and an application. The modularity in the architecture allows extending the network, for example by adding multiple GWs covering a larger area. A well-supported open-source LoRaWAN network server was implemented by ChirpStack[2]. The ChirpStack network server implements Adaptive Data Rate (ADR) [4], authentication, multicasting, device class management, GW management, logging, etc. Furthermore, it allows integration using an exposed API targeting the Network server and Application server.

2.2   Network Simulator 3

Complex network technologies such as LoRaWAN are often evaluated and tested by means of network simulation, which allows to investigate how the protocol behaves depending on its different parameters, to test it on complex scenarios at a cost lower than physical implementation, and to measure properties that are not usually readily accessible on testbeds.

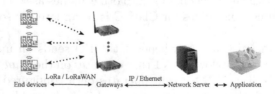

Fig. 2. LoRaWAN architecture

---

[2] https://www.chirpstack.io/network-server/.

Network simulators typically use the discrete-event paradigm, modelling the system's behavior as a (discrete) sequence of timed events where each change (event) in the systems happens at a specific time in the simulation timeline. This enables the simulator to jump to the next scheduled operation, with the assumption that no state of the system changes in the time in-between the events.

Network Simulator 3 (ns-3) is an open-source discrete network simulator licensed under the GNU GPLv2 license and is free for research, development, and commercial use [13]. The ns-3 platform provides models to simulate how different packet data technologies work, all driven by a general simulation engine [1]. ns-3 has a substantial [15] community which contributes to the platform and the many modules found in their ns-3 App Store.

The LoRaWAN ns-3 module [14] provides support for most of the basic functionalities of the protocol. The module supports a network server implementation with multiple GWs and Class A EDs. In [9], the authors used the module to evaluate LoRaWAN's scalability in a smart-city scenario with many EDs (up to 10^4). However, the module currently supports Class A EDs only. In [6], the authors evaluate the scalability of LoRaWAN Class B. The authors implemented an ns-3 module to simulate Class B EDs and investigated the limitations of Class B for uplink and downlink frames. They conclude that the limiting factor for Class B is the Duty Cycle Restrictions.

In this work, we will expand the ns-3 LoRaWAN module to support basic multicast operation and Class C operations.

2.3   Related Work

In [5] the authors consider downlink transmission issues for LoRaWAN Class A, and in particular the limits of downlink communication, namely, the downlink frames scheduled to be received by EDs in RX1 or RX2 receive windows (see Fig. 1). They propose three solutions to mitigate packet loss in networks with low, medium, and high amounts of downlinks: (a) using multiple GWs with overlapping coverage to be able to mitigate packet loss due to Duty Cycle Restrictions, (b) Allowing GWs to send and receive frames at the same time, and (c) implementing a balancing GW selection algorithm to select the best GW for the next downlink frame.

[2] investigates the throughput of different LoRaWAN GW deployments for downlink communication, and compares three algorithms for selecting the best GW for downlink communication. It appears that balancing the load (number of EDs) per GW increases the throughput of the system with respect to choosing a GW based on signal quality only.

In [3], the authors review the LoRa alliance's FUOTA specifications, and provide simulations of FUOTA scenarios using Class B and C. Via their simulations, they conclude that doing FUOTA via Class B takes 17% more time, but uses 550 times less energy than Class C.

In [8], authors discuss the requirements for FUOTA to work for LPWANs, and propose three key requirements, namely (i) Efficient multicasting, (ii) Packet

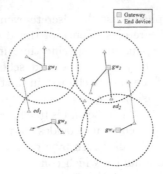

Fig. 3. A schematic overview of the reference scenario considered in this paper.

recovery, and (iii) Verification of authenticity and integrity of the update binaries. The authors developed a reference implementation of a FUOTA scenario with LoRaWAN, where EDs switch from Class A to C, perform firmware update, then switch back to Class A. However, as the authors point out, this approach is good for stationary EDs only, since data rates and device groups need to be defined before doing the update, which clashes with the dynamicity of mobility scenarios.

Bottom line, all these surveyed approaches work well when selecting GWs for stationary EDs, but do not take into account mobility, and it can be argued that they would be challenged when considering moving EDs.

3   Extensive Downlink Communication in LoRaWAN

The purpose of this work is to evaluate the feasibility of extensive downlink communication with moving EDs and to study how to enhance current approaches to deliver a large quantity of data to EDs, for example, to perform FUOTA. We assume that data is subject to linear coding, and that a fixed amount of packets are needed to reconstruct the firmware update correctly. [7]

The scenario is roughly represented in Fig. 3, where multiple GWs are sending downlink messages to moving EDs concurrently. First of all, the network needs to be able to orchestrate multiple GWs to efficiently send downlink messages without interference. When moving devices are part of the picture, the quality of the communication link to the GW changes in correlation to the devices' movement. For example, in Fig. 3 the network needs to know which gateway(s) should be activated. EDs can use any packets they receive to recompose their update.

In a LoRaWAN network with unconfirmed downlink communication, the GWs do not get any indication of the signal strength perceived by the EDs, which in turn does not allow the GWs to adapt to the evolution of the scenario. Thus, to provide better support for moving EDs, we consider the need for an ED to signal the network. The network then uses the feedback regarding the link quality to estimate which GWs are currently able to reach a given ED with their data, and if there is the need for a handover.

The communication strategies that we consider are:

- Out of Signal (OOS): EDs only send packets when their Received Signal Strength Indication (RSSI) is below a certain threshold or when they are not receiving any packets, and the network server selects which GWs to activate based on the information;
- Periodic: EDs send UL data periodically, and the network server selects which GWs to activate based on the information;
- Bulk: EDs never send UL data, and all GWs are always active.

In the simulations (described in Sect. 5), EDs move according to the RandomWalk2dMobilityModel ns-3 mobility model, moving within a rectangular area of side of 2000 m, and pick a random direction after either 10 min or 500 m; speed is chosen from an uniform random distribution between 2 and 6 m/s.

4 Real World Data Collection

In this section, we describe the implementation of the test setup and how the GW, network server, and application server worked together. The testbed made use of two Multitech Conduit Gateways [12] with LoRa extension cards. The GWs were running the latest firmware (5.3.3) and were configured as packet forwarders. A B-L072Z-LRWAN1 board [19] (LoRaWAN discovery board) is used as ED. The board contains a Semtech SX1276 LoRa chip [18]. The board runs Mbed OS[3] version 6.9, which implements a LoRaWAN connectivity stack complying with the specifications of LoRa [16] and supports the embedded discovery platform "B-L072Z-LRWAN1". The application executed on Mbed OS implements the following 3 steps. (i) A **Join procedure** connects the ED to the LoRaWAN network and is triggered by a power cycle or reset of the device. (ii) As soon as the ED is connected, it sends an uplink message with the ADR flag true that starts the **ADR process**. (iii) Once the optimal connectivity setting is found, the ED **switches to Class C** to receive a large quantity of data, and logs information regarding every message sent or received.

For the network to be fully functional, we installed the ChirpStack Network server and Application server from Sect. 2.1 on a central server. This implementation of the network server was chosen due to the ability to change GW based on the latest uplink transmission. The test application used to send FUOTA packets was written in python. It establishes a connection to the application server using gRPC[4], which is a high-performance universal remote procedure call framework.

The studied scenario featured an urban environment populated with buildings in Aalborg, Denmark. Given the nLoS nature of the scenario, the range

---

[3] https://os.mbed.com/mbed-os/.
[4] https://www.grpc.io/.

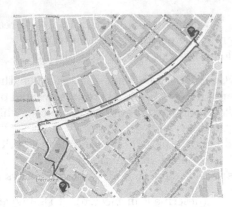

Fig. 4. Map of gateway deployment in Aalborg, Denmark

of the GWs was reduced, which resulted in a signal dead zone. The GWs were placed in two apartment buildings approximately one kilometer apart, one located on the 6th floor and the second on the 3rd floor. The GW deployment showing the approximate range and location of each GW can be seen in Fig. 4, which also shows the route taken to move by bicycle from the coverage of one GW to the other. Conceptually, we considered that the experiments involved travelling by bicycle on the same route at approximately the same speed. However, this is a limitation of the experimental setting, since the route contains four intersections that disturb the continuity of the test runs.

The test setup consisted of two scenarios where two different strategies were used for signalling to the GW that an ED is moving out of range. GPS and RSSI data are recorded as they are acquired (periodically for the GPS, with each packet transmission for the RSSI).

4.1   Test Scenario 1 - Out of Signal

The first test scenario made use of an "Out of signal" message from the ED. After receiving each downlink message, the ED (i) changes its state to an

Table 1. Test result for "Out of signal" scenario.

RSSI value:	*-140*	*-130*	*-120*
MIN SNR	−79	−82	−63
MIN RSSI	−128	−127	−128
AVG RSSI	−90,7	−87,3	−92,7
Packet loss %	42,1	39,4	6,9
Number of packets sent	140	155	188
Number of packets received	81	94	175

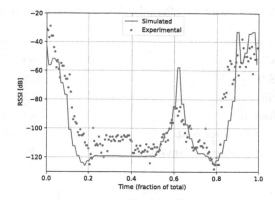

Fig. 5. Rssi for "out-of-signal" threshold: −120, and simulated RSSI.

out-of-signal state if the RSSI is under a given threshold, or (ii) changes its state back to under-coverage if the RSSI is over the threshold. When the ED is in the out-of-signal state, it sends every 10 s an uplink message to request a connection to any GW in range.

We experimented with 3 different RSSI thresholds, namely −120, −130, and −140 based on the nominal sensitivities [18] for the LoRa chip used. The results (see Table 1) show that for thresholds of −140 and −130 the minimum RSSI value is higher than the threshold, resulting in no out-of-signal packets sent and 42, 1% and 39, 4% packet loss. This suggests that the test setup is not able to yield the maximum range. However, for an RSSI value just above the minimum observed RSSI (−120), the approach yields a better result of 6, 9% packet loss. The RSSI value throughout this test run is shown in Fig. 5, which was also used to set the parameters characterizing the propagation model for the simulations of Sect. 5 (the solid line in the figure). Choosing a value even higher could result in missing some packets that the ED could have received.

4.2 Test Scenario 2 - Periodic Acknowledgement

The second test scenario consists of periodic confirmed downlink messages, having the EDs respond with an uplink acknowledgment packet allowing the network server to select the closest GW for transmitting further. This allows the network server to evaluate the signal strength between GW and EDs to select a gateway for the next downlink message. Three test runs were done with a periodicity of every 3rd, 6th, and 9th downlink packet.

The results of the tests (see Table 2) show that sending confirmed messages as often as every 3rd or 6th packet yields a packet loss of 43, 4% and 26, 4%. This can be due to a collision between downlink and uplink messages. Sending confirmed messages less frequently yields a better result of 14, 9% packet loss. This can also be a matter of better timing in terms of being in and out of the signal dead zone at the right moment.

Table 2. Test result for "Periodic Acknowledgement" scenario.

Confirmed message every:	3rd packet	6th packet	9th packet
MIN SNR	−51	−69	−63
MIN RSSI	−122	−128	−127
AVG RSSI	−92,5	−98,3	−99,0
Packet loss %	43,4	26,4	14,9
Number of packets sent	159	121	161
Number of packets received	90	89	137

5   Simulation of LoRaWAN Class C

A LoRaWAN module [14] for ns-3 was developed, to further study the scenario at hand. To the aim of evaluating the feasibility of FUOTA-like applications with extensive downlink communication, Prior to our work, the existing LoRaWAN module implemented both PHY and MAC for Class A of LoRaWAN only. The module implements the architecture seen in Fig. 2, which consists of EDs, gateways, and a network server.

The Class C implementation was developed on top of the current LoRaWAN ns-3 module, mainly by modifying the MAC layer implementation for GWs and EDs to accommodate Class C. The Class C End Device can switch from Class A to Class C to simulate a FUOTA-like application (see Fig. 6). When the downlink communication is finished, another command is sent by the GW, which tells the MAC layer on the ED to switch back to Class A.

When in Class C, the ED behaves as per the LoRaWAN Class C specification (see Sect. 2.1) and in particular whenever a transmission (TX) is performed, the RXC is opened and closed again after the RX1 delay. If nothing is received in

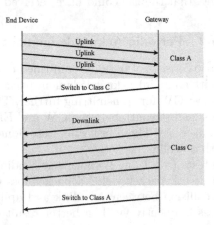

Fig. 6. Simulation scenario: Switch from Class A to Class C

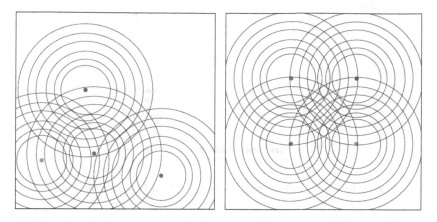

Fig. 7. Examples of a Random and Grid Gateways deployment. Dots represent Gateways, while circles represent the achievable range with each value of the Spreading Factor parameter.

RX1 the RXC is open again and is kept open until the next transmission, i.e.: the ED is always ready to receive packets whenever it is not transmitting.

As a preliminary step, we tuned the propagation loss model used in ns-3 to match our experimental data. In particular, we chose to rely on a Log-distance path loss model with $n = 4$ to capture the densely built environment of Aalborg, and a reference path loss of 60 dB at 2 m. In order to ensure this model matches the actual data, we re-created the experimental scenario in simulation, using the GPS measurements of the test route of the ED and the GW locations. The resulting path loss estimate can be seen in the solid line in Fig. 5, and the resemblance between the collected data and the simulated received power turned out to be satisfyingly close and motivated us to keep the aforementioned path loss model for the simulations described in the remainder of this work.

Figure 7 shows two examples of GW deployments, the left with GWs placed randomly, the right featuring a "grid" placement. While the grid configuration clearly provides the best coverage of the entire deployment area, it might not always be possible to achieve such a GW placement in the real world. In fact, actual deployments, especially when crowdsourced as in the case of The Things Networks, might look closer to the random deployment, where some relatively large areas have no coverage. We also remark that GWs are assumed to be transmitting FUOTA packets sequentially in time, and thus any overlap in the coverage area of GWs in this work does not lead to interference between downlink packets.

The Empirical Cumulative Distribution Function (ECDF) of the time needed to download the entire update (i.e., the 100 packets representing a firmware update) is shown in Fig. 8 for both the cases of a random deployment and a grid deployment. These plots were obtained using SF 12 and the Bulk strategy to transmit the FUOTA packets. As expected, random and grid placement yield

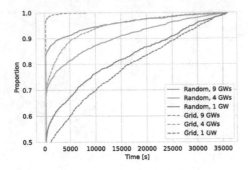

Fig. 8. ECDF of Firmware Update Download Completion Times.

similar results when a single GW is used. As the number of employed GWs grows, however, the grid placement is clearly superior: when 9 GWs are used, all EDs correctly receive the update within three hours, with 95% of the EDs within few minutes. In the random deployment with 9 GWs, instead, only 90% of the EDs are able to collect all the required packets within the first few minutes of the update, while the other 10% needs more than 7 h (25200 s) to roam back within a coverage area and be able to complete the download.

The left side of Fig. 9 compares different policies, and it shows that the Bulk strategy is the best performer for the grid deployment of 4 GWs. The right side of Fig. 9 compares the Bulk strategy in the same scenario with different SF parameter. The results hint that SF 11 is too slow, while a higher data rate allows most of the device to complete the FUOTA faster, but by having a shorter range it leads to having a small number of EDs ending up with slower updates.

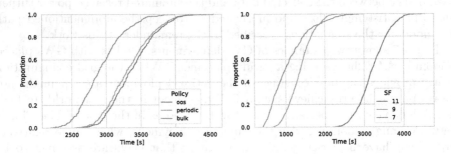

Fig. 9. ECDF of time to complete the update. On the left, we show different policies with SF 11. On the right, we use the bulk policy, various values of Data Rate.

6   Conclusion and Future Work

This paper addressed the usage of LoRaWAN Class C communication for extensive downlink communication in a mobility scenario. A Class C ns-3 component was developed on top of the ns-3 LoRaWAN module, as well as a reference application. The resulting framework was showcased by testing two simple strategies that EDs can use to provide feedback regarding their link quality to GWs. The results showed the choice of the signalling strategy between EDs and GWs and the parameters of the LoRaWAN communication has a huge impact on packet loss.

Several future works can be considered as immediate follow-ups on this work. First, more complex strategies can be proposed to cope with the scenario at hand. Moreover, the LoRaWAN ns-3 module can be used to simulate a large network of mobile devices, to study the system's behavior when the network scales to hundreds of EDs. Since the firmware update is broadcast, we will investigate rateless coding schemes that could work better than linear coding. Furthermore, the ns-3 LoRaWAN module should be expanded with a Class B implementation to compare its performance to Class C, and also to create a module that can simulate all three classes of the LoRaWAN protocol. To be able to test different GW selection algorithms, the network server implementation in ns-3 should be expanded with the ability to "install" different applications to control the GWs. Finally, we plan to experiment with more complex GW placements to investigate if they can yield better results, for example with and without overlap in GW ranges.

Acknowledgment. This work was partly funded by the ERC Advanced Grant LASSO; and by the Villum Investigator Project "4OS: Scalable analysis and Synthesis of Safe, Small, Secure and Optimal Strategies for Cyber-Physical Systems".

References

1. ns 3 consortium: ns-3 tutorial. Tech. rep., ns-3 consortium (January, 2009)
2. Abboud, S., El Rachkidy, N., Guitton, A., Safa, H.: Gateway selection for downlink communication in Lorawan. In: 2019 IEEE Wireless Communications and Networking Conference (WCNC), pp. 1–6. IEEE (2019)
3. Abdelfadeel, K., Farrell, T., McDonald, D., Pesch, D.: How to make firmware updates over lorawan possible. In: 2020 IEEE 21st International Symposium on" A World of Wireless, Mobile and Multimedia Networks" (WoWMoM), pp. 16–25. IEEE (2020)
4. Coutaud, U., Heusse, M., Tourancheau, B.: High reliability in lorawan. In: 2020 IEEE 31st Annual International Symposium on Personal, Indoor and Mobile Radio Communications, pp. 1–7. IEEE (2020)
5. Di Vincenzo, V., Heusse, M., Tourancheau, B.: Improving downlink scalability in lorawan. In: ICC 2019–2019 IEEE International Conference on Communications (ICC), pp. 1–7. IEEE (2019)
6. Finnegan, J., Brown, S., Farrell, R.: Evaluating the scalability of lorawan gateways for class b communication in ns-3. In: 2018 IEEE Conference on Standards for Communications and Networking (CSCN), pp. 1–6. IEEE (2018)
7. Fujimura, A., Oh, S.Y., Gerla, M.: Network coding vs. erasure coding: Reliable multicast in ad hoc networks. In: MILCOM 2008–2008 IEEE Military Communications Conference, pp. 1–7. IEEE (2008)

8. Jongboom, J., Stokking, J.: Enabling firmware updates over lPWANs. In: Embedded World Conference(2018)
9. Magrin, D., Centenaro, M., Vangelista, L.: Performance evaluation of LoRa networks in a smart city scenario. In: 2017 IEEE International Conference on Communications (ICC), pp. 1–7. IEEE (2017)
10. Mekki, K., Bajic, E., Chaxel, F., Meyer, F.: Overview of cellular lPWAN technologies for IoT deployment: Sigfox, Lorawan, and NB-IoT. In: 2018 IEEE International Conference on Pervasive Computing and Communications Workshops (Percom Workshops), pp. 197–202. IEEE (2018)
11. Meulen, R.: Gartner says 8.4 billion connected "things" will be in use in 2017, up 31 percent from 2016. Gartner Letzte Aktualisierung 7 (2017)
12. Multitech gateway. https://www.multitech.com/models/94557602LF (July, 2021)
13. ns-3 network simulator. https://www.nsnam.org/ (July, 2021)
14. An ns-3 module for simulation of lorawan networks. https://apps.nsnam.org/app/lorawan/ (July 2021)
15. ns-3 statistics. https://www.nsnam.org/about/statistics/ (July 2021)
16. N. Sornin, A. Yegin, e.a.: Lorawan 1.1 specification. Tech. rep., Lora Alliance (October 2017)
17. Popli, S., Jha, R.K., Jain, S.: A survey on energy efficient narrowband internet of things (NBIoT): architecture, application and challenges. IEEE Access 7, 16739–16776 (2018)
18. Semtech   sx1276.   https://www.semtech.com/products/wireless-rf/lora-core/sx1276 (July 2021)
19. Stm32l0 discovery kit lora, sigfox, low-power wireless. https://www.st.com/en/evaluation-tools/b-l072z-lrwan1.html (July 2021)
20. Wenyan, Z.: Technical overview on LORA physical layer and mac layer. Mob. Commun. 2017, 17 (2017)
21. Zuniga, J.C., Ponsard, B.: Sigfox system description. LPWAN@ IETF97, November 14th 25 (November 2016)

Mobile and Human Computer Interactions

Microbenchmarking Documents in the Air

Dragoş Ştefan Niculescu$^{(\boxtimes)}$, Laura Ruse , and Costin Carabaş

University Politehnica of Bucharest, Bucharest, Romania
`suotiuqibom.dragos@0sg.net`

Abstract. *Documents in the Air* is a middleware system that allows placing and retrieving virtual objects or documents at different indoor locations **without requiring a positioning system**. It consists of an Android application and an intranet or cloud server, and only makes use of existing WiFi or BLE infrastructure to produce location specific signatures. We evaluate the performance of the system and study signature behavior with respect to: WiFi network characteristics, dissimilarity and real distances, and various collection methods. Using our own measurements, as well as publicly available data from several buildings, we show that the document retrieval process is accurate under conditions of signature impairment, signature aging, reduced AP density, and heterogeneous devices.

Keywords: WiFi fingerprints · Location centric services · Performance evaluation

1 Introduction

One of the main driving forces of the IoT is the desire to connect everything to the network, and the hope to access and control everyday life's processes. With cluttered environments in homes, and institutions, one of the challenges is the management of the Internet connected objects. Physical object databases come with significant challenges in management of devices, topologies, inter-operation, security, privacy, portability, and context awareness. The concept of context is central for pervasive computing and IoT, so that ongoing research still requires extensive surveying effort and building of taxonomies [6,15,18,28,32,33]. Context is heavily overloaded concept, and while position is certainly a context, obtaining it, especially indoors requires nontrivial effort. Indoor location will no doubt play an important role in the quest for context awareness, and research in locating and tracking devices, which has ramped up significantly in the last decade [16,20,21,23], has shown that obtaining indoor location is costly in several ways: necessary infrastructure (specialized measurement hardware), low accuracy (WiFi, BLE), effort (training and maintaining location databases), battery consumption (GPS, WiFi, 4G methods), erosion of privacy (Google tracking).

Work supported in part by the Romanian National Authority for Scientific Research and Innovation, UEFISCDI project PN-III-P2-2.1-PED-2019-5413.

© ICST Institute for Computer Sciences, Social Informatics and Telecommunications Engineering 2023
Published by Springer Nature Switzerland AG 2023. All Rights Reserved
S. Longfei and P. Bodhi (Eds.): MobiQuitous 2022, LNICST 492, pp. 471–493, 2023.
https://doi.org/10.1007/978-3-031-34776-4_25

Documents in the Air(*AirDocs*) is a recently proposed [26] middleware system that avoids the use of Cartesian location, relying instead on context specific signatures to allow placing and retrieving virtual documents at different indoor locations. It relies on WiFi/Bluetooth infrastructure existing in most homes and institutions, requiring a single additional server visible in the intranet, and an application that can be installed on any mobile device. Collecting this information in a **signature of the context**, which includes the WiFi fingerprint and other context specific information, enables retrieval of information based on signatures. *AirDocs* enables many applications that involve natural placing and retrieving of documents at locations, but without actually requiring a location system. In this article, we experiment with a dissimilarity measure as a proxy for Euclidean distance, that allows for several operations in signal space to enable placing and retrieving virtual objects using **only** context derived from wireless fingerprints. We benchmark the behavior of the signatures in signal space, and Cartesian locations are never used in the operation of the system, except for reporting purposes. The contributions of the papers are:

- implement a proof of concept for the middleware, which includes a simple Android application that places and retrieves signatures, and a server that implements searches in signature space.
- propose mapping between Euclidean distance and signature dissimilarity
- benchmark the main part of signatures, namely the WiFi fingerprints, with respect to creation, classification, collision behavior, aging
- show that object retrieval is robust with respect to: infrastructure density, time variation, methods of fingerprint collection, and device variability.

2   System Architecture

The *AirDocs* architecture is shown in Fig. 1: the middleware provides an API for scanning for Wi-Fi APs, cellular networks, Bluetooth Low Energy (BLE) devices, GPS information, and sound, in order to build signatures. Also, it includes methods for sending documents to the server along with the associated signature, and for retrieving documents from the server for a recently collected signature. This middleware can then be used by actual applications in order to store and retrieve documents depending on their specific.

The server is responsible with storing documents and their associated signatures, and also with identifying the appropriate document for a certain signature. It does this by comparing the collected signature with other signatures stored in the database, by using a (dis)similarity function. The most similar signature is identified and the associated document is retrieved and displayed in the application.

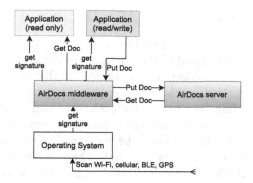

Fig. 1. AirDocs architecture: the middleware module on the mobile collects signatures from the environment. Th server indexes document databases and answers queries based on signatures.

The unique rich signatures obtained can then be used to manage a document collection without mapping them to geographical locations, but in fact obtaining an association between a document and its location in the building, but not physical position. The data-structure obtained provides many functionalities of a location indexed database. The middleware will offer three main primitives to the applications:

- $S = CreateSgn()$ collects a location specific signature from the phone sensors(WiFi, BLE, 4G, sound, etc.) and creates a multidimensional signature that is unique from any other location signature in the building;
- $Put(S, document)$ stores a document on the server associated with the signature S; The signature is created by a phone, but the indexing of the signatures and the document storage happen on a server in the intranet (or Internet).
- $Get(S)$ - a phone harvests its current signature, and asks the server for a list of documents that have "close" signatures, meaning documents that have been stored at nearby locations. The server **searches in the signature space, and real geographical coordinates are never needed.**

On the server, documents are indexed by their signatures, based on their similarities between them. For a given signature query, the server may: 1. retrieve the document with the lowest dissimilarity with the query, or 2. retrieve all documents with dissimilarities below a threshold. Since real physical positions are not known, the database of signatures on the server needs to be organized using clustering and labeling methods.

2.1   Usage Scenarios

The system is akin to augmented reality with the users having the illusion of the virtual objects being spread in the physical environment, visible only at certain locations. Leaving an object or a document "in the air" allows for a natural way to use it as a virtual wireless post-it for museums explanations, navigation in complex buildings like universities, airports and malls, advertising, lab door announcements, restaurant menus, office pin-boards, refrigerator post-its, general reminders, and notices around the house and office. Many of these applications would usually require location, and a building-wide indoor coordinate system, but if the *AirDocs* service is available, the functionality of placing and retrieving documents can be used right away requiring only the installation of the Android application.

Since the WiFi coverage is often associated with administrative control of the physical space, the placement of the document server may be in the intranet. In this case, the server can be accessible on a standard port once the mobile joins the building WiFi, as any other service that runs inside a home or institution. Applications using the *AirDocs* API would detect local servers using a name discovery (e.g. DNS-SD, zeroconf, or UPnP) and interact with them in an application specific fashion.

As we will show in Sect. 4.1, the resolution of the system is currently around $2\,m^1$. This allows for placing documents at higher density, but at query time they will be reported as being in the same place. As the performance of the system will improve by enriching signatures (Sect. 6.1, more applications would become possible. In a shopping mall for example, signatures are based on all visible and fixed WiFi infrastructure, and the documents are placed for announcement or for advertisement purposes. The system would be read-only for shoppers, and a document could contain a floor map, a sale, a coupon, or any other digital object that could be useful to the shoppers. A museum would have a similar setup in that documents placing and contents are curated by the institutions and the visitors would only read them when the appropriate locations. An university, on the other hand, may allow limited posting by the students in certain areas, or for a maximum document size, or limited lifetime imposed by weekly cleanups. Conferences could place maps, programs, and other pointers at hotel entrances and in appropriate presentation rooms.

Full-blown applications based on this API will have to consider actual institution specific virtual object types (pdf, gif, URLs, multimedia), document policies (their maximum size and life length), security (who can create documents), visibility (certain user-groups might see different sets of documents), scalability, and an appropriate GUI (simple browser refresh, or full augmented reality) to facilitate production and consumption of spatial data that are all application specific. If *AirDocs* is run in the intranet on a standardized port, a common smartphone app would cover many usage cases, and the user would not need to

---

[1] Limited by the Android WiFi throttling procedure taking about 3–4 s for a full scan of both 2.4 GHz and 5 GHz WiFi bands.

install a new one when attending a conference, visiting an exhibit, or browsing a brick and mortar store.

The *AirDocs* API can be used even without ownership of the physical space or of the WiFi infrastructure, with a server in the cloud, as long as the collected signatures are stable (see Sect. 6, whitelists). Since connectivity to the visible APs is not needed, signatures can be collected anywhere and stored on an application specific, or group specific private server that allows *Put*-ting and *Get*-ting documents to create a private document collection embedded in any WiFi rich physical space.

3   Dissimilarity of Signatures

In this section, we explore the behavior of signatures collected from the WiFi infrastructure, called fingerprints, which are most readily available, and present in ever increasing AP (access point) densities. Since the system does not use any Cartesian location and distances, we first look at the mapping between signature dissimilarity and Cartesian distance.

As far as indoor positioning based on radio fingerprints is concerned, accuracy is predictable [3], and can be quantified in terms of *meters per dBm* of RSSI (received signal strength indicator) measurement accuracy. The organizers of several editions of Microsoft Indoor Location Competition mention that for the infrastructure-free mode, the expected indoor positioning accuracy was around 2 m in most years, but was as high as 4 m in tough environments [16]. Some improvements implemented for these wining methods could be employed by *AirDocs*, but not the ones that require extensive setup, training, and calibration. We next propose a dissimilarity measure that employs methods that have been validated by other researchers, and exhibit a monotonic behavior with real distance.

3.1   Dissimilarity Measure

Generally, positioning using fingerprints uses some function of distance in signal space, with Euclidean used in the RADAR paper [1], and many others tested in the literature. Caso et al. [4] tests Minkowski, cosine, Pearson correlation, and Shepard, finding that Euclidean and Pearson correlation provide the best results. In other studies, Mahalanobis is found to have the best performance, but for our setup it cannot be applied, since Android only gives one RSSI per 3 s reading, therefore a covariation matrix between RSSI distributions of different APs cannot be obtained without extensive waiting. Torres-Sospedra et al. [34] explore many others distances ad dissimilarities used in the literature, and found Sørensen (BrayCurtis coefficient) to perform best. In addition, we adopted some other improvements proposed in [34]: zero-to-one normalized representation (Eq. 1) of a RSSI value x_i in dBm:

$$X_i = normalized(x_i) = \alpha(1 - \frac{x_i}{min})^e \tag{1}$$

We chose the scale value α so that the range of x_i observed values -99 dBm .. -30 dBm get mapped to X_i in the interval $[0,1]$. The purpose of this normalization is double: it maps negative power reading in dBm to positive values that are needed by some similarity measures, but also discounts more differences between low power readings. The latter means that differences in stronger signals are penalized, for example a -90 dBm to -85 dBm difference is less important than a -40 dBm to -35 dBm difference, as RSSI readings are known to be much noisier at low power values.

The Bray-Curtis dissimilarity (Sørensen distance) relies on APs common between the two fingerprints:

$$BCurtis(X,Y) = \frac{\sum_{i=1}^{c} |X_i - Y_i|}{\sum_{i=1}^{c} (X_i + Y_i)} \qquad (2)$$

Most dissimilarity measures consider only common APs between two signatures, but as stated by Beder and Klepal [2], non common APs are a critical factor in reducing false similarities.

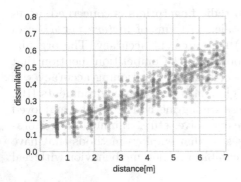

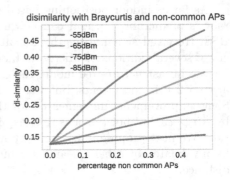

Fig. 2. Braycurtis dissimilarity vs real distance for all pairs of points on a square floor with 46 signatures.

Fig. 3. Braycurtis dissimilarity (Eq. (2)) when a high percentage of non common APs received at different powers. Low power APs have sporadic reception, but have low effect on dissimilarity.

Device Variability. Another issue to be considered when evaluating dissimilarity is the harvesting of signatures with different devices, which might have different receiving characteristics. These are caused by different antenna patterns, and different RF chains. In order to mitigate the RSSI differences introduced by device heterogeneity, we use robust fingerprints that include differences of RSSIs corresponding to pairs of APs from the same WiFi fingerprint. The method is derived from [7] and [17], and has been evaluated in [9] to be effective in dealing with device heterogeneity.

For a WiFi fingerprint, **only** for common APs $X = \{X_i\}$, the device invariant fingerprint is represented by differentiating power for consecutive APs:

$$X_{invariant} = \{(X_1 - X_2), (X_2 - X_3), ..., (X_{n-1} - X_n), (X_n - X_1)\} \qquad (3)$$

In *AirDocs* we use Bray-Curtis based dissimilarity function with all the mentioned features, and compare its monotonicity against real distance on data collected in an eight-story building, dataset 1a (described in Sect. 4.1). In Fig. 2, we consider all pairs of points on a floor that are 15 m or closer. We can see that dissimilarity increases linearly with actual distance, and beyond the 13 m mark, which is the length of a corridor, we begin to see values of 1.0 in dissimilarity, and a higher deviation due to more wall attenuation.

For APs missing between the two signatures, we consider them visible at −100 dBm (−99 dBm is the minimum observed value in datasets in this article), so that they contribute to the dissimilarity. To quantify the contribution of non common APs, we increase the percentage of non common APs between compared signatures to understand how they affect dissimilarity. As will be detailed later in the paper (Sect. 4.1), these are typical ratios of non common APs between spots that can be meters away from each other, and a dissimilarity of 0.25 will be later used as a threshold for selecting nearby documents. In Fig. 3, we see that weak APs that are not common do not affect the dissimilarity much, as it is common for mobile phones not to reliably pick them. In contrast, strong missing APs are a clear indicator of a faraway spot. In addition to that, we simply set the dissimilarity to 1.0 if the fraction of common APs is lower than a threshold (25%).

4   Dissimilarity Microbenchmarks

We evaluate the behaviour of the dissimilarity function and of the retrieval process on three different setups: one that we produced in our building, which will be made available as supporting material [27], and two which are publicly available [19], and [22]. In all the following sections, we use the real position of the documents only for reporting purposes, that is, to quantify the distance at which documents would be found, but **the real position is not used in the calibration of the system, indexing of the database, or anywhere in the search and retrieval process**, as it will not be available or necessary for the users of the system.

4.1   Building 1 Results

Datasets 1a and 1b were collected in our own office building with methodologies described in Sect. 3. The documents are spread across a square corridor (Fig. 4)

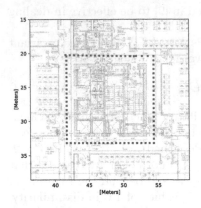

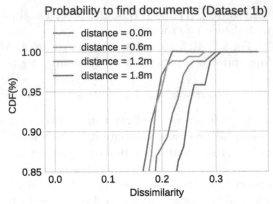

Probability to find documents (Dataset 1b)

Fig. 4. Dataset 1a contains 8 floors with similar collection trajectory, and dataset 1b one floor.

Fig. 5. Searching the document with a different device at the same point, or at points closeby. Increasing the dissimilarity threshold guarantees that the document is found even if searching some distance from it.

consisting of true position and signature. For dataset 1a, eight floors were collected with collection points 2 steps apart (approximately 1.2 m), holding two Android devices (Google Pixel 4A and Redmi Note 8) at waist level close to the body. For each collection point 4 directions were collected, rotating 90° after each scan. Dataset 1b contains the ground floor, sampled along the same trajectory, but at one step (0.6 m) resolution, and with the devices held at face level, away from the body. The building has an infrastructure WiFi, and a measurement point receives a median of 32 APs (minimum 20 APs, 95% = 49 APs). The collection methodology is described in more detail in Sect. 6.

We use documents placed in the environment (Fig. 4) to validate the searching process in several ways. First we search with a different device at the same physical point where the document was placed, and by using a large enough threshold we can guarantee that the document is found with high probability. In Fig. 5 we see that using a dissimilarity threshold of 0.22 guarantees that the document would be found in 99.5% of the cases. When searching at a distance from where the document was placed, an increasingly higher value of the threshold is necessary. As shown in Fig. 5, for dataset 1b, a search tolerance of 0–1.8 m would require a dissimilarity threshold of 0.22–0.3.

An alternate way of looking at the problem is to compute for each query signature the distance to the closest document in the database. This can be zero when a document collected with the other device is found at that same location, or non-zero for nearby documents. In Fig. 6, we see that in 72% of the cases the closest document (in signal space) returned is the one taken at the query spot, and in the rest of the cases is a spot 0.6 m away. The closer the response document, the more discriminate the signature is, and fewer faraway documents

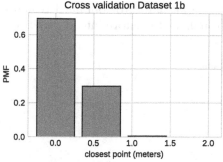

Fig. 6. Distance to the closest point: *Put* and *Get* devices are different. In 72% of the cases, the same point (collected with the other device) is returned. Sample documents are 0.6 m apart.

dataset 1b		
dissim thresh	50% of documents	95% of documents
0.20	0.63 m	2.54 m
0.25	1.21 m	3.13 m
0.30	1.52 m	3.81 m
0.35	1.88 m	4.45 m

Fig. 7. Document queries based on dissimilarity thresholds in signature space will also return some further away documents.

will be returned. For the rest of the experiments in the paper, we will use this measure of distance to closest document reported as a performance for all the datasets we explore.

As shown in Fig. 2, the relation between dissimilarity and real distance will make any decision based on a threshold in signal space to return several documents that have similar signatures, but are far from the query point. In Fig. 7, increasing the dissimilarity threshold returns, in addition to the desired document, other documents that have similar signatures. Whether these are considered as false positives depends on the actual application *Air Docs* is used for.

Simulated Impairments. Knowing that devices used by the system may vary in their antenna characteristics, we stress test the searching process to better understand higher diversity in devices.

We add Gaussian $\mathcal{N}(\mu, \sigma)$ noise to the database taken with the Pixel smartphone. The Redmi device queries for the closest point in the signal space from the database. As mentioned in Sect. 6, Fig. 19, the Pixel device already receives a $\mathcal{N}(-4.4\,\mathrm{dBm}, 3.5\,\mathrm{dBm})$ lower power. To explore a wider range of impairments, we add noise with $\mu = -5$ dBm, and σ increased from 1 dBm to 8 dBm, and compute through cross-validation the all the obtained distances. In Fig. 8, we plot the 50%, 90% and 99% percentiles of the CDF for the obtained closest distances. The system degrades gracefully, even for a standard deviation of 8 dBm, with the resulted median distance to the closest point increasing from 0.6 m to 0.9 m.

Then, we alter the database with a fixed deviation of $\sigma = 3$ dBm, and a varying offset $\mu = -1$ dBm .. -10 dBm. Due to the differentiating feature of the proposed dissimilarity used (Sect. 3.1), the median error obtained remains constant at 0.6m, and the 95% at 1.8 m throughout the entire interval studied.

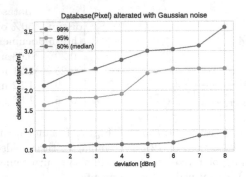

Fig. 8. Adding Gaussian (−5 dBm, stddev) noise to RSSI measurements, dataset 1b.

Another issue to explore is AP density, which has been increasing in recent years, even if sometimes the APs are virtual, being emitted from the same physical card. We eliminate fractions of APs from the query (Redmi) before querying the database (Pixel), and summarize the results in Fig. 9. The performance degrades gracefully and maintains performance even with one third of the existing APs. Please see the Sect. 6 for further discussion about AP density.

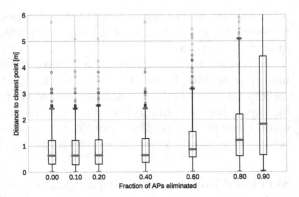

Fig. 9. Distance to closest point obtained when removing a fraction of APs (dataset 1b).

4.2 Building 2 Results

We use a dataset published by Indoor Location Competition, 2020 edition [22]. It contains data from two shopping mall buildings, that have been sampled at walking speed with the collector facing the necessary direction to complete the desired path. The collector stopped and marked certain points in the measurement trips, but WiFi and BLE beacon collection went on continuously. We post-processed the data to interpolate linearly the position of the collector at the time of each WiFi scan based on the timestamped positions logged during collection. The first floor of the first site is shown in Fig. 10, together with the resulted sampled points.

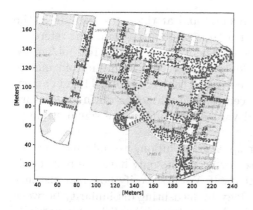

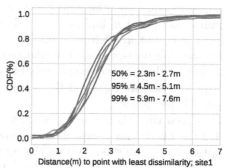

Fig. 10. Dataset 2 floor topology   **Fig. 11.** Dataset 2 closest point

The first site has a high density of APs with a total of 4053 unique MAC addresses for the entire building, with 1452–2524 APs per floor, and 130–401 APs collected on average for each point. Despite this density, collecting at high speed and with the collector facing only one direction, yields a closest point that is higher than for datasets 1a and 1b (Fig. 11). Dissimilarities of these closest points appear invariant to density. *AirDocs* is usable even with these relaxed collection methods, but the operating circle around the user would be larger, which could be appropriate for malls, with larger spaces and higher mobility patterns.

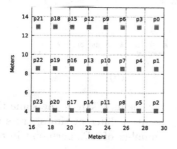

Fig. 12. UJI 3rd floor topology, 25 complete sets of WiFi signatures taken at the same points over a span of 11 months

On the server side, the implication of high density and variability is that $q = 9$ offers 99% retrieval rate and $q = 20$ is necessary to achieve 100% document retrieval rate, where we consider documents all the WiFi sampled points. This result shows that high AP density is not always a blessing, since variability in the strongest AP received increases the search time on the server. This situation can be partially mitigated by identification and merging of virtual APs.

4.3   Building 3 Results

The third dataset used is based on data from the UJI repository at [19], from which we select one particular floor that has been measured repeatedly over a period of almost one year. The topology is depicted in Fig. 12 and consists of

24 points visited sequentially by the collector, and at the end returning in the opposite sense over the same points after a time of about 10 min. The reference points have rather high distances between them 1.8 m, respectively 4.2 m on each axis, but at each location 6 samples were collected with Android mobile devices. We post-processed the data so we merged the two readings 10 min apart, assuming that the collectors probably faced opposite direction during the return trip, and also averaged all the collected values resulting in one signal strength per AP per point.

Given that the dataset has a lower spatial resolution, we only used points 3–20 as queries for cross-validation since corner points only have one reasonable option to be returned, besides the point itself. We first verify how real distance and dissimilarity are linked for this topology by measuring dissimilarity between points taken in the same session (Fig. 13a, blue dots and line fit). This partially resembles the behavior for dataset 1 (Fig. 2), with the collection lattice binning of possible distances. Then for each collection point, we computed all dissimilarities to its past and future measurements, and collected all the values in the gray boxplot. The boxplot is manually placed horizontally based on its median value and the line fit to give an estimation of the error resulted from fingerprint aging.

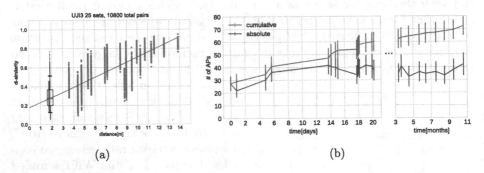

(a)   (b)

Fig. 13. (a) Blue: dissimilarity vs distance for measurements taken at the same time; Boxplot: dissimilarities between scans of the same point at different times, cross validated across all times and all sets. (b) UJI 3rd floor number of APs per point in time. (Color figure online)

To understand better the behavior of fingerprints in time, we look at a timeline of the number of APs available for a point at different moments. In Fig. 13b, each point represents a measurement set, and the actual number of APs is averaged across all 24 points, with the standard deviation indicated at each point. As the collecting device does not pick up all APs at all times, even if the instantaneous number of APs is relatively stable, the total number of APs that are historically available is substantially higher. This mismatch behaves like an aging effect, but can be countered either by taking more measurements, using more collector orientations, or using a different stances for the device.

To evaluate how retrieving of documents works with old databases, we cross validate fingerprints against entire database of 24 points taken at future or past time, and compute the closest point returned. In Fig. 14, we see that in 67% of the cases, the same location would result, and the rest distributed between the two available candidates, at 1.8 m and 4.2 m. The dissimilarities associated to these closest points are higher than the ones resulted in dataset 1, due to both fingerprint aging, and the actual spatial resolution of the sample points.

5   App and Server Implementation

The *AirDocs* middleware consists of an Android module that collects signatures, and a server that stores documents indexed by signatures and responds to queries based on signatures.

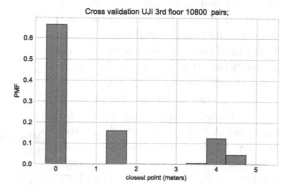

Fig. 14. UJI 3rd floor dissimilarity of the closest point across time

The Android module performs WiFi scans every 3 s, which is a limitation imposed by the operating system, as mentioned by other works as well [14]. The operating system provides a list of APs and the associated RSSI in dBm, which constitutes the WiFi fingerprint, the main part of the context signature. The module also scans cellular networks, BLE devices, obtains the GPS location when possible and records the background sound. All this is performed in the 3 s frame and all information is included in the signature.

From Android version 8, an additional throttling mechanism was included in the operating system, in order to limit the frequency of scans and reduce power consumption. In Android 8, a background application can only perform one scan in 30 min. However, this is mitigated by using a foreground service, which is not limited by the throttling mechanism. In Android 9, each foreground application can scan 4 times in 2 min. This problem can not be circumvented and it limits the scanning capabilities of *AirDocs* middleware on this version of Android. From Android 10 and above, the throttling mechanism can be disabled from Settings, so it does not affect the scanning procedure of our middleware.

The *AirDocs* server communicates with the *AirDocs* smartphone module and is responsible for two scenarios. First, it receives a new document together with an associated signature and stores them in a database associated with the building, institution, or group. Second, it responds to searches based on signatures, identifying documents with low dissimilarities. The most similar signatures and their associated documents are sent to the mobile and then displayed in the application.

With a naive linear database implementation, insertions would take $O(1)$, and searches $O(n)$, where n is the number of documents stored on the server. *AirDocs* stores a spatial database, in the sense that documents are tied to location, but the actual locations of documents is not known. Therefore, most of the methods to index spatial information, such as *M-trees* and *R*trees*, or others used optimize databases of position labeled fingerprints are not applicable.

However, dissimilarities between documents impose some structure in the signal space. A natural spatial clusterization should produce hierarchical structure into buildings, floors, rooms. This would allow for searching in a tree like structure that uses spatial relationships of inclusion and adjacency.

We use a multi-labeling system, where clusters are headed by the strongest AP observed, which imposes locality to the search process. When receiving a document, the server assigns q labels, where q is the number of the strongest APs visible in the WiFi fin-

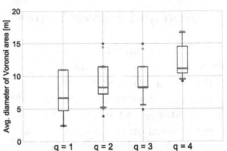

Fig. 15. Diameter of Voronoi-like regions. Multi label based searching will only query documents inside a diameter of 11m(median) for dataset 1b.

gerprint. For every query, the server then searches only in q lists associated with the strongest APs. Due to instabilities of indoor WiFi, the strongest AP might not always be the same and the question is *how to determine the minimum value of q required to retrieve any document?* If we had perfectly regular signal propagation, and $q = 1$, APs in a plane would divide space among them in Voronoi regions. The strongest AP would be the Voronoi seeds, and the documents points in the Voronoi cells, based on their strongest RSSI value. In reality, due to irregular indoor propagation, these regions are not Voronoi shaped, and do not have definite borders, but are partially overlapping. The shape and the amount of overlap depend on the building, AP density, and the collection method.

The search complexity of this data-structure is therefore $O(q*n_V)$, where n_V is the number of documents inside a Voronoi region. The areas of Voronoi regions depend on the density of APs (as Voronoi vertices), but because of varying RSSI values for the strongest APs, the size of the region will be larger in practice. This search process is trivial to parallelize since a fingerprint can be searched in parallel in each of the q lists. In Sect. 4.1 we will estimate typical values for q, and for the size of the regions.

For dataset 1b, we now characterize the data structures necessary on the server, given that they are a function of AP density and of indoor propagation specifics. As detailed in Sect. 5, searches on the server are performed in q lists of documents, corresponding the q strongest APs for a fingerprint. We tested increasing values of q to determine the minimum value that allows retrieval of all documents. We considered all 85 measured points in this dataset as potential documents, since the resolution is of 0.6m. If for $q = 1$ the associated region is akin to a Voronoi region, for increasing q, this region is enlarged, and we measure the size of the region by measuring the longest distance between two points in such a region, calling it a diameter. In Fig. 15 we plot diameters for values of $q = 1..4$. For $q = 4$ all documents are retrieved successfully for dataset 1b, querying regions 11m wide on average.

6 Discussion

In previous sections we validated the fact that WiFi signatures can discriminate between close-by points in a variety of operating conditions, but there are still a number of open questions remaining:

Tunables: while the target is for the system to work out of the box for both users and sysadmins, there are still a few values that need to be calibrated: The dissimilarity threshold that governs the area around the user is invariant on the density of APs but the actual values that correspond to a given radius in meters tend to be different depending on the collection density. For the server part, the q value that governs the efficiency of the document search depends on AP density and on collection method ($q = 4$ for dataset 1, and $q = 20$ for dataset 2).

AP density affects the performance of the system in more than one way: on one hand many APs means more ways to discriminate between close locations, on the other hand unstable AP picked up by Android scanning introduces additional noise in the dissimilarity. More study is needed to understand whether certain APs contribute positively or negatively to the signatures.

Whitelists: in many setups there will be temporary APs, or APs that change location. If these are a small fraction of the total, their effect will not be visible, as shown in Sect. 4.1. However, for low AP density it is indicated that the system only use APs in a whitelist with MAC addresses that belong to the infrastructure. Also, most modern APs create virtual SSIDs, so the same physical card would broadcast under MAC addresses differing by one byte (Cisco), therefore a whitelist would be beneficial in unifying these readings. For searching on the server q value is also affected by virtual APs since the physically strongest AP might appear with several MACs, thus artificially increasing the search complexity.

Better harvesting: We target an app that is usable on most Android phones, and decided to rely on a default scanning procedure that takes 3–4 s, only getting one RSSI reading per AP. But using monitor mode on a laptop would allow receiving 10 beacons/second from most APs, which could allow using the entire sampled distribution of received power, enabling richer signatures and better dissimilarity measures (Mahalanobis). Unfortunately, the use of laptops would decrease the accessibility of the project, but could be used for anchor documents or other high quality signatures.

Bad spots are those where document resolution is weaker, the WiFi fingerprint is not discriminate enough, or measurement is insufficient for retrieval of the document within a reasonable radius. More study is needed on how to identify these situations when needed, and either alert the user to take extra measurements, or prompt the sysadmin to improve the density of APs (physical, not virtual).

Curating documents: since documents are not placed on a map, a method to manage document collections by the server administration is needed. The proxy of distance used provides good clustering properties, in that documents beyond a certain distance, on different floors, or not having enough common APs have their dissimilarity set to 1. This allows for some organization of documents on buildings and floors, but management of documents in signal space is needed to perform periodic cleanup (because of institution policy for example), retrieving of lost/non-accessible documents, refreshing of fingerprints with changes in WiFi infrastructure, or addition of maps if they are available.

Signature Collection Methods. Since mobile phones have downsized antennas, the collector's body orientation with respect to the building, and the relative position of the phone with respect to the collector are factors affecting the sampling of the signal strength. We explore both aspects of collecting, by having the collector gather one sample in four consecutive directions, 90° apart. The collector holds the phone either near to the body, at hip level, or at the face level, arm length away from the body. Data is collected simultaneously with two different phones - Google Pixel 4A, and Redmi Note 8, both running Android 10.

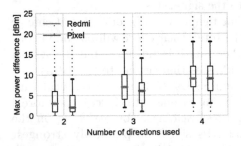

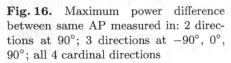

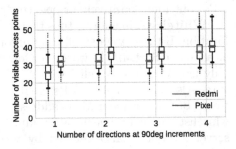

Fig. 16. Maximum power difference between same AP measured in: 2 directions at 90°; 3 directions at −90°, 0°, 90°; all 4 cardinal directions

Fig. 17. APs gained when harvesting several samples with collector body rotating around 90°.

In Fig. 16 we can see that the maximum power difference for the same AP ranges from 2.5 dBm when rotating 90°, 7 dBm when rotating 180°, and 9 dBm when considering all 4 directions. Boxplots[2] represent distribution of results gathered across spots and directions in the entire building (dataset 1a, described in Sect. 4.1). For comparison, Beder and Klepal [3] mention 2 m (best case) to 15 m (worst case) of positioning error per dBm RSSI measurement accuracy.

The effect of collecting data facing different directions can be seen in Fig. 17 as we count the number of APs that are cumulatively collected with 1–4 poses 90° apart. When rotating, Redmi keeps 75% of the APs, and drops/gains another 25%, when compared to the number of APs seen before rotation. For Pixel, the same figures are 87% and 13% respectively. This statistics are gathered for all consecutive 90° rotations, for all points in the dataset. By comparing all same AP readings in all the spots and in all directions (a total of 13000 measurements), we found that the Pixel - Redmi power difference is −4.3 dBm with a deviation of 3.6 dBm (Gaussian shaped). The interpretation of these numbers is that Redmi has a more directional antenna, and sees more of a power difference when rotating, but number of APs gathered is lower since it only gathers in the preferred direction.

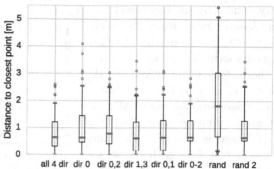

Fig. 18. All 4 dir: average of four samples measured in 4 directions 90° apart; dir 0: the direction along the walk; dir 0,2: experimenter uses direction 0, and opposite 180°; dir 1,3: two orientations sideways, also 180° apart; dir 0,1: two directions 90° apart; dir 0–2: three directions sweeping from left to right, 90° apart; rand: one random direction; rand 2: average of two random directions (out of 4 possible). Measuring in two random directions either 90 or 180° apart is invariant on actual orientation of sampling and reduces measurement time.

To better quantify all these factors, we search for a given fingerprint taken with Pixel among all fingerprints taken with Redmi, considering the dissimilarity measure presented in Sect. 3.1. We cross validate using all the points on the floor (dataset 1b, described in Sect. 4.1), and report the real distance to the fingerprint with the minimum dissimilarity. In Fig. 18 boxplots summarize distances to the closest point in signal space for several combinations of directions used during collection (*Put*) and testing (*Get*). The best case is when we use all 4 directions collected, and the worse when selecting a random directions out of the 4. An acceptable performance is obtained using any two directions, including random. Since one measurement takes 3s in Android, we conclude that measuring at least

---

[2] Boxplots in this article indicate middle quartiles (25%–75%), median, and whiskers at 5% and 95%. Outliers are shown outside the whiskers.

two different angles provides a good balance between the collection latency and the accuracy of the results. King et al. [11] also reports that measuring in two directions is enough for positioning purposes.

Phone Position Relative to the Body. We collected two datasets: 1a) at waist level and close to the body, and 1b) at face level and arm length away from the body. In Fig. 19, we summarize the findings comparing these two collection methods. Collecting away from the body, and at a higher pose brings several advantages: more APs are gathered by either phone by 18%-31%; There is less of a difference in number of APs gathered as the effect of rotating about; Less of a difference in power gathered as the effect of rotating about, therefore less variability; The consistent power difference between devices is reduced.

All these factors show that collecting high and away from the body is beneficial, as it reduces measurement variability for the three factors that affect dissimilarity: absolute power, number of APs, and device difference. These recommendations have an impact on the way the user collects the fingerprint whenever documents are placed or queried.

direc-tions	Pixel		Redmi	
	Waist	Face	Waist	Face
	Median # of APs			
1	41	52	29	38
2	48	60	39	46
4	54	64	45	54
	Power difference[dBm]			
2	2.0	3.0	3.0	3.0
3	6.0	6.0	7.0	6.0
all	9.0	8.0	10.0	8.0
	APs after rotation			
common gain/ loss	64%	87%	64%	82%
	36%	13%	33%	18%
	RSS power diff. Pixel-Redmi			
	Waist		Face	
mean	-4.4 dBm		-1.8 dBm	
stddev	3.5 dBm		3.8 dBm	

Fig. 19. Improvements obtained with signal harvesting stance: Collecting high and away from the body improves: power, number of APs collected, and reduces effect of device variation.

6.1 Future Work

One method to obtain increased resolution for the dissimilarity of the signatures is to use of additional sensors besides WiFi. BLE infrastructures are not as prevalent as WiFi, but all the issues explored in this paper for WiFi apply directly when beacons are available (datasets 1 and 2 also have BLE information but their density is not operational).

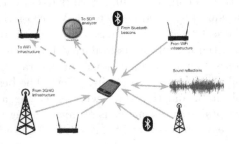

Fig. 20. Location specific signatures built using signals received to or from the smartphone.

Figure 20 shows several possible sources of data to enrich signatures making them more discriminate with respect to location. 4G/5G has a rather low positioning accuracy, but is available in all smartphones, and could be used to speed up the searching structures in the server. Sound reflections (as used in project EchoTag [36]) are another source of enriching the signature that does not require deploying of additional infrastructure. Basically, any context information that is *stable, available, and easily collectable* by the phone can become part of the signature.

Contact tracing [24,25,35] has recently seen a surge of interest, and has similar requirements with our system: no additional infrastructure, and simple operation with existing smartphones. *AirDocs* explores the same idea of proximity based on dissimilarity, and can be used as support for a contact tracing app, since the 1 m–4 m proximity detection is within range of current heath advisories.

Finally, as part of future work, we plan to open-source the client app (in public Application Stores) and the server, as well as publish all the measured data on *Zenodo* [27].

7   Related Work

Several systems were proposed to achieve positioning based solely on the existing wireless infrastructure using propagation properties, but many of them require extensive training and updating to maintain a positioning service [10,39]. In contrast, *AirDocs* proposes management of documents in a context aware fashion, but not linked to geographic locations which are natural contexts. Association of documents with locations has been explored—web documents are being geo-tagged and geo-referenced [29], and in the database community there are efforts to formalize searches for objects distributed in space [37].

Use of fingerprints for positioning has began in 2000 with the seminal paper by Padmanabhan [1], but has since developed into a rich research area in which several engineering approaches are possible. For a taxonomy, see [12], which describes choices of types of measurements, estimation methods, radio maps, collection methods, types of collectors. Collection effort, also called training, or war driving, is the main disadvantage for fingerprint based location, and some researchers have proposed the use of monitors [13] to minimize the training process. Yang et al. [38] tries to reduce training effort using an informal site survey by untrained users. Signatures are recorded with gait measurements and mapped to real space using MDS (multi dimensional scaling) and ground truth points obtained by GPS or manually. Google uses undisclosed methods to crowdsource data from all the users, and offers sparsely available indoor positioning, but does not have a public API, and comes with serious privacy concerns.

The EchoTag project [36] uses the microphone and speaker of the mobile phone to create a sound signature specific to the location. We plan to explore this direction with the purpose of creating an even richer signature for *AirDocs*.

Augmented reality is an emerging technology that "supplements the real world with virtual (computer-generated) objects that appear to coexist in the same space as the real world" [5]. [30] mentions projects spawned from MIT Media Lab's project sixth sense, that achieves a form of augmented reality by requiring the user to carry a projector and a camera to recognize hand gestures. *AirDocs* is an enabler of augmented reality in the sense that documents are embedded in physical space, but without requiring positioning, head mounted displays, or instrumentation of the environment.

Dousse et al. [8] develop a purely fingerprint-based place learning method. Its core is a density-based clustering algorithm that works directly on the raw WiFi fingerprints. They also study the behavior of fingerprints with respect to space and time, but their focus on learning about stationary *places* by using 60s sampling, manually labeled sets, and an unspecified spatial resolution of these places. Also, locations are visited for more than 5 min, in contrast with *AirDocs*, which aims for a more fluid user experience.

Proximity based on fingerprint comparison has been explored both for the purpose of privacy implication [31], and contact tracing [35]. *AirDocs* exploits more the resolution available in the dissimilarity - distance function, and can be used as a primitive for both problems.

8   Conclusion

We benchmarked *AirDocs*, a system that makes use of signatures composed of stable information about the location, that is easily collectable by smartphones. Documents are managed spatially, but without the use of a location system, which usually requires extra infrastructure, training, or crowd-sourcing of measurements. We explore the use of WiFi fingerprints as the main component of a location dependent signature, and define a measure of dissimilarity that is mostly monotonic with real distance. We show that typical WiFi deployments enable reliable retrieval of documents in areas with radius 0.6 m–2 m (median values), and characterize the behavior of dissimilarity with respect to: impairments and differences between measuring devices, collection methods, density of APs, and signature aging.

References

1. Bahl, P., Padmanabhan, V.N.: Radar: an in-building RF-based user location and tracking system. In: Proceedings IEEE INFOCOM 2000, vol. 2, pp. 775–784. IEEE (2000)
2. Beder, C., Klepal, M.: Fingerprinting based localisation revisited a rigorous approach for comparing RSSI measurements coping with missed access points and differing antenna attenuations. In: 2012 International Conference on Indoor Positioning and Indoor Navigation, IPIN 2012 (2012). https://doi.org/10.1109/IPIN. 2012.6418940
3. Beder, C., McGibney, A., Klepal, M.: Predicting the expected accuracy for fingerprinting based wifi localisation systems. In: 2011 International Conference on Indoor Positioning and Indoor Navigation, pp. 1–6 (2011). https://doi.org/10. 1109/IPIN.2011.6071939

4. Caso, G., De Nardis, L., Di Benedetto, M.G.: A mixed approach to similarity metric selection in affinity propagation-based wifi fingerprinting indoor positioning. Sensors **15**(11), 27692–27720 (2015). https://doi.org/10.3390/s151127692. https://www.mdpi.com/1424-8220/15/11/27692

5. Chatzopoulos, D., Bermejo, C., Huang, Z., Hui, P.: Mobile augmented reality survey: from where we are to where we go. IEEE Access **5**, 6917–6950 (2017)

6. de Matos, E., et al.: Context information sharing for the internet of things: a survey. Comput. Netw. **166**, 106988 (2020). https://doi.org/10.1016/j.comnet.2019.106988. https://www.sciencedirect.com/science/article/pii/S1389128619310400

7. Dong, F., Chen, Y., Liu, J., Ning, Q., Piao, S.: A calibration-free localization solution for handling signal strength variance. In: Fuller, R., Koutsoukos, X.D. (eds.) MELT 2009. LNCS, vol. 5801, pp. 79–90. Springer, Heidelberg (2009). https://doi.org/10.1007/978-3-642-04385-7_6

8. Dousse, O., Eberle, J., Mertens, M.: Place learning via direct wifi fingerprint clustering. In: 2012 IEEE 13th International Conference on Mobile Data Management, pp. 282–287. IEEE (2012)

9. Fang, S.H., Wang, C.H., Chiou, S.M., Lin, P.: Calibration-free approaches for robust wi-fi positioning against device diversity: a performance comparison. In: 2012 IEEE 75th Vehicular Technology Conference (VTC Spring), pp. 1–5 (2012). https://doi.org/10.1109/VETECS.2012.6240088

10. He, S., Chan, S.H.G.: Wi-fi fingerprint-based indoor positioning: recent advances and comparisons. IEEE Commun. Surv. Tutor. **18**(1), 466–490 (2016). https://doi.org/10.1109/COMST.2015.2464084

11. King, T., Kopf, S., Haenselmann, T., Lubberger, C., Effelsberg, W.: Compass: a probabilistic indoor positioning system based on 802.11 and digital compasses. In: Proceedings of the 1st International Workshop on Wireless Network Testbeds, Experimental Evaluation and Characterization, WiNTECH 2006, pp. 34 40. Association for Computing Machinery, New York (2006). https://doi.org/10.1145/1160987.1160995

12. Kjærgaard, M.B.: A taxonomy for radio location fingerprinting. In: Hightower, J., Schiele, B., Strang, T. (eds.) LoCA 2007. LNCS, vol. 4718, pp. 139–156. Springer, Heidelberg (2007). https://doi.org/10.1007/978-3-540-75160-1_9

13. Lim, H., Kung, L.C., Hou, J.C., Luo, H.: Zero-configuration indoor localization over IEEE 802.11 wireless infrastructure. Wirel. Netw. **16**(2), 405–420 (2010)

14. Liu, H.H., Liu, C.: Implementation of wi-fi signal sampling on an android smartphone for indoor positioning systems. Sensors **18**(1) (2018). https://doi.org/10.3390/s18010003. https://www.mdpi.com/1424-8220/18/1/3

15. Lohiya, R., Thakkar, A.: Application domains, evaluation data sets, and research challenges of IoT: a systematic review. IEEE Internet Things J. **8**(11), 8774–8798 (2021). https://doi.org/10.1109/JIOT.2020.3048439

16. Lymberopoulos, D., Liu, J.: The microsoft indoor localization competition: experiences and lessons learned. IEEE Signal Process. Mag. **34**(5), 125–140 (2017). https://doi.org/10.1109/MSP.2017.2713817

17. Mahtab Hossain, A., Jin, Y., Soh, W.S., Van, H.N.: SSD: a robust RF location fingerprint addressing mobile devices' heterogeneity. IEEE Trans. Mob. Comput. **12**(1), 65–77 (2013). https://doi.org/10.1109/TMC.2011.243

18. Makris, P., Skoutas, D.N., Skianis, C.: A survey on context-aware mobile and wireless networking: on networking and computing environments' integration. IEEE Commun. Surv. Tutor. **15**(1), 362–386 (2012)

19. Mendoza-Silva, G.M., Richter, P., Torres-Sospedra, J., Lohan, E.S., Huerta, J.: Long-term wi-fi fingerprinting dataset and supporting material. Zenodo (2017). https://doi.org/10.5281/zenodo.1066041

20. Microsoft: Microsoft indoor localization competition (2017). https://www. kaarta.com/kaarta-wins-microsoft-indoor-localization-competition-for-second-consecutive-year/

21. Microsoft: Microsoft indoor localization competition (2018). https://www. microsoft.com/en-us/research/event/microsoft-indoor-localization-competition-ipsn-2018/

22. Microsoft: Indoor location competition dataset (2020). https://github.com/ location-competition/indoor-location-competition-20. gitHub repository

23. Microsoft: Microsoft indoor localization competition (2020). https://github.com/ location-competition/indoor-location-competition-20

24. Nguyen, C., et al.: A comprehensive survey of enabling and emerging technologies for social distancing-Part I: fundamentals and enabling technologies. IEEE Access 8, 153479–153507 (2020)

25. Nguyen, C., et al.: A comprehensive survey of enabling and emerging technologies for social distancing-Part II: emerging technologies and open issues. IEEE Access 8, 154209–154236 (2020)

26. Niculescu, D.S., Ruse, L., Carabas, C.: Documents in the air. In: 2022 IEEE International Conference on Pervasive Computing and Communications Workshops and other Affiliated Events (PerCom Workshops), pp. 1–4 (2022). https://doi.org/10. 1109/PerComWorkshops53856.2022.9767318

27. Niculescu, D., Ruse, L., Carabas, C.: Documents in the air dataset and supporting materials. Zenodo (2021). https://doi.org/10.5281/zenodo.4999707

28. Perera, C., Zaslavsky, A., Christen, P., Georgakopoulos, D.: Context aware computing for the internet of things: a survey. IEEE Commun. Surv. Tutor. 16(1), 414–454 (2013)

29. Poese, I., Uhlig, S., Kaafar, M.A., Donnet, B., Gueye, B.: IP geolocation databases: unreliable? ACM SIGCOMM Comput. Commun. Rev. 41(2), 53–56 (2011)

30. Sanchez-Vives, M.V., Slater, M.: From presence to consciousness through virtual reality. Nat. Rev. Neurosci. 6(4), 332–339 (2005)

31. Sapiezynski, P., Stopczynski, A., Wind, D.K., Leskovec, J., Lehmann, S.: Inferring person-to-person proximity using wifi signals. Proc. ACM Interact. Mob. Wearable Ubiquitous Technol. 1(2) (2017). https://doi.org/10.1145/3090089

32. Sezer, O.B., Dogdu, E., Ozbayoglu, A.M.: Context-aware computing, learning, and big data in internet of things: a survey. IEEE Internet Things J. 5(1), 1–27 (2018). https://doi.org/10.1109/JIOT.2017.2773600

33. Shit, R.C., Sharma, S., Puthal, D., Zomaya, A.Y.: Location of things (LoT): a review and taxonomy of sensors localization in IoT infrastructure. IEEE Commun. Surv. Tutor. 20(3), 2028–2061 (2018)

34. Torres-Sospedra, J., Montoliu, R., Trilles, S., Óscar Belmonte, Huerta, J.: Comprehensive analysis of distance and similarity measures for wi-fi fingerprinting indoor positioning systems. Expert Syst. Appl. 42(23), 9263–9278 (2015). https://doi.org/10.1016/j.eswa.2015.08.013. https://www.sciencedirect. com/science/article/pii/S0957417415005527

35. Trivedi, A., Zakaria, C., Balan, R., Becker, A., Corey, G., Shenoy, P.: Wifitrace: network-based contact tracing for infectious diseases using passive wifi sensing. Proc. ACM Interact. Mob. Wearable Ubiquitous Technol. 5(1) (2021). https://doi. org/10.1145/3448084

36. Tung, Y.C., Shin, K.G.: Echotag: accurate infrastructure-free indoor location tagging with smartphones. In: Proceedings of the 21st Annual International Conference on Mobile Computing and Networking, pp. 525–536 (2015)
37. Wu, D., Cong, G., Jensen, C.S.: A framework for efficient spatial web object retrieval. VLDB J. **21**(6), 797–822 (2012)
38. Yang, Z., Wu, C., Liu, Y.: Locating in fingerprint space: wireless indoor localization with little human intervention. In: Proceedings of the 18th Annual International Conference on Mobile Computing and Networking, pp. 269–280 (2012)
39. Zhu, X., Qu, W., Qiu, T., Zhao, L., Atiquzzaman, M., Wu, D.O.: Indoor intelligent fingerprint-based localization: principles, approaches and challenges. IEEE Commun. Surv. Tutor. **22**(4), 2634–2657 (2020). https://doi.org/10.1109/COMST.2020.3014304

InnerEye: A Tale on Images Filtered Using Instagram Filters - How Do We Interact with them and How Can We Automatically Identify the Extent of Filtering?

Gazi Abdur Rakib[1], Rudaiba Adnin[1(✉)] (iD), Shekh Ahammed Adnan Bashir[1],
Chashi Mahiul Islam[1], Abir Mohammad Turza[1], Saad Manzur[1],
Monowar Anjum Rashik[1], Abdus Salam Azad[1,2], Tusher Chakraborty[3],
Sydur Rahaman[1], Muhammad Rayhan Shikder[1], Syed Ishtiaque Ahmed[4],
and A. B. M. Alim Al Islam[1]

[1] Bangladesh University of Engineering and Technology, Dhaka, Bangladesh
1505032.ra@ugrad.cse.buet.ac.bd
[2] University of California, Berkeley, USA
[3] Microsoft, Redmond, USA
[4] University of Toronto, Toronto, Canada

Abstract. Even though digitally filtered images are taking over the Internet for their aesthetic appeal, general people often feel betrayed if they are dealt with filtered images. Our study, comprising a series of structured surveys over images filtered using Instagram filters, reveals that different people perceive the filtered images differently. However, people have a common need for an automated tool to help them distinguish between original and filtered images. Accordingly, we develop an automated tool named 'InnerEye', which is capable of identifying how far an image is filtered or not. InnerEye utilizes a novel analytical design of a Neural Network Model that learns from a diverse set of images filtered using Instagram filters. Rigorous objective and subjective evaluations confirm the efficacy of InnerEye in identifying the extent of filtering in the images.

Keywords: Images · Filters · Survey · Deep Learning

1 Introduction

With the rise of social media, the world has witnessed an influx of images shared on the Internet. As of January 2022, an average of more than 100 million images are uploaded, and more than 4.2 billion likes are accumulated each day on Instagram alone [33], and these values are ever-rising. Part of the reason for having the images to be predominating on social media is associated with the availability

S. Longfei and P. Bodhi (Eds.): MobiQuitous 2022, LNICST 492, pp. 494–514, 2023.
https://doi.org/10.1007/978-3-031-34776-4_26

of mobile cameras and mobile applications specializing in image editing. Digital image processing is categorized into two classes such as pixel-level editing and parametric editing [36]. Using both of the classes of image editing, mobile 'apps' provide different preset ways to edit images reflecting the choice of a user. These preset ways are called 'Filters'. People use filters to achieve a stylized appearance of images without having any prior knowledge about digital image processing [27]. The filters are considered a type of parametric image editing system, which changes the outlook of an image while preserving the context and original objective content. As the notion of image filtering is extensively used nowadays and people are now substantially experiencing outcomes of image filtering, there arise several aspects related to real-life interactions with filtered images. The aspects include how people perceive the filtered images, how far they are confident in their ability to distinguish whether a filter has been applied to an image or not, and so on. Several related studies have focused on users' ability to find out image manipulation [19,32], however, very few studies focused specifically on the perspectives of users while interacting with filtered images. Therefore, this study focuses specifically on the perceptions of users with filtered images.

In this research, we performed a chronological series of online surveys to uncover the different aspects of people's perceptions of filtered images. To overcome the demographic variations that unavoidably occur in our chronological series of surveys and to verify whether the results of our surveys hold value over time, we performed a consolidated survey ensuring consistent demography of the participants. Analyzing the results of our surveys, we discovered people's experiences with filtered images. The results demonstrate significant variability in public opinions on categorization and quantification over original and filtered images. Irrespective of this variability, analysis of the survey results implies the need for an automated tool for detecting and measuring the extent of applying a filter to an image. Accordingly, we designed and developed a new web tool-based solution that employed a Neural Network Model specially crafted for predicting whether an input image is edited with filters or not. Here, our consideration of filtering mostly subsumes applying Instagram filters, as Instagram is the largest photo-sharing social media network that has a huge collection of built-in filters [37,38]. We present our solution to the public and sought out public opinion through yet another survey to evaluate the efficacy of our solution and its acceptability to the users. As a result, we encountered the following set of research questions in this study.

- *RQ1:* Is there any prevalence of filtered images shared on social media? Can users perceive the extent of applying filters over images with bare eyes?
- *RQ2:* Will general users appreciate the help of an automated tool in identifying the extent of applying filters over an image, and if so, why?
- *RQ3:* What are the components of an automated tool for identifying whether an image is filtered or not? Do people appreciate using such a tool?

Working with the above-mentioned research questions, we make the following set of contributions to this paper.

Fig. 1. The user interface of InnerEye

- We conducted a comprehensive series of chronological surveys that present an in-depth look into users' perspectives on interacting with filtered images, their preferences in interacting with specific types of filtered images, and their ability to distinguish between an original image and a filtered image. The findings of the surveys reveal salient aspects of users' experience with filtered images. This will help HCI researchers to better understand users' interaction with filtered images.
- Being inspired by the findings of our surveys, we developed a novel solution called *'InnerEye'* (Fig. 1) for detecting the extent of applying filters over an image. InnerEye is a web tool implemented with a Neural Network Model specializing in predicting the originality of an image in terms of being edited with image filters. Our implemented tool, InnerEye, informs the HCI community of a method regarding how a filtered image detection tool can be designed and implemented for users.
- We conducted a user evaluation with a survey presented within the InnerEye tool. This survey uncovers users' feedback on the performance of InnerEye as well as their appreciation of identifying the extent of image filtering with an automated tool. The user evaluation will assist HCI researchers to understand users' preferences for filtered image detection tools and facilitate the development of solutions in the realm of image filtering in novel ways.

2   Related Work

In this section, we provide an in-depth discussion of the prior research work pertaining to our study.

2.1   Social and News Media, and Edited Images

The upsurge in social media usage has led us to a world where images are shared across the globe and edited images play a significant role in people's interaction with social media. A study [26] takes an in-depth look at how social media shaped people's perception of images and how it has affected their day-to-day life. Another study [23] investigates the factors that influence Facebook users' intentions to post digitally altered self-images. However, manipulated images lead to significant personal or societal impact [6]. Gupta et al., show how edited images are prevalent in prominent social media sites like Twitter, especially during disastrous events such as Hurricane Sandy, misleading the general users to believe in fake news, and how automated techniques can be used to detect fake images with adequate accuracy [14]. Boididou et al., explored the challenges of building an automatic detection framework for fake multimedia content in social media posts [5]. Another study [30] talked about a broad case study of Hurricane Sandy and the Instagram images shared over Twitter. They explored how news propagates among citizens in a post-newspaper era where uncontrolled access to images shapes people's viewpoints toward various groundbreaking incidents differently. Additionally, exposure to manipulated images directly led to lower confidence related to physical appearance [20], especially, girls with higher social comparison tendencies [20].

In addition, some research studies [7,32] investigate how well people can identify image tampering. Farid et al. [7] focus on people's ability to identify photo manipulations by creating a series of computer-generated scenes consisting of basic geometrical shapes. Furthermore, an exploratory focus group study [19] was done to discover how individuals react and evaluate the authenticity of images that accompany online stories in communications channels.

However, we know little about how people assess filtered images specifically and their judgments about the authenticity of such images. Therefore, we investigate the experiences of people with filtered images.

2.2 Image Forgery and Fake Image Detection

The field of image forgery detection has become of paramount importance in recent years. Jang et al. [17], theorized an apparatus capable of detecting fake images by learning the background information from input images and building a learned background and comparing it to the present background to detect discrepancies. The performance comparison between various novel passive techniques concludes that they need automation, i.e., removal of human intervention in output analysis [4]. In digital images, sometimes image portions are edited to cover up a major feature of the original image, which contributes to deceiving people. Fridrich et al. [9], studied detecting what is known as copy-move forgery, which involved copying a segment of an image to cover up another part. Several other studies also worked on dealing with the same problem. Some studies focus on detecting re-sampling [24] and interpolation [10] in digital images. Another recent work [25] addresses the problem of tampering localization. Another study [34] uses contextual cues to detect image forgery. With the recent development of generative neural network architectures, the world has begun witnessing the prevalence of DeepFake, which describes the phenomena of replacing one person's face with another's realistically in images or videos. Nguyen et al. [31] talk about the existing DeepFakes technology and how to detect DeepFakes in-depth.

Rössler et al. [35] showed us in their dataset collection work how excessive the growth of generated face images has been in recent years. Agarwal et al. [1] show us why detection cannot keep up with the generation of DeepFake and what is hindering the current development of DeepFake detection. Xuan et al. [42], show how preprocessing both real and fake training data can lead to a better generalization across DeepFakes generated using various technologies. In a more recent work [28] by Marra et al., it has been shown that Neural Network Models can achieve higher efficiency in detecting machine-generated images with variable properties. Tariq et al. [39], show how preprocessing and employing ensemble methods can achieve far greater success in GAN-generated fake images than edited images. Frank et al. [8], show us how analyzing images in the frequency domain could lead to a groundbreaking change in the sector of GAN-generated face images. Belkasoft's [3] forgery detection module is a comprehensive payware that can perform automatic detection of alteration, modification, and forgery, providing a confidence percentage score on the originality of an image. The tool employs error level analysis, clone detection, quantization table analysis, double compression artifacts analysis, double quantization effect analysis, and foreign artifact detection.

Due to the extreme prevalence of edited and fabricated images online, there has been a lot of development in the sector of building user-friendly software that can perform qualitative and forensic analysis on digital images. Jonas Wagner [40] built the tool Forensically that can perform a multitude of levels of forensic operation on digital images, such as digital magnification with three types of enhancement: histogram equalization, and auto contrast by channel; similar region detection through operations regarding minimal similarity, minimal detail, minimal cluster size, block-size, and maximal image size; error level analysis through comparison of the original and re-compressed image for manipulation detection; Level sweep for histogram analysis; principal component analysis; metadata analysis; and string extraction for hidden ASCII content in the image. Dr. Neal Krawetz [21] built a similar forensic analysis tool called FotoForensics that can perform metadata analysis, error level analysis, hidden content analysis, and service information extraction. Zampoglou et al. [43], built a tool for an image originality verification system, featuring a multitude of image tampering detection algorithms, along with metadata analysis, geolocation tagging, and reverse image searching through Google. In a study [13], we see how analyzing image histograms can reveal the statistical differences of the Hue and Saturation channel, and designing a histogram-based and feature-based detection system can lead to a decent performance in detecting fake colorization of images.

Analyzing the previously annotated research studies, we can observe that a limited number of studies focused on filtered images. Therefore, we uncover the perspectives of users with filtered images and a filtered image detection tool.

3 Methodology of Our Study

We recruited participants for a chronological series of online surveys to gather public opinion on the prevalence of image sharing and filtered images over social media as per their experiences and practices. Analyzing the survey result, we performed the task of filtered image detection. We built a web tool *'InnerEye'* by analyzing the alteration of the inherent color distribution of an image with a custom Neural Network model. Deploying our automated web tool, we performed a user evaluation to find out whether people appreciate using InnerEye which assists them by detecting filtered images online and quantifying the extent of filtering applied to images. Figure 2 shows our methodology (Fig. 3).

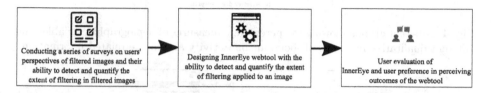

Fig. 2. An overview of the methodology of our work

Fig. 3. A series of surveys conducted in our study in a chronological manner

4 Perception About Interacting with Alterations of Shared Filtered Images

During the rudimentary stages of our research, we designed three consecutive online surveys to understand how people perceive image sharing on social media, and what is the general experience while interacting with shared filtered images. All the questionnaires of the surveys were designed to attain the perspectives of users on how they interact with filtered images on social media. The participants of the surveys were recruited through open online communication via publicly available emails and public social media groups. This study was approved by the Ethics Committee of the institution of the corresponding author.

4.1 Surveying Users About Their Experiences with Interacting Through Images on Social Media

We designed this questionnaire to analyze the social media usage of the participants and their experiences while interacting with filtered images shared on

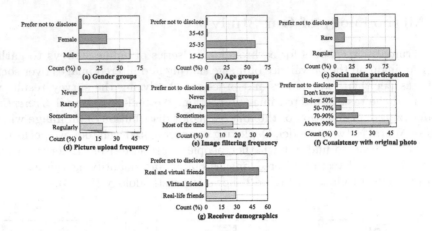

Fig. 4. Different graphs showing the percentage measures of demographic variables and different qualitative measures of social media activity and image-related information

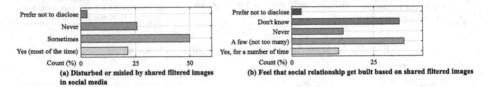

Fig. 5. Different graphs showing the general opinion about different aspects of relationships in social media

social media. From the results in Fig. 4, we observe that participants from different demographics use social media regularly and a lot of these social media users interact with filtered images, in the forms of uploading, and filtering. A considerable amount of participants filter images to be shared online and they have different tastes in filtering frequency and deciding the extent to which the filters will alter the images. The receivers of these filtered images are not convergent towards a specific category, which emphasizes more on the varied taste of general users when it comes to filtered images. Additionally, from the results in Fig. 5, we notice that many feel disturbed by filtered images shared on social media. Some of them further think that social relationships frequently get built based on filtered images.

In addition, from the results in Fig. 6, we observe that majority of the participants claim to be able to determine whether an image has been filtered or not with their own eyes, but at the same time, a vast majority will appreciate using an automated tool to detect filtering in images. These imply that users are not confident in their ability to detect image alterations by applying filters while interacting with images. Therefore, an objective opinion about the originality of images will assist them in their interaction with filtered images.

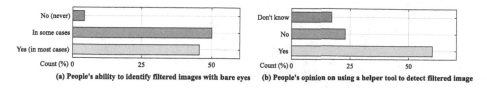

(a) People's ability to identify filtered images with bare eyes   (b) People's opinion on using a helper tool to detect filtered image

Fig. 6. Different graphs showing the confidence of people's ability to distinguish filtered images and opinion on automated tools to help in differentiating between filtered and original images

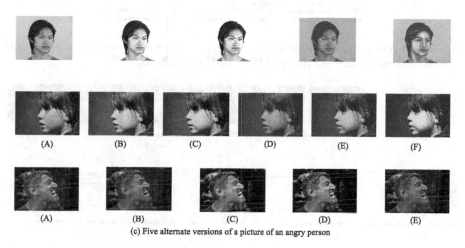

(c) Five alternate versions of a picture of an angry person

Fig. 7. Different images used to quantify user preference for image filtering

4.2 Surveying Social Media Users About Their Preferences Towards Interacting with Types of Image Filtering

We designed this questionnaire with inspiration from the previous survey, to find an objective view of the preferences of the participants regarding filtered images. The first part of the survey collected demographic data. The second part of the survey showed the participants different filtered variants of the same images, shown in Fig. 7, filtered in terms of brightness, contrast, color saturation, and temperature, and asked which variant of effect in each image would they choose most likely when filtering an image. We decided to perform the same test on three images to present a subjective variability to the contents of the images so that we do not see any sort of subjective bias in the preference of the participants.

If we look at the results of this survey (Fig. 8), we observe that participants have varied tastes when it comes to image filtering preferences, across filters and subjective variables. Additionally, there is no universal agreement on what types

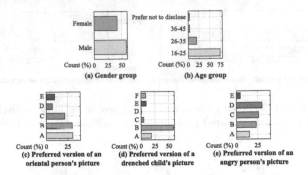

Fig. 8. Different graphs showing the demographic information, and the variability of preference between different filtered versions of three images

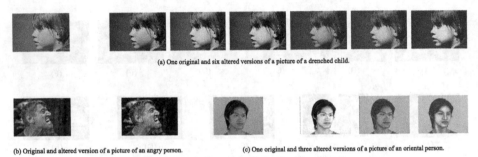

Fig. 9. All ten examples of the original image and their edited counterpart, used in the survey on quantification of image alteration

of filters participants will use. Thus, the user's preference varies when choosing a filter to apply to images. These imply that the task of detecting whether an image has been filtered or not is a vast problem space.

4.3 Surveying Capability of General Users in Quantifying Extent of Image Alteration

We designed this questionnaire to test out whether participants can come to an agreement when quantifying different extents of image filtering and whether they have any objective measurements of the properties of the images when they are considering the extent of filtering. The first section of the questionnaire served to collect demographic information. The second part aimed to judge the participants' ability to come to an agreement while quantifying the extent of filtering of different filtered versions of three images, as shown in Fig. 9. The third part extracted the qualitative information about the specifics of components based on which participants reported their quantification of filtering of the images in

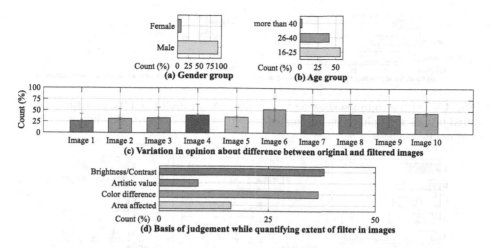

(a) Gender group

(b) Age group

(c) Variation in opinion about difference between original and filtered images

(d) Basis of judgement while quantifying extent of filter in images

Fig. 10. Five graphs showing the demographic information, one graph showing median and standard deviation of the general perception towards the level of editing of 10 images, and one graph showing the basis of the judgment of quantifying image editing level

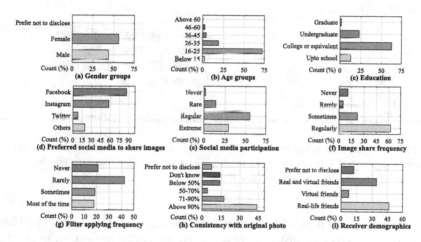

(a) Gender groups

(b) Age groups

(c) Education

(d) Preferred social media to share images

(e) Social media participation

(f) Image share frequency

(g) Filter applying frequency

(h) Consistency with original photo

(i) Receiver demographics

Fig. 11. Different graphs showing the percentage measures of demographic variables and different qualitative measures of social media activity and image-related information

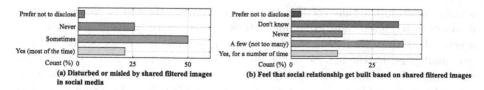

(a) Disturbed or misled by shared filtered images in social media

(b) Feel that social relationship get built based on shared filtered images

Fig. 12. Different graphs showing the general opinion about different aspects of relationships in social media

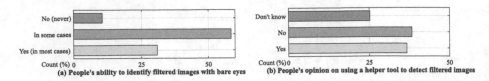

(a) People's ability to identify filtered images with bare eyes

(b) People's opinion on using a helper tool to detect filtered images

Fig. 13. Different graphs showing the confidence of people's ability to distinguish filtered images and opinion on automated tools to help in differentiating between filtered and original images

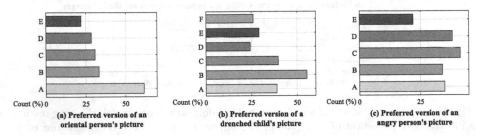

(a) Preferred version of an oriental person's picture

(b) Preferred version of a drenched child's picture

(c) Preferred version of an angry person's picture

Fig. 14. Different graphs showing the variability of preference between different filtered versions of three images

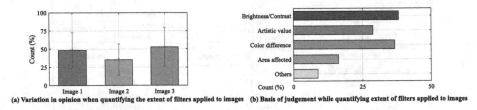

(a) Variation in opinion when quantifying the extent of filters applied to images

(b) Basis of judgement while quantifying extent of filters applied to images

Fig. 15. One graph showing median and standard deviation of the general perception towards the level of editing of three images, and one graph showing the basis of the judgment of quantifying image editing level

the second part. We decided to present ten different variations of three different images to overcome the subjective bias due to regularity or pattern in questions that would arise if we presented the same number of variations of each image.

The participants had to answer some numeric value that quantified the level of image alteration in each instance. For all such items, the responses almost uniformly varied in the range of 10% to 90%. They were allowed to choose multiple answers if they used more than one criterion to compare two images. Therefore, when calculating, we used a weighted percentage manner. Each person's choice was multiplied by the inverse of the number of choices they made. Delving into the results of the questionnaire (Fig. 10), we observe that users perceive the same filtered versions of images to a varying degree and it is hard for them to achieve agreement while quantifying the extent of filters applied to images. Even when identifying image components that were changed during filtering the images in our questionnaire, there is a vast divergence among participants. Therefore, we can hypothesize that users' opinions toward a tool that can detect a wide variety of filters are divergent similar to divergent opinions towards filtered images.

4.4 Consolidated Survey to Verify Our Findings Across Demographic and Temporal Variations

Due to conducting an open online series of chronological surveys designed respectively, we noticed a demographic variation in the three questionnaires. We understand that open online surveys have their limitations when it comes to capturing a wide range of demography. Additionally, we sequentially collected the results, which raises some questions about the validity of the surveys, as participants observed shifts in their online presence between the time they answered the three questionnaires. To verify the results of our series of surveys, we designed a consolidated one and we recruited participants in a manner that preserves the demographic proportion of the participants.

In this consolidated survey, we brought in a few changes compared to the previous ones while keeping all the questions similar to the previous three consecutive surveys. We collected more detailed demographic information, and we further presented the participants with three filtered images, compared to ten in the previous survey, as we noticed the consolidated survey would be rather time-consuming if we presented the participants with ten filtered images, which might discourage participants to complete the survey. After analyzing the results (Fig. 11, 12, 13, 14, 15) of our consolidated survey, we can see the results are comparable even in the presence of demographic and temporal variation.

5 Implementation of an Automated Solution to Detect Extent of Image Alteration: InnerEye

We developed a web tool, 'InnerEye' to enable users to interact with filtered images by detecting filtered images automatically. InnerEye makes use of an image classifier to distinguish between unfiltered and filtered images and provides a confidence value (chance of being filtered) of the input image. We deployed the tool online and made it open for public use.

Table 1. Dataset division into train, validation, and test set for updated dataset

Dataset Description			
	Sampled Images	Filtered Images	Total Images
Train	7001	203029	210030
Validation	251	7279	7530
Test	501	14529	15030

(a) Original Image   (b) Edited Image

(c) Edited Image   (d) Edited Image

Fig. 16. An original and three filtered versions of a single image that our tool can successfully distinguish between

5.1 Developing a Neural Network Model for Detecting Filtered Images

We implemented a classifier to classify input images into two types: Filtered and Unfiltered. The challenge was to recognize how the appearance of colors of the objects present in a filtered image is different from those in its unfiltered counterpart. Further, while constructing such a classifier, we had to consider the fact that, under different illumination conditions, e.g., early morning, mid-afternoon, and evening, the color appearance of the objects in an image changes. However, the real color of the objects in an image does not change over the day. Therefore, if we can have the classifier learn to recognize the invariant properties each color posses under all-natural illumination conditions, our classifier learns the features present in the unfiltered images. We refer to the invariant properties each color posses under all-natural illumination conditions to be the style of an image. The classifier can classify filtered and unfiltered images following the

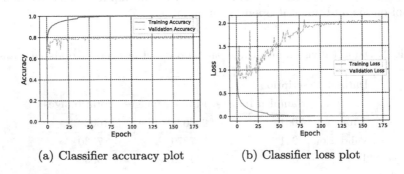

(a) Classifier accuracy plot   (b) Classifier loss plot

Fig. 17. Classification performance of the sequential Neural Network-based classifier on the larger, more varied dataset

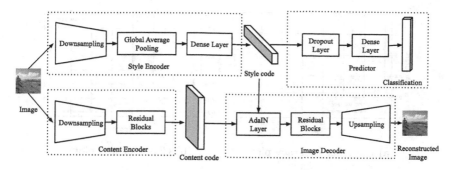

Fig. 18. Architecture of the analytical classifier

prescribed knowledge. Therefore, we are using supervised Learning to build the classifier. We compiled a dataset of Filtered and Unfiltered images to train the InnerEye classifier from the Google Landmarks dataset [12]. We included the image filters *Gotham, Lomo,* and *Sepia, Aden, Brannan, Brooklyn, Clarendon, Earlybird, Gingham, Hudson, Inkwell, Kelvin, Lark, Lofi, Maven, Mayfair, Moon, Nashville, Perpetua, Reyes, Rise, Slumber, Stinson, Toaster, Valencia, Walden, Willow,* and *Xpro2.* Description of these filters are given in [29] and we used the Python package [18] to generate the newly filtered images. Our compiled dataset description is given in Table 1.

After training our sequential classifier with the dataset, we can observe a larger case of overfitting due to the high variance in the dataset from our training log in Fig. 17. Thus We looked more closely into the problem of the classification of filtered and unfiltered images. We note that the application of an image filter only alters the color of the objects in an image, however, it does not alter the semantic content. Therefore, if we can have our classifier ignore the semantic content of images as much as possible, it can better learn the style and hence yield a better accuracy on the classes. Moreover, this approach is likely to reduce the variance that used to arise in the previous classifiers due to a large number of different filters. InnerEye classifier consists of a style encoder module, a content encoder module, an image decoder module, and a style predictor module. Inner-Eye classifier is co-trained for both image classification and image reconstruction tasks. This classifier does not overfit the training data, as evidenced in Fig. 19,

Table 2. Accuracy report on train, validation and test set

Accuracy Report	
	Accuracy
Train	91.39%
Validation	80.32%
Test	96.02%

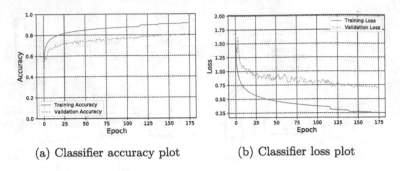

(a) Classifier accuracy plot   (b) Classifier loss plot

Fig. 19. Classification performance of the analytical classifier.

as there is a convergence tendency among the training loss and validation loss curve in the training logs.

In one recent work, Huang et al. described a mechanism, which the authors call MUNIT [15], for image-to-image translation. In image-to-image translation, some aspects of an image, which may be only style or only semantic content, or both, are preserved entirely or to some degree, and the rest are filtered according to those described in a different image. In MUNIT, the authors assumed that an image consists of domain-invariant semantic content code and domain-invariant style code. In the case of InnerEye, we can make the same assumption on the images and can work with the style code only to have the classifier learn better than before. Based on this assumption, we design a classifier, presented in Fig. 18, for InnerEye. We call such a classifier an *analytical classifier* because it analyzes and decomposes the image into content code and style code. The training logs are shown in Fig. 19. The accuracy reports are given in Table 2.

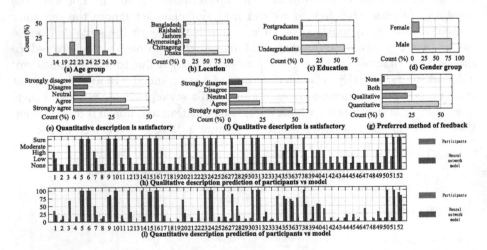

Fig. 20. Four graphs showing the demographic information, three graphs showing the general consensus about chances of being filtered, summary, and the preferred method of feedback, and two graphs showing contrast between the human prediction and the machine one

5.2   Developing a Web Tool to Deploy the Neural Network Model

We deployed our newly designed neural network model in the form of a web tool, InnerEye. The tool consists of two components, the Predictor and the Survey. The predictor serves to give an objective measurement in the form of a quantitative percentage value of the extent of a filter applied to an image and a qualitative message about the possibility of an image being filtered.

The left part of the web tool contains the predictor. It takes an image as an input and outputs two results: a quantitative description, a percentage score of the extent of any filter applied to the input image, and a qualitative description, a brief message about the possibility that the input image is filtered. The qualitative description has five values: None, Low, Moderate, High, and Sure. The message is delivered in the form of a sentence, for example, 'InnerEye thinks there is no chance of the image being filtered' if the output is None. We showed three examples of filtered images our system can detect, as shown in Fig. 16. The web tool contains a survey through which we collected feedback about our tool from our users. The survey starts with a section for collecting demographic information such as gender, age, education, and location. Consecutively, the survey collected user opinions regarding the quantitative and qualitative descriptions, the preference between the qualitative description and quantitative one, and the user-proposed values for quantitative and qualitative descriptions.

6   Evaluation of Performance of Our Solution

We made the web tool online after finishing development and made it public. We distributed the tool among participants (n = 52) recruited through open online participation via emailing to publicly available email addresses. We collected the user experiences through the survey integrated into the tool. The survey results can be observed in Fig. 20.

We observe that the general agreement and disagreement towards our solution are nearly equalized, which is undesirable but quite expected. We hypothesized that as the opinions of users towards filtered images are very divergent, their opinions toward a filtered image detection tool will be divergent. We analyzed the survey results on our baseline and verified this hypothesis. The results reflect this hypothesis. We see the general agreement towards the qualitative and quantitative description of our improved solution. We further observe the correlation between the model's prediction and the participant's predictions from the bar charts. Consequently, we can conclude that the participants prefer the results of our tool in a quantitative manner.

7   Discussion

In this section, we answer the key research questions of our study.

7.1   Users and Filtered Images

We identify that users frequently share images on social media and edit those images using filters. However, they have varied tastes when it comes to image filtering preferences. As a result, there is no fixed type of filters that users use. These extend prior work [23] where the intention of users to post edited images was studied.

As an unavoidable consequence, users frequently come across filtered images shared by others. They further perceive that some social relationships are built based on filtered images. Additionally, whilst some users prefer filtered images shared by others, many showed detest to such images probably because they often feel that those images can be misleading. This contributes to prior work [14,20,30] on how edited images can mislead people.

In addition, as found in our study, users feel somewhat confident about their capability of identifying filtered images with their bare eyes. However, that does not stop them from seeking assistance from a technological solution such as a tool to detect filtered images. This proves the dependency of users on technology to support their confidence [22].

Several prior studies [7,32] investigate the capability of users in identifying image manipulations. We extend these prior researches by uncovering that users perceive that they can detect filtered images with bare eyes even though different users quantify the extent of filters used on images in a substantially different manner. This indicates that users cannot uniformly (and perhaps accurately) identify filtered images or the extent of filters used on those images with bare eyes.

7.2   Variability in General Perception Towards Filtered Images

Users are often confident in their ability to distinguish filtered images shared on social media. This thought of users is reflected in our survey results as about 46% of the participants are highly confident and 50% of the participants are somewhat confident. However, while we let the users quantify the extent of image alteration for the same sets of images, we get a completely different story. We noticed that the quantification of the extent of filtering over the same image substantially deviates for different users. This suggests that the opinions of users about a filtered image can highly vary and they do not generally agree (or even somewhat agree) on a single value of quantification for the extent of image filtering.

This result, along with the confidence of users, demonstrates that users perceive filtered images differently, which complies with individuals' cognitive differences on visual images [2,11,30]. Thus, the same image that appeared to be highly filtered to one person may appear to be mostly untouched to another. The variability of users to quantify the extent of filters used on images and their desire for detecting filtered images point out a need for technological solutions enabling the detection of filtered images. In this context, most of the users in our study further expressed the need for an automated tool for detecting filtered images. Thus, analysis of our survey results implied a common need for an automated tool for the purpose of detecting and measuring the extent of filtering to an image.

7.3 Appreciation of Automated Tools in Detecting Filtered Images

Although users feel that they can distinguish filtered images with their bare eyes, when asked whether they would appreciate an automated tool to detect a filtered image, 60% of the participants answered positively and about 17% of the participants were unsure (Fig. 6). We can further observe a different trend in our consolidated survey - about 37% of the participants were sure and about 25% of the participants were unsure. It sheds light on the fact that with the progression of time, users are perhaps turning indifferent toward filtered images. Accordingly, they are potentially becoming less conscious about the potential harms engendered from disturbing filtered images over social media.

When presented with an automated tool that specializes in detecting whether an image is filtered or not, the results obtained from the user evaluation shed light on some new interesting facts. Here, 37% of the participants strongly agreed with the chances of being filtered, and 35% agreed, compared to 11% disagreement and 12% strong disagreement (Fig. 20). Based on these results, we observe that users appreciate automated tools for detecting filtered images. Therefore, we provide a novel solution to detect filtered images by following a user-centric approach. This extends previous studies [3, 21, 40, 43], where different online tools were proposed to detect edited and fabricated images.

In addition, we designed our tool with the option for both types of prediction, i.e. quantitative prediction based on chances of being filtered, and qualitative prediction based on the summary comment. We put an option in our survey (integrated with our tool) to check which one of the two ways users find preferable while receiving predictions from the tool. While analyzing the collected survey data, we noticed a phenomenon that users generally prefer quantitative assessments over qualitative ones (Fig. 20).

7.4 Limitations of Our Study

The values we obtained from the surveys were self-reported values collected from the participants. Determining the objective viability of these self-reported values is another challenging research topic. Additionally, considering the reality of having computational resource constraints, we used a subset of filters for training our implemented tool from a huge number of existing filters on Instagram. Despite these limitations, the findings of our study will be useful for technology design in the context of image filtering.

8   Avenues for Further Research

This study focuses on image filtering, which is a particular way of performing image editing. Other ways of image editing could be cropping, color adjustment, removal of objects from images, selective color change, etc., which have not been covered in this study. We are aware of recent research studies [16,41,44], where the authors addressed cropping, cloning, and other types of forgeries. In future work, we plan to address these ways of image editing along with our considered image filtering in a single pipeline to detect clever frauds ever. Moreover, in this study, we built a classifier by decomposing an image into style and content. However, we want to explore how can we implement the decomposition in a better way to achieve more classifier accuracy. Therefore, in the future, we intend to study the construction and the properties of the image filters in-depth and make changes to the Neural Network architecture accordingly to enhance the classifier.

9 Conclusion

Image filtering presents a process of changing the style of the components of an image through various mathematical operations. Our survey results showed how the participants could not provide a unified view on the quantification of the extent of the filter of different images pointing out that users cannot agree on an objective value of the extent of image filtering and how they would appreciate the help of an automated tool in this regard. Inspired by the results of the surveys, we built a custom web tool, InnerEye, using a Neural Network Model that can detect images processed or filtered with popular social media filters. We conducted a user evaluation after deploying the tool online, which demonstrates the efficacy of InnerEye and its acceptance among users. Thus, our study contributes to the field of identifying the extent of image filtering and shows that an automated tool can assist in improving user experience substantially in this domain.

Acknowledgements. The work was conducted at and supported by the Bangladesh University of Engineering and Technology (BUET), Dhaka, Bangladesh.

References

1. Agarwal, S., Varshney, L.R.: Limits of deepfake detection: a robust estimation viewpoint (2019)
2. Bandura, A.: Social cognitive theory of personality. In: Handbook of Personality, vol. 2, pp. 154–96 (1999)
3. Belkasoft: Belkasoft forgery detection module (2021). http://reveal-mklab.iti.gr/reveal/
4. Birajdar, G.K., Mankar, V.H.: Digital image forgery detection using passive techniques: a survey. Digit. Investig. **10**(3), 226–245 (2013)
5. Boididou, C., Papadopoulos, S., Kompatsiaris, Y., Schifferes, S., Newman, N.: Challenges of computational verification in social multimedia. In: Proceedings of the 23rd International Conference on World Wide Web, pp. 743–748 (2014)
6. Dearden, L.: The fake refugee images that are being used to distort public opinion on asylum seekers. Independent **16**(9), 15 (2015)

7. Farid, H., Bravo, M.J.: Image forensic analyses that elude the human visual system. In: Media Forensics and Security II, vol. 7541, pp. 52–61. SPIE (2010)

8. Frank, J., Eisenhofer, T., Lea, S., Fischer, A., Kolossa, D., Holz, T.: Leveraging frequency analysis for deep fake image recognition (2020)

9. Fridrich, J.A., Soukal, D.B., Lukáš, J.A.: Detection of copy-move forgery in digital images. In: Proceedings of Digital Forensic Research Workshop. Citeseer (2003)

10. Gallagher, A.C.: Detection of linear and cubic interpolation in jpeg compressed images. In: The 2nd Canadian Conference on Computer and Robot Vision (CRV 2005), pp. 65–72. IEEE (2005)

11. Gartus, A., Klemer, N., Leder, H.: The effects of visual context and individual differences on perception and evaluation of modern art and graffiti art. Acta Physiol. (Oxf) **156**, 64–76 (2015)

12. Google: Google landmarks dataset (2020). https://www.kaggle.com/google/google-landmarks-dataset

13. Guo, Y., Cao, X., Zhang, W., Wang, R.: Fake colorized image detection. IEEE Trans. Inf. Forensics Secur. **13**(8), 1932–1944 (2018)

14. Gupta, A., Lamba, H., Kumaraguru, P., Joshi, A.: Faking sandy: characterizing and identifying fake images on twitter during hurricane sandy. In: Proceedings of the 22nd International Conference on World Wide Web, pp. 729–736 (2013)

15. Huang, X., Liu, M.Y., Belongie, S., Kautz, J.: Multimodal unsupervised image-to-image translation. In: Proceedings of the European Conference on Computer Vision (ECCV), pp. 172–189 (2018)

16. Huh, M., Liu, A., Owens, A., Efros, A.A.: Fighting fake news: image splice detection via learned self-consistency. In: Proceedings of the European Conference on Computer Vision, pp. 101–117 (2018)

17. Jang-Hee, Y., Kim, Y., Kyoungho, C., Soonyoung, P., Moon, K.Y.: Method and apparatus for determining fake image (2013). US Patent 8,515,124

18. Kamakura, A.: pilgram 1.1.0 (2019). https://pypi.org/project/pilgram/

19. Kasra, M., Shen, C., O'Brien, J.F.: Seeing is believing: how people fail to identify fake images on the web. In: Extended Abstracts of the 2018 CHI Conference on Human Factors in Computing Systems, pp. 1–6 (2018)

20. Kleemans, M., Daalmans, S., Carbaat, I., Anschütz, D.: Picture perfect: the direct effect of manipulated instagram photos on body image in adolescent girls. Media Psychol. **21**(1), 93–110 (2018)

21. Krawetz, D.N.: Fotoforensics (2021). http://fotoforensics.com/

22. Lee, Y., Lee, J., Lee, Z.: Social influence on technology acceptance behavior: self-identity theory perspective. ACM SIGMIS Database DATABASE Adv. Inf. Syst. **37**(2–3), 60–75 (2006)

23. Lowe-Calverley, E., Grieve, R.: Self-ie love: predictors of image editing intentions on Facebook. Telematics Inform. **35**(1), 186–194 (2018)

24. Luo, W., Huang, J., Qiu, G.: Robust detection of region-duplication forgery in digital image. In: 18th International Conference on Pattern Recognition (ICPR 2006), vol. 4, pp. 746–749. IEEE (2006)

25. Maigrot, C., Kijak, E., Claveau, V.: Context-aware forgery localization in social-media images: a feature-based approach evaluation. In: 2018 25th IEEE International Conference on Image Processing (ICIP), pp. 545–549. IEEE (2018)

26. Manovich, L.: Instagram and contemporary image. CUNY, Nova Iorque (2017)

27. Marques, O.: Innovative Technologies in Everyday Life. Springer, Cham (2016). https://doi.org/10.1007/978-3-319-45699-7

28. Marra, F., Gragnaniello, D., Cozzolino, D., Verdoliva, L.: Detection of GAN-generated fake images over social networks. In: 2018 IEEE Conference on Multimedia Information Processing and Retrieval (MIPR), pp. 384–389 (2018)
29. Messieh, N.: How instagram filters work, and can you tell the difference? (2018). https://www.makeuseof.com/tag/instagram-filters-work-can-tell-difference/
30. Murthy, D., Gross, A., McGarry, M.: Visual social media and big data. Interpreting instagram images posted on twitter. Digit. Cult. Soc. **2**(2), 113–134 (2016)
31. Nguyen, T., Nguyen, C.M., Nguyen, T., Nguyen, D., Nahavandi, S.: Deep learning for deepfakes creation and detection: a survey (2019)
32. Nightingale, S.J., Wade, K.A., Watson, D.G.: Can people identify original and manipulated photos of real-world scenes? Cogn. Res. Principles Implications **2**(1), 1–21 (2017). https://doi.org/10.1186/s41235-017-0067-2
33. Omnicore: Instagram statistics (2022). https://www.omnicoreagency.com/instagram-statistics/
34. Papadopoulou, O., Zampoglou, M., Papadopoulos, S., Kompatsiaris, Y.: Web video verification using contextual cues. In: Proceedings of the 2nd International Workshop on Multimedia Forensics and Security, pp. 6–10 (2017)
35. Rössler, A., Cozzolino, D., Verdoliva, L., Riess, C., Thies, J., Nießner, M.: Faceforensics: a large-scale video dataset for forgery detection in human faces. arXiv (2018)
36. Russotti, P., Anderson, R.: Digital Photography Best Practices and Workflow Handbook: A Guide to Staying Ahead of the Workflow Curve. Taylor & Francis, Milton Park (2010)
37. Statista: Instagram number of daily active instagram stories statistics (2021). https://www.statista.com/statistics/730315/instagram-stories-dau/
38. Statista: Instagram number of monthly active user statistics (2021). https://www.statista.com/statistics/253577/number-of-monthly-active-instagram-users/
39. Tariq, S., Lee, S., Kim, H., Shin, Y., Woo, S.S.: Detecting both machine and human created fake face images in the wild. In: Proceedings of the 2nd International Workshop on Multimedia Privacy and Security, pp. 81–87 (2018)
40. Wagner, J.: Forensically (2021). https://29a.ch/photo-forensics/
41. Wu, Y., AbdAlmageed, W., Natarajan, P.: Mantra-net: manipulation tracing network for detection and localization of image forgeries with anomalous features. In: Proceedings of the IEEE Conference on Computer Vision and Pattern Recognition, pp. 9543–9552 (2019)
42. Xuan, X., Peng, B., Wang, W., Dong, J.: On the generalization of GAN image forensics. In: Sun, Z., He, R., Feng, J., Shan, S., Guo, Z. (eds.) CCBR 2019. LNCS, vol. 11818, pp. 134–141. Springer, Cham (2019). https://doi.org/10.1007/978-3-030-31456-9_15
43. Zampoglou, M.: Reveal - image verification assistant (2021). http://reveal-mklab.iti.gr/reveal/
44. Zhou, P., Han, X., Morariu, V.I., Davis, L.S.: Learning rich features for image manipulation detection. In: 2018 IEEE/CVF Conference on Computer Vision and Pattern Recognition, vol. 9, pp. 1053–1061 (2018)

An Interactive Visualization System for Streaming Data Online Exploration

Fengzhou Liang[1], Fang Liu[2(✉)], Tongqing Zhou[3], Yunhai Wang[4], and Li Chen[5]

[1] Sun Yat-sen University, Guangzhou 510000, China
`liangfzh@mail2.sysu.edu.cn`
[2] Hunan University, Changsha 410000, China
`fangl@hnu.edu.cn`
[3] National University of Defense Technology, Changsha 410000, China
`zhoutongqing@nudt.edu.cn`
[4] Shandong University, 250000 Jinan, China
[5] University of Louisiana at Lafayette, Lafayette, LA 70503, USA
`li.chen@louisiana.edu`

Abstract. The practices of understanding real-world data, in particular the high dynamic streaming data (e.g., social events, COVID tracking), generally relies on both human and machine intelligence. The use of mobile computing and edge computing brings a lot of data. However, we identify that existing data structures of visualization systems (a.k.a., data cubes) are designed for quasi-static scenarios, thus will experience huge efficiency degradation when dealing with the ever-growing streaming data. In this work, we propose the design and implementation of an enhanced interactive visualization system (i.e., Linkube) based on novel structure and algorithms support, for efficiently and intelligibly data exploration. Basically, Linkube is designed as a multi-dimensional and multi-level tree with spatiotemporal correlated knowledge units linked into a chain. Interested knowledge aggregations are thus attained via efficient and flexible sequential access, instead of dummy depth-first searching. Meanwhile, Linkube also involves a smart caching mechanism that adaptively reserves some beneficial aggregations. We implement Linkube as a web service and evaluate its performance with four real-world datasets. The results demonstrate the superiority of Linkube on response time ($\sim 25\% \downarrow$) and structure updating time ($\sim 45\% \downarrow$), compared with state-of-the-art designs.

Keywords: Man-computer interactions · Streaming data · Interactive visualization · Data analysis · Data structure

1 Introduction

Discovering phenomena and essence from real-world data relies on both machine intelligence for tremendous parsing tasks and human intelligence for subjective decision-making. To seamlessly integrate both intelligence, we have practically seen a lot efforts devote to interactive visualization for semi-automatic

S. Longfei and P. Bodhi (Eds.): MobiQuitous 2022, LNICST 492, pp. 515–534, 2023.
https://doi.org/10.1007/978-3-031-34776-4_27

and explainable data exploration in intelligent systems [12,24]. For example, Tableau [25], a famous visualization software, has won unanimous praise from customers by elaborating data statistics visually with interaction interfaces for various applications [15,27] (e.g., pollution monitoring, COVID tracking, city planning).

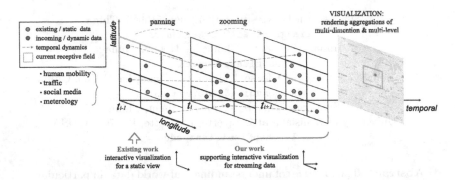

Fig. 1. A toy example of interactive visualization for streaming data. Along with continuous incoming data, statistics (e.g., density of a focused region) that an expert is interested in need to be dynamically re-calculated. Existing work handles such dynamics in an offline manner, while we investigate online visualization to reactively update statistics and respond to interactions with incoming knowledge.

The brain behind these applications is dedicated data structures that support interactive (e.g., spatial and temporal zooming, panning) knowledge searching and querying (e.g., density, numbers), known as data cubes. As a pioneering work, Nanocubes [13] adopts a tree-like structure to organize data and provides comprehensive operation strategies for finding and calculating knowledge aggregations or statistics (these two terms are used interchangeably in this paper). Given that storing all the aggregations in prior would consume significant memory resources, researchers bring forth the Hashedcubes and Smartcube structures in the follow-up work, which manage to identify and only reserves partial aggregations in advance for memory efficiency. However, we emphasize that the existing proposals are all **designed to be constructed offline on quasi-static scenarios**. As shown in the example of Fig. 1, these data cubes are built on data collected in specific spatiotemporal intervals, so the visualized views are in fact static, although the interactions are performed in real-time. That is, the inherent structure intelligence of them only supports experts to explore stale data.

This can be problematic when coming to the cases of streaming data, particularly for dynamic urban data [22]. For example, massive Twitter data are dynamically gathered to examine the evacuation response of residents during Hurricane Matthew in 2017 [18], which can be illustratively depicted in Fig. 1. In this example, for the experts to accurately understand the evolving situations, it is essential for the underlying data cubes to absorb the continuous incoming event data and update the corresponding aggregations of different regions and levels. Unfortunately, traditional data cubes (e.g., [9,13,14]) cannot properly respond to such frequent updates, as they depend heavily on static knowledge aggregation in advance, which is, however, not possible because streaming data are collected online. As a result, experts would have to experience unexpected latency (far beyond the empirical threshold 500 ms [16]) to get responses for their interactive queries, seriously hampering the exploration.

In this work, we propose to enhance interactive visualization with novel data structure and algorithm support for efficiently and intelligibly exploring streaming data. The systematic design, Linkube, attempts to attain efficient response on interactions by adapting the data cube structure to temporal dynamics. For this, it basically maintains certain structure information to simplify the dummy traversal process (i.e., depth-first searching) for finding aggregation in the built tree. In particular, it constructs a linked list [2] for the spatial or temporal correlated root nodes (i.e., knowledge units) in the tree. Having these structural basics, we further maintain an index for each aggregation (i.e., nodes in the middle layers) to the corresponding first children root node, which facilitates Linkube with the advantages of sequential access for arbitrary knowledge. In this way, the response time of Linkube will be significantly reduced when performing queries on the incoming new data, because it can **update the tree structure and search for and calculate the queried aggregations online at the same time**.

Furthermore, to avoid proactively calculating large numbers of unnecessary aggregations, we design **a smart caching mechanism that reserves beneficial aggregation for dynamic reuse**. It measures the utility of aggregations based on the frequency they are queried, as well as the estimated traversal time for attaining them. We then propose to adaptively cache the pre-accessed values with the highest utility. Finally, the main contributions of this work can be summarized as follows:

- We identify the structural drawbacks of existing data cubes on dealing with streaming data, and propose the design of a novel data structure and its corresponding searching strategies for flexible data exploration. It can adaptively maintain the structure online and provide fast query/search responses simultaneously.
- Technically, Linkube introduces linked lists and vertical indices to retain multi-dimensional structure information of streaming data for sequential data access and efficient knowledge aggregation computation; A smart caching mechanism is also designed to quantify the utility of reserving certain aggregations and further reduce the response time.
- We implement Linkube as a web-based prototype and test its performance on four real-world datasets. The results demonstrate Linkube's superiority on three state-of-the-art data cubes, in terms of both response time and structure updating time.

2   Related Work

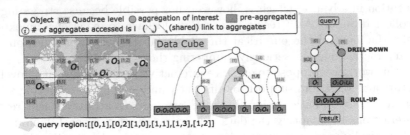

Fig. 2. The above map is divided into four sub-regions and indexed. The data cube builds a tree structure to support efficient searching of objects. An example on conducting a query: finding all objects in query region ▰ .

Streaming Visualization. Streaming data is a continuous flow of data, according to the definition by [1]. An obvious feature is that the system cannot control the time of the arriving data also the number of updates. The system generally does not know the scale of data, needing to constantly update to accommodate new data. Streaming visualization is more concerned with showing significant changes in the context of the past data [8]. For example, how to add or remove elements from the visualization based on layout choice. Streaming data visualization is also widely used, such as dynamic network visualization [23], spatiotemporal data analysis [5] and event detection techniques [26].

As a method to deal with the aggregation of stream, sliding window is widely used to filter data in valid spatiotemporal domain. StreamSqueeze [17] use flexible sliding windows, the problem of the data accumulation in stream data is avoided. ScatterBlogs2 [4] takes advantage of the sampling, the topic filtering of documents is carried out in real time to extract the information that users are interested in. These methods can support streaming visualization within a limited range of data, but are difficult to manage massive amounts of data and respond to interaction in real-time. In addition, they pay attention to handling online incoming data, lacking management of entire data in the time domain.

Data Cube. Data cube, as a data management architecture, has gained attractions among researchers in recent years. It is well suited to the handling of multi-dimensional datasets.

There are two basic operations in data cube: **drill-down** and **roll-up**. Drill-down refers to the process of viewing data at a level of increased detail, while roll-up refers to the process of viewing data with decreasing detail. The traversal path ▰ in Fig. 2 shows how the data cube responds to queries with the drill-down and roll-up. The aggregates of O_1, O_2, O_3, and O_4 are found after the drill-down can be applied roll-up to produce the result of query. As you can see from figure, data cube will get the aggregate ▰ directly instead of ▰ and ▰ during the drill-down, that is why the data cube have well query performance. Queries have low latencies due to pre-aggregation ▆ , supporting interactive visualization in real-time.

There is a lot of work that use data cubes today [3,11,20,28]. Among all the relevant efforts, Nanocubes [13] is considered to be the baseline. It first takes advantage of the shared links to reduce memory overhead. The query in the temporal domain often requests a period of time rather than a specific time point. Summed-Area table [7] is widely applied to the structure of stored time series. Time Lattice [19] leverages the partial order relation of time to reduce the memory cost but only applies to the temporal domain and does not support spatial data exploration.

To solve the problem of aggregations using a lot of memory, array-based structure Hashedcubes [9,11] achieves low memory usage by sorting multi-dimensional arrays and recording pivots for each dimension. Smartcube [14] supports the creation and deletion of cuboids to support dynamic partial aggregation, and a dynamic adaptive algorithm is designed to maintain the valuable cuboids in the structure. They both introduces a way to adapt to user interaction habits and focus on dimensions of interest to users. In fact, the user's points of interest are variable during the interaction. When a query hits a non-existent cuboid, the Smartcube takes time to drill-down, causing a burst of high latency. Falcon [21], a Linked Visualization of big data. It utilizes data cube to build complete indexes, which is a low-latency solution for the exploration of cold start dataset.

Data cube-based methods have proven themselves to be good at interactive visualization, able to respond to user queries in milliseconds, even with millions or even billions of pieces of Data. This excellent interaction performance is due to the aggregations that are built at the expense of memory. However, they all focus on a static view. When considering dynamically incoming data, they are constrained by longer updating times.

3 Challenges and Motivation

In this section, we briefly point out the shortcomings of the data cube for visualization of streaming data and how do we get inspired to solve these problems.

3.1 Limitations of Data Cube

The data cube uses two key technologies to support real-time interaction. One is to structure data in way to improve the speed of the query path, and the other is to store pre-aggregations to avoid dynamic calculating. As the dataset scale gets larger in recent years, the overhead of data cubes has become the focus of much work. It's hard to implement data cube with both **high retrieval speed** and **low memory overhead,** that we often have to trade off between them. When the visualization task is picky about the data structure and overhead, such as streaming data, meeting challenges.

Firstly, in the previous work, datasets were static and structures were often built only once. Dynamically appended data introduces additional latencies for data cubes, which is especially problematic for array-based data cubes. Because arrays need to be sorted, it is expensive to resort all existing data every time data arrives. Besides, when the volume of data is large enough, and there are many aggregations stored in the structure, even the tree-based data cubes also significantly degrade performance. Because all involved aggregations also need to be rebuilt during updating.

Secondly, though reducing the number of aggregations alleviates the above problem, too few aggregations will hurt interaction performance. In particular, without pre-aggregations, the tree-based data cubes will drill down to the deeper nodes of the tree to search for results, and the overhead of recursively traversing the tree can be worrying.

As mentioned, it is difficult to solve these two problems simultaneously in streaming data visualization. The key is **how to use fewer aggregations to speed up structure updating while maintaining high query performance.**

3.2   Motivation

In response to any queries immediately, the ideal approach is to calculate all possible aggregations in advance. It inevitably leads to more memory cost and more time spent to build data cubes. Actually, aggregations can be calculated in real time by merging aggregations of child nodes. For example, a query, "How many tweets have been sent?", can be equivalent to the combinations of the following queries: "How many tweets have been sent with Android?" and "How many tweets have been sent with iPhone?", assuming the device can only be one of Android or iPhone.

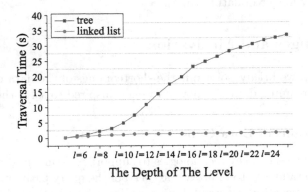

Fig. 3. The comparison of the time traversing all leaves of a tree and a linked list, with increasing depth of the tree. The tree structure consists of 10,000 objects that follow a Gaussian distribution and each node has UP to five branches.

Instead of calculating all possible combinations as aggregations, we can achieve the same effect by merging queries of partial aggregations. It is a universal idea to reduce building time and memory cost in existing studies [9,14].

With a tree-based data cube, multiple queries require the depth-first traversal of the tree. Such recursive operations are expensive. We want to avoid recursive traversal and access aggregations to be merged directly. Intuitively, additional links can be built to increase the retrieval speed, introducing some extra storage overhead but is far less than required for storing many aggregations.

More specifically, a naive solution would be for all nodes to hold links, pointing directly to the aggregations to be merged. Consider a quadtree with N layers, with the number of 4^N leaves for the full tree. The cost for all nodes linking to leaves can be derived as:

$$\sum_{i=1}^{N-2} 4^N = (N-2) \cdot 4^N \tag{1}$$

On the other hand, we propose to link leaves using a linked list like the B+ Tree, so that all nodes with same aggregations can share one linked list. The cost of building such a linked list is $4^N - 1$. Adding the cost of all nodes' links, we get the overall overhead as:

$$\sum_{i=1}^{N-2} \left(4^i\right) + 4^N - 1 = \frac{13}{12} \cdot 4^N - \frac{7}{3} \tag{2}$$

Compared with the naive solution, the traversal speed is the same, while our solution incurs less overhead, with the cost of $\Theta(4^N)$ (Eq. 2) that is smaller than $\Theta(N \cdot 4^N)$ (Eq. 1) for the naive one. As shown in Fig. 3, when the depth of the tree grows large, the cost of accessing linked lists is still small, while accessing the same amount of objects recursively becomes time-consuming.

Based on the observation and motivation, we propose the design and implementation of Linkube that improves retrieval efficiency by linking aggregations with linked lists to reduce tree traversals. Linkube avoids storing many aggregations, which increases update speed and reduces memory overhead. It also speeds up the drill-down, which reduces response time.

4   Design of Linkube

With an observation on the traversal time of existing methods based on trees and linked lists, we are motivated to propose Linkube to accelerate the query process. We expect an approach that query efficiency without building new aggregations.

4.1   Basic Definitions

Attributes in a dataset can be defined with a dimension set $D = \{d_1, d_2, ..., d_n\}$, where $d_i \in D$ refers to a specific attribute. Each object o has a separate label of $d_i(o)$ in dimension d_i.

We index the label value of each dimension. To support the subdivision of dimensions, each dimension can be represented by multiple levels [13]. An object label value $d_i(o)$ will be denoted as a **chain** $C_i = [l_1, l_2, ..., l_n]$, where the levels satisfy the partial order $l_1 \succcurlyeq l_2 \succcurlyeq ... \succcurlyeq l_n$. We say l_{n-1} is coarser than l_n or that l_n is finer than l_{n-1} if for the same dimension of any two objects $d_i(o), d_i(o')$ have $l_{n-1}(o) = l_{n-1}(o') \Rightarrow l_n(o) = l_n(o')$. The chain can be regarded as the granularity of label value.

Data are stored in structure according to the dimension of each attribute. A dataset can be formulated as **schema** $\{C_1, C_2, C_3, ..., C_n\}$. Following above definitions, **path** of chains $P = \{[l_{11}, l_{12}, l_{13}...], [l_{21}, l_{22}, l_{23}...], ..., [l_{n1}, l_{n2}, l_{n3}...]\}$ refers to the traversal path during the execution of a query, where each chain is defined by the attribute itself.

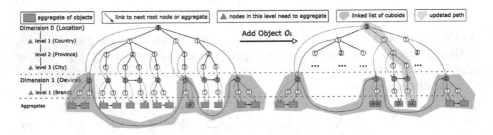

Fig. 4. An illustration of the structure of Linkube and an example of updating a linked list when a new object o_2 is added.

4.2 Linked List-Optimized Structure

As Linkube stores only partial aggregations, queries involving unaggregated nodes need to drill-down. Taking advantage of the linked list, Linkube achieves high query efficiency when accessing unaggregated nodes, by the linking of adjacent nodes that avoids recursively traversing the tree.

Structure Building. Figure 4 illustrates the structure of Linkube, which utilizes shared links to avoid unnecessary node generation and does not calculate all aggregations. The root node can be regarded as the beginning of the aggregation of each dimension. In general, aggregations at the branch node result in the creation of new root nodes in the next dimension. Linkube will chain ↘ the root nodes (the next dimension) as a linked list. When accessing unaggregated nodes, Linkube can perform a drill-down operation by traversing a linked list.

The linked list chains adjacent root nodes of the same dimension. We describe the root node in dimension $i + 1$ pointed ↘ (↘) by the node in dimension i as **content**, which is the first aggregation of the node at the beginning of the arrow. Thus, each node needs to record a number that indicates the number of aggregations to be read in the linked list. As shown in the figure, when querying the aggregation of all objects, such as $\{[all, all, all], ...\}$, Linkube will access the linked list pointed by the node at level 0 in dimension 0 based on the number recorded. The light blue area in the figure represents a linked list of aggregated results, which is the aggregation of three adjacent child nodes linked.

Structure Updating. Since Linkube actually uses lists instead of storing aggregations, it only needs to update the linked list when receiving new data, which is much faster than recursively updating aggregations. Figure 4 shows an example of the structural change when a new object is added to Linkube. The new object generates a new branch at level 2 of dimension 0. Since the nodes of level 2 do not need to maintain aggregation, the number it records and the linked list pointed to by node needs to be updated. The root node created is inserted into the linked list. The node at level 1 of dimension 0 needs to maintain aggregation, pointing to the new aggregation. The previous root node of the subtree with only o_1 as a singleton aggregate has to be removed from the list. As shown in the light blue area ▼ , after adding a new object, the structure is rebuilt, and the linked list where the aggregation resides needs to be updated.

Query Engine. Considering queries that involve aggregations which are built with linked-lists, such as a query "How many tweets in the dataset were sent from iPhone?" Since we don't care about the location information of each record, we don't have to drill-down to a specific country or city. The query will be interpreted as the path $\{[all, all, all], [iPhone]\}$. Based on the path $[all, all, all]$, Linkube looks for aggregations of the root node of dimension 0. As shown, find the three aggregations ▼ in the linked list according to the number recorded by the root node ❸ . Since we are interested in iPhone, Linkube will drill-down to search device records of the corresponding brand according to path $[iPhone]$ after three aggregations found.

Linkube significantly speeds up the calculating of aggregations in real-time with almost no aggregation nodes built. For a comparison with the state-of-the-arts on data cube, please refer to Table 1.

Table 1. Comparison of our Linkube with the state-of-the-arts.

	structure	drill-down	aggregation	dataset
Linkube	flexible	ordinal	flexible	spatiotemporal
Smartcube	flexible	recursive	flexible	spatiotemporal
Nanocubes	fixed	recursive	all	spatiotemporal
Hashedcubes	fixed	ordinal	partial	spatiotemporal
Time Lattice	fixed	ordinal	partial	temporal

4.3   Smart Caching Mechanism

In the scenario of streaming data, as the structure is constantly updated, it is inevitable that some queries involve a large amount of data. Even Linkube calculates aggregation efficiently, there are still some queries have high latency. Furthermore, it is typical that only partial aggregations are actually accessed, and only a few ones frequently accessed. Accordingly, We want to build aggregations cache for a few nodes with high response time, increasing the interactive experience without slowing down the updating.

Because of the uncertainty of user behavior, it is difficult to define which aggregations are the most valuable. But we know which aggregation in the past queries were expensive to retrieve. Nodes of the same level have a similar distribution, so nodes with the same level tend to have similar costs. Besides, We notice that aggregations at partial resolution levels are sufficient to support efficient queries, and the aggregated levels can feed back to the parent nodes to reduce the traversal length of the linked list. As such, we introduce an adaptive caching mechanism during the query process to help find which levels of aggregations are worth being built and reserved.

Initialization. An initial threshold k_d for each dimension is given, which is the number of aggregated levels where aggregations of all nodes will be calculated and maintained. l_d indicates the index of levels subdivided in dimension d. During the building process, aggregations are generated at every level by checking:

$$(|l_d| - l_d) \, Mod \left\lceil \frac{|l_d|}{k_d} \right\rceil = 0 \tag{3}$$

where $|l_d|$ is the number of levels that dimension d contains. For nodes at other levels, linked lists are applied to link aggregations.

Updating the Utility. A set $U = \{u_1, u_2, ..., u_d\}$ records each level's utility in each dimension, where $u_d = \{r_{d1}, r_{d2}, ..., r_{dl}\}$. As the utility record of level l, r_{dl} indicates the benefit of maintaining aggregations for nodes at level l. Linkube finds levels with the greatest utility in the same dimension and stores their aggregations. When the query arrives, r_{dl} is updated as follows:

$$r_{dl} = r_{dl} + l_d \times n \tag{4}$$

where n is the number of nodes accessed and may change next time after updating. That is, when new aggregations are calculated and stored for level l', all the parent nodes in levels $l_d(l_d < l')$ will adjust the linked list for their root nodes to partially use the aggregations already stored.

In this way, the latencies for these upper level nodes are shortened and their utilities would also be decreased according to Eq. 4. We also clean up the global record U to avoid possible overflows. Whenever the maximum value of r_{dl} reaches the threshold that we set (half of the MAX INTEGER value), if the minimum value of u_d is 0 then $r_{dl} = \frac{r_{dl}}{2}$ otherwise $r_{dl} = r_{dl} - Min(u_d)$. This operation still ensures the validity of the utility estimate because the existing aggregation state is maintained.

Updating the Aggregation. After u_d gets updated, if r_{dl} is the top k_d terms of set u_d and nodes at level l_d have no aggregations, aggregations for all nodes at level l_d will be calculated. Simultaneously, aggregations of nodes beyond the top k_d are removed from memory and links are rebuilt by pointing to linked lists.

The updating process can be regarded as (1) recording the query overhead of the specific level and (2) keeping aggregations of the more expensive ones stored in memory. Updating process can be done in parallel and it's done very quickly, thanks to existing linked lists that speed up drill-down.

Algorithm 1. REMAKECHAIN(*stack, content*)

```
 1: child ← POP(stack), node ← POP(stack), pop_size ← 1
 2: while node does not need to aggregate and stack is not empty do
 3:     if child is LEFTMOSTCHILD(node) then
 4:         child ← node, node ← POP(stack), pop_size ← pop_size + 1
 5:     else
 6:         left_child ← LEFTSIBLING(child)
 7:         if ISCHILDSHARED(node,left_child) then
 8:             origin_node ← node, copy ← SHALLOWCOPOY(left_child)
 9:             REPLACECHILD(node,copy), PUSH(stack,node), PUSH(stack,copy)
10:             node ← copy
11:             for k = 1 to pop_size do
12:                 copy ← SHALLOWCOPY(RIGHTMOSTCHILD(node))
13:                 REPLACECHILD(node,copy), PUSH(stack,copy), node ← copy
14:             end for
15:             content_copy ← SHALLOWCOPY(CONTENT(node))
16:             INSERTNEXTNODE(content_copy,content)
17:             SETPROPERCONTENT(node,content_copy)
18:             REMAKECHAIN(stack,content)
19:             POP(stack)
20:             while true do
21:                 last_node ← POP(stack)
22:                 SETSHAREDCONTENT(last_node,CONTENT(LEFTMOSTCHILD(last_node)))
23:                 if last_node is origin_node then
24:                     break
25:                 end if
26:             end while
27:         else
28:             node ← left_child
29:             for k = 1 to pop_size do
30:                 node ← RIGHTMOSTCHILD(node)
31:             end for
32:             INSERTNEXTNODE(CONTENT(node),content)
33:         end if
34:     end if
35: end while
```

---

5 Algorithm

The key technologies addressed in Linkube are how to build the linked list and how to alter the aggregation state of nodes. We introduce the design details with the pseudo-code in this section.

5.1 Building the Linked List

The building process of Linkube is the insertion of data, allowing data to be added at run-time. When a new data is added, there are two cases: (1) inserted into an existing aggregate; (2) inserted into a new branch created. There is no need to modify any structure in the first case, and the existing structure is still correct. In the second case, a new branch means a new aggregation of the node is created. Linkube needs to update the linked list to ensure the correctness of the structure.

As illustrated in Algorithm 1, the function **RemakeChain** is designed to insert root nodes into linked lists, which is called whenever the structure is changed. *content* and a *stack* of path to access node are given as input. The main idea of the algorithm is for all nodes on the updated path to find the nearest branch on the path while the left sibling node *left_child* exists (line 3–4). Then, it looks for the deepest, rightmost child of *left_child* (line 28–31). The content is inserted after the content of the rightmost child of *left_child* (line 34). Note that some of the nodes may be *shared_node* which will be replaced by cloned nodes during the traversal (line 7–26).

Algorithm 2. UPDATEAGGREGATION(*stack*)

1: $node \leftarrow$ POP(*stack*)
2: **if** *node* needs to aggregate **then**
3:      SETCOUNT(*root*,1)
4:      **if** *node* has single child with count is 1 **then**
5:          SETSHAREDCONTENT(*node*,CONTENT(CHILD(*node*)))
6:      **else if** $[c_1, c_2, ..., c_n]$ is not empty **then**
7:          SETPROPERCONTENT(*node*,AGGREGATECONTENT($[c_1, c_2, ..., c_n]$))
8:      **end if**
9:      REMAKECHAIN(PUSH(COPY(*stack*),*node*),CONTENT(*node*))
10: **else**
11:     UPDATECOUNT(*node*)
12:     SETSHAREDCONTENT(*node*,CONTENT(LEFTMOSTCHILD(*node*)))
13:     REMAKECHAIN(PUSH(COPY(*stack*),*node*),CONTENT(*node*))
14: **end if**
15: **while** *stack* is not empty **do**
16:     $node \leftarrow$ POP(*stack*)
17:     **if** *node* need to aggregate **then**
18:         *break*
19:     **end if**
20:     UPDATECOUNT(*node*)
21:     SETSHAREDCONTENT(*node*,CONTENT(LEFTMOSTCHILD(*node*)))
22: **end while**

5.2   Aggregation State Updating

Updating the aggregation state is a process of depth traversal of the tree. Specifically, for **UpdateAggregation** in Algorithm 2, a stack that stores nodes of a path is used as input, and the node at the top of the stack is the one that needs to update the aggregation state. For nodes that need to be aggregated, the new content is aggregated and inserted into the linked list (line 3–9). Otherwise, Linkube will update the recorded number and set aggregation as the content of the leftmost child node (line 11–13).

6   Evaluation

In this section, we evaluate our Linkube, in comparison with existing visualization methods on four public-available datasets.

6.1   Implementation

We implement Linkube as a web service, using a simple client-server architecture. It exposes the updating API via Socket for data producer and the querying API via HTTP for user. For intuitively displaying Linkube, we implement the

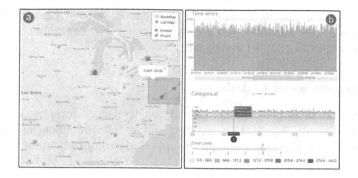

Fig. 5. The prototype of the Linkube. (a) A heatmap case with a dataset of 5 million tweets. (b) A large scale bar chart shows time series, filtering for the time range. The categorical chart of the twitter dataset provides intuitive comparison of device type.

prototype of Linkube using a simple web page as shown in Fig. 5. Users can visually access massive data of different dimensions in real time with Linkube, supporting general interactions (Zooming, Panning, Brushing, and Linking). We make a video for to illustrates our system, which provides more details (link: https://www.youtube.com/watch?v=V8IEywu9qHc).

6.2 Experimental Setup

The four datasets used in our experiments are **BrightKite**, **Flight**, **Twitter**, and **Taxi**. The contained data covers spatial, temporal, and specific categorical dimensions. The amount of data varies from millions to hundred of millions.

- **BrightKite**. BrightKite includes over **4.5 million** items from April 2008 to October 2010. BrightKite is a former location-based social network that recorded location and time when users checked in. [6].
- **Flight**. Airline On-Time Performance covers over **121 million** flights data in a 20-year period. The records include the airport of a flight, departure and arrival time, carrier, delay and other related information. [10]
- **Twitter**. Twitter contains over **5.5 million** tweets between year 2014 and 2015. Using Twitter API to collect the information about tweets, we collected data on the location, time, and device type of tweets sent over time.
- **Taxi**. Taxi includes over **17.6 million** records, which is a sample of T-Drive taxi trajectory dataset which was generated by over 10,000 taxis in a period of one week in Beijing [29,30].

The experiments are performed on an Intel Core i7-9750 CPU with 32 GB RAM. We choose Nanocubes, Smartcube and Hashedcubes as our baselines for different evaluations. We implement them in Java for a fair comparison. Smartcube is set to build aggregations when $\frac{S_{C_{bsc}}}{S_C}$ is greater than the threshold value of 1.5. To evaluate the scalability of Linkube with different utility strategies, we test the performance of different k_d values. Linkube is considered equivalent to Nanocubes when k_d is set to $|l_d|$. For experiments without k_d legend, we set k_d as 2 for all dimensions.

6.3   Effectiveness of Linkube

We first evaluated the performance of Linkube, focusing on the two main latency causing processes in visualization, building and interaction. Especially in the case of streaming data, the major computation is updates of data cube and queries.

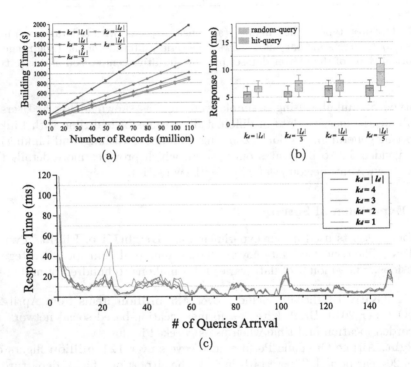

Fig. 6. Performance on the building time and response time. (a) Linkube's building time on the Flight dataset. (b) The response time of 10,000 queries on the Twitter dataset. (c) The response time of Linkube with the arrival of queries.

Building Time. To demonstrate the experimental results of building Linkube, we measured the building time of Linkube with the largest dataset, Flight. Linkube has different construction costs for different values of k_d, indicating that the structure of Linkube is scalable.

As shown in Fig. 6(a), the building time of Linkube is much lower than that of Nanocubes, effectively reducing building time by more than 45%. The building time increases steadily because data objects are inserted during the building process, which can be viewed as a linear function. The greater k_d is set, the more time it takes to build the structure. When k_d is less than $\frac{|l_d|}{3}$, the difference in drop rate becomes less obvious and tends to be stable.

Interaction. We measure the performance of random-query and hit-query in the experiment, elaborated as follows. Random-query indicates that all query inputs are random, requesting aggregated values for any data depth and distribution. In this form, the query engine returns immediately when it finds that the required aggregation does not exist. For example, suppose we query for the tweets sent from area A with the Android device during March. When the query engine traverses the tree and finds that the node with label A does not exist, it does not need to continue with the deeper dimension (device type and period of time). Hit-query refers to valid queries with the aggregation certain to be found in Linkube. Random-query is more realistic, while hit-query is better to characterize the cost of traversing the tree.

Figure 6(b) shows the response time on the Twitter dataset, corresponding to 10,000 aggregates of both random-queries and hit-queries. Linkube optimizes the drill-down process with sequential access. Linkube's response time increases as k_d decreases, but the increased overhead is acceptable, thus maintaining high query efficiency with fewer aggregation nodes. As shown, the hit-query latencies fluctuate wildly, but random-query performance is similar to Nanocubes which is closer to the real query case, and its. Since all aggregations have been calculated, Nanocubes shows the best and most stable performance of response. We can consider Linkube to have near-optimal query performance.

Caching Mechanism. To evaluate the caching mechanism of Linkube, we compare the response time when a set of queries arrived. Figure 6(c) illustrate the performance with caching mechanism in different settings and domains. In this experiment, 1ms is the lowest possible resolution of the used timing framework.

The result shows the response time with the same queries arrival. We note that partial levels of aggregates can respond to arbitrary queries quickly. The larger the value of k_d, the more levels are aggregated. Upon query arrival, the aggregation state of each level is updated to achieve the best utility. When k_d is set greater than 3, Linkube has almost the same performance as Nanocubes. Even in the early stages, Linkube is able to respond quickly, due to the linked lists built. Thanks to the utility model, Linkube's performance is stable when the state of aggregations converges, and has similar performance to Nanocubes.

6.4 Performance on Streaming Data

The study of streaming data visualization lacks qualitative or quantitative formal evaluation methods. Due to differences in the dataset and the visualization task, the evaluation varies for different scenarios. In order to understand the changes of the data cube in different streaming data, we first test the performance of each method against data with different attributes and granularity. Similar to Fig. 3, data conforming to Gaussian distribution is generated to simulate datasets of different dimensions and levels. We assume that there are 50 times of incoming data, each with a volume ranging from 500 to 1000, and 1000 queries to respond to after each update.

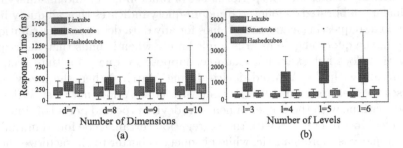

Fig. 7. The influence of different dimensions and levels on the data cube. (a) The average response time of each method in different dimension settings. (b) The average response time of each method in different levels settings.

Figure 7(a) shows the impact of different dimension settings. As datasets tend to be higher dimensional, it is inevitable that the overhead of calculating aggregations and traversing during queries increases. The result demonstrated that Linkube is stable and performs better. Hashedcubes is also stable, but takes much time to update as it needs to rebuild the entire structure with each update. Smartcube is more sensitive, and its performance degrades more significantly as the number of dimension increase. Through analysis, it is found that with the update of streaming data, new aggregations are constantly constructed, and the more aggregations there are, the higher the update cost will be when new data arrives. In addition, Smartcube's updating strategy requires traversing a large number of nodes, which is another reason for the high response time. Figure 7(b) shows the impact of different dimensions set. When l is larger, the query granularity supported by this dimension is larger. Basically the result is the same as the dimension evaluation. The Smartcube performance degrades more at finer granularity (higher l). Nanocubes builds too many aggregations that runs out of memory to complete the test. Nanocubes performs worse after building a large number of aggregations, so that it takes several times than the other methods.

As shown in Fig. 8, we show the update process when $d = 7$. The response time of Nanocubes is much higher than that of other methods. Although Nanocubes has a low query time, the number of aggregations has a significant impact on performance. Similarly, Smartcube is also affected by the number of aggregates and has a larger latency fluctuation, even if Smartcube has a heuristic update strategy. In contrast, Linkube and Hashedcubes are more stable.

To test the performance of our work in a real-world scenario, we adopted a stream dataset of Beijing traffic and Tweets sending. The results are shown in Fig. 9. Intuitively, Linkube performs better than the others. Especially in the Taxi dataset (figure a), Linkube's novel structure supports it to load the

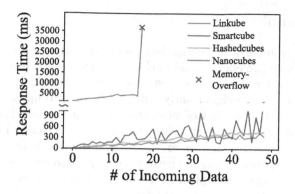

Fig. 8. The response time during stream data update process when dimension is 7.

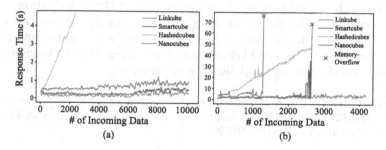

Fig. 9. Performance comparison of different methods under real data. As data arrives, the response time of updating of the structure and queries. (a) The response time of the Taxi dataset. (b) The response time of the Twitter dataset.

entire stream completely, and is the only method to complete the test. Due to hardware limitations, other comparison methods cannot complete the test. Both Smartcube and Nanocubes run out of memory at some point due to building too many aggregations, which is unacceptable for scenarios with large amounts of data. Prior to this, SmartCube performance was close to Linkube, but the response time increased more as the incoming data updated. In contrast, Hashed-cubes generally does not have overflow problems because it uses arrays to build finite aggregations. However, it brings up worse problems. When the data volume is large enough, the delay caused by each update is too long. The Hashedcubes performs poorly in the actual streaming data scenario compared to the previous experiment. Due to the higher dimensional of the real spatiotemporal dataset, the data distribution is more dispersed, greatly increasing the rebuilding cost of Hashedcubes. Hence, in both experiments, we did not measure the complete time spent by Hashedcubes.

7 Conclusion

To address the problem of streaming data processing brought by massive devices, we propose Linkube, an efficient and intelligible system with corresponding maintaining algorithms for visualization of streaming data. Briefly, Linkube maintains few knowledge units and significantly reduces the time to update the structure. In order to ensure the efficiency of query response, a novel linked list is applied to replace the dummy depth-first searching strategy for accelerated traversing. For better interactive experience, a smart caching mechanism is designed according to a utility model to determine whether to keep aggregations in memory for flexible resource usage. We implement it as a web-based interactive visualization tool to answer queries from real-world datasets.

For future work, data parallel processing methods in distributed system paradigm can be introduced into Linkube to support the visualization of larger and more complex datasets. The memory cost can be further reduced by utilizing simplifying coding. Machine learning techniques can be integrated into Linkube for user queries prediction and helping decision making, thereby providing more intelligent and efficient data visualization experience.

Acknowledgment. This work is supported by the National Natural Science Foundation of China (62172155, 62072465, 62102425), the Science and Technology Innovation Program of Hunan Province (2021RC2071).

References

1. Babcock, B., Babu, S., Datar, M., Motwani, R., Widom, J.: Models and issues in data stream systems. In: Proceedings of the Twenty-First ACM SIGMOD-SIGACT-SIGART Symposium on Principles of Database Systems, PODS 2002, pp. 1–16. Association for Computing Machinery, New York (2002). https://doi.org/10.1145/543613.543615
2. Bayer, R., McCreight, E.M.: Organization and maintenance of large ordered indices. Acta Informatica **1**, 173–189 (1972). https://doi.org/10.1007/BF00288683
3. Beyer, K.S., Ramakrishnan, R.: Bottom-up computation of sparse and iceberg cubes. In: Delis, A., Faloutsos, C., Ghandeharizadeh, S. (eds.) SIGMOD 1999, Proceedings ACM SIGMOD International Conference on Management of Data, 1–3 June 1999, Philadelphia, Pennsylvania, USA, pp. 359–370. ACM Press (1999). https://doi.org/10.1145/304182.304214
4. Bosch, H., et al.: Scatterblogs2: real-time monitoring of microblog messages through user-guided filtering. IEEE Trans. Vis. Comput. Graph. **19**(12), 2022–2031 (2013). https://doi.org/10.1109/TVCG.2013.186
5. Cao, N., Lin, Y.R., Sun, X., Lazer, D., Liu, S., Qu, H.: Whisper: tracing the spatiotemporal process of information diffusion in real time. IEEE Trans. Visual Comput. Graphics **18**(12), 2649–2658 (2012). https://doi.org/10.1109/TVCG.2012.291
6. Cho, E., Myers, S.A., Leskovec, J.: Friendship and mobility: user movement in location-based social networks. In: Apté, C., Ghosh, J., Smyth, P. (eds.) Proceedings of the 17th ACM SIGKDD International Conference on Knowledge Discovery and Data Mining, San Diego, CA, USA, 21–24 August 2011, pp. 1082–1090. ACM (2011). https://doi.org/10.1145/2020408.2020579

7. Crow, F.C.: Summed-area tables for texture mapping. In: Christiansen, H. (ed.) Proceedings of the 11th Annual Conference on Computer Graphics and Interactive Techniques, SIGGRAPH 1984, Minneapolis, Minnesota, USA, 23–27 July 1984, pp. 207–212. ACM (1984). https://doi.org/10.1145/800031.808600

8. Dasgupta, A., Arendt, D.L., Franklin, L.R., Wong, P.C., Cook, K.A.: Human factors in streaming data analysis: challenges and opportunities for information visualization. Comput. Graph. Forum **37**(1), 254–272 (2018). https://doi.org/10.1111/cgf.13264. https://onlinelibrary.wiley.com/doi/abs/10.1111/cgf.13264

9. de Lara Pahins, C.A., Stephens, S.A., Scheidegger, C., Comba, J.L.D.: Hashedcubes: simple, low memory, real-time visual exploration of big data. IEEE Trans. Vis. Comput. Graph. **23**(1), 671–680 (2017). https://doi.org/10.1109/TVCG.2016.2598624

10. Levine, R.A., Sampson, E., Lee, T.C.M.: Journal of computational and graphical statistics. WIREs Comput. Stat. **6**(4), 233–239 (2014). https://doi.org/10.1002/wics.1307

11. Li, M., Choudhury, F.M., Bao, Z., Samet, H., Sellis, T.: Concavecubes: supporting cluster-based geographical visualization in large data scale. Comput. Graph. Forum **37**(3), 217–228 (2018). https://doi.org/10.1111/cgf.13414

12. Li, Q., Wei, X., Lin, H., Liu, Y., Chen, T., Ma, X.: Inspecting the running process of horizontal federated learning via visual analytics. IEEE Trans. Visual. Comput. Graphics **28**(12), 4085–4100 (2021)

13. Lins, L.D., Klosowski, J.T., Scheidegger, C.E.: Nanocubes for real-time exploration of spatiotemporal datasets. IEEE Trans. Vis. Comput. Graph. **19**(12), 2456–2465 (2013). https://doi.org/10.1109/TVCG.2013.179

14. Liu, C., Wu, C., Shao, H., Yuan, X.: Smartcube: an adaptive data management architecture for the real-time visualization of spatiotemporal datasets. IEEE Trans. Vis. Comput. Graph. **26**(1), 790–799 (2020). https://doi.org/10.1109/TVCG.2019.2934434

15. Liu, G., Zhang, Q., Cao, Y., Tian, G., Ji, Z.: Online human action recognition with spatial and temporal skeleton features using a distributed camera network. Int. J. Intell. Syst. **36**(12), 7389–7411 (2021). https://doi.org/10.1002/int.22591. https://onlinelibrary.wiley.com/doi/abs/10.1002/int.22591

16. Liu, Z., Heer, J.: The effects of interactive latency on exploratory visual analysis. IEEE Trans. Visual Comput. Graphics **20**(12), 2122–2131 (2014)

17. Mansmann, F., Krstajic, M., Fischer, F., Bertini, E.: StreamSqueeze: a dynamic stream visualization for monitoring of event data. In: Wong, P.C., et al. (eds.) Visualization and Data Analysis 2012, vol. 8294, pp. 13–24. International Society for Optics and Photonics, SPIE (2012). https://doi.org/10.1117/12.912372

18. Martín, Y., Li, Z., Cutter, S.L.: Leveraging twitter to gauge evacuation compliance: spatiotemporal analysis of Hurricane Matthew. PLoS ONE **12**(7), 1–22 (2017). https://doi.org/10.1371/journal.pone.0181701

19. Miranda, F., et al.: Time lattice: a data structure for the interactive visual analysis of large time series. Comput. Graph. Forum **37**(3), 23–35 (2018). https://doi.org/10.1111/cgf.13398

20. Miranda, F., Lins, L.D., Klosowski, J.T., Silva, C.T.: Topkube: a rank-aware data cube for real-time exploration of spatiotemporal data. IEEE Trans. Vis. Comput. Graph. **24**(3), 1394–1407 (2018). https://doi.org/10.1109/TVCG.2017.2671341

21. Moritz, D., Howe, B., Heer, J.: Falcon: balancing interactive latency and resolution sensitivity for scalable linked visualizations. In: Proceedings of the 2019 CHI Conference on Human Factors in Computing Systems, CHI 2019, Glasgow, Scotland, UK, 04–09 May 2019, p. 694 (2019). https://doi.org/10.1145/3290605.3300924

22. Moshtaghi, M., Bezdek, J.C., Erfani, S.M., Leckie, C., Bailey, J.: Online cluster validity indices for performance monitoring of streaming data clustering. Int. J. Intell. Syst. **34**(4), 541–563 (2019). https://doi.org/10.1002/int.22064. https://onlinelibrary.wiley.com/doi/abs/10.1002/int.22064

23. Ponciano, J.R., Linhares, C.D.G., Rocha, L.E.C., Faria, E.R., Travençolo, B.A.N.: A streaming edge sampling method for network visualization. Knowl. Inf. Syst. **63**(7), 1717–1743 (2021). https://doi.org/10.1007/s10115-021-01571-7

24. Sacha, D., et al.: What you see is what you can change: human-centered machine learning by interactive visualization. Neurocomputing **268**, 164–175 (2017)

25. Tableau Software: Tableau-interactive-visualization-examples (2003). https://www.tableau.com/learn/articles/interactive-map-and-data-visualization-examples

26. Steed, C.A., et al.: Web-based visual analytics for extreme scale climate science. In: 2014 IEEE International Conference on Big Data (Big Data), pp. 383–392 (2014). https://doi.org/10.1109/BigData.2014.7004255

27. Tang, J., Liu, J., Zhang, M., Mei, Q.: Visualizing large-scale and high-dimensional data. In: Proceedings of the 25th International Conference on World Wide Web, WWW 2016, pp. 287–297. International World Wide Web Conferences Steering Committee, Republic and Canton of Geneva, CHE (2016). https://doi.org/10.1145/2872427.2883041

28. Wang, Z., Ferreira, N., Wei, Y., Bhaskar, A.S., Scheidegger, C.: Gaussian cubes: real-time modeling for visual exploration of large multidimensional datasets. IEEE Trans. Vis. Comput. Graph. **23**(1), 681–690 (2017). https://doi.org/10.1109/TVCG.2016.2598694

29. Zheng, Y., Xie, X., Ma, W.Y.: Understanding mobility based on GPS data. In: Proceedings of the 10th ACM Conference on Ubiquitous Computing (Ubicomp 2008) (2008). https://www.microsoft.com/en-us/research/publication/understanding-mobility-based-on-gps-data/

30. Zheng, Y., Xie, X., Ma, W.Y.: Mining interesting locations and travel sequences from GPS trajectories. In: Proceedings of International conference on World Wide Web 2009 (2009). https://www.microsoft.com/en-us/research/publication/mining-interesting-locations-and-travel-sequences-from-gps-trajectories/

RF-Eye: Training-Free Object Shape Detection Using Directional RF Antenna

Weiling Zheng[1,2], Dian Zhang[2(✉)], Peng Ji[2], and Tao Gu[3]

[1] RMIT University, 124 La Trobe Street, Melbourne, VIC 3000, Australia
[2] Shenzhen University, Nanhai Avenue 3688, Shenzhen, China
zhangd@szu.edu.cn
[3] Macquarie University, Balaclava Road, North Ryde, NSW 2109, Australia

Abstract. Detecting object shape presents significant values to applications such as Virtual Reality, Augmented Reality and surveillance. Traditional solutions usually deploy camera on site and apply image processing algorithms to obtain object shape. Wearable solutions require target to wear some devices, and apply machine learning algorithms to train and recognize object behaviors. The recent advances in Radio Frequency (RF) technology offer a device-free solution to detect object shape, however a number of research challenges exist. This paper presents RF-Eye, a novel RF-based system to detect object shape without training in indoor environments. We design and implement Linear Frequency Modulated baseband signal, making it suitable for detecting object shape. We also apply the narrow pulse signal reflections and Doppler Frequency Shift to detect the full image of object shape. We implement RF-Eye on a Universal Software Radio Peripheral device. Our experimental results show that RF-Eye achieves 100% successful rate, and it performance is reliable in complicated cases.

Keywords: Directional Antenna · Device-free · Line-of-Sight · Radio Frequency

1 Introduction

Detecting object shape such as human body in a device-free manner, also known as transceiver-free, plays a significant role in applications such as Virtual Reality (VR), Augmented Reality (AR) and surveillance. One of the most common technology used for detecting objects shape is video due to its stability and simplicity [11,12,14,28,31,40]. However, video technique usually require suitable light condition and the line-of-sight (LoS) from camera to object. Otherwise, the object is hard to be isolated from the background. And it may therefore result in failure of detecting object shape. Moreover, vision-based solutions introduce an unavoidable problem of user privacy violation, especially in indoor environment. Radio Frequency (RF) technology would help fill this shortfall in

---

This research was supported in part by NSFC 61872247.

S. Longfei and P. Bodhi (Eds.): MobiQuitous 2022, LNICST 492, pp. 535–555, 2023.
https://doi.org/10.1007/978-3-031-34776-4_28

demand. Although RF-based detection method is comparatively mature in an outdoor environment. It remains challenges in indoor environment where can be complicated due to multi-path effect, i.e., wireless signals will be reflected, refracted and scattered by indoor objects. Radar and Sonar systems [9] are able to detect and capture the figure of inanimate object outdoors, e.g., planes. However, they operate at a very high frequency (i.e., millimeter or sub-millimeter wave), requiring expensive equipment which can be bulky in size. It also requires strong transmission power which it may be harmful to human health, making it almost inapplicable in indoor environments.

The lower frequency RF-based signal will most likely to be chosen in indoor environment. Most of the existing RF-based technologies in indoor can only localize and track objects. Several recent attempts [32,41] apply machine learning algorithms to recognize human behaviors such as waving hand and falling down. However, since these solutions leverage heavily on proper training, and the training cost arises with environment or target changes. Dina Katabi et al. [1] propose to capture human figure by designing a multi-antenna Frequency Modulated Carrier Wave (FMCW) radio system. But the whole figure will be stitched together from a number of segments, i.e., sub figures, requiring multiple operations to combine partial segments to obtain the full image.

In this paper, we propose RF-Eye, an RF-based system to object shape detection in indoor environments. In our design, we face three major challenges.

First, commodity wireless signal such as WiFi is not suitable for detecting object shape due to the limitation of its narrow bandwidth (i.e., 20 MHz) [29]. Study shows that the image resolution depends much on bandwidth [29]. The most straightforward way to improve the accuracy of object shape detection is to deploy higher bandwidth wireless signal. However, indoor wireless radio usually has limited bandwidth, hence it is tricky to design a wireless radio system with bandwidth limitation. We implement Linear Frequency Modulated (LFM) baseband signal on Universal Software Radio Peripheral (USRP) device operates at 5.8 GHz. The instantaneous frequency of this signal is a linear function of time and the transmitted signal is a narrow pulse. As a result, both bandwidth and time-width will be improved since they are determined by frequency- and time-domain characteristics of the signal, respectively. Moreover, we leverage Quadrature Amplitude Modulation (QAM) to expand the effective bandwidth to 120 MHz. Therefore, it is able to capture relatively clear object shape.

Second, existing methods [1] to detect object shape usually utilize image mosaic. These approaches typically deploy multiple antennas where each antenna is responsible of capturing a partial segment, and then combine all the segments into the full image. However, the assembly process is error prone, and it often results in assembling segments in wrong positions. Our design principle is to obtain the full image one time to avoid such error. This task will become more challenging with only one antenna. In RF-Eye, we use the Doppler frequency change to achieve the full coverage of object with one antenna. Hence, it is able to capture object shape in one time.

Third, indoor environments are suffered from multi-path phenomenon, which means the signals indoors are easily reflected, refracted and scattered by indoor objects, making the signal at the receiver is the combination of signals along multiple paths. We aim to apply one directional antenna with a narrow angle. Thus, signals from other paths not existing in the angle area are easily filtered out. It has advantages to reduce the effect of multi-path phenomenon, so as to improve the results. Based on them, we use image processing algorithms to obtain a more fine-grained object shape.

We implement RF-Eye on USRP device, and conduct extensive experiments to evaluate system performance on different objects. Our results show that RF-Eye is able to achieve 100% successful rate to detect object shape. Even for complicate object such as human body, RF-Eye is able to obtain the shape.

In summary, this paper makes the following contributions.

- We present a novel low frequency RF-based system to detect object shape in indoor environments without training.
- Our system is able to detect object shape in one go, avoiding the segment combination problem and reducing multi-path effect. We use one directional antenna instead of an antenna array to detect complex object shape based on the narrow pulse signal reflections and Doppler frequency change caused by object.
- We design Linear Frequency Modulated (LFM) baseband signal based on USRP operates at 5.8 GHz, which essentially leverages on QAM to expand the effective bandwidth to 120 MHz. We leverage image processing algorithm to improve the results. Results show that RF-Eye is able to detect contoured shapes of common indoor objects.

The rest of the paper is organized as follows. We first introduce the related work. In Sect. 3, we give an overview of our system design and describe the proposed algorithms. We present our implementation and experiments in Sect. 4. Finally, we conclude the paper and point out our future work in Sect. 5.

2   Background

In this section, we discuss various approaches of object shape detection. We divide the related work into three categories as follows.

Camera-Based Approach. Much work [11,12,14,28,31,40] has been done using various cameras, e.g., Multi-View cameras, Moving cameras, and Time-of-Flight cameras, and they typically utilize image processing algorithms to capture human figure. Kinect et al. [37] propose to detect human image by integrating with some infrared sensors when the light is dim. They design a $2 - D$ head contour model and a $3 - D$ head surface model. However, this approach is able to obtain coarse-grained human skeleton only. In general, camera-based approaches have a limited range of line of sight, and also they do not work in dark area. In addition, user privacy can be a big concern preventing them from being widely adopted.

Device-Based Approach. Some existing work requires to carry a device by target. Their main purpose is to track the moving target or identify target behaviors [25,27,30,33], rather than obtain target shape. Xsens MVN [27] can track the motion of human full body using biomechanical models and sensor fusion algorithms, but it requires the target to wear inertial and magnetic sensors. The study in [30] can recognize human motion both indoors and outdoors. It also requires the target to wear ultrasonic and inertial sensors on the garment. Prakash et al. [25] measure three dimensional motion and orientation of the target, but the target has to carry RFID passive tags.

Device-Free Tracking and Behavior Identification. Several device-free systems have been proposed to track or analyze target without the requirement of carrying any device. E-eyes [33] is able to identify human activities in a device-free manner using WiFi in indoor environments. The work in [38] proposes a software-base system to obtain high resolution power delay profiles by splicing the CSI measurements. The work in [2,3] introduce a system called WiTrack, which tracks a user's indoor location by using wireless signal reflections from human body, even when the user is not in line of sight. However, these systems aim for tracking user location and activities, not target shape.

Radar and Related Systems. Existing objection imaging systems such as radar, SAR, ISAR, X-ray, CT, MRI, B-scan [13, 19–21, 35, 36, 42, 43] use a special equipment with bulky size and high cost. For example, Radar systems [4, 6, 9, 43] are able to image the figure of inanimate object outdoors, e.g., planes. However, they operate at a very high frequency (i.e., millimeter or sub-millimeter wave), and use professional equipment which is very expensive and big in size. Furthermore, it requires strong transmission power that it may be harmful to human health, making it almost inapplicable indoors. X-ray and CT although can detect human shape indoors, it is harmful to human body [26] as well.

Device-Free Target Shape Capturing Systems. Huang et al. [15] explore the feasibility of imaging with Wi-Fi signal by leveraging the multipath propagation method. This approach results in wireless signals light up the objects. Then, the reflection of untagged objects is used for imaging. However, due to the limitations of WiFi signal such as the narrow band property, their work can only distinguish whether there is a target or not without imaging a rough picture. Dina et al. [1] propose an approach to capture the human's coarse skeleton figure when they stand behind a wall without wearing any device. Their system firstly collects the reflection signal from the target, then catches the different segments of human body parts. Finally, it stitches every part to form a whole image. However, the target figure cannot be figured out in one go as the entire target image is concatenated by several sub-images. How to assemble sub-images correctly remains unsolved. Tyler et al. [24] propose to image low Radar Cross Section (RCS) objects, fast moving objects in free-space and a human-shape object behind a 10 cm-thick solid concrete wall with an Ultra Wide Band (UWB) Multiple-Input Multiple-Output (MIMO) phased array radar system. However, it aims to track a moving human target, not capture human shape.

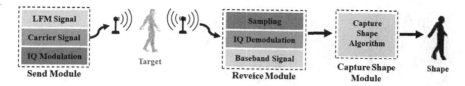

Fig. 1. Design overview

3 Methodology

In this section, we first point out the challenges of capturing target shape by using RF-based technologies. We then introduce our solution to address each of the challenges. We finally present the detail algorithms to implement our ideas.

3.1 Challenge

We discover two key challenges: 1) how to choose and implement radio signal, making it applicable to capture target shape in indoor environments, and 2) how to design an algorithm which is able to obtain fine-grained target shape in one go.

Challenge 1. We first consider how to select radio signal. It is known that different radio signals have different roles [29]. Only when high frequency wavelength is comparable to the roughness of the surface, the human body becomes a scatter as opposed to a reflector [5,8,16]. However, it is difficult and costly to apply high frequency wave in indoor environments.

On the other hand, commodity WiFi signal is originally designed for effective data transmission by using specific modulation methods, e.g., Orthogonal Frequency Division Multiplexing (OFDM) [38,39]. Studies show that the effectiveness of capturing target shape depends much on bandwidth [29]. Due to its narrow bandwidth of WiFi, it is hence not suitable for capturing target shape.

Challenge 2. It is difficult to capture target shape using RF reflected signals. Although human skeleton figure can be captured in [1], their system needs to concatenate several sub-image to assembly the entire target image. We aim to design a system which is able to obtain target shape in one go without training.

3.2 Our Design Principles

We now present the proposed design principles in this section.

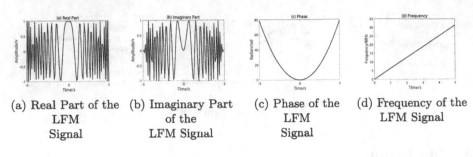

(a) Real Part of the   (b) Imaginary Part   (c) Phase of the   (d) Frequency of the
   LFM   of the   LFM   LFM Signal
   Signal   LFM Signal   Signal

Fig. 2. LFM signal

Linear Frequency Modulation. According to signal and system theory [23], the product of time-width and bandwidth is a constant. The range resolution of capturing target shape depends on bandwidth B, which is $(C/2B)$ (C is the speed of light). The bandwidth of the signal is a constant. In order to achieve both large time-width and bandwidth, we use Linear Frequency Modulation (LFM), i.e., a pulse compression method [18,34]. In LFM, the radio frequency will increase with time. In order to expand the effective bandwidth, we also leverage Quadrature Amplitude Modulation (QAM), which is an amplitude modulation on two orthogonal carriers.

Doppler Frequency Shift. When LFM signal is transmitted, different parts of the target will reflect the narrow pulse signal. Since target rotation/moving will cause Doppler frequency shift, such changes can be used to capture target shape. With Doppler effect, we are able to capture fine-grained target shape with different states, provided the target rotates or moves during capturing. If the target is moving, we can apply moving compensation to capture its shape. If the target is static, we may move the antenna and apply a similar approach to obtain its shape.

3.3   Design Overview

Figure 1 gives an overview of our system design. We first implement the LFM signal, and each LFM pulse signal contains a number of sub-pulse signals. We then leverage Quadrature Amplitude Modulation (QAM) to modulate the LFM signal. QAM is an amplitude modulation on two orthogonal carriers. The quadrature amplitude modulation signal has two carriers of the same frequency, but the phase difference is 90°. One signal is called I signal, which represents in phase. Another signal is called Q signal, which represents orthogonal to I signal. When the radio signal is transmitted, it will be reflected by the target and received by the receiver. After demodulation by the receiver, we use Nyquist sampling [29] on the base frequency signal to obtain IQ data. Finally, we design our algorithm to obtain target shape.

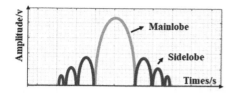
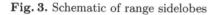
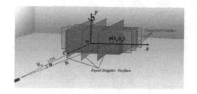

Fig. 3. Schematic of range sidelobes

Fig. 4. Basic idea of capturing target shape

3.4   Linear Frequency Modulated (LFM) Signal Implementation

In Linear Frequency Modulated (LFM) signal, the instantaneous frequency is a linear function of time. The LFM signal $S(t)$ can be represented as follows.

$$S(t) = rect(\frac{t}{T})e^{j(2\pi f_0 t + \pi k t^2)} \tag{1}$$

where t is the time variable, T is the total time length, k is the linear frequency modulation parameter and f_0 is the starting frequency, and its value is set to 5.68 GHz.

Figure 2 depicts the LFM signal. We can see that the real and imaginary parts of the signal function are both the oscillatory functions of time, and the oscillation frequency increases gradually as the time increases. The signal pulse phase is represented by $\phi(t) = \pi k t^2$, which is a quadratic function of time. The instantaneous frequency f after the time is differentiated is depicted as

$$f = \frac{1}{2\pi}\frac{d\phi(t)}{dt} = \frac{1}{2\pi}\frac{d(\pi k t^2)}{dt} \tag{2}$$

Therefore, the frequency is a linear function of time t, the slope is k, as shown in Fig. 2(d).

3.5   Reduce the Effect of Sidelobe

The presence of the sidelobes, as shown in Fig. 3 will obscure the resolution of the neighboring target, resulting in decreasing the signal detection capability and increasing false alarm.

When the desired narrow pulse is obtained by LFM, which is one of the pulse compression methods, the received pulse strength will decrease significantly due to strong clutter, noise and other factors. A series of range sidelobes, whose amplitude is lower than narrow pulse, often appear on both sides of the mainlobe [17] as a result of these factors. The presence of range sidelobes will obscure the resolution of the neighboring target, and reduce the signal detection capability of small target. The false alarm rate will be high without suppressing sidelobes disturbance. A matched filter based on weighted processing, i.e., a window technique, can be used to suppress high range sidelobes. Window techniques

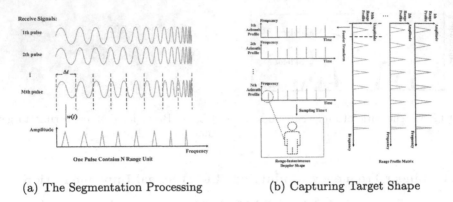

(a) The Segmentation Processing   (b) Capturing Target Shape

Fig. 5. Illustration of algorithm

can reduce the spectral leakage when the digital signal is processed for discrete spectrum analysis.

Both the Hamming Window and the Hanning Window are improved ascending cosine window but with different Weighting Coefficient. The Hamming Window has a better inhibition of spectral leakage than the Hanning Window [17]. Therefore, we utilize the Hamming Window to suppress high range sidelobes.

The time domain of the Hamming Window function can be expressed as follows.

$$w(k_h) = 0.54 - 0.46\cos(\frac{2\pi k_h}{N-1}) \quad k_h = 1, 2, \ldots, N \tag{3}$$

where N is the length of the window.

3.6   Modulation and Demodulation

In the design of signal modulation and demodulation, we leverage Quadrature Amplitude Modulation (QAM) to modulate LFM signal. QAM is an amplitude modulation on two orthogonal carriers of the same frequency, but the phase difference is 90° (quarter cycle, from the integral term). One signal is called I signal, which represents in phase. Another signal is called Q signal, which represents orthogonal to I signal. From a mathematical point of view, these two signals can be expressed as a sine function and a cosine function, respectively. Therefore, Eq. 1 can also be expressed as follows.

$$I(t) = cos(2\pi f_0 t + \pi k t^2)rect(\frac{t}{T})$$
$$Q(t) = sin(2\pi f_0 t + \pi k t^2)rect(\frac{t}{T}) \tag{4}$$

Figure 6 illustrates the procedure for both modulation and demodulation. The two orthogonal signals are obtained from after the LFM signals multiply by in-phase signal and quadrature signal of the carrier signal, respectively. They are

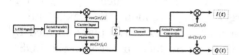
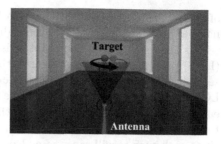

Fig. 6. Schematic of IQ modulation and demodulation

Fig. 7. Illustration of our experiments

stacked as modulated signal at the time of transmission. After reflecting from the target, the time-domain sampling signals will be obtained by quadrature demodulation to received signal, and recorded as digital data (Fig. 7).

In detail, in the modulation step, the signal $S_b(t) = I(t) + jQ(t)$ is modulated on the frequency carrier. I signal is multiplied by $cos(2\pi f_0 t)$, while Q signal is multiplied by $sin(2\pi f_0 t)$. The output signal is then

$$
\begin{aligned}
S_c(t) &= I(t)cos(2\pi f_0 t) - Q(t)sin(2\pi f_0 t) \\
&= I(t)cos(\omega_0 t) - Q(t)sin(\omega_0 l)
\end{aligned}
\tag{5}
$$

When the receiver receives $S_c(t) = I(t) + jQ(t)$, the I signal can be obtained by multiplying $cos(2\pi\omega_0 t)$. Then the I signal can be calculated by the integral result as follows.

$$
\begin{aligned}
&\frac{2}{T}\int_{-\frac{T}{2}}^{\frac{T}{2}}[I(t)cos(\omega_0 t) - Q(t)sin(\omega_0 t)cos(\omega_0 t)]dt \\
&= \frac{2}{T}\int_{-\frac{T}{2}}^{\frac{T}{2}}I(t)cos^2(\omega_0 t) - Q(t)sin(\omega_0 t)cos(\omega_0 t)dt \\
&= \frac{2}{T}\cdot\frac{I(t)}{2}\cdot T \\
&= I(t)
\end{aligned}
\tag{6}
$$

The other Q signal can be calculated similarly.

3.7 Algorithm to Capture Target Shape

In this subsection, we present our algorithm to capture target shape.

Based on the radio implementation, the transmitted signal is a narrow pulse. A certain part of the target object will reflect or scatter the narrow pulse signal. We refer such point as the target reflection (scattering) point. If the target rotates, it will produce a micro-Doppler shift. Accordingly, for one reflected (scattered) narrow pulse signal received by the receiver, we may form one point of the target shape. Since there are a large number of such reflected (scattered) narrow pulse signals, we can eventually obtain the entire target shape.

As shown in Fig. 4, the point T is the transmitter. Along the Line-of-Sight (LOS) path from the transmitter to the target two-dimensional plane, the intersection point on the plane is the center of the coordinates, which is (x_0, y_0). The LOS distance is R_0. Suppose that the target will rotate along the y axis (can be easily extended to other direction), the surface parallel to the plane formed by the y axis and the z axis is called Equal-Doppler Surface (parallel to the LOS), since each surface will cause same Doppler frequency change for the signals. Also, the surface parallel to the plane formed by the x axis and the y axis is called Equidistant Surface (vertical to the LOS).

For a certain reflection (scattering) point $P(x_p, y_p)$ on the target, the distance R from transceiver to this point can be represented below.

$$R \cong R_0 + x_0 sin\omega t + y_0 cos\omega t \tag{7}$$

The Doppler Frequency f_d is calculated as

$$f_d = \frac{2\nu}{\lambda} = \frac{2dr}{\lambda dt} = \frac{2x\omega}{\lambda} cos\omega t - \frac{2y\omega}{\lambda} sin\omega t \tag{8}$$

According to Eqs. 7 and 8, when either t or the rotation angle $\triangle \varphi = \omega t$ is very small, we can do the following linear approximation.

$$R \cong R_0 + y f_d = \frac{2x\omega}{\lambda} \tag{9}$$

From the above equation, suppose $\triangle x$ is the required Azimuth resolution (target capturing accuracy), we can conclude that the Doppler resolution should reach

$$\triangle f_d = \frac{2\omega}{\lambda} \triangle x \tag{10}$$

The real Doppler resolution determined by coherent processing time $\triangle f_d = \frac{1}{T}$, combining Eq. 10, we have real Azimuth resolution ρ_0 as

$$\rho_0 = \frac{\lambda}{2\omega T} = \frac{\lambda}{2\triangle \varphi} = \triangle x \tag{11}$$

$\triangle \varphi$ is the rotation angles within the coherent processing time T, wavelength λ is determined by the carrier frequency. From this Azimuth resolution is directly proportional to carrier frequency and rotation angles $\triangle \varphi$. Azimuth resolution improved with the coherent accumulative rotation angles increases within the limit in the range-doppler imaging method. Excessive rotation angles $\triangle \varphi$ may cause a blurring effect to the image of target shape since the reflection (scattering) point which has long distance to the reference rotation center moves over a resolution unit.

The signals to a discrete Doppler domain by Fourier transform. Thus, we can obtain the one-dimensional Doppler spectrum of the target. When the wavelength is fixed, the Doppler frequency change caused by the different position i of target can be used to achieve the ranging profile of signals at position i.

Our algorithm of capturing target shape is based on Short-time Fourier Transform [23]. It can use the time-frequency joint function to describe the density and intensity of the signal at each time and frequency point. The detail is listed as follows.

We therefore use the time-domain analysis method in the shape capturing process since range-Doppler shape can be obtained by analysing the frequency component of the giving signal at various time based on time-frequency transform without compensating for complex translational components. Our algorithm of capturing target shape is based on Short-time Fourier Transform [23]. We use the time-frequency joint function to describe the density and intensity of the signal at each time and frequency point. The detail is described as follows.

Suppose we capture the target shape into two-dimensions, and in a time period P in total we have received M number of reflected (scattered) narrow pulse signals. For each signal i, there are N number of sub pulse signals. We divide the time period P into several shorter series, whose time length is Δt. Then we use the Fourier transform method to describe the frequency component of the signal. This segmentation is achieved by multiplying the sliding window $w(t)$ and the signal $s(t)$, which can be represented as follows.

$$S(t,\omega) = \int_{-\infty}^{+\infty} s(\tau)w(\tau - t)e^{-j\omega\tau}dt \tag{12}$$

During each sampling period Δt, The time-frequency distribution of different pulse are combined together. Thus, we can obtain the instantaneous ranging profile of each reflection (scattering) point. As shown in Fig. 5, in total, we have M number of ranging profiles corresponding to M number of reflected (scattered) narrow pulse signals. For each ranging profile in each sampling period Δt, there are N number of ranging units (Azimuth Profiles) corresponding to N sub-pulse signals. Then the azimuth Doppler analysis of each ranging profile is carried out, we may get the two-dimensional image of the target.

Through the above solution, the two-dimensional ranging-Doppler image is transformed into a three-dimensional time-ranging-Doppler stereogram. Then we take the sample time into account, you can get a ranging-Doppler image along the time series. Thus, in each of the individual time sample, we may provides a high-resolution image. Then we sort the reflection (scattering) signal according to its ranging profile, time-frequency distribution of signal s is $s(t)$.

Then we combine all the Doppler spectra of the signals at one time, to achieve the target shape.

In coherent processing time, the object has a center of rotation, then the reflection (scattering) signal is received in the range unit z could be expressed as follows:

$$S_R(t)|_z = \sum_{k=1}^{N_k} A_k e^{-j4\pi(Bw(n-1)/N+f_0)r(t)/c} \tag{13}$$

where N_k is the number of reflection (scattering) points of this range unit, A_k is the amplitude of the Kth reflection (scattering) point (x_k, y_k) on the target.

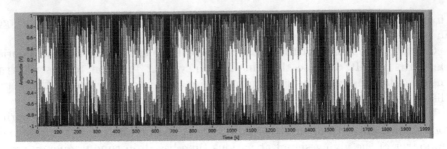

Fig. 8. Implementation result of LFM signal

As Fig. 5 depicted, the reflection (scattering) signal can be divided into a range of short time series, then its frequency components can be described by using Fourier Transform. The segmentation processing is implemented by multiplying a sliding window $w(t)$ and signal. On one hand, the length of the window function determines the resolution of time-domain frequency; on the other hand, the shape of the window function determines the sidelobe level and the resolution of frequency-domain. Here, the Hamming window is more adaptable to a further experiment [17,29].

According to Eq. 10, the Doppler of reflection (scattering) wave is independent of temporal variations, hence we can get time-domain distribution of current range unit signal by performing the following windowed fourier transform, combining Eq. 12.

$$S(t,\omega) = \int_{-\infty}^{+\infty} s_R(\tau)w(\tau - t)e^{-j\omega\tau}dt \tag{14}$$

For moment t, the STFT to the signal $S_R(t)|_z$ is tantamount to Fourier Transform to the value of signal multiply by moment t-centred Window Function $w(\tau - t)$. Because of the signal at this window segment can be approximated as steady and time-invariant. The time-frequency distribution of the signal could be obtained using Eq. 13. There are considerable time-frequency distribution of pulse at the same moment. We will get the instantaneous range profile of each reflection (scattering) signal at different moment if we grouping these time-frequency distribution. In the final step, Doppler analysis of the instantaneous range profile uses Fourier Transform along the range unit can display the two-dimensional shape of the target object.

3.8 Operator Selection to Detect Image Edge

According to previous approach, we may get the target's RF shape. The capturing image of target object has a relatively clear center and a hazy outer edge. Using edge detection operators can adaptively estimate the edge points of target shape so as to extract and clarify the edge. The operator we have chosen is Prewitt Operator [22].

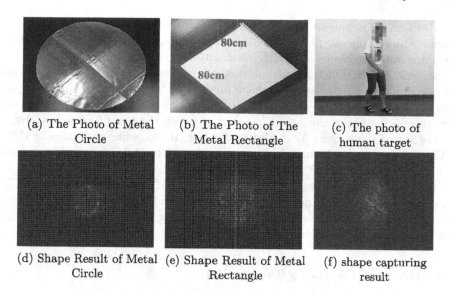

(a) The Photo of Metal Circle

(b) The Photo of The Metal Rectangle

(c) The photo of human target

(d) Shape Result of Metal Circle

(e) Shape Result of Metal Rectangle

(f) shape capturing result

Fig. 9. RF-eye result of different target shape

Mathematically, the operator uses two kernels, which are convolved with the original image, to calculate approximations of the derivatives. Suppose I_a is the source image. G_x and G_y contain horizontal and vertical derivative approximations of I_a, respectively.

$$G_x = \begin{bmatrix} -1 & 0 & +1 \\ -1 & 0 & +1 \\ -1 & 0 & +1 \end{bmatrix} * I_a G_y = \begin{bmatrix} -1 & -1 & -1 \\ 0 & 0 & 0 \\ +1 & +1 & +1 \end{bmatrix} * I_a \qquad (15)$$

At each point in the image, the resulting gradient approximations can be combined to give the gradient magnitude, using

$$G = \sqrt{G_x{}^2 + G_y{}^2} \qquad (16)$$

Therefore, edge detection of the target can be realized.

4   Evaluation

We now move to implement and evaluate RF-Eye. In this section, we first introduce our experimental setup and the LFM radio implementation. We the present the result of LFM signal and also the result of capturing different target shapes. Finally, we discuss the impact of key factors affecting system performance.

4.1   Experiment Setup and Radio Implementation

Our prototype system consists of two components: hardware and software components.

Hardware Component: We implement our system on a USRP (Universal Software Radio Peripheral) platform with a directional antennas. $NIUSRP-2953R$ software radio generates a 5.8 GHz modulated signal with the maximum bandwidth of 120 MHz. The transmission power is set to 30 mW. In our experiments, we use only one off-the-shelf parabolic antenna. The antenna has a 32 dbi gain and 6° horizontal beam width and vertical beam width. Our RF-Eye system generates a frequency chip which repeatedly sweep the band 5.68 ~ 5.8 GHz.

Software Component: We implement the signal processing algorithm in MATLAB on a commercial Lenovo desktop computer with a 3.3 Ghz Intel $i5$ processor and 16 GB of RAM.

Radio Implementation: We implement the LFM signal based on the USRP platform. Figure 8 shows our implementation results. The x axis in the figure is the time domain, and the y axis is the amplitude of the signal. We observe that the frequency increases with time.

4.2   Result of Capturing Target Shape

In this section, we show the result of our first experiment to capture the target shape, concerning both regular and complex target shapes.

In total, we perform 20 rounds of different target tests, including different targets with different shapes. Figure 9(a) shows one original shape of the test target: a mental circle with a diameter of 65 cm. Figure 9(b) shows another original shape of test target: a mental rectangle with a side length of 80 cm. Figure 9(d) and Fig. 9(e) show the RF-Eye results, respectively. We observe that our system perform accurately to identify the shapes.

Next, we perform an experiment with complex shape. Human body is widely regarded as an irregular object with complex geometry shape, and Fig. 9(c) shows the result of a human target. From the image result shown in Fig. 9(f), we see that RF-Eye is able to identify the complete human image successfully. The imaging result clearly present the complete human shape with clear body parts, e.g., the head, arms and legs. We may even observe the gesture from the imaging obtained.

In summary, our RF-Eye system is able to successfully recognize target shape, even its shape is complex.

4.3   The Impact of Sampled Signal Pulse Number

The number of pulse signals M is a key parameter in our algorithm to decide the target shape resolution. If this value is set too low, the accuracy will be affected. If this value is set too high, the latency will increase.

Therefore, for each target shape, we test the signal sample numbers from 1000 to 15000, to obtain the capturing result. Figure 10(a)–Fig. 10(f) shows the imaging results of the circle with different sampled signal pulse number, respectively. We can observe, when the sampled number increases, the edge is more clear. Similarly, Fig. 11(a)–Fig. 11(f) shows the imaging results of the rectangle

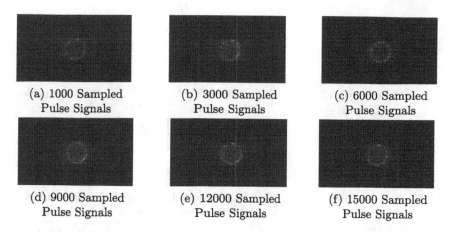

(a) 1000 Sampled
Pulse Signals

(b) 3000 Sampled
Pulse Signals

(c) 6000 Sampled
Pulse Signals

(d) 9000 Sampled
Pulse Signals

(e) 12000 Sampled
Pulse Signals

(f) 15000 Sampled
Pulse Signals

Fig. 10. Impact of sampled pulse signal number on circular target

with different sampled signal pulse number, respectively. We can see that, the rectangle result is more influenced by sampled signal pulse number since it is harder to get a very clear edge at the corner of the rectangle compared to other parts. The reason may be due to that less reflected signals by the sharp corner will enter the acceptable range of the directional antenna.

For more complex human target, we increase the sample range accordingly. The sampled signal pulse number varies from 1000 to 30000. Figure 12(a)–Fig. 12(e) show the imaging results of the human target with 1000, 5000, 10000, and 30000 signal sample numbers, respectively. We can see that, as the sampled signal pulse number increase, the body part becomes more clearly, especially for the limbs. When the sampled number is 1000 as shown in Fig. 12(a), we may roughly recognize it is a human, but limb parts are blurry. When the sampled number increases to 30000 as shown in Fig. 12(d), we are able to see the head, arms and legs very clearly.

4.4   Impact of Window Functions

In this section, we investigate how window functions will influence the experiment results. Choosing an appropriate window function may reduce the size of the side lobe of leakage and improve the frequency resolution capability, resulting in more clear images.

In order to investigate how the window functions will influence the results, we perform several experiments based on the imaging result of human target, utilizing four typical window functions, Kaiser Window, Hanning Window, Hamming Window and Blackman Window. Figure 13 shows the imaging results after processing by these four windows, respectively. We observe that, actually there are no big difference for the results. Therefore, in our experiment, we utilize Hamming Window by default.

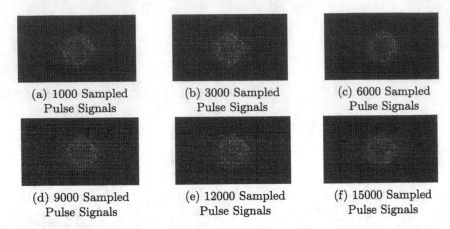

(a) 1000 Sampled
Pulse Signals

(b) 3000 Sampled
Pulse Signals

(c) 6000 Sampled
Pulse Signals

(d) 9000 Sampled
Pulse Signals

(e) 12000 Sampled
Pulse Signals

(f) 15000 Sampled
Pulse Signals

Fig. 11. Impact of sampled pulse signal number on rectangular target

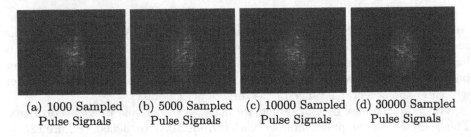

(a) 1000 Sampled
Pulse Signals

(b) 5000 Sampled
Pulse Signals

(c) 10000 Sampled
Pulse Signals

(d) 30000 Sampled
Pulse Signals

Fig. 12. Impact of sampled pulse signal number on human target

4.5   Edge Detection Algorithm Comparison

To capture the image of a target shape in one go, we perform the Prewitt algorithm to highlight the edge of the shape and obtain a clearer contour shape of the target. In this section, we compare our algorithm with others such as Roberts and Sobel algorithm [7,10]. Figure 14 and Fig. 15 show the circle and rectangle results before and after using image processing algorithms, respectively. It is obvious to see that, when leveraging Prewitt and Sobel Operator, the contour shape presents the clearest image. The Roberts Operator does not work as good as Sobel and Prewitt. And Prewitt operator is a little bit better. Therefore, we choose Prewitt operator by default to obtain the shape edge of the RF-Eye image.

4.6   Latency

The latency of RF-Eye depends on the time of both signal sampling acquisition and target shape capturing. The time cost of the signal sampling acquisition can be negligible since RF-Eye captures millions of sampling data within 1 ms through the USRP based system. The time cost of the second part depends

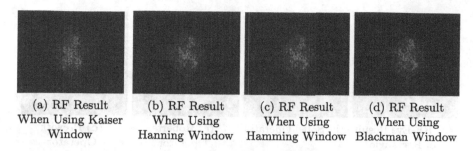

(a) RF Result
When Using Kaiser
Window

(b) RF Result
When Using
Hanning Window

(c) RF Result
When Using
Hamming Window

(d) RF Result
When Using
Blackman Window

Fig. 13. Comparison of different window function

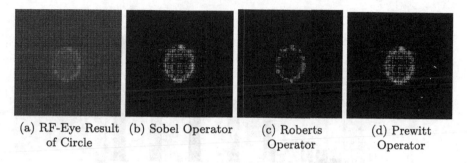

(a) RF-Eye Result
of Circle

(b) Sobel Operator

(c) Roberts
Operator

(d) Prewitt
Operator

Fig. 14. Comparison of different edge operator (circle

on the number of sampling data and the performance of the system. Figure 16 shows the latency of RF-Eye. As shown in the figure, based on the hardware we introduced before in the experimental setup section, the latency of RF-Eye is about 23s when the number of sampling data is 1000. The latency of RF-Eye is about 237s while the number of sampling data is 10000. The latency surely will decrease if we use a high-performance computer or reduce the number of sampling data.

In order to get a clear trade-off between accuracy and latency, in real-world scenarios, users may choose preferred number of sampling data to achieve their desired results.

5   Discussion

In this section, we review several critical decisions in our current design, and also discuss the limitations of our system.

5.1   How to Choose Carrier Frequency

Actually, RF-Eye is adaptive to other carrier frequency like the 2.4 GHz. In such scenario, the bandwidth also can be expanded far greater than 20 MHz. The current upper bound is 120 MHz, which is limited by the USRP hardware features.

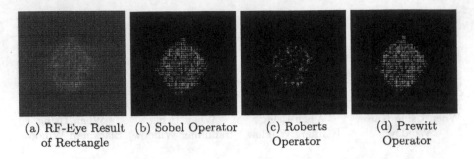

(a) RF-Eye Result   (b) Sobel Operator   (c) Roberts   (d) Prewitt
    of Rectangle   Operator   Operator

Fig. 15. Comparison of different edge operator (rectangle)

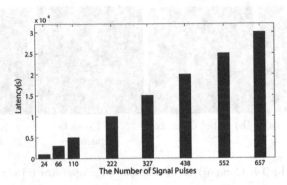

Fig. 16. The latency of RF-Eye

It can be further expanded using other hardware. Why in this work we choose the carrier frequency as 5.8 GHZ, is due to the following reason. Compare to the wavelength 11.6 cm of 2.4 GHz, the wavelength of 5.8 GHZ is 4.8 cm, making it not so easier to diffract small size targets or the small parts of the target, e.g., the human hand or limb. The signal can be reflected effectively and we can get the shape results more accurately. If users aim to capture the target with larger size, they may choose 2.4 GHz to apply our approach similarly.

5.2 Antenna Rotation

RF-Eye uses the narrow pulse signal reflections and Doppler frequency change caused by the rotate target to get the target shape. The limitation is the target will rotate in the real scenario. In reality, there are many possible ways to overcome such limitation. For example, if moving compensation are considered, our system is easily to be extend to moving target. Even for the static target, we may choose to move the antenna instead and apply the same approach. But this work is our first try, it can be further investigated in our future work.

6 Conclusion and Future Work

This paper presents RF-Eye, an RF-based system to capture complete target shape in indoor environments without training. Different from existing systems, RF-Eye exploits the basic characteristics of electromagnetic waves and implements a customized radio to efficiently capture complete target shape in one go. We use the narrow pulse signal reflections and Doppler frequency shift by the target to get the target image, and utilize image processing approach to obtain the shape of the target. Our experimental results show that RF-Eye successfully recognizes target shape (i.e., the successful recognition ratio reaches 100%). We also demonstrate that even for complicate targets our system is able to recognize and obtain its shape.

In our future work, we will investigate the impact of the bandwidth on the shape result. Second, we may change to other carrier frequency. At last, we will perform experiment to capture the shape of static target, we can move the antenna instead by applying the similar approach.

References

1. Adib, F., Hsu, C.Y., Mao, H., Katabi, D., Durand, F.: Capturing the human figure through a wall. ACM Trans. Graphics **34**(6), 1–13 (2017)
2. Adib, F., Kabelac, Z., Katabi. D.: Multi-person localization via RF body reflections. In: USENIX Conference on Networked Systems Design and Implementation, pp. 279–292 (2015)
3. Adib, F., Kabelac, Z., Katabi, D., Miller, R.C.: 3D tracking via body radio reflections. In: 11th USENIX Symposium on Network Systems design and Implementation, pp. 317–329 (2014)
4. Appleby, R., Anderton, R.N.: Millimeter-wave and submillimeter-wave imaging for security and surveillance. Proc. IEEE **95**(8), 1683–1690 (2007)
5. Biot, M.A.: Some new aspects of the reflection of electromagnetic waves on a rough surface. J. Appl. Phys. **28**(12), 1455–1463 (1957)
6. Cooper, K.B., et al.: Penetrating 3-d imaging at 4- and 25-m range using a submillimeter-wave radar. IEEE Trans. Microw. Theory Tech. **56**(12), 2771–2778 (2008)
7. Davis, D.: A real-time regenerative response method of equalizing a sound system. J. Audio Eng. Soc. **23**, 300–2 (1975)
8. Davies, H.: The reflection of electromagnetic waves from a rough surface. Proc. IEE Part III: Radio Commun. Eng. **101**(70), 118 (2010)
9. Dengler, R.J., et al.: 600 GHz imaging radar with 2 cm range resolution. In: Microwave Symposium, 2007. IEEE/MTT-S International, pp. 1371–1374 (2007)
10. Farid, H., Simoncelli, E.P.: optimally rotation-equivariant directional derivative kernels. In: Sommer, G., Daniilidis, K., Pauli, J. (eds.) CAIP 1997. LNCS, vol. 1296, pp. 207–214. Springer, Heidelberg (1997). https://doi.org/10.1007/3-540-63460-6_119
11. Gall, J., Stoll, C., De Aguiar, E., Theobalt, C., Rosenhahn, B., Seidel, H.P.: Motion capture using joint skeleton tracking and surface estimation. In: 2009 IEEE Conference on Computer Vision and Pattern Recognition, pp. 1746–1753 (2009)

12. Ganapathi, V., Plagemann, C., Koller, D., Thrun, S.: Real time motion capture using a single time-of-flight camera. In: Computer Vision and Pattern Recognition, pp. 755–762 (2010)
13. Goertz, D.E., Cherin, E., Needles, A., Karshafian, R., Brown, A.S., Burns, P.N., Foster, F.S.: High frequency nonlinear b-scan imaging of microbubble contrast agents. IEEE Trans. Ultrason. Ferroelectr. Frequ. Control **52**(1), 65–79 (2005)
14. Hasler, N., Rosenhahn, B., Thormahlen, T., Wand, M.: Markerless motion capture with unsynchronized moving cameras. In: IEEE Conference on Computer Vision and Pattern Recognition, 2009. CVPR 2009, pp. 224–231 (2009)
15. Huang, D., Nandakumar, R., Gollakota, S.: Feasibility and limits of Wi-Fi imaging. In: Proceedings of the 12th ACM Conference on Embedded Network Sensor Systems, pp. 266–279 (2014)
16. Katzin, M.: The Scattering of Electromagnetic Waves From Rough Surfaces. Pergamon Press (1963)
17. bibitemch28Kraus2002Antennas Kraus, J.D., Marhefka, R.J.: Antennas For All Applications. Mcgraw, -1 (2002)
18. Lin, Q.I., Ran, T., Zhou, S., Yue, W.: Detection and parameter estimation of multicomponent LFM signal based on the fractional Fourier transform. Sci. China **47**(2), 184–198 (2004)
19. bibitemch28Lustig2007Sparse Lustig, M., Donoho, D., Pauly. J.M.: Sparse MRI: the application of compressed sensing for rapid MR imaging. Mag. Reson. Med. **58**(6):1182C1195 (2007)
20. Moses, R.L., Potter, L.C., Chiang, H.C., Koets, M.A., Sabharwal, A.: A parametric attributed scattering center model for SAR automatic target recognition. In: Proceedings of the Image Understanding Workshop, pp. 849–860 (1998)
21. Mozzo, P., Procacci, C., Tacconi, A., Martini, P.T., Andreis, I.A.: A new volumetric CT machine for dental imaging based on the cone-beam technique: preliminary results. Eur. Radiol. **8**(9), 1558 (1998)
22. Prewitt, J.: Object enhancement and extraction. In: Object Enhancement and Extraction. Picture Processing and Psychopictorics, vol. 10, pp. 15–19 (1970)
23. Proakis, J.G., Salehi, M.: Digital communications. Digit. Commun. **73**(11), 3–5 (2015)
24. Ralston, T.S., Charvat, G.L., Peabody, J.E.: Real-time through-wall imaging using an ultrawideband multiple-input multiple-output (MIMO) phased array radar system. In: IEEE International Symposium on Phased Array Systems and Technology, pp. 551–558 (2010)
25. Raskar, R., et al.: Prakash:lighting aware motion capture using photosensing markers and multiplexed illuminators. Acm Trans. Graphics **26**(3), 36 (2007)
26. Ratnapalan, S., Bentur, Y., Koren. G.: Doctor, will that x-ray harm my unborn child?. Can. Med. Assoc J. l'Association medicale canadienne, **179**(12), 1293 (2008)
27. Roetenberg, D., Luinge, H., Slycke, P., Xsens MVN: full 6DOF human motion tracking using miniature inertial sensors. Xsens Motion Technologies Bv (2009)
28. Shotton, J., et al.: Real-time human pose recognition in parts from single depth images. Commun. ACM **56**(1), 116–124 (2013)
29. Tse, D., Viswanath, P.: Fundamentals of Wireless Communications, vol. 3, pp. B6–1 - B6–5 (2005)
30. Vlasic, D., Adelsberger, R., Vannucci, G., Barnwell, J., Gross, M., Matusik, W.: Practical motion capture in everyday surroundings. In: ACM SIGGRAPH, pp. 35 (2007)
31. Vlasic, D., Baran, I., Matusik, W.: Articulated mesh animation from multi-view silhouettes. Acm Trans. Graphics **27**(3), 1–9 (2008)

32. bibitemch28Wang:2014:WHY:2639108.2639112 Wang, G., Zou, Y., Zhou, Z., Wu, K., Ni, L.M.: We can hear you with Wi-Fi! In: Proceedings of the 20th Annual International Conference on Mobile Computing and Networking, MobiCom 2014, pp. 593–604, New York, NY, USA. ACM (2014)

33. Wang, Y., Liu, J., Chen, Y., Gruteser, M., Yang, J., Liu, H.; E-eyes: device-free location-oriented activity identification using fine-grained Wi fi signatures. In: International Conference on Mobile Computing and NETWORKING, pp. 617–628 (2014)

34. Wang, Y., Jiang, Y.C.: Detection and parameter estimation of multicomponent LFM signal based on the cubic phase function. Eur. J. Adv. Sig. Proces. **2008**(1), 743985 (2008)

35. White, D.A., Jones, C., Forman, W.: An investigation of cooling flows and general cluster properties from an x-ray image deprojection analysis of 207 clusters of galaxies. Mon. Not. R. Astron. Soc. **292**(2), 419 (1997)

36. Woodward, R.M., et al.: Terahertz pulse imaging in reflection geometry of human skin cancer and skin tissue. Physi. Med. Biol. **47**(21), 3853–3863 (2002)

37. L. Xia, C., Chen, C., Aggarwal, J.K.: Human detection using depth information by Kinect. In: CVPR 2011 Workshops, pp. 15–22, June 2011

38. Xie, Y., Li, Z., Li. M.: Precise power delay profiling with commodity Wi fi. In: International Conference on Mobile Computing and Networking, pp. 53–64 (2015)

39. Xie, Y., Li, Z., Li, M., Jamieson, K.: Augmenting wide-band 802.11 transmissions via unequal packet bit protection. In: IEEE INFOCOM 2016 - the IEEE International Conference on Computer Communications, pp. 1–9 (2016)

40. Ye, M., Wang, H., Deng, N., Yang, X., Yang, R.: Real-time human pose and shape estimation for virtual try-on using a single commodity depth camera. IEEE Trans. Visual. Comput. Graphics **20**(4), 550–9 (2014)

41. Wu, K., Wang, Y., Ni, L.M.: Wifall: device-free fall detection by wireless networks. IEEE Trans Mob. Comput. **16**(2), 581–594 (2017)

42. Zhang, L., Xing, M., Qiu, C.W., Li, J., Bao, Z.: Achieving higher resolution ISAR imaging with limited pulses via compressed sampling. IEEE Geosci. Remote Sens. Lett. **6**(3), 567–571 (2009)

43. Zhu, Y., Zhu, Y., Zhao, B.Y., Zheng, H.: Reusing 60 GHz radios for mobile radar imaging. In: International Conference on Mobile Computing and NETWORKING, pp. 103–116 (2015)

Technology for Health

Identification of Abnormal Behavior in Activities of Daily Life Using Novelty Detection

Mauricio Freitas[1], Vinicius de Aquino Piai[1], Rudimar Dazzi[1], Raimundo Teive[1], Wemerson Parreira[5], Anita Fernandes[1], Ivan Miguel Pires[2], and Valderi Reis Quietinho Leithardt[3,4][✉]

[1] Artificial Intelligence Laboratory, University of Vale do Itajai, Itajai 88302-901, Brazil
{mauriciopasetto,vinicius_paiai}@edu.univali.br, {rudimar, rteive,anita.fernandes}@univali.br
[2] Instituto de Telecomunicações, Universidade da Beira Interior, 6200-001 Covilhã, Portugal
impires@it.ubi.pt
[3] VALORIZA, Research Center for Endogenous Resources Valorization, Instituto Politécnico de Portalegre, 7300-555 Portalegre, Portugal
valderi@ipportalegre.pt
[4] COPELABS, Universidade Lusófona de Humanidades e Tecnologias, 1749-024 Lisbon, Portugal
[5] Laboratory of Embedded and Distributed Systems, University of Vale do Itajai, Itajai 88302-901, Brazil
parreira@univali.br

Abstract. The world population is aging at a rapid pace. According to the WHO (World Health Organization), from 2015 to 2050, the proportion of elderly people will practically double, from 12 to 22%, representing 2.1 billion people. From the individual's point of view, aging brings a series of challenges, mainly related to health conditions. Although, seniors can experience opposing health profiles. With advancing age, cognitive functions tend to degrade, and conditions that affect the physical and mental health of the elderly are disabilities or deficiencies that affect Activities of Daily Living (ADL). The difficulty of carrying out these activities within the domestic context prevents the individual from living independently in their home. Abnormal behaviors in these activities may represent a decline in health status and the need for intervention by family members or caregivers. This work proposes the identification of anomalies in the ADL of the elderly in the domestic context through Machine Learning algorithms using the Novelty Detection method. The focus is on using available ADL data to create a baseline of behavior and using new data to classify them as normal or abnormal daily. The results obtained using the E-Health Monitoring database, using different Novelty Detection algorithms, have an accuracy of 91% and an F1-Score of 90%.

Keywords: Novelty Detection · Anomaly Detection · Activities of Daily Living · Machine Learning · One-Class Support Vector Machine (OC-SVM) · Local Outlier Factor (LOF)

© ICST Institute for Computer Sciences, Social Informatics and Telecommunications Engineering 2023
Published by Springer Nature Switzerland AG 2023. All Rights Reserved
S. Longfei and P. Bodhi (Eds.): MobiQuitous 2022, LNICST 492, pp. 559–570, 2023.
https://doi.org/10.1007/978-3-031-34776-4_29

1 Introduction

The world population is aging at a rapid pace. According to the WHO, from 2015 to 2050. The proportion of people over 60 will practically double, from 12% to 22% of the population, representing 2.1 billion people. The number of people over 80 is expected to triple and reach 526 million [24].

From the individual's point of view, aging brings a series of challenges, mainly related to health conditions. Although seniors can experience opposite health profiles, several conditions are common at this stage of life [25]. The most common are chronic diseases affecting 80% of the elderly, such as hypertension, heart disease, heart failure, ischemic heart disease/coronary diabetes, chronic obstructive pulmonary disease, depression, Alzheimer's disease, and dementia [26].

Other conditions that affect the physical and mental health of the elderly are disabilities or impairments, which affect activities of daily living (ADL) [9]. It is estimated that more than 56% of the elderly suffer from moderate to severe disability, representing more than 256 million people [27]. The difficulty of carrying out these activities within the domestic context and which prevent the individual from living independently in their own home are minimized through Ambient Assisted Living (AAL) technologies.

AAL technologies aim to develop personal health and remote monitoring systems [8]. Thus, monitoring the ADL is essential to identify abnormalities in activities [2, 11]. It is because significant changes in the elderly's routine can represent a decline in physical or mental health. This detection allows family members and caregivers to be aware of the need for intervention [19]. The recognition of ADL is done by Human Activity Recognition (HAR) techniques [1, 14]. Recognizing these activities in a period defines a pattern of typical behavior, and, from this pattern, abnormalities can be detected [3, 22, 23].

In this context, the Novelty Detection technique can be used to identify abnormalities in ADL. Novelty Detection is a Machine Learning technique for the classification task. It is used when the target class is well characterized in the training data, and the data of the other class has few samples or is not well defined. This technique is also known as a class classification, and its use is related to identifying rare events and anomalies in [18]. Among the novelty detection algorithms are One-Class Support Vector Machine (OC-SVM) [12] and Local Outlier Factor (LOF) [5]. These algorithms were selected for this experiment because they are used in similar works.

OC-SVM is a powerful machine learning algorithm that can be used to build a model from only available normal data to learn its normal behavior. OC-SVM classifies any deviation from this normal behavior as anomalous [5, 36]. OC-SVM is very sensitive to the initial values of its hyperparameters [32, 33, 37] and this affects its generalization performance.

LOF is a density-based technique, that can be considered as a classical local outlier detection algorithm, widely used in network intrusion detection and processing of classification benchmark data [5, 38].

The main objective of this work is to identify ADL abnormalities in the elderly using the Novelty Detection technique. Where available, ADL data represent the individual's normal behavior, and subsequent data are analyzed to identify abnormal behaviors. This means predicting whether the newly observed data is within the pattern learned by the model, normal class, or is out of this pattern, characterizing an abnormality or, in the context of Novelty Detection, a novelty [18].

Although the focus and objective of the research carried out and the results obtained have no focus and relationship with the treatment of patient data privacy, we based our work on different works [6, 13, 15, 16, 34, 35]. These works present research and useful contributions to data privacy management in different concepts and scenarios.

The rest of the article is structured as follows: Sect. 2 shows the related works, Sect. 3 presents the methodology, Sect. 4 the results found, and Sect. 5 concludes the article.

2 Related Work

Through the search in the literature, four related works were identified. They all present the use of Machine Learning in conjunction with several algorithms for detecting anomalies in Activities of Daily Living. Also, one to three databases are used for analysis in conjunction with the algorithms.

Yahaya, Lofti, and Mahmud [23] used an ensemble of one-class support vector machine, isolation forest, robust covariance estimator and local outlier factor is utilized for the anomaly detection achieving an accuracy of 98%. Bozdog et al. [4] used five algorithms and two databases, one generated synthetically. The results were based on three quantities, each with an algorithm obtaining a better result.

Erfanmanesh, Tahayori, and Visconti [7] use four algorithms to detect and predict user actions and one to detect anomalies. The AdaBoost learning algorithm had the best performance and was used for detecting the anomalies and modeling normal/abnormal behavior. In conjunction with only one database, it obtained an accuracy of 100% and an approximate recall value of 83% in detecting abnormalities.

Finally, Fouquet, Faraut, and Lesage [10] use only one algorithm and database. The results were determined based on three scenarios: the inhabitant is in good health, lacks appetite, and has a urinary tract infection.

3 Methodology

The proposed workflow to identify ADL abnormalities is shown in Fig. 1. The steps presented in Fig. 1, are described below. The initial set of daily ADL data, which represents the baseline behavior of the elderly, is used to train the model. This model uses the following daily data to identify deviant daily routines that constitute an abnormality. The result for each new day observed is considered normal (1) or abnormal (-1).

This work has secondary objectives: (i) to identify the predictive attribute that presents the best model generalization analyzing activities' duration and duration/frequency attributes. (ii) identify the minimum number of weeks to obtain an accuracy above 85%; (iii) identify and select among the OC-SVM and LOF algorithms the one with the best performance; (iv) select the predictive parameter, training weeks, and the algorithm for the proposed anomaly identification model.

Among the ADL databases found in the literature [20, 21, 28–31], the eHealth Monitoring Open Data Project [28] was selected. This presents monitoring the elderly's ADL activity in the domestic context, where 21 activities are observed in one year. Each observation includes the day of the observation, the activity, and the start and end times. Activities include Eating, Laundry, Sleep, making coffee, Watching TV, and Cell Use, among others. On this basis, the monitoringP1HRversion dataset was selected. It contains 14297 records and presents the monitoring of the elderly's ADL on the one dependency profile of SMAF (Functional Autonomy Measurement System). This profile corresponds to an autonomous individual with some level of supervision and helps needed [17].

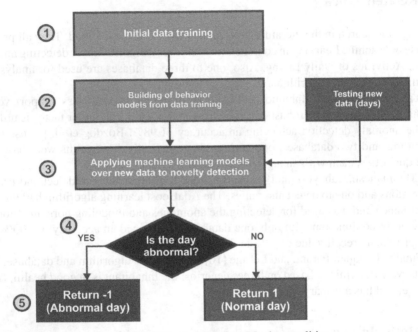

Fig. 1. Workflow to identify ADL abnormalities.

The development and pre-processing of data were done using the Python 3.10.7 programming language, using the Machine Learning library Scikit Learn 1.1.2.

3.1 Pre-processing

To use the E-Health monitoringP1HRversion dataset, it was necessary two steps to pre-processing data. Table 1 shows the dataset partially in raw format. In the first stage, the data were organized into a CSV file, presenting the same information as the original file, adding the duration of each activity (Table 2).

Table 1. Original dataset [28]

day_begin	day_end	begin_time	end_time	begin_time_seconds	end_time_seconds	activity_name	activity_number
1	1	08:03:32	08:22:40	29012	30160	Washing (take shower)	3
1	1	08:23:46	08:26:53	30226	30413	Hair dray	5
1	1	08:28:50	08:38:39	30530	31119	Change clothes	2
1	1	08:40:37	08:50:24	31237	31824	Toileting	7
1	1	08:52:12	08:55:38	31932	32138	Washing hand/face	4

Table 2. Pre-processing First Stage

day	activity_number	activity_name	duration	frequency	duration/frequency
1	1	Eating	73.450000	2	36.725000
1	2	Change clothes	21.983333	3	7.327778
1	3	Washing (take shower)	19.133333	1	19.133333
1	4	Washing hand/face	49.516667	10	4.951667
1	5	Hair dray	3.116667	1	3.116667

The second pre-processing stage included the creation of two distinct datasets using pivoting the dataset resulting from the second pre-processing stage. Both use activities as predictive attributes (columns), the first using the duration attribute as content (Table 3) and the second duration/frequency (Table 4). In both, the day of the task was kept. The creation of these two datasets is necessary for the generalization evaluation of the duration and duration/frequency predictive attributes. Nine activities were selected arbitrarily for this work to facilitate experiments and analysis. The selected activities were Change clothes, Eating, Make hot food, Sleep, Take M., Toileting, Take shower, Washing hand/face, Watching TV.

Table 3. Pre-processing result with the Duration predictive attribute

Activities

day	Change clothes	Eating	Make hot food	Sleep	Take M	Toileting	Take shower	Washing hand/face	Watching TV
1	21.98	73.45	44.73	415.65	2.80	47.33	19.13	49.52	172.77
2	20.70	123.48	78.50	786.10	2.50	32.28	19.28	44.32	94.65
3	25.22	64.08	102.88	726.72	2.10	46.67	12.65	39.32	184.33
4	15.98	116.83	97.00	620.42	3.07	40.02	10.87	47.70	206.72
5	15.78	133.78	97.05	734.07	3.42	23.82	11.08	17.77	181.07

Table 4. Pre-processing result with the Duration/Frequency predictive attribute

Activities

day	Change clothes	Eating	Make hot food	Sleep	Take M	Toileting	Take shower	Washing hand/face	Watching TV
1	7.33	36.73	44.73	207.83	2.80	7.89	19.13	4.96	86.38
2	6.90	41.16	39.25	262.03	2.50	8.07	19.28	4.43	47.33
3	8.41	32.04	51.44	242.24	2.10	6.67	12.65	4.91	36.87
4	7.99	38.94	48.50	206.81	3.07	8.00	10.87	4.34	68.91
5	7.89	44.59	48.53	244.69	3.42	7.94	11.08	4.44	36.21

3.2 Machine Learning for Novelty Detection

The novelty detection step predicts whether a given day is normal or abnormal. The OC-SVM and LOF algorithms were applied to the datasets resulting from the last pre-processing step. In both datasets, the data were separated into training, validation, and testing. For training data, the first 20 weeks of observations were selected. For validation data, the next eight weeks were determined. The same validation data were used for the training data, adding abnormalities. This addition obeyed the following rules: in the first 4 weeks, 1 to 9 activities were selected, in 50% of the data an increase from 20% to 200% was applied, and in the remaining 50% a decrease from 20% to 200%. Both the selection of activities and the changes in values were done randomly. In the remaining 4 weeks, no changes were applied to the data, maintaining the proportion of 50% between days with and without abnormalities. In this process, negative values were imputed, replacing them with zero. It is important to say that expansion and decreased values follow a normal error distribution Fig. 2 shows the graph of fluctuations applied to the dataset that uses the predictive attribute duration. Similarly, Fig. 3 shows the dataset that uses the duration/frequency predictive attribute.

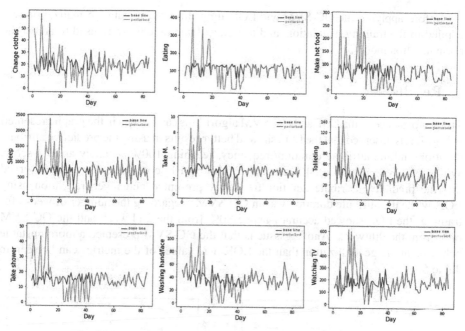

Fig. 2. Validation and test data with predictive attribute: duration.

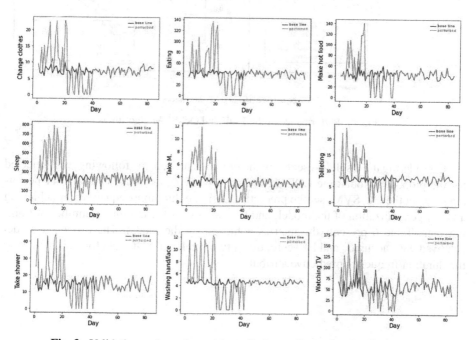

Fig. 3. Validation and test data with predictive attribute: duration/frequency.

Before applying the OC-SVM and LOF algorithms to the data, normalization was applied to the training, validation, and test data. Training data were used to adjust the normalization model.

4   Results

The performance of the LOF and OC-SVM algorithms can be seen in the graph presented in Fig. 4. It is observed that the LOF showed better results in using the predictive attribute duration and the attribute duration/frequency, reaching 100% accuracy and F1-score. While OC-SVM achieved 84% accuracy and 86% F1-score. However, it is observed that the predictive attribute duration/frequency presented better generalization using LOF, while the attribute duration was in OC-SVM. Regarding the number of weeks for training, the LOF showed accuracy above 80% from the 2nd week and the OC-SVM only from the 9th week. Another issue is that the OC-SVM presented a more unstable behavior in the generalization than the LOF. The values of the metrics can be seen in Table 5.

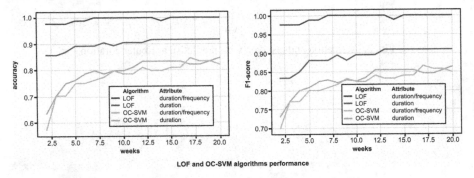

Fig. 4. Performance of the LOF and OC-SVM algorithms.

Considering the results presented in the previous section, the following were selected for the proposed model: the LOF algorithm, for having demonstrated a better performance than the OC-SVM; set the predictive attribute duration/frequency, for achieving a better generalization of the model; and two weeks for the minimum number of training data. Table 6 presents the metrics achieved by the model. The proposed model achieved 98% accuracy and F1-score, using two weeks of ADL data for training, using the duration/frequency predictive attribute.

Table 5. Performance of the LOF and OC-SVM algorithms by predictive attributes.

LOF				OC-SVM			
duration		duration/frequency		duration		duration/frequency	
accuracy	F1score	accuracy	F1score	accuracy	F1score	accuracy	F1score
0.857	0.833	0.976	0.976	0.631	0.73	0.571	0.7
0.857	0.833	0.976	0.976	0.702	0.771	0.702	0.771
0.869	0.849	0.976	0.976	0.75	0.8	0.702	0.771
0.893	0.88	0.988	0.988	0.762	0.808	0.75	0.8
0.893	0.88	0.988	0.988	0.786	0.824	0.75	0.8
0.893	0.88	1	1	0.798	0.828	0.762	0.808
0.905	0.895	1	1	0.786	0.82	0.774	0.816
0.893	0.88	1	1	0.798	0.828	0.798	0.832
0.905	0.895	1	1	0.798	0.825	0.786	0.824
0.905	0.895	1	1	0.81	0.833	0.786	0.824
0.905	0.895	1	1	0.833	0.854	0.81	0.84
0.917	0.909	1	1	0.833	0.854	0.798	0.832
0.917	0.909	0.988	0.988	0.833	0.854	0.798	0.832
0.917	0.909	1	1	0.833	0.854	0.81	0.84
0.917	0.909	1	1	0.833	0.854	0.81	0.84
0.917	0.909	1	1	0.821	0.845	0.843	0.866
0.917	0.909	1	1	0.821	0.845	0.833	0.857
0.917	0.909	1	1	0.833	0.854	0.833	0.857
0.917	0.909	1	1	0.845	0.863	0.821	0.848

Table 6. Proposed method performance for the evaluated metrics.

True Positive	True Negative	False Positive	False Negative	Accuracy	Precision	Recall	F1-score
40	42	2	0	0.976	0.952	1	0.976

5 Conclusion

This work proposed a model to identify abnormalities in the Activities of Daily Living of the Elderly using the Novelty Detection method. And it had as sub-objectives: to evaluate the LOF and OC-SVM algorithms; identify the predictive attribute with the best generalization, considering the duration and duration/frequency attributes; determine the minimum number of training weeks to obtain an accuracy greater than or equal to 85%; and select the best configuration for the proposed model based on the results.

The E-Heath database was used to train the model. The first 20 weeks were used as training data and the subsequent 8 weeks for validation and test data. In addition, over 50% of the test data, 1 to 9 activities were selected, adding variations from 20 to 200% for plus and minus, maintaining the 50% ratio between data with and without variances.

The novelty detection algorithms OC-SVM and LOF were used and evaluated in the detection of anomalies. As a result, the LOF performed better, with an F1-score accuracy of 97% from the second week onwards and 100% from the seventh week onwards. The OC-SVM presented its highest accuracy and F1-Score in the twentieth week, respectively 84% and 86%. However, OC-SVM presented better generalization with the use of the duration predictive attribute, and the LOF with the duration/frequency attribute.

Considering the results presented, the following were selected for the predictive model: the LOF algorithm, for achieving a better performance in relation to the OC-SVM; the predictive attribute duration/frequency, for presenting a greater generalization with the LOF; and two weeks for model training data. The proposed model achieved an accuracy and F1-Score of 98%.

Acknowledgments. We would like to thank the Fundação de Amparo a Pesquisa e Inovação do Estado de Santa Catarina - FAPESC, for supporting the projects promoted: Public Notice 15/2021 TO 2021TR001236 and Public Notice 29/2021 TO 2021TR001758.

This work is funded by FCT/MEC through national funds and co-funded by FEDER—PT2020 partnership agreement under the project **UIDB/50008/2020**.

This work is also supported by national funds through the Foundation for Science and Technology, I.P. (Portuguese Foundation for Science and Technology) by the project **UIDB/05064/2020** (VALORIZA—Research Center for Endogenous Resource Valorization), and Project UIDB/04111/2020, ILIND—Lusophone Institute of Investigation and Development, under project **COFAC/ILIND/COPELABS/3/2020**.

This article is based upon work from COST Action IC1303-AAPELE— Architectures, Algorithms, and Protocols for Enhanced Living Environments and COST Action CA16226–SHELD-ON—Indoor living space improvement: Smart Habitat for the Elderly, supported by COST (European Cooperation in Science and Technology). COST is a funding agency for research and innovation networks. Our Actions help connect research initiatives across Europe and enable scientists to grow their ideas by sharing them with their peers. It boosts their research, career, and innovation. More information on www.cost.eu.

References

1. Abdulhussein, A.A., Hassen, O.A., Gupta, C., Virmani, D., Nair, A., Rani, P.: Health monitoring catalogue based on human activity classification using machine learning. Int. J. Electr. Comput. Eng. **12**(4), 3970 (2022)
2. Acuña, S.A., Tyler, M.E., Danilov, Y.P., Thelen, D.G.: Abnormal muscle activation patterns are associated with chronic gait deficits following traumatic brain injury. Gait Posture **62**, 510–517 (2018). https://doi.org/10.1016/j.gaitpost.2018.04.012
3. Arifoglu, D., Bouchachia, A.: Detection of abnormal behaviour for dementia sufferers using Convolutional Neural Networks. Artif. Intell. Med. **94**, 88–95 (2019)
4. Bozdog, I.A., et al.: Human behavior and anomaly detection using machine learning and wearable sensors. In: 2021 IEEE 17th International Conference on Intelligent Computer Communication and Processing (ICCP), pp. 383–390. IEEE (2021)

5. Budiarto, E.H., Permanasari, A.E., Fauziati, S.: Unsupervised anomaly detection using K-means, local outlier factor and one class SVM. In: 2019 5th International Conference on Science and Technology (ICST), pp. 1–5. IEEE (2019)
6. Cesconetto, J., Augusto Silva, L., Bortoluzzi, F., Navarro-Cáceres, M., Zeferino, C.A., Leithardt, V.R.Q.: PRIPRO—privacy profiles: user profiling management for smart environments. Electronics 9, 1519 (2020). https://doi.org/10.3390/electronics9091519
7. Erfanmanesh, M., Tahayori, H., Visconti, A.: Elderly action prediction and anomalous activity detection in smart homes through profiling residents' behavior. Mod. Care J. 16(3), e94661 (2019). https://doi.org/10.5812/modernc.94661
8. Ferreira, J.M., et al.: Activities of daily living and environment recognition using mobile devices: a comparative study. Electronics 9, 180 (2020). https://doi.org/10.3390/electron-ics 9010180
9. Foti, D., Koketsu, J.S.: Activities of daily living. Pedretti's Occup. Ther. Pract. Skills Phys. Dysfunction 7, 157–232 (2013)
10. Fouquet, K., Faraut, G., Lesage, J.-J.: Model-based approach for anomaly detection in smart home inhabitant daily life. In: 2021 American Control Conference (ACC), pp. 3596–3601. IEEE (2021)
11. Guo, J., Zhou, X., Sun, Y., Ping, G., Zhao, G., Li, Z.: Smartphone-based patients' activity recognition by using a self-learning scheme for medical monitoring. J. Med. Syst. 40(6), 1–14 (2016). https://doi.org/10.1007/s10916-016-0497-2
12. Jin, B., Chen, Y., Li, D., Poolla, K., Sangiovanni-Vincentelli, A.: A one-class support vector machine calibration method for time series change point detection. In: 2019 IEEE International Conference on Prognostics and Health Management (ICPHM), pp. 1–5. IEEE (2019)
13. Leithardt, V., et al.: A privacy taxonomy for the management of ubiquitous environments. J. Commun. Comput. 10, 1529–1553 (2013)
14. Leithardt, V.R., et al.: Mobile architecture for identifying users in ubiquitous environments focused on Percontrol. In: The Seventh International Conference on Mobile Ubiquitous Computing, Systems, Services and Technologies, UBICOMM, pp. 145–151 (2013)
15. Leithardt, V.R., et al.: Mechanism for privacy management based on data history (UbiPri-His). J. Ubiquit. Syst. Pervasive Netw. 10, 11–19 (2018)
16. Leithardt, V.R., Nunes, D., Rossetto, A.G., Rolim, C.O., Geyer, C.F., Silva, J.S.: Privacy management solution in ubiquitous environments using percontrol. J. Ubiquit. Syst. Pervasive Netw. 5, 21–28 (2014)
17. Mshali, H., Lemlouma, T., Magoni, D.: Analysis of dependency evaluation models for eHealth services. In: 2014 IEEE Global Communications Conference, Austin, TX, USA, pp. 2429–2435. IEEE (2014)
18. Ouafae, B., Oumaima, L., Mariam, R., Abdelouahid, L.: Novelty detection review state of art and discussion of new innovations in the main application domains. In: 2020 1st International Conference on Innovative Research in Applied Science, Engineering and Technology (IRASET), pp. 1–7. IEEE (2020)
19. Pires, I.M., et al.: Mobile 5P-medicine approach for cardiovascular patients. Sensors 21, 6986 (2021). https://doi.org/10.3390/s21216986
20. Pires, I.M., Garcia, N.M., Zdravevski, E., Lameski, P.: Activities of daily living with motion: a dataset with accelerometer, magnetometer and gyroscope data from mobile devices. Data Brief 33, 106628 (2020). https://doi.org/10.1016/j.dib.2020.106628
21. Pires, I.M., Garcia, N.M., Zdravevski, E., Lameski, P.: Daily motionless activities: a dataset with accelerometer, magnetometer, gyroscope, environment, and GPS data. Sci Data 9, 105 (2022). https://doi.org/10.1038/s41597-022-01213-9
22. Saha, S.S., Rahman, S., Rasna, M.J., Mahfuzul Islam, A.K.M., Rahman Ahad, Md.A.: DU-MD: an open-source human action dataset for ubiquitous wearable sensors. In: 2018 Joint

7th International Conference on Informatics, Electronics & Vision (ICIEV) and 2018 2nd International Conference on Imaging, Vision & Pattern Recognition (icIVPR), Kitakyushu, Japan, pp. 567–572. IEEE (2018)

23. Yahaya, S.W., Lotfi, A., Mahmud, M.: Detecting anomaly and its sources in activities of daily living. SN Comput. Sci. **2**(1), 14 (2020). https://doi.org/10.1007/s42979-020-00418-2

24. Ageing and health. https://www.who.int/news-room/fact-sheets/detail/ageing-and-health. Accessed 5 Aug 2020

25. 10 facts on ageing and health. https://www.who.int/news-room/fact-sheets/detail/10-facts-on-ageing-and-health. Accessed 2 Sept 2022

26. The Top 10 Most Common Chronic Diseases for Older Adults. https://www.ncoa.org/article/the-top-10-most-common-chronic-conditions-in-older-adults. Accessed 2 Sept 2022

27. Ageing and disability: United Nations Enable. https://www.un.org/development/desa/disabilities/disability-and-ageing.html. Accessed 2 Sept 2022

28. eHealth Monitoring Open Data Project. SourceForge. https://sourceforge.net/projects/ehealthmonitoringproject/. Accessed 2 Sept 2022

29. Welcome to CASAS. http://casas.wsu.edu/datasets/. Accessed 2 Sept 2022

30. DaLiAc: Daily Life Activities. https://www.mad.tf.fau.de/research/activitynet/daliacdaily-life-activities/. Accessed 2 Sept 2022

31. UCI Machine Learning Repository: Activities of Daily Living (ADLs) Recognition Using Binary Sensors Data Set. https://archive.ics.uci.edu/ml/datasets/Activities+of+Daily+Living+(ADLs)+Recognition+Using+Binary+Sensors. Accessed 2 Sept 2022

32. Xiao, Y., Wang, H., Xu, W.: Parameter selection of Gaussian kernel for one-class SVM. IEEE Trans. Cybern. **45**(5), 941–953 (2015)

33. Zou, X., Cao, J., Guo, Q., Wen, T.: A novel network security algorithm based on improved support vector machine from smart city perspective. Comput. Electr. Eng. **65**, 67–78 (2018)

34. Silva, L.A., Leithardt, V.R.Q., Rolim, C.O., González, G.V., Geyer, C.F.R., Silva, J.S.: PRISER: managing notification in multiples devices with data privacy support. Sensors **19**(14), 3098 (2019). https://doi.org/10.3390/s19143098

35. Apolinário, V.A., Dal Bianco, G., Duarte, D., Leithardt, V.R.Q.: Exploring feature extraction to vulnerability prediction problem. In: de la Iglesia, D.H., de Paz, J.F., Santana, A.J., Rivero, L. (eds.) New Trends in Disruptive Technologies, Tech Ethics and Artificial Intelligence: The DITTET 2022 Collection, pp. 79–90. Springer, Cham (2023). https://doi.org/10.1007/978-3-031-14859-0_7

36. Klikowski, J., Woźniak, M.: Employing one-class SVM classifier ensemble for imbalanced data stream classification. In: Krzhizhanovskaya, V.V., et al. (eds.) ICCS 2020. LNCS, vol. 12140, pp. 117–127. Springer, Cham (2020). https://doi.org/10.1007/978-3-030-50423-6_9

37. Khraisat, A., Gondal, I., Vamplew, P., Kamruzzaman, J., Alazab, A.: Hybrid intrusion detection system based on the stacking ensemble of C5 decision tree classifier and one class support vector machine. Electronics **9**(1), 173 (2020). https://doi.org/10.3390/electronics9010173

38. Alghushairy, O., Alsini, R., Soule, T., Ma, X.: A review of local outlier factor algorithms for outlier detection in big data streams. Big Data Cogn. Comput. **5**, 1 (2021). https://doi.org/10.3390/bdcc5010001

Behavioral Anomaly Detection of Older People Living Independently

Carlos A. S. Cunha$^{(\boxtimes)}$ ⓘ, Rui Pedro Duarte ⓘ, and David Mota

Polytechnic Institute of Viseu, Viseu, Portugal
{cacunha,pduarte,dmota}@estgv.ipv.pt

Abstract. Older people living independently represent one significant part of the population nowadays. Most of them have family or friends interested in being informed about changes in their routine. Considering these changes signal some physical or mental problem, they can trigger a contact or action from the interested persons to provide support. This paper presents an approach for non-intrusive monitoring of older people to send alerts after detecting anomalous behaviors. An analysis of seven months of data gathered using PIR sensors in a couple's living house has shown regularities in their presence in compartments along the day. We validated the adequacy of an outlier detection algorithm to build a model of the persons' behavior, exhibiting just 3.6% of outliers interpreted as false positives.

Keywords: Autonomous Living · Anomaly Detection · Behavioral Analysis

1 Introduction

According to the report of the United Nations [14], the number of older persons over the next three decades is predicted to more than double compared to 2020, reaching over 1.5 billion in 2050. The same report shows that older persons often live independently when their health is good enough. Nevertheless, they rely on the support of children, siblings, and other kin (friends, neighbors) not residing with them.

Older persons need to be able to perform activities of daily living (ADLs) [9] unassisted to live independently (e.g., eating, bathing, and mobility). ADLs represent the elements forming each person's routine. The spatiotemporal distribution of ADLs models a regular behavior pattern, which identifies behavioral

This work is funded by National Funds through the FCT—Foundation for Science and Technology, I.P., within the scope of the project Ref. UIDB/05583/2020. Furthermore, we would like to thank the Research Centre in Digital Services (CISeD) and the Polytechnic of Viseu for their support. Moreover, the authors greatly thank IPV/CGD-Polytechnic Institute of Viseu/Caixa Geral de Depositos Bank, within the scope of the projects PROJ/IPV/ID&I/002 and PROJ/IPV/ID&I/007.

S. Longfei and P. Bodhi (Eds.): MobiQuitous 2022, LNICST 492, pp. 571–582, 2023.
https://doi.org/10.1007/978-3-031-34776-4_30

anomalies. People's families and friends are interested in these anomalies because they express alerts to conditions that may require their intervention.

Previous work on monitoring ADLs of the elderly focuses mainly on long-term behavioral analysis—e.g., for detection of dementia [11,13]. Some techniques are intrusive (e.g., video-vigilance) [10] or change the person's routine (e.g., wearables [3,8]). This paper presents the infrastructure based on low-cost PIR sensors installed in older adults' homes living alone to gather data and a machine learning approach to detect behavioral anomalies in their everyday behaviors.

This paper addresses the following research questions:

- How to gather data required for detecting anomalous behaviors in older adults living independently?
- Are there regularities in the daily living behaviors captured by the permanence of individuals in house compartments of a couple living together?
- How to model anomalous events from data representing temporal permanence of individuals in house compartments?

This remaining of this paper is structured as follows. Section 2 presents the related work. Section 3 describes the data gathering and preprocessing methodology. Section 4 analyses behavioral patterns from the data and presents the anomaly detection model. Section 5 discusses experimental results. Finally, Sect. 6 presents the conclusion.

2   Related Work

Most work on behavioral analysis explores data gathered in the context of ADLs. In [11] ADLs are studied for diagnosis of dementia. Statistical methods and machine learning techniques have shown accuracy higher than 90% from sensor data – door, motion, temperature, humidity, vibration and lidar sensors, and smart plugs. The use of household appliances during late-night hours has revealed an essential feature in predicting early-stage dementia patients. Also, in [13], the authors explore anomalies as a predictor of dementia. They perform pattern extraction over activity vectors of whole days. The Hamming distance and Levenshtein distance determine the distance between two sequences of activities, while the entropy measures the activity uncertainty at each time slot. The approach showed the presence of regularities in the dataset used in the experimental work. In [2], the authors present a simulation tool to create normal and wandering trajectories and related sensor activities to detect overnight wandering in patients with dementia in home environments. The resultant simulation datasets created a decision tree classifier to perform binary classification of normal and wandering pathways. An unobtrusive activity recognition classifier employing deep convolutional neural networks (DCNNs) is studied in [6]. The approach uses anonymous binary sensors to recognize different ADLs. The approach was evaluated with high accuracy using a single older woman living inside for eight months. In [15] the authors address detection of anomalous days for ADLs and evolution trends. They propose a similarity index to measure deviations from maps of pheromone distributions, entailing the activity intensity, the places where the activities occur, and relative weights of places related to the spatial distribution of activity. Another work [5] studies unsupervised machine learning to cluster users' behavioral patterns. Evaluation using inexpensive and unlabelled sensors in a community-based housing with 17 residents exhibited accuracy higher than 85%.

Root cause analysis pursues the problem behind the anomaly. Understanding the cause of anomalies unveils the problem behind ADL patterns. The authors of [17] investigated a similarity measure approach to identify single anomaly sources.

A review of techniques for abnormal human activity recognition based on an analysis of video surveillance is presented in [4]. Deep learning dominates this area, focusing mainly on fall detection. The review pointed to vision-based single-person behavior recognition as an area not yet explored due to the non-availability of large datasets to train deep networks.

The work presented in this paper distinguishes itself from previous work as it addresses the detection of behavioral anomalies based just on the position of persons in the house to ensure their privacy. Moreover, it analyzes the regularities of a couple instead of individuals.

3   Data Gathering and Preprocessing

The testbed used to gather data was deployed at a husband and wife's house for approximately seven months – from February until September of 2021. They live alone in a village in the center of Portugal. Their ages are between 68 and 70 years old, and they have a college education. They rarely receive regular family visits and are often at the house. Participants consented and accepted their participation in this study, as long as the data are used for scientific research.

3.1   Data Gathering

The placement of sensors followed the criteria of covering as much monitoring area as possible and reducing intrusiveness in people's daily activities to a minimum. The PIR sensors used in the testbed are small enough (30 mm × 30 mm × 33 mm) to be ingrained in the environment without being intrusive to the aesthetics or functionality of house compartments. They provide a maximum coverage distance of seven meters (Fig. 1(a)) and angle of 170° (Fig. 1(b)).

Sensors were installed in house compartments where people perform their normal daily activities. Exceptions are transition zones between compartments. Following that criteria, we considered the room (Fig. 2(b)), WC (Fig. 2(a)), living room (Fig. 2(d)), and kitchen (Fig. 2(c)). Also, each sensor location was chosen to avoid undesired displacement (e.g., during cleaning activities), leading to erroneous data.

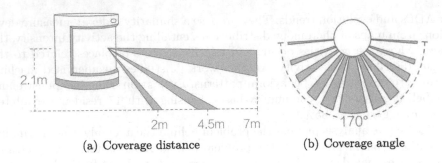

(a) Coverage distance   (b) Coverage angle

Fig. 1. PIR sensors specification.

3.2 Data Integration

The sensor data gathered by the hub is only accessible through third-party applications. We adopted OpenHab [1] for that purpose. This platform provides connectors specific to several IoT sensor types, including those used in our testbed.

The Linux OpenHabian image installed in the Raspberry PI (version 3) with 512 Mb, contains the openHAB platform. This platform configures each sensor connected to the hub as a *thing*, through a specific *channel* responsible for transmitting the respective sensor data. These data are incrementally written in logs in text format, as shown in Listing 1.1.

Listing 1.1. OpenHab event

```
"$oid":"60284c135ed15f380a0c35ab",
"date":"2021-01-30",
"time":"17:07:55.544",
"sensorID":"XiaomiMiMotionSensor4",
"event":"ON"
```

A Python script performs data preprocessing. It starts by querying the MongoDB database and transforming the openHAB log into an accessible format for data processing. Then it labels each record with the compartment name, removes incomplete data blocks (days with records missing), and aggregates data temporally (Listing 1.2).

3.3 Incomplete Data Removal

Each record in the dataset represents an event triggered by a sensor at a specific time. Thus, residents' absence of movement or failure periods explain periods of lacking data. To shield the model performance, the preprocessing activity must remove the records associated with failure periods from the training dataset. However, discriminative separation of failure periods from the absence of movement is complex just from data analysis.

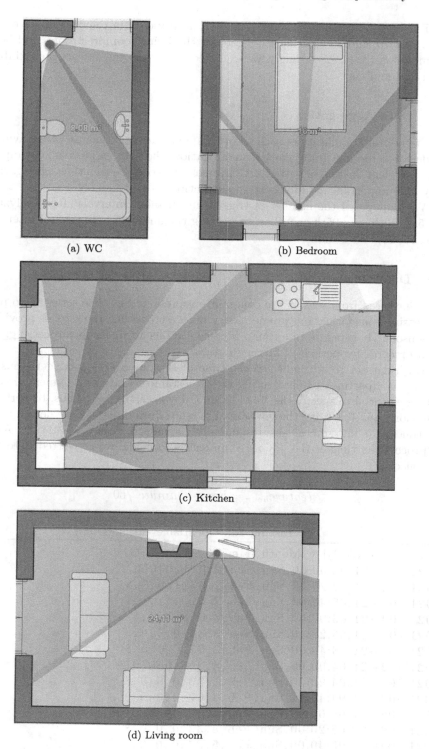

(a) WC

(b) Bedroom

(c) Kitchen

(d) Living room

Fig. 2. Placement of Sensors

Empirical data analysis shows that only faulty days in the dataset have less than 200, 70, and 20 movement triggers for the living room, restroom, and bedroom, respectively. Accordingly, we excluded days from the dataset not exhibiting these minima.

3.4 Data Aggregation

The temporal granularity of each record impacts the performance of behavioral models. For too fine-grain temporal aggregation, the data variance may compromise the identification of patterns. Conversely, too coarse-grain time aggregation may hide important data for pattern extraction.

We aggregated the number of triggers in one-hour intervals after analyzing the 5th, 50th, and 95th quantiles, respecting the number of triggers for intervals of 1, 15, 30, and 60 min.

3.5 Data Formatting

Data gathered from sensors are commonly represented as time series. Two pre-processing transformations are necessary before processing the records provided by sensors: (1) generate timestamp representations adequate for processing; (2) create records for periods of missing data.

Each dataset record indicates the time of the day a person triggers sensors inside a compartment. Representing the timestamp feature as a numerical variable is essential to specify the time distance between triggers. Thus, to perform behavioral analysis using the position of persons during the day, we decomposed the timestamp into several features, namely, the month, weekday, and time. Also, to process the time of the day as a numerical variable, we converted it to the format of (1).

$$feature_{hour} = hour + minutes/60 \qquad (1)$$

Listing 1.2. OpenHab event

```
Date ,Time ,Weekday ,Month ,Time ,C1 ,C2 ,C3 ,C4
2021 −02 −21 ,02:00:00 ,Sun ,Feb ,2.0 ,1 ,0 ,0 ,0
2021 −02 −21 ,02:20:00 ,Sun ,Feb ,2.33 ,1 ,0 ,0 ,8
2021 −02 −21 ,02:40:00 ,Sun ,Feb ,2.67 ,1 ,1 ,1 ,1
2021 −02 −21 ,03:00:00 ,Sun ,Feb ,3.0 ,8 ,0 ,1 ,1
2021 −02 −21 ,03:20:00 ,Sun ,Feb ,3.33 ,0 ,0 ,0 ,8
2021 −02 −21 ,03:40:00 ,Sun ,Feb ,3.67 ,0 ,0 ,0 ,8
2021 −02 −21 ,04:00:00 ,Sun ,Feb ,4.0 ,8 ,0 ,0 ,0
2021 −02 −21 ,04:20:00 ,Sun ,Feb ,4.33 ,0 ,0 ,0 ,8
2021 −02 −21 ,04:40:00 ,Sun ,Feb ,4.67 ,0 ,0 ,0 ,8
2021 −02 −21 ,05:00:00 ,Sun ,Feb ,5.0 ,8 ,0 ,0 ,0
2021 −02 −21 ,05:20:00 ,Sun ,Feb ,5.33 ,0 ,0 ,0 ,8
2021 −02 −21 ,05:40:00 ,Sun ,Feb ,5.67 ,0 ,0 ,0 ,8
```

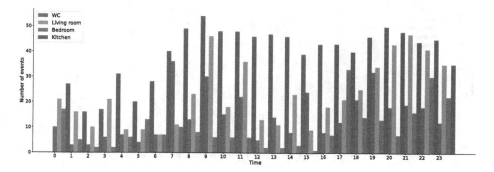

Fig. 3. Number of triggered events per hour.

```
2021-02-21,06:00:00,Sun,Feb,6.0,8,0,0,0
2021-02-21,06:20:00,Sun,Feb,6.33,0,0,0,8
2021-02-21,06:40:00,Sun,Feb,6.67,0,0,0,8
2021-02-21,07:00:00,Sun,Feb,7.0,0,0,0,0
```

4 Analysis of Results

The research objectives described in this paper depend on behavioral regularities in house inhabitants. We start by analyzing the number of triggers for each period and compartment to evaluate these regularities. Then, we perform the same analysis for the lower and higher limits, exposed by the percentile 5th and 95th. These percentiles filter the 5% bottom and top values, which are susceptible to representing outliers that compromise the identification of patterns. Finally, we evaluate the occupation probability of each compartment, indicating the likelihood of an inhabitant being present there at a specific time.

4.1 Analysis of Events Per Hour

Figure 3 presents the number of events registered in the house compartments per hour. The periods with a higher presence in all compartments are observable from the graphics analysis. These values expose the regularities of the presence of persons in each compartment.

4.2 Occupation Probability

The probability of compartments occupation by persons represents another valuable analysis perspective since it exhibits the occupation likelihood of a compartment during a specified period. Hence, a behavioral anomaly results from an unlikely presence in a compartment.

Some events in the data represent transient activity filtered from the analysis since they represent temporary presence in the compartment (e.g., when

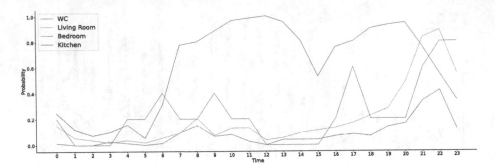

Fig. 4. Probability of occupation of each compartment during the day.

somebody passes by a compartment) instead of effective permanence. Since each sensor triggers a new event at each minute, we consider five events (i.e., five minutes) as the threshold for events to account for the presence in the compartment at the corresponding hour, as specified in (2).

$$Prob_t = \frac{\#Days\{\#triggers_t >= 5\}}{\#Days} \tag{2}$$

Figure 4 presents the presence probability in each house compartment. It reveals the following patterns:

- from midnight to 6 am, the likelihood of presence in any compartment is low;
- the presence in the kitchen is high between 7 am and 2 pm and between 4 pm and 9 pm;
- occupation in the living room is higher between 9 pm and 11 pm;
- the room is inhabited at 5 pm, and after 10 pm – the location of the sensor position (close to the room's entrance) explains the low activity registered after midnight;
- regarding the occupation of WC, there is more occupation at the end of the day, reaching its peak around 10 pm.

4.3   Outlier Detection

A visual analysis of patterns shows regularities in the use of house compartments. However, building an outlier detection model able to predict unusual behaviors exposed by the occupation of spaces in the house requires combining the presence of persons in all compartments at a specific time. Additionally, the error created by hourly data aggregating can compromise the model prediction performance. These constraints lead the solution to an anomaly detection model combining data from several compartments that exploits time as a numerical variable calculated as in (1), to avoid the error originating in temporal data aggregations.

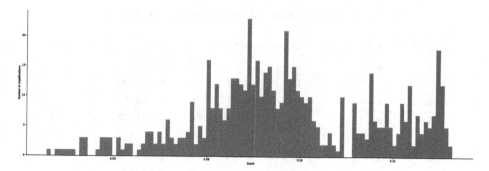

Fig. 5. Outlier classification using Isolation Forests.

Machine learning algorithms classification is two-fold: supervised and unsupervised. Supervised learning algorithms build models from samples of all classes (e.g., normal and anomalous behaviors). In contrast, unsupervised algorithms model one class (normal samples) and classify anomalous samples when they unfit the model. Unsupervised algorithms suit the problem addressed in this paper since the expected behavior is observable, but the anomalous behavior space is practically unlimited.

We decided on the Isolation Forest algorithm [12] to create an anomaly detection model due to its exemplary performance in several domains [7,16]. This algorithm isolates anomalies based on the characteristics that make them unique. Accordingly, it fits a decision tree on all the observations and regards outliers as those instances close to the root of trees.

The Isolation Forest requires parameterization of the contamination factor. This parameter sets the sensitivity of the algorithm to outlier classification. We evaluated several contamination factors and decided on 0.1 (10%) due to its lowest number of outliers with the training dataset, showing the best model adjustment to the data. The resultant model has 3.6% of outliers – shown in Fig. 5 as the number of samples classified with a score inferior to zero. Table 1 lists these outliers, representing false positives if used in an alert system.

5   Discussion of Results

Section 4 presents ADL regularities defined in the context of people's temporal occupation of house compartments. Inference of fine-grain ADLs (e.g., reading a book, drinking water) demands intrusive appliances with low impact on the answer to our research questions. Informal caretakers or familiars of older adults may want to be notified of changes in their daily routine without interfering and disrespecting their privacy. A marker signaling an abnormal condition that requires attention is a change in an individual's home routine, described in terms of the temporal distribution of permanence in house compartments.

Detection of abnormal conditions explores patterns of two older adults' presence in house compartments. However, ordinary people's routine outliers may

Table 1. Outliers identified during the training process.

weekday	hour	kitchen	living-room	room	wc	score	prediction
4	23.0	1	0	1	0	−0.004654	−1
6	2.0	0	1	1	1	−0.016904	−1
6	14.0	0	1	1	0	−0.015443	−1
6	23.0	0	0	1	0	−0.021297	−1
7	5.0	0	1	1	0	−0.027471	−1
7	17.0	1	0	1	1	−0.025279	−1
7	23.0	1	1	1	0	−0.014824	−1
5	5.0	0	1	0	1	−0.006145	−1
6	4.0	0	1	0	1	−0.009018	−1
7	0.0	1	0	1	0	−0.002024	−1
7	5.0	0	1	1	1	−0.035581	−1
6	23.0	1	0	1	0	−0.001213	−1
5	5.0	0	1	1	1	−0.003214	−1

lead to false notifications. That may happen because they change their routine for some reason not explained by a problem that requires attention from their family.

False positives leading to false notifications may impact the trust of the system. Experimental results showed 3.6% of outliers respecting the period of analysis. Since the main system goal is to trigger notifications to familiars interested in being informed about abnormal conditions, the consequence of an anomaly would be an unnecessary contact. However, the value of an accurate notification may compensate for the cost of unnecessary notifications respecting false positives when they are rare.

The observed regularities in the data may depend on the couple's activities rather than the individuals. Patterns in data produced by PIR sensors mean that a couple's routine can be exploited to trigger alerts for anomalous conditions.

6   Conclusion

The increasing percentage of older persons living independently nowadays makes monitoring their ADLs valuable, allowing alerts to family or friends not living with them when something goes wrong. However, sensors attached to the person and other physical objects can simplify ADLs identification and processing but create intrusiveness issues.

This paper presents a solution based on simple PIR sensors placed in house compartments to gather information about the presence of persons in those compartments without compromising their daily routine. The events generated by these sensors are used to build a model of the location of persons in the house.

Deviations from the expected behavior (e.g., going to the kitchen several times during the night) provide the basis to trigger notifications.

We gathered and analyzed the activity of an older couple during seven months of living together in the same house. Experimental results unveiled behavioral regularities in the routine of persons that can be explored to detect abnormal conditions.

We plan to design the solution to trigger notifications based on the model created in future work. Despite being rare, the number of false positives may lead to distrust by the most demanding users. Combining several detected irregularities would potentially reduce the number of unnecessary alerts. A significant problem is determining how to explore the combination of some outliers detected without extending the notification latency.

References

1. openHAB. https://www.openhab.org
2. Casaccia, S., Rosati, R., Scalise, L., Revel, G.M.: Measurement of Activities of Daily Living: a simulation tool for the optimisation of a Passive Infrared sensor network in a Smart Home environment. In: 2020 IEEE International Instrumentation and Measurement Technology Conference (I2MTC), pp. 1–6 (2020). https://doi.org/10.1109/i2mtc43012.2020.9128409
3. Cunha, C.A., Duarte, R.P.: Multi-device nutrition control. Sensors **22**(7), 2617 (2022)
4. Dhiman, C., Vishwakarma, D.K.: A review of state of-the-art techniques for abnormal human activity recognition. Eng. Appl. Artif. Intell. **77**, 21–45 (2010). https://doi.org/10.1016/j.engappai.2018.08.014
5. Fiorini, L., Cavallo, F., Dario, P., Eavis, A., Caleb-Solly, P.: Unsupervised machine learning for developing personalised behaviour models using activity data. Sensors **17**(5), 1034 (2017). https://doi.org/10.3390/s17051034
6. Gochoo, M., Tan, T.H., Liu, S.H., Jean, F.R., Alnajjar, F.S., Huang, S.C.: Unobtrusive activity recognition of elderly people living alone using anonymous binary sensors and DCNN. IEEE J. Biomed. Health Inform. **23**(2), 693–702 (2018). https://doi.org/10.1109/jbhi.2018.2833618
7. He, Y., Zhu, X., Wang, G., Sun, H., Wang, Y.: Predicting bugs in software code changes using isolation forest. In: 2017 IEEE International Conference on Software Quality, Reliability and Security (QRS), pp. 296–305 (2017). https://doi.org/10.1109/QRS.2017.40
8. Kantoch, E., Augustyniak, P., Markiewicz, M., Prusak, D.: Monitoring activities of daily living based on wearable wireless body sensor network. In: 2014 36th Annual International Conference of the IEEE Engineering in Medicine and Biology Society, pp. 586–589. IEEE (2014)
9. Katz, S.: Assessing self-maintenance: activities of daily living, mobility, and instrumental activities of daily living. J. Am. Geriatr. Soc. **31**(12), 721–727 (1983). https://doi.org/10.1111/j.1532-5415.1983.tb03391.x
10. König, A., et al.: Validation of an automatic video monitoring system for the detection of instrumental activities of daily living in dementia patients. J. Alzheimers Dis. **44**(2), 675–685 (2015)

11. Kwon, L.N., et al.: Automated classification of normal control and early-stage dementia based on activities of daily living (ADL) data acquired from smart home environment. Int. J. Environ. Res. Public Health **18**(24), 13235 (2021). https://doi.org/10.3390/ijerph182413235

12. Liu, F.T., Ting, K.M., Zhou, Z.H.: Isolation forest. In: 2008 Eighth IEEE International Conference on Data Mining, pp. 413–422 (2008). https://doi.org/10.1109/ICDM.2008.17

13. Maučec, M.S., Donaj, G.: Discovering daily activity patterns from sensor data sequences and activity sequences. Sensors **21**(20), 6920 (2021). https://doi.org/10.3390/s21206920

14. United Nations: World population ageing 2020. Technical report (2020). https://www.un.org/development/desa/pd/sites/www.un.org.development.desa.pd/files/undesa_pd-2020_world_population_ageing_highlights.pdf

15. Susnea, I., Dumitriu, L., Talmaciu, M., Pecheanu, E., Munteanu, D.: Unobtrusive monitoring the daily activity routine of elderly people living alone, with low-cost binary sensors. Sensors **19**(10), 2264 (2019)

16. Xu, S., Zhu, J., Jiang, J., Shui, P.: Sea-surface floating small target detection by multifeature detector based on isolation forest. IEEE J. Sel. Top. Appl. Earth Obs. Remote Sens. **14**, 704–715 (2021). https://doi.org/10.1109/JSTARS.2020.3033063

17. Yahaya, S.W., Lotfi, A., Mahmud, M.: Detecting anomaly and its sources in activities of daily living. SN Comput. Sci. **2**(1), 1–18 (2020). https://doi.org/10.1007/s42979-020-00418-2

Making Everyday Objects More Inclusive: A Case Study via Remote Participatory Design

Barbara Leporini[1,4](✉), Marina Buzzi[2], and Luca Baldini[3]

[1] ISTI-CNR, via Moruzzi 1, 56124 Pisa, Italy
`barbara.leporini@isti.cnr.it`
[2] IIT-CNR, via Moruzzi 1, 56124 Pisa, Italy
`marina.buzzi@iit.cnr.it`
[3] Editoriale Campi, via San Giuseppe, 1, 06038 Spello, PG, Italy
`l.baldini@barbanera.it`
[4] I.Ri.Fo.R., via Borgognona 38, 00187 Roma, Italy

Abstract. Interacting with everyday objects remains a challenge for blind and visually impaired people who rely on assistive technology. This study investigates how to exploit Information and Communication Technology (ICT) to make everyday objects more accessible for people with visual disabilities, and help create a more inclusive society. A participatory design process including five blind and two visually impaired users was carried out in Italy, exploiting video conferencing tools with the aim of increasing the usability of everyday objects, based on visual interfaces, usually poorly accessible to sightless people. As a case study, a well-known traditional paper-based calendar was selected, since it is a very popular object used at home, at work and in social life. Although digital calendars are very popular nowadays, a tangible paper-based calendar may be more suitable or preferred by users, in specific contexts. Due to people's various needs and preferences, a set of suggestions emerged from this valuable experience in co-design sessions with technical teams and end users, which can be applied in other contexts where additional information is required.

Keywords: Visually-impaired users · everyday objects · Tangible interfaces · QR-code · accessibility · inclusive society

1 Introduction

As digital solutions pervade our life, new access modes are needed to make tools, artefacts and apps accessible to all, regardless of disability. One of the most popular objects is the calendar, paper-based as well as digital format, including date pickers, interactive or personal calendars [1]. Many studies indicate that the inclusion of people with disabilities is a key factor in those individuals' psychological and social wellbeing [2] as well as a powerful learning motivation factor [3]. Exploiting technology to make everyday objects more accessible is a valuable step toward individual autonomy, in a lifelong pathway of inclusion.

© ICST Institute for Computer Sciences, Social Informatics and Telecommunications Engineering 2023
Published by Springer Nature Switzerland AG 2023. All Rights Reserved
S. Longfei and P. Bodhi (Eds.): MobiQuitous 2022, LNICST 492, pp. 583–597, 2023.
https://doi.org/10.1007/978-3-031-34776-4_31

This study was carried out jointly with the Institute for Research, Training and Rehabilitation (I.Ri.Fo.R.), which as a branch of the Italian Union of the Blind and Visually Impaired seeks solutions to improving the independence of visually impaired people in everyday life. The willingness of the Campi publishing house to make its calendar accessible provided an opportunity to investigate this study's solutions to designing a paper-based calendar for everyone, including people with visual impairments. In particular, the aim of this study was to enable a multimodal and multimedia use of the paper calendar so that it is also usable through the assistive technologies used by people with visual disabilities. Co-design with blind and visually impaired users was applied in our case study.

The participatory design process proved to be fundamental for increasing accessibility and usability of any physical or digital object or artefacts, including applications. In this study, a participatory design approach was applied to making a paper-based calendar more inclusive by exploiting technology to enrich it with additional digital accessible contents. From the beginning this approach involved visually impaired and blind people, who have first-hand experience with the problems they face every day and can propose solutions as co-designers on a technical team.

The most famous Italian lunar calendar is the Barbanera Calendar, in print ever since 1762 [4]. It has always been widely used by families since it offers information about lunar phases linked to the stages of raising crops: sowing, cultivating, harvesting, etc. This is why we decided to select this calendar as a case study, to render it more accessible and inclusive.

The final solution is based on the combined use of the following technologies:

- traditional Braille code to mark the day
- QR (quick response) code to enrich the information with audio or textual descriptions
- Audio (mp3) content that can be triggered via a QR code
- Digital web-based content and pages to choose a specific day (web page with the list of days)

Two main questions emerged in our case study:

- How many QR codes can be placed on a page and at what distance?
- How can a blind user identify the position of a QR code to be detected via smartphone?

In the following we describe in detail the design phases of our work and answer these two questions. The paper is organized into seven sections. Section 2 introduces the Related Work and Sect. 3 the methodology that drives the project. Section 4 describes the participatory design process of the Accessible Calendar. Section 5 discusses the results and Sect. 6 suggests a set of guiding principles for designers. Conclusions end the paper.

2   Related Work

Nowadays ICT technologies and the Internet network enable the automatic association of additional content to (everyday) objects. Thanks to the ability to identify univocally an object in the Internet network, it is possible to augment the object by showing or announcing additional information and content. Radio Frequency Identification (RFID) tags and readers [5], Near-field communication (NFC) labels with smartphones (reader) [6], and more recently beacons and bi-dimensional QR codes with mobile applications are examples of enabling technologies that can trigger dynamic (web) content uploading [7, 8].

Previous research focused on making Web calendars more accessible for screen reader users. Calendar widgets can pose accessibility problems. Although accessible, the calendar is poorly usable via screen reader since arrow keys enable sequential exploring of dates (one by one), the announced content can be unclear ("M" instead of "Monday"), and table shortcuts might not work [9].

Other authors have investigated the problem of audio access to calendars by designing a non-visual interface for selecting dates on web-based forms in order to provide audio access to date selection while automating the formatting of dates. The proposed calendar date entry system reduced errors in date format when a user has to insert a date [10].

WebbIE is an example of a calendar app specifically designed for blind users [11]. It is a desktop application with a simple user interface with just a few buttons and menus that can easily be navigated by keyboard and screen reader. However, it is very simple and does not deliver important functions such as location, additional information, and confirmations of deleted events and was not recently updated. More recent apps are designed to be used on mobile devices. An accessible and usable interface for a dynamic web-based calendar was proposed by [12].

A collection of common mobile Apps (such as phone, contacts, messages, calendars, notes) accessible for visually impaired users has been organized in an accessible mobile portal designed for easy interaction and customization for low vision users (icon size, colors, screen contrast, voice speed) [13].

Recently companies such as Google, Microsoft, and Apple provide users with their calendars integrated into the OS. For instance, the sophisticated Google Calendar provides APIs to incorporate its digital calendar functions in apps. The Calendar API lets developers integrate their apps with Google Calendar, created for engaging users (https://developers.google.com/calendar/api). Thus developers can save resources, by reusing components (API libraries) without the burden of development and maintenance over time. These components have to provide support for use with a screen reader to make interaction comfortable and satisfying for blind users.

Analogously, mobile phones and tablets (Android, iOS) integrate their own calendars. Date pickers and calendar applications are available today on touch-screen devices. Users can interact with gestures and finger touch. This modality was a revolution for blind users enabling easy interaction with mobile phones [14].

With the rapid evolution of technology, people with special needs such as blind and visually impaired (BVI) people can especially benefit from using voice assistants such as Siri or Alexa. They are very useful for BVI people thanks to the vocal interaction and the audio information exploited in everyday-life tasks. By conducting an online survey with 145 participants, authors discovered that common voice assistants are used by most BVI people and are considered helpful; especially in everyday life practical tasks like checking for weather, setting an alarm clock, checking calendar entries and taking notes are particularly useful and frequently used [15].

However, to the best of the authors' knowledge, a hybrid modality of the tangible and digital calendar has not yet been described. Moreover, the experience of co-design with BVI people, exploiting video conferencing tools that may pose accessibility and usability problems for blind users [16] has been tackled in the project by collecting valuable user feedback and suggestions.

3 Method

Participatory Design (PD) exploits different tools and strategies to make users become designers in order to improve the usability of designed artefacts. "We can make user experience the source of inspiration and ideation for design. And by making user experience the source of inspiration, we are better able to design for experiencing" [17]. A change is required in this approach with the awareness of the value of designing with users instead of designing for users (a method prone to subjective interpretations during the design process, negatively impacting the artefact's usability). To this aim, appropriate tools to express the user's full design potential must be provided. As participants in the PD are from different and not homogenous domains, it might be necessary to establish a common language to be shared between all design team participants to facilitate communication and comprehension.

Participatory design implies investigating, reflecting, understanding, modeling, developing, and stimulating and sustaining mutual learning processes during the design process. The interplay between competence, skills, experiences, emotions enhance mutual learning through a synergic cooperative process [18].

A participatory design approach has been applied since the beginning of the study. The design of an accessible calendar was carried out in collaboration with the Barbanera publishing house, which was interested in making their paper-based calendar accessible also to people with vision impairments, and with the Italian Association for the Blind, which participated in the design of the proposed solution. End users who have experienced interaction problems can provide crucial cues and guidance to create products simple to use, easy to understand and able to deliver a satisfying experience [18].

The participatory design approach with incremental steps led to the multimodal and multimedia solutions described in the following. Traditional and digital technologies have been exploited to develop the solution proposed in this study, as described in the next sections.

The design team was composed of a group of people with various skills, experiences and abilities: a designer from the Barbanera calendar Publishing House, two technicians, and one expert in graphic design (sighted). The blind participants were recruited by the Italian Association for the Blind. Seven users with visual impairments (five men and two women aged 32 to 67 years) took part; five were totally blind and two were visually impaired. Users were comfortable with technology and the use of computers and smartphones. In addition, a researcher expert in accessibility – the blind author of this work -- was included in the team, thus resulting in a total of eight blind people involved from the start of the design process. Although not statistically significant due to the low cardinality of this sample, in our opinion they could represent the experienced problems, feelings and the ideas of the visually impaired since the eight blind team participants ranged from very expert to novice, including both young and older people, and comprising three females and five males.

Once the paper-based initial prototype was ready, a preliminary printing of a limited edition of the calendar was carried out by the editor, as a pilot test. The publishing house then sent the first calendar prototype to all participants to perform a preliminary evaluation and share feedback and suggestions. User feedback was collected and analyzed to prepare a new version of the calendar prototype. Finally, a focus group was held in attendance at the association's headquarters with all participants for testing the new version of the prototype.

4 Participatory Design: Case of the Barbanera Calendar

In this section, we describe the design phases and the development of the calendar in an accessible version following the indications of the visually impaired members of the team.

4.1 Barbanera Calendar

Barbanera has been a famous Italian almanac and calendar since 1762. In its paper format, it offers valuable daily advice according to the seasons and the Moon phases. The Barbanera tradition is a UNESCO 'Memory of the World' [4].

The calendar is presented in a paper format with an eye-catching and rich graphic look for the reader. In addition to the cover, each page of the month shows: (1) the days' dates with an indication of the saint of the day (on the front of the page), and (2) advice regarding the harvest, how to sow, useful tips for the home, horoscope, etc. (on both the front and the back of the page). All this information is written on the calendar itself. The calendar thus not only provides an overview of the days of the month, but also offers useful information for all the members of a family.

We chose this type of calendar not only because of its popularity in Italy, but because it offers a lot of information, which can therefore be made more accessible in digital format.

4.2 Designing the First Prototype

The two-step participatory design carried out by the team enabled the development of an accessible technology-enhanced version of the Barbanera paper-based Calendar. As previously mentioned, the team comprised two researchers (one totally blind), the Barbanera technical team (sighted people), and seven visually impaired people with different technical skills.

Due to the Covid-19 pandemic, the team worked remotely in a collaborative way exploiting video conferencing tools. Specifically, Zoom was used since it was preferred by visually impaired participants. In the first meeting, with the other members of the team the participants analyzed the main features and the graphic appearance of the calendar in paper form. As a result, the main issues experienced by the visually impaired in accessing paper-based calendars as well as the user requirements were collected during the focus group meeting. A second meeting with the participants allowed the team to develop possible strategies to apply in order to work out a format enriched with digital content, to make it accessible also to people with visual impairments. Accessibility principles drove the design of the first draft of the prototype.

Usually, co-design sessions are performed in presence by using visual based tools to favour creativity and collaboration. In this study, the collaboration and cooperation relied first and foremost on voice interaction based on in-depth descriptions.

In the first remote meeting, the visually impaired participants shared information about the main issues faced when carrying out everyday activities, as well as the assistive technologies usually used to overcome them. The members of the publishing house shared information about the graphical rendering of the calendar. The accessibility expert researcher (who is a computer scientist) introduced accessibility principles and current technology solutions to the group. Participants with visual impairments expressed interest in a solution that on one hand included tactile elements that may be more familiar to the blind, and on the other hand exploited the most popular technologies in the blind community for accessing digital content.

The first prototype of the accessible Barbanera calendar was conceived and took shape over several meetings. In the design, four parts of the paper-based calendar content were digitally expanded: a) Cover information b) Contents of the month c) The phases of the moon and d) The information of the day. This suggests exploiting ICT to augment the information associated with the object.

The QR code was acknowledged by all team members to be a suitable tool for enriching the calendar information with digital content. When scanned via a mobile app, the QR code triggers the opening of an URL in the browser, and the page can contain text and/or multimedia objects. Some accessibility aspects of using QR codes and the applications needed to be discussed with the visually-impaired participants:

- *QR code Detection.* Visually, the QR code is easily recognizable. For a blind person, it is not easy (I) to know whether QR codes are present and if so (II) where they are located in order to be framed by the camera.
- *Number and positioning of QR codes.* It was necessary to figure out how many codes to apply and where to place them.
- *Marking of days.* To facilitate the consultation of the paper calendar by a blind person, it was necessary to understand how to mark the days so that the blind person can identify the days and thus the information associated with them.

The first prototype included the use of the QR codes to tag the following elements: day information (for all days), cultivation descriptions, horoscope and partners' websites. For the day information, specific written or audio content about the day was added. The cover page and an example of a month (January) are shown in Fig. 1 (a) and (b).

In the first page prototype, each day was marked with a QR code linked to the day's description loaded on the publishing house's website, for a total of 31 QR codes for the month of January. Two links were placed at the bottom of the page for the horoscope and cultivation descriptions.

When the user scans a QR code with a smartphone camera via an app, the corresponding URL can be triggered. However, scanning the QR code can be a difficult task for a screen reader user. QRBlind is an app specifically designed to handle QR codes

Fig. 1. Accessible calendar first prototype – a) Cover page b) Month of January

by visually impaired users, available in the Apple Store. It is fully accessible via screen reader and provides five push buttons that enable the functions: Go to the Web address, Add or Modify a QR Code, Play Audio, Create a new Label, Share QR Code. The app enables a blind person to create a QR code in a simple way. This is very important for their autonomy since it enables the creation of personalized labels that can be scanned via QR code for reproducing stored audio descriptions. This app was used to test the page prototype. Figure 2 shows the blind user scanning the Barbanera calendar month page via QRBlind. Analogous apps are available for the android platform such as VIP Code Reader - Blind scanner.

Fig. 2. QR code scanning with QRBlind

4.3 The Pilot Test and Second Design Iteration

In the second Participatory Design iteration, issues highlighted by the pilot test were addressed by the multidisciplinary team, in order to make the calendar more accessible and usable.

The pilot test was performed over a 3-week period to ensure that any participants received the calendar prototype via postal mail. Three tasks were assigned to the user via email and WhatsApp group:

1) explore the cover page and read the info about the Barbanera. This task evaluates the use of the QR code on the left at the top of the cover page
2) explore the page for January and read the information on day 6. This task evaluates the usability of the QR codes associated with each day (i.e., QR code detectability and distance)
3) Count the number of QR codes on the cover page. QR codes on the cover have been manually embossed with one point in relief in order to make the tactile detection of the QR code easier.

The test was performed autonomously by each participant, while the feedback was shared through written comments or audio messages via WhatsApp. Feedback was read (or listened to) during the next meeting and then commented on by all the team participants. Researchers annotated those comments for better analysis.

Problems and technical solutions to be addressed were mostly discussed during the meetings until a consensus was reached among the team. The most significant issues that emerged were related to:

- QR code activation. Having many QR codes too close together on the page may cause some difficulties since the camera may trigger the first detected QR code as soon as the user moves the camera focus over the day dates. To resolve this issue, a digital solution was implemented: using just one QR Code to refer to a single web page including all the days. Thus, the user can select the desired date to listen to the description of the day. Thus, in this way the solution includes a digital list of the days that can be navigated via smartphone/computer and assistive technology. When the day is selected on the page, the user can listen to/read the associated information (audio files in mp3 format). The days could be arranged in various ways, such as a list (solution applied to the prototype), a link or a button for each day, or alternatively a combo-box or a dropdown menu.
- Limiting the use of Braille labels. Since Braille requires coding each character with a sequence of dots in relief, the Braille translation of textual documents may need too much space to fit on the calendar page. Thus only a few labels were reproduced in the paper-based calendar, while additional information was delivered throughout the audio/digital channel.
- Color, contrast and fonts. Difficulties related to the rendering features were experienced by the low-vision users in reading the days and the related writings. Fortunately, after having removed the QR codes from each day (using just one), some space was saved and so the graphical appearance was rearranged by changing some layout features (font type and size).

4.4   Final Prototype

In the Barbanera calendar all suggestions were taken into consideration except the shapes in relief which had been suggested by users for the lunar phases, due to the difficulty of reproducing it on paper. More specifically:

- *Braille labels.* Each day was marked in Braille code. For this purpose, traditional Braille printing was used in order to keep the page unchanged. In fact, the Braille dots cause tiny holes on the opposite side of the sheet. For this reason, the technique applied by the publishing house consisted in reproducing the Braille character by composing the same dot by dot with an embossing material. In this way, the back of the page was been altered. This made it possible to write text on the back of the month page to make the content available to sighted people (i.e., maintaining the format of the original calendar).
- *QR code detection.* One dot on the left side of the QR code was introduced to make it easily detectable by touch.
- *Number of QR codes.* The cover page of the new version of the accessible calendar is shown in Fig. 3. Four QR codes were placed at the bottom of the cover page. The QR code on the left refers to the Barbanera website and particularly by reproducing the current day's info (see Fig. 4). The 2022 QR code links to the event page (see Fig. 4). Figure 5 shows the month page. Due to problems detecting the QR codes when they are too close together, it was decided to insert only one QR code referring to the whole list of days. This was placed on the top left. Scanning this QR code, the user accesses the list of all audio content related to all days of that month (Fig. 6). In addition, to quickly obtain info related to the current day, a specific QR code was added to the top right-hand side linking to the day info (Fig. 6). It is important to note that the QR code on the top right of the page links to the info about today's day (regardless of the month page that the user is exploring).

Fig. 3. Barbanera calendar – Cover page 2022

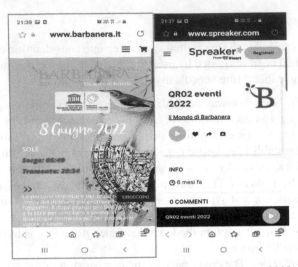

Fig. 4. Scanning the cover page: a) Day Info (top left QR code) b) Event 2022 page (middle right QR code)

Fig. 5. Barbanera calendar: Month page

As in the first prototype, the two QR codes placed at the bottom of the page refer to the horoscope and agricultural information related to phases of the moon (Fig. 5).

As previously mentioned, the QR code in the top left corner brings the users to a web page navigable by flick left & right screen gestures, enabling listening and the navigation of all the month's audio files (one for each day) (Fig. 6a) Please note that with respect to the possible solutions, the most usable was selected since moving up and down with one's finger is the easiest and best-known option for blind people. The QR code in the top right corner activates the day's textual content (Fig. 6b).

Fig. 6. Scanning the month page: a) Audio Files List (QR code top left) b) Info of the day (QR code top right)

Considering the final version of the calendar, the feedback received from (sighted) readers was very positive. Five thousand copies were distributed for Christmas 2021 (to associates, politicians, etc.). Considering both calendars and almanacs, about 3,000,000 in all -- of which more than 2,000,000 calendars have been sold in 2022 -- were distributed throughout the commercial network (both online and in newsstands). The accessible format has been confirmed for the 2023 version (as shown in Fig. 7).

Fig. 7. Barbanera calendar – Cover page 2023

5 Discussion

The experience of codesigning the augmented calendar with sightless end users enabled us to test the video conferencing tools as a means for remote collaboration. The results are encouraging. Blind people were very active and interested in exploiting technology.

We learned that people with visual impairments reacted positively to this collaboration via video conferencing tools. Users stated that these two years of pandemic allowed them to learn about the new remote communication tools and that they can now be used for many purposes. They also stated that in these two years, the opportunities for remote meetings have increased thanks to the new tools, allowing more participation and more activities.

Herein we focus on visually impaired users but the augmented content (which can be perceived through different senses) can benefit any person, including children, elderly, students and so on.

This case study of making the paper calendar more inclusive for all is a clear demonstration of how simple existing technologies can be combined to make content more accessible in a variety of ways and with a variety of devices. Augmented content can thus be useful assistive technologies for many categories of users. This approach could be better investigated in the design of other everyday objects to disseminate a methodology that can contribute to a more inclusive society. In the next section, some early design suggestions are proposed, to be further investigated in similar situations.

6 Design Suggestions

After analyzing the feedback regarding interaction with the calendar prototypes by blind and visually impaired, the multidisciplinary team proposed a set of suggestions to design a more inclusive format. These suggestions are easily generalized for all disabilities, not only the visual.

1. **Exploit tactile sensing to deliver information**. Braille letters and relief shapes can deliver information since they are easily recognizable by touch. Two features have been suggested to be easily and rapidly detectable by touch:
   a. *Tactile cues*. The idea is to exploit Braille dots to localize QR codes. The tactile dots enable the user to correctly and rapidly identify the QR codes. For example, the same can be placed in the upper left corner of each QR code.
   b. *Tangible icons*. If icons relating to the lunar phase are inserted (full moon, first quarter, etc.), in order to make moon phases tactilely perceivable, the outline of the moon icon can be marked in relief. In the case of a full moon, the same could be highlighted with a full circle, while in the case of a new moon, the circle could be empty.
2. **Maintain consistency between tactile cues**. It is important that for each QR code, the tactile dot is always inserted in the same position in order to maintain consistency and allow the blind person to know exactly where the QR code is located.
3. **Optimize QR Code Positioning**. Having QR codes too close on the page may cause difficulties since the camera triggers the description of the first detected code as soon as the user moves the camera focus over the dates of the days. A blind person might not

be very precise when focusing on an item. To resolve this issue, a digital solution can be implemented: only one QR Code can be used to refer to a single digital page showing a list of the days, which can be selected by the user via a smartphone/computer and an assistive technology. When the day is selected on the page, the user can listen to/read the associated information (audio files in mp3 format). Various technical design solutions can be applied: e.g., using a link or a button corresponding to each day, or alternatively a combo-box or a dropdown menu where the user can edit (or select from the list) the desired day. For the day's info, specific written or audio content can be assigned and thus triggered.

4. **Optimize calendar graphic format for readability**.

   a. The standard format with a single list of days placed one under the other would make much more space available to write the information that is more visible even for visually impaired people. To keep information readable, the more compact grid format requires an app to enrich content and information not only for the blind but also for the visually impaired.

   b. Whenever possible, avoid paper that is too glossy. Better mark the number of days with a more full-bodied font (https://www.letturagevolata.it/). Concerning fonts, colors, and contrast for facilitating reading for visually impaired people see the World Wide Web (W3C) resources [19].

In conclusion, making everyday objects more accessible to blind and visually impaired people is crucial to making a more inclusive society.

7 Conclusions

In this paper we describe a remote participatory design process which drove the design of an inclusive paper calendar exploiting QR codes, Braille labels, audio descriptions and web pages.

The proposed approach can be replicated in all contexts including paper-based objects such as a diary, map or personal organizer. Furthermore, this approach can be useful for addressing the needs of other disabilities such as neurodevelopmental or hearing, augmenting objects with pictures or AAC (Augmentative and alternative communication) or videos.

From this study, we can conclude that participatory design using video conferencing tools deserves further investigation. Future work can assess this remote modality vs traditional participatory design in presence for visually-impaired people.

Moreover, it would be important to explore the accessibility of calendar and schedule apps such as Google calendar and Doodle, which by now have become essential tools for supporting and organizing daily work.

Acknowledgment. We thank the "Istituto per la Ricerca, la Formazione e la Riabilitazione" (IRIFOR), Unione Italiana dei Ciechi e degli Ipovedenti (UICI) for their role in leading this study, and all participants for the time they devoted to the design of the Accessible Calendar and for providing their valuable feedback and suggestions.

References

1. Huang, D., Tory, M., Bartram, L.: A field study of on-calendar visualizations. arXiv preprint arXiv:1706.01123 (2017)
2. Eisenman, L.T., Freedman, B., Kofke, M.: Focus on friendship: relationships, inclusion, and social well-being. In: Handbook of Positive Psychology in Intellectual and Developmental Disabilities, pp. 127–144. Springer, Cham (2017). https://doi.org/10.1007/978-3-319-590 66-0
3. Dickinson, H., Smith, C., Yates, S., Tani, M.: The importance of social supports in education: survey findings from students with disability and their families during COVID-19. Disabil. Soc. 1–23 (2021). https://doi.org/10.1080/09687599.2021.1994371
4. Barbanera calendar. http://www.barbanera.it/
5. Sedighi, P., Norouzi, M.H., Delrobaei, M.: An RFID-Based assistive glove to help the visually impaired. IEEE Trans. Instrum. Meas. **70**, 1–9 (2021). https://doi.org/10.1109/TIM.2021.306 9834
6. Lim, K.Y., Ho, Y.L.: NFC label tagging smartphone application for the blind and visually impaired in IoT. In: Kim, H., Kim, K.J., Park, S. (eds.) Information Science and Applications. LNEE, vol. 739, pp. 305–315. Springer, Singapore (2021). https://doi.org/10.1007/978-981-33-6385-4_29
7. Dabke, R.B., Harrell, M., Melaku, S., Ray, L., Turner, H.: QR code labels and audio commentaries for commonly used chemistry laboratory apparatus: an assisted learning experience for visually impaired students. J. Chem. Educ. **98**(10), 3395–3399 (2021). https://doi.org/10.1021/acs.jchemed.1c00058
8. Senjam, S.S., Souvik, M., Covadonga, B.: Smartphones-based assistive technology: accessibility features and apps for people with visual impairment, and its usage, challenges, and usability testing. Clin. Optom. **13**, 311 (2021). https://doi.org/10.2147/OPTO.S336361
9. Ashok, V., Puzis, Y., Borodin, Y., Ramakrishnan, I.V.: Web screen reading automation assistance using semantic abstraction. In: Proceedings of the 22nd International Conference on Intelligent User Interfaces, pp. 407–418 (2017). https://doi.org/10.1145/3025171.3025229
10. Brown, A., Jay, C., Harper, S.: Audio access to calendars. In: Proceedings of the 2010 International Cross Disciplinary Conference on Web Accessibility (W4A), pp. 1–10 (2010). https://doi.org/10.1145/1805986.1806028
11. King, A.: WebbIE Calendar. https://www.webbie.org.uk/calendar/
12. Wentz, B., Lazar, J.: Usable web-based calendaring for blind users. In: Proceedings of HCI 2011 the 25th BCS Conference on Human Computer Interaction, vol. 25, pp. 99–103 (2011). https://doi.org/10.14236/ewic/HCI2011.33
13. Sierra, J.S., Togores, J.: Designing mobile apps for visually impaired and blind users. In: The Fifth International Conference on Advances in Computer-Human Interactions, pp. 47–52 (2012)
14. Leporini, B., Buzzi, M.C., Buzzi, M.: Interacting with mobile devices via VoiceOver: usability and accessibility issues. In: Proceedings of the 24th Australian Computer-Human Interaction Conference, pp. 339–348 (2012). https://doi.org/10.1145/2414536.2414591
15. Mehta, Y., Joshi, A., Joshi, M., Jadhav, C.: Accessibility of date picker for touchscreens. In: Proceedings of the 8th Indian Conference on Human Computer Interaction, pp. 64–69 (2016). https://doi.org/10.1145/3014362.3014368
16. Leporini, B., Buzzi, M., Hersh, M.: Distance meetings during the covid-19 pandemic: are video conferencing tools accessible for blind people?. In: Proceedings of the 18th International Web for All Conference, pp. 1–10 (2021). https://doi.org/10.1145/3014362.3014368
17. Sanders, E.B.N.: From user-centered to participatory design approaches. In: Design and the Social Sciences, pp. 18–25. CRC Press (2002)

18. Robertson, T., Simonsen, J.: Challenges and opportunities in contemporary participatory design. Des. Issues **28**(3), 3–9 (2012). https://doi.org/10.1162/DESI_a_00157
19. W3C: Accessibility Requirements for People with Low Vision. W3C First Public Working Draft 17 March 2016 (2016). https://www.w3.org/TR/low-vision-needs/

The Journey Through Illness of the Type 1 Diabetes Caregiver, from Disruption to Positive Coping

Silvia Torsi[1]([⊠]), Fausto Giunchiglia[2], Sole Ayala[2], and Cristina Rebek[3]

[1] Department of Computer Science, University of Pisa, Pisa, Italy
silvia.torsi@unipi.it
[2] DISI, University of Trento, Trento, Italy
giunchiglia@unitn.it
[3] Free University of Bozen, Bozen, Italy
crebek@unibz.it

Abstract. Type 1 Diabetes is a chronic autoimmune disease that affects mainly children and teenagers. The life, feelings, thoughts and thinking patterns of their parental caregivers must be taken in consideration as they are severely affected by this illness. In the following qualitative study, we are drawing a timeline inspired by mythology aimed to locate the different phases in a universal narrative of the caregivers. Thus, this timeline is used to create a conceptual tool for understanding, forecasting, and designing technological devices for them.

Keywords: Human-Computer Interaction (HCI) · Type 1 Diabetes · Parental caregivers · Hero's journey

1 Introduction

The experience of the caregiver of a child with Type 1 Diabetes (T1D) is very close to a first-hand experience of the illness. Especially in the beginning, the parent totally identifies herself with the condition of her child and experiences disruptive feelings such as anxiety, distress, and they lose interest in many things they considered important before. They also have negative thoughts for the threat of the son's night hypoglycemia of the son that are affecting their sleeping pattern. Therefore, it is possible to draw a path across this chronic condition for the carer as well. This path that started with heartache ends with achieving a balance in the inner and outer world of the carer, an improvement in their daily life and a newly found openness toward the external environment. This considerable improvement in the life of the parents occurs at the same time with an improvement in the life of the cared, because of the tight relationship between hyperglycemia and mood. The rationale of our contribution lies in providing a temporal and causal sequence of what happens to the caregivers by following the sequence of myths [4]. Our research question is "How can the tool we create help the caregivers?". To support our reasoning, we will bring forth an analysis of a set of interviews with T1D caregivers.

© ICST Institute for Computer Sciences, Social Informatics and Telecommunications Engineering 2023
Published by Springer Nature Switzerland AG 2023. All Rights Reserved
S. Longfei and P. Bodhi (Eds.): MobiQuitous 2022, LNICST 492, pp. 598–606, 2023.
https://doi.org/10.1007/978-3-031-34776-4_32

We organize the paper as follows. We begin with a brief definition and history of the illness followed by a literature review of the topic. Next, we expand on the methodology and data analysis. We then proceed with a discussion of the findings of our research and an answer to our research question. We conclude the paper with a short conclusion drawing a summry of the results of this research.

2 What T1D is

Diabetes is a metabolic disease characterized by the fact that the body either does not produce enough insulin or cannot use it efficiently [5, 22]. There are three different types of diabetes: Type 1, Type 2, and gestational diabetes [11]. Since 2019, 9.3% of the global population has been diagnosed with diabetes [13, 19]. In particular, Type 1 diabetes (T1D) is a complex chronic disease in which the body does not produce insulin or produces it in insufficient quantities [5]. Worryingly, rates of incidence of Type 1 diabetes are continuously rising around the world [17]. At the moment, there is no cure for T1D [5]. It is possible, however, to manage the disease by following healthy-living strategies like eating well-balanced meals, doing sport activities, checking blood sugar levels and balancing insulin doses [11, 12]. As documented in several studies, regularly keeping up with these daily routines is challenging for the T1D patients. This rigorous life-style is especially trying for young kids [19] and adolescents that have been diagnosed with T1D. Both patients and their families, may experience a great degree of difficulty in accepting and managing this condition. They go through different behavioral stages before being able to fully adopt, for the rest of their lives, these positive routines.

3 Related Work and Research Gap

Taking into account the existing literature and the analysis of the database we have collected, it emerged that, even with different research approaches to the question, to the transcripts and using a different qualitative analysis, the results tend to coincide. Therefore, we can affirm that the most relevant events of the life story of the caregivers have been triangulated, offering relevance to the study. From our own analysis and from the literature we reviewed, despite the social and geographical differences, the monologues of the T1D parents look very similar in content. Thus, they show a common thread that we would like to set as a narrative for this paper. This model is grounded in the collective unconscious, and, therefore, has properties of universality [4]. In the literature, there are reliable qualitative studies on the topic. For instance, [20] describes the emotional work of the T1D parental caregivers that is twofold: on the one hand, they need to embrace the complexity of their children's condition, continuously looking for patterns to rely on and forecast short term and long term consequences. On the other hand, they need to prevent their offspring from experiencing negative feelings related to their illness, preserve their positive attitude and progressively build "normal" family routines for all of them. Also, a consistent work on their emotions has a positive effect on their glycemic levels, due to the tight relationship between those emotions and the patients' mood. [9] explores the embodiment aspects of parental caregiving as it is assumed that "thoughts, feelings, and behaviors are grounded in bodily interaction with the environment" [16].

Research shows that, even though T1D patients do not show visible specific physical changes, they can still experience social stigma and exclusion. That happens because the child does not completely understand his condition, which requires the parent to exhibit constant vigilance and struggle to protect the child. [I5] is a phenomenological analysis touching the main points of the life story of parental caregiving. This contribute focuses on the life and feelings that parents live, like the constant alertness that leaves no room for relaxation, the isolation from the external world that cannot understand the never ending battle they are fighting, loss of spontaneity, freedom, and interest for life. [8] reviews the existing literature, up to 2019, on the consequence of T1D on family life. It draws a picture of the parental stress following the diagnosis, the partial adjustment of routines, perspectives and mood, and finally the long term work towards the independence of the young T1D patient across adolescence and finally, maturity. [9] makes use of inductive qualitative content analysis and provides a rich explanation of the topic, in particular the work of parents and children on learning to cope with this lifelong illness, from the struggle to understand the condition to the organization of daily life, from the difficulty to manage work to the collaboration with the school staff. [15] focuses on the concept of burnout in order to model the events occurring when parental caregiving, therefore applying already existing paradigms coming from the work environment. At the forefront of this prosperous qualitative literature on parenting a T1D child, there is a lack of a unifying paradigm that can allow meanings to be organized across a temporal full-fledged, coherent and explicit model, that can be used for forecasting, explaining, or providing ICT support. Therefore, we propose our qualitative analysis contextualizing it in existing narratives in order to draw a path from diagnosis of the T1D child toward positive coping. This paper fills this gap and offers a temporal, logical and causal sequence, by following the steps of the hero's journey [4].

4   Method

We interviewed 9 caregivers (8 mothers and 1 father; 1 in person and 8 over the phone [10]) of teenagers and young adults with T1D and tried to understand how their daily life and their feelings towards the events related to the illness unfold. The interviewees were recruited, on a voluntary basis, from a Facebook page dedicated to T1D and come from all over Italy. We interviewed all the people who answered to our request and the interviews were anonymized. The interviews were semi-structured allowing the respondents to reveal their personal narrative by answering our open-ended questions [1]. The interviews were transcribed, analyzed, and coded by the authors, using Grounded Theory [6]. After reading and re-reading the transcripts, the authors understood that there was a lot that was left unsaid by the interviewees. It was up to the researchers making sense of the narratives [3]. In the search of a Gestalt inside the transcripts we reviewed the related literature in order to find a pattern to organize the transcripts. This was found in [4]'s and in [14]'s modelling of collective unconscious.

5 The Hero's Journey in Mythology

We made use of mythology to map out our study. Mythology is a privileged way to get in contact with one's own psyche in a poetic and transcendent way, as it condenses human imagination and concretize it into the collective unconscious. Mythologies are canvases that define strategies and provide meanings to human experiences; in this sense, they look like a cognitive device [21]. For example, in his extensive work, Campbell analyzed, the worldwide similarities based on the hero's journey, the "monomyth" that is pervasive across many cultures of the humankind. Just like Campbell's hero's adventure, the journey of the caregiver begins in the ordinary world. He must depart from the ordinary world, when he receives a call to commence his adventure. The adventure of the hero starts with a request to leave his community (the "departure"); although reluctant at first, he starts a lonely travel across an enchanted and sinister region in which he will be guided by a mentor, who will guide him across "a guarded threshold, leading him to a supernatural world, where familiar laws and order do not apply". The mentor gives him advice and supernatural powers. After a long search, and an encounter with allies that will help him, and enemies he will defeat (the "Initiation"), he returns from this challenging venture to his community and is rewarded (the "return"). This monomyth used for reading the transcripts gives access to a narrative grounding in the collective unconscious as it was described by the classic psychologist Gustav Jung [14]. It also adds an advantaged access to consciousness, agency, and a spiritual dimension that were noticed in the story of the interviewed people. The monomyth allows to map their thoughts, actions, and events into a narrative that empowers and provides meanings to their life story.

6 The Journey

In the following sub-chapters we draw a comparison between The Campbell monomyth and the results of the qualitative studies. From the Hero's journey we isolated 4 phases: the departure, the road of trials, the victory and the acquisition of new powers. In Fact, the Campbell framework can be applied by recognizing even few phases from the original sequence.

6.1 The Departure

T1D enters in the life of a family often abruptly, with the child having a few symptoms revealed by blood tests, whose results often come as a shock to the parents. This is a traumatic experience and one of the worst memories in the life of a caregiver. Often, during the interview, after this question, the tone of the voice becomes sadder and the speaking is decelerated. There is a sharp line dividing life before – without the diabetes - and after the illness -with diabetes. This bleak revelation spurs negative feelings such as disruption, guilt, and fear inside the parent. Disruption comes from not knowing what the illness entails, thus, ignoring the impact it will have upon their lives. The guilt, however, originates from the thought of having an ill child, the fear is caused by a sinister and subtle, yet constant threat to the child's life. This is the beginning of the journey through the illness. The transformation from parent to parent-caregiver begins here.

C09: [...] *Therefore, I measured his glycemic level and it was more than 300...I don't remember exactly how much because I blocked out most of that night...*

The departure of the caregiver-hero, starts from the exordium of the condition, when the physician discovers the illness of the young one. This is a negative event that the parent tends to go through with great heart-ship. This is the call for the departure: abrupt, shocking, unpleasant, throwing the hero in an unknown and hostile world, and leaving him in confusion and chaos [18]. The hero, then, lives a separation from his previous life that does not interest him anymore. The work life of the caregiver is affected as well. Their work efficiency is lowered, some caregivers quit their occupation, some others go back to work, but perform it without motivation or energy.

C09: [...] *In the beginning, I never went out of the house without my son, [...] I went back to work, unwillingly, I forced myself to do it, because it was the right thing to do, wasn't it?....*

This is one of the most relevant effects of the initial life of the caregiver, losing interest for the outside world and totally devoting themselves to the ill child. The decrement of passion for the working life is only one of the signs of depression of the caregiver in the beginning, and in a certain sense his/her previous life will never return to normal.

6.2 The Road of Trials

After the initial shock, the path continues with the caregiver looking for information about the illness, in order to understand what it means and what it implies in term of self-management. The moment the caregiver starts gathering information, balancing doses of insulin while counting carbohydrates, is the moment when he slowly starts making sense of this new aspect of his family life. Thus, the caregiver begins to create his own strategies of self-management on behalf of his son, who is obviously too young to manage T1D on his own.

CO3: [...] *I had to do a lot of studying, [there were] a lot of notions that I had to learn, a lot of conferences to go to, travels to take [...] in order to perfectly know this pathology, the progress the scientific research was making, to personally know the researchers, the doctors... I immersed myself into this world...*

The world of the carer is populated by a lot of learning about the condition, in the beginning, and the continuous trials aimed to balance the blood levels of their child, later on. In this setting, the healthcare staff, offering information and support, has the role of mentors in the monomyth. There is a lot of inferential reasoning starting from several elements involved in the illness (food, physical activity, mood, etc.) and suffering from negative emotions, like the threat of night hypoglycemia (that can kill the young patient). After each trial, the hero starts being more and more confident in doing what he considered impossible in the life before diabetes [20].

The inner life of the caregiver is turned upside down. His/her cognitive load is seriously affected by the anxiety related to the illness and the modification of the routines. Everything looks new and potentially harmful, the caregiver is overwhelmed by this new, unexpected, and unknown thing related to his son, therefore, affecting also parental identity and their self-confidence. They never know if what they are doing is right or wrong; from the doses of insulin to inject, to the food to administer, or the physical activity to advise there is a lot of unknown territory. Above all, however, he has to learn how to correctly relate with the young patient regarding issues about the illness. Also, the fear of a son's nightly hypoglycemia affects their sleep, and they start living only for the ill child.

C08: *[Often] I didn't know how many units [of insulin] I had to give him, because it is obvious that you have anxieties, if it is too early, if it is too late, if everything went well. It is a job you have to learn how to do, how to manage your anxieties [...] the job of the parent is huge, because, it is obvious, the more you do, the more the child is relieved [of the burden]...*

This is the new environment of the hero-caregiver, a world populated by risks, hazards, and pitfalls; in this phase, there is the need to both practice inferential reasoning (from the health parameters, the carbohydrates intake, the physical activity and the way to guess the doses of insulin to inject) and manage distress and negative thoughts, while not forgetting to reassure and tranquillize the ill child. There is a detachment from the world in the sense that the majority of people do not understand the struggle and often criticize the parents for being too dedicated and fail to comprehend the real problem this condition represents.

6.3 The Victory

Then routines begin settle in, and there is a growing, yet unstable and dynamic balance in the daily life of the patient and of the carer. The cognitive burden, the worries, and a pervasive feeling of sadness still mark their life; anyway, there is a slight but constantly ascending positive mood.

C07: *[...] it has been a change, but not a total change, if I think about it... if before we could wait till the last minute to prepare lunch...now I always try to have some pasta in the fridge, so, if he has an episode of a low glycemic level, he can find it ready... medical visits are every 3 months [..], then, of course, you have always the telephone close by [...] but I have to say, recently I feel quite calm, I don't live with the fear that he calls me anymore. Of course, there is always the state of alert in the background...*

Self-management becomes a bond between the patient and the carer. This newly formed bond increases s their feeling of belonging together. This newly formed facet of their relationship is marked by ties of companionship and alliance to the extent that they share an important parts of their life much more than an average parent shares with their son. This is one of the most important life skills that the caregiver acquires across this path.

CO3: *[...] The dialogues have changed during our daily life, because you enter in a different world, and your dialogues are now: how much is it?, is it high?, is it low?, did you get your insulin shot?, did you eat anything strange?...*

In time, living with T1D becomes a routine, and a new balance is gradually settled. It takes some time to make sense of the condition, accepting it and incorporate it in the daily life, in few words reducing it to just one more thing to think about. The illness becomes like an additional member of the family to take into consideration. There is a struggle in the family to seek normality, to reduce the burden of the condition as much as possible in order to consider itself as normal. This joint effort increases the components' synchronization and reinforces bonds. In particular, the special relationship between the parent caregiver and the ill child is tightened.

C08: *[…] Diabetes actually becomes a part of your routine, it is not difficult to have a routine, it becomes part of your life, you stick it into your own routine: When they are young, you wake up and measure their the glycemic level, you prepare lunch with the right food, you check the glycemic level again, if it is high, you take a walk…in the end, it becomes your own routine…*

M08: *[…] When he was younger, we always tried to make him understand that he was normal, that he did some things that were different from what the other children were doing, but normal nevertheless […], we tried to make him consider diabetes a normal thing, and, if managed in a certain way, his life could be like everyone else's…*

6.4 The Acquisition of New Powers

This phase of positive coping and the mastering of T1D brings some constructive consequences in the lives of caregivers, like appreciating good moments more intensely, searching and valuing authentic relationships, opening themselves to the world, optimizing time and being selective towards people and experiences. Life can never be like before the initial episode, but there are specific improvements that can make their life not so different from that of a non-caregiver.

M08: *[…] This illness, like any other illness, or like difficulties, strengthens you, in the sense that it gives you the capacity, that everybody has without knowing, of interacting with other people in order to survive…*

C09: *One thing that [S09]'s diabetes has taught me […] is to keep it simple and cut unnecessary relationships out of my life. It is useless to waste so many words: you either understand that I need you or you go away, if you are here only to cause troubles, you'd better go. I do not need you. This was our life change, even with family, once diabetes entered this house.*

The hero demonstrates he can master novel competences. Based on our data, we can affirm that the caregiver is able to manage not only the illness, but also all the negative feelings it brings along with it. Therefore, rationality and inferential reasoning as well as unconscious emotions like fear, anguish, guilt, or anxiety become more manageable for them. As a consequence, they regain interest for life. There is also a component of self-realization, the hero discovery of his unrealized, unused potential and his self-actualization [21], this, in turn, provides a new level of understanding about how the relationship with life could be.

7   Discussion

From the qualitative analysis, we learnt that caregivers gained, after much pain and trials, a privileged access to their irrational feelings that they have to accept, discipline, and turn into assets for caregiving. Caregivers fight against sugar fluctuations, and, in order to do this, they need to master both the unconscious and the rationality. These elements need to be managed, accepted and employed continuously. The work of Campbell [4] can be considered a canvas to make sense of parental carers' life stories and provides an interpreting tool that paints the whole picture of the story of parental caregivers. These men and women find understanding, inspiration, prediction and consciousness, intended as a deep sense of being present in one's own time and space, when facing a life-altering situation. In this sense, the mythology put forth by [4] is an organized narrative giving a meaningful structure to a set of symbols meant to organize a human experience. In fact, heroism is an approach to read intelligence as it is unfolding in daily life. The carer faces their problems in a transformative way that changes one's view on life, environment, and inner consciousness in the direction of an expansion, that is deeply restorative and generative. Accordingly, heroic behavior can be seen as a form of intelligent behavior that is embodied in everyday life, and proposes a reading of those "heroes". Thus, they are capable of heightened cognitive, psychological, and "transcendent" actions exhibiting increased awareness, the use of the body to modify the external world, and the acceptance of death [7]. Finally, as a possible future direction of this contribute, the Hero's journey in [4] can be considered in Healthcare HCI in terms of providing a broad and detailed canvas for the modelling of users and stakeholders in the phase of User Studies in the User-Centered Design process.

8 Conclusion

In this paper, we describe the strenuous journey of parental caregivers of T1D children and teenagers towards a complete management of the illness. We conducted a qualitative study based on narrative interviews that were analyzed and interpreted in the respective parts of the study. We used mythology [4] as a model for our narrative. In particular, we took inspiration from the journey of the hero that can be retrieved in numerous folk tales and myths and whose framework belongs to the collective imagination of most of the worldwide cultures and in the end to individual unconscious. Hence, we draw a path starting from a negative event, that is the kick-off point of a journey full of adventures due to which the hero learns and becomes stronger. From the qualitative analysis, some other minor steps of the Campbell paradigm emerged, like the help of the healthcare staff, that in the myth give the hero the instruments to win the battles, and the return to the original community with additional skills available for his members. The voyage ends with the hero having gained a novel balance in his life, as his travel through the illness has helped him to achieve novel levels of wisdom and understanding.

Acknowledgements. Acknowledgements. This work has been supported by the European Union's Horizon 2020 FET Proactive project "WeNet - The Internet of us" grant agreement No 823783 and the "DELPhi - DiscovEring Life Patterns" project funded by the MIUR Progetti di Ricerca di Rilevante Interesse Nazionale (PRIN) 2017 - DD n. 1062 del 31.05.2019.

References

1. Anderson, C., Kirkpatrick, S.: Narrative interviewing. Int. J. Clin. Pharm. **38**(3), 631–634 (2015). https://doi.org/10.1007/s11096-015-0222-0
2. Beyond Type 1: Type 1 Diabete Statistics. https://beyondtype1.org/type-1-diabetes-statistics/. 2021 February 10
3. Braun,V.Reflecting on reflexive thematic analysis. Qualitative Research in Sport, Exercise and Health, Volume 11, 2019 - Issue 4

4. Campbell, E.: The hero with a thousand faces. Princeton University Press, Princeton, NJ (1968)
5. CDC - Centers for Disease Control and Prevention: What is Diabetes?. https://www.cdc.gov/diabetes/basics/diabetes.html. (2020, June 11)
6. Charmaz, K.: Constructing Grounded Theory: a Practical Guide through qualitative analysis. Sage, Thousand Oaks, CA (2006)
7. Efthimiou, O., Franco, Z.E.: Heroic intelligence: The hero's journey as an evolutionary and existential blueprint. Journal of Genius and Eminence 2(2), 33–44 (2017)
8. Fornasini, S., Miele, F., Piras, E.M.: The Consequences of Type 1 Diabetes Onset on Family Life. An Integrative Review. Journal of Child and Family Studies, 29, pp. 1467–1483 (2019)
9. Holmström, M.R., Häggström, M., Söderber, S.: Experiences from Parents to Children with diabetes Type 1. JSM Health Education Primary Health Care, 3(2) (2018)
10. Holt, A.: Using the telephone for narrative interviewing: a research note. Qual. Res. 10(1), 113–121 (2010)
11. IDF Europe organization ©: Type 1 diabetes. https://www.idf.org/aboutdiabetes/type-1-diabetes.html, 2021, February 10
12. IDF Europe organization ©: What is diabetes. https://www.idf.org/aboutdiabetes/what-is-diabetes.html. 2021, February 10
13. IDF Europe organization: Diabetes in Italy statistics. https://www.idf.org/our-network/regions-members/europe/members/142-italy.html" International Diabetes Federation, 2021
14. Jung, C.G.: The Archetypes and the Collective Unconscious, 2nd edn. Princeton University Press, Princeton (1969)
15. Lindström, C., Åman, J., Norberg, A.L., Forssberg, M., Anderzén-Carlsson, A.: "Mission impossible": the mothering of a child with type 1 diabetes—from the perspective of mothers experiencing burnout. J. Pediatr. Nurs. 36, 149–156 (2017)
16. Meier, B.P., Schnall, S., Schwarz, N., Barghd, J.A.: Embodiment in Social Psychology. Topics in Cognitive Science, 1–12 (2012)
17. Patterson, C.C., Karuranga, S., Salpea, P., Saeedi, P., Dahlquist, G., Soltesz, G.D. Ogle, G. D.: Worldwide estimates of incidence, prevalence and mortality of type 1 diabetes in children and adolescents: Results from the International Diabetes Federation Diabetes Atlas, 9th edition. Diabetes Research and Clinical Practice, Vol. 157, 107842, Nov 01, 2019
18. Rifshana, F., Breheny, M., Taylor, J.E., Ross, K.: The parental experience of caring for a child with type 1 diabetes. J. Child Fam. Stud. 26(11), 3226–3236 (2017)
19. Saeedi, P., Petersohn, I., Salpea, P., Malanda, B., Karuranga, S., Unwin, N. Colagiuri, S. Guariguata, L., Motala, A.A., Ogurtsova, K., . Shaw, J.E., . Bright, D., Williams, R.: Global and regional diabetes prevalence estimates for 2019 and projections for 2030 and 2045: Results from the International Diabetes Federation Diabetes Atlas, 9th edition. Diabetes Research and Clinical Practice, Vol. 157 (2019)
20. Watt, L.: "Her life rests on your shoulders": Doing worry as emotion work in the care of children with diabetes. Global Qualitative Nursing Research 4, 1–11 (2017)
21. Williams, C.: The hero's journey: A creative act. Journal of Genius and Eminence 2(2), 70–78 (2017)
22. Chen, T.: Diabetes. In: Jackson, M.B., Huang, R., Kaplan, E., Mookherjee, S. (eds.) The Perioperative Medicine Consult Handbook, pp. 107–118. Springer, Cham (2020). https://doi.org/10.1007/978-3-030-19704-9_13

Author Index

Printed in the United States
by Baker & Taylor Publisher Services